SIXTH EDITION

INTERNATIONAL ACCOUNTING

Frederick D. S. Choi

New York University

Gary K. Meek

Oklahoma State University

PEARSON
Prentice
Hall

Upper Saddle River, New Jersey 07458

Library of Congress Cataloging-in-Publication Data

Choi, Frederick D. S., 1942-
    International accounting / Frederick D. S. Choi, Gary K. Meek.— 6th ed.
        p. cm.
    Includes bibliographical references and index.
    ISBN-13: 978-0-13-158814-1 (alk. paper)
    ISBN-10: 0-13-158814-1 (alk. paper)
    1. International business enterprises—Accounting.   I. Meek, Gary K., 1949-
II. Title.
    HF5686.I56C53 2008
    657'.96—dc22

                                            2007042113

Acquisitions Editor: Steve Sartori
Editor in Chief: Eric Svendsen
Product Development Manager: Ashley Santora
Editorial Project Manager: Kierra Kashickey
Marketing Manager: Jodi Bassett
Marketing Assistant: Ian Gold
Senior Managing Editor: Judy Leale
Permissions Coordinator: Charles Morris
Operations Specialist: Michelle Klein
Cover Design: Bruce Kenselaar
Composition: Laserwords
Full-Service Project Management: Laserwords
Printer/Binder: Courier/Westford
Typeface: Times 10/12

Credits and acknowledgments borrowed from other sources and reproduced, with permission, in this textbook appear on appropriate page within text.

Pearson Education LTD.
Pearson Education Singapore, Pte. Ltd
Pearson Education, Canada, Ltd
Pearson Education–Japan

Pearson Education Australia PTY, Limited
Pearson Education North Asia Ltd
Pearson Educación de Mexico, S.A. de C.V.
Pearson Education Malaysia, Pte. Ltd.

10 9 8 7 6 5 4 3 2 1
ISBN-13: 978-0-13-158814-1
ISBN-10: 0-13-158814-1

To Lois, Michele, Marisa, Alexa, Sharon,
Janet, Alana and Kaily.

Brief Contents

Contents

CHAPTER 8   Global Accounting and Auditing Standards   282

CHAPTER 11 Financial Risk Management   422

Preface

This book is written with the express purpose of introducing students to the international dimensions of accounting, financial reporting, and financial control. The world in which they will pursue their professional careers is a world dominated by global business and cross-border investing. As these activities require decisions premised on financial data, a knowledge of international accounting is crucial for achieving proper understanding in external and internal financial communications. While ideal for upper division undergraduate students and masters students, we are pleased that the contents of this award-winning effort have also benefited practicing accountants, financial executives, investment managers, university educators and professional administrators around the world.

This revision of a work that has spanned three decades features a number of enhancements. These include:

- Expanded coverage of corporate governance and related legislation. See chapters 4, 5, 8, and 9.
- Examination of international auditing, both external and internal. See chapters 8 and 9.
- Reorganized and updated discussion of comparative accounting emphasizing developments in Europe, the Americas, and Asia in Chapters 3 and 4.
- Capital market, managerial, taxation, and institutional updates reflective of current trends and issues throughout most chapters.
- Discussion of international accounting convergence and the major players in this important effort. See chapters 3, 5 and 8.
- Revised discussion of reporting and disclosure practices spanning both developed and emerging market countries. See Chapters 3, 4, 5 and 7.
- Expanded listings of relevant international Web site addresses and data sources.
- New and updated discussion questions, exercises, and cases.

We have benefited from the professional literature and from many of our students and faculty colleagues whose thoughtful comments have triggered new ideas for us to consider. In addition, we wish to acknowledge the following individuals for reviewing, providing data, or offering constructive suggestions for improving our work:

Nils Crasselt, Ruhr-Universität Bochum
Timothy A. Farmer, University of Missouri – St. Louis
Katerina Hellström, Stockholm School of Economics
Elmen Li, Hong Kong Polytechnic University
Thorston Sellhorn, Ruhr-Universität Bochum

Hervé Stolowy, HEC School of Management
Ann Tarca, University of Western Australia

Many individuals furnished able assistance in producing the manuscript. We especially thank Shevon Estwick and Cyril Martinez at New York University, and Cindy Conway at Oklahoma State University for their assistance with Web searches and exhibits and Wendy Craven, Steve Sartori, and Kerri Tomasso at Prentice–Hall for their encouragement and editorial support.

However hard one tries to avoid them, errors are bound to occur in a work of this type. As authors, we accept full responsibility for all errors and omissions in the manuscript. As always we welcome constructive comments from all who use this book as students are the ultimate beneficiaries of your thoughtfulness.

F. D. S. Choi
New York, N.Y.

G. K. Meek
Stillwater, OK

CHAPTER 1

Introduction

Accounting plays a vital role in society. As a branch of economics, it provides information about a firm and its transactions to facilitate resource allocation decisions by users of that information. If the information reported is reliable and useful, scarce resources are allocated in an optimal fashion, and conversely, resource allocations are less than optimal when information is less reliable and useful.

International accounting, the subject of this text, is no different in its intended role. What makes its study distinctive is that the entity being reported on is either a multinational company (MNC) with operations and transactions that cross national boundaries, or an entity with reporting obligations to users who are located in a country other than that of the reporting entity.

Recall that accounting entails several broad processes: measurement, disclosure, and auditing. Measurement is the process of identifying, categorizing, and quantifying economic activities or transactions. These measurements provide insights into the profitability of a firm's operations and the strength of its financial position. Disclosure is the process by which accounting measurements are communicated to their intended users. This area focuses on such issues as what is to be reported, when, by what means, and to whom. Auditing is the process by which specialized accounting professionals (auditors) attest to the reliability of the measurement and communication process. Whereas internal auditors are company employees who answer to management, external auditors are nonemployees who are responsible for attesting that the company's financial statements are prepared in accordance with generally accepted standards.

An understanding of the international dimensions of the accounting processes that were just described is important to those engaged in importing or exporting activities, as well as those seeking to manage a business or to obtain or supply financing across national borders. Even a company operating solely within the confines of a single country is no longer insulated from the international aspects of accounting, because reliance on international vendors to contain production costs and remain globally competitive is a common feature of present-day business. Accounting amounts may vary significantly depending on the principles that govern them. Differences in culture, business practices, political and regulatory structures, legal systems, currency values, local inflation rates, business risks, and tax codes all affect how the MNC conducts its operations and financial reporting around the world. Financial statements and other disclosures are impossible to understand without an awareness of the underlying accounting principles and business culture.

The importance of studying international accounting has grown over the years. We begin with a brief history of the subject.

HISTORICAL PERSPECTIVE

The history of accounting is an international history. The following historical summary demonstrates that accounting has been remarkably successful in its ability to be transplanted from one national setting to another while allowing for continued development in theory and practice worldwide.

To begin, double-entry bookkeeping, generally thought of as the genesis of accounting as we know it today, emanated from the Italian city-states of the 14th and 15th centuries. Its development was spurred by the growth of international commerce in northern Italy during the late Middle Ages and the desire of government to find ways to tax commercial transactions. "Bookkeeping in the Italian fashion" then migrated to Germany to assist the merchants of the Fugger era and the Hanseatic League. At about the same time, business philosophers in the Netherlands sharpened ways of calculating periodic income, and government officials in France found it advantageous to apply the whole system to governmental planning and accountability.

In due course, double-entry accounting ideas reached the British Isles. The development of the British Empire created unprecedented needs for British commercial interests to manage and control enterprises in the colonies, and for the records of their colonial enterprises to be reviewed and verified. These needs led to the emergence of accounting societies in the 1850s and an organized public accounting profession in Scotland and England in the 1870s. British accounting practices spread not only to North America but throughout the British Commonwealth as it then existed.

Parallel developments occurred elsewhere. The Dutch accounting model was exported to Indonesia, among other places. The French accounting system found a home in Polynesia and French-administered territories in Africa, while the reporting framework of the Germans proved influential in Japan, Sweden, and czarist Russia.[1]

As the economic might of the United States grew during the first half of the 20th century, its sophistication in matters of accounting grew in tandem. Business schools assisted in this development by conceptualizing the subject matter and eventually having it recognized as an academic discipline in its own right on college and university campuses. After World War II, U.S. accounting influence made itself felt throughout the Western world, particularly in Germany and Japan. To a lesser extent, similar factors are directly observable in countries like Brazil, Israel, Mexico, the Philippines, Sweden, and Taiwan.

The paradox of the international heritage of accounting is that in many countries, accounting remains a nationalistic affair, with national standards and practices deeply anchored in national laws and professional regulations. (Examples of comparative accounting practices are provided in Chapters 3 and 4.) There is little understanding of parallel requirements in other countries. Nonetheless, accounting serves people and organizations whose decisions are increasingly international in scope.

---

[1]For a revisionist account of this summary, see Sy Aida and Tony Tinker, "Bury Pacioli in Africa: A Bookkeepers Reification of Accountancy," *Abacus*, Vol. 42, March 2006, pp. 105–127.

Resolving the historical paradox of accounting has long been a concern of both users and preparers of accounting information. In recent years, institutional efforts to narrow differences in measurement, disclosure, and auditing processes around the world have intensified. A description of this effort and the major players with an important stake in attaining convergence of global accounting systems is the focus of Chapter 8.

CONTEMPORARY PERSPECTIVE

While the effort to reduce international accounting diversity is important in its own right, there are today a number additional factors that are contributing to the growing importance of studying international accounting. These factors stem from significant and continuing reductions in national trade barriers and capital controls together with advances in information technology.

National controls on capital flows, foreign exchange, foreign direct investment, and related transactions have been dramatically liberalized in recent years, reducing the barriers to international business. Appendix 1-1 presents selected information on changes in financial sector policy in a sample of developed and developing countries during the last three decades, and illustrates efforts by national governments to open their economies to private enterprise and international investors and business. It shows that, with a few exceptions, there has been a strong trend worldwide during this period to privatize government-owned financial enterprises (especially banks) and to reduce or eliminate foreign exchange controls and limits on cross-border investment. As accounting is the language of business, cross-border economic interactions mean that accounting reports prepared in one country must increasingly be used and understood by users in another.[2]

Advances in information technology are also causing a radical change in the economics of production and distribution. Vertically integrated production is no longer an efficient mode of operation. Real-time global information linkages mean that production, including accounting services,[3] is increasingly being outsourced to whatever firm of whatever size wherever in the world can best do the job, or portions of the job. The adversarial, arm's-length relationships that have characterized companies' relations with their suppliers, middle persons, and customers are being replaced by cooperative global linkages with suppliers, suppliers' suppliers, middle persons, customers, and customers' customers.

Exhibit 1-1 provides an illustration of the outsourcing phenomenon.[4] In producing the ProLiant ML150, a small box that helps companies manage customer databases and run e-mail systems, among other things, Hewlett-Packard (H-P) turned to the usual sources of low-cost labor: China and India. However, it decided to also

---

[2]For a recent study on the association between economic interactions and financial reporting practices, see Tarun Khanna, Krishna G. Palepu, and Suraj Srinivasan, "Disclosure Practices of Foreign Companies Interacting with U.S. Markets, *Journal of Accounting Research* 42, no. 2 (May 2004): 475–508.
[3]For example, see Gary S. Shamis, M. Cathryn Green, Susan M. Sorensen, and Donald L. Kyle, "Outsourcing, Offshoring, Nearshoring: What to Do?" *Journal of Accountancy* (June 2005), pp. 1–7.
[4]Rebecca Buckman, "H-P Outsourcing: Beyond China," *Wall Street Journal*, February 23, 2004, p. A14.

EXHIBIT 1-1   Outsourcing Process for Hewlett-Packard's ProLiant ML150

make some ML150s in higher-cost locations such as Singapore and Australia, which were closer to targeted customers. Initial design for the ML150 was done in Singapore, approved in Houston, and then handed off to an outside contractor in Taiwan. Although China possesses the lowest wage rates, it is but one part of a highly specialized manufacturing system. Considerations ranging from logistics to tariff policies reportedly kept H-P from putting all of its production lines in China. It would take too long for machines manufactured in China to reach customers in other Asian markets. Moreover, shipping goods to India triggered steep tariffs, so it made sense to produce some ML150s in India with imported parts for the local market. All of the links in this outsourcing example are associated with accounting issues discussed in the following pages of this chapter.

Spurred by the twin developments we have just described, there are several factors that are contributing to the growing importance of the subject matter of this text. We describe each in turn.

GROWTH AND SPREAD OF MULTINATIONAL OPERATIONS

International business has traditionally been associated with foreign trade. This activity, rooted in antiquity, continues unabated. While trade in services has traditionally palled in comparison with trade in merchandise, the former is gaining in significance and growing at a faster rate than the latter. Current trends in exports and imports of both goods and services by region and selected economy are depicted in Exhibit 1-2.

What is not shown in Exhibit 1-2 is the composition of each region's exports and imports. To obtain a better picture of the pattern of global trade at the micro level, one need simply examine the foreign-operations disclosures of any major MNC. Exhibit 1-3 shows the geographic distribution of sales of Heineken, one of the world's leading international brewers. As can be seen, the company's sales literally blanket every continent in the world. Unisys, the U.S.-based information technology services company, provides its expertise to clients in over 100 countries, while Sweden's Volvo Group sells both automotive products and financial services in some 185 countries. An aggregation of such disclosures for all MNCs in all countries would confirm that trade today is neither bilateral nor regional, but truly global.

EXHIBIT 1-2   World Trade by Region

Total Merchandise Trade			Unit: U.S. dollar at current prices (millions)				
Region	**Activity**	**Partner**	**1985**	**1990**	**1995**	**2000**	**2005**
Africa	Exports	World	83,700	106,000	112,000	147,800	297,700
Africa	Imports	World	75,600	99,600	126,700	129,400	249,300
Asia	Exports	World	416,400	792,400	1,446,800	1,836,200	3,050,900
Asia	Imports	World	386,600	761,500	1,403,300	1,677,100	2,871,000
Europe	Exports	World	846,245	1,684,940	2,335,635	2,633,930	4,371,915
Europe	Imports	World	862,075	1,750,925	2,334,760	2,774,755	4,542,675
Middle East	Exports	World	102,200	138,400	151,000	268,000	538,000
Middle East	Imports	World	87,800	101,300	132,500	167,400	322,100
North America	Exports	World	336,560	562,035	856,550	1,224,975	1,477,530
North America	Imports	World	452,660	684,460	1,015,760	1,687,580	2,284,735
South/ Central America	Exports	World	81,800	106,000	148,900	195,800	354,900
South/ Central America	Imports	World	65,400	85,900	176,900	206,300	297,600
World	Exports	World	1,954,000	3,449,000	5,164,000	6,452,000	10,431,000
World	Imports	World	2,015,000	3,550,000	5,284,000	6,724,000	10,783,000

Total Trade in Commercial Services			Unit: U.S. dollar at current prices (millions)				
Region	**Activity**	**Partner**	**1985**	**1990**	**1995**	**2000**	**2005**
Africa	Exports	World	11,100	18,600	25,700	31,300	56,900
Africa	Imports	World	20,700	26,500	34,400	37,400	69,300
Asia	Exports	World	60,800	131,500	257,800	309,500	525,300
Asia	Imports	World	77,400	178,800	328,100	367,900	573,500
Europe	Exports	World			597,100	721,900	1,244,800
Europe	Imports	World			560,200	674,100	1,120,100
Middle East	Exports	World				33,100	54,900
Middle East	Imports	World				48,800	85,400
North America	Exports	World	75,700	135,500	171,200	268,200	366,300
North America	Imports	World	75,700	135,500	171,200	268,200	366,300
South/ Central America	Exports	World	13,600	22,400	34,600	47,100	68,200
South/ Central America	Imports	World	16,700	24,900	45,300	54,600	70,500
World	Exports	World	381,600	780,500	1,185,100	1,491,000	2,414,300
World	Imports	World	401,100	820,500	1,200,700	1,474,600	2,347,400

EXHIBIT 1-3   Heineken's 2005 Geographic Distribution of Sales (millions of hectolitres)

Western Europe		32.2
Netherlands	5.8	
Spain	10.9	
France	6.8	
Italy	5.7	
Other	3	
Central and Eastern Europe		45.5
Poland	10.2	
Russia	7.2	

(continued)

EXHIBIT 1-3   Heineken's 2005 Geographic Distribution of Sales (millions of hectolitres)
(continued)

Germany	8.7	
Austria	4.6	
Greece	3.2	
Other	11.6	
Americas		15.1
U.S.	6.9	
Latin America	6.9	
Other	1.3	
Africa and Middle East		15
Nigeria	5.4	
Egypt	1	
Other	8.6	
Asia Pacific	10.8	

A major accounting issue associated with export and import activities relates to accounting for foreign currency transactions. Assume, for example, that Heineken exports a certain quantity of beer to a Brazilian importer and invoices the sale in Brazilian reals. Should the real devalue relative to the euro prior to collection, Heineken will experience a foreign exchange loss because reals will yield less in euros upon conversion after the devaluation than before. The measurement of this transaction loss is not straightforward and is a subject that is dealt with in Chapter 6.

Today, international business transcends foreign trade and is increasingly associated with foreign direct investments, which involve operating production or distribution systems abroad by way of a wholly- or majority-owned affiliate, a joint venture, or a strategic alliance.

While there is clearly a developed-country bias among foreign direct investors, the boom of foreign direct investment flows to developing countries since the early 1990s indicates that MNCs are increasingly finding these host countries to be attractive investment locations.[5]

At the level of the firm, foreign direct investment activities are captured by a company's segmental disclosures and its roster of shareholdings in affiliated companies. Exhibit 1-4 provides operating statistics by region for AKZO Nobel, a multinational company headquartered in the Netherlands and concentrating on healthcare products, coatings, and chemicals.

Exhibit 1-5 illustrates the extensive holdings in operating group companies of Nestlé, one of the world's largest food and beverage companies, headquartered in Vevy, Switzerland. While both AKZO and Nestlé's foreign operations are extensive, the numbers relating to capital expenditures, invested capital, production sold locally,

---

[5]The World Bank's chief economist, Francois Bourguignon, predicts that over the next 25 years, developing countries will move to the center stage in the global economy; see "Global Economic Prospects 2007: Managing the Next Wave of Globalization" (World Bank Panel Discussion sponsored by the Global Business Institute), New York University, Stern School of Business, December 12, 2006.

EXHIBIT 1-4 Foreign Operations Disclosures of AKZO NOBEL[*]

	Net Sales by Destination	Net Sales by Origin	Operating Income	Capital Expenditures	Invested Capital	Number of Employees
Netherlands	862	2,459	474	179	2,229	11,600
Germany	1,238	1,152	144	25	539	4,100
Sweden	516	1,237	137	65	604	3,900
U.K.	809	754	(59)	31	492	4,100
Other Europe	4,075	3,069	527	81	1,264	12,900
U.S./Canada	2,400	2,116	(67)	51	1,534	8,200
Latin America	830	626	85	42	448	4,400
Asia	1,590	1,231	192	32	661	9,800
Other regions	680	356	53	8	236	2,300

[*]*These figures are based on IFRS.*

EXHIBIT 1-5 Countries in Which Nestlé Owns One or More Majority-Owned Companies[*]

Europe

Germany	14
Austria	4
Belgium	8
Bulgaria	1
Croatia	1
Denmark	3
Spain	10
Finland	3
France	18
Greece	2
Hungary	5
Italy	8
Lithuania	1
Malta	1
Norway	3
Netherlands	6
Poland	5
Portugal	7
Ireland	1
Czech Republic	3
Romania	1
U.K.	9
Russia	12
Serbia	1
Slovakia	1
Sweden	7
Switzerland	8
Turkey	3
Ukraine	3

Africa

South Africa	4
Cameroon	1
Cote d'Ivoire	1
Egypt	2
Gabon	1
Ghana	1
Guinea	1
Kenya	1
Mauritius	2
Morocco	1
Mozambique	1
Niger	1
Nigeria	1
Senegal	1
Tunisia	1
Zimbabwe	1

Americas

Argentina	3
Bolivia	1
Brazil	5
Canada	2
Chile	2
Colombia	5
Costa Rica	1
Cuba	2
Salvador	2
Ecuador	2
U.S.	9
Guatemala	1
Honduras	1
Jamaica	1
Mexico	8
Nicaragua	2
Panama	2
Paraguay	1
Peru	1
Puerto Rico	2
Dominican Republic	1
Trinidad	2
Uruguay	1
Venezuela	3

Asia

Saudi Arabia	3
Bangladesh	1
Cambodia	1
UAE	1
India	2
Indonesia	1
Israel	1
Japan	9
Jordan	1
Kuwait	1
Lebanon	3
Malaysia	7
Pakistan	1
Philippines	4
South Korea	4
China	21
Singapore	1
Sri Lanka	1
Syria	2
Thailand	9
Vietnam	2

Oceana

Australia	3
Fiji	1
New Zealand	1
New Guinea	1
French Polynesia	1
New Caledonia 1	1

[*]*This list is conservative in that it does not include affiliated companies for which proportionate consolidation is employed, associated companies for which the equity method is used, subholding financial and property companies, and technical assistance, research, and development companies.*

and number of foreign employees understate the extent of their foreign operations, for they do not reflect either company's joint ventures, strategic alliances, or other cooperative arrangements.

Operations conducted in foreign countries expose financial managers and accountants alike to an additional set of problems that they do not encounter when solely engaged in international trade. As one example, how should an MNC like Nestlé report the results of its operations, both domestic and international, to its Swiss investors? Each affiliate listed in Exhibit 1-5 must prepare its accounts according to the generally accepted accounting principles of the country in which it is domiciled for statutory and tax purposes. As Chapters 3 and 4 will attest, national financial reporting principles can vary significantly from country to country because they are shaped by different socio-economic environments. Environmental influences that impinge on accounting development are examined in Chapter 2. Nestlé's domestic shareholders are accustomed to seeing reports on the basis of Swiss reporting conventions. Examination of Nestlé's accounting policies on consolidation suggests that the company first restates all of its foreign accounts to the reporting framework of the parent company prior to consolidation. The report of Nestlé's auditors states that the consolidated financial statements comply with Swiss law and are in accordance with International Financial Reporting Standards (IFRS) issued by the International Accounting Standards Board (IASB) and with the interpretations issued by the International Financial Reporting Interpretations Committee (IFRIC). But in restating from one set of principles to another, does something get lost in the translation? To illustrate, Mexican companies adjust their financial statements for changing prices (a subject that we cover in Chapter 7) owing to serious bouts of inflation in the past. Their adjustment for changing prices utilizes a methodology that incorporates changes in specific prices or replacement costs. Nestlé, on the other hand, restates assets located in hyperinflationary countries for changes in the general purchasing power of the local currency prior to consolidation. Since general price changes seldom move in tandem with specific price changes, does Nestlé's methodology reduce the information content of the Mexican subsidiary's inflation-adjusted accounts? Yamaha, producer of world-renowned musical instruments and other lifestyle products, expresses this concern in the first footnote to its consolidated financial accounts:

> Yamaha Corporation (the Company) and its domestic subsidiaries maintain their accounting records and prepare their financial statements in accordance with accounting principles and practices generally accepted in Japan, and its foreign subsidiaries maintain their books of account in conformity with those of their countries of domicile. The Company and all consolidated subsidiaries are referred to as the "Group." The accompanying consolidated financial statements have been prepared from the financial statements filed with the Ministry of Finance as required by the Securities and Exchange Law of Japan. Accordingly, the accompanying consolidated financial statements may differ in certain significant respects from accounting principles and practices generally accepted in countries and jurisdictions other than Japan.

Then there is the choice of exchange rate to use in converting foreign accounts to a single reporting currency. As Chapter 6 explains, there are a variety of rates that an MNC can use. As foreign exchange rates are seldom constant, restating accounts using exchange rates that gyrate almost daily produces gains and losses that can have a significant effect on the reported profitability and perceived riskiness of multinational operations. As you might suspect, accounting treatments for these gains and losses are far from uniform internationally.

Domestic readers are not the only audience that reporting entities must address. What about statement readers who are domiciled abroad? Their information needs must be considered when a firm seeks access to foreign sources of capital and at reasonable costs. Market access and cost-of-capital considerations are, in turn, related to the nature and quality of a firm's external financial communications. Should a company send the same set of accounts that it prepares for its domestic readers to its foreign readers? Or should the reporting entity restate its reports to the language, currency, and/or accounting principles of the reader's country? This is not a trivial consideration, because foreign readers are generally not accustomed to providing money capital on the basis of an unfamiliar currency, language, and measurement framework. Evidence suggests that some institutional investors exhibit a home-country bias in their portfolio choices and tend to invest in nondomestic firms whose accounting and reporting methods conform to the GAAP framework that they are accustomed to.[6] Would you be interested in investing in the shares of a Chinese company if the numbers in the annual report you received were expressed in renmenbi, the text writen in Mandarin, and the accounting measurements based on Chinese GAAP?

Both AKZO and Nestlé, mentioned earlier, accommodate their foreign readers by restating their financial statements to International Financial Reporting Standards (IFRS). AKZO's initiative is in compliance with a European Union (EU) Directive that mandates all EU-listed companies to follow IASB standards. Nestlé's decision is voluntary, because its decision to conform to IFRS predates the EU requirement. Issues associated with management's use of special disclosures for nondomestic readers of financial statement is covered in Chapter 5.

In addition to external reporting, a firm's internal users of accounting information (i.e., financial managers and accountants) must also understand the effects of the environmental complexities of an MNE's accounting measurements. Discussion of these topics begins in Chapter 10. For example, understanding the effects of changes in foreign exchange and inflation rates is critical in such areas as the preparation of short- and long-term budgets for parent companies and their subsidiaries (or branches), measuring and evaluating the performance of local business units and managers, and making corporate-wide decisions on the allocation of investment capital and retained earnings, among others. To make matters more complex, foreign exchange and inflation rates do not work in tandem. The effect on accounting measurements of changes in foreign exchange rates and foreign inflation is so pervasive that domestic financial-control systems cannot serve managers well in the absence of appropriate environmental adaptation. Then there are issues of management control. While companies often expand operations abroad to take advantage of low-cost labor or untapped markets, productivity and decision-making styles can be so different that company

---

[6]See Mark T. Bradshaw, Brian J. Bushee, and Gregory S. Miller, "Accounting Choice, Home Bias and U.S. Investments in Non-U.S. Firms," *Journal of Accounting Research* 42, no. 5 (December 2004): 795–841.

expectations are often met with disappointment. Imposing culturally inappropriate control systems on foreign managers only magnifies such disappointments.[7] Managerial accounting from an international perspective includes possibly the most complex and detailed material in this book.

Chapter 12 addresses the important issues of international taxation and transfer pricing. Businesses that operate in more than one country need to carefully examine and manage their tax exposure. Knowledge of tax codes and currency values is only the beginning. It is very possible that steps taken by management to lower taxes in one place will raise taxes elsewhere, possibly by an amount greater than the original reduction. The effects of tax strategies on corporate budgeting and control procedures must be considered carefully. For example, a good strategy to reduce taxes might have unintended effects on the performance-evaluation system. Transfer prices—the prices charged to business units for internal transactions that cross national borders—frequently are set with tax minimization in mind. The basic idea is to concentrate expenses (as far as possible) in high-tax countries and to concentrate revenues in low-tax countries, thus maximizing overall profit. Governments are well aware of this strategy and have adopted complex rules to prevent abusive use of it. While the notion of the arm's-length price is widespread, its definition and the methods for calculating it have many variations. On top of all this, unexpected changes in exchange rates or inflation rates can wreak havoc on tax-planning strategy. Managerial accountants must often devise complex computer models to calculate the overall expected impact of a company's tax strategy.

FINANCIAL INNOVATION

Risk management has become a buzzword in corporate and financial circles. The reason is not hard to find. With continued deregulation of financial markets and capital controls (see Appendix 1-1), volatility in the price of commodities, foreign exchange, credit, and equities has become the order of the day. These price gyrations do not simply impact internal reporting processes; they also expose the firm to the risk of economic losses. This has spurred a host of managerial activities aimed at identifying a firm's exposure to this volatility, deciding which risks to hedge against, and evaluating the results of its risk-management strategy. The rapid growth of risk-management services suggests that management can enhance firm value by managing market risks. Investors and other corporate stakeholders expect financial managers to identify and actively manage such exposures. At the same time, advances in financial technology have made it possible to shift market risks to someone else's shoulders. However, the burden of assessing counterparty risk—the risk that this someone else will not default on the obligation—cannot be transferred and is now placed on the shoulders of a larger pool of market participants, many of whom may be located thousands of miles apart. The dependence on international reporting practices this creates and the resulting confusion caused by diversity in accounting for financial risk products is onerous. Those with risk-management skills are highly valued by the market. Hence we devote the entirety of Chapter 11 to the topic of financial risk management.

---

[7]Stephen B. Salter, Philip A. Lewis, and Luis Felipe Juarez Valdes, "Aqui No Se Habla Agencia: An Examination of the Impact of Adverse Selection and Framing in Decision-Making: A US/Mexico Comparison," *Journal of International Financial Management and Accounting* 15, no. 2 (June 2004): 93–117.

GLOBAL COMPETITION

Another factor contributing to the growing importance of international accounting is the phenomenon of global competition. Benchmarking, the act of comparing one's performance against an appropriate standard, is not new. What is new is that standards of comparison now transcend national boundaries. The relevant question today is not "How am I doing relative to my competitor who may be right across the street?" but "Am I adding more value to my customer base than my counterpart who may be located in another country?"

In benchmarking against international competitors, one must be careful to ensure that the comparisons are really comparable. For example, one frequently used performance metric is return on equity (ROE). In comparing the ROE of an American consumer durables manufacturer with Sweden's Electrolux, are you comparing apples to apples, or are you really comparing apples to oranges?

Exhibit 1-6 suggests that comparing a U.S. ROE against the Swedish ROE would be comparing apples to oranges. Exhibit 1-6 begins with the net income of Electrolux

---

EXHIBIT 1-6   Adjusting Electrolux's Consolidated Earnings and Equity from IFRS to U.S. GAAP

Consolidated net income

SEKm	2005	2004
Net income per IFRS	1,763	3,259
Adjustments before taxes:		
Development costs	–217	–367
Restructuring and other provisions	172	178
Pensions	–316	–312
Derivatives and hedging	–143	–158
Discounted provisions	–78	
Securities		2
Share-based compensation	71	–40
Taxes on these adjustments	266	226
Net income per U.S. GAAP	1,518	2,788

Equity

SEKm	2005	2004
Equity per IFRS	25,888	23,636
Minority interest	–1	–10
Acquisitions	–589	–546
Goodwill and intangibles	414	373
Development costs	–1,089	–819
Restructuring	340	167
Pensions	422	1,102
Discounted provisions	–78	
Derivatives and hedging		143
Securities	–20	3
Revaluation of assets	–134	–132
Share-based compensation	–36	–143
Taxes on these adjustments	–60	–207
Equity per U.S. GAAP	25,057	23,567

as reported in its recent consolidated financial statements. Since Sweden is a member of the European Community, Electrolux now presents its financial statements in conformity with international financial reporting standards (IFRS). This net income figure is followed by a series of adjustments that would be required to restate those numbers to a basis consistent with U.S. GAAP. A comparable series of adjustments is provided for stockholders' equity. A comparison of the unadjusted ROE 2005 with the adjusted ROE 2005 yields return statistics of 7.1 percent versus 6.2 percent. While adjusting from IFRS to U.S. GAAP did not have a significant effect on equity, it did have a 16.1 percent effect on reported earnings. Statement readers who are not aware of national measurement differences and required accounting adjustment algorithms are obviously at a disadvantage. These and related statement-analysis considerations are the subject of Chapter 9.

CROSS-BORDER MERGERS AND ACQUISITIONS

As the global trend toward industrial consolidation continues, news about international mergers and acquisitions is practically a daily occurrence. While mergers are normally rationalized in terms of operating synergies or economies of scale, accounting plays a crucial role in these mega-consolidations because accounting numbers are fundamental in the corporate valuation process. Differences in national measurement rules can complicate the corporate valuation process (see Chapter 9).

For example, corporate valuations are often based on price-based multiples, such as the price-to-earnings (P/E) ratio. The approach here is to derive an average P/E multiple for comparable firms in the industry and apply this multiple to the reported earnings of the firm being valued to arrive at a reasonable offering price. A major concern of the acquiring firm when bidding for a foreign acquisition target is to determine the extent to which the E in the P/E metric is a true reflection of the attribute being measured, as opposed to the result of an accounting measurement difference!

Differences in accounting measurement rules could also create an unlevel playing field in the market for corporate control. Thus, if Company A in Country A is allowed to take purchased goodwill directly to reserves, while Company B in Country B must amortize purchased goodwill to earnings, Company A may very well enjoy a bidding advantage over B when seeking to acquire a common target company. Company A could offer a higher purchase price, knowing that its earnings will not be penalized by the hit to earnings of any excessive premiums paid.

INTERNATIONALIZATION OF CAPITAL MARKETS

The factor that has perhaps contributed most to the growing interest in international accounting among corporate executives, investors, market regulators, accounting standard setters and business educators alike is the internationalization of the world's capital markets. Statistics indicate that the dollar volume of cross-border equity flows has increased more than twenty-fold since 1990, while the value of international securities offerings has more than quadrupled during the same time period, exceeding $1.5 trillion today. International offerings in bonds, syndicated loans, and other debt instruments have also grown dramatically since the 1990s. Investment banks Russel,

Greenwich Associates, Morgan Stanley, Merrill Lynch, and Grail Partners estimate that global retail hedge fund investments will grow to $2.5 trillion by 2010, representing a 14.3 percent compounded annual growth rate since 2005.

As financial markets become more integrated, we are also witnessing an increase in the number of companies listed on the world's stock exchanges. Exhibit 1-7 discloses the number of domestic and foreign companies listed on the world's major exchanges. Over the last ten years, global market capitalization more than doubled to well over $40 trillion. The World Federation of Exchanges reports that while the number of domestic companies with shares listed increased in some markets and decreased in others during the early part of this decade, the average sizes and annual

EXHIBIT 1-7   Number of Listed Companies 2005

Exchange	Total	Domestic Companies	Foreign Companies
Americas			
American SE	595	495	100
Bermuda SE	56	19	37
Buenos Aires SE	104	100	4
Colombia SE	98	98	0
Lima SE	224	193	31
Mexican SE	326	150	176
NASDAQ	3,164	2,832	332
NYSE	2,270	1,818	452
Santiago SE	246	245	1
São Paulo SE	381	379	2
TSX Group	3,758	3,719	39
Asia-Pacific			
Australian SE	1,714	1,643	71
Bombay SE	4,763	4,763	0
Bursa Malaysia	1,019	1,015	4
Colombo SE	239	239	0
HK Exchanges	1,135	1,126	9
Jakarta SE	336	336	0
Korea Exchange	1,616	1,616	0
NSE India	1,034	1,034	0
NZ Exchange	185	153	32
Osaka SE	1,064	1,063	1
Philippine SE	237	235	2
Shanghai SE	833	833	0
Shenzhen SE	544	544	0
Singapore Exchange	686	564	122
Taiwan SE	696	691	5
Thailand SE	504	504	0
Tokyo SE	2,351	2,323	28
Europe- Africa- Middle East			
Athens Exchange	304	302	2
Borsa Italiana	282	275	7
Budapest SE	44	44	0
Cairo SE	744	744	0
Cyprus	119	119	0

(continued)

EXHIBIT I-7   Number of Listed Companies 2005 *(Continued)*

Exchange	Total	Domestic Companies	Foreign Companies
Deutsche Börsee	764	648	116
Euronext	1,259	966	293
Irish SE	66	53	13
Istanbul SE	304	304	0
JSE	373	348	25
Ljubljana SE	116	116	0
London SE	3,079	2,757	334
Luxembourg SE	245	39	206
Malta SE	13	13	0
Mauritius SE	30	30	0
OMX	678	656	22
Oslo Bors	219	191	28
Swiss Exchange	400	284	116
Tehran SE	408	408	0
Tel Aviv SE	584	NA	NA
Warsaw SE	241	234	7
Wiener Börse	111	92	19

trading volumes of listed companies have grown substantially, in part due to mergers and acquisitions, which have also resulted in delistings of some of the entities involved.

Some of the most impressive growth is taking place in emerging markets. Exhibit 1-8 details stock market index performance for the year ended 2005 in local currency by international time zones. As can be seen, exchanges located in emerging economies generally outperformed those in the more industrialized countries. As a result, the traditional preference for investing in one's back yard is beginning to give way to investors exploiting the most attractive investment opportunities wherever they may be located.

The three largest equity market regions are the Americas, Asia-Pacific, and Europe, including Africa and the Middle East.[8] Since the tragic events of 9/11, markets

EXHIBIT I-8   Top Five Performing Broad Stock Market Indexes in Local Currency Terms by International Time Zones

Americas	% Change 2005/2004	Asia-Pacific	% Change 2005/2004	Europe/Africa Middle East	% Change 2005/2004
1. Colombia	118.90%	1. Korea	54.00%	1. Cairo & Alexandria	146.30%
2. Mexican	37.80%	2. Osaka	50.60%	2. Cyprus	68.40%
3. Lima	29.40%	3. Tokyo	43.50%	3. Malta	63.40%
4. São Paulo	27.70%	4. Bombay	42.30%	4. Istanbul	59.30%
5. American	22.60%	5. NSE India	36.30%	5. JSE	43.00%

[8]Each equity market region comprises equity markets in multiple countries, and some of these national equity markets comprise several stock exchanges as well as off-exchange trading systems. (For example, four stock exchanges operate in Spain, and eight stock exchanges operate in the United States.) A stock exchange is an entity that plays a central role in the regulation of trading markets and develops, operates, and manages those markets.

in all three regions have grown significantly. In terms of domestic equity market capitalization, the Americas experienced an annual compounded growth rate of 13 percent, rising from $11,931 trillion in 2002 to 19,458 trillion in 2005; Europe, 17.2 percent, rising from $6,465 to $12,206 trillion; and Asia-Pacific a whopping 20 percent, rising from $4,437 trillion to $9,310 trillion.

Americas

The U.S. economy and its stock market had unprecedented growth during the 1990s. Today the NYSE and NASDAQ dominate other stock exchanges worldwide in terms of market capitalization, value of trading in domestic shares, value of trading in foreign shares (except for the London Stock Exchange [LSE]), number of domestic listed companies, and number of foreign listed companies. The relative importance of the Americas in the global equity market has also increased. Market capitalization in the Americas as a percentage of the global total stood at 47.5 percent at the start of 2006. But even here, the forces of global competition are making themselves felt. The Committee on Capital Market Regulation, whose members are appointed by the SEC in consultation with the Federal Reserve Board of Governors and the U.S. Treasury, has concluded that the United States could lose its dominance in the global capital markets unless it streamlines its regulatory provisions, which the market feels are onerous. This issue is discussed further in Chapter 8 in conjunction with the topic of corporate governance and the U.S. Sarbanes-Oxley Act.

Western Europe

Europe is the second-largest equity market region in the world in terms of market capitalization and trading volume. Economic expansion significantly contributed to the rapid growth in European equity markets during the second half of the 1990s. A related factor in continental Europe has been a gradual shift to an equity orientation that long has characterized the London and North American equity markets.[9] Privatizations of large government entities have made European equity markets more prominent and have attracted noninstitutional investors, who until recently were not active in continental Europe. Finally, confidence in European markets has grown with the success of the European Monetary Union (EMU).

European equity markets will continue to grow. Pension reforms, for one, are creating new demand for investment opportunities.[10] Also, more and more foreign investors are entering European equity markets. Cross-border equity flows are

---

[9]Developed countries around the world can be divided roughly into those having a common law (English) orientation and those having a code law (continental Europe) orientation (see Chapter 2). Common law countries include the United Kingdom, Canada, the United States, and Australia. In these countries, equity investors are widely dispersed and are the most important suppliers of capital. As a result, capital markets in many common law countries have evolved credible and open disclosure and accounting systems, and relatively stringent market regulation. In code law countries such as France, Germany, and Japan, banks provide most of the financing, and ownership tends to be concentrated among small groups of insiders. Demand for detailed public disclosure is generally lower in these countries than in common law countries, but is increasing.

[10]With aging populations causing the numbers of pensioners to increase, a major initiative across much of Europe has been to move toward the private funding of pensions. The goal is to relieve the strain on "pay-as-you-go" state pension schemes. The growing numbers of private pension funds are allocating more of their assets to equities to increase returns. Also, some countries are liberalizing restrictions on pension fund investment.

increasing as a percentage of cross-border bond flows, in part because equity has proved to be a profitable investment. In addition, the advent of the euro has prompted a rush of cross-border mergers that is expected to continue.

Intense rivalry among European stock exchanges has contributed to the development of an equity culture. During the 1990s, continental European markets became more investor oriented to increase their credibility and attract new listings. External investors, in particular foreign investors and institutional investors, are demanding expanded disclosure and improved corporate governance. In addition, equity market development has become increasingly important to national governments and regulators, who also compete for recognition and prestige. Many European securities regulators and stock exchanges have implemented more stringent market rules and are strengthening their enforcement efforts.

Asia

Many experts are predicting that Asia will become the second-most-important equity market region. The People's Republic of China (China) has emerged as a major global economy, and the "Asian Tiger" nations continue to experience phenomenal growth and development.

Critics argue that Asian accounting measurement, disclosure, and auditing standards are weak, and so too the monitoring and enforcement of these standards.[11] Some Asian governments periodically announce that they will intervene in equity markets to boost share prices, and market manipulation is not uncommon.[12]

However, the prospects for continued growth in Asian equity markets are strong. Market capitalization as a percentage of gross domestic product (GDP) is lower in Asia than in the United States and several major European markets. This suggests, however, that equity markets can play a much larger role in many Asian economies. Also, Asian governments and stock exchanges appear eager to improve market quality and credibility to attract investors.[13] As mentioned earlier, Asian-Pacific markets (e.g., China, India, Korea, Taiwan, Hong Kong) have grown rapidly, and are experiencing heavy trading volume relative to market capitalization.

Cross-Border Equity Listing and Issuance

The current wave of interest in cross-border listings on major world exchanges is not a chance phenomenon. Evidence suggests that issuers seek cross-border listings to broaden their shareholder base, promote awareness in their products, and/or build public awareness of the company, especially in countries where the company has significant operations and/or major customers.

National regulators and stock exchanges compete fiercely for foreign listings and trade volume, both of which are necessary for any stock exchange that seeks to

---

[11]These attributes are neither good nor bad. Each market develops in response to economic conditions, the nature of its investors, its sources of financing, and other factors. In Japan, for example, banks have long been the primary sources of finance. Japanese banks have full access to inside information about Japanese companies, and so there is less demand for credible external financial reporting.

[12]For example, Taiwan announced in November 2000 that it would institute emergency action to support share prices after a recent, dramatic fall.

[13]The Singapore Exchange, for example, has moved aggressively to position itself as the premier financial exchange in Asia outside of Japan. It recently implemented new listing rules and more stringent disclosure requirements to attract new domestic and foreign listings.

become or remain a global leader. In response, organized exchanges and market regulators have worked to make access faster and less costly for foreign issuers and at the same time increase their markets' credibility. As capital markets become more specialized, they can each can offer unique benefits to foreign issuers.

Many companies have difficulty deciding where to raise capital or list their shares. Knowledge of many equity markets with different laws, regulations, and institutional features is now required. Also required is an understanding of how issuer and stock exchange characteristics interact. The issuer's home country, industry, and offering size are just some of the factors to be considered.[14] In addition, the costs and benefits of different market combinations need to be understood. One entrepreneur planning to raise capital said, "I spoke to three investment banks about it, and I had three different answers about which would be the right market for me." Exhibit 1-9 presents a detailed list of the factors companies consider in choosing a foreign capital market.[15]

The pace of change in the world's capital markets show no signs of slowing. One example is the growing importance of stock exchange alliances and consolidation. In a strategic move, the New York Stock Exchange recently acquired Euronext, the pan-European stock exchange created by a merger of the Amsterdam, Brussels, Lisbon, and Paris exchanges. This business combination creates the world's first transatlantic stock market. Some observers predict that financial markets and trading will be dominated by two or three global exchange groups operating across continents within the not-too-distant future.[16] This will increase significantly the exposure of international investors to international companies. Similarly, the emergence of newer markets, such as London's Alternative Investment Market (AIM), France's Alternext, and Germany's Entry Standard, expands the pool of companies that can now break the bonds of local debt financing. All of these developments present a highly complex setting for financial-reporting regulation.

WHERE ARE WE?

The rapid growth of global capital markets and cross-border investment activity means that the international dimensions of accounting are more important than ever for professionals who have to deal with these areas in one way or another. Accounting plays a critical role in the efficient functioning of capital markets. Lenders, investors, financial analysts,

---

[14]Home country is relevant because companies can raise capital more easily in foreign countries that have legal and regulatory environments similar to their own. For example, an Australian company can probably access the U.K. equity market more easily than the French equity market. Industry is important because, other things equal, issuers seek to raise capital in markets where other companies in the same industry are listed in order to improve the chances for adequate attention by financial analysts. For example, the SWX Swiss Exchange's New Market is attractive to biotechnology companies in part because Novartis and Roche (two of the world's largest pharmaceutical companies) are listed on the SWX Swiss Exchange and have attracted many pharmaceutical/biotech analysts to Zurich. Offering size is important because only relatively large offerings attract sufficient attention in the United States. Much smaller IPOs are common in Europe's new markets.

[15]Appendix 1-2 presents Web site addresses for stock exchanges in more than 50 countries. Many stock exchange Web sites include information on unique stock exchange features that may attract foreign companies considering listing or raising capital in those markets.

[16]Alistair McDonald, "Euronext Head Sees Markets Dominated by Global Exchanges," *WSJ Online,* January 22, 2007.

EXHIBIT 1-9   Factors Relevant in Choosing an Overseas Market

1. What is the extent of interest in a company shown by financial analysts and investors who normally participate in a market?

2. What is the level of trading activity on the exchange? Higher trading volume means more potential buyers of a company's securities.

3. How easy is it to raise capital? Some jurisdictions have complex listing or ongoing reporting requirements that may be difficult or impossible for a smaller company to meet.

4. What is the availability of capital in a market?

5. What is the reputation of the exchange? A growing international company may want the increased credibility and recognition that come with listing on a preeminent market such as the New York Stock Exchange.

6. To what extent does the company desire to raise its profile and establish its brand identity in a particular market? A stock exchange listing can benefit companies that operate or plan to operate in an overseas country.

7. To what extent are the market's regulatory environment and language similar to those in the company's home market? For example, a company from an English-speaking country with a common law (British-American) legal and regulatory system, such as Australia, might find it easier to list in the United Kingdom than in continental Europe.

8. To what extent do institutional investors face statutory or self-imposed restrictions on the proportion of their investment portfolio that they can hold in securities of foreign companies? Sometimes such restrictions force a large international company to list on many stock exchanges to have access to sufficient institutional capital. These restrictions are difficult to overcome in some jurisdictions.

9. What are the nature and activities of investors in the market? For example, large pension funds in the Netherlands, Switzerland, and the United Kingdom invest heavily in equities of both domestic and foreign companies.

10. What is the likelihood that the company will be required to have locally listed shares to carry out a merger or acquisition in a particular country?

11. Will there be a need for locally listed shares to be used in employee stock option plans?

---

regulators, and stock exchanges require information about the financial performance, position, and future prospects of companies seeking financing. In turn, the needs of capital market participants have strongly shaped the development of accounting practice, as discussed in Chapter 2. Demands of market participants strongly influence companies' accounting and disclosure choices and national and international efforts to harmonize accounting measurement, disclosure, and auditing practices around the world.

How, for example, does a British or American investor make sense of Japanese accounts or Swiss accounts where measurement and transparency rules are very different from what they are accustomed to? Should they attempt to restate Japanese or Swiss accounts to a more familiar set of reporting norms, such as U.S., UK, or IASB measurement rules, prior to analysis? Or should they put themselves in the shoes of a Japanese or Swiss shareholder and conduct their analysis from a local perspective? These and other, related issues are covered in Chapter 9.

On the other side of the coin, a major factor motivating many corporations to raise monies abroad is to increase their access to funds and lower their capital costs. The challenge here is to ensure that the foreign reader receives the same intended message as the domestic reader. This challenge is significant in a world where firms compete for funds, an issue explored in Chapter 5.

LEARNING OBJECTIVES

Having set the stage for your study of international accounting, we identify below the essential ideas that you should get out of each chapter. We invite you to revisit this section before you begin reading each chapter and also upon completion of each chapter to be sure that you understand the essential ideas it conveyed. This text is intended to sensitize you to the important concepts and issues in the field of international accounting and reporting, and, in so doing, to enable you to ask the right questions as a reader of international financial statements, whether you opt for a career in the corporate, legal, financial services, or not-for-profit world.

After studying Chapter 1, you should be able to:

1. Explain how international accounting is different from domestic accounting.
2. Define the term *accounting diversity*.
3. Identify the factors that are contributing to the internationalization of accounting.
4. Understand how foreign direct-investment activities differ from international trade and the implications of this difference for accounting.
5. Appreciate, in general terms, the historical development of international accounting.
6. Understand why the study of international accounting is so important.
7. Identify several internal and external reporting issues that arise when business and investments transcend national borders.
8. Explain what is meant by *global capital markets* and what this development means for capital market participants.

After studying Chapter 2, you should be able to:

1. Identify and understand the importance of the eight factors that have a significant influence on accounting development.
2. Understand the four approaches to accounting development found in market-oriented Western economies and identify countries in which each approach is prevalent.
3. Have a basic working knowledge of accounting classifications and how they compare with one another.
4. Explain the difference between the "fair presentation" and "legal compliance" orientations of accounting and identify nations in which each is prevalent.
5. Explain why distinctions of accounting at the national level are becoming blurred.

After studying Chapter 3, you should be able to:

1. Understand how financial reporting is regulated and enforced in five European countries: France, Germany, the Czech Republic, the Netherlands, and the United Kingdom.
2. Describe the key similarities and differences among the accounting systems of these five countries.
3. Identify the use of International Financial Reporting Standards at the levels of the individual company and the consolidated financial statements in these five countries.
4. Describe the audit-oversight mechanisms in these five countries.

After studying Chapter 4, you should be able to:

1. Understand how financial reporting is regulated and enforced in five countries of the Americas and Asia: the United States, Mexico, Japan, China, and India.
2. Describe the key similarities and differences among the accounting systems of these five countries.
3. Describe the auditor-oversight mechanisms in these five countries.
4. Explain the difference between principles-based and rules-based accounting standards.

After studying Chapter 5, you should be able to:

1. Distinguish voluntary and mandatory disclosure and the applicable regulatory measures.
2. Identify the broad objectives for accounting disclosure systems in investor-oriented equity markets.
3. Discuss "triple bottom line" reporting and why it is a growing tendency among large multinational corporations.
4. Have a basic understanding of the following selected corporate financial-disclosure practices: (a) disclosures of forward-looking information, (b) segment disclosures, (c) social responsibility reporting, (d) special disclosures for nondomestic financial statement users, and (e) corporate governance disclosures.

After studying Chapter 6, you should be able to:

1. Describe the nature of foreign currency transactions done in the spot, forward, and swap markets.
2. Understand the foreign currency translation terms set forth in Exhibit 6-1.
3. Explain the difference between a translation gain or loss and a transaction gain or loss.
4. Understand alternative foreign currency translation methods and their rationales.
5. Evaluate which of the available foreign currency translation methods are best under which specific business and currency market conditions.
6. Compare and contrast the financial statement effects of the temporal versus the current rate method of foreign currency translation.
7. Understand the relationship between foreign currency translation and inflation.
8. Appreciate how foreign currency translation is handled outside the United States.

After studying Chapter 7, you should be able to:

1. Understand why financial statements may be misleading during periods of changing prices.
2. Define the inflation accounting terms listed in Exhibit 7-1.
3. Understand the effect of general price-level adjustments on financial statement amounts.
4. Describe how the current cost-accounting framework differs from conventional accounting.
5. Appreciate how and why adjustments for changing prices may vary from country to country.
6. Have a basic understanding of the IASB's pronouncement on changing prices in "hyperinflationary economies."

7. Discuss whether constant dollars or current costs better measure the effects of changing prices.
8. Understand how changing prices and foreign exchange rates are related and their financial statement effects.

After studying Chapter 8, you should be able to:

1. Define and understand the distinction between "harmonization" and "convergence" as they apply to accounting standards.
2. State the pros and cons of adopting international accounting standards.
3. Understand what is meant by "reconciliation" and "mutual recognition" of different sets of accounting standards.
4. Identify the six organizations that have leading roles in setting international accounting standards and promoting international accounting convergence.
5. Describe the structure of the International Accounting Standards Board and how it sets International Financial Reporting Standards.
6. Understand the major provisions of the U.S. Sarbanes-Oxley Act and why similar legislation is being enacted in other countries.

After studying Chapter 9, you should be able to:

1. Understand the special difficulties involved in undertaking international business strategy analysis.
2. Identify basic approaches to information gathering.
3. Describe the steps involved in conducting an accounting analysis.
4. Appreciate the impact on accounting analysis of (a) cross-country variations in accounting measurement, disclosure, and auditing quality (both external and internal) and (b) the difficulty of obtaining necessary information.
5. Understand the several coping mechanisms available to deal with cross-country accounting measurement differences.
6. Explain the specific difficulties and pitfalls involved in doing an international prospective analysis.
7. Undertake a more intelligent approach to international financial ratio analysis.
8. Use the World Wide Web to obtain information for company research.

After studying Chapter 10, you should be able to:

1. Identify four critical dimensions of business modeling.
2. Understand the difference between standard and Kaizen costing concepts.
3. Measure the expected returns of a foreign investment.
4. Calculate (in general fashion) a firm's cost of capital in a multinational framework.
5. Understand the basic issues and complexities involved in designing multinational information and financial control systems.
6. Perform an exchange rate variance analysis.
7. State the unique difficulties involved in designing and implementing performance evaluation systems in multinational companies.
8. Deal with the effects of inflation and exchange rate fluctuation on performance measurement of multinational companies.

After studying Chapter 11, you should be able to:

1. Explain what Enterprise Risk Management (ERM) entails.
2. Define market risk and provide an example of this risk with a foreign exchange example.
3. State four tasks involved in managing foreign exchange risk.
4. Define and calculate translation exposure.
5. Define and calculate transaction exposure.
6. Understand the difference between accounting exposure and economic exposure.
7. Explain what a financial derivative is and the accounting issues associated with it.
8. Understand the types of foreign currency hedges recognized by IAS 39 and FAS 133 and their accounting treatments.

After studying Chapter 12, you should be able to:

1. Identify the major types of tax systems that exist around the world.
2. Understand what determines a multinational entity's effective tax burden.
3. Understand concepts relating to the taxation of foreign source income and the rationale behind the foreign tax credit.
4. Identify the major variables that complicate international transfer pricing.
5. Explain the meaning of *arm's-length price* and the transfer pricing methods designed to achieve it.
6. Explain what an advance pricing arrangement is.

APPENDICES

APPENDIX 1-1

EXHIBIT 1-10 Changes in Financial Sector Policy in 34 Nations, 1973–1996

Country	Privatization	International Capital Flows
Industrialized Countries		
United States	None	Limited controls imposed in the 1960s, abolished in 1974
Canada	None	None
Japan	Government controls roughly 15% of financial assets through the postal savings system.	Controls on capital inflows eased after 1979. Controls on capital outflows eased in the mid-1980s. Foreign exchange restrictions eased in 1980. Remaining restrictions on cross-border transactions removed in 1995.
United Kingdom	None	All remaining controls on foreign exchange purchase eliminated in 1979.
France	Some banks nationalized since 1945. All larger banks nationalized in 1982. Several French banks privatized in 1987 and 1993, including Banque Nationale de Paris.	Capital flows in and out of the country largely liberalized during 1986–1988. Liberalization was completed in 1990.
Germany	None	Most capital controls dismantled in 1973.
Italy	Credito Italiano and some other public banks privatized in 1993–1994.	Foreign exchange and capital controls eliminated by May 1990.
Australia	Some state-owned banks privatized in the 1990s. Commonwealth Bank of Australia privatized in 1997.	Capital and exchange controls tightened in late 1970s after the move to indirect monetary policy increased capital inflows. Capital account liberalized in 1984.
New Zealand	Bank of New Zealand (one of the four largest banks) privatized in the early 1990s. Development Finance Corporation closed. Government sold all remaining shares in state-owned banks by 1992.	All controls on inward and outward foreign exchange transactions removed in 1984. Controls on outward investment lifted in 1985. Restrictions on foreign-owned companies' access to domestic financial markets removed in late 1984. Controls on foreign direct and portfolio investment and repatriation of profits eased in 1985.
East Asia		
Hong Kong	None	None
Indonesia	Stock exchange privatized in 1990.	Most transactions on the capital account liberalized in 1971. Some restrictions on inflows remain. The

(continued)

EXHIBIT 1-10   Changes in Financial Sector Policy in 34 Nations, 1973–1996 (Continued)

Country	Privatization	International Capital Flows
		regulation requiring exporters to sell their foreign-exchange holdings to banks abolished in 1982. Foreign direct investment regulations eased further in 1992.
Korea	Government divested its shares in commercial banks in the early 1980s. State-owned banks' share of total assets 13% in 1994.	Controls on foreign borrowing under US$200,000 with maturities of less than 3 years eased in 1979. Restriction on foreign borrowing under US$1 million eased in 1982. Controls on outward and inward foreign investment gradually eased since 1985. Significant restrictions on inward investment in place until 1998.
Malaysia	Share of state-owned banks in total assets of the financial sector 8% in 1994 (BIS estimate). Government is the majority shareholder in the country's largest bank and wholly owns the second largest bank.	Capital account mostly liberalized in the 1970s. Inward foreign direct and portfolio investment deregulated further in the mid-1980s. Controls on short-term and portfolio inflows temporarily reimposed in 1994.
Philippines	Government took over some failed financial institutions during the early 1980s. Government's share of total bank assets was lowered to 22% by 1996. Government reduced its stake in PNB to 47% in December 1995.	Foreign exchange and investment channeled through government in the 1970s. Interbank foreign exchange trading limited to 30 minutes per day after 1983. Off-floor trading introduced in 1992. Restrictions on all current and most capital transactions eliminated over 1992–1995.
Singapore	None	Government freed exchange and capital controls by 1978. (Exception: Offshore banks may not transact in Singapore dollars.)
Taiwan	Privatization effort blocked by controlling interests in 1989.	Foreign-exchange controls removed in 1987. Inward and outward capital flows limited to US$5 million per person per year.
Thailand	Share of state-owned banks in total assets 8% in 1994 (BIS estimate).	Restrictions on inward long-term investment eased in the mid-1980s. Controls on short-term flows and outward investment eased in the 1990s. The reserve requirement on short-term foreign borrowing is 7%. Currency controls introduced in May and June 1997 to deter currency speculators. Limits on foreign ownership of domestic financial institutions relaxed in October 1997.
Latin America Argentina	Fifteen percent of the loan market privatized since 1992. Government	Multiple exchange rate system unified between 1976 and 1978.

(continued)

EXHIBIT 1-10   Changes in Financial Sector Policy in 34 Nations, 1973–1996 *(Continued)*

Country	Privatization	International Capital Flows
	still owns the largest commercial bank, Banco de la Nación Argentina.	Foreign loans at market exchange rates permitted in 1978. Controls on inward and outward capital flows loosened in 1977. Liberalization measures reversed in 1982. Capital and exchange controls eliminated in 1991.
Brazil	None	System of comprehensive foreign exchange controls abolished in 1984. Most capital outflows restricted in the 1980s. Controls on capital inflows strengthened and controls on outflows loosened in the 1990s.
Chile	Nineteen domestic commercial. banks privatized in 1974. Banks nationalized during the 1982 crisis were reprivatized in the mid-1980s	Capital controls gradually eased since 1979. Controls reimposed in 1982 and eased again in mid-1980s. Foreign direct and portfolio investment subject to a 1-year minimum holding period. Foreign loans subject to a 30% reserve requirement.
Colombia	Two large banks and a large finance company nationalized in 1982. Government intervened in over 20 financial institutions between 1982 and 1986. 30% of loan market privatized by 1995.	Controls on capital inflows relaxed in 1991. Exchange controls also reduced. Large capital inflows in the early 1990s led to the reimposition of reserve requirements on foreign loans in 1993.
Mexico	Authorities nationalized 18 commercial banks in 1982. Nationalized banks privatized in 1991.	Government given discretion over foreign direct investment in 1972. Ambiguous restrictions on foreign direct investment rationalized in 1989. Portfolio flows decontrolled further in 1989.
Peru	All five public development banks closed in early 1990s. All seven public commercial banks liquidated or divested over 1991–1995.	Capital controls removed in December 1990.
Venezuela	Four small public commercial banks liquidated or privatized in 1989. Public sector banks' share of total deposits 9% in 1993. Share increased to 29% after the nationalization of several banks during 1994–1996.	Foreign direct investment regime largely liberalized over 1989–1990. Exchange controls on all current and capital transactions imposed in 1994. System of comprehensive foreign exchange controls abandoned in April 1996.
Middle East and Africa		
Egypt	Some privatization of smaller state banks. The four largest public banks not slated for privatization as of 2004.	Foreign exchange system decontrolled and unified in 1991. Some controls on inward portfolio and direct investment lifted in 1990s.
Israel	Government nationalized leading banks in 1983. Union Bank (part of	Capital controls eliminated in 1977 and reimposed in 1979. After 1987,

(continued)

EXHIBIT 1-10   Changes in Financial Sector Policy in 34 Nations, 1973–1996 *(Continued)*

Country	Privatization	International Capital Flows
	Bank Leumi) privatized in 1990s. 43% of Bank Hapoalim sold to Israeli-American consortium in 1997.	restrictions on capital inflows gradually eliminated and restrictions on capital outflows gradually eased.
Morocco	The Casablanca stock market is state owned. One state-owned bank was privatized in 1995.	Current account convertibility achieved in the 1990s. Surrender requirements or export revenue and outward investment restrictions relaxed in the early 1990s. Restrictions on inward foreign direct and portfolio investment and external borrowing by residents eased after 1993.
South Africa	None	Capital controls tightened in 1985. Exchange controls on nonresidents eliminated in 1995. Controls on residents relaxed in 1995.
Turkey	State-owned banks' share in total assets of the bank system remained constant over 1980–1990, at approximately 52%.	Capital flows liberalized in 1989.
South Asia		
Bangladesh	Commercial banks nationalized in the 1970s. Two state-owned banks sold back to original owners in early 1980s. (These banks remain uncompetitive.)	Foreign exchange markets unified in 1991–1992. Restrictions on current transactions eliminated in 1994. Controls on capital inflows eased after 1991.
India	All large banks nationalized in 1969. Government divested part of its equity position in some public banks in the 1990s.	Regulations on portfolio and direct investment eased since 1991. The exchange rate was unified in 1993–1994. Current account convertibility achieved in 1994.
Nepal	Two large public-sector banks hold over half of total bank deposits. Government share of Nepal Bank Limited reduced to 41%.	Dual exchange rate system introduced in 1992. Current account became fully convertible in 1994. Some capital transactions liberalized in the 1990s, but restrictions remain.
Pakistan	Muslim Commercial Bank privatized in 1991. Allied Bank privatized in stages between 1991 and 1993. First Women Bank privatized in 1997.	Rupee convertible for current transactions since July 1994. Capital controls eased in the 1990s.
Sri Lanka	Two development finance banks privatized in 1990s.	Exchange rate unified in 1978. Rupee made convertible for current transactions in 1994. Capital controls on inflows eased in 1978. Foreign portfolio investment restrictions eased further in 1991. Restrictions on capital outflows remain.

SOURCE: John Williamson and Molly Mahar, *A Survey of Financial Liberalization* (Princeton, NJ: Princeton University International Finance Section, Essays in International Finance #211).

APPENDIX I-2

Stock Exchange Web Sites

Country	Stock Exchange	Web Site
Argentina	Buenos Aires	www.bcba.sba.com.ar
Australia	Australia	www.asx.com.au
Austria	Vienna	www.wbag.at
Azerbaijan	Baku	www.az/bicex
Belgium	Euronext—Belgium	www.euronext.com
		www.stockexchange.be/enindex.htm
Bermuda	Bermuda	www.bsx.com
Brazil	Rio de Janeiro	www.bvrj.com.br (Portuguese only)
Brazil	São Paulo	www.bovespa.com.br (Portuguese only)
Canada	Montréal	www.me.org
Canada	Toronto	www.tse.com
Canada	Canadian Venture	www.cdnx.ca
Chile	Santiago	www.bolsadesantiago.com
China	Schenzhen	sse.org.cn
Colombia	Bogotá	www.bolsabogata.com.co/ (Spanish only)
Colombia	Medellín	www.bolsamed.com.co (Spanish only)
Croatia	Zagreb	www.zse.hr
Czech Republic	Prague	www.pse.cz
Denmark	Copenhagen	www.xcse.dk
Finland	Helsinki	www.hex.fi
France	Paris	www.euronext.com
		www.bourse-de-paris.fr/defaultgb.htm
Germany	Deutsche Böerse	deutsche-boerse.com/
Greece	Athens	www.ase.gr
Hong Kong	Hong Kong	www.hkex.com.hk
India	National Stock Exchange	www.nseindia.com
India	Surabaya	www.bes.co.id
Indonesia	Jakarta	www.jsx.co.id
Iran	Tehran	www.tse.or.ir
Israel	Tel-Aviv	hebrew.tase.co.il/www/intro.asp
Italy	Italy	www.borsaitalia.it
Japan	Osaka	www.ose.or.jp
Japan	Tokyo	www.tse.or.jp
Jordan	Amman	www.access2arabia.com/AFM/
Luxembourg	Luxembourg	www.bourse.lu
Macedonia	Macedonian	www.mse.org.mk
Malaysia	Kuala Lumpur	www.klse.com.my
Mexico	Mexico	www.bmv.com.mx
Netherlands	Euronext—Netherlands	www.euronext.com
		www.aex.nl/aex.asp?taal=en
New Zealand	New Zealand	www.nzse.co.nz
Norway	Oslo	www.ose.no

(continued)

Country	Stock Exchange	Web Site
Pakistan	Lahore	www.lse.brain.net.pk
Peru	Lima	www.bvl.com.pe
Philippines	Philippines	www.pse.org.ph
Poland	Warsaw	www.gpw.com.pl
Portugal	Lisbon	www.bvl.pt
Russia	Siberian	www.sse.nsk.su (Russian only)
Singapore	Singapore	www.ses.com.sg
Slovakia	Bratislava	www.bsse.sk
Slovenia	Ljubljana	www.ljse.si
South Africa	Johannesburg	www.jse.co.za
South Korea	Korea	www.kse.or.kr
Spain	Barcelona	www.borsabcn.es
Spain	Bilbao	www.bolsabilbao.es
Spain	Madrid	www.bolsamadrid.es
Sweden	Stockholm	www.xsse.se
Switzerland	Swiss	www.swx.ch
Taiwan	Taiwan	www.tse.com.tw
Thailand	Thailand	www.set.or.th
Turkey	Istanbul	www.ise.org
United Kingdom	London	www.londonstockexchange.com
United States	American (Amex)	www.amex.com
United States	Chicago	www.chicagostockex.com
United States	Nasdaq	www.nasdaq.com
		www.nasdaqnews.com
		www.nasdr.com
		www.nasdaqtrader.com
United States	New York	www.nyse.com

Note: All Web site addresses here begin with the prefix http://

APPENDIX 1-3

Financial Statements and Selected Notes from the Annual Report of INFOSYS.

Please refer to pages 86–89, 96–103, and 142–175 of the annual report of Infosys. Log on to www.infosys.com/investor/reports/annual/ and select *annual report for 2006.*

SELECTED REFERENCES

Bradshaw, Mark T., Brian J. Bushee, and Gregory S. Miller, "Accounting Choice, Home Bias, and U.S. Investment in Non-U.S. Firms," *Journal of Accounting Research* 42, no. 5 (2004): 795–841.

Bradsher, Keith, "Hong Kong Set to Be No. 1 in 2006 Offerings, Surpassing London and New York," *nytimes.com*, 10/20/2006.

Buckley, Peter J., and M. Casson, "The Future of the Multinational Enterprise in Retrospect and in Prospect," *Journal of International Business Studies* 34, no. 2 (2003): 219–222.

Cowen, David, Ranil Salgado, Hemant Shah, Leslie Teo, and Alessandro Zanello, "Financial Integration in Asia: Recent Developments and Next Steps," IMF Working Paper No. 06/196, August 1, 2006.

Donaldson, William H., "Remarks Before the International Organization of Securities Commissions," New York: U.S. Securities and Exchange Commission, October 28, 2004.

Gannon, D. J., and Alex Ashwal, "Financial Reporting Goes Global," *Journal of Accountancy Online*, September 2004.

Hubbard, Glenn R., and John L. Thornton, "Action Plan for Capital Markets," *Wall Street Journal Online*, November 30, 2006, p. A16.

Jiang, Li, and Jeong-Bon Kim, "Foreign Equity Ownership and Information Asymmetry: Evidence from Japan," *Journal of International Financial Management and Accounting* 15, no. 3 (2004): 185–211.

Kazarian, Elias, "Integration of the Securities Market Infrastructure in the European Union: Policy and Regulatory Issues," IMF Working Paper No. 06/241, October 1, 2006.

Faruqee, Hamid, Shujing Li, and Isabel K. Yan, "The Determinants of International Portfolio Holdings and Home Bias," IMF Working Paper No. 04/34, February 1, 2004.

Khanna, Tarun, Krishna G. Palepu, and Suraj Srinivasan, "Disclosure Practices of Foreign Companies Interacting with U.S. Markets," *Journal of Accounting Research* 42, no. 2,(2004): 475–508.

Madison, Angus, *The World Economy, Vol. 1: A Millennial Perspective,* OECD Development Centre Studies, Paris: OECD, 2006.

Narayan, Paresh, Russell Smyth, and Mohan Nandha, "Interdependence and Dynamic Linkages Between the Emerging Stock Markets of South Asia," *Accounting and Finance* 44, no. 3 (2004): 419–439.

Salter, Stephen B., Philip A. Lewis, and Luis Felipe Juarez Valdes, "Aqui No Se Habla Agencia: An Examination of the Impact of Adverse Selection and Framing in Decision-Making: A US/Mexico Comparison," *Journal of International Financial Management and Accounting* 15, no. 2 (2004): pp. 93–117.

Shamis, Gary S., M. Cathryn Green, Susan M. Sorensen, and Donald L. Kyle," "Outsourcing, Offshoring, Nearshoring: What to Do?" *Journal of AccountancyOnline*, June 2005.

Stulz, Rene M. "The Limits of Financial Globalization," *Journal of Finance* 60, no. 4 (2006): 1595–1638.

Sy, Aida, and Tony Tinker, "Bury Pacioli in Africa: A Bookkeeper's Reification of Accountancy," *Abacus* 42 (March 2006): 105–127.

Tarca, Ann, "International Convergence of Accounting Practices: Choosing Between IAS and US GAAP," *Journal of International Financial Management and Accounting* 15, no. 1 (2004): 60–91.

"What the Upsurge in Global Capital Flows Indicates," *Business Line*, June 13, 2006.

Zarb, Bert J., "The Quest for Transparency in Financial Reporting: Should International Financial Reporting Standards Replace U.S. GAAP?" *CPA Journal Online*, September 2006.

DISCUSSION QUESTIONS

1. Explain how international accounting differs from purely domestic accounting.
2. Accounting may be viewed as having three components: measurement, disclosure, and auditing. What are the advantages and disadvantages of this classification? Can you suggest alternative classifications that might be useful?

3. What contemporary factors are contributing to the internationalization of the subject of accounting.

4. Describe in two short paragraphs how foreign direct-investment activities differ from international trade and the implications of this difference for accounting.

5. Given the international heritage of accounting, do you feel that efforts to harmonize global accounting standards is a good thing? Why or why not?

6. Why have international accounting issues grown in importance and complexity in recent years?

7. Identify several internal and external reporting issues that arise when business and investments transcend national borders.

8. Explain the term *global capital markets*. This chapter primarily discusses global equity markets. What other types of financial instruments are traded in these markets? How important are global capital markets in the world economy?

9. Some have advocated that a single widely spoken language be designated as the formal international accounting language. Write a two-paragraph statement in favor of choosing English as the designated language.

10. Capital markets often are grouped into two categories: those in developed countries and those in emerging market countries. Give your own definitions of developed and emerging market countries. Which stock exchanges shown in Appendix 1-3 are in emerging market countries? What characteristics do they share?

11. Appendix 1-1 shows that over time, national governments in many countries sold shares in state-owned financial institutions to nongovernmental entities. Discuss how these privatizations might affect the capital markets as well as the accounting systems of these companies.

12. Outsourcing, especially from vendors located abroad, has become a politically sensitive issue, especially in the United States. Do you think this argument has merit? What are the consequences of this debate for international accounting?

EXERCISES

1. Re-examine Exhibit 1-1, which describes the outsourcing process for HP's production of the Proliant ML150. For each leg of the production chain, identify the various accounting and related issues that might arise.

2. Revisit Appendix 1-1, which chronicles the trend toward privatization of state-owned enterprises and reductions in national barriers to cross-border investments. From an investors' perspective, prepare a country index in which you would assign a numerical rating of 1 for the countries that appear most receptive to investors, 2 for the countries that appear receptive but where the risks of reimposing controls appear to be non-zero, and 3 for countries that you would not find attractive at the present time.

3. Examine Exhibit 1-2 and compute the compounded annual growth rate of merchandise trade versus the global trade in services. What implication does your finding have for accounting as a service activity?

4. Examine the Web sites of five of the exchanges listed in Appendix 1-2 that you feel would be most attractive to foreign listers. Which exchange in your chosen set proved most popular during the last two years? Provide possible explanations for your observation.

5. Does the geographic pattern of merchandise exports in Exhibit 1-2 correlate well with the pattern of Heineken's geographic distribution of sales shown in Exhibit 1-3? What might explain any differences you observe?

6. What international reporting issues are triggered by AKZO NOBEL's foreign operations disclosure in Exhibit 1-4 for investors? For managerial accountants?

7. Exhibit 1-5 lists the number of majority-owned foreign affiliates in each country that Nestlé includes in its consolidated results. What international accounting issues are triggered by this exhibit?

8. Revisit Exhibit 1-6 and show how the ROE statistics of 7.1 percent and 6.2 percent for 2005 were derived. Which of the two ROE statistics is the better performance measure to use when comparing Electrolux's performance with that of Maytag, the U.S. parent company of Hoover, which makes vacuum cleaners and other household products?

9. The World Wide Web provides low-cost access to a vast amount of information about financial reporting requirements and practices worldwide.
    Required: Refer to Appendix 1-2, which provides Web site addresses for stock exchanges in more than 50 countries. Select a stock exchange and do a Web search for information about the financial reporting requirements for listed companies in that market. (Many stock exchange Web sites provide information on their own financial reporting requirements, such as those related to annual and interim reporting, and links to national securities regulatory bodies.) Present a brief overview of financial reporting regulation of the stock exchange you select. (Note: The IASB Web site, at www.iasb.org, also presents information about accounting-principle requirements at stock exchanges around the world.)

10. Stock exchange Web sites vary considerably in the information they provide and their ease of use.
    Required: Select any two of the stock exchanges presented in Appendix 1-2. Explore the Web sites of each of these stock exchanges. Prepare a table that compares and contrasts the sites for type and quality of information presented and ease of using the Web site. Are English-language press releases of listed companies available? Links to listed companies' Web sites? Listing requirements? Price and volume data for listed securities? Helpful information for investors?

11. Referring to Exhibit 1-7, which geographic region is experiencing the most activity in foreign listings: the Americas, Asia-Pacific, or Europe–Africa–Middle East? Do you expect this pattern to persist in the future? Explain.

12. If you had a nontrivial sum of money to invest and decided to invest it in a country index fund, in which country or countries identified in Exhibit 1-8 would you invest your money ? What accounting issues would play a role in your decision?

Case 1-1   E-Centives, Inc.—Raising Capital In Switzerland

On October 3, 2000, E-centives, incorporated in the United States, made an initial public offering on the Swiss Stock Exchange's New Market. The company raised approximately US$40 million. The E-centives offering circular stated that no offers or sales of the company's common stock would be made in the United States, and that there would be no public market for the common stock in the United States after the offering.

THE SWISS EXCHANGE'S NEW MARKET

The Swiss Exchange launched the New Market in 1999. The New Market is designed to meet the financing needs of rapidly growing companies from Switzerland and abroad. It provides firms with a simplified means of entry to Swiss capital markets. Listing requirements for the New Market are simple. For example, companies must have an operating track record of 12 months, the initial public listing must involve a capital increase, and to ensure market liquidity, a bank must agree to make a market in the securities.

E-centives

E-centives, Inc., is a leading online direct-marketing infrastructure company. The company offers systems and technologies that enable businesses to build large, rich databases of consumer profiles and interests. In return, consumers receive a free personalized service that provides them with promotional offers based on their interests. At the time of the public offering, E-centives maintained over 4.4 million online accounts for members. The company does not charge members a fee for its service. Instead, it generates revenue primarily from marketers whose marketing matter is delivered to targeted groups of E-centives members. E-centives currently employs more than 100 people in its Bethesda, Maryland, headquarters, and its offices in Redwood City, New York, and Los Angeles.

As of the offering date, the company had little revenue and had not been profitable. Revenue for the year ended December 31, 1999, was US$740,000, with a net loss of about US$16 million. As of June 30, 2000, the company had an accumulated deficit of about US$39 million. E-centives' growth strategy is to expand internationally. To date, the company has focused on pursuing opportunities in the United States. E-centives intends to expand into Europe and other countries. The company is currently considering expanding into Switzerland, the United Kingdom, and Germany.[17] ∎

---

[17]From the E-centives offering circular dated October 2, 2000.

REQUIRED

1. Refer to Exhibit 1-9, which lists factors relevant for choosing an overseas market for listing or raising capital. Which factors might have been relevant in E-centives' decision to raise capital and list on the Swiss Exchange's New Market?

2. Why do you believe E-centives chose not to raise public equity in the United States? What are the potential drawbacks related to the decision not to raise capital in the U.S. public markets?

3. What are the advantages and disadvantages for E-centives of using U.S. GAAP?

4. Should the SWX Swiss Exchange require E-centives to prepare its financial statements using Swiss accounting standards?

5. Learn more about the New Market at the SWX Swiss Exchange's Web site (www.swx.com). What are the listing requirements for the New Market? What are the financial reporting requirements? Does E-centives appear to fit the profile of the typical New Market company?

Case 1-2 Global Benchmarks: Infosys Technologies Limited

Investors, whether individual, corporate, or institutional, are increasingly investing beyond national borders. The reason is not hard to find. Returns abroad, even after allowing for foreign currency exchange risk, often exceed those offered by domestic investments. Information provided in a firm's annual report is often the major source of information available to those seeking to sample foreign equities. In attempting to assess the risk and return attributes of a given company, readers must answer questions like the following: What accounting principles were employed? Would the financial statements be more useful if restated to a different set of accounting principles? What types of information are not provided that one would expect to find in financial statements of

companies from the investor's home country? How would one compensate for limited disclosure? What does the audit report reveal about the level of audit quality? What auditing standards were used? Are they acceptable? Does the audit report mean the same thing as it does in the reader's home country?

Appendix 1-3 refers you to the financial statements (including selected notes) and auditor's report for Infosys Technologies Limited. Infosys was incorporated in 1981 as Infosys Consultants Private Limited, a private company under the Indian Companies Act. Its name eventually evolved into Infosys Technologies Limited in 1992, when the company went public. Its mission is to provide high-quality and cost-competitive technology solutions for companies around the world. It has grown into a $2 billion company with a market capitalization in excess of $21 billion.

In examining the information referred to in Appendix 1-3, comment on how the statements of Infosys stack up to other companies in the industry in meeting the information needs of a nondomestic investor such as yourself. Specifically: What reporting practices raise issues for you? What reporting practices do you find helpful? In preparing your critique, compare the reporting practices of Infosys to a service provider in your country that maintains a corporate Web site on the Internet. ∎

CHAPTER 2

Development and Classification

Accounting must respond to society's ever-changing informational needs and reflect the cultural, economic, legal, social, and political conditions within which it operates. The history of accounting and accountants reveals continuing change. At first, accounting was little more than a recording system for certain banking services and tax-collection schemes. Double-entry bookkeeping systems were later developed to meet the needs of trading ventures. Industrialization and division of labor made cost-behavior analysis and managerial accounting possible. The rise of the modern corporation stimulated periodic financial reporting and auditing. In keeping with society's increased concerns about the environment and about corporate integrity, accountants have found ways to measure and report environmental remediation liabilities and to uncover money laundering and other white-collar crimes. Accounting provides decision information for huge domestic and international public securities markets. It extends into management consulting and incorporates ever-increasing information technology within its systems and procedures.

Why should we want to know how and why accounting develops? The answer is the same as for developmental studies in other fields. We can better understand a nation's accounting by knowing the underlying factors that have influenced its development. Accounting differs around the world, and knowledge of the developmental factors helps us see why. In other words, they can explain the observable differences as well as the similarities. Because accounting responds to its environment, different cultural, economic, legal, and political environments produce different accounting systems, and similar environments produce similar systems.

This leads us to classification. Why should we classify (compare) national or regional financial accounting systems? Classification is fundamental to understanding and analyzing why and how national accounting systems differ. We can also analyze whether these systems are converging or diverging. The goal of classification is to group financial accounting systems according to their distinctive characteristics. Classifications reveal fundamental structures that group members have in common and that distinguish the various groups from each other. By identifying similarities and differences, our understanding of accounting systems is improved. Classifications are a way of viewing the world.

DEVELOPMENT

Every nation's accounting standards and practices result from a complex interaction of economic, historical, institutional, and cultural factors. Diversity among nations is to be expected. The factors that influence national accounting development also help explain the accounting diversity among nations.

The following eight factors have a significant influence on accounting development. The first seven are economic, sociohistorical, and/or institutional in nature, and they have occupied most of the attention of accounting writers. The relationship between culture (the eighth item) and accounting development ends the discussion in this section.

1. ***Sources of Finance.***   In countries with strong equity markets, such as the United States and the United Kingdom, accounting profits measure how well management is running the company. Accounting is designed to help investors assess future cash flows and the associated risks, and to value the firm. Disclosures are extensive to meet the requirements of widespread public share ownership. By contrast, in credit-based systems, where banks are the dominant source of finance, accounting focuses on creditor protection through conservative earnings measures to minimize dividend payouts and retain sufficient funds for the protection of lenders. Because financial institutions have direct access to any information they want, extensive public disclosures are not considered necessary. Japan and Switzerland are examples.[1]

2. ***Legal System.***   The legal system determines how individuals and institutions interact. The Western world has two basic orientations: code (or civil) law and common (or case) law. Code law derives mainly from Roman law and the Code Napoléon.[2] In code law countries, laws are an all-embracing set of requirements and procedures. Codification of accounting standards and procedures is natural and appropriate. Thus, in code law countries, accounting rules are incorporated into national laws and tend to be highly prescriptive and procedural.[3] By contrast, common law develops on a case-by-case basis with no attempt to cover all cases in an all-encompassing code. Statute law exists, of course, but it tends to be less detailed and more flexible than in a code law system. This encourages experimentation and permits the exercise of judgment.[4] Common law derives

---

[1]For further discussion of this point, see C. Nobes, "Towards a General Model of the Reasons for International Differences in Financial Reporting," *Abacus* (September 1998): 162–187. He points out that outsiders (e.g., individual and institutional shareholders) normally dominate ownership in strong equity countries, causing a demand for high levels of disclosure. Insiders (families, other companies, government, and banks) usually dominate ownership in credit-based countries, which is why low levels of disclosure are usually found there. Germany is an exception. Although Germany is a credit-based country, German-listed companies have high disclosures because of Germany's unusually large market in listed debt (p. 169).

[2]There are three major families in the code law tradition: French, German, and Scandinavian. French and German code law, like the common law, spread around the world through conquest, imperialism, or borrowing.

[3]There are exceptions to this generalization; for example, the Netherlands (Chapter 3) and Mexico (Chapter 4), where accounting is like that in common law countries.

[4]Irving Fantl, "The Case Against International Uniformity," *Management Accounting* (May 1971): 13–16.

from English case law. In most common law countries, accounting rules are established by private sector professional organizations. This allows them to be more adaptive and innovative. Except for broad statutory requirements, most accounting rules are not incorporated directly into statute law.[5] Code law accounting tends to focus on legal form, whereas common law accounting tends to focus on economic substance. For example, leases are normally not capitalized under code law. In contrast, under common law leases are capitalized when they are, in substance, the purchase of property. Exhibit 2-1 lists code and common law countries.

3. *Taxation*   In many countries, tax legislation effectively determines accounting standards because companies must record revenues and expenses in their accounts to claim them for tax purposes. In other words, financial and tax accounting are the same. This is the case, for example, in Germany and Sweden. In

EXHIBIT 2-1	Code and Common Law Countries		

Code law — French origin

Africa
Egypt

Americas
Argentina
Brazil
Chile
Colombia
Ecuador
Mexico
Peru
Uruguay
Venezuela

Asia
Indonesia
Jordan
Philippines
Turkey

Europe
Belgium
France
Greece
Italy
Luxembourg

The Netherlands
Portugal
Spain

Code law — German origin

Asia
Japan
South Korea
Taiwan

Europe
Austria
Czech Republic
Germany
Hungary
Slovak Republic
Switzerland

Code law — Scandinavian origin

Europe
Denmark
Finland
Iceland
Norway
Sweden

Common law

Africa
Kenya
Nigeria
South Africa
Zimbabwe

Americas
Canada
United States

Asia
Hong Kong
India
Israel
Malaysia
Pakistan
Singapore
Sri Lanka
Thailand

Australasia
Australia
New Zealand

Europe
Ireland
United Kingdom

SOURCE: Adapted from Rafael La Porta, Florencio Lopez-de-Salines, Andrei Shleifer, and Robert W. Vishny, "Law and Finance," *Journal of Political Economy* 106, no. 6 (1998): 1142–1143; and David Alexander and Simon Archer, *European Accounting Guide, 5th ed.,* New York: Aspen, 2003.

[5]Under martial law or other national emergency situations, all aspects of the accounting function may be regulated by a central governmental court or agency. This was the case, for instance, in Nazi Germany, where intensive war preparations and World War II itself required a highly uniform national accounting system for total control of all national economic activities.

other countries, such as the Netherlands, financial and tax accounting are separate: Taxable profits are essentially financial accounting profits adjusted for differences with the tax laws. Of course, even where financial and tax accounting are separate, tax legislation may occasionally require the application of certain accounting principles. Last in, first out (LIFO) inventory valuation in the United States is an example.

4. ***Political and Economic Ties***   Accounting ideas and technologies are transferred through conquest, commerce, and similar forces. Double-entry bookkeeping, which originated in Italy in the 1400s, gradually spread across Europe along with other ideas of the Renaissance. British colonialism exported accountants and accounting concepts throughout the empire. German occupation during World War II led France to adopt its Plan Comptable (see Chapter 3). The United States imposed U.S.-style accounting regulatory regimes on Japan after World War II. Many developing economies use an accounting system that was developed elsewhere, either because it was imposed on them (e.g., India) or by their own choice (e.g., countries of Eastern Europe that modeled their accounting systems after European Union [EU] regulations). As discussed more generally in Chapter 8, economic integration through the growth of international trade and capital flows is a powerful motivator for the convergence of accounting standards in individual countries around the world.

5. ***Inflation***   Inflation distorts historical cost accounting by understating asset values and related expenses, and overstating income. Countries with high inflation often require that companies incorporate price changes into the accounts. Mexico and certain countries of South America use general price-level accounting because of their experiences with hyperinflation.[6] In the late 1970s, in response to unusually high rates of inflation, both the United States and the United Kingdom experimented with reporting the effects of changing prices. Accounting responses to inflation are explored in Chapter 7.

6. ***Level of Economic Development***   This factor affects the types of business transactions conducted in an economy and determines which ones are most prevalent. The type of transactions, in turn, determines the accounting issues that are faced. For example, stock-based executive compensation or asset securitization makes little sense in economies with underdeveloped capital markets. Today, many industrial economies are becoming service economies. Accounting issues relevant in manufacturing, such as valuing fixed assets and recording depreciation, are becoming less important. New accounting challenges, such as valuing intangibles and human resources, are emerging.

7. ***Educational level***   Highly sophisticated accounting standards and practices are useless if they are misunderstood and misused. For example, a complex technical report on cost behavior variances is meaningless unless the reader understands cost accounting. Disclosures about the risks of derivative securities are not informative unless they can be read competently. Professional accounting education is difficult to achieve where general educational levels are low. Mexico is a country where this difficulty has been overcome. In other situations, a country must

---

[6]Israel discontinued inflation-adjusted accounting in 2004 after drastic reductions in inflation.

import accounting training or send its citizens elsewhere to get it, something that China is now doing. (Mexico and China are discussed in Chapter 4.)

Several of these first seven variables are closely associated. For example, the common law legal system originated in Britain and was exported to such countries as Australia, Canada, and the United States. These four countries all have highly developed capital markets that dominate the orientation of their financial reporting. Financial and tax accounting are separate. By contrast, most of continental Europe and Japan have code law legal systems and rely on banks or the government for most of their finance. Thus their accounting rules generally conform to tax laws.

Establishing cause and effect is difficult. The type of legal system may predispose a country toward its system of finance. A common law legal system emphasizes shareholder rights and offers stronger investor protection than a code law system. The outcome is that strong equity markets develop in common law countries and weak ones develop in code law countries.[7] Taxation is an important function of accounting in any country with a corporate income tax. Whether it dominates the orientation of accounting may depend on whether accounting has a major competing purpose, namely, informing outside shareholders. (Tax accounting is not suitable for this purpose.) If common law results in strong equity markets, taxation will not dominate. There will be two sets of accounting rules: one for taxation and another for financial reporting. Tax rules will dominate in code law/credit-based countries, and accounting for taxation and financial reporting will be the same.[8]

Two basic orientations of accounting have evolved out of these circumstances. One is oriented toward a fair presentation of financial position and results of operations; the other is designed to comply with legal requirements and tax law. The *fair presentation* versus *legal compliance* distinction is further discussed at the end of the chapter.

8. *Culture*   Culture encompasses the values and attitudes shared by a society. Cultural variables underlie nations' legal systems and other institutional arrangements. Hofstede identified four national cultural dimensions (or societal values): (1) individualism, (2) power distance, (3) uncertainty avoidance, and (4) masculinity. His analysis is based on data from employees of a large U.S. multinational corporation operating in 40 different countries.[9]

Briefly, *individualism* (versus *collectivism*) is a preference for a loosely knit social fabric over an interdependent, tightly knit fabric (*I* versus *we*). *Power distance* is the extent to which hierarchy and an unequal distribution of power in institutions and organizations are accepted. *Uncertainty avoidance* is the degree to which

---

[7]R. La Porta, F. Lopez-de-Silanes, A. Shleifer, and R.W. Vishny, "Legal Determinants of External Finance," *Journal of Finance* (July 1997): 1131–1150.
[8]C. Nobes, "Towards a General Model of the Reasons for International Differences in Financial Reporting," *Abacus* (September 1998): 162–187.
[9]G. Hofstede, *Culture's Consequences: International Differences in Work-Related Values* (Beverly Hills, CA: Sage Publications, 1980).

society is uncomfortable with ambiguity and an uncertain future. *Masculinity* (versus *femininity*) is the extent to which gender roles are differentiated and performance and visible achievement (traditional masculine values) are emphasized over relationships and caring (traditional feminine values). Some scholars now call this *achievement orientation.*[10]

Drawing on Hofstede's analysis, Gray proposed a framework linking culture and accounting.[11] He suggests that four *accounting value dimensions* affect a nation's financial reporting practices. They are:

1. Professionalism vs. statutory control: a preference for the exercise of individual professional judgment and professional self-regulation, as opposed to compliance with prescriptive legal requirements.

   > A preference for independent professional judgment is consistent with a preference for a loosely knit social framework where there is more emphasis on independence, a belief in fair play and as few rules as possible, and where a variety of professional judgments will tend to be more easily tolerated. . . . [P]rofessionalism is more likely to be accepted in a small power-distance society where there is more concern for equal rights, where people at various power levels feel less threatened and more prepared to trust people, and where there is a belief in the need to justify the imposition of laws and codes.[12]

2. Uniformity vs. flexibility: a preference for uniformity and consistency over flexibility in reacting to circumstances.

   > A preference for uniformity is consistent with a preference for strong uncertainty avoidance leading to a concern for law and order and rigid codes of behaviour, a need for written rules and regulations, a respect for conformity and the search for ultimate, absolute truths and values. [Uniformity] is also consistent with a preference for collectivism . . . with its tightly knit social framework, a belief in organization and order, and respect for group norms. . . . [U]niformity is more easily facilitated in a

---

[10]Later work documents a fifth cultural dimension, *Confucian dynamism* (also called *long-term orientation*). This later work contends that only individualism, power distance, and masculinity are universal across all cultures. Uncertainty avoidance is a unique characteristic of Western societies, whereas Confucian dynamism is unique to Eastern societies. See G. Hofstede and M.H. Bond, "The Confucian Connection: From Cultural Roots to Economic Growth," *Organizational Dynamics* 16, no. 1 (1988): 4–21; G. Hofstede, *Cultures and Organizations: Softwares of the Mind* (London: McGraw-Hill, 1991). The existence of this fifth dimension has been contested. See R. Yeh and J .J. Lawrence, "Individualism and Confucian Dynamism: A Note on Hofstede's Cultural Root to Economic Growth," *Journal of International Business Studies* (third quarter 1995): 655–669. These authors note a data problem in Hofstede's subsequent work. Once an outlier is removed, Confucian dynamism no longer emerges as an independent construct; it reflects the same cultural dimension as individualism. It should also be pointed out that there are other cultural dimensions that are not considered by Hofstede. For example, religion, which extends beyond national boundaries, underlies business practices, institutional arrangements, and, by extension, accounting. Language is another cultural input. For a critique of Hofstede, see B. McSweeney, "Hofstede's Model of National Cultural Differences and Their Consequences," *Human Relations* (January 2002): 89–118.

[11]S. J. Gray, "Towards a Theory of Cultural Influence on the Development of Accounting Systems Internationally," *Abacus* (March 1988): 1–15.

[12]Ibid., 9.

large power-distance society in that the imposition of laws and codes of a uniform character are [*sic*] more likely to be accepted.[13]

3. Conservatism vs. optimism: a preference for a cautious approach to measurement to cope with the uncertainty of future events instead of a more optimistic, risk-taking approach.

> A preference for more conservative measures of profits is consistent with strong uncertainty avoidance following from a concern with security and a perceived need to adopt a cautious approach to cope with uncertainty of future events. . . . [A]n emphasis on individual achievement and performance is likely to foster a less conservative approach to measurement.[14]

4. Secrecy vs. transparency: a preference for confidentiality and the restriction of business information on a need-to-know basis versus a willingness to disclose information to the public.

> A preference for secrecy is consistent with strong uncertainty avoidance following from a need to restrict information disclosures so as to avoid conflict and competition and to preserve security. . . . [H]igh power-distance societies are likely to be characterized by the restriction of information to preserve power inequalities. Secrecy is also consistent with a preference for collectivism . . . with its concern for those closely involved with the firm rather than external parties. . . . [S]ocieties where more emphasis is given to the quality of life, people, and the environment, will tend to be more open especially as regards socially related information.[15]

Exhibit 2-2 shows how Gray's accounting values relate to Hofstede's cultural dimensions.[16]

EXHIBIT 2-2   Relationships Between Accounting Values and Cultural Dimensions

	Accounting Values			
Cultural Dimensions	*Professionalism*	*Uniformity*	*Conservatism*	*Secrecy*
Individualism	+	−	−	−
Uncertainty Avoidance	−	+	+	+
Power Distance	−	+	•	+
Masculinity	•	•	−	−

Note: + indicates a direct relationship between the variables; − indicates an inverse relationship; • indicates no relationship. Gray hypothesizes that individualism and uncertainty avoidance will influence accounting the most, followed by power distance, then masculinity.

[13]Ibid., 9–10.

[14]Ibid., 10.

[15]Ibid., 11.

[16]The empirical work testing Gray's framework is reviewed in T.S. Doupnik and G. T. Tsakumin, "A Critical Review of Gray's Theory of Cultural Relevance and Suggestions for Future Research," *Journal of Accounting Literature* 23 (2004): 1–48.

CLASSIFICATION

International accounting classifications fall into two categories: judgmental and empirical. Judgmental classifications rely on knowledge, intuition, and experience.[17] Empirically derived classifications apply statistical methods to databases of accounting principles and practices around the world.[18]

Four Approaches to Accounting Development[19]

The pioneering classification is the one proposed by Mueller in the mid-1960s. He identified four approaches to accounting development in Western nations with market-oriented economics systems. (1) Under the *macroeconomic* approach, accounting practices are derived from and designed to enhance national macroeconomic goals. Firm goals normally follow rather than lead national economic policies as business firms coordinate their activities with national policies. Thus, for example, a national policy to maintain stable employment by avoiding big swings in business cycles would result in accounting practices that smooth income. As another example, a nation that wished to promote the development of certain industries could permit them to rapidly write off capital expenditures. Accounting in Sweden developed from the macroeconomic approach. (2) Under the *microeconomic* approach, accounting develops from the principles of microeconomics. The focus is on individual firms whose main goal is to survive. To accomplish this goal, firms must maintain their physical capital. It is also critical that they clearly separate capital from income to evaluate and control their business activities. Accounting measurements based on replacement cost best fit this approach. Accounting developed from microeconomics in the Netherlands. (3) Under the *independent discipline* approach, accounting derives from business practices and develops on an ad hoc, piecemeal basis from judgment and trial-and-error. Accounting is viewed as a service function that derives its concepts and principles from the business process it serves, not from a discipline such as economics. Businesses cope with real-world complexities and ever-present uncertainties through experience, practice, and intuition. Accounting develops the same way. For example, income is simply what seems to be the most useful in practice, and disclosures respond pragmatically to user needs. Accounting developed as an independent discipline in the United Kingdom and the United States. (4) Under the *uniform* approach, accounting is standardized by the central government and employed as a tool for administrative control. Uniformity in measurement, disclosure, and presentation makes it easier for government planners, tax authorities, and even managers to use accounting information to control all types of

---

[17]Examples are C. W. Nobes, "A Judgmental International Classification of Financial Reporting Practices," *Journal of Business Finance & Accounting* (spring 1983): 1–19; idem, "Towards a General Model of the Reasons for International Differences in Financial Reporting," *Abacus* (September 1998): 162–187.

[18]Examples are R. D. Nair and W. G. Frank, "The Impact of Disclosure and Measurement Practices on International Accounting Classifications," *Accounting Review* (July 1980): 426–450; T. S. Doupnik and S. B. Salter, "External Environment, Culture, and Accounting Practice: A Preliminary Test of a General Model of International Accounting Development," *International Journal of Accounting* 30, no. 3 (1995): 189–207.

[19]The concepts underlying these developmental patterns were first proposed in G. Mueller, *International Accounting* (New York: Macmillan, 1967). This work is the basis for most of the classifications of accounting systems worldwide.

businesses. In general, the uniform approach is used in countries with strong governmental involvement in economic planning where accounting is used to measure performance, allocate resources, collect taxes, and control prices, among other things. France, with its national uniform chart of accounts, is the leading exponent of the uniform approach.[20]

Legal Systems: Common Law vs. Code Law Accounting

Accounting can also be classified by a nation's legal system.[21] This view has dominated accounting thinking for the last 25 years or so. (1) Accounting in *common law* countries is characterized as oriented toward "fair presentation," transparency and full disclosure, and a separation between financial and tax accounting. Stock markets dominate as a source of finance, and financial reporting is aimed at the information needs of outside investors. Setting accounting standards tends to be a private sector activity, and the accounting profession plays an important role. Common law accounting is often called "Anglo-Saxon," "British-American," or "micro-based." Common law accounting originated in Britain and was exported to such countries as Australia, Canada, Hong Kong, India, Malaysia, Pakistan, and the United States. (2) Accounting in *code law* countries is characterized as legalistic in orientation, opaque with low disclosure, and an alignment between financial and tax accounting. Banks or governments ("insiders") dominate as a source of finance, and financial reporting is aimed at creditor protection. Setting accounting standards tends to be a public sector activity, with relatively less influence by the accounting profession. Code law accounting is often called "continental," "legalistic," or "macro-uniform." It is found in most of the countries of continental Europe and their former colonies in Africa, Asia, and the Americas.

This characterization of accounting parallels the so-called stockholder and stakeholder models of corporate governance in common and code law countries, respectively. As noted earlier in this chapter, a nation's legal system and its system of finance may be linked in a cause-and-effect way.[22] A common law legal system emphasizes shareholder rights and offers stronger investor protection than a code law system. Laws protect outside investors and are generally well enforced. The outcome is that strong capital markets develop in common law countries and weak ones develop in code law countries. Relative to code law countries, firms in common law countries raise substantial amounts of capital through public offerings to numerous investors.

---

[20]European academics like K. Käfer (Switzerland), L. L. Illetschko (Austria), E. Schmalenbach (Germany), and A. ter Vehn (Sweden) are largely identified with generalizing accounting processes from comprehensive charts of accounts.

[21]See, for example, C. W. Nobes, "A Judgmental International Classification of Financial Reporting Practices," *Journal of Business Finance & Accounting* (spring 1983): 1–19; I. Berry, "The Need to Classify Worldwide Accountancy Practices," *Accountancy* (October 1987): 90–91; T. S. Doupnik and S. B. Salter, "An Empirical Test of a Judgmental International Classification of Financial Reporting Practices," *Journal of International Business Studies* 24, no. 1 (1993): 41–60.; R. Ball, S. P. Kothari, and A. Robin, "The Effect of International Institutional Factors on Properties of Accounting Earnings," *Journal of Accounting and Economics* 29, no. 1 (2000): 1–51.

[22]R. La Porta, F. Lopez-de-Salines, A. Shleifer, and R.W. Vishny, "Legal Determinants of External Finance," *Journal of Finance* (July 1997): 1131–1150; R. La Porta, F. Lopez-de-Salines, A. Shleifer, and R.W. Vishny, "Law and Finance," *Journal of Political Economy* 106, no. 6 (December 1998): 1113–1155; R. La Porta, F. Lopez-de-Salines, A. Shleifer, and R.W. Vishny, "Investor Protection and Corporate Governance," *Journal of Financial Economics* 58, nos. 1–2 (2000): 3–27.

Because investors are at arm's length to the firm, there is a demand for accounting information that accurately reflects the firm's operating performance and financial position. Public disclosure resolves the information asymmetry between the firm and investors.

By contrast, ownership of firms in code law countries tends to be concentrated in the hands of families, other corporations, and large commercial banks. Firms satisfy substantial fractions of their capital needs from the government or through bank borrowing. Debt as a source of finance is relatively more important in code law countries than in common law countries. Conservative accounting measurements provide a cushion to lenders in the event of default. Major lenders and significant equity investors may occupy seats on boards of directors, along with other stakeholders, such as labor and important suppliers and customers. Because information demands are satisfied by private communication, there is less demand for public disclosure. Accounting income is the basis for income taxes owed and often, as well, for dividends and employee bonuses, resulting in pressures for smooth income amounts from year to year.

Practice Systems: Fair Presentation vs. Legal Compliance Accounting

Many accounting distinctions at the national level are becoming blurred. There are several reasons for this. (1) The importance of stock markets as a source of finance is growing around the world. Capital is increasingly global, creating pressure for a world standard of corporate reporting. For many companies, global convergence of financial reporting standards will reduce the costs of complying with different accounting rules and may also reduce their costs of capital. The integration of the world's capital markets is arguably the most important reason why the International Accounting Standards Board has emerged as the focal point for accounting standard setting in Australia, Japan, Europe, Singapore, South Africa, the United States, and elsewhere (see Chapter 8). Stock market development is also a top priority in many countries, especially those emerging from centrally planned to market-oriented economies. Two such countries are the Czech Republic and China, discussed in Chapters 3 and 4, respectively. (2) Dual financial reporting is becoming more common. One set of financial statements complies with local, domestic financial reporting requirements, while the other set uses accounting principles and contains disclosures aimed at international investors. Starting in 2005, all European listed companies were required to adopt International Financial Reporting Standards in their consolidated financial statements.[23] However, some EU code law countries, such as France and Germany, sanctioned a duality whereby individual company financial statements comply with national legal standards and consolidated financial statements comply with IFRS. In other words, it is necessary to distinguish accounting practice at the *national* level from that at the *transnational* level. (3) Some code law countries, in particular Germany and Japan (Chapters 3 and 4, respectively), are shifting responsibility for setting accounting standards from the government to independent professional, private-sector groups. This change makes the standard-setting process more like that in common law countries such as Australia, Canada, the United Kingdom, and the

---

[23]Approximately 7,000 companies were affected by this requirement.

United States, and is seen as a way to more actively influence the agenda of the IASB. These points indicate that another framework besides legal systems is needed to classify accounting worldwide.[24]

We believe that a classification based on *fair presentation* versus *legal compliance* describes accounting in the world today.[25] The distinction between fair presentation and legal compliance has pervasive effects on many accounting issues, such as (1) depreciation, where the expense is determined based on the decline in an asset's usefulness over its economic useful life (fair presentation) or the amount allowed for tax purposes (legal compliance); (2) leases that are in substance a purchase of property are treated as such (fair presentation) or are treated like regular operating leases (legal compliance); and (3) pensions with costs accrued as earned by employees (fair presentation) or expensed on a pay-as-you-go basis (legal compliance). In addition, the issue of deferred income taxes never arises when tax and financial accounting are the same.

Another issue is the use of discretionary reserves to smooth income from one period to the next. Generally, these reserves work the following way. In good years extra expenses are provided for, with the corresponding credit going to a reserve account in shareholders' equity. In lean years reserves are dissolved to boost income. This process irons out year-to-year fluctuations in income. Because this practice jeopardizes a fair presentation, it is less common under fair presentation and more common under legal compliance. Of course, if such manipulations are fully disclosed, investors can undo the effects on income. This may not be the case; reserves often are secret.

Fair presentation and *substance over form* characterize common law accounting described above. It is oriented toward the decision needs of external investors. Financial statements are designed to help investors judge managerial performance and predict future cash flows and profitability. Extensive disclosures provide additional information relevant for these purposes. IFRS are also aimed at fair presentation. IFRS are particularly relevant for companies relying on international capital markets for finance. Fair presentation accounting is found in the United Kingdom, the United States, the Netherlands, and other countries influenced by political and economic ties to them (such as British influence throughout the former British Empire and U.S. influence

---

[24]The common law vs. code law distinction can be criticized on other grounds. First, there are exceptions. The Netherlands (Chapter 3) and Mexico (Chapter 4) are code law countries with fair presentation accounting. Some observers doubt that legal systems are the sole cause of differences in accounting systems worldwide, but one of several contributing factors, including sources of finance and colonial or cultural influence. They say that there are too many exceptions for causality to run from legal system to accounting system. See, in particular, C. Nobes and A. Roberts, "Towards a Unifying Model of Systems of Law, Corporate Financing, Accounting and Corporate Governance," *Australian Accounting Review* 10, no. 1 (2000): 26–34. Enforcement is another significant point. If laws and accounting standards are not enforced, they exist on paper only. Distinctions based on legal systems are less clear in countries where standards are not enforced. See C. Leuz, D. Nanda, and P. Wysocki, "Investor Protection and Earnings Management: An International Comparison," *Journal of Financial Economics* (September 2003): 505–527.

[25]For completeness, *inflation-adjusted* accounting should also be considered. Accounting in Mexico is fair presentation/full disclosure with general price level accounting added on. (Chapter 4 discusses accounting in Mexico.) Certain countries in South America have legal compliance accounting, but with inflation adjustments. Countries also abandon inflation adjustments once inflation is tamed, as happened in Brazil and Israel. Islamic accounting, which has a theological base, is also omitted from this framework. It prohibits recognizing interest on money, and current market values are favored as measures of assets and liabilities. Islamic accounting has not yet evolved to the point where it represents a comprehensive pattern of accounting.

on Canada, Mexico, and the Philippines). All listed European companies follow fair presentation accounting in their consolidated statements since they now use IFRS. Further, IFRS are the benchmark for standards now being developed in China and Japan (Chapter 4).

Legal compliance accounting is designed to satisfy government-imposed requirements, such as calculating taxable income or complying with the national government's macroeconomic plan. The income amount may also be the basis for dividends paid to shareholders and bonuses paid to managers and employees. Conservative measurements ensure that prudent amounts are distributed. Smooth patterns in income from year to year mean that tax, dividend, and bonus payouts are more stable. Legal compliance accounting will probably continue to be used in individual-company financial statements in those code law countries where consolidated statements adopt fair presentation reporting. In this way, consolidated statements can inform investors while individual-company accounts satisfy legal requirements.

We believe that the integration of the world's capital markets will be the most significant influence shaping accounting development in the future. This development is the reason behind the trend toward fair presentation accounting, at least for consolidated financial statements. It is also the key driver behind the activities of the International Accounting Standards Board and the European Union's "IFRS 2005" decision, and it is why financial statement analysis is increasingly global in nature.

SELECTED REFERENCES

Ball, R., S.P. Kothari, and A. Robin, "The Effect of International Institutional Factors on Properties of Accounting Earnings," *Journal of Accounting and Economics* 29, no. 1 (2000): 1–51.

Bartov, E., S. R. Goldberg, and M-S Kim, "The Valuation-Relevance of Earnings and Cash Flows: An International Perspective," *Journal of International Financial Management and Accounting* 12, no. 2 (summer 2001): 103–132.

Baydoun, N., and R. Willett, "Cultural Relevance of Western Accounting Systems to Developing Countries," *Abacus* (March 1995): 67–92.

Beck, T., A. Demirgüç-Kunt, and R. Levine, "Law and Finance: Why Does Legal Origin Matter?" *Journal of Comparative Economics* 31 (2003): 653–675.

Bushman, R. M., and J. D. Piotroski, "Financial Reporting Incentives for Conservative Accounting: The Influence of Legal and Political Institutions," *Journal of Accounting and Economics* 42, nos. 1–2 (2006): 107–148.

Bushman, R.M., J. D. Piotroski, and A. J. Smith, "What Determines Corporate Transparency?" *Journal of Accounting Research* 42, no. 2 (2004): 207–252.

Chanchani, S., and A. MacGregor, "A Synthesis of Cultural Studies in Accounting," *Journal of Accounting Literature* 18 (1999): 1–30.

Doupnik, T.S., and G. T. Tsakumis, "A Critical Review of Tests of Gray's Theory of Cultural Relevance and Suggestions for Future Research," *Journal of Accounting Literature* 23 (2004): 1–48.

Gray, S. J., "Towards a Theory of Cultural Influence on the Development of Accounting Systems Internationally," *Abacus* (March 1988): 1–15.

Hope, O.-K., "Firm-Level Disclosures and the Relative Roles of Culture and Legal Origin," *Journal of International Financial Management and Accounting* 14, no. 3 (2003): 218–248.

La Porta, R., F. Lopez-de-Silanes, A. Shleifer, and R.W. Vishny, "Law and Finance," *Journal of Political Economy* 106, no. 6 (1998): 1113–1155.

Meek, G. K., and S. M. Saudagaran, "A Survey of Research on Financial Reporting in a Transnational Context," *Journal of Accounting Literature* 9 (1990): 145–182.

Nobes, C. W., *Developments in International Accounting: General Issues and Classification*, Cheltenham: Edward Elgar, 2004.

Nobes, C. W., *International Accounting: General Issues and Classification*, Cheltenham: Edward Elgar, 1996.

Nobes, C., "Towards a General Model of Reasons for International Differences in Financial Reporting," *Abacus* (September 1998): 162–187.

Nobes, C., and A. Roberts, "Towards a Unifying Model of Systems of Law, Corporate Financing, Accounting and Corporate

Governance," *Australian Accounting Review* 10, no. 1 (2000): 26–34.

Parker, R. H., "European Languages of Account," *European Accounting Review* 10, no. 1 (2001): 133–147.

Roberts, A., "The Very Idea of Classification in International Accounting," *Accounting, Organizations and Society* 20, nos. 7/8 (1995): 639–664.

Saudagaran, S. M., and J. G. Diga, "Evaluation of the Contingency-Based Approach in Comparative International Accounting: A Case for Alternative Research Paradigms," *Journal of Accounting Literature* 18 (1999): 57–95.

Sellhorn, T., and S. Gornik-Tomaszewski, "Implications of 'IAS Regulation' for Research into the International Differences in Accounting Systems," *Accounting in Europe* 2 (2006): 187–217.

DISCUSSION QUESTIONS

1. The chapter identifies seven economic, sociohistorical, and institutional factors believed to influence accounting development. Explain how each one affects accounting practice.

2. Referring to the seven factors in Question 1, rank them from most to least important as far as accounting development is concerned, then justify both the top and bottom items in your ranking.

3. How do cultural values influence accounting? Are there parallel influences between the factors identified in Question 1 and the cultural factors identified here?

4. Are national differences in accounting practice better explained by culture or by economic and legal factors? Why?

5. The four approaches to accounting development discussed in the chapter were originally outlined in 1967. Do you think these patterns will persist in the future? Why or why not?

6. Countries that have relatively conservative measurement practices also tend to be secretive in disclosure, while countries that have less conservative measurement practices tend to be transparent in disclosure. Why is this so?

7. What is the purpose of classifying systems of accounting?

8. What is the difference between a judgmental and an empirical classification of accounting?

9. What are the major accounting classifications in the world? What are the distinguishing features of each model?

10. Why does the chapter contend that many accounting distinctions at the national level are becoming blurred? Do you agree? Why or why not?

11. The authors contend that a classification based on fair presentation vs. legal compliance describes accounting in the world today better than one based on common law and code law legal systems. Do you agree? Why or why not?

12. What are the prospects of a convergence or harmonization of national systems of accounting and financial reporting? What factors might be influential in promoting or inhibiting change?

EXERCISES

1. The chapter identifies seven economic, historical, and/or institutional variables that influence accounting development: sources of finance, legal system, taxation, political and economic ties, inflation, level of economic development, and education level.

   Required:
   a. Consider the case of Taiwan. Describe it on the basis of these seven dimensions. Web sites include the *Encyclopaedia Britannica Online* (www.eb.com) and *The World Factbook* (www.cia.gov/cia/publications/factbook/).
   b. Using this description, predict a general profile of financial accounting in Taiwan.
   c. Go to the library and find a reference that describes accounting in Taiwan. Is your prediction accurate? Why or why not?

2. Consider the following countries: (1) Belgium, (2) China, (3) the Czech Republic, (4) Gambia, (5) India, (6) Mexico, (7) Senegal, and (8) Taiwan.

   Required: Where would they be classified based on legal system? Where would they be classified based on accounting practice systems? Justify your answers. (*Hint:* Web sites with information on countries of the world include the *Encyclopaedia Britannica Online* (www.eb.com) and *The World Factbook* (www.cia.gov/cia/publications/factbook/).)

3. The text distinguishes four approaches to accounting development. Naturally, these four approaches overlap and are not found in completely pure forms. Under the generally accepted accounting principles in the United States, LIFO inventory-pricing methods are available for financial purposes only if they are also applied in parallel fashion for tax accounting purposes. This scenario is a good example of the uniform approach to accounting development.

   Required: For each of the other three approaches to accounting development, identify two specific financial accounting standards, principles, or practices in your home country that illustrate the respective pattern.

4. Consider the following countries classified according to legal system:

Common law	Code law
Australia	France
Canada	Germany
Ireland	Italy
New Zealand	Japan
United Kingdom	The Netherlands
United States	Sweden

   Required:
   a. Obtain an annual report from a company headquartered in one of the six common law countries listed above and another one from one of the six code law countries. Two sources are www.carolworld.com and www.corporateinformation.com.
   b. Compare and contrast the two annual reports along measurement and disclosure dimensions.
   c. Do the similarities and differences conform to your expectations?

5. Go to the World Federation of Exchanges Web site (www.world-exchanges.org) and obtain the latest annual report. The statistics section on equity markets has information on the numbers of domestic and foreign companies listed on member stock exchanges.

Required: Which five stock exchanges have the most foreign listed companies? Which five stock exchanges have the highest proportion of foreign to total listed companies? Discuss possible reasons for this.

6. The European Union (EU)—formerly known as the European Community and, at its start, as the European Common Market—was founded in 1957 and had 15 members at the end of 2003: Austria, Belgium, Denmark, Finland, France, Germany, Greece, Ireland, Italy, Luxembourg, the Netherlands, Portugal, Spain, Sweden, and the United Kingdom. To encourage capital movement and capital formation, the EU has issued various *Directives* designed to harmonize the generally accepted accounting principles of its member countries.

Required: Which of the factors affecting accounting development are likely to be the most serious obstacles to the EU harmonization effort? What factors indicate that the EU harmonization effort can succeed?

7. Refer to Exercise 6. In May 2004 the EU expanded to incorporate 10 Central and East European nations: Cyprus, the Czech Republic, Estonia, Hungary, Latvia, Lithuania, Malta, Poland, Slovakia, and Slovenia. Bulgaria and Romania joined in January 2007.

Required: Which factors affecting accounting development are likely to be the most serious obstacles to achieving accounting harmonization with the other 15 member nations?

8. Gray proposed a framework linking culture and accounting. He predicts four accounting values (professionalism, uniformity, conservatism, and secrecy) based on Hofstede's four cultural dimensions (individualism, uncertainty avoidance, power distance, and masculinity). Exhibit 2-2 has Gray's predictions and also notes that individualism and uncertainty avoidance are expected to have the most significant influence on accounting values.

Required:

a. Go to Hofstede's Web site (www.geert-hofstede.com/hofstede_dimensions.php) and find the individualism scores for the following 10 countries: China, the Czech Republic, France, Germany, India, Japan, Mexico, the Netherlands, the United Kingdom, and the United States.

b. Characterize the individualism scores as high, medium, or low.

c. Based on your characterizations in the preceding item, predict Gray's four accounting values for the 10 countries.

9. Refer to Exercise 8.

Required:

a. Go to Hofstede's Web site (www.geert-hofstede.com/hofstede_dimensions.php) and find the uncertainty avoidance scores for the same 10 countries.

b. Characterize the uncertainty avoidance scores as high, medium, or low.

c. Based on your characterizations in the preceding items, predict Gray's four accounting values for the 10 countries.

d. Are these predictions consistent with those in Exercise 8?

10. Many countries permit or require their domestic listed companies to use International Financial Reporting Standards (IFRS) in their consolidated financial statements for investor reporting.

Required: Consider the following 10 countries: China, the Czech Republic, France, Germany, India, Japan, Mexico, the Netherlands, the United Kingdom, and the United States. For which countries are IFRS (a) not permitted, (b) permitted, (c) required for some, or (d) required for all domestic listed companies? Discuss the possible reasons for the observed patterns. (*Hint:* Refer to the IAS Plus Web site, www.iasplus.com).

11. Consider the development factors in the following five countries: France, India, Japan, the United States, and the United Kingdom:

Development Factor	France	India	Japan	United Kingdom	United States
Main source of finance	Banks; government	Government; Stock market	Banks	Stock market	Stock market
Legal system	Code law	Common law	Code law	Common law	Common law
Taxation (link to accounting)	Linked	Separate	Linked	Separate	Separate
Political and economic ties	Europe	U.K., U.S., China	U.S., China	U.S., Europe	Canada, Mexico
Inflation	Low	Low	Low	Low	Low
Level of economic development	High	Low	High	High	High
Educational level	High	Low	High	High	High

Required: Based on the information provided in this chapter, prepare a profile of accounting in each of the countries.

12. Think ahead 10 years from now. Prepare a classification of accounting systems that you think will exist then. What factors motivate your classification?

CASES

Case 2-1   Are Classifications of Accounting Outmoded?

Consider the following statements by David Cairns, former secretary-general of the International Accounting Standards Committee.[26]

> When we look at the way that countries or companies account for particular transactions and events, it is increasingly difficult to distinguish in a systematic way so-called Anglo-American accounting from Continental European accounting or American accounting from, say, German accounting.[27]
>
> I am increasingly persuaded . . . that the distinction between Anglo-American accounting and Continental European accounting is becoming less and less relevant and more and more confused. In reaching this conclusion, I do not dispute that different economic, social and legal considerations have influenced the development of accounting in different countries. I also do not dispute the fact that there have been, and still are, differences in the means by which different countries determine accounting requirements and the form of the resulting requirements. I do believe, however, that those who continue to favour these classifications are ignoring what is happening in the world and how companies actually account for transactions and events.
>
> It is increasingly apparent that the different economic, social and legal considerations which have influenced national accounting do not necessarily result in different accounting and that countries are reaching the same answers irrespective of their different cultural backgrounds (or reaching different answers in spite of the similar cultural backgrounds). In fact, there are now probably far more similarities between American and German accounting than there are between American and British accounting. There are many reasons for this not least the increasing practice of standard setting bodies and other regulators to share ideas and learn from one another. They do this in the IASC, the UN, the OECD, the EU, and such groupings as G4. This cross-fertilization of ideas is not surprising because standard setting bodies in all countries are having to address the same accounting problems.[28] ∎

---

[26]D. Cairns, "The Future Shape of Harmonization: A Reply," *European Accounting Review* 6, no. 2 (1997): 305–348.

[27]Ibid., 306.

[28]Ibid., 316.

REQUIRED

1. Do you agree with Cairns's assertion that classifications of accounting are simplistic and of little relevance in today's world? Are attempts to classify accounting futile and outmoded? Why or why not?

2. Some observers contend that financial reporting is becoming more and more alike among "world-class" companies—the world's largest multinational corporations—and especially those listed on the major stock exchanges, such as London, New York, and Tokyo. What is the relevance of this contention for classifications of accounting, and what are the factors that would cause this to happen?

Case 2-2   Volkswagen Group

The Volkswagen Group adopted International Accounting Standards (IAS, now International Financial Reporting, or IFRS) for its 2001 fiscal year. The following is taken from Volkswagen's 2001 annual report. It discusses major differences between the German Commercial Code (HGB) and IAS as they apply to Volkswagen.

GENERAL

In 2001 VOLKSWAGEN AG has for the first time published its consolidated financial statements in accordance with International Accounting Standards (IAS) and the interpretations of the Standing Interpretations Committee (SIC). All mandatory International Accounting Standards applicable to the financial year 2001 were complied with. The previous year's figures are also based on those standards. IAS 12 (revised 2000) and IAS 39, in particular, were already complied with in the year 2000 consolidated financial statements. The financial statements thus give a true and fair view of the net assets, financial position and earning performance of the Volkswagen Group.

The consolidated financial statements were drawn up in Euros. Unless otherwise stated, all amounts are quoted in millions of Euros (million €).

The income statement was produced in accordance with the internationally accepted cost of sales method.

Preparation of the consolidated financial statements in accordance with IAS requires assumptions regarding a number of line items that affect the amounts entered in the consolidated balance sheet and income statement as well as the disclosure of contingent assets and liabilities.

The conditions laid down in Section 292a of the German Commercial Code (HGB) for exemption from the obligation to draw up consolidated financial statements in accordance with German commercial law are met. Assessment of the said conditions is based on German Accounting Standard No. 1 (DSR 1) published by the German Accounting Standards Committee. In order to ensure equivalence with consolidated financial statements produced in accordance with German commercial law, all disclosures and explanatory notes required by German commercial law beyond the scope of those required by IAS are published.

TRANSITION TO INTERNATIONAL ACCOUNTING STANDARDS

The accounting valuation and consolidation methods previously applied in the financial statements of VOLKSWAGEN AG as produced in accordance with the German Commercial Code have been amended in certain cases by the application of IAS.

Amended accounting, valuation and consolidation methods in accordance with the German Commercial Code

- Tangible assets leased under finance leases are capitalized, and the corresponding liability is recognized under liabilities in the balance sheet, provided the risks and rewards of ownership are substantially attributable to the companies of the Volkswagen Group in accordance with IAS 17.

- As a finance lease lessor, leased assets are not capitalized, but the discounted leasing installments are shown as receivables.

- Movable tangible assets are depreciated using the straight-line method instead of the declining balance method; no half-year or multi-shift depreciation is used. Furthermore, useful lives are now based on commercial substance and no longer on tax law. Special depreciation for tax reasons is not permitted with IAS.

- Goodwill from capital consolidation resulting from acquisition of companies since 1995 is capitalized in accordance with IAS 22 and amortized over its respective useful life.

- In accordance with IAS 2, inventories must be valued at full cost. They were formerly capitalized only at direct cost within the Volkswagen Group.

- Provisions are only created where obligations to third parties exist.

- Differences from the translation of financial statements produced in foreign currencies are not recorded in the income statement.

- Medium- and long-term liabilities are entered in the balance sheet including capital take-up costs, applying the effective interest method.

Amended accounting, valuation and consolidation methods that differ from the German Commercial Code

- In accordance with IAS 38, development costs are capitalized as intangible assets provided it is likely that the manufacture of the developed products will be of future economic benefit to the Volkswagen Group.

- Pension provisions are determined according to the Projected Unit Credit Method as set out in IAS 19, taking account of future salary and pension increases.

- Provisions for deferred maintenance may not be created.

- Medium- and long-term provisions are shown at their present value.

- Securities are recorded at their fair value, even if this exceeds cost, with the corresponding effect in the income statement.

- Deferred taxes are determined according to the balance sheet liability method. For losses carried forward deferred tax assets are recognized, provided it is likely that they will be usable.

- Derivative financial instruments are recognized at their fair value, even if it exceeds cost. Gains and losses arising from the valuation of financial instruments serving to hedge future cash flows are recognized by way of a special reserve in equity. The profit or loss from such contracts is not recorded in the income statement until the corresponding due date. In contrast, gains and losses arising from the valuation of derivative financial instruments used to hedge balance sheet items are recorded in the income statement immediately.

- Treasure shares are offset against capital and reserves.
- Receivables and payables denominated in foreign currencies are valued at the middle rate on the balance sheet date, and not according to the imparity principle.

- Minority interests of shareholders from outside the Group are shown separately from capital and reserves.

The adjustment of the accounting and valuation policies to International Accounting Standards with effect from January 1, 2000 was undertaken in accordance with SIC 8, with no entry in the income statement, as an allocation to or withdrawal from revenue reserves, as if the accounts had always been produced in accordance with IAS.

The reconciliation of the capital and reserves to IAS in shown in the following table: ■

	million €
Capital and reserves according to the German Commercial Code as at January 1, 2000	**9,811**
Capitalization of development costs	3,982
Amended useful lives and depreciation methods in respect of tangible and intangible assets	3,483
Capitalization of overheads in inventories	653
Different treatments of leasing contracts as lessor	1,962
Differing valuation of financial instruments	897
Effect of deferred taxes	−1,345
Elimination of special items	262
Amended valuation of pension and similar obligations	−633
Amended accounting treatment of provisions	2,022
Classification of minority interests not as part of equity	−197
Other changes	21
Capital and reserves according to IAS as at January 1, 2000	**20,918**

SOURCE: Volkswagen AG Annual Report 2001, pp. 84–86.

REQUIRED

1. Based on the information provided in the chapter, describe the basic features of German accounting at the time Volkswagen adopted IAS. What developmental factors cause these features?
2. What differences between the accounting requirements in the HGB and IAS are highlighted in Volkswagen's disclosure? Are the German requirements consistent with your characterizations in requirement 1?
3. What is the relevance of Volkswagen's adoption of IAS to the classifications studied in this chapter?

CHAPTER 3

Comparative Accounting: Europe

In Chapter 2 we learned about the factors that affect the development of a nation's accounting system, including its sources of finance, legal system, taxation, political and economic ties, and inflation. Chapter 2 went on to classify accounting systems according to their common elements and distinctive features.

Chapters 3 and 4 more closely examine accounting in a few selected countries. Specific knowledge of accounting in a country is needed to analyze financial statements from that country. Chapter 3 deals with five European countries. Chapter 4 deals with five countries from the Americas and Asia. Background information for each country is provided in both chapters, along with a discussion of each country's institutional framework for regulating and enforcing accounting. Financial reporting based on local generally accepted accounting principles (GAAP) is also discussed. The global convergence toward International Financial Reporting Standards (IFRS) (Chapter 8), notwithstanding, we believe that analysts need to have knowledge about local GAAP and institutional arrangements. That's because many companies are simply unaffected by the convergence movement. For example, some 7,000 to 8,000 listed European companies must now prepare their consolidated financial statements according to IFRS. But the estimated 3 million nonlisted European companies are not directly affected by the IFRS requirement. As another example, U.S., Japanese, and Mexican companies must follow their respective national GAAP, not IFRS. Even though financial reporting standards and practices are converging for many companies around the world, differences remain for many others.

Chapter 3 focuses on five members of the European Union (EU): the Czech Republic, France, Germany, the Netherlands, and the United Kingdom. France, Germany, and the Netherlands were original members of the European Economic Community when it was established in 1957. The United Kingdom joined in 1973. All four of these countries have highly developed economies and are home to many of the world's largest multinational corporations. They were among the founders of the International Accounting Standards Committee (now the International Accounting Standards Board, or IASB), and they have a major role in directing its agenda. The Czech Republic is an "emerging" economy.[1] Until 1989 a member of the now defunct Soviet bloc, it is converting from a planned to a market economy. Accounting developments there are representative of those in other former Soviet bloc countries. The Czech Republic joined the EU in 2004.

Exhibit 3-1 contains some comparative economic data about the five countries discussed in this chapter. The contrast between the Czech Republic and the other four

---

[1]The term emerging economy refers loosely to newly industrialized countries (NICs) and countries in transition from planned to free-market economies. NICs have experienced rapid industrial growth, but their economies are not yet rich in terms of per capita gross domestic product. India, discussed in Chapter 4, is a NIC. The Czech Republic has an economy in transition.

EXHIBIT 3-1 Economic Data for Selected Countries

	France	Germany	Czech Republic	Netherlands	United Kingdom
Area: sq. km.(in thousands)	544	358	79	42	243
Population (in millions)	60.4	82.5	10.2	16.2	59.4
Gross Domestic Product (in billions)	$2,047	$2,741	$107	$579	$2,124
GDP per Capita	$33,890	$33,220	$10,490	$35,740	$35,760
GDP by sector					
Agriculture	2%	1%	3%	3%	1%
Industry	22%	29%	38%	24%	26%
Services	76%	70%	59%	73%	73%
Imports (in billions)	$440	$718	$68	$284	$460
Exports (in billions)	$417	$912	$67	$318	$350
Market Capitalization (in billions), end 2005	$1,710	$1,221	$38	$728	$3,058
Major Trading Partners	Germany, Spain, Italy	France, U.S.A.; U.K.	Germany, Slovakia, Austria	Germany, Belgium, U.K.	U.S.A., Germany, France

SOURCE: Compiled from *Pocket World in Figures, 2007 Edition* (London: The Economist, 2006) and *The World Factbook,* www.cia.gov/cia/publications/factbook/, January 2007.

countries is apparent. Its gross domestic product (both in absolute terms and per capita), imports and exports, and stock market capitalization are significantly smaller than those of the other four countries. It also has more of an industrial and less of a service economy than the other countries.

SOME OBSERVATIONS ABOUT ACCOUNTING STANDARDS AND PRACTICE

Accounting standards are the regulations or rules (often including laws and statutes) that govern the preparation of financial statements. *Standard setting* is the process by which accounting standards are formulated. Thus, accounting standards are the outcome of standard setting. However, actual practice may deviate from what the standards require. There are at least three reasons for this. First, in many countries the penalties for noncompliance with official accounting pronouncements are weak or ineffective. Companies don't always follow standards when they are not enforced. Second, companies may voluntarily report more information than required. Third, some countries allow companies to depart from accounting standards if doing so will better represent a company's results of operations and financial position. To gain a complete picture of how accounting works in a country, we must pay attention to the accounting standard-setting process, the resulting accounting standards, and actual practice. *Auditing* adds credibility to financial reports. Thus, we also discuss the role and purpose of auditing in the countries we examine.

Accounting standard setting normally involves a combination of private- and public-sector groups. The private sector includes the accounting profession and other groups affected by the financial reporting process, such as users and preparers of financial statements and employees. The public sector includes such agencies as tax authorities, government agencies responsible for commercial law, and securities commissions. Stock exchanges may influence the process and may be in either the private or public sector, depending on the country. The roles and influence of these groups in setting accounting standards differ from country to country. These differences help explain why standards vary around the world.

The relationship between accounting standards and accounting practice is complex, and does not always move in a one-way direction. In some cases, practice derives from standards; in others, standards are derived from practice. Practice can be influenced by market forces, such as those related to the competition for funds in capital markets. Companies competing for funds may voluntarily provide information beyond what is required in response to the demand for information by investors and others. If the demand for such information is strong enough, standards may be changed to mandate disclosures that formerly were voluntary.

Chapter 2 distinguished the fair presentation and legal compliance orientations of accounting. Fair presentation accounting is usually associated with common law countries, whereas legal compliance accounting is typically found in code law countries. This distinction applies in standard setting, in that the private sector is relatively more influential in fair presentation, common law countries, while the public sector is relatively more influential in legal compliance, code law countries. Auditing parallels the type of legal system and the role and purpose of financial reporting. The auditing profession tends to be more self-regulated in fair presentation countries, especially those influenced by the United Kingdom. Auditors also exercise more judgment when the purpose of an audit is to attest to the fair presentation of financial reports. By contrast, in code law countries the accounting profession tends to be more state regulated. In such countries, the main purpose of an audit is to ensure that the company's records and financial statements conform to legal requirements.

IFRS IN THE EUROPEAN UNION

The trend in financial reporting is toward fair presentation, at least for consolidated financial statements. This trend is particularly true in the European Union. In 2002, the EU approved an accounting regulation requiring all EU companies listed on a regulated market to follow IFRS in their consolidated financial statements, starting in 2005. Member states are free to extend this requirement to all companies, not just listed ones, including individual company financial statements. Exhibit 3-2 summarizes the EU requirements for using IFRS in the five countries surveyed in this chapter. Convergence in financial reporting can be expected where IFRS are required, but differences remain where they are not.

To understand accounting in Europe, one must understand both IFRS and local accounting requirements. Many companies will choose to follow local requirements in instances where IFRS are permitted. For example, they may view IFRS as not relevant for their needs or too complicated. Thus, we provide an overview of IFRS in this section. The rest of the chapter looks at accounting in the five countries surveyed.

EXHIBIT 3-2   IFRS Requirements

	Czech Republic	France	Germany	Netherlands	United Kingdom
Listed companies — consolidated financial statements	Required	Required	Required	Required	Required
Listed companies — individual company financial statements	Required	Prohibited[a]	Permitted, but for informational purposes only[a]	Permitted	Permitted
Nonlisted companies — consolidated financial statements	Permitted	Permitted	Permitted	Permitted	Permitted
Nonlisted companies — individual company financial statements	Prohibited[b]	Prohibited[a]	Permitted, but for informational purposes only[a]	Permitted	Permitted

[a] French and German individual company financial statements must be prepared using local accounting require-ments because these statements are the basis for taxes and dividends.
[b] IFRS are not allowed in individual company financial statements of Czech nonlisted companies because it is thought that IFRS would be too complex and costly for these small, privately owned firms.

Financial Reporting

IFRS financial statements consist of the consolidated balance sheet, income statement, cash flow statement, a statement of changes in equity (or a statement of recognized income and expense), and explanatory notes. Note disclosures must include:

- Accounting policies followed
- Judgments made by management in applying critical accounting policies
- Key assumptions about the future and other important sources of estimation uncertainty

Comparative information is only required for the preceding period. There is no IFRS requirement to present the parent entity's financial statements in addition to the consolidated financial statements. There are also no IFRS requirements to produce interim financial statements. Consolidation is based on control, which is the power to govern the financial and operating activities of another entity. Generally, all subsidiaries must be consolidated even if control is temporary or the subsidiary operates under severe long-term funds-transfer restrictions. Fair presentation is required. IFRS may be overridden in extremely rare circumstances to achieve a fair presentation. When they are, the nature, reason, and financial impact of the departure from IFRS must be disclosed.

Accounting Measurements

Under IFRS, all business combinations are treated as purchases. Goodwill is the dif-ference between the fair value of the consideration given and the fair value of the subsidiary's assets, liabilities, and contingent liabilities. Goodwill is tested annually for impairment. Negative goodwill should be immediately recognized in income. Jointly controlled entities may be accounted for either by proportional consolidation (preferred) or the equity method. Investments in associates are accounted for by the equity method. An associate is an entity in which the investor has significant influence, but which is neither a subsidiary nor a joint venture. Significant influence is the power to participate in the financial and operating policy decisions of the investee but not to control those policies. It is presumed to exist when the investor holds at least 20 percent of the investee's voting power and not to exist when less than 20 percent is held; these presumptions may be rebutted if there is clear evidence to the contrary.

Translation of the financial statements of foreign operations is based on the functional currency concept. The functional currency is the currency of the primary economic environment in which the foreign entity operates. It can be either the same currency that the parent uses to present its financial statements or a different, foreign currency. (a) If the foreign entity has a functional currency different from the reporting currency of the parent, the financial statements are translated using the current rate method with the resulting translation adjustment included in stockholders' equity. (Under the current rate method, assets and liabilities are translated at the year-end, or current, exchange rate; revenues and expenses are translated at the transaction rates [or, in practice, the average rate]). (b) If the foreign entity has the same functional currency as the reporting currency of the parent, financial statements are translated as follows:

- Year-end rate for monetary items
- Transaction-date exchange rates for nonmonetary items carried at historical cost
- Valuation-date exchange rates for nonmonetary items carried at fair value

Translation adjustments are included in current period income. (c) If a foreign entity has the functional currency of a hyperinflationary economy, its financial statements are first restated for the effects of inflation, then translated using the current rate method described above.

Assets are valued at either historical cost or fair value. If the fair value method is used, revaluations must be carried out regularly and all items of a given class must be revalued. Revaluation increases are credited to equity. Depreciation is charged systematically over the asset's useful life, reflecting the pattern of benefit consumption. Research costs are charged to expense when incurred. Development costs are capitalized after the technical and commercial feasibility of the resulting product or service has been established. Inventories are valued at the lower of cost or net realizable value. FIFO and weighted average are acceptable cost bases under IFRS, but LIFO is not.

Finance leases are capitalized and amortized, while operating leases are expensed on a systematic basis, usually expensing the lease payments on a straight-line basis. The cost of providing employee benefits is recognized in the period in which the benefit is earned by the employee rather than when it is paid or payable. Provisions are liabilities of uncertain timing or amount. They are recognized when a past event has created a legal or constructive obligation, an outflow of resources is probable, and the amount of the obligation can be estimated reliably. Contingent liabilities are a possible obligation, an obligation that will probably not require an outflow of resources, or an obligation that cannot be reliably estimated. They are not recognized as liabilities, but are instead disclosed in the notes. Contingent assets are also not recognized. Deferred taxes are provided in full, using the liability method, for temporary differences between the carrying amount of an asset or liability and its tax base. Deferred tax assets and liabilities should be measured at the tax rates that are expected to apply when the asset is realized or the liability is settled. They are not discounted.

FIVE NATIONAL FINANCIAL ACCOUNTING SYSTEMS.[2]

France

France is the world's leading advocate of national uniform accounting. The Ministry of National Economy approved the first formal Plan Comptable Général (national accounting code) in September 1947. A revised plan came into effect in 1957. A further revision of the plan was enacted in 1982 under the influence of the Fourth Directive of the European Union (EU). In 1986 the plan was extended to implement the requirements of the EU's Seventh Directive on consolidated financial statements, and it was further revised in 1999.

The Plan Comptable Général provides:

- objectives and principles of financial accounting and reporting
- definitions of assets, liabilities, shareholders' equity, revenues, and expenses
- recognition and valuation rules
- a standardized chart of accounts, requirements for its use, and other bookkeeping requirements
- model financial statements and rules for their presentation

The mandatory use of the national uniform chart of accounts does not burden French businesses because the plan is widely accepted in practice. Moreover, various schedules required for income tax returns are based on the standardized models of the income statement and balance sheet, and the state statistical office produces macroeconomic information by aggregating the financial statements of enterprises.

French accounting is so closely linked to the plan that it is possible to overlook the fact that commercial legislation (i.e., the Code de Commerce) and tax laws dictate many of France's actual financial accounting and reporting practices. Both of these predate the plan. The Code de Commerce has its roots in the 1673 and 1681 ordinances of Colbert (finance minister to Louis XIV) and was enacted by Napoleon in 1807 as a part of the legal system he created, based on written law. The first income tax law was passed in 1914, thereby linking taxation and the need to keep accounting records.

The main bases for accounting regulation in France are the 1983 Accounting Law and 1983 Accounting Decree, which made the Plan Comptable Général compulsory

---

[2]The discussion in this section draws on the references cited at the end of the chapter and on references cited in earlier editions of this book.

for all companies. Both texts are inserted in the Code de Commerce.[3] Commercial legislation in the Code de Commerce has extensive accounting and reporting provisions. Annual inventories of assets and liabilities are required. The true and fair view for financial reporting must be evidenced, and certain accounting records are granted a privileged role in specified judicial proceedings. Accounting records, which legally serve purposes of proof and verification, are increasingly considered sources of information for decision-making.

Each enterprise must establish an accounting manual if it believes that this is necessary to understand and control the accounting process. At a minimum, the manual includes a detailed flow chart and explanations of the entire accounting system, descriptions of all data-processing procedures and controls, a comprehensive statement of the accounting principles underlying annual financial statements, and the procedures used in the mandatory annual counting of inventory.

Tax laws also significantly influence accounting in France. Business expenses are deductible for tax purposes only if they are fully booked and reflected in annual financial statements.

Accounting Regulation and Enforcement

Five major organizations are involved in setting standards in France:[4]

1. Counseil National de la Comptabilité, or CNC (National Accounting Board)
2. Comité de la Réglementation Comptable, or CRC (Accounting Regulation Committee)
3. Autorité des Marches Financiers, or AMF (Financial Markets Authority)[5]
4. Ordre des Experts-Comptables, or OEC (Institute of Public Accountants)
5. Compagnie Nationale des Commissaires aux Comptes, or CNCC (National Institute of Statutory Auditors)

The CNC consists of 58 members representing the accounting profession, civil servants, and employer, trade union, and other private-sector groups. Attached to the Ministry of Economy and Finance, the CNC issues rulings and recommendations on accounting issues and has major responsibility for keeping the plan current. It is consulted on accounting matters requiring regulation, but has no regulatory or enforcement powers. Most of the CNC's technical work is done by committees of CNC members and staff. An Urgent Issues Committee is attached to the CNC to address accounting issues needing quick resolution. Appointments to the CNC are highly prestigious, and its recommendations carry much weight.

Due to a need for a flexible and expeditious means of providing regulatory authority for accounting standards, the CRC was established in 1998. The CRC converts CNC rulings and recommendations into binding regulations. Under the jurisdiction of the

---

[3]The legal framework for accounting includes laws passed by Parliament, government decrees dealing with the application of these laws, and ministerial orders by the Ministry of Economy and Finance.
[4]The Web site addresses are: CNC and CRC: www.minefi.gouv.fr/directions_services/CNCompta; AMF: www.amf-france.org; OEC: www.experts-comptables.com; CNCC: www.cncc.fr.
[5]The AMF was established in 2003 from the merger of the Commission des Operations de Bourse (COB), the Conseil des Marchés Financiers, and the Conseil de Discipline de la Gestion Financière. The COB was the previous organization with authority over the stock exchanges.

Ministry of Economy and Finance, it has 15 members, among them representatives of different ministries, the CNC, AMF, OEC, and CNCC, and judges from the two highest courts in France. CRC regulations are published in the *Official Journal of the French Republic* after ministerial approval. Thus, the CRC has real regulatory power.

French companies traditionally have relied less on capital markets than on other sources of finance.[6] The French equivalent of the U.S. Securities and Exchange Commission—the AMF—has important but limited influence on accounting standard setting. The AMF supervises the new-issues market and the operations of regional and national stock exchanges. It has authority to issue additional reporting and disclosure rules for listed companies. The president of France appoints the chair of the AMF, and the commission reports annually to the president. This arrangement provides independence from other government departments.[7] The AMF is responsible for enforcing compliance with reporting requirements by French listed firms. Two divisions verify compliance. The Division of Corporate Finance (SOIF) conducts a general review of the legal, economic, and financial aspects of documents filed with the AMF (including annual reports). The Accounting Division (SACF) verifies compliance with accounting standards. The AMF has broad powers to require companies to modify questionable items in their filings. If necessary, the AMF can take administrative action against a company to force compliance.[8]

In France the accounting and auditing professions have historically been separate. French accountants and auditors are represented by two bodies, the OEC and the CNCC, despite substantial overlap in their memberships. Indeed, 80 percent of France's qualified accountants hold both qualifications. The two professional bodies maintain close links and cooperate on issues of common interest. Both participate in the development of accounting standards through the CNC and CRC, and they represent France on the IASB.

The practice of public accounting and the right to the title *expert-comptable* is restricted to OEC members, who contract with clients to maintain and review accounting records and prepare financial statements. They may also provide tax, information systems, and management advisory services. The OEC is under the jurisdiction of the Ministry of Economy and Finance. Most of its effort is devoted to professional-practice issues, although before the CRC was established it issued interpretations and recommendations on the application of accounting legislation and regulations.

By contrast, the CNCC (professional association of statutory auditors, *commissaires aux comptes*) is under the jurisdiction of the Ministry of Justice. By law, only statutory auditors may audit and give an opinion on financial statements.[9] The CNCC publishes a member handbook that contains extensive professional standards. It also publishes

---

[6]France has a tradition of family businesses and nationalized industries, both of which rely on debt financing.
[7]A predecessor body to the AMF, the Commission des Opérations de Bourse (COB), was an early advocate of consolidation requirements for French companies and, in general, sought French acceptance of world-class accounting and reporting standards—at least for larger publicly listed French companies. The COB pressed for better accounting and disclosure, and successfully improved the quality of information in French consolidated financial statements.
[8]For further information, see T.H.P Dao, "Monitoring Compliance with IFRS: Some Insights from the French Regulatory System," *Accounting in Europe* 2 (2005): 107–135.
[9]The same person can practice both accounting and auditing. However, independence rules prohibit the statutory auditor from also providing accounting services to the same client firm.

information bulletins that provide technical assistance. Audits in France are generally similar to their counterparts elsewhere. However, French auditors must report to the state prosecutor any criminal acts that they become aware of during an audit. The Haut Conseil du Commissariat aux Comptes (High Council of External Auditors) was established in 2003 to monitor the audit profession, particularly in the areas of ethics and independence. Like the CNCC, it is under the Ministry of Justice. The 2003 law also requires an auditor's report on internal controls.[10]

The AMF is responsible for overseeing the audits of listed companies. However, the AMF relies on a committee of the CNCC (the Comité de l'Examen National des Activités, or CENA) to conduct audit-quality reviews on its behalf. By arrangement with the AMF, CENA examines the audit of each listed company at least once every six years.[11] Follow-up examinations are also done in cases where the auditor's work is found to be deficient.

Financial Reporting

French companies must report the following:

1. Balance sheet
2. Income statement
3. Notes to financial statements
4. Directors' report
5. Auditor's report

The financial statements of all corporations and other limited liability companies above a certain size must be audited. Large companies also must prepare documents relating to the prevention of business bankruptcies and a social report, both of which are unique to France. There are no requirements for a statement of changes in financial position or a cash flow statement. However, the CNC recommends a cash flow statement, and nearly all large French companies publish one. Individual company and consolidated statements are both required, but small groups are exempt from the consolidation requirement. The Code de Commerce allows simplified financial statements for small and medium-sized companies.

To give a true and fair view (*image fidèle*), financial statements must be prepared in compliance with legislation (*régularité*) and in good faith (*sincérité*). A significant feature of French reporting is the requirement for extensive and detailed footnote disclosures, including the following items:

• Explanation of measurement rules employed (i.e., accounting policies)
• Accounting treatment of foreign currency items
• Statement of changes in fixed assets and depreciation
• Details of provisions
• Details of any revaluations
• Breakdown of receivables and liabilities by maturity
• List of subsidiaries and share holdings

---

[10]The heightened oversight of the auditing profession and the new report on internal controls are in part a response to the same accounting scandals that gave rise to the Sarbanes-Oxley Act in the United States (Chapter 4).
[11]The normal period for an audit contract of a listed company in France is six years.

- Amount of commitments for pensions and other retirement benefits
- Details of the impact of taxes on the financial statements
- Average number of employees listed by category
- Analysis of turnover by activity and geographically

The directors' report includes a review of the company's activities during the year, the company's future prospects, important post–balance sheet events, research and development activities, and a summary of the company's results for the past five years. The financial statements of commercial companies must be audited, except for small, limited liability companies and partnerships.

Listed companies must provide half-yearly interim reports and, starting in 2003, the results of their environmental activities. Among other items, information must be given on:

- Water, raw material, and energy consumption, and actions taken to improve energy efficiency
- Activities to reduce pollution in the air, water, or ground, including noise pollution, and their costs
- Amount of provisions for environmental risks

French law also contains provisions aimed at preventing bankruptcies (or mitigating their consequences). The idea is that companies that have a good understanding of their internal financial affairs and prepare sound projections can better avoid financial difficulties. Accordingly, larger companies prepare four documents: a statement of cash position, a statement of changes in financial position or cash flow statement, a forecast income statement, and a business plan. These documents are not audited, but are given a limited examination by the auditors. They are submitted only to the board of directors and employee representatives; they are not made available to the shareholders or the general public unless provided voluntarily (such as the cash flow statement). Thus, this information is designed as an internal early-warning signal for management and workers.

A social report also is required for all companies with 300 or more employees. This report describes, analyzes, and reports on matters of training, industrial relations, health and safety conditions, wage levels and other employment benefits, and many additional relevant work-environment conditions. The report is required for individual companies, not consolidated groups.

Accounting Measurements

Listed French companies follow IFRS in their consolidated financial statements, and nonlisted companies also have this option. However, all French companies must follow the fixed regulations of the plan at the individual company level. Accounting for individual companies is the legal basis for distributing dividends and for calculating taxable income. Exhibit 3-3 provides an example of financial reporting by French listed firms. Saint-Gobain, a materials and construction products company listed in Paris and on other European stock exchanges, explains its accounting policies for its consolidated and nonconsolidated financial statements.

Tangible assets are normally valued at historical cost. Although revaluations are allowed, they are taxable and, therefore, are seldom found in practice. Fixed assets are depreciated according to tax provisions, normally on a straight-line or declining balance

EXHIBIT 3-3   Saint-Gobain Accounting Policies

Note to consolidated financial statements

These consolidated financial statements of Compagnie de Saint-Gobain and its subsidiaries (together "the Group") have been prepared in accordance with International Financial Reporting Standards (IFRS), as adopted by the European Union at December 31, 2005.

Note to parent company financial statements

The financial statements of Compagnie de Saint-Gobain have been drawn up in accordance with the accounting principles set out in the 1999 French Chart of Accounts.

SOURCE: 2005 Saint-Gobain Annual Report, pp. 120 and 175.

basis. Extra tax depreciation is sometimes available, in which case the additional amount taken is shown as an exceptional charge on the income statement and the corresponding credit as a tax-related provision in equity. Inventory must be valued at the lower of cost or realizable value using either First in, First Out (FIFO) or weighted-average methods.

Research and development costs are expensed as incurred, but may be capitalized in restricted circumstances. If capitalized, research and development costs must be amortized over no more than five years. Leased assets are not capitalized, and the rent paid is expensed. Pension and other retirement benefits are normally expensed when paid, and future commitments are seldom recognized as liabilities. Probable losses whose amounts can be determined with reasonable accuracy are accrued. Many other risks and uncertainties may be provided for, such as those relating to litigation, restructurings, and self-insurance; these allow income-smoothing opportunities. Given the link between book and tax income, companies do not account for deferred taxes in individual company financial statements. Legal reserves must be created by appropriating 5 percent of income each year until the reserve equals 10 percent of legal capital.

With a few exceptions, French rules regarding consolidated financial statements follow the fair presentation approach of reporting substance over form. Two exceptions are that liabilities for post-employment benefits do not have to be recognized and finance leases do not have to be capitalized. (In both cases, the fair presentation treatment of accrual and capitalization is recommended, but still optional.) Deferred taxes are accounted for using the liability method, and are discounted when the reversal of timing differences can be reliably estimated. The purchase method is normally used to account for business combinations, but the pooling method is allowed in some circumstances. Goodwill normally is capitalized and amortized to income, but no maximum amortization period is specified. Goodwill is not required to be impairments tested. Proportional consolidation is used for joint ventures and the equity method is used to account for investments in nonconsolidated entities over which significant influence is exercised. Foreign currency translation practice is consistent with IFRS, as previously described.

Germany

The German accounting environment has changed continuously and remarkably since the end of World War II. At that time, business accounting emphasized national and sectional charts of account (as in France). The Commercial Code stipulated various principles of "orderly bookkeeping," and independent auditing barely survived the war.

In a major turn of events, the 1965 Corporation Law moved the German financial reporting system toward British-American ideas (but only for larger corporations). More disclosure, limited consolidation,[12] and a corporate management report were required. The management report and additional audit requirements became legal requirements through the 1969 Corporate Publicity Law.

In the early 1970s the European Union (EU) began issuing its harmonization directives, which member countries were required to incorporate into their national laws. The Fourth, Seventh, and Eighth EU Directives all entered German law through the Comprehensive Accounting Act of December 19, 1985. This legislation is remarkable because (1) it integrates all existing German accounting, financial reporting, disclosure, and auditing requirements into a single law; (2) this single law is specified as the *third book* of the German Commercial Code (HGB), thus becoming applicable to all business entities, from limited partnerships to private and publicly held corporations; and (3) the legislation is based predominantly on European concepts and practices.

Two new laws were passed in 1998. The first added a new paragraph in the third book of the German Commercial Code allowing companies that issue equity or debt on organized capital markets to use internationally accepted accounting principles in their consolidated financial statements. The second allowed the establishment of a private-sector organization to set accounting standards for consolidated financial statements.

Creditor protection is a fundamental concern of German accounting as embodied in the Commercial Code. Conservative balance sheet valuations are central to creditor protection. This creates a tendency to undervalue assets and overvalue liabilities. Reserves are seen as protection against unforeseen risks and possible insolvency. These practices also result in a conservative income amount that serves as the basis for dividends to owners. Thus, German accounting is designed to compute a prudent income amount that leaves creditors unharmed after distributions are made to owners.

Tax law also largely determines commercial accounting. The *determination principle* (*Massgeblichkeitsprinzip*) states that taxable income is determined by whatever is booked in a firm's financial records. Available tax provisions can be used only if they are fully booked. This means, among other things, that any special or highly accelerated depreciation used for tax purposes must also be booked for financial reporting purposes. The dominance of tax accounting means that no distinction is made between financial statements prepared for tax purposes and those published in financial reports.

The third fundamental characteristic of German accounting is its reliance on statutes and court decisions. Nothing else has any binding or authoritative status. To understand German accounting, one must look to both HGB and a considerable body of case law.

Accounting Regulation and Enforcement

Before 1998, Germany had no financial accounting standard-setting function, as it is understood in English-speaking countries. The German Institute provided consultation in various processes of lawmaking that affected accounting and financial reporting, but legal requirements were absolutely supreme. Similar consultation was

---

[12]For example, the law only required consolidation of German subsidiaries.

given by the Frankfurt Stock Exchange, German trade unions, and accounting academics. The 1998 law on control and transparency (abbreviated KonTraG) introduced the requirements for the Ministry of Justice to recognize a private national standard-setting body to serve the following objectives:

- Develop recommendations for the application of accounting standards for consolidated financial statements.
- Advise the Ministry of Justice on new accounting legislation.
- Represent Germany in international accounting organizations such as the IASB.

The German Accounting Standards Committee (GASC), or in German, the *Deutsches Rechnungslegungs* Standards Committee (DRSC), was founded shortly thereafter, and duly recognized by the Ministry of Justice as the German standard-setting authority.[13]

The GASC oversees the German Accounting Standards Board (GASB), which does the technical work and issues the accounting standards. The GASB is made up of seven independent experts with a background in auditing, financial analysis, academia, and industry. Working groups are established to examine and make recommendations on the issues before the board. As a rule, these working groups have representatives from trade and industry and the auditing profession, a university professor, and a financial analyst. GASB deliberations follow a due process and meetings are open. Once issued, the standards must be approved and published by the Ministry of Justice.

The new German accounting standard-setting system is broadly similar to the systems in the United Kingdom (as discussed in this chapter) and the United States (Chapter 4), and to the IASB (Chapter 8). It is important to emphasize, however, that GASB standards are authoritative recommendations that only apply to consolidated financial statements. They do not restrict or alter HGB requirements. The GASB was created to develop a set of German standards compatible with international accounting standards. Since its founding, the GASB has issued German Accounting Standards (GAS) on such issues as the cash flow statement, segment reporting, deferred taxes, and foreign currency translation. However, in 2003, the GASB adopted a new strategy that aligned its work program with the IASB's efforts to achieve a convergence of global accounting standards. These changes recognized the EU requirement for IFRS for listed companies.

The Financial Accounting Control Act (abbreviated BilKoG) was enacted in 2004 to improve compliance with German financial reporting requirements and IFRS by listed companies. The law established a two-tiered enforcement system. A private-sector body, the Financial Reporting Enforcement Panel (FREP), reviews suspected irregular financial statements that come to its attention. It also conducts random reviews of financial statements. The FREP relies on companies to voluntarily correct any problems it finds. The FREP refers matters that are not resolved to the Federal Financial Supervisory Authority (German abbreviation BaFin), the public-sector regulatory body that oversees securities trading (stock exchanges) and the banking and insurance industries. BaFin will then take authoritative action to resolve the issue. BaFin refers questionable auditing to the *Wirtschaftsprüferkammer*, discussed next.

---

[13]The GASC Web site is www.drsc.de.

Certified public accountants in Germany are called *Wirtschaftsprüfer* (WPs), or enterprise examiners.[14] All WPs are legally required to join the official Chamber of Accountants (*Wirtschaftsprüferkammer*). The Auditor Oversight Commission, which reports to the Ministry of Economics and Labor, is responsible for overseeing the Chamber of Accountants. By international standards, the German auditing (accounting) profession is small. The 1985 Accounting Act extended the audit requirement to many more companies. As a result, a second-tier body of auditors was created in the late 1980s. These individuals, known as sworn book examiners (*Vereidigte Buchprüfer*), are only allowed to audit small and medium-sized companies, as defined in the act. Thus, two classes of auditors are legally sanctioned to conduct independent audit examinations of companies. German audit reports emphasize compliance with requirements over the "true and fair view." Exhibit 3-4, the opinion paragraph of KPMG on the 2005 financial statements of the BMW automobile company, is illustrative.

Financial Reporting

German law specifies different accounting, auditing, and financial reporting requirements depending on company size rather than the form of business organization.[15] There are three size classes—small, medium, and large—defined in terms of balance sheet totals, annual sales totals, and numbers of employees. Companies with publicly traded securities are always classified as large. The law specifies the content and format of financial statements, which include the following:

1. Balance sheet
2. Income statement
3. Notes
4. Management report
5. Auditor's report

EXHIBIT 3-4   Audit Opinion on BMW Financial Statements

In our opinion, based on the findings of our audit, the consolidated financial statements comply with IFRS, as adopted by the EU, the additional requirements of German Commercial Law pursuant to §315 a Abs. 1 HGB and give a true and fair view of the net assets, financial position, and results of operations of the Group in accordance with these requirements. The group management report is consistent with the consolidated financial statements and as a whole provides a suitable view of the Group's position and suitably presents the opportunities and risks of future development.

Munich, 24 February 2006
KPMG Deutsche Treuhand-Gesellschaft

SOURCE: 2005 BMW Annual Report, p. 125.

---

[14]The Institute der Wirtschaftsprüfer's Web site is www.wpk.de.
[15]The three major forms of business organizations in Germany are (1) *Aktiengesellschaft* (AG), (2) *Kommanditgesellschaft auf Aktien* (KGaA), and (3) *Gesellschaft mit beschränkter Haftung* (GmbH).

AGs are typically large corporations with two senior boards: a management board and a supervisory board. The supervisory board appoints and dismisses members of the management board, supervises the management board, and reviews and approves annual financial statements. The KGaA is a mixture of the limited partnership and the corporate form of business organization. It must have at least one shareholder who is personally liable for the company's indebtedness (the remaining shareholders are liable only to the extent of their investments in the company). KGaAs are unknown in English-speaking countries. GmbHs are privately held companies. Most medium and small businesses operate in this form.

Small companies are exempt from the audit requirement and may prepare an abbreviated balance sheet. Small and medium-sized companies may prepare abbreviated income statements. Small and medium-sized companies also have fewer disclosure requirements for their notes. A cash flow statement and a statement of changes in owners' equity are required for consolidated financial statements but not individual company statements.

The notes section of the financial statements is usually extensive, especially for large companies. Disclosures include the accounting principles used, the extent to which results are affected by claiming tax benefits, unaccrued pension obligations, sales by product line and geographic markets, unaccrued contingent liabilities, and average number of employees. The management report describes the financial position and business developments during the year, important post-balance sheet events, anticipated future developments, and research and development activities. Publicly traded companies are required to provide additional segment disclosures. They must also provide abbreviated half-yearly financial statements that are reviewed by an auditor and accompanied by an interim management report.

A feature of the German financial reporting system is a private report by the auditors to the company's managing board of directors and supervisory board. This report comments on the company's future prospects and, especially, factors that may threaten its survival. The auditor must describe and analyze items on the balance sheet that have a material impact on the company's financial position. The auditor also has to evaluate the consequences of and pass judgment on all significant accounting choices. This report can run several hundred pages for large German companies. As noted, it is private information, not available to shareholders.

Consolidated financial statements are required for enterprises under unified management and with a majority of voting rights, dominant influence by virtue of control contracts, or the right to appoint or remove a majority of the board of directors. For purposes of consolidation, all companies in the group must use identical accounting and valuation principles. However, they need not be the same as those used in individual company statements. In this way, tax-driven accounting methods in individual accounts can be eliminated in the group accounts. Consolidated accounts are not the basis for either taxation or profit distributions.

All companies, not just listed ones, may use IFRS in preparing their consolidated financial statements. However, individual company financial statements must follow HGB requirements. Companies have the option of also publishing individual company financial statements according to IFRS for informational purposes.

Accounting Measurements

Under the Commercial Code (HGB), the purchase (acquisition) method is the primary consolidation method, but pooling of interests is acceptable in limited circumstances. Two forms of the purchase method are permitted: the book-value method and the revaluation method (they essentially differ in the treatment of minority interests).[16] Assets and liabilities of acquired enterprises are brought up to current value, and any amount left over is goodwill, which can either be offset against reserves in equity or amortized

---

[16]Dieter Ordelheide, "Germany: Group Accounts," in *Transnational Accounting,* ed. Dieter Ordelheide (London: Macmillan Press, 1995): 1599–1602.

systematically over its economic life. The law mentions four years as the regular amortization period, but ranges up to 15 years are common. The equity method is used for associates that are owned 20 percent or more, but only in consolidated financial statements. Joint ventures may be accounted for using either proportional consolidation or the equity method. Since the HGB has no requirements for foreign currency translation, German companies use a number of methods. Translation differences are also dealt with in many ways.

GAS are more restrictive than the HGB regarding consolidated financial statements. Under GAS 4, the revaluation method must be used, whereby assets and liabilities acquired in a business combination are revalued to fair value, and any excess allocated to goodwill. Goodwill is tested annually for impairment. GAS 14 adopts the functional currency approach to foreign currency translation, in line with IFRS, as previously described.

Historical cost is the basis for valuing tangible assets. (Germany is one of the world's staunchest adherents to the historical cost principle. Its strong anti-inflation attitudes are the result of the ravages of the two debilitating inflationary periods it went through in the 20th century.) Inventory is stated at the lower of cost or market; FIFO, LIFO, and average are acceptable methods of determining cost. Depreciable fixed assets are subject to tax depreciation rates.

Research and development costs are expensed when incurred. Finance leases typically are not capitalized, but pension obligations are accrued based on their actuarially determined present value consistent with tax laws. Deferred taxes do not normally arise in individual company accounts, because these are tax determined. However, they may arise in consolidated statements if accounting methods used for consolidations are different from those used for the individual accounts. In this case, deferred taxes must be set up using the liability method.

Provisions as estimates of future expenses or losses are used heavily. Provisions must be set up for deferred maintenance expenses, product guarantees, potential losses from pending transactions, and other uncertain liabilities. Optional provisions, such as those for future major repairs, are also allowed. Most companies make provisions as large as possible because legally booked expenses directly affect the determination of taxable income. Provisions give German companies many opportunities to manage income. Portions of retained earnings often are allocated to specific reserves, including a mandated legal reserve and those resulting from the provisions just described.

As noted earlier, listed German companies must prepare their consolidated financial statements in accordance with IFRS. Other companies have a choice of using either IFRS or German rules described above for consolidation purposes. Both choices are found in practice, and the reader of German financial statements should be careful to know which accounting standards are being followed.

Czech Republic

The Czech Republic (CR) is located in Central Europe with Germany to the west and northwest, Austria to the south, the Slovak Republic to the east, and Poland to the north. Its territory was a part of the Austro-Hungarian Empire for nearly 300 years (from 1620 to 1918), ruled by the Austrian monarchy, the Hapsburgs. The empire collapsed at the end of World War I, and the independent nation of Czechoslovakia was founded in 1918. Between the two world wars, Czechoslovakia was a prosperous parliamentary democracy with universal voting rights. This ended in 1938, when Britain and France allowed Nazi Germany to annex Czechoslovakia's ethnically German border territories. Within a year, Hitler controlled the rest of the nation and the Nazi occupation began. After the end of World War II, the 1946 elections and subsequent political maneuvering brought the Communist Party to power. This began the Soviet Union's domination over Czechoslovakia, which lasted until 1989. The internal disintegration of the Soviet regime and the collapse of the Czechoslovak Communist government in that year led to the so-called Velvet Revolution and the establishment of a new government. In 1993 Czechoslovakia peacefully split into two nations, the Czech Republic and the Republic of Slovakia.

Accounting in the Czech Republic has changed direction several times, reflecting the country's political history. Accounting practice and principles reflected those of the German-speaking countries of Europe until the end of World War II. Then, with the construction of a centrally planned economy, accounting practice was based on the Soviet model. The administrative needs of various central government institutions were satisfied through such features as a uniform chart of accounts, detailed accounting methods, and uniform financial statements, obligatory for all enterprises. A focus on production and costing, based on historical costs, was emphasized over external reporting. A unified system of financial and cost accounting used the same pricing and other principles.

Of course, prices did not reflect the market forces of supply and demand. They were centrally determined and controlled, primarily on a *cost plus* basis. Losses were normally subsidized. Accounting was of limited importance in managing an enterprise. Furthermore, accounting information was considered to be secret and financial statements were not published. While accounting information was inspected, it was not independently audited.[17]

After 1989 Czechoslovakia moved quickly toward a market-oriented economy. The government revamped its legal and administrative structure to stimulate the economy and attract foreign investments. Commercial laws and practices were adjusted to fit Western standards. Price controls were lifted. Accounting again turned westward, this time reflecting the principles embodied in the European Union Directives.

The division of Czechoslovakia did not appreciably affect this process. In 1993 the Prague Stock Exchange began regular operations. Considering the high level of economic and political development achieved in pre-1938 Czechoslovakia, these events were more a matter of returning to previously held norms than discovering new ones.[18]

Privatization of the economy involved the return of property to former owners, small privatizations in which more than 20,000 shops, restaurants, and other small businesses were sold to Czech citizens at public auction, and a series of large privatizations. A key element of the latter was a coupon voucher system allowing adult Czech citizens to buy investment vouchers for a nominal price. These vouchers were used to acquire shares of newly privatized large industrial concerns. However, many Czechs,

---

[17]Rudolf Schroll, "The New Accounting System in the Czech Republic," *European Accounting Review* 4, no. 4 (1995): 827–832; Jan Dolezal, "The Czech Republic," in *European Accounting Guide*, 2nd ed., ed. David Alexander and Simon Archer (San Diego: Harcourt Brace Jovanovich, 1995).
[18]Willie Seal, Pat Sucher, and Ivan Zelenka, "The Changing Organization of Czech Accounting," *European Accounting Review* 4, no. 4 (1995): 667.

with no experience as shareholders, sold their shares to investment funds owned by state-controlled Czech banks. One result was a conflict of interest for the banks, which ended up owning the same companies to which they were lending money. A second round of privatizations involved auctions or direct sales, often to the companies' own managers. Many of these newly privatized businesses subsequently failed, leaving little or no collateral and overloading the court system with business cases. Both waves of privatization are now viewed as a mistake of trying to do too much at once.[19] A few remaining state-owned enterprises are still to be privatized. The economic reforms are ongoing. Among the more pressing issues are improving the openness and transparency of stock market operations through tighter regulations, and restructuring enterprises.[20]

In 1995 the Czech Republic became the first post-Communist member of the Organization for Economic Cooperation and Development (OECD). The Czech Republic joined NATO in 1999 and the European Union in 2004.[21]

Accounting Regulation and Enforcement

The new Commercial Code was enacted by the Czech parliament in 1991 and became effective on January 1, 1992.[22] Influenced by the Austrian roots of the old commercial code and modeled on German commercial law, it introduced a substantial amount of legislation relating to businesses. (Czech law is based on the civil code law system of continental Europe.) This legislation includes requirements for annual financial statements, income taxes, audits, and shareholders meetings.

The Accountancy Act, which sets out the requirements for accounting, was passed in 1991 and became effective on January 1, 1993. Based on the EU's Fourth and Seventh Directives, the act specifies the use of a chart of accounts for record keeping and the preparation of financial statements.[23] It was significantly amended with effect from January 1, 2002 and 2004, primarily to bring Czech accounting closer to IFRS. The Ministry of Finance is responsible for accounting principles. Ministry of Finance

---

[19]The first wave of coupon privatization occurred in 1992 and involved 1,491 state-owned companies. The second round ended in 1994, privatizing a further 861 companies.

[20]U.S. Department of State, "Background Notes: Czech Republic" (September 2006); U.S. Central Intelligence Agency, "The World Factbook—Czech Republic" (2006); Daniel Michaels and John Reed, "Halfway There," *Wall Street Journal Interactive Edition* (September 18, 1997): 1–6; Mark Andress, "Czech, Please!," *Accountancy* (September 2000): 60–61; Zuzana Kawaciukova, "Privatization Theft," *Prague Post Online* (July 24, 2003).

Czech capital markets are largely illiquid. In 1995 and 1996, after the initial large privatizations, there were over 1,600 Czech companies listed on the Prague Stock Exchange. However, in 1997 the exchange started delisting securities that were rarely traded. By the end of 1999, the Prague Stock Exchange had approximately 200 listed companies and there were less than 35 at the end of 2006. The Czech stock market is not seen as a place to raise new capital. For example, there have only been three initial public offering of shares since it began operations in 1993 through the end of 2006. Transparent reporting, tight regulations, investor protection, and judicial enforcement are still lacking. See Pat Sucher, Peter Moizer, and Marcela Zarova, "The Images of the Big Six Audit Firms in the Czech Republic," *European Accounting Review* 8, no. 3 (1999): 503, 519; "After the Chaos: A Survey of Finance in Central Europe," *Economist* (September 14, 2002): 5–7, 10–11.

[21]The Czech Republic is scheduled to adopt the euro in 2010.

[22]In 1991 legislation was passed by the then-Czechoslovak parliament. The Czech Republic carried forward its provisions after the division.

[23]Charts of accounts are not new to the Czech Republic because their use was required under communism. The Czechs based their new system on the French Plan Comptable and received substantial help from the French Ministry of Finance and the French accounting profession in developing their new charts of account.

decrees set out acceptable measurement and disclosure practices that companies must follow. Thus, accounting in the CR is influenced by the Commercial Code, the Accountancy Act, and Ministry of Finance decrees. The stock exchange has so far had little influence, and, despite the German origins of the Commercial Code, tax legislation is not directly influential. As discussed in the following section, the true and fair view embodied in the Accountancy Act and taken from EU Directives is interpreted to mean that tax and financial accounts are treated differently.[24] Nevertheless, legal form takes precedence over economic substance in some cases. The Ministry of Finance also oversees the Czech Securities Commission, responsible for supervising and monitoring the capital market and enforcing the Securities Act.

Auditing is regulated by the Act on Auditors, passed in 1992. This act established the Chamber of Auditors, a self-regulated professional body that oversees the registration, education, examination, and disciplining of auditors, the setting of auditing standards, and the regulation of audit practice, such as the format of the audit report. An audit of financial statements is required for all corporations (joint stock companies) and for large limited liability companies (those exceeding two of the following three criteria: turnover of CzK80 million, net assets of CzK40 million, 50 employees).[25] The audit is designed to assure that the accounts have been kept according to applicable legislation and decrees and that the financial statements present a true and fair view of the company's financial position and results. The Chamber of Auditors has adopted International Standards on Auditing (see Chapter 8).

Financial Reporting

Financial statements must be comparative, consisting of:

1. Balance sheet
2. Profit and loss account (income statement)
3. Notes

Consistent with the requirements of the EU Directives, the notes include a description of the accounting policies and other relevant information for assessing the financial statements. Examples of the latter include employee information, revenues by segment, and contingencies. The notes must also include a cash flow statement. Consolidated financial statements are required for groups meeting at least two of the following criteria: (1) assets of CzK350 million, (2) revenues of CzK700 million, (3) 250 employees. Controlling interest in a subsidiary is based on either owning a majority of shares or having a direct or indirect dominant influence. Small and other companies not subject to audit have abbreviated disclosure requirements. Financial statements are approved at the annual meeting of shareholders. Listed Czech companies must use IFRS for both their consolidated and individual company financial statements. Nonlisted companies have the option of using IFRS or Czech accounting standards for their consolidated statements, but must use Czech standards in their individual company statements. Listed companies are also required to present quarterly income statements.

---

[24]Pat Sucher, Willie Seal, and Ivan Zelenka, "True and Fair View in the Czech Republic: A Note on Local Perceptions," *European Accounting Review* 5, no. 3 (1996): 551.
[25]Corporations issue shares, whereas limited liability companies do not. The latter are similar to limited partnerships.

Accounting Measurements

The acquisition (purchase) method is used to account for business combinations. Goodwill arising from a business combination is written off in the first year of consolidation or capitalized and amortized over no more than 20 years. The equity method is used for associated companies (those over which the company exercises significant influence but which are not consolidated), and proportional consolidation is used for joint ventures.[26] The year-end (closing) exchange rate is used to translate both the income statement and balance sheet of foreign subsidiaries. There are no guidelines for reporting foreign currency translation adjustments.

Tangible and intangible assets are valued at cost and written off over their expected economic lives. Inventory is valued at the lower of cost or net realizable value, and FIFO and weighted average are allowable cost-flow assumptions (LIFO is not). Research and development costs may be capitalized if they relate to projects completed successfully and capable of generating future income. Leased assets are typically not capitalized—an example of form over substance. Deferred income taxes are provided in full for all temporary differences. Contingent losses are recorded when they are probable and can be reliably measured. Companies may also take provisions for future repairs and maintenance expenditures. Legal reserves are required: Profits are appropriated annually until they reach 20 percent of equity for corporations and 10 percent for limited liability companies.

The Netherlands

Dutch accounting presents several interesting paradoxes. The Dutch have relatively permissive statutory accounting and financial reporting requirements but very high professional practice standards. The Netherlands is a code law country, yet accounting is oriented toward fair presentation. Financial reporting and tax accounting are two separate activities. Further, the fairness orientation developed without a strong stock market influence. The United Kingdom and the United States have influenced Dutch accounting as much (or more) than other continental European countries. Unlike the norm elsewhere in continental Europe, the accounting profession has had a significant influence on Dutch accounting standards and regulations.[27]

Accounting in the Netherlands is considered a branch of business economics. As a result, much economic thought has been devoted to accounting topics and especially to accounting measurements. Highly respected professional accountants are often part-time professors. Thus, academic thought has a major influence upon ongoing practice.

Dutch accountants are also willing to consider foreign ideas. The Dutch were among the earliest proponents of international standards for financial accounting and reporting, and the statements of the IASB receive substantial attention in determining

---

[26]In individual company statements, either the equity or cost method may be used to account for associated companies.

[27]The idea that the business community is capable of adequate financial reporting is well entrenched in Dutch thinking. The first limited liability companies were formed in the 17th century without a clear legal framework on the matter. The first commercial code, introduced in the 19th century, viewed shareholders as responsible for management, which prompted little need for extensive accounting requirements in the law. As in the United Kingdom, the Dutch accounting profession emerged in the 19th century and has had a substantial influence on accounting. By the time an income tax on corporations was introduced (in 1940), financial reporting was already too well developed to be dominated by tax accounting. See Kees Canfferman, "The History of Financial Reporting in the Netherlands," in *European Financial Reporting: A History*, ed. Peter Walton (London: Academic Press, 1995).

acceptable practice. The Netherlands is also home to several of the world's largest multinational enterprises, including Philips, Royal Dutch Shell, and Unilever.[28] These enterprises have been internationally listed since the 1950s and have been influenced by foreign (particularly U.K. and U.S.) accounting. Through example, these large multinationals have influenced the financial reporting of other Dutch companies. The influence of the Amsterdam Stock Exchange, however, has been minimal because it does not provide much new business capital.

Accounting Regulation and Enforcement

Accounting regulations in the Netherlands remained liberal until the passage of the Act on Annual Financial Statements in 1970. The act was a part of an extensive program of changes in company legislation and was introduced partly to reflect the coming harmonization of company law within the EU. Among the major provisions of the 1970 act are the following:

- Annual financial statements shall show a fair picture of the financial position and results of the year, and all items therein must be appropriately grouped and described.
- Financial statements must be drawn up in accordance with sound business practice (i.e., accounting principles acceptable to the business community).
- The bases of stating assets and liabilities and determining results of operations must be disclosed.
- Financial statements shall be prepared on a consistent basis, and the material effects of changes in accounting principles must be properly disclosed.
- Comparative financial information for the preceding period shall be disclosed in the financial statements and accompanying footnotes.

The 1970 act introduced the mandatory audit. It also set into motion the formation of the Tripartite Accounting Study Group[29] and gave birth to the Enterprise Chamber. The act, incorporated into the civil code in 1975, was amended by legislation in 1983 to incorporate the EU Fourth Directive, and further amended in 1988 to incorporate the EU Seventh Directive.

The Dutch Accounting Standards Board (DASB) issues guidelines on generally acceptable (not accepted) accounting principles.[30] The board is composed of members from three different groups:

1. Preparers of financial statements (employers)
2. Users of financial statements (representatives of trade unions and financial analysts)
3. Auditors of financial statements[31]

The DASB is a private organization financed by grants from the business community and the auditing profession. Its activities are coordinated by the Foundation for Annual Reporting (FAR). FAR appoints the members of the DASB and ensures adequate

---

[28]Unilever is a binational (British and Dutch) concern. Royal Dutch Shell is headquartered in the Netherlands but incorporated in Britain.

[29]The Tripartite Accounting Study Group was replaced in 1981 by the Council on Annual Reporting (CAR). The CAR changed its name to the Dutch Accounting Standards Board in 2005.

[30]The DASB Web site is www.rjnet.nl.

[31]Neither the Amsterdam Stock Exchange nor shareholder representatives participate in the board.

funding. Even though the board's guidelines do not have the force of law, they have traditionally been followed by most companies and auditors.[32] The guidelines are comprehensive in scope and incorporate as far as possible the standards of the IASB. (As an aid in drafting new or revised guidelines, the DASB uses a conceptual framework that is a translation of the IASB framework.) Nevertheless, the only legally enforceable accounting rules are those specified in the accounting and financial reporting provisions of the Dutch civil code.

The Netherlands Authority for the Financial Markets (AMF) supervises the operations of the securities markets. Although it falls under the Ministry of Finance, the AMF is an autonomous administrative authority. Among the responsibilities given it in 2006 is the oversight of annual reporting and auditing of listed companies. Its Financial Reporting Supervision Division examines financial statements filed with the AMF to ensure that they comply with applicable standards and the law. Its Audit Firm Oversight Division ensures that applicable audit standards are followed. The 2006 Supervision of Auditors' Organizations Act also provides for AMF oversight of the audit profession.

The Enterprise Chamber, a specialist court connected with the High Court of Amsterdam, is a unique feature of the Dutch system of enforcing compliance with accounting requirements. Any interested party may complain to this chamber if it believes that a company's financial statements do not conform to applicable law. Shareholders, employees, trade unions, and even the public prosecutor (but not independent auditors) may bring proceedings to the chamber. The chamber is composed of three judges and two expert accountants, and there is no jury. Chamber decisions may lead to modifications of financial statements or various penalties. Even though the rulings apply only to defendant companies, they sometimes state general rules that may influence the reporting practices of other companies.

Auditing is a self-regulated profession in the Netherlands. Its governing body is the Netherlands Institute of Registeraccountants (NIvRA), which has approximately 14,000 members.[33] It is autonomous in setting auditing standards, and its strong professional code of conduct has statutory status.

Until 1993, only members of NIvRA could certify financial statements, but changes were made that year to incorporate the EU Eighth Directive. In the Netherlands there are two kinds of auditors: registeraccountants (RAs, or chartered accountants) and administrative accountants (AAs).[34] The 1993 changes allowed AAs to also certify financial statements if they undergo additional training. Over time, educational and training qualifications for RAs and AAs will be standardized, and the code of conduct will be the same in relation to audit work, the auditor's responsibilities, and independence. One set of disciplinary rules will apply. However, NIvRA is likely to continue to dominate auditing and accounting in the Netherlands.

NIvRA is involved in everything that is accounting related in the Netherlands. It participates in the Dutch Accounting Standards Board and in commissions charged with revising the accounting statutes of the civil code. NIvRA members serve on the Enterprise Chamber, as accounting faculty at leading Dutch universities, on the IASB, and on committees of the EU, the OECD, the UN, and the International Federation of Accountants.

---

[32]However, auditors can issue an unqualified opinion when there is noncompliance with a guideline, as long as the financial statements still convey a true and fair view.

[33]The NIvRA Web site is www.nivra.nl.

[34]The Nederlandse Orde van Accountants-Administratieconsultenen (NovAA) Web site is www.novaa.nl.

Financial Reporting

The quality of Dutch financial reporting is uniformly high. Statutory financial statements should be filed in Dutch, but English, French, and German are also acceptable. The financial statements must include the following:

1. Balance sheet
2. Income statement
3. Notes
4. Directors' report
5. Other prescribed information

A cash flow statement is recommended, and most Dutch companies provide one. The notes must describe the accounting principles used in valuation and the determination of results, and the reasoning behind any accounting changes. The directors' report reviews the financial position at the balance sheet date, and performance during the financial year. It also provides information about the expected performance during the new financial year and comments on any significant post-balance sheet events. "Other prescribed information" must include the auditor's report and profit appropriations for the year.

Annual financial reports must be presented on both a parent-company-only and a consolidated basis. Group companies for the purpose of consolidation are companies that form an economic unit under common control. Consistent with EU Directives, reporting requirements vary by company size. Small companies are exempt from the requirements for an audit and for consolidated financial statements, and they may file an abbreviated income statement and balance sheet. Medium-sized companies must be audited, but may publish a condensed income statement. Small, medium-sized, and large companies are defined in the civil code. Listed Dutch companies must prepare IFRS consolidated statements. Their parent-company statements may also be prepared using IFRS, Dutch accounting guidelines, or a mixture of the two. All Dutch companies are allowed to use IFRS instead of Dutch guidelines.

Accounting Measurements

Although the pooling-of-interests method of accounting for business combinations is allowed in limited circumstances, it is rarely used in the Netherlands. The purchase method is the normal practice. Goodwill is the difference between the acquisition cost and the fair value of the assets and liabilities acquired. It is capitalized and amortized over its estimated useful life, up to a maximum of 20 years. The equity method is required when the investor exercises significant influence on business and financial policy. Joint ventures may be accounted for using either the equity method or proportional consolidation. Foreign currency translation is similar to IFRS. The balance sheet of a "foreign entity" is translated at the closing (year-end) rate, while the income statement is translated at the closing or average rate. Translation adjustments are charged to shareholders' equity. The temporal method is used for "direct foreign activities," with the translation adjustment charged to income.

The Dutch flexibility toward accounting measurements is most evident in permitting the use of current values for tangible assets such as inventory and depreciable assets. When current values are used for these assets, their corresponding income-statement amounts, cost of goods sold, and depreciation are also stated at current values. Current value can be replacement value, recoverable amount, or net realizable value. Current value accounting is expected to be consistently applied; piecemeal revaluations normally are not allowed. Revaluations are offset by a revaluation reserve in shareholders' equity. Companies using current values should provide additional historical cost information in the notes. Historical cost is also acceptable. While much has been made of current value accounting in the Netherlands, few companies actually use it. Philips, arguably the most conspicuous example, started using current value accounting in 1951, but abandoned it in 1992 in the interests of international comparability. Nevertheless, current values have a place in Dutch accounting because companies that use historical cost for the balance sheet and income statement are expected to disclose supplemental current cost information in their notes. Current cost accounting is discussed more fully in Chapter 7.

When historical cost is used for inventory, it is generally stated at the lower of cost or net realizable value, with cost determined by FIFO, LIFO, or average methods. All intangibles are assumed to have a finite life, normally no more than 20 years. Intangibles with lives longer than 20 years must be impairments tested each year. Research and development costs are capitalized only when the amounts are recoverable and sufficiently certain. Leases, contingencies, and pension costs are generally measured as they are in the United Kingdom and United States, although the applicable rules are more general. Deferred income taxes are recognized on the basis of the comprehensive allocation concept (full provision) and measured according to the liability method. They may be valued at discounted present value. Current value accounting is not acceptable for tax purposes, so when current values are used for financial reporting, permanent rather than timing differences arise.

Because Dutch companies have flexibility in applying measurement rules, one would suspect that there are opportunities for income smoothing. In addition, there is flexibility in providing for probable future obligations. For example, provisions for periodic maintenance and major overhauls are allowed.[35]

United Kingdom

Accounting in the United Kingdom developed as an independent discipline, pragmatically responding to the needs and practices of business.[36] Over time, successive companies laws added structure and other requirements, but still allowed accountants considerable flexibility in the application of professional judgment. Since the 1970s, the most important source of development in company law has been the EU Directives, most notably the Fourth and Seventh Directives. At the same time, accounting standards and the standard-setting process have become more authoritative.

The legacy of British accounting to the rest of the world is substantial. The United Kingdom was the first country in the world to develop an accountancy profession as we know it today.[37] The concept of a fair presentation of financial results and position

---

[35]For evidence that Dutch firms use provisions to smooth earnings, see Erik Peek, "The Use of Discretionary Provisions in Earnings Management," *Journal of International Accounting Research* 3, no. 2 (2004): 27–43.

[36]The United Kingdom of Great Britain and Northern Ireland is a union of England, Scotland, Wales, and Northern Ireland. Even though the United Kingdom has an integrated system of laws, monetary and fiscal policies, and social rules and regulations, important individual differences remain among these four countries. The term Britain is often used for the United Kingdom. "British, " "Anglo," and "Anglo-Saxon" are often used interchangeably to describe accounting in the United Kingdom.

[37]The first recognized accounting society was the Society of Accountants in Edinburgh, which was granted a royal charter in 1854. Similar societies were officially recognized in Glasgow in 1855 and in Aberdeen in 1867. Professional accounting began with these early professional societies. The United Kingdom has less than 1 percent of the world's population, yet has more than 13 percent of its accountants. See Bob Parker, "Accountants Galore," *Accountancy* (November 2001): 130-131.

(the true and fair view) is also of British origin. Professional accounting thinking and practice were exported to Australia, Canada, the United States, and other former British possessions including Hong Kong, India, Kenya, New Zealand, Nigeria, Singapore, and South Africa.

Accounting Regulation and Enforcement

The two major sources of financial accounting standards in the United Kingdom are companies law and the accounting profession. Activities of companies incorporated in the United Kingdom are broadly governed by statutes called companies acts. Companies acts have been updated, extended, and consolidated through the years. For example, in 1981 the EU Fourth Directive was implemented, adding statutory rules regarding formats, accounting principles, and basic accounting conventions. This introduced standardized formats for financial statements into Britain for the first time. Companies may choose from alternative balance sheet formats and four profit and loss account formats. The 1981 act also sets out five basic accounting principles:

1. Revenues and expenses are matched on an accrual basis.
2. Individual asset and liability items within each class of assets and liabilities are valued separately.
3. The principle of conservatism (prudence) is applied, especially in the recognition of realized income and all known liabilities and losses.
4. Consistent application of accounting policies from year to year is required.
5. The going concern principle is applicable to the entity being accounted for.

The act contains broad valuation rules in that the accounts may be based on either historical or current cost.

The Companies Act 1985 consolidated and extended earlier legislation and was amended in 1989 to recognize the EU Seventh Directive. This act requires the consolidation of financial statements, although consolidation was already standard practice.[38] The legal stipulations are general and allow considerable flexibility in case-by-case applications.

The following six accountancy bodies in the United Kingdom are linked through the Consultative Committee of Accountancy Bodies (CCAB), organized in 1970.[39]

1. The Institute of Chartered Accountants in England and Wales
2. The Institute of Chartered Accountants in Ireland
3. The Institute of Chartered Accountants of Scotland
4. The Association of Chartered Certified Accountants
5. The Chartered Institute of Management Accountants
6. The Chartered Institute of Public Finance and Accountancy

British standard setting evolved from recommendations on accounting principles (issued by the Institute of Chartered Accountants in England and Wales) to the 1970 formation of the Accounting Standards Steering Committee, later renamed the

---

[38]The Companies Act 1985 (as amended by the Companies Act 1989) applies to England, Scotland, and Wales. Similar legislation for Northern Ireland is embodied in the Companies (Northern Ireland) Order 1986.

[39]The Web site addresses are: ICAEW: www.icaew.co.uk; ICAI: www.icai.ie; ICAS: www.icas.org.uk; ACCA: www.acca.co.uk; CIMA: www.cimaglobal.com; CIPFA: www.cipfa.org.uk.

Accounting Standards Committee (ASC). The ASC promulgated Statements on Standard Accounting Practice (SSAPs). SSAPs were issued and enforced by the six accounting bodies, any one of which could effectively veto the standard. The veto power of these organizations often led to excessive delays and compromises in developing SSAPs. In addition, SSAPs were more in the nature of recommendations than compulsory requirements, and had little authority.

The Dearing Report, issued in 1988, expressed dissatisfaction with the existing standard-setting arrangement.[40] It recommended a new structure for setting accounting standards and more authoritative support for them. The Companies Act 1989 was important not only for incorporating the EU Seventh Directive but also for enacting the recommendations of the Dearing Report. The 1989 act created a new Financial Reporting Council (FRC) with the duty of overseeing its three offshoots: the Accounting Standards Board (ASB), which replaced the ASC in 1990, an Urgent Issues Task Force (UITF), and a Financial Reporting Review Panel.[41]

The FRC sets general policy. It is an independent body whose members are drawn from the accounting profession, industry, and financial institutions. The ASB has a full-time chair, a technical director, and up to eight paid part-time members, and is empowered to issue accounting standards. The ASB issues Financial Reporting Standards (FRSs) after considering comments on Discussion Papers and Financial Reporting Exposure Drafts (FREDs). The ASB is guided by a Statement of Principles for Financial Reporting, a conceptual framework for setting accounting standards.[42] The ASB also established the UITF to respond quickly to new problems and issue clarifications of the accounting standards and other regulations (called UITF Abstracts). Because listed British (and other EU) companies must now use IFRS in their consolidated financial statements, the ASB has turned its attention away from developing U.K. GAAP to gradually converging U.K. accounting standards with IFRS. Another major role of the ASB is partnering with the IASB and other standard setters in the development of IFRS.

The 1989 act enacted legal sanctions for companies that do not comply with accounting standards. Both the Financial Reporting Review Panel and the Department of Trade and Industry can investigate complaints about departures from accounting standards. They can go to court to force a company to revise its financial statements. Companies must adopt the accounting policies most appropriate to their specific circumstances in order to give a true and fair view, and they must regularly review their policies to ensure that they remain appropriate.

All but small limited liability companies must be audited. Of the six accountancy bodies listed earlier, only members of the first four are allowed to sign audit reports. The audit report affirms that the financial statements present a true and fair view and comply with the Companies Act 1985. For example, the opinion paragraph of PricewaterhouseCoopers on the 2005 financial statements of BG Group, the British natural gas company, is reproduced in Exhibit 3-5.

Until 2000, auditing standards were the responsibility of a board of the CCAB. In that year the Accountancy Foundation was set up to regulate and oversee the auditing profession. Following a review of the accounting profession by the Department of

---

[40]Sir Ron Dearing, (The Dearing Report) "The Making of Accounting Standards, Report of the Review Committee," presented to the Consultative Committee of Accountancy Bodies, 1988.

[41]Web sites are: Financial Reporting Council: www.frc.org.uk; Accounting Standards Board and Urgent Issues Task Force: www.frc.org.uk/asb/; Financial Reporting Review Panel: www.frc.org.uk/frrp.

[42]Work on the Statement of Principles began soon after the ASB was formed and was completed in 1999.

EXHIBIT 3-5   Audit Opinion on BG Group Financial Statements

In our opinion:

- The Group Financial Statements give a true and fair view, in accordance with IFRSs as adopted by the European Union, of the state of the Group's affairs as at 31 December 2005 and of its profit and cash flows for the year then ended;

- The parent company Financial Statements give a true and fair view, in accordance with IFRSs as adopted by the European Union as applied in accordance with the provisions of the Companies Act 1985, as of the state of the parent company's affairs as at 31 December 2005 and cash flows for the year then ended; and

- The Financial Statements and the part of the remuneration report to be audited have been properly prepared in accordance with the Companies Act 1985 and Article 4 of the IAS Regulation.

PricewaterhouseCoopers LLP
8 March 2006

SOURCE: 2005 BG Group Annual Report, p. 62.

Trade and Industry in 2003, the Accountancy Foundation was dissolved and its functions transferred to the FRC. A newly established Professional Oversight Board (POB) oversees the regulation of the auditing profession by monitoring the activities of the professional accounting bodies, including education and training, standards, professional conduct, and discipline. The POB also oversees an independent Audit Inspection Unit (AIU), which monitors the audits of listed companies and other public interest entities. The Auditing Practices Board (APB) was transferred from the Accountancy Foundation to the FRC. It prescribes the basic principles and practices that an auditor must follow when conducting an audit, and is responsible for ethical standards and standards on audit independence. Finally, the Accountancy Investigation and Discipline Board (AIDB) was established as a mechanism to investigate and discipline accountants or accounting firms for professional misconduct. All of these reforms were designed to strengthen the accounting and audit profession, and provide a more effective system of regulation of the profession. Thus, the Financial Reporting Council has responsibility for both accounting and auditing standards, and their enforcement.

Financial Reporting

British financial reporting is among the most comprehensive in the world. Financial statements generally include:

1. Directors' report
2. Profit and loss account and balance sheet
3. Cash flow statement
4. Statement of total recognized gains and losses
5. Statement of accounting policies
6. Notes referenced in the financial statements
7. Auditor's report

The directors' report addresses principal business activities, review of operations and likely developments, important post-balance sheet events, recommended dividends, names of the directors and their shareholdings, and political and charitable contributions.

Listed companies must include a statement on corporate governance with disclosures on directors' remuneration, audit committees and internal controls, and a declaration that the company is a going concern. Financial statements must present a true and fair view of a company's state of affairs and profits. To achieve this, additional information may be necessary, and in exceptional circumstances requirements may be overridden. The latter is known as the "true and fair override."

Group (consolidated) financial statements are required in addition to a parent-only balance sheet. Control of subsidiary "undertakings" occurs when the parent has power to exercise dominant influence or control over the undertaking, or the parent and subsidiary are managed in a unified basis. The London Stock Exchange requires that listed companies provide half-year interim reports. Listed companies must also report basic and diluted earnings per share.

Another feature of U.K. financial reporting is that small and medium-sized companies are exempt from many financial reporting obligations. The Companies Act sets out size criteria. In general, small and medium-sized companies are permitted to prepare abbreviated accounts with certain minimum prescribed information. Small and medium-sized groups are exempt from preparing consolidated statements.

Accounting Measurements

The United Kingdom allows both the acquisition and merger methods of accounting for business combinations. However, the conditions for the use of the merger method (*pooling-of-interests* in the United States) are so narrow that it is almost never used. Under the acquisition method, goodwill is calculated as the difference between the fair value of the consideration paid and the fair value of the net assets acquired. FRS 7 specifies that fair values are assigned to identifiable assets and liabilities that exist at the date of acquisition, reflecting the conditions at that time. Future operating losses and reorganization costs cannot be considered in the calculation of goodwill, but must be reflected in post-acquisition income. Goodwill is capitalized and amortized over 20 years or less; however, a longer period or an indefinite period (resulting in no amortization) is possible if goodwill is subject to an annual impairment review. Proportional consolidation is only permitted for unincorporated joint ventures. The equity method is used for *associated* undertakings and for joint ventures that are companies. FRS 23 deals with foreign currency translation and requires the closing rate (current rate) method for independent subsidiaries and the temporal method for integrated subsidiaries. Under the former, translation differences are included in shareholders' equity reserves; under the latter, they are included in the profit and loss account. The financial statements of subsidiaries operating in hyperinflationary countries must be adjusted to reflect current price levels before translation. FRS 23 is aligned with IFRS.

Assets may be valued at historical cost, current cost, or (as most companies do) using a mixture of the two. Thus, revaluations of land and buildings are permissible. Depreciation and amortization must correspond to the measurement basis used for the underlying asset. Research expenditures are written off in the year of the expenditure, and development costs may be deferred under specific circumstances. However, in practice, few British companies capitalize any development costs. Inventory (referred to as "stocks") is valued at the lower of cost or net realizable value on a FIFO or average cost basis; LIFO is not acceptable.

Leases that transfer the risks and rewards of ownership to the lessee are capitalized and the lease obligation is shown as a liability. The costs of providing pensions and other retirement benefits must be recognized systematically and rationally over the period during which the employees' services are performed. Contingent losses are accrued when they are probable and can be estimated with reasonable accuracy. Deferred taxes are calculated under the liability method on a full provision basis for most timing differences. Long-term deferred tax balances may be valued at discounted present value. Income smoothing opportunities exist given the flexibility that exists in asset valuation and other measurement areas. Concern has been expressed in the United Kingdom over "creative accounting," and whether its use to mislead rather than inform has increased in recent years.[43] Indeed, the ASB focused much of its early attention on remedying abuses in U.K. accounting.

All U.K. companies are permitted to use IFRS instead of U.K. GAAP just described. Thus, the EU 2005 initiative for listed companies is extended to nonlisted U.K. companies as well.

Exhibit 3-6 summarizes the significant accounting practices in the countries surveyed in this chapter.

---

[43]For an interesting case history, see A. K. Shah, "Exploring the Influences and Constraints on Creative Accounting in the United Kingdom," *European Accounting Review* 7, no. 1 (1998): 83–104.

EXHIBIT 3-6 Summary of Significant Accounting Practices

	IFRS	France	Germany	Czech Republic	Netherlands	United Kingdom
1. Business combinations: purchase or pooling	Purchase	Purchase[a]	Purchase[a]	Purchase	Purchase[a]	Purchase[a]
2. Goodwill	Capitalize and impairments test	Capitalize and amortize	Capitalize and amortize[b]	Capitalize and amortize[b]	Capitalize and amortize	Capitalize and amortize[c]
3. Associates	Equity method	Equity method	Equity method	Equity method	Equity method	Equity method
4. Asset valuation	Historical cost & fair value	Historical cost	Historical cost	Historical cost	Historical cost & fair value	Historical cost & fair value
5. Depreciation charges	Economic based	Tax based	Tax based	Economic based	Economic based	Economic based
6. LIFO inventory valuation	Not permitted	Not permitted	Permitted	Not permitted	Permitted	Not permitted
7. Probable losses	Accrued	Accrued	Accrued	Accrued	Accrued	Accrued
8. Finance leases	Capitalized	Not capitalized	Not capitalized	Not capitalized	Capitalized	Capitalized
9. Deferred taxes	Accrued	Not accrued	Not accrued	Accrued	Accrued	Accrued
10. Reserves for income smoothing	No	Used	Used	Some	Some	Some

[a]Pooling also allowed in narrow circumstances, but not widely used.
[b]May also be written off to reserves.
[c]Nonamortization permitted if subject to annual impairment review.

SELECTED REFERENCES

Aisbitt, S., and L. Evans, eds., *Development in Country Studies in International Accounting – Europe*, Cheltenham, U.K.: Edward Elgar, 2004.

Alexander, D., and S. Archer, eds., *European Accounting Guide*, 5th ed., New York: Aspen Publishers, 2003.

Baker, C.R., A. Mikol, and R. Quick, "Regulation of the Statutory Auditor in the European Union: A Comparative Survey of the United Kingdom, France and Germany," *European Accounting Review* 10, no. 4 (2001): 763–786.

Brown, P., and A. Tarca, "A Commentary on Issues Relating to the Enforcement of International Financial Reporting Standards in the EU," *European Accounting Review* 14, no. 1 (2005): 181–212.

Dao, T.H.P., "Monitoring Compliance with IFRS: Some Insights from the French Regulatory System," *Accounting in Europe* 2 (2005): 107–135.

Deloitte, "Country Accounting Standards Update," IAS Plus Web site(www.iasplus.com).

Del Vaille, P., G. Ebbers, and C. Saccon, "International Financial Reporting Convergence: Evidence from Three Continental European Countries," *Accounting in Europe* 2 (2005): 137–164.

Ding, Y., H. Stolowy, and M. Tenenhaus, "Shopping Around for Accounting Practices: The Financial Statement Presentation of French Groups," *Abacus* 39, no. 1 (February 2003): 42–65.

Haller, A., and B. Eierle, "The Adaptation of German Accounting Rules to IFRS: A Legislative Balancing Act," *Accounting in Europe* 1 (2004): 27–50.

Institute of Chartered Accountants of Scotland, *Principles-Based or Rules-Based Accounting Standards? A Question of Judgment*, 2006 (www.icas.org.uk).

Jindrichovska, I., "The Relationship Between Accounting Numbers and Returns: Some Empirical Evidence from the Emerging Market of the Czech Republic," *European Accounting Review* 10, no. 1 (2001): 107–131.

KPMG, *IFRS Compared to Dutch GAAP: An Overview*, July 2006 (www.kpmgifrg.com/pubs/pub_gaapc.cfm).

Nobes, C., and R. Parker, *Comparative International Accounting*, 9th ed., Harlow, U.K.: Pearson Education, 2006.

Ordelheide, D., and KPMG, eds., *Transnational Accounting*, 2nd ed., Hampshire and New York, Palgrave 2001.

Peek, E., "The Use of Discretionary Provisions in Earnings Management: Evidence from the Netherlands," *Journal of International Accounting Research* 3, no. 2 (2004): 27–43.

PricewaterhouseCoopers, *IFRS and Czech GAAP: Similarities and Differences*, August 2004 (www.pwc.com/extweb/pwcpublications.nsf/dfeb71994ed9bd4d802571490030862f/d50e7fb32dcf33bb80257026005023ef/$FILE/PwC_IFRS-CzechGAAP_Similarities-Differences.pdf).

PricewaterhouseCoopers, *Similarities and Differences: A Comparison of IFRS, US GAAP, and German GAAP*, May 2004 (www.pwc.com/gx/eng/about/svcs/corporatereporting/GermanSandD.pdf).

Sellhorn, T., and S. Gornik-Tomaszewski, "The Implications of the 'IAS Regulation' for Research into the International Differences in Accounting Systems," *Accounting in Europe* 3 (2006): 187–17.

Sucher, P., and I. Jindrichovska, "Implementing IFRS: A Case Study of the Czech Republic," *Accounting in Europe* 1 (2004): 109–141.

"A Survey of Finance in Central Europe," *Economist* (September 14, 2002): 1–16.

DISCUSSION QUESTIONS

1. Compare and contrast the mechanisms for regulating and enforcing financial reporting in the five countries discussed in this chapter.
2. Compare and contrast the main features of financial reporting in the five countries discussed in this chapter.
3. Auditor oversight bodies have recently been established in several countries discussed in this chapter. Identify the auditor oversight bodies discussed in the chapter. What is the reason for this recent trend?

4. What is the role of tax legislation on financial accounting practices in each of the five countries discussed in this chapter?
5. What is the difference between consolidated and individual company financial statements? Why do some EU countries prohibit IFRS in individual company financial statements while others permit or require IFRS at the individual company level?
6. Code law countries typically have portions of their financial accounting and reporting requirements anchored in the law itself and other portions derived from professional standards or recommendations. Explain whether extensive formal legal requirements lead to high-quality levels of financial reporting.
7. Consider the following statement: "Experience shows that the needs of national and international markets, for international harmonization in particular, are better served by self-regulation and development than by government regulation." Do you agree? Why or why not?
8. In France, financial accounting standards and practices originate primarily from three authoritative sources: (a) companies legislation (Plan Comptable Général and Code de Commerce), (b) professional opinions and recommendations (CNC, CRC, OEC, and CNCC), and (c) stock exchange regulations (AMF). Which of these three has the greatest influence on day-to-day French accounting practice?
9. Consider the following statement: "The German Accounting Standards Committee is modeled on Anglo-American and international practice." Do you agree? Why or why not?
10. How have accounting requirements and practices in the Czech Republic been influenced by European Union requirements?
11. The most novel feature of the Dutch accounting scene is the Enterprise Chapter of the Court of Justice of Amsterdam. What is the mission of the Enterprise Chamber? How is this mission carried out?
12. A feature of British accounting is the "true and fair override." What is the meaning of this term? Why is the true and fair override found in the United Kingdom but almost nowhere else?

EXERCISES

1. This chapter provides synopses of national accounting practice systems in five European countries.

    Required:
    For each country, list:
    a. the name of the national financial accounting standard-setting board or agency
    b. the name of the agency, institute, or other organization charged with supervising and enforcing financial accounting standards
2. Refer to your answer to Exercise 1.

    Required: Which country discussed in this chapter appears to have the most effective accounting and financial reporting supervision mechanism for companies whose securities are traded in public financial markets? Should each country that has a stock exchange (and therefore a public financial market) also have a regulatory agency that enforces accounting and financial reporting rules? Write a concise paragraph to support your answer.
3. The International Federation of Accountants (IFAC) is a worldwide organization of professional accounting bodies. IFAC's Web site (www.ifac.org) has links to a number of accounting bodies around the world.

    Required: Visit IFAC's Web site. List the accounting organizations discussed in this chapter that are linked to IFAC's Web site.
4. Reread Chapter 3 and its discussion questions.

    Required:
    a. As you go through this material, prepare a list of five expressions, terms, or short phrases that are unfamiliar or unusual in your home country.
    b. Write a concise definition or explanation of each item.

5. Analyze the five national accounting practice systems summarized in this chapter.

    Required:
    a. For each of the five countries discussed in this chapter, select the most important financial accounting practice or principle at variance with international norms.
    b. For each selection you make, state briefly your reasons for its inclusion on your list.
    c. How does this variance affect reported earnings and the debt to asset ratio?
    d. How likely is it that an analyst could adjust for this variance to achieve an "apples to apples" comparison with companies from other countries?

6. The world's stock exchanges differ in terms of the number of domestic versus foreign listed firms.

    Required: Go to the World Federation of Stock Exchanges Web page (www. world-exchanges.org) (Statistics). For each country discussed in this chapter, identify the number of domestic and foreign listed firms. How do the countries compare and what are the implications of the observed patterns?

7. Refer to Exhibit 3-6.

    Required: Which country's GAAP appears to be the most oriented toward equity investors? Which country's GAAP appears to be the least oriented toward equity investors? Why do you say so?

8. Several companies from the five countries discussed in this chapter are listed on the New York Stock Exchange (NYSE).

    Required: Go to the NYSE Web site (www.nyse.com). Identify the companies listed on the NYSE from each of the five countries discussed in this chapter. How do the numbers of listed companies from these countries compare to the numbers from other European countries? What are the implications of the observed patterns?

9. The role of government in developing accounting and auditing standards differs in the five countries discussed in this chapter.

    Required: Compare the role of government in developing accounting and auditing standards in France, Germany, the Czech Republic, the Netherlands and the United Kingdom.

10. Countries of the European Union are establishing oversight bodies to regulate the activities of statutory auditors. These national bodies are also coordinated at the EU level.

    Required: Go to the European Union Web site (europa.eu) and find information on the European Group of Auditors' Oversight Bodies (EGAOB). Discuss the role of the EGAOB. Identify the European countries with a public oversight body for auditing and name the country's related body.

11. In most countries, accounting standard setting involves a combination of private- and public-sector groups. The private sector includes the accounting profession and other groups affected by the financial reporting process, such as users and preparers of financial statements, and organized labor. The public sector includes government agencies, such as tax authorities, ministries responsible for commercial law, and securities commissions. The stock market is another potential influence.

    Required: Complete a matrix indicating whether each of the above groups significantly influences accounting standard setting in the five countries discussed in this chapter. List the groups across the top and the countries down the side; indicate the influence of each group with a yes or a no.

12. Listed below are certain financial ratios used by analysts:
    * *Liquidity:* current ratio; cash flow from operations to current liabilities
    * *Solvency:* debt to equity; debt to assets
    * *Profitability:* return on assets; return on equity

    Required: Assume that you are comparing the financial ratios of companies from two countries discussed in this chapter. Discuss how the accounting practices identified in Exhibit 3-6 would affect your comparison for each of the six ratios in the list.

CASES

Case 3-1   Old Habits Die Hard

"The ethical climate in the Czech Republic has improved since the early days, but we still have a long way to go," said Josef Machinka, an economic adviser to the Ministry of Finance, while attending an investment seminar sponsored by the Prague Stock Exchange. "We really lack an established ethical framework."

Adds Charles University professor Jana Vychopeň, "Ethical problems still exist, but they stem from 40 years under a system that promoted corruption. Under the communists it was all political influence. There wasn't an economy—corruption sustained the system back then, but now chokes it. We were shocked into a market economy and our coupon privatization was racked with scandal. Even the word 'tunneling,' meaning asset stripping, was coined here."

"Ethics hangs over the market but so does a lack of transparency," states Pavel Kraus, analyst for Merta Investment Management. "Many of today's managers forged their attitudes in the 70s and 80s. Under communism, secrecy—not transparency—was the watchword. They just don't think it's important to keep investors informed, so how do you know they're not a bunch of shady managers trying to hide something?"

He goes on to give the example of Bednar, a large chemical company that was one of the first state-owned enterprises to be privatized. "Bednar is run by old dogs who can't—or won't—learn new tricks. Like a lot of Czech companies, Bednar didn't come to the stock market, but found itself on the stock exchange because of the privatization. The managers found themselves in a publicly traded company against their will.

"Still, it's better than the old days. Back in the 90s I asked to meet with them to discuss their business plan and was told, 'Sure—for CzK 400 an hour.' I kept phoning them for several weeks and finally wore them down. They ended up meeting me for free!"

Agreeing with Kraus is Jiři Michalik, a broker with Habova Securities. "Things are getting better. Czech companies are finally realizing that they have to let investors know what they're getting into if they are going to attract more investment. They looked around and realized that our Polish and Hungarian rivals were leaving us in the dust. Right after privatization most managers didn't have experience at quickly compiling and disseminating their financial information. Even if they had good intentions, it was hard for them to do. But now more and more of them have the experience."

The conversation comes back to Jana Vychopeň. "I put a lot of the blame on the Prague Stock Exchange. It's still not seen as a place to raise capital. Three IPOs between 1993 and 2006 is not a good track record. We have the rules in place and managers' attitudes are changing, if slowly. But poor enforcement means that investors don't always get what they need or they get it too late to be of any good." ∎

REQUIRED

1. Describe the problems characterized in this case.
2. What are the likely causes of these problems?
3. What are consequences of these problems for investors, Czech companies, and the Prague Stock Exchange?
4. Outline a program of changes needed to correct the problems identified.

Case 3-2A   What Difference Does It Really Make?

As an analyst for a securities firm, you are aware that accounting practices differ around the world. Yet you wonder whether these differences really have any material effect on companies' financial statements. You also know that the SEC in the United States requires non-U.S. registrants to reconcile key financial data from the GAAP used in their financial statements to U.S. GAAP. You obtain the reconciliation from the 2005 Form 20F SEC filing for Lafarge (a French cement and construction materials company).

LAFARGE

Note 36 - Summary of Differences Between Accounting Principles Followed by the Group and U.S. GAAP

Until December 31, 2004, the Group consolidated financial statements were prepared in accordance with the provisions of French accounting standards ("Previous GAAP"). The 2005 consolidated financial statements of the Group are prepared in accordance with accounting principles described in Note 2 above ("IFRS"), which require 2004 comparative data to be presented on the same basis. In order to provide this comparative data, the Group established an opening balance sheet prepared in accordance with IFRS, as of January 1, 2004. Accounting principles under IFRS differ in certain significant respects from those applicable in the United States of America ("U.S. GAAP"). These differences relate mainly to the items which are described below and which are summarized in the following tables.

1. Differences in accounting for business combinations under IFRS and U.S. GAAP. As permitted by IFRS 1, the Group has not restated the business combinations, which were entered into prior to January 1, 2004 (IFRS transition date). Business combinations entered into subsequent to January 1, 2004 have been accounted for in accordance with the accounting principles described in Note 2(e).

(a) Determination of the purchase price in case of share consideration. Under Previous GAAP, as under U.S. GAAP, the purchase price of a transaction accounted for as an acquisition was based on the fair value of the consideration exchanged. In the case of acquisitions involving the issuance of the Group's shares, under Previous GAAP the fair value of such consideration was based on the agreed-upon share price at completion of the acquisition or at the date when the transaction became unconditional. Under U.S. GAAP, the fair value of the share consideration is based on the average share price on the date of and the two trading days prior to and subsequent to the announcement of the proposed acquisition. This difference in valuation of the shares resulted in a difference in the fair value of consideration and consequently in the amount of goodwill capitalized and amortized. As of January 1, 2002, goodwill is no longer amortized under U.S. GAAP.

Under IFRS, the fair value of the consideration exchanged is measured for acquisitions after January 1, 2004 based on the share price on the date of acquisition. No acquisition involving the issuance of Group's shares has occurred since January 1, 2004.

(b) Fair value adjustments related to minority interests. Under both Previous GAAP and IFRS, when the Group initially acquires a controlling interest in a business, any portion of the assets and liabilities considered retained by minority shareholders is recorded at fair value. Under U.S. GAAP, only the portion of the assets and liabilities

acquired by the Group is recorded at fair value. This gives rise to two differences:

(i) Operating income was different between Previous GAAP and U.S. GAAP, and continues to be different under IFRS because of the difference in basis of assets that are amortized. This difference is offset entirely by a difference in the minority interest's participation in the income of the subsidiary.

(ii) After an initial acquisition of a subsidiary, if an additional portion of that subsidiary was subsequently acquired, under both Previous GAAP and IFRS, the purchase consideration in excess of the net assets acquired was recorded as goodwill. Under U.S. GAAP, the incremental portion of the assets and liabilities was recorded at fair value, with any excess being allocated to goodwill, thus creating a difference in the carrying value of both assets and goodwill.

(c) Impairment of goodwill.   Impairment analysis under IFRS is described in Note 2(l). Under U.S. GAAP, the Group measures goodwill impairment as the difference between the implied fair value and carrying value of goodwill, in accordance with Statement of Financial Accounting Standards ("SFAS") 142, "Goodwill and other Intangible Assets" ("SFAS 142"). These two methods did not give rise to any material differences between the U.S. GAAP fair value and the IFRS recoverable amount of goodwill for the periods presented.

The carrying value of goodwill under IFRS and U.S. GAAP is different due to the items described above and below. As a consequence, impairment losses recognized on goodwill have been different in some circumstances, creating a reconciling item between IFRS and U.S. GAAP financial statements.

(d) Business combinations prior to January 1, 2004 – specific treatment related to first-time adoption of IFRS.   As permitted by IFRS 1, the Group has not restated the business combinations,

which were entered into prior to January 1, 2004 (IFRS transition date). The differences described below relate to business combinations accounted for under Previous GAAP before the transition to IFRS, which now create differences between IFRS and U.S. GAAP.

(i) *Goodwill recorded as a reduction of shareholders' equity before January 1, 1989.*   Before January 1, 1989, as described in Note 2 (e), under Previous GAAP, the excess of the purchase price over the fair value of the net assets acquired was written off directly to shareholders' equity upon acquisition. Under U.S. GAAP, these goodwill amounts have been recognized as an asset, and as of January 1, 2002 are no longer amortized based upon the provisions of SFAS 142.

Such difference would not arise on acquisitions after January 1, 2004 under IFRS.

(ii) *Goodwill and market share amortization.*   Under Previous GAAP, acquired goodwill was amortized over the expected period of benefit, which did not exceed forty years. SFAS 142 requires that goodwill acquired in a purchase business combination completed after June 30, 2001 not be amortized. Subsequent to January 1, 2002, all previously recorded goodwill is no longer amortized but is tested for impairment at least annually under U.S. GAAP. Subsequent to January 1, 2004, all previously recorded goodwill is no longer amortized but is tested for impairment at least annually under IFRS.

Under Previous GAAP, market share, separately identified on the acquisition of subsidiaries, was not amortized. Under IFRS, market share is not recognized as a separate intangible asset but is considered as a component of goodwill. As permitted by IFRS 1, the Group did not revise past business combinations as part of its transition process but simply reclassified the carrying amount of market share to goodwill on January 1, 2004. Under U.S. GAAP, market share is not considered as a separately identifiable intangible asset, but as a component of goodwill as of the date of acquisition. Therefore, it was amortized until the provisions of SFAS 142 were applied.

(iii) *Negative goodwill arising on acquisitions.* Under Previous GAAP, negative goodwill was amortized into income on a rational systematic basis based upon estimates of future operating results of the acquiree. Negative goodwill was presented as a liability on the balance sheet. Under U.S. GAAP, negative goodwill was recorded as a reduction in the fair value of long-lived assets acquired and the related depreciation expense was adjusted accordingly. Such a difference will not arise on acquisitions after January 1, 2004 under IFRS.

(iv) *Depreciation period for goodwill related to the aggregates businesses prior to January 1, 2002.* The difference between the purchase price of the aggregates businesses and the underlying fair value of net assets is mainly allocated to mineral reserves acquired based on their fair values at the time of acquisition. Under Previous GAAP, the remaining goodwill was generally amortized over 40 years whereas under U.S. GAAP, this goodwill was accounted for based upon the provisions of SFAS 142, as described above. Prior to January 1, 2002, under U.S. GAAP, this goodwill was amortized over the residual lives of the quarries acquired, which approximated the expected future benefit of the goodwill. Such difference will not arise on acquisitions after January 1, 2004 under IFRS.

(v) *Determination of goodwill.* The carrying amount of goodwill is substantially different under U.S. GAAP and under Previous GAAP due to the fact that certain transactions were accounted for differently between the two standards as described below

Lafarge Roofing GmbH (formerly Lafarge Braas) minority interests acquisition in 1999 and 2000. The acquisition by the Group of the 43.5% minority interests in Lafarge Braas through a share for share exchange was accounted for under Previous GAAP from the date of the contract signing which was December 22, 1999. Approximately 44% of the total share consideration for this transaction was issued in December 1999. The remainder was issued on June 20, 2000 after an authorized increase in share capital. For purposes of U.S. GAAP, the transaction was accounted for as a two-step acquisition based upon the dates the shares were exchanged with the minority shareholders. Consequently, an additional goodwill was recorded under U.S. GAAP based upon the different methodologies used to determine the purchase price under Previous and U.S. GAAP (Note 36-1 (a)).

Accounting for deferred income taxes before January 1, 2000. Before January 1, 2000, the Group's deferred tax provision was calculated using the partial allocation method. Effective January 1, 2000, as required under Previous GAAP, the Group adopted the balance sheet liability method, which among other changes, requires that deferred taxes be recorded on all temporary differences between the tax basis of assets and liabilities and their carrying amount in the balance sheet. The adoption of this methodology required that all deferred tax assets or liabilities be accounted for with the offsetting amount recorded as an adjustment to equity. Under U.S. GAAP, which also applies the balance sheet liability method, temporary differences arising in connection with fair value adjustments on business combinations typically result in deferred taxes and a corresponding adjustment to goodwill. Consequently, an adjustment is required in the reconciliation to U.S. GAAP to record goodwill arising from deferred tax liabilities related to past business combinations and charged to equity under Previous GAAP upon adoption of the balance sheet liability method. Such differences will not arise on acquisition after January 1, 2004 under IFRS.

Restructuring costs related to business combinations.　　Previous GAAP provided that where a business combination results in regional over capacity, costs associated with restructuring the acquirer's operations should be included as a cost of the acquisition. As a result of certain acquisitions, the Group has closed certain of its own operations in regions where it has determined that over capacity will result from the duplication of its operations with those of the acquired operations. U.S. GAAP specifically excludes from costs of an acquisition those costs associated with closing duplicate facilities and restructuring operations of the acquirer. Such costs are charged to income as a period cost under U.S. GAAP. Such difference will not arise on acquisitions after January 1, 2004 under IFRS.

For the purpose of the U.S. GAAP reconciliation, the Group has applied Emerging Issues Task Force ("EITF") 95-3, "Recognition of Liabilities in Connection with a Purchase Business Combination" ("EITF 95-3"), in accounting for restructuring costs associated with businesses it has acquired. As discussed below, the requirements for recording restructuring costs and liabilities were more specific under U.S. GAAP. Therefore, certain restructuring

provisions included in the fair value of businesses acquired under Previous GAAP were not accruable under U.S. GAAP, generating a difference in goodwill, and liabilities acquired for restructuring costs charged against goodwill under Previous GAAP. Those restructuring charges originally charged to goodwill under Previous GAAP are subsequently expensed under U.S. GAAP once the U.S. GAAP criteria have been satisfied for recording the costs. For the years prior to January 1, 2002, reduction in amortization of goodwill is created between the Previous and U.S. GAAP treatment (as described above).

Under Previous GAAP, prior to January 1, 2002, the Group recorded restructuring liabilities during the period when the appropriate level of management has approved decisions. Commencing January 1, 2002, except for the recognition of restructuring charges related to business combinations, there is no longer a difference in the recognition of restructuring liabilities between Previous and U.S. GAAP. Under U.S. GAAP, the Group has applied the provisions of SFAS 112, "Employer's Accounting for Post employment Benefits" ("SFAS 112") and EITF 94-3, "Liability Recognition for Certain Employee Termination Benefits and Other Costs to Exit an Activity" ("EITF 94-3"), in accounting for its employee layoffs and restructuring costs. Under EITF 94-3, a provision for restructuring can only be recorded during the period when certain conditions are satisfied, including the specific identification and approval by the appropriate level of management of the operations and activities to be restructured, and notification to the employees of the benefit arrangement. In addition, costs associated with an exit plan are recognized as restructuring provisions only if the related costs are not associated with or do not benefit continuing activities of the Group. The foregoing creates a timing difference between (i) the recording of provisions of new Previous GAAP charges to the extent that such provisions are not accrued for U.S. GAAP purposes, (ii) restructuring charges accrued under U.S. GAAP that were expensed for Previous GAAP purposes in a prior period, and (iii) changes in estimates on prior year Previous GAAP provisions that did not qualify for accrual under U.S. GAAP. Starting January 1, 2003, the Group applied prospectively and for all new plans initiated after this date SFAS 146, "Accounting for Costs Associated with Exit or Disposal Activities". This statement requires that a liability for costs associated with exit or disposal activities to be recognized at fair value when the liability is incurred rather than at the date an entity commits to a plan of restructuring. Adoption of these provisions did not have a material impact on our financial positions or results of operations.

2. Pension obligations.

Accounting for pensions. Under U.S. GAAP, pension costs are accounted for in accordance with SFAS 87, "Employers' Accounting for Pensions" ("SFAS 87"), SFAS 88, "Employers' Accounting for Settlements and Curtailments of Defined Benefit Plans and for Termination Benefits" ("SFAS 88") and SFAS 106, "Employers' Accounting for Post retirement Benefits Other than Pensions" ("SFAS 106"). IAS 19 is the corresponding standard applicable to employee benefits under IAS / IFRS. A limited number of discrepancies between these two sets of standards have been identified. They concern:

- the minimum liability adjustment mechanism not authorized by IAS 19;

- the limitations applicable, under IAS 19 (asset ceiling), to prepaid pension costs to be recognized on the employer's balance sheet for the overfunding of a plan's liabilities by its dedicated assets, which have no direct equivalent under U.S. GAAP;

- the recognition of prior service costs (under U.S. GAAP, the effects of plan amendments can be recognized over the average remaining active life of plans participants, whereas IAS 19 requires the immediate recognition, in the profit and loss account, of any effect of plan amendments on benefits already vested);

- the valuation of death and disability benefits covering active employees (IAS 19 does not require to provide for these types of benefits as long as they do not relate to services rendered by beneficiaries; costs are then expensed as incurred);

- the valuation of dedicated plan assets (U.S. GAAP authorize the smoothing of the fair value of plans assets over time, whereas IAS 19 requires the use of year end fair value for assets);

- measurement dates for liabilities and dedicated assets (under U.S. GAAP, valuation dates can be set before year end, whereas IAS 19 requires the use of year-end measurement dates). The measurement date used to determine liabilities and dedicated assets under US GAAP is December 31 for all plans except for our North American plans for which the date is November 30;

- transitional provisions which are specific to each set of standards;

- the allocation method for defined benefit costs over the periods of service rendered by beneficiaries (under certain circumstances, U.S. GAAP allows for an allocation of costs over the entire expected active career of beneficiaries, whereas IAS 19 requires the recognition of these costs over the periods of service over which benefits become vested, occasionally shorter than the entire expected active career);

* the valuation of "constructive" obligations which is explicitly required by IAS 19, whereas U.S. GAAP valuation requirements are limited to obligations for formal benefit plans.

Specific treatment related to first-time adoption of IFRS. The Group has elected to use the option available in IFRS 1 under which any difference existing as of January 1, 2004 between defined benefit plan liabilities and the fair value of dedicated assets can be recognized in equity, except the non-vested portion of unrecognized prior service costs. As a consequence, at January 1, 2004 the Group does not carry any unamortized actuarial gains or losses relating to post-employment benefits. The corridor method has been applied prospectively beginning January 1, 2004. The impact of this election creates a difference between IFRS and U.S. GAAP of 1,183 million euros at January 1, 2004 in shareholders' equity.

Reconciliation. The difference between the net pension obligation recorded under U.S. GAAP and IFRS can be summarized as follows:

	Pension benefits		Other benefits		Total	
(million euros)	2005	2004	2005	2004	2005	2004
NET AMOUNT RECOGNIZED UNDER U.S. GAAP	**4**	**18**	**(239)**	**(213)**	**(235)**	**(195)**
Minimum liability adjustment (MLA)	**(377)**	(659)	-	-	**(377)**	(659)
NET AMOUNT ACCRUED FOR UNDER U.S. GAAP	**(373)**	**(641)**	**(239)**	**(213)**	**(612)**	**(854)**
Prepaid benefit cost (including MLA)	**488**	168	-	-	**488**	168
Accrued benefit liability (including MLA)	**(861)**	(809)	**(239)**	(213)	**(1,100)**	(1,022)
Minimum liability adjustment (MLA)	**377**	659	-	-	**377**	659

(continued)

(million euros)	Pension benefits		Other benefits		Total	
	2005	2004	2005	2004	2005	2004
Other U.S. GAAP adjustments	**(1,056)**	(1,099)	**(61)**	(38)	**(1,117)**	(1,137)
Change in scope of consolidation	**(7)**	(8)	**-**	(12)	**(7)**	(20)
NET AMOUNT ACCRUED IN CONSOLIDATED FINANCIAL STATEMENTS UNDER IFRS	**(1,059)**	**(1,089)**	**(300)**	**(263)**	**(1,359)**	**(1,352)**
Prepaid	**15**	3	**-**	-	**15**	3
Accrued	**(1,074)**	(1,092)	**(300)**	(263)	**(1,374)**	(1,355)

Additional U.S. GAAP Disclosure Information. The following table provides the amounts recognized in the accompanying balance sheet:

(million euros)	Pension benefits		Other benefits		Total	
	2005	2004	2005	2004	2005	2004
ACCUMULATED BENEFIT OBLIGATION AT END OF THE PERIOD	**4,635**	**3,858**	**-**	**-**	**4,635**	**3,858**
Prepaid asset	**488**	168	**-**	-	**488**	168
Accrued liability	**(861)**	(809)	**(239)**	(213)	**(1,100)**	(1,022)
Intangible asset *	**23**	14	**-**	-	**23**	14
Accumulated other comprehensive loss *	**354**	645	**-**	-	**354**	645
NET AMOUNT RECOGNIZED AT DECEMBER 31	**4**	**18**	**(239)**	**(213)**	**(235)**	**(195)**

* Minimum pension liability related to the accumulated benefit obligation in excess of the fair value of plan assets; the portion recorded in intangible asset reflects the portion of minimum pension liability generated from unamortized prior service costs and transition obligation.

The following table provides additional U.S. GAAP disclosure:

(million euros)	At December 31,	
	2005	2004
PROJECTED BENEFIT OBLIGATION, ACCUMULATED BENEFIT OBLIGATION AND FAIR VALUE OF ASSETS INFORMATION IN RESPECT OF PENSION PLANS WITH ACCUMULATED BENEFIT OBLIGATIONS IN EXCESS OF THE FAIR VALUE OF PLAN ASSETS:		
Projected benefit obligation	**1,706**	3,850
Fair value of plan assets	**769**	2,758
Accumulated benefit obligation	**1,525**	3,467
PROJECTED BENEFIT OBLIGATION AND FAIR VALUE OF ASSETS INFORMATION IN RESPECT OF PENSION PLANS WITH PROJECTED BENEFIT OBLIGATIONS IN EXCESS OF THE FAIR VALUE OF PLAN ASSETS:		
Projected benefit obligation	**5,164**	4,310
Fair value of plan assets	**3,831**	3,109

3. Income taxes

(a) Accounting for deferred taxes in hyperinflationary economies. IAS 12 requires us to recognize deferred tax assets and liabilities for temporary differences related to assets and liabilities that are remeasured at each balance sheet date in accordance with the provisions of IAS 29, *Financial Reporting in Hyperinflationary Economy* as described in Note 2(d).

Pursuant to SFAS 109, "Accounting for Income Tax" ("SFAS 109"), U.S. GAAP prohibits recognition of a deferred tax liability or asset for differences related to assets and liabilities that are remeasured at each balance sheet date. Deferred taxes recorded in entities in hyperinflationary economies have been reversed for U.S. GAAP purposes.

(b) Accounting for deferred tax on tax-free reserves. Under Greek tax legislation, non-taxed or specially-taxed income may be transferred to special reserves under various tax incentive laws. The amounts transferred to these reserves are taxable upon their distribution, capitalization, offsetting of losses carried forward or ultimately upon the dissolution of the Company. Under IFRS, no tax liability is recorded. Under U.S. GAAP, a deferred tax liability should be recognized for the entire balance of the above reserves at the current prevailing tax rate, in the case of tax-free income, or at the difference between the general tax rate and privileged tax rates in each case for the specially-taxed income.

(c) Valuation allowance on deferred tax assets. As described in Note 2(u), under IFRS the Group offsets deferred tax assets and liabilities

in the balance sheet if the entity has a legally enforceable right to offset current tax assets against current tax liabilities and the deferred tax assets and deferred tax liabilities relate to income taxes levied by the same taxing authority. Deferred tax assets are recognized and their recoverability is then assessed. If it is not reasonably certain that they will be recovered in future years, a valuation allowance is recorded to reduce the deferred tax asset to the amount that is reasonably certain to be recovered. The impact of U.S. GAAP adjustments resulted in additional deferred tax assets recognition and a related valuation allowance on deferred tax assets.

(d) Accounting for tax contingencies in business combinations.   Under IAS 12, if tax contingencies of the acquiree, which were not recognized at the time of the combination are subsequently recognized, the resulting debit is taken to income for the period. Under U.S. GAAP, the Group adjusts goodwill to reflect revisions in estimates and/or the ultimate disposition of these contingencies with the provisions of SFAS No. 109 "Accounting for Income Taxes" and EITF 93-7, "Uncertainties Related to Income Taxes in a Purchase Business Combination".

4. Stock based compensation and employee stock plans.

(a) Employee stock option plans.   As described in Note 2(v), under IFRS, the Group records in its financial statements a compensation expense for all share-based compensation granted to its employees. The fair value is recognized in profit and loss on a linear basis over the vesting period (generally 4 years for stock options). In accordance with IFRS 2, "Share Based Payments", only options granted after November 7, 2002 and not fully vested at January, 1 2004 are measured and accounted for as employee costs.

Under U.S. GAAP, the Group accounts for stock based compensation awards pursuant to Accounting Principles Board Opinion 25, *Accounting for Stock Issued to Employees* ("APB 25") which requires that compensation expense be recorded when the market price of the stock at the measurement date exceeds the amount the employee is required to pay upon exercise of the option. The stock options granted to employees have been repriced in situations where there would be a theoretical dilution of the option holder's percentage interest in the Group. Typically, these repricing events arise from the Group's issuance of common stock or warrants. Under U.S. GAAP, the repricing of the Group's stock option plan causes the plan to be considered a variable plan under APB 25. As such, the difference between the exercise price of the option and the market price of the shares is recorded in profit and loss until the option is exercised or forfeited.

As of December 31, 2002, the Group adopted the disclosure requirements of SFAS 148, *Accounting for Stock-Based Compensation - Transition and Disclosure.* The costs associated with options granted in each of the two years ended December 31, 2005 and 2004 are 25 million euros and 46 million euros, respectively. The pro forma amounts below reflect the fair value effect as if the options granted had been charged to income for the years presented.

	Years ended December 31,	
	2005	2004
NUMERATOR (MILLION EUROS)		
NET EARNINGS UNDER U.S. GAAP (NOTE 37(C)) - BASIC EARNINGS PER SHARE	**1,097**	987
NET EARNINGS U.S. GAAP (NOTE 37(C)) - DILUTED EARNINGS PER SHARE	**1,112**	1,017
Stock-based employee compensation (recovery) expense included in net earnings, net of tax	**9**	2
Stock-based employee compensation expense determined under fair value based method for all awards, net of tax	**(25)**	(46)
NET EFFECT ON BASIC AND DILUTED EARNINGS	**(16)**	(44)
NET EARNINGS PRO FORMA - BASIC EARNINGS PER SHARE	**1,081**	943
NET EARNINGS PRO FORMA - DILUTED EARNINGS PER SHARE	**1,096**	973
DENOMINATOR (THOUSANDS))		
Weighted average number of shares outstanding - basic	**171,491**	167,204
Weighed average number of shares outstanding - fully diluted	**180,216**	178,548
BASIC EARNINGS PER SHARE (EUROS)		
As reported under U.S. GAAP (Note 37(c))	**6.40**	5.90
Pro forma	**6.30**	5.64
DILUTED EARNINGS PER SHARE (EUROS)		
As reported under U.S. GAAP (Note 37(c)	**6.17**	5.70
Pro forma	**6.08**	5.45

The pro forma compensation cost may not be representative of that to be expected in future years.

(b) Employee stock plans. In conjunction with the Group's stock purchase plan described above, the Group has granted a two-year loan to employees for the purpose of subscribing to the offered shares. Under U.S. GAAP, such loans are recorded as a reduction of shareholders' equity. For the year ended December 31, 2005, an amount of 13 million euros remains outstanding on this loan.

5. Other items. Other differences between accounting principles followed by the Group and U.S. GAAP are not individually significant, and are presented in the aggregate in the reconciliation of net income and shareholders' equity.

Compound instruments. On June 29, 2001 the Group issued 10,236,221 bonds convertible into common shares (non-detachable conversion option) for 1,300,000,067 euros, bearing interest at an annual rate of 1,5% (OCEANEs). The maturity of this convertible bond is January 1, 2006. As described in Note 2(r), IAS 32 requires that compound instruments with characteristics of both liabilities and equity be classified separately as component parts according to the nature of the components. Therefore, a separate presentation of liabilities and equity for this convertible loan is required. The equity component is assigned the residual amount after deducting from the compound instrument the value of the liability component. U.S. GAAP does not permit the split accounting for this instrument.

6. Items affecting the presentation of consolidated financial statements.

(a) Differences in the consolidation method.

Accounting for joint-venture investments and use of proportionate consolidation method.   Companies that are accounted for using the proportionate consolidation method under IFRS are accounted for by the equity method for U.S. GAAP purposes.

The tables disclosed in Note 13 present contributive amounts consolidated in the IFRS financial statements for those entities that are accounted for using the equity method under U.S. GAAP.

Related party transactions.   Related party transactions in the ordinary course of business with those entities that are accounted for using the equity method under U.S. GAAP (using the proportionate method under IFRS) are not significant. Such amounts have been eliminated in the IFRS financial statements as intercompany transactions, on the basis of the Group's interest in the entities involved.

(b) Presentation of minority interests.   Under IFRS, minority interests are presented within equity, but separate from the parent shareholders' equity. In contrast, U.S. GAAP requires minority interests to be presented outside equity, between liabilities and equity.

(c) Deferred tax assets and liabilities.   IFRS prohibits separate accounting for deferred taxes between current and non-current. Under IFRS, deferred tax accounts are classified as non-current in the balance sheet.

(d) Intangible assets.   Under IFRS, mineral rights are classified as "Intangible assets". In accordance with EITF 04-2, "Whether Mineral Rights Are Tangible or Intangible Assets", mineral rights should also be reclassified to quarries, within tangible assets, for purposes of U.S. GAAP.

(e) Put options on shares of subsidiaries.   Note 2(r.4) describes the Groups' accounting treatment under IFRS related to put options on the shares of its subsidiaries. The Group records the face value of the put as debt in the IFRS balance sheet in the line-item "put options on shares of subsidiaries" by (1) reclassifying the carrying value of the underlying minority interests and (2) recording goodwill in an amount equal to the difference between the carrying value of minority interests previously reclassified and the value of the debt. U.S. GAAP does not require equivalent treatment.

Thus, for U.S. GAAP reporting purposes, the Group has reversed the aforementioned IFRS accounting which has decreased debt related to put options granted to minority interests.

(f) Securitization arrangement.   The Group was involved in two major receivable securitization programs (in France and in the United States) to provide a cost-effective source of working capital and short-term financing. Under the programs, the subsidiaries agree to sell, on a revolving basis,

certain of their accounts receivable. Under the terms of the arrangements, the subsidiaries involved in these programs do not maintain control over the assets sold and there is neither entitlement nor obligation to repurchase the sold receivables. In these agreements, the purchaser of receivables holds a subordinated retained interest in the receivables not sold to third parties as usually granted in similar commercial transactions. Consequently, the receivables securitization transactions have been accounted for under U.S. GAAP as sales (with the subordinated interest being classified as long-term financial asset) and as a result, the related receivables and debt have been excluded from the consolidated balance sheets.

Under revised IAS 39, which the Group has applied for the purpose of its transition to IFRS effective January 1, 2004, financial assets can be derecognized only if substantially all risks and rewards attached to the assets have been transferred. The subordinated retained interest held by the purchaser in the receivables not sold to third parties represents a breach in the transfer of all risks and rewards. As a consequence, these accounts receivable should not be derecognized in the IFRS consolidated balance sheets and these operations should be treated as secured financings.

(g) Cumulative translation adjustments. As described in Note 2(d), the Group, as permitted by IFRS 1, elected to "reset to zero" previous cumulative translation differences arising from the translation into euros of foreign subsidiaries' financial statements denominated in foreign currency. The amount of 2,335 million euros recorded in the Previous GAAP accounts at January 1, 2004 has thus been reclassified to retained earnings as of January 1, 2004. This reclassification has no impact on consolidated shareholder's equity. For U.S.

GAAP purposes, this reclassification has been reversed in order to maintain historical amounts of cumulative translation adjustments. Translation adjustments which predate IFRS transition will therefore generate a difference between IFRS and U.S. GAAP in the calculation of gains and losses arising from future disposal of consolidated subsidiaries, joint-venture and associates.

7. Recently issued accounting pronouncements.

SFAS No. 123(R) "Share-Based Payment". In December 2004, the Financial Accounting Standards Board (the "FASB") issued SFAS 123 (revised 2004), *Share-Based Payment* ("SFAS 123(R)"), which is a revision of SFAS 123, *Accounting for Stock-Based Compensation.* SFAS 123(R) supersedes APB Opinion No. 25, *Accounting for Stock Issued to Employees,* and amends FASB Statement No. 95, *Statement of Cash Flows.* Generally, the approach in SFAS 123(R) is similar to the approach described in SFAS 123. However, SFAS 123(R) requires all share-based payments to employees, including grants of employee stock options, to be recognized in the income statement based on their fair values. Pro forma disclosure is no longer an alternative. The Group adopted SFAS 123(R) on January 1, 2006 using the "modified prospective" method. Under this method, compensation cost is recognized beginning with the effective date (a) based on the requirements of SFAS 123(R) for all share-based payments granted after the effective date and (b) based on the requirements of SFAS 123 for all awards granted to employees prior to the effective date of SFAS 123(R) that remain unvested on the effective date. Had we adopted SFAS 123(R) in prior periods, the impact of that standard would have approximated the impact of SFAS 123 as described in the disclosure of pro forma net income and income per share presented in Note 36-4.

EITF 04-6 "Accounting for Stripping Costs in the Mining Industry".   In March 2005, the Emerging Issues Task Force reached a consensus on Issue 04-6, *Accounting for Stripping Costs in the Mining Industry* ("EITF 04-6") which we are required to adopt on January 1, 2006. EITF 04-6 states that stripping costs incurred after the first saleable minerals are extracted from the mine (i.e. post-production stripping costs) should be considered costs of the extracted minerals and recognized as a component of inventory to be recognized in costs of sales in the same period as the revenue from the sale of the inventory. In June 2005, the EITF modified the consensus requiring entities to now recognize any cumulative effect adjustment in retained earnings. In accordance with the transition provisions of EITF 04-6, the Group will write off these deferred costs to retained earnings on January 1, 2006, and prospectively recognize the costs of all post-production stripping activity as a cost of the inventory produced during the period the stripping costs are incurred. As the impact of EITF 04-6 on post-adoption income statements will depend, in part, on the future level of post-production stripping activity and sales, both of which vary from period to period, the Group has not yet estimated any material effect on the financial condition or results of operations.

FASB Interpretation No. 47 "Accounting for Conditional Asset Retirement Obligations".   In March 2005, the FASB issued FASB Interpretation No. 47, *Accounting for Conditional Asset Retirement Obligations* ("FIN 47"). FIN 47 clarifies that an entity must record a liability for a "conditional" asset retirement obligation if the fair value of the obligation can be reasonably estimated. The adoption of FIN 47 did not have a material effect on our financial condition or results of operations.

SFAS No. 151, "Inventory Costs an amendment of ARB No. 43, Chapter 4".   In November 2004, the FASB issued SFAS No. 151, *"Inventory Costs an amendment of ARB No. 43, Chapter 4."* SFAS No. 151 clarifies that abnormal amounts of idle facility expense, freight, handling costs, and wasted materials (spoilage) should be recognized as current-period charges and requires the allocation of fixed production overheads to inventory based on the normal capacity of the production facilities. SFAS No. 151 is effective for fiscal years beginning after June 15, 2005. The Group does not expect the adoption of SFAS No. 151 to have a material effect on our consolidated financial position or results of operations.

Note 37 - Reconciliation of IFRS to U.S. GAAP.

The following is a summary reconciliation of net income as reported in the consolidated statements of income to net income as adjusted for the approximate effects of the application of U.S. GAAP for the years ended December 31, 2005 and 2004 and shareholders' equity, as reported in the consolidated balance sheets to shareholders' equity as adjusted for the approximate effects of the application of U.S. GAAP at December 31, 2005 and 2004.

(a) Reconciliation of net income.

(million euros)	Years ended December 31, 2005	2004
NET INCOME AS REPORTED IN THE CONSOLIDATED STATEMENTS OF INCOME	**1,424**	**1,334**
(less) Minority interests	**(328)**	(288)
NET INCOME – GROUP SHARE	**1,096**	**1,046**
1 - Business combinations	**74**	10
2 - Pension obligations	**(85)**	(83)
3 - Income taxes	**(42)**	(11)
4 - Stock based compensation and employee stock plans	**14**	13
5 - Other items	**20**	(16)
TOTAL U.S. GAAP ADJUSTMENTS BEFORE INCOME TAX AND MINORITY INTERESTS	**(19)**	**(87)**
Tax effects of the above U.S. GAAP adjustments	**20**	23
Minority interests on the above U.S. GAAP adjustments, net of taxes	**-**	5
NET INCOME ACCORDING TO U.S. GAAP	**1,097**	**987**

(b) Summarized Statements of income according to U.S. GAAP. For purposes of presenting summarized consolidated statements of income for the years ended December 31, 2005 and 2004 consistent with U.S. GAAP, the Group has reflected the financial statement impact of the above reconciling items between IFRS and U.S. GAAP presented in the above mentioned Notes.

(million euros)	Years ended December 31, 2005	2004
Revenue	**15,104**	13,371
Operating income	**2,052**	1,811
Minority interests	**(311)**	(241)
NET INCOME	**1,097**	**987**

(c) Earnings per share according to U.S. GAAP. In accordance with Statement of Financial Accounting Standards 128, *Earnings per Share* ("SFAS 128"), basic earnings per share is computed by dividing income available to common shareholders by the weighted average number of common shares outstanding. The computation of diluted earnings per share is adjusted to include any potential common shares. Potential common shares include stock options, warrants, and convertible securities issued by the Group on its own stock.

The computation and reconciliation of basic and diluted earnings per share for the years ended December 31, 2005 and 2004 prepared in accordance with U.S. GAAP are as follows:

	Years ended December 31,	
	2005	2004
NUMERATOR (IN MILLION EUROS)		
NET EARNINGS - BASIC EARNINGS PER SHARE	**1,097**	987
Interest expense on convertible debt ("OCEANE")	**15**	30
NET EARNINGS - DILUTED EARNINGS PER SHARE	**1,112**	**1,017**
DENOMINATOR (IN THOUSANDS)		
WEIGHTED AVERAGE NUMBER OF SHARES OUTSTANDING - BASIC	**171,491**	**167,204**
Weighted average of dilutive effect of:		
- *Stock options*	*590*	*575*
- *Assumed conversion of convertible debt ("OCEANE")*	*8,135*	*10,769*
Total potential dilutive shares	**8,725**	11,344
WEIGHTED AVERAGE NUMBER OF SHARES OUTSTANDING - FULLY DILUTED	**180,216**	**178,548**
BASIC EARNINGS PER SHARE (EUROS)	**6.40**	**5.90**
DILUTED EARNINGS PER SHARE (EUROS)	**6.17**	**5.70**

For purposes of computing diluted earnings per share, 3,267 and 4,727 thousand stock options were excluded from the calculation, for 2005 and 2004, respectively, as the effect of including such options would have been antidilutive.

(d) Reconciliation of shareholders' equity.

	At December 31,	
(million euros)	2005	2004
EQUITY AS REPORTED IN THE CONSOLIDATED BALANCE SHEETS	**12,329**	**9,901**
(less) Minority interests	**(2,571)**	(2,119)
SHAREHOLDERS' EQUITY – PARENT COMPANY	**9,758**	**7,782**
1 - Business combinations	**243**	136
2 - Pension obligations	**763**	477
3 - Income taxes	**(26)**	(14)
4 - Stock based compensation and employee stock plans	**(13)**	-
5 - Other items	**(8)**	(47)
TOTAL U.S. GAAP ADJUSTMENTS BEFORE INCOME TAX AND MINORITY INTERESTS	***959***	***552***
Tax effects of the above U.S. GAAP adjustments	**(232)**	(108)
Minority interests on the above U.S. GAAP adjustments, net of taxes	**38**	35
SHAREHOLDERS' EQUITY ACCORDING TO U.S. GAAP	**10,523**	**8,261**

The information below discloses the items affecting shareholders' equity under U.S. GAAP.

(million euros)	2005	2004
BALANCE AT JANUARY 1,	**8,261**	**7,500**
Net income	1,097	987
Dividends paid	(408)	(383)
Issuance of common stock (dividend reinvestment plan)	248	207
Exercise of stock options	22	10
Employee stock purchase plan	33	-
Purchase (sale) of treasury shares	4	2
Deferred stock based compensation	10	4
Employee stock purchase loans	(13)	7
Changes in other comprehensive income	299	85
Changes in translation adjustments	970	(158)
BALANCE AT DECEMBER 31,	**10,523**	**8,261**

(e) Comprehensive income for the years ended December 31, 2005 and 2004 under U.S. GAAP. Under U.S. GAAP, comprehensive income is the term used to define all non-owner changes in shareholders' equity. Comprehensive income includes, in addi-tion to net income, net unrealized gains and losses arising during the period on available for sale securites, movements in cumulative translation adjustments and additional mini-mum pension liability.

(million euros)	2005	2004
NET INCOME	**1,097**	**987**
Net unrealized gain (loss) on available for sale securities, net of income taxes	28	5
Net unrealized gain (loss) on derivative instruments, net of income taxes	10	39
Additional minimum pension liability adjustment, net of income taxes	261	41
Changes in cumulative translation adjustments	970	(158)
COMPREHENSIVE INCOME (LOSS) FOR THE YEAR ENDED DECEMBER 31,	***2,366***	***914***

(f) Summarized Balance sheets according to U.S. GAAP. For purposes of presenting sum-marized consolidated balance sheets at December 31, 2005 and 2004 in a format consistent with U.S. GAAP, the Group has reflected the financial statement impact of the reconciling items between IFRS and U.S. GAAP presented in the above men-tioned notes. ∎

(million euros)	At December 31, 2005	At December 31, 2004
Cash and cash equivalents	1,529	1,344
Accounts receivable-trade, net	2,296	1,878
Other receivables	943	836
Inventories	1,748	1,395
Deferred taxes – current portion	38	45
Goodwill	6,485	5,909
Intangible assets, net	241	54
Property, plant and equipment, net	11,182	9,861
Investments in associates	1,506	1,436
Other financial assets	1,201	815
Deferred taxes	218	54
TOTAL ASSETS	*27,387*	*23,627*
Accounts payable-trade	1,582	1,284
Other payables	1,691	1,398
Short-term bank borrowings and current portion of long-term debt	1,523	1,053
Deferred taxes	707	500
Pension liability	1,100	1,022
Provisions	1,060	989
Long-term debt	6,676	6,876
Minority interests	2,525	2,244
Shareholders' equity	10,523	8,261
TOTAL LIABILITIES AND SHAREHOLDERS' EQUITY	*27,387*	*23,627*

REQUIRED:

1. Document the effects of the GAAP differences in the 20F by doing the following:

   a. For the current year, calculate the percentage change for net income and for total shareholders' equity indicated by the reconciliation and using the non-U.S. GAAP (i.e., IFRS) numbers as a base.

   b. Repeat the same calculations for the preceding year. Are the percentage changes approximately the same? What is significant about your findings?

   c. For the current year, identify the two income statement items and the two balance sheet items that exhibit the relatively largest differences. Would

you expect other French multinational companies to be subject to similar item-by-item differences?

2. Should a U.S. reader of non-U.S. financial statements find this SEC-mandated reconciliation useful?

3. Various corporate management and financing decisions are made with the consequences for corporate financial statements in mind. If a given management had to report under a different set of GAAP, it might make different business decisions. If we accept this assertion, then GAAP reconciliations have only limited informational value. Suggest a procedure that would represent a better solution to international financial reporting difficulties.

Case 3-2B Do the Differences Really Matter?

As an analyst for a securities firm, you are aware that accounting practices differ around the world. Yet you wonder whether these differences really have any material effect on companies' financial statements. You also know that the SEC in the United States requires non-U.S. registrants to reconcile key financial data from the GAAP used in their financial statements to U.S. GAAP. You obtain the reconciliation from the 2005 Form 20F SEC filing for BASF (a German chemicals company).

BASF

Reconciliation of net income and stockholders' equity to U.S. GAAP.

The Consolidated Financial Statements comply with U.S. GAAP as far as permissible under IFRS. The remaining differences concern the following adjustments:

Reconciliation of net income to U.S. GAAP	Note	2005	2005	2004
			(Million € and Million $, Except Per Share Amounts)	
Income after taxes and minority interests according to IFRS		**$3,560.5**	**€ 3,006.7**	**€ 2,004.3**
Adjustments required to conform with U.S. GAAP				
Accounting for pensions	(a)	(86.0)	(72.6)	(24.6)
Accounting for provisions	(b)	7.7	6.5	6.1
Valuation adjustments relating to companies accounted for using the equity method	(e)	—	—	(108.4)
Acquisitions	(f)	(25.8)	(21.8)	
Other adjustments	(g)	197.6	166.9	(11.0)
Deferred taxes	(h)	(31.0)	(26.2)	(2.4)
Minority interests	(i)	1.3	1.1	(1.2)
Adjustments to U.S. GAAP		**63.8**	**53.9**	**(141.5)**
Net income in accordance with U.S. GAAP		**3,624.4**	**3,060.6**	**1,862.8**
Cumulative effect of change in accounting for major overhauls	(g)	(90.0)	(76.0)	—
Net income in accordance with U.S. GAAP before cumulative effect of change in accounting		**3,534.4**	**2,984.6**	**1,862.8**

(continued)

Reconciliation of net income to U.S. GAAP	Note	2005	2005	2004
			(Million € and Million $, Except Per Share Amounts)	
Earnings per share in accordance with U.S. GAAP		6.90	5.83	3.39
Cumulative effect of change in accounting for major overhauls		(0.17)	(0.14)	—
Earnings per share in accordance with U.S. GAAP before cumulative effect of change in accounting		6.73	5.69	3.39
Dilutive effect		—	—	—
Diluted earnings per share in accordance with U.S. GAAP		6.90	5.83	3.39

Reconciliation of stockholders' equity to U.S. GAAP	Note	2005	2005	2004
		(Million € and Million $,Except Per Share Amounts)		
Stockholders' equity in accordance with IFRS as of December 31		$20,751.3	€ 17,523.5	€ 16,602.2
Minority interests		(570.5)	(481.8)	(328.5)
Stockholders' equity excluding minority interests		20,180.8	17,041.7	16,273.7
Adjustments required to conform with U.S. GAAP				
Accounting for pensions	(a)	1,089.6	920.1	1,020.1
Accounting for provisions	(b)	133.8	113.0	105.0
Accounting for financial instruments	(c)	(14.3)	(12.1)	—
Reversal of goodwill amortization and write-offs due to impairment	(d)	408.0	344.5	325.7
Valuation adjustments relating to companies accounted for using the equity method	(e)	46.2	39.0	39.0
Acquisitions	(f)	(25.8)	(21.8)	—
Other adjustments	(g)	(0.1)	(0.1)	(145.7)
Deferred taxes	(h)	(548.8)	(463.4)	(441.7)
Minority interests	(i)	(19.1)	(16.1)	(17.0)
Adjustments to U.S. GAAP		1,069.5	903.1	885.4
Stockholders' equity in accordance with U.S. GAAP as of December 31		21,250.3	17,944.8	17,159.1

Earnings per share	2005	2005	2004
	(Million € and Million $, Except Per Share Amounts)		
Net income in accordance with U.S. GAAP	**$3,624.4**	**€3,060.6**	**€1,862.8**
Number of shares (1,000)			
Weighted-average undiluted number of shares	525,125	525,125	548,714
Dilutive effect	—		
Weighted-average diluted number of shares	525,125	525,125	548,714
Basic earnings per share in accordance with U.S. GAAP	**6.90**	**5.83**	**3.39**
Dilutive effect	—	—	—
Diluted earnings per share in accordance with U.S. GAAP	**6.90**	**5.83**	**3.39**
Cumulative effect of change in accounting for major overhauls	(0.17)	(0.14)	—
Earnings per share in accordance with U.S. GAAP before cumulative effect of change in accounting	**6.73**	**5.69**	**3.39**

The calculation of earnings per share is described in detail in Note 4.

(a) Accounting for pensions.   Pension provisions and expenses which fall under the scope of SFAS 87 are based on the same actuarial assumptions as under IFRS (see Note 23).

BASF exercises the option allowing actuarial gains and losses to be offset directly against retained earnings outside of profit and loss in the year in which they are incurred. According to SFAS 87, these items are charged to income as soon as they exceed 10% of the greater of the Projected Benefit Obligation (PBO) and pension plan assets. In addition, a difference results because an Additional Minimum Liability reduces stockholders' equity according to U.S. GAAP.

The Accumulated Benefit Obligation (ABO) amounted to €11,398.0 million in 2005 compared with €9,419.9 million in 2004. The pension plans whose plan assets do not completely cover the ABO are shown below.

Current funding situation (Million €)	2005		2004	
	ABO	Plan Assets	ABO	Plan Assets
Unfunded pension plans	582.2	—	3,563.1	—
Partially funded pension plans	6,954.6	6,756.6	1,727.5	1,686.3
Total of pension plans that are not fully funded	**7,536.8**	**6,756.6**	**5,290.6**	**1,686.3**
Fully funded pension plans	3,861.2	4,258.6	4,129.3	4,518.0
Total	**11,398.0**	**11,015.2**	**9,419.9**	**6,204.3**

The balance of the expected return on plan assets and the interest costs pertaining to the pension obligation is recognized in the financial results (see Note 9) as an allowable IFRS option. According to U.S. GAAP, these items are considered in personnel costs. As a result, income from operations, according to U.S. GAAP would be lower in 2005 by € 120.8 million (2004: € 134.8 million), and the financial result accordingly higher.

Actuarial losses amounted to € 2,587.1 million as of December 31, 2005 and € 1,505.8 million as of December 31, 2004. Based on these amounts, € 62.2 million was amortized in 2005 and € 15.4 million in 2004 in the income statement. As of December 31, 2005, unrecognized prior service costs existed in the amount of € 54.2 million and as of December 31, 2004, € 64.3 million. Based on these amounts, € 10.4 million was amortized in 2005 and € 9.2 million in 2004 in the income statement. Information required according to SFAS 132 "Employers' Disclosures about Pensions and Other Postretirement Benefits" (revised 2003) are contained in Note 23.

(b) Accounting for provisions.   The reconciliation item contains the following deviations:

> ***Provisions for part-time programs for employees nearing retirement age:***   In these financial statements agreed upon top-up payments within the pre-retirement part-time programs are immediately accrued in their full amount, and discounted at a rate of 3.0%. A provision is also recorded for the expected costs for agreements that are anticipated to be concluded during the term of the collective bargaining agreements, taking into consideration the ceilings on the number of employee participants provided in such collective bargaining agreements. In accordance with U.S. GAAP, provisions may only be recorded for employees who have accepted an offer, and the supplemental payments are accrued over the employee's remaining service period. This

resulted in a decrease in income under U.S. GAAP of € 29.4 million in 2005 and € 22.3 million in 2004. Stockholders' equity increased by € 125.3 million in 2005 and by € 154.7 million in 2004.

Provisions for restructuring measures: SFAS 146, "Accounting for Costs Associated with Exit and Disposal Activities" requires expected costs associated with the exit or disposal of business activities to be accrued only when a liability against a third party exists. In case of a retention period, severance payments to employees are accrued over the term of this period.

Discounting of provisions and liabilities: According to IFRS, long-term provisions and liabilities are to be discounted to their present value if the effect from discounting is material. Under U.S. GAAP, however, discounting is only permissible for specific types of provisions and liabilities when the amount and timing of the cash flows can be reliably predicted. This resulted in an income effect of € 10.8 million in 2005 and € 47.0 million in 2004, and a decrease in equity of € 30.5 million in 2005 and of € 41.3 million in 2004.

(c) Accounting for financial instruments.   The guidelines for accounting for financial instruments according to IAS 39 "Financial Instruments: Recognition and Measurement" and SFAS 133 "Accounting for Derivatives and Hedging Activities" are very similar in concept. The reconciliation items relate to the differing treatment of fair value changes of derivatives within equity, which are a component of a cash flow hedge for a future transaction. According to IAS 39, for hedging future transactions, there is an option regarding the accounting treatment of these fair value changes. BASF has chosen the option to net these changes in valuation against the acquisition costs of the non-financial assets or debts. The other option allows the valuation changes to be charged to the income

statement in the same period in which the hedged transaction flows through the income statement. According to SFAS 133, only the second method is allowed, while netting against acquisition costs is prohibited. This timing difference leads to a difference in equity and has no impact on income.

(d) Reversal of goodwill amortization and write-offs due to impairment. Goodwill is only written down if an impairment exists according to SFAS 142 as of January 1, 2002. According to IFRS 1 "First-time Adoption" in conjunction with IFRS 3 "Business Combinations," regularly scheduled amortization of goodwill has been replaced by impairment testing effective as of January 1, 2004. The amortization on goodwill in 2002 and 2003 has been reversed and increases stockholders' equity.

(e) Valuation adjustments relating to companies accounted for using the equity method. This item contains differences from companies accounted for using the equity method that result from different dates on which the scheduled amortization for goodwill was discontinued under U.S. GAAP (2002) and IFRS (2004).

(f) Acquisitions. A difference between U.S. GAAP and IFRS with respect to the first-time consolidation involves the treatment of in-process research and development projects of acquired businesses. Whereas these costs are expensed in the first year of consolidation under U.S. GAAP, IFRS requires that these costs are capitalized as intangible assets and amortized over their useful lives. This resulted in a decrease of income of € 25.5 million. Stockholders' equity decreased similarly by € 25.5 million in 2005. There were no in-process research and development costs in connection with acquisitions in 2004.

According to U.S. GAAP, contingent purchase price adjustments of acquisitions are only accounted for at the time of payment of the contingent price adjustment. IFRS 3, however, requires the recognition of these purchase price adjustments at estimated values in the first consolidation of an acquired business. If the purchase price is less than the fair value of assets and liabilities acquired as a result of these differing practices, the difference is to be booked immediately to the income statement according to IFRS, whereas according to U.S. GAAP it reduces the values assigned to the acquired assets. This resulted in an income effect of € 3.7 million in 2005. Stockholders' equity increased correspondingly by € 3.7 million in 2005. There were no such differences in 2004 as a result of contingent price adjustments.

(g) Other adjustments. This item primarily includes the elimination of provisions for the fair value of stock options granted, differences arising from the accounting of sale and leaseback transactions as well as provisions for major overhauls of large scale plants.

Following a resolution by the Board of Executive Directors, stock options are to be settled in cash. Under U.S. GAAP, such obligations are to be accounted for as stock appreciation rights based on the intrinsic value of the options on the balance sheet date. However, options granted in prior years, for which cash settlement was not foreseen, are to be accounted for in accordance with SFAS 123 as equity instruments based upon the fair value on the grant date. In the present Financial Statements, all obligations resulting from stock options are accounted for based upon the fair value on the balance sheet date. A provision is accrued over the vesting period of the options. The different accounting methods led to an increase in net income in accordance with U.S. GAAP of € 6.1 million in 2005, and € 16.1 million in 2004.

In the present Financial Statements, obligations resulting from stock options are shown as provisions. In accordance with U.S. GAAP, options for which cash settlement was not originally foreseen are recorded as additions to stockholders' equity. Overall, the accounting for stock options resulted in a decrease in stockholders' equity of € 17.4 million in 2005, and € 9.4 million in 2004.

Under IFRS, anticipated costs necessary for the major overhaul of large scale plants prescribed at certain intervals are capitalized as a part of the respective asset and depreciated on a straight-line basis over the period until the next regularly scheduled major overhaul. According to U.S. GAAP, provisions for such costs were established. In 2005, this accounting method was changed to comply with IFRS. The pre-tax cumulative effect of € 117.0 million was

recognized in income. The net effect after taxes amounted to € 76.0 million.

Gains from the sale of assets, which continue to be used under operating leases are to be recognized in income under IFRS, if the sale is an arm's-length transaction. U.S. GAAP requires the deferral of the gain and its recognition in income over the useful life of the asset.

(h) Deferred taxes. The adjustments required to conform with U.S. GAAP would result in taxable temporary differences between the valuation of assets and liabilities in the Consolidated Financial Statements and the carrying amount for tax purposes. Resulting adjustments for deferred taxes primarily relate to the following:

	Note	Stockholders' equity		Net Income	
		2005	2004	2005	2004
		(Million €)			
Accounting for pensions	(a)	(348.5)	(384.2)	27.4	10.2
Accounting for provisions	(b)	(51.6)	(46.0)	(5.2)	10.7
Accounting for financial instruments	(c)	4.3	—	(5.3)	—
Reversal of goodwill amortization and write-offs due to impairment	(d)	(96.2)	(86.9)	—	—
Acquisitions	(f)	9.3	—	9.3	—
Other adjustments	(g)	19.3	75.4	(52.4)	(23.3)
Total		**(463.4)**	**(441.7)**	**(26.2)**	**(2.4)**

(i) Minority interests. The portion of U.S. GAAP valuation adjustments applying to minority interests is shown separately.

Consolidation of majority-owned subsidiaries: First-time consolidations of subsidiaries require the restatement of the figures of the previous year. The effect of first-time consolidated companies on the net worth, financial position

and results was immaterial; an adjustment was therefore not performed.

New U.S. GAAP accounting standards not yet adopted: SFAS 123R "Share-Based Payment" revised 2004 replaces SFAS 123 "Accounting for Stock-Based Compensation." This disallows the former optional treatments contained in APB 25 "Accounting for Stock Issued to

Employees." According to SFAS 123R all listed companies must recognize stock-based payment as an expense during the vesting period. Equity instruments granted as payment are valued at their market value at the time of granting. The market value at reporting date is calculated to value share-based payment, which is to be settled in cash. SFAS 123R applies to all reporting years commencing after June 15, 2005. As BASF already recognizes share-based payment as an expense, SFAS 123R will have no material effects on BASF's Consolidated Financial Statements.

SFAS 154, governing the accounting and reporting of voluntary changes in accounting methods, replaces APB Opinion Nr. 20 "Accounting Changes" and FASB Statement No. 3 "Reporting Accounting Changes in Interim Financial Statements." According to SFAS 154, impacts on income as a result of voluntary changes in accounting methods will no longer be shown as a separate item "cumulative change in accounting principle" on the income statement of the current period but rather as an adjustment of the financial statements for all previously published periods as if the new method had always been used.

EITF 04-13 "Inventory Exchanges" determines when a purchase and sale of inventory is to be seen as a barter transaction. According to APB Opinion No. 29 "Accounting

Million €	2005	2004
Net income in accordance with U.S. GAAP (before other comprehensive income)	**3,060.6**	**1,862.8**
Change of foreign currency translation adjustments		
Gross	765.6	(291.3)
Deferred taxes	(33.1)	17.2
Changes in unrealized holding gains on securities		
Gross	66.7	95.6
Deferred taxes	4.5	0.3
Changes in unrealized losses from cash flow hedges		
Gross	(21.2)	(54.0)
Deferred taxes	11.6	18.7
Additional minimum liability for pensions		
Gross	(1,179.7)	(514.7)
Deferred taxes	457.1	197.0
Other comprehensive income (loss), net of tax	**71.5**	**(531.2)**
Comprehensive income, net of tax	**3,132.1**	**1,331.6**

for Non-monetary Transactions," barter transactions are not to be included in income. The key criterion is whether the purchase and sale are closely connected. EITF 04-13 clearly states that no sales revenues may be recognized from these transactions if sale and purchase of inventories are clearly connected. Furthermore, EITF 04-13 has specified the scope of FASB Statement No. 153 "Exchanges of Non-monetary Assets." EITF 04-13 is to be applied to all new transactions that were concluded in the reporting years beginning after March 15, 2006. No revenue was recognized for barter transactions as defined in these standards.

Other changes in stockholders' equity.   The option allowed by IFRS 1 to offset currency translation adjustments against retained earnings as of January 1, 2004 was exercised. Under U.S. GAAP, the translation adjustment is to be carried forward unchanged.

According to U.S. GAAP, specifically SFAS 130, certain expenses and income are recognized outside of profit or loss (Other Comprehensive Income):

Million €	2005	2004
Stockholders' equity in accordance with U.S. GAAP (before accumulated other comprehensive income) on January 1	**19,408.9**	**18,694.7**
Accumulated other comprehensive income		
Foreign currency translation adjustments		
Gross	(603.4)	(1,369.0)
Deferred taxes	36.1	69.2
Unrealized holding gains on securities		
Gross	262.9	196.2
Deferred taxes	(40.9)	(45.4)
Unrealized losses from cash flow hedges		
Gross	(79.3)	(58.1)
Deferred taxes	31.7	20.1
Additional minimum liability for pensions		
Gross	(1,730.7)	(551.0)
Deferred taxes	659.5	202.4
Accumulated other comprehensive income	**(1,464.1)**	**(1,535.6)**
Total stockholders' equity in accordance with U.S. GAAP including comprehensive income on December 31	**17,944.8**	**17,159.1**

REQUIRED

1. Document the effects of the GAAP differences in the 20F by doing the following:

   a. For the current year, calculate the percentage change for net income and for total shareholders' equity indicated by the reconciliation and using the non-U.S. GAAP (i.e., IFRS) numbers as a base.

   b. Repeat the same calculations for the preceding year. Are the percentage changes approximately the same? What is significant about your findings?

   c. For the current year, identify the two income statement items and the two balance sheet items that exhibit the relatively largest differences. Would you expect other German multinational companies to be subject to similar item-by-item differences?

2. Should a U.S. reader of non-U.S. financial statements find this SEC-mandated reconciliation useful?

3. Various corporate management and financing decisions are made with the consequences for corporate financial statements in mind. If a given management had to report under a different set of GAAP, it might make different business decisions. If we accept this assertion, then GAAP reconciliations have only limited informational value. Suggest a procedure that would represent a better solution to international financial reporting difficulties.

CHAPTER 4

Comparative Accounting: The Americas and Asia

Chapter 4 looks at accounting in five countries, two in the Americas (Mexico and the United States) and three in Asia (China, India, and Japan). The United States and Japan have highly developed economies, whereas Mexico, China, and India are "emerging" economies.[1] The United States is the largest economy in the world and home to more large multinational corporations than any other nation. Japan has the second-biggest economy in the world and is also home to many of the world's largest businesses. Both countries were founders of the International Accounting Standards Committee (now the International Accounting Standards Board, or IASB), and they have a major role in directing the IASB's agenda. In addition, the standard-setting bodies in both countries have committed to converging their national generally accepted accounting principles (GAAP) with International Financial Reporting Standards (IFRS).

Why were the other countries chosen for this chapter? We picked Mexico because we wanted to include a Latin American country. Free-market reforms accelerated in the 1990s throughout much of Latin America. These reforms involved removing protectionist barriers to imports, welcoming foreign investment, and privatizing state-owned companies. The reforms have gone furthest in Argentina, Chile, Mexico, and Peru.[2] The 1994 North American Free Trade Agreement (NAFTA) created much new interest in Mexican accounting in Canada, the United States, and elsewhere. Accounting in Mexico has many features in common with accounting in other Latin American countries. The choice of China may be obvious: It is the largest and most populous country in the world. Companies from all around the world are eager to do business there. Like the Czech Republic, discussed in Chapter 3, China is converting from a centrally planned economy to one that is more market oriented. However, the extent to which these two countries are embracing market reforms is different. The Czech Republic is moving toward a complete market economy, while China is taking a middle course in moving to a *socialist market economy*, that is, a planned economy with market adaptations. Accounting developments are an important part of the structural changes in the Chinese economy. India, the second most populous country in the world, has been described a "the next big thing. . . . No big international company can do without an India strategy."[3] Reforms that began in 1991 have resulted in a remarkable transformation of its economy, and most observers feel that the next decade and half will see equally dramatic changes.

---

[1]As noted in Chapter 3, the term emerging economy refers loosely to newly industrialized countries (NICs) and to countries in transition from planned to free-market economies. NICs have experienced rapid industrial growth, but their economies are not yet rich in terms of per capita gross domestic product. Mexico and India are NICs; China has an economy in transition.

[2]"Back on the Pitch: A Survey of Business in Latin America," *Economist* (December 6, 1997): 3–4.

[3]*Economist*, "Now for the Hard Part: A Survey of India," (June 3, 2006): 3.

Mexico and India are capitalist countries but with traditionally heavy central-government intervention and government ownership of key industries. Historically, their economies have been somewhat closed to foreign investment and international competition. This relative isolation is now changing, because both governments are privatizing their industry holdings and opening up to the global economy. Their financial accounting systems are more developed than China's in terms of standard setting, requirements, and practices. Naturally, accounting is evolving in these two countries as well, but not as rapidly as in China.

Exhibit 4-1 contains some comparative economic data about the five countries that are the focus of this chapter. China's area dwarfs the others. Another contrast is gross domestic product (GDP) per capita and by sector. Overall, China and India are significantly poorer than the other three nations, and their economies are much more agricultural. Both of these factors are indicators of significant development potential. The United States is at the other end of the economic spectrum. Its GDP (in absolute terms and per capita) and stock market capitalization exceed the other countries. Its economy is also more service oriented than the others. The United States is a major trading partner of the other four. In fact, the United States is the largest trading partner of Japan, Mexico, and India.[4] Japan also has an advanced economy, as evidenced by its GDP (in absolute terms, per capita, and by sector) and stock market capitalization. Japan is also a major trading partner of China and Mexico, in addition to the United States.

Political and economic ties have been an important influence on accounting in these five countries. U.S. accounting was originally imported from Great Britain (along with the English language and the common law legal system). Most of the first accountants in the United States were British expatriates. However, as a result of the growth of U.S. economic and political power in the 20th century, U.S. ideas on accounting and financial reporting have had substantial influence on the rest of the world for some time now. Mexico's close economic ties with the United States are why it has fairness-oriented accounting despite being a code law country. India was once part of the British Empire. Like the United States, India imported its accounting from Great Britain. In China, the effect of political and economic ties is more anticipatory than historical. China is basing its new accounting standards on IFRS because it hopes to better communicate with the foreign investors so vital to its economic development plans.

FIVE NATIONAL FINANCIAL ACCOUNTING SYSTEMS[5]

United States

Accounting in the United States is regulated by a private-sector body (the Financial Accounting Standards Board, or FASB), but a governmental agency (the Securities and Exchange Commission, or SEC) underpins the authority of its standards. The key

---

[4]The United States accounts for more than three-fourths of Mexico's imports and imports.
[5]The discussion in this section draws on the references cited at the end of the chapter and on references cited in earlier editions of this book.

EXHIBIT 4-1   Economic Data for Selected Countries

	United States	Mexico	Japan	China	India
Area: sq. km. (in thousands)	9,373	1,973	378	9,561	3,287
Population (in millions)	297	105	128	1,313	1,081
Gross Domestic Product (in billions)	$11,712	$677	$4,623	$1,932	$691
GDP Per Capita	$39,430	$6,450	$36,170	$1,470	$640
GDP by Sector					
Agriculture	1%	4%	1%	15%	22%
Industry	18%	26%	30%	53%	27%
Services	81%	70%	69%	32%	51%
Imports (in billions)	$1,470	$197	$455	$561	$107
Exports (in billions)	$819	$188	$566	$593	$80
Market Capitalization (in billions), end 2005	$16,998	$239	$4,737	$781	$553
Major Trading Partners	Canada, Mexico, China	U.S.A., China, Germany	U.S.A., China, S. Korea	U.S.A., Japan, S. Korea	U.S.A., China

SOURCE: Compiled from *Pocket World in Figures, 2007 Edition* (London: The Economist, 2006) and *The World Factbook*, www.cia.gov/cia/publications/factbook/, January 2007.

link allowing this shared-power system to work effectively is the 1973 SEC Accounting Series Release (ASR) No. 150. This release states:

> The Commission intends to continue its policy of looking to the private sector for leadership in establishing and improving accounting principles. For purposes of this policy, principles, standards, and practices promulgated by the FASB in its statements and interpretations, will be considered by the Commission as having substantial authoritative support, and those contrary to such FASB promulgations will be considered to have no such support.[6]

Until 2002, the American Institute of Certified Public Accountants (AICPA), another private-sector body, set auditing standards. In that year, the Public Company Accounting Oversight Board (PCAOB) was established, with broad powers to regulate audits and auditors of public companies. The PCAOB, discussed later, is a private organization overseen by the SEC.[7]

Accounting Regulation and Enforcement

The U.S. system has no general legal requirements for the publication of periodic audited financial statements. Corporations in the United States are formed under state law, not federal law. Each state has its own corporate statutes; in general, these contain minimal requirements for keeping accounting records and publishing periodic financial statements. Many of these statutes are not rigorously enforced, and reports

---

[6]Securities and Exchange Commission, *Statement of Policy on the Establishment and Improvement of Accounting Principles and Standards*, Accounting Series Release No. 150. Reprinted in *The Development of SEC Accounting*, G. J. Previts, ed., Reading, MA: Addison-Wesley, 1981, 228. The SEC reaffirmed the FASB as the designated accounting standard setting body in April 2003. This reaffirmation followed an SEC study of the U.S. accounting standards setting process, as mandated by the 2002 Sarbanes-Oxley Act (discussed later).
[7]The Web sites of these organizations are: Securities and Exchange Commission: www.sec.gov; Financial Accounting Standards Board: www.fasb.org; American Institute of Certified Public Accountants: www.aicpa.org; and Public Company Accounting Oversight Board: www.pcaobus.org.

rendered to local agencies are often unavailable to the public. Thus, annual audit and financial reporting requirements realistically exist only at the federal level as specified by the SEC. The SEC has jurisdiction over companies listed on U.S. stock exchanges and companies traded over-the-counter.[8] Other limited-liability companies have no such compulsory requirements for financial reporting, making the United States unusual by international norms.

The SEC has the legal authority to prescribe accounting and reporting standards for public companies but relies on the private sector to set the standards. It works with the FASB and exerts pressure when it believes the FASB is moving too slowly or in the wrong direction. At times, the SEC has delayed or overruled pronouncements or has imposed its own requirements.

Since the SEC is an independent regulatory agency, Congress and the president have no direct influence over its policies. However, the five full-time SEC commissioners are appointed by the president and confirmed by the Senate, and the SEC has only those powers that Congress has granted it by statute. As part of the regulatory process, the SEC issues Accounting Series Releases, Financial Reporting Releases, and Staff Accounting Bulletins. Regulations SX and SK contain the rules for preparing financial reports that must be filed with the SEC. Annual filings by U.S. and Canadian companies are on Form 10K, while those from non-Canadian foreign companies are on Form 20F.[9]

The FASB was established in 1973[10] and as of December 2006 issued 158 Statements of Financial Accounting Standards (SFASs). The objective of the SFASs is to provide information that is useful to present and potential investors, creditors, and others who make investment, credit, and similar decisions. The FASB has seven full-time members, representing accounting firms, academia, corporations, and the investor community. Board members must sever all economic and organizational ties to prior employers or ownership in order to serve. The FASB's use of a conceptual framework is a significant feature of accounting standard setting in the United States. Statements of Financial Accounting Concepts set forth the fundamentals on which financial accounting and reporting standards are based.

The FASB goes through lengthy due-process procedures before issuing an SFAS. In developing its work agenda, it listens to individuals, professional firms, courts of law, companies, and government agencies. It also relies on an emerging-issues task force and an advisory council to help identify accounting issues that need attention. Once a topic is added to the agenda, the FASB's technical staff does research and analysis, and an advisory task force is appointed. A Discussion Memorandum or other discussion document is disseminated for comment, and public hearings are held. The FASB considers oral and written comments in meetings open to the public. Next, an Exposure Draft is issued and further public comments are considered. The process

---

[8]There are approximately 14,000 companies that must report to the SEC, including 1,200 foreign companies (of which 500 are from Canada). Companies traded on the "pink sheets" over-the-counter market are exempt from the SEC's periodic filing requirements if they meet a minimum-size test and certain other requirements.

[9]The SEC rigorously enforces its filing requirements. Over half of SEC filers had their disclosures reviewed by the SEC in 2005, twice the percentage from a few years earlier.

[10]Two other private-sector bodies established U.S. generally accepted accounting principles (GAAP) before the FASB. These were the Committee on Accounting Procedure (1938 to 1959) and the Accounting Principles Board (1959 to 1973).

ensures that standard setting in the United States is both political and technical. An SFAS must be approved by four of the seven members.

Generally accepted accounting principles (GAAP) comprise all the financial accounting standards, rules, and regulations that must be observed in the preparation of financial reports. The SFASs are the major component of GAAP. The accounting and auditing regulations are probably more voluminous in the United States than in the rest of the world combined and substantially more detailed than in any other country. For this reason, the FASB and SEC are considering moving U.S. GAAP away from rules-based standards toward principles-based standards.

The FASB did not seriously engage itself internationally until the 1990s. In 1991, the FASB developed its first strategic plan for international activities. In 1994, the FASB added the promotion of international comparability to its mission statement. The FASB is now a major cooperative international player, committed to converging U.S. GAAP and IFRS. In 2002, the FASB and IASB formalized their commitment to convergence by signing the so-called Norwalk Agreement. Under this agreement, the two boards pledge to remove existing differences between their standards and coordinate future standard setting agendas so that major issues are worked on together. The commitment to convergence was reaffirmed in 2005, with several significant convergence goals to be reached by 2008.[11]

The Sarbanes-Oxley Act was signed into law in 2002, significantly expanding U.S. requirements on corporate governance, disclosure and reporting, and the regulation of the audit profession. Among its more important provisions is the creation of the PCAOB, a nonprofit organization overseen by the SEC. The PCAOB is responsible for:

- Setting auditing, quality control, ethics, independence, and other standards relating to the preparation of audit reports on companies issuing securities to the public
- Overseeing the audit of public companies subject to the securities laws
- Inspecting registered public accounting firms
- Conducting investigations and disciplinary proceedings
- Sanctioning registered public accounting firms, and referring cases to the SEC or other enforcement bodies for further investigation

Previously, the AICPA issued auditing standards, was responsible for the Code of Professional Ethics, and disciplined auditors. The PCAOB effectively assumed these responsibilities from the AICPA.[12]

The Sarbanes-Oxley Act was passed in the wake of numerous corporate and accounting scandals, such as Enron and WorldCom. The act limits the services that audit firms can offer clients and prohibits auditors from offering certain nonaudit services (including types of consulting services) to audit clients. It also requires that lead audit partners rotate off audits every five years. Section 302 of the act requires a company's chief executive officer and chief financial officer to certify

---

[11]For example, in July 2006 the FASB and IASB issued a joint discussion paper on improving their conceptual frameworks. The intention is to develop a common conceptual framework.

[12]The act is the most substantial piece of U.S. business legislation since the 1934 Securities Exchange Act established the SEC.

each quarterly and annual report. Section 404 requires management's assessment of internal control over financial reporting, along with a related report by the independent auditor.[13]

Thus, the auditor's report covers both the financial statements and internal controls. For example, the auditor's report on the financial statements in Colgate-Palmolive's 2005 annual report says the following:

> In our opinion, the consolidated financial statements . . . present fairly, in all material respects, the financial position of Colgate-Palmolive Company and its subsidiaries at December 31, 2005 and 2004, and the results of their operations and their cash flows for each of the three years in the period ended December 31, 2005 in conformity with accounting principles generally accepted in the United States of America.

The auditor's report on internal controls over financial reporting says the following:

> [I]n our opinion, the Company maintained, in all material respects, effective internal control over financial reporting as of December 31, 2005, based on criteria established in *Internal Control—Integrated Framework* issued by the COSO [Committee of Sponsoring Organizations of the Treadway Commission].

Financial statements are supposed to "present fairly" the financial position of the company and the results of its operations "in conformity with generally accepted accounting principles." Compliance with GAAP is the test for fair presentation. There is no subjective override, such as the "true and fair" override in the United Kingdom. The SEC also expects compliance with GAAP and will not accept an auditor's report with an "adverse" opinion.

Financial Reporting

A typical annual financial report of a large U.S. corporation includes the following components:

1. Report of management
2. Report of independent auditors
3. Primary financial statements (income statement, balance sheet, statement of cash flows, statement of comprehensive income, statement of changes in stockholders' equity)
4. Management discussion and analysis of results of operations and financial condition

---

[13]Section 404 is viewed by many observers as the most burdensome (and costly) provision of the act. The PCAOB has five board members, two CPAs and three non-CPAs. Board members are appointed by the SEC after consultation with the Chairman of the Federal Reserve Board and the Secretary of the Treasury. They serve five-year terms. The PCAOB is funded by fees assessed against SEC-registered public companies and registered accounting firms.

5. Disclosure of accounting policies with the most critical impact on financial statements[14]
6. Notes to financial statements
7. Five- or ten-year comparison of selected financial data
8. Selected quarterly data

Consolidated financial statements are required, and published U.S. financial reports typically do not contain parent-company-only statements. Consolidation rules require that all controlled subsidiaries (i.e., ownership of more than 50 percent of the voting shares) be fully consolidated, including those with nonhomogeneous operations.[15] Interim (quarterly) financial reports are required for companies listed on major stock exchanges. These reports typically contain only abbreviated, unaudited financial statements and a concise management commentary.

Accounting Measurements

Accounting measurement rules in the United States assume that a business entity will continue as a going concern. Accrual basis measurements are pervasive, and transactions and events-recognition rules rely heavily on the matching concept. A consistency requirement insists on uniformity of accounting treatment of like items within each accounting period and from one period to the next. If changes in practices or procedures occur, the changes and their effects must be disclosed.

Business combinations must be accounted for as a purchase. Goodwill is capitalized as the difference between the fair value of the consideration given in the exchange and the fair value of the underlying net assets acquired (including other intangibles). It is reviewed for impairment annually and written off and expensed to earnings when its book value exceeds its fair value.[16] Proportional consolidation is not practiced. Joint ventures are accounted for using the equity method, as are investments nonconsolidated, 20 percent– to 50 percent–owned affiliated companies. Foreign currency translation follows the requirements of SFAS No. 52, which relies on the foreign subsidiary's functional currency to determine translation methodology (Chapter 6).

The United States relies on historical cost to value tangible and intangible assets. Revaluations are permitted only after a business combination (accounted for as a purchase). Both accelerated and straight-line depreciation methods are permissible. Estimated economic usefulness determines depreciation and amortization periods. All research and development costs are typically expensed as incurred, though there are special capitalization rules for computer software costs.

---

[14]A study of 65 of the Fortune 100 companies revealed that these were policies affecting contingencies, goodwill and intangibles, revenue recognition, pension benefits, and derivative securities. See Shearman and Sterling, "Survey: Fortune 100 Critical Accounting Policies Disclosure" (www.realcorporatelawyer.com).

[15]The FASB has proposed extending the consolidation requirement to other entities that a company controls based on its ability to direct the entity's policies and management.

[16]Both the purchase and pooling-of-interests (merger) methods were previously used to account for business combinations. They were not alternatives: pooling-of-interests was used when the combination met specified criteria. Under the purchase method, goodwill was capitalized and amortized on a straight-line basis over a maximum of 40 years and the amortization amount was included in current period income. SFAS 141 and 142, issued in 2001, changed how business combinations were accounted for, as described above.

LIFO, FIFO, and average cost methods are permissible and widely used for inventory pricing. LIFO is popular because it can be used for federal income tax purposes. However, if LIFO is used for tax purposes, it must also be used for financial reporting purposes. Marketable securities are valued at market unless they are classified as held-to-maturity and valued at historical cost.[17]

When financial leases are in substance the purchase of property, the value of the property is capitalized and a corresponding liability is booked. The costs of pensions and other postretirement benefits are accrued over the periods in which employees earn their benefits, and unfunded obligations are reported as a liability. Contingent losses/liabilities are accrued when they are probable and the amount can be reasonably estimated. Income-smoothing techniques are not allowed.

Finally, there is the issue of deferred taxes, because (except for LIFO) financial and tax reporting are distinct. Income taxes are accounted for using the liability method. Deferred taxes are accrued for the tax effects of temporary differences between financial and tax accounting methods, and are measured based on the future tax rates that will apply when these items reverse. Comprehensive income tax allocation is required.

Mexico

Before the Spanish conquest in the 1500s, Mexico was home to several highly advanced cultures, including the Olmecs, Mayas, Toltecs, and Aztecs. Hernando Cortés conquered Mexico in 1521 and founded a Spanish colony that lasted for nearly 300 years. Mexico declared independence in 1810, and an 1821 treaty recognized its independence from Spain. Except for 30 years of internal peace under General Porfírio Díaz (1877 to 1880 and 1884 to 1911), Mexico experienced political and military strife until 1929, when what is now known as the Institutional Revolutionary Party (PRI) was formed. The PRI controlled Mexico's government continuously for 70 years. The 2000 presidential election was won by the National Action Party (PAN), a center-right opposition party, thus ending the supremacy of the PRI in Mexican politics.[18]

Mexico is the most populous Spanish-speaking country in the world and the second most populous country in Latin America (after Portuguese-speaking Brazil).[19] Mexico has a largely free-market economy: Government-owned or controlled companies dominate petroleum and public utilities, but private enterprise dominates manufacturing, construction, mining, entertainment, and the service industries. In recent years, the government has been privatizing its holdings in nonstrategic industries. Free-market economic reforms during the 1990s helped reduce inflation, increase the rate of economic growth, and deliver healthier economic fundamentals. The reforms included dismantling protectionist trade barriers, opening up to foreign investment, and signing regional trade agreements. The most important agreement for Mexico is the North American Free Trade Agreement (NAFTA), signed with Canada and the United States in 1994. The United States accounts for nearly 60 percent of Mexico's

---

[17]Unrealized gains and losses from value changes on trading securities are recognized in current income while unrealized gains and losses on available-for-sale securities are taken to equity.
[18]For a history of the 2000 election, see J. Preston and S. Dillon, *The Making of Democracy* (New York: Farrar, Straus, & Giroux, 2004). The PAN also won the divisive, and contested, 2006 election.
[19]The capital, Mexico City, is the second most populous city in the world.

imports and 90 percent of Mexico's exports. Mexico has the world's twelfth-largest economy (in terms of gross domestic product).[20]

Family-controlled conglomerates dominate Mexico's private sector and, by world standards, are relatively small.[21] Although Mexico's stock market is the second largest in Latin America, it is still relatively small by international standards, because firms prefer to raise capital through debt rather than equity. This is changing, however, and more and more Mexican firms are entering U.S. capital markets.

Given the dominance of family-controlled enterprises, Mexican companies traditionally guarded their information and were secretive in their financial reporting. This too is changing. Disclosure practices of Mexican companies are increasingly influenced by the expectations of the U.S. market. Another significant feature of Mexican accounting is the use of comprehensive general price level accounting as a measurement basis, discussed more fully in Chapter 7.

The U.S. influence on Mexico's economy extends to accounting. "[M]any of the early leaders of the Mexican profession grew up on 'American accounting,'"[22] and U.S. textbooks and professional literature (either in the original English or translated into Spanish) are used extensively in the education of accountants and as guidance on accounting issues. NAFTA accelerated a trend toward closer cooperation between professional accounting organizations in Mexico, Canada, and the United States. Today, the accounting standard setting bodies in these three countries[23] are committed to a program of harmonization and are attempting to work in concert wherever possible. As a founding member of the International Accounting Standards Committee (now the International Accounting Standards Board), Mexico is also committed to convergence with IFRS. Mexico now looks to the IASB for guidance on accounting issues, especially in cases where there is no corresponding Mexican standard.

Accounting Regulation and Enforcement

The Mexican Commercial Code and income tax laws contain requirements for keeping certain summary accounting records and preparing financial statements, but their influence on financial reporting is generally minimal. Accounting standards are issued by the Council for Research and Development of Financial Information Standards (Consejo Mexicano para la Investigación y Desarrollo de Normas de Información Financiera, or CINIF). CINIF is an independent public/private-sector partnership patterned after the U.S. Financial Accounting Standards Board and the International Accounting Standards Board. Its specific aim is to align Mexican GAAP with IFRS.[24] The Mexican Institute of

---

[20]*Pocket World in Figures, 2007 Edition* (London: *The Economist*, 2006), p. 179.

[21]It is estimated that up to 95 percent of Mexican businesses are family owned. Over 40 percent of the value of the Mexican stock market is in firms controlled by one family. See "Still Keeping It in the Family," *Business Week* (March 20, 2004): 63–64.

[22]Stephen A. Zeff, *Forging Accounting Principles in Five Countries: A History and an Analysis of Trends* (Champaign, IL: Stipes Publishing, 1971), pp. 96–97.

[23]The Instituto Mexicano de Contadores Públicos, Canadian Institute of Chartered Accountants, and the Financial Accounting Standards Board, respectively.

[24]The Web site is www.cinif.org.mx. CINIF was established in 2004 and took over from the Mexican Institute of Public Accountants' Accounting Principles Commission, which had been responsible for developing accounting standards since 1968. CINIF was created by a mutual agreement of organizations representing financial executives, securities brokers, financial institutions, the stock exchange, and the accounting profession, among others. It is backed by government agencies such as the National Banking and Securities Commission, discussed later.

Public Accountants (Instituto Mexicano de Contadores Públicos) issues auditing standards through its Auditing Standards and Procedures Commission. The institute, a federation of state and other local associations of registered public accountants, is an independent nongovernmental professional association representing the overwhelming majority of public accountants. The Mexican accounting profession is mature, well organized, and highly regarded by the business community.

Despite a legal system based on civil law, accounting standard setting in Mexico takes a British-American, or Anglo-Saxon, approach rather than a continental European one. The standard-setting process is well developed. Before standards are finalized, exposure drafts of proposed standards are issued for review and public comment. Accounting standards are recognized as authoritative by the government, and in particular by the National Banking and Securities Commission, which regulates the Mexican Stock Exchange. Mexican accounting principles do not distinguish between large and small companies, and so are applicable to all business entities. In some cases the National Banking and Securities Commission issues rules for listed companies that limit certain options in generally accepted accounting principles.

Requirements for preparing financial statements and having them audited vary by type and size of company. All companies incorporated under Mexican law (*sociedades anónimas*) must appoint at least one statutory auditor to report to the shareholders on the annual financial statements. Statutory auditors do not have to be public accountants, but when a firm uses independent auditors, a member of the auditing firm frequently acts as statutory auditor. Companies or consolidated groups that meet certain size criteria must file a tax-compliance audit report every year with the Federal Tax Audit Department of the Ministry of Finance. The report consists of audited financial statements, additional schedules, and a statement by the auditor that no irregularities were observed regarding compliance with tax laws. This audit must be done by a Mexican public accountant. Finally, companies listed on the Mexican Stock Exchange must submit annual consolidated financial statements audited by a Mexican public accountant both to the exchange and to the National Banking and Securities Commission.

Financial Reporting

The fiscal year of Mexican companies must coincide with the calendar year. Comparative consolidated financial statements must be prepared, consisting of:

1. Balance sheet
2. Income statement
3. Statement of changes in stockholders' equity
4. Statement of changes in financial position
5. Notes

Financial statements must be adjusted for inflation. The effects of the adjustment are shown in the statement of changes in stockholders' equity. The format of the statement of changes in financial position is similar to the statement of cash flows and is divided into operating, investing, and financing activities. However, because it is also prepared in constant pesos, the resulting amounts do not represent cash flows as understood under historical cost accounting. Exhibit 4-2 illustrates the difference for CEMEX, the Mexican cement company. The 2005 20F report filed with the SEC

EXHIBIT 4-2 CEMEX Statement of Changes in Financial Position and Cash Flow Disclosures

	2005	*2004*	*2003*
Statement of Changes in Financial Position (adjusted for inflation)			
• Net resources provided by operating activities	Ps 36,300	23,811	17,937
• Resources provided by (used in) financing activities	8,937	(7,287)	(5,349)
• Resources used in investing activities	(42,507)	(16,204)	(13,471)
Cash Flows (historical cost)			
• Net cash provided by operating activities	Ps 28,909	21,885	9,772
• Net cash provided by (used in) financing activities	12,502	(3,723)	(4,874)
• Net cash used in investing activities	(38,818)	(17,734)	(5,419)

SOURCE: 2005 CEMEX 20F, pp. F-6 and F-53.

reports amounts in the statement of changes in financial position (adjusted for inflation) as well as cash flow amounts (under historical cost).[25]

Notes are an integral part of the financial statements (covered by the auditor's report) and include the following:

- Accounting policies of the company
- Material contingencies
- Commitments for substantial purchases of assets or under lease contracts
- Details of long-term debt and foreign currency exposure
- Limitations on dividends
- Guarantees
- Employees' pension plans
- Transactions with related parties
- Income taxes.

Accounting Measurements[26]

Consolidated financial statements are prepared when a parent company controls another company. Control is indicated by the ability to determine a company's operating and financial policies. Control normally exists when more than 50 percent of a company's common stock is owned, but it can be obtained in other ways, including the ability to appoint management or a majority of the board of directors. The equity method is used when there is influence but not control, normally meaning an ownership level between 10 and 50 percent. Joint ventures may be proportionally consolidated or accounted for using the equity method. Mexico has adopted International Accounting Standard No. 21 on foreign currency translation.[27]

---

[25]CEMEX is listed on the New York Stock Exchange and must therefore file Form 20F with the SEC.
[26]Because of the long-time influence of the United States and the more recent influence of the IASB, Mexican financial reporting practices have always been fairness oriented.
[27]General price level accounting (described later) is integrated with foreign currency translation: (1) the financial statements of integrated operations are adjusted by the National Consumer Price Index after translation into pesos; (2) financial statements of "foreign entities" (i.e., subsidiaries that are not integrated operations) are first adjusted to reflect the purchasing power of the home currency, then translated into pesos using the closing exchange rate.

The purchase method is used to account for business combinations. Goodwill is the excess of purchase price over the current value of the net assets acquired. It is not amortized, but subject to an annual impairments test.

General price level accounting is used in Mexico. The historical costs of nonmonetary assets are restated in pesos of current purchasing power by applying factors derived from the National Consumer Price Index (NCPI). The components of stockholders' equity are also restated using the NCPI. The gain or loss from holding monetary assets and liabilities is included in current period income, but the effects of other restatements are in stockholders' equity. A tangible fixed asset is depreciated over its useful life. An intangible asset is amortized over its useful life (normally no more than 20 years) unless the life is indefinite, in which case it is not amortized but subject to an annual impairment test.

Research costs are expensed as incurred, while development costs are capitalized and amortized once technological feasibility has been established. Leases are classified as financing or operating. Financing leases—those transferring substantially all the benefits and risks of ownership of the asset—are capitalized, while rents from operating leases are expensed on the income statement. Contingent losses are accrued when they are likely and measurable. General contingency reserves are not acceptable under Mexican GAAP. Deferred taxes are provided for in full, using the liability method. The costs of employee pensions, seniority premiums,[28] and termination pay are accrued currently when they can be reasonably estimated based on actuarial calculations. Statutory (legal) reserves are created by allocating 5 percent of income each year until the reserve equals 20 percent of the value of the outstanding capital stock.

Japan

Japanese accounting and financial reporting reflect a mixture of domestic and international influences. Two separate government agencies have responsibility for accounting regulations, and there is the further influence of Japanese corporate income tax law. In the first half of the 20th century, accounting thinking reflected German influences; in the second half, U.S. ideas were pervasive. More recently, the effects of the International Accounting Standards Board have been felt, and in 2001 a profound change occurred with the establishment of a private-sector accounting standard setting organization.[29]

To understand Japanese accounting, one must understand Japanese culture, business practices, and history. Japan is a traditional society with strong cultural and religious roots. The group consciousness and interdependence in personal and corporate relationships in Japan contrast with the independent, arm's-length relationships among individuals and groups in Western nations. Japanese companies hold equity interests in each other, and often jointly own other firms. These interlocking investments yield giant industrial conglomerates—notably the *keiretsu*. Banks are often a part of these industrial groups. The widespread use of bank credit and debt capital to

---

[28]Seniority premiums are compensation amounts paid at the termination of employment based on how long the employee has worked. Generally, employees who voluntarily retire must work at least 15 years, but there is no minimum number of years for other types of termination, such as redundancy layoffs, or if an employee dies.

[29]Until the late 1990s, external influences came to bear only gradually. In terms of what we would consider world-class reporting, accounting was slow to develop in Japan. For example, consolidated financial statements date from 1976 and requirements for segment reporting began in 1990.

finance large enterprises is unusually great from a Western perspective, and corporate managers must primarily answer to banks and other financial institutions rather than shareholders. Central government also exerts tight control on many activities in Japan, which means a strong bureaucratic control over business affairs, including accounting. Knowledge of corporate activities is primarily limited to the corporation and other insiders, such as the banks and the government.

This *keiretsu* business model is being transformed as the Japanese undertake structural reforms to counteract the economic stagnation that began in the 1990s.[30] The financial crisis that followed the bursting of Japan's "bubble economy" also prompted a review of Japanese financial reporting standards. It became clear that many accounting practices hid how badly Japanese companies were doing. For example:

1. Loose consolidation standards allowed Japanese companies to bury loss-making operations in affiliates. Investors could not see whether a company's entire operations were really profitable.
2. Pension and severance obligations were only accrued to 40 percent of the amount owed because that was the limit of their tax deductibility. This practice led to substantial underfunding of pension obligations.
3. Securities holdings were valued at cost, not market prices. Designed to reinforce the cohesion of the *keiretsu*, these cross-holdings are vast. Companies held on to the ones with losses, but sold those with gains to prop up sagging profits.

An accounting "Big Bang" was announced in the late 1990s to make the economic health of Japanese companies more transparent and to bring Japan more in line with international standards. These accounting reforms are described later.[31]

Accounting Regulation and Enforcement

The national government has a significant influence on accounting in Japan. Accounting regulation is based on three laws: the Company Law, the Securities and Exchange Law, and the Corporate Income Tax Law. These three laws are linked and interact with each other. A leading Japanese scholar refers to the situation as a "triangular legal system."[32]

The Company Law is administered by the Ministry of Justice (MOJ). Developed from German commercial law, the original code was enacted in 1890 but not implemented until 1899. Creditor and shareholder protection is its fundamental principle, with an unequivocal reliance on historical cost measurements. Disclosures on creditworthiness and the availability of earnings for dividend distribution are of primary importance. All companies incorporated under the Company Law are required to meet its accounting provisions.

---

[30]For example, in 1992, 46 percent of listed equities were held as cross-shareholdings by related companies. By 2004, cross-shareholdings accounted for 24 percent of shares.

[31]"Japan on the Brink," *Economist* (April 11, 1999): 15–17; "Japan Restructures, Grudgingly," *Economist* (February 6, 1999): 63–65; "The Secrets Pour Out," *Business Week* (August 2, 1999): 50–51; "Reshaping Standards," *Accountancy* (June 2000): 110; "Japan: Restoring Investor Confidence," *IASC Insight*(September 2000): 8; "Going International," *Accountancy* (March 2002): 102–103; "The Sun Also Rises: A Survey of Japan," *Economist* (October 8, 2005): 1–18.

[32]Kiyomitsu Arai, *Accounting in Japan* (Tokyo: Waseda University, Institute for Research in Business Administration, 1994), p. 5.

Publicly owned companies must meet the further requirements of the Securities and Exchange Law (SEL), administered by the Financial Services Agency (FSA).[33] The SEL is modeled after the U.S. Securities Acts and was imposed on Japan by the United States during the U.S. occupation following World War II. The main objective of the SEL is to provide information for investment decision-making. Although the SEL requires the same basic financial statements as the Company Law, the terminology, form, and content of financial statements are more precisely defined under the SEL; certain financial statement items are reclassified for presentation, and additional detail is provided. Net income and shareholders' equity are, however, the same under the Company Law and the SEL.

Until recently, a special advisory body to the FSA was responsible for developing accounting standards under the SEL. Called the Business Accounting Deliberation Council (BADC), and now the Business Accounting Council (BAC), it was arguably the major source of generally accepted accounting principles in Japan.[34] However, a major change in accounting standard setting occurred in 2001 with the establishment of the Accounting Standards Board of Japan (ASBJ) and its related oversight foundation, the Financial Accounting Standards Foundation (FASF). The ASBJ now has sole responsibility for developing accounting standards and implementation guidance in Japan. It has 13 members, three of whom are full-time. It also has a full-time technical staff to support its activities. The FASF is responsible for funding and naming its members. Funding comes from companies and the accounting profession, not the government. As an independent private-sector organization, the ASBJ is stronger and more transparent than the BAC, and subject to fewer political and special-interest pressures.[35] The ASBJ collaborates with the IASB in developing IFRS and in 2005 launched a joint project with the IASB to reduce differences between IFRS and Japanese accounting standards. The BAC still advises the FSA on accounting standards and, as discussed later, is responsible for establishing auditing standards. Japanese accounting standards cannot be at variance with commercial law (or tax law, as discussed next). Thus, the triangulation of accounting standards, company law, and tax law is still a feature of Japanese financial reporting.

Finally, the influence of the tax code is significant. As in France, Germany, and elsewhere, expenses can be claimed for tax purposes only if they are fully booked. Taxable income is based on the amount calculated under the Company Law, but if the law does not prescribe an accounting treatment, the one in the tax law is often followed.

Under the Company Law, the financial statements and supporting schedules of small and medium-sized companies are subject to audit only by statutory auditors. Both statutory and independent auditors must audit large corporations. Independent auditors must audit financial statements of publicly held companies in accordance with the Securities and Exchange Law. Statutory auditors do not need any particular

---

[33]The FSA is the government regulatory agency responsible for supervising private-sector financial institutions, such as banks, insurance companies, and the securities exchanges. It took over the administration of the SEL from the Ministry of Finance when it was established in 2000. As discussed later, it also oversees the Certified Public Accountant and Auditing Oversight Board. The FSA Web site is www.fsa.go.jp/en.

[34]Before 2000, the BADC reported to the Ministry of Finance (see preceding footnote).

[35]The standard setting framework is similar to that of the U.S. Financial Accounting Foundation and Financial Accounting Standards Board, as discussed in this chapter. The FASF and ASBJ Web site is www.asb.or.jp.

professional qualifications and are employed by the company on a full-time basis. Statutory audits focus mainly on the managerial actions of the directors and whether they perform their duties in compliance with legal statutes. Independent audits involve examining the financial statements and records, and must be performed by certified public accountants (CPAs).

The Japanese Institute of Certified Public Accountants (JICPA) is the professional organization of CPAs in Japan. All CPAs must belong to the JICPA.[36] In addition to providing guidance on the conduct of audits, the JICPA publishes implementation guidelines on accounting matters, and provides input to the ASBJ in developing accounting standards. Generally accepted auditing standards are promulgated by the BAC rather than the JICPA. The Certified Public Accountant and Auditing Oversight Board was established in 2003. A government agency, it is designed to monitor and oversee the auditing profession and improve the quality of Japanese audits. It was put under the FSA in 2004.

Financial Reporting

Companies incorporated under the Company Law are required to prepare a statutory report for approval at the annual shareholders' meeting, consisting of the following:

1. Balance sheet
2. Income statement
3. Statement of changes in shareholders' equity
4. Business report
5. Supporting schedules

Notes accompanying the balance sheet and income statement describe the accounting policies and provide supporting details, as is typical in other countries. The business report contains an outline of the business and its internal control systems, and information about its operations, financial position, and operating results. A number of supporting schedules are also required, separate from the notes, including:

- Changes in bonds and other short- and long-term debt
- Changes in fixed assets and accumulated depreciation
- Collateralized assets
- Debt guarantees
- Changes in provisions
- Amounts due to and from the controlling shareholders
- Equity ownership in subsidiaries and the number of shares of the company's stock held by subsidiaries
- Receivables due from subsidiaries
- Transactions with directors, statutory auditors, controlling shareholders and third parties that create a conflict of interest
- Remuneration paid to directors and statutory auditors

---

[36]The Web site is www.jicpa.or.jp.

This information is prepared for a single year on a parent-company basis and is audited by the statutory auditor. The Company Law does not require a statement of cash or funds flow.

Listed companies also must prepare financial statements under the Securities and Exchange Law, which generally requires the same basic statements as the Company Law plus a statement of cash flows. However, under the SEL, consolidated financial statements, not the parent-company statements, are the main focus. Additional footnotes and schedules are also required.[37] Financial statements and schedules submitted under the SEL must be audited by independent auditors. Beginning in 2008, listed companies must issue quarterly financial reports. Also beginning in 2008, managements of listed companies must submit an annual assessment of the company's internal controls and a letter certifying the accuracy of the annual report. The internal control report must be audited.[38]

A cash flow forecast for the next six months is included as supplemental information in filings with the FSA. Other forecast information is also reported, such as forecasts of new capital investments and production levels and activities. Overall, the amount of corporate forecast reporting is extensive in Japan. However, this information is reported in statutory filings and rarely appears in the annual report to shareholders.

Accounting Measurements

The Company Law requires large companies to prepare consolidated financial statements. In addition, listed companies must prepare consolidated financial statements under the Securities and Exchange Law. Individual company accounts are the basis for the consolidated statements, and normally the same accounting principles are used at both levels. Subsidiaries are consolidated if a parent directly or indirectly controls their financial and operational policies. The pooling-of-interest method for business combinations is used in limited situations where no party obtains control over the other. Otherwise, business combinations are accounted for as a purchase. Goodwill is measured on the basis of the fair value of the net assets acquired and is amortized over 20 years or less and is subject to an impairments test. The equity method is used for investments in affiliated companies when the parent and subsidiaries exert significant influence over their financial and operational policies. The equity method is also used to account for joint ventures; proportional consolidation is not allowed. Under the foreign currency translation standard, assets and liabilities of foreign subsidiaries are translated at the current (year-end) exchange rate, revenues and expenses at the average rate, and translation adjustments are in stockholders' equity.

Inventory must be valued at cost or the lower of cost or net realizable value. FIFO, LIFO, and average are all acceptable cost-flow methods, with average the most popular. Investments in securities are valued at market. Fixed assets are valued at cost and depreciated in accordance with the tax laws. The declining-balance method is the most common depreciation method. Fixed assets are also impairments tested.

---

[37]Additional footnotes include information about such things as subsequent events and liabilities for employee retirement and severance benefits. Additional schedules detail items on the financial statements, such as marketable securities, tangible and intangible assets, investments in and loans to or from affiliated companies, bonds payable and other long-term borrowings, and reserves and allowances.

[38]The law requiring an internal control assessment and certification of the financial statements is based on the U.S. Sarbanes-Oxley Act and is informally called the "J-Sox rule." However, unlike Sarbanes-Oxley it does not require the auditor's direct assessment of the company's internal control. Rather, the auditor's opinion covers management's assessment of internal controls.

Research and development costs are expensed when incurred. Leases that transfer ownership to the lessee are capitalized. Other finance leases may be either capitalized or treated as operating leases.[39] Deferred taxes are provided for all timing differences using the liability method. Contingent losses are provided for when they are probable and can be reasonably estimated. Pension and other employee retirement benefits are fully accrued as employees earn them, and unfunded obligations are shown as a liability. Legal reserves are required: Each year a company must allocate an amount equal to at least 10 percent of cash dividends and bonuses paid to directors and statutory auditors until the legal reserve reaches 25 percent of capital stock.

Many of the accounting practices described above were implemented in the last several years as a result of the accounting Big Bang referred to earlier. These recent changes include: (1) requiring listed companies to report a statement of cash flows; (2) extending the number of subsidiaries that are consolidated based on control rather than ownership percentage; (3) extending the number of affiliates accounted for using the equity method based on significant influence rather than ownership percentage; (4) valuing investments in securities at market rather than cost; (5) valuing inventory at the lower of cost or net realizable value rather than cost; (6) full provisioning of deferred taxes; and (7) full accrual of pension and other retirement obligations. Accounting in Japan is being reshaped to bring it in line with IFRS.

China

China has a quarter of the world's population, and market-oriented reforms have helped generate rapid economic growth.[40] In the late 1970s, Chinese leaders began to move the economy from Soviet-style central planning to a system that is more market-oriented but still under Communist Party control. [41] To achieve this, they switched to a system of household responsibility in agriculture instead of the old collectivization, increased the authority of local officials and plant managers in industry, permitted a wide variety of small-scale enterprises in services and light manufacturing, and opened the economy to increased foreign trade and investment. In 1993 China's leadership approved additional long-term reforms aimed at giving more flexibility for market-oriented institutions. Central features include the share system of ownership, privatizations, the development of organized stock exchanges, and the listing of shares in Chinese companies on Western exchanges. Nevertheless, state-owned enterprises still dominate many key industries in what the Chinese call a "socialist market economy," that is, a planned economy with market adaptations.[42]

---

[39]An exposure draft issued in 2006 would require the capitalization of all finance leases.

[40]In 1997, Great Britain ceded control of Hong Kong to China. Under the agreement between China and Britain, China has guaranteed to operate a "one country, two systems" arrangement in which Hong Kong's lifestyle will be unchanged for 50 years and basic freedoms and rights will be guaranteed by law.
Accounting in Hong Kong is similar to accounting in the United Kingdom, described in Chapter 3. The discussion of China in this chapter refers to mainland China and excludes Hong Kong.

[41]China's real gross domestic product grew at an average annual rate of 9.1 percent between 1994 and 2004, one of the highest growth rates of any nation. See *The Economist Pocket World in Figures, 2007 Edition* (London: *The Economist*, 2006), p. 32. For much of recorded history, China was the largest economy in the world. Until the 15th century, China had the highest income per head and was the world's technological leader. Even as late as 1820, it still accounted for 30 percent of the world's GDP. However, by 1950, its share of world output had fallen to less than 5 percent. See "The Dragon and the Eagle," *Economist* (October 2, 2004): 1–26.

[42]The Chinese economy is now the sixth-largest in the world. A central feature of China's reforms is a gradualist approach to economic liberalization. See Robert J. Barro, "China's Slow Yet Steady March to Reform, *Business Week* (September 30, 2002): 28; Fareed Zakaria, "The Big Story Everyone Missed," *Newsweek* (January 6, 2003): 52.

Accounting in China has a long history. Its functioning in a stewardship role can be detected as far back as 2200 B.C. during the Hsiu Dynasty, and documents show that it was used to measure wealth and compare achievements among dukes and princes in the Xia Dynasty (2000 to 1500 B.C.). The young Confucius (551 to 479 B.C.) was a manager of warehouses, and his writings mention that the job included proper accounting—keeping the records of receipts and disbursements up-to-date. Among the teachings of Confucius is the imperative to compile a history, and accounting records are viewed as part of history.

The principal characteristics of accounting in China today date from the founding of the People's Republic of China in 1949. China installed a highly centralized planned economy, reflecting Marxist principles and patterned after the system in the Soviet Union. The state controlled the ownership, the right to use, and the distribution of all means of production, and enacted rigid planning and control over the economy. Production was the top priority of state-owned enterprises. Their sales and pricing were dictated by the state's planning authorities, and their financing and product costing were administered by the state's finance departments. Under this system, the purpose of accounting was to serve the needs of the state for economic planning and control. A uniform set of standardized accounts was developed to integrate information into the national economic plan. The uniform accounting system contained all-inclusive accounting rules that were mandatory for state-owned enterprises across the country.

Financial reporting was frequent and detailed. The main feature was a fund-management orientation where *funds* meant the property, goods, and materials used in the production process. Financial reporting emphasized the balance sheet, which reflected the source and application of funds. It focused on stewardship and accountability, or the fulfilling of production and other goals, as well as compliance with governmental policies and regulations. Accounting emphasized counting quantities and comparing costs and quantities. Although accounting focused more on managerial than financial objectives, its role in decision-making by the managers of individual enterprises was nevertheless subordinated to the central authorities.

China's economy today is best described as a hybrid economy in which the state controls strategic commodities and industries, while other industries, as well as the commercial and private sectors, are governed by a market-oriented system. The recent economic reforms involve privatizations, including the conversion of state-owned enterprises into share-issuing corporations. New accounting rules have had to be developed for newly privatized companies and other independent limited liability companies, as well as for foreign business entities, such as joint ventures. The role of the government has been changing from managing both the macro- and microeconomy to one managing at the macro level only.[43] Accounting standards were needed to reflect this new reality.

---

[43]The ownership relationship between the government and state-owned enterprises has been redefined. Regulations issued by the Ministry of Finance in 1994 announced for the first time that the state is an investor in the enterprise and is responsible for the enterprise's debts limited to the amount of its capital; the enterprise has its own legal status, enjoying its own property rights and bearing independent civil responsibilities. See Zezhong Xiao and Aixiang Pan, "Developing Accounting Standards on the Basis of a Conceptual Framework by the Chinese Government," *International Journal of Accounting* 32, no. 3 (1997): 282. For further discussion of China's reforms of state-owned enterprises, see "The Longer March," *Economist* (September 30, 2000): 71–73. China has nearly 170,000 state-owned enterprises.

Accounting Regulation and Enforcement

The Accounting Law, last amended in 2000, covers all enterprises and organizations, including those not owned or controlled by the state. It outlines the general principles of accounting and defines the role of the government and the matters that require accounting procedures. The State Council (an executive body corresponding to a cabinet) has also issued Financial Accounting and Reporting Rules for Enterprises (FARR). These focus on bookkeeping, the preparation of financial statements, reporting practices, and other financial accounting and reporting matters. FARR apply to all enterprises other than very small ones that do not raise funds externally. The Ministry of Finance, supervised by the State Council, formulates accounting and auditing standards. Besides accounting and auditing matters, the ministry is responsible for a wide range of activities affecting the economy. Generally, these activities include formulating long-term economic strategies and setting the priorities for the allocation of government funds. More specifically, the ministry's responsibilities include:

- formulating and enforcing economic, tax, and other finance-related policies
- preparing the annual state budget and fiscal report
- managing state revenue and expenditure
- developing the financial management and tax system[44]

Accounting and auditing matters fall into the last category.

In 1992 the Ministry of Finance issued Accounting Standards for Business Enterprises (ASBE), a conceptual framework designed to guide the development of new accounting standards that would eventually harmonize domestic practices and harmonize Chinese practices with international practices. The ASBE was a landmark event in China's move to a market economy. Before the ASBE, more than 40 different uniform accounting systems were in use, varying across industries and types of ownership. Although each one of these could individually be labeled as *uniform*, taken together they resulted in inconsistent practices overall. Thus, one motive for issuing the ASBE was to harmonize domestic accounting practices. Moreover, existing practices were incompatible with international practices and unsuited for a market-oriented economy. Harmonizing Chinese accounting to international practices served to remove barriers of communication with foreign investors and helped meet the needs of the economic reforms already under way.

After the issuance of the ASBE, the Ministry of Finance replaced the more than 40 uniform accounting systems mentioned previously with 13 industry-based and two ownership-based accounting systems. These systems were viewed as transitional until specific accounting standards could be promulgated that would apply to all enterprises operating in China. A revised ASBE was issued in 2001.

The China Accounting Standards Committee (CASC) was established in 1998 as the authoritative body within the Ministry of Finance responsible for developing accounting standards.[45] The standard-setting process includes assigning necessary research to task forces, the issuance of exposure drafts, and public hearings. CASC members are experts drawn from academia, accounting firms, government, professional accounting associations, and other key groups concerned with the development of

---

[44]"Role of the Ministry of Finance," Ministry of Finance Web site (www.mof.gov.cn), December 16, 2000.
[45]The CASC Web site is www.casc.gov.cn.

accounting in China. After it was formed, the CASC began issuing standards on such issues as the cash flow statement, debt restructuring, revenue, nonmonetary transactions, contingencies, and leases. All of these standards were aimed at converging Chinese accounting standards with International Financial Reporting Standards.

Finally, in 2006, in a Big Bang approach to convergence, a new set of Accounting Standards for Business Enterprises was issued. This new ASBE consists of one basic ASBE and 38 specific ASBE. The basic standard established the framework, and the specific standards set out broad principles and detailed implementation guidance on such areas as fixed and intangible assets, inventories, leases, income taxes, consolidations, and segment reporting. Together they represent a comprehensive set of Chinese accounting standards that are substantially in line with IFRS. The new ASBE applies to listed companies and will gradually extend to all Chinese companies (except small ones), phasing out the industry and ownership standards referred to above. Exhibit 4-3 summarizes the basic ASBE. Forty-eight new auditing standards, similar to the International Standards on Auditing issued by the International Auditing and Assurances Standards Board (see Chapter 8), were issued at the same time. All Chinese accounting firms and CPAs are required to follow these audit standards.

The China Securities Regulatory Commission (CSRC) regulates China's two stock exchanges: Shanghai, which opened in 1990, and Shenzhen, which opened in 1991.[46] It sets regulatory guidelines, formulates and enforces market rules, and authorizes initial public offers and new shares. A code of corporate governance was introduced in 2002. The CSRC also issues additional disclosure requirements for listed companies. Thus, disclosure requirements for listed companies are established by two government bodies, the Ministry of Finance and the CRSC.[47]

EXHIBIT 4-3   China's Accounting Standards for Business Enterprises—Basic Standard

- **General provisions:** stewardship, economic decision-making, going concern, accrual basis.
- **Qualitative requirements of accounting information:** faithful representation, relevance, understandability, comparability, substance over form, prudence.
- **Definitions of elements:** assets, liabilities, owners' equity, revenue, expenses, profit.
- **Accounting measurement:** Generally, historical cost; if elements are measured at replacement cost, net realizable value, present value, or fair value, the enterprise shall ensure that such amounts are available and can be reliably measured.
- **Financial reports:** balance sheet, income statement, cash flow statement, and notes.

---

[46]The CSRC Web site is www.csrc.gov.cn.

[47]China's stock markets rank twelfth in the world (and third in Asia behind Japan and Hong Kong) in terms of market capitalization. Around 1,400 companies are listed, and there are officially nearly 70 million individual investors. Nevertheless, the state holds roughly two-thirds of the shares of listed companies, meaning that two-thirds of the market capitalization is not traded. Most companies are listed for political rather than economic reasons, and almost all of them benefit from government favoritism. Since the state is the dominant shareholder of most listed companies, there are few incentives for managers to maximize shareholder value, and thus managers have relatively little market discipline. Controlling shareholders tend to engage in related-party transactions that are not in the interest of minority shareholders. (China has a *guanxi* ["relationship"] culture based on mutuality and mutual duties. *Guanxi* creates obligations for a continual exchange of favors, which in the extreme can lead to corruption.) Disclosures are still poor, and enforcement of market rules is weak. Much of the individual trading is based on rumor rather than reliable information. The stock markets are not yet effective as a way to allocate capital. See "Fools in Need of Institutions," *Economist* (June 30, 2001): 65–66; "Banking on Growth," *Economist* (January 18, 2003): 67–68; "A Survey of Asian Finance: Casino Capital," *Economist*(February 8, 2003): 10–12; P. Lupton, "Corporate Governance and Business Ethics in the Asia-Pacific Region," *Business and Society* (June 2005): 178–210.

Until 1995 China had two professional accounting organizations. The Chinese Institute of Certified Public Accountants (CICPA), established in 1988 under the jurisdiction of the Ministry of Finance, regulated the audit of private-sector enterprises. The Chinese Association of Certified Public Auditors (CACPA) was responsible for auditing state-owned enterprises and was under the authority of a separate agency, the State Audit Administration. In 1995 CICPA and CACPA merged, keeping the name of the CICPA. The CICPA sets the requirements for becoming a CPA, administers the CPA examination, develops auditing standards, and is responsible for the code of professional ethics.

Financial Reporting

The accounting period is required to be the calendar year. Financial statements consist of:

1. Balance sheet
2. Income statement
3. Cash flow statement
4. Statement of changes in equity
5. Notes

Additional statements are required disclosing asset impairments, changes in capital structure, appropriations of profits, and business and geographical segments. The notes include a statement of accounting policies. As applicable, they discuss such matters as contingencies, important post-balance sheet events, and related-party transactions. A management discussion and analysis is required discussing the enterprise's operations, financial position, results, cash flows, and items affecting them. Financial statements must be consolidated, comparative, in Chinese, and expressed in the Chinese currency, the renminbi. The annual financial statements must be audited by a Chinese CPA. Listed companies must assess their internal controls and engage an external auditor to evaluate the controls and comment on the self-assessment report.[48] A quarterly balance sheet, income statement, and notes are required for listed companies.

Accounting Measurements

The purchase method must be used to account for business combinations. Goodwill is the difference between the cost of the acquisition and the fair values of the assets and liabilities acquired. It is tested for impairment on an annual basis. The equity method is used for investments in associates, those over which the investee has significant influence. The equity method is also used to account for joint ventures. All subsidiaries under the control of the parent are consolidated. The financial statements of an overseas subsidiary are translated based on the primary economic environment in which it operates. If it is the local (overseas) environment, the balance sheet is translated at the year-end exchange rate, the income statement is translated at the average-for-the-year exchange rate, and any translation difference is shown in equity. If it is the parent's environment, monetary items are translated at the year-end exchange rate, nonmonetary items are translated at the relevant transaction-date exchange rate, and revenues and expenses are translated at the transaction-date rate (or the appropriate average rate for the period). The translation difference is included in income.

---

[48]This requirement is similar to Section 404 of the Sarbanes-Oxley Act discussed in the section on the United States.

Historical cost is the basis for valuing tangible assets; revaluations are not allowed. They are depreciated over their expected useful lives, normally on a straight-line basis. Accelerated and units-of-production depreciation are also acceptable. FIFO and average are acceptable costing methods, and inventory is written down for price declines and obsolescence. Acquired intangibles are also recorded at cost. Those with a finite life are amortized over the periods benefited based on the pattern in which the benefits are consumed. Intangibles with an indefinite life are not amortized but are impairments tested at least annually. Because land and much of the industrial property in China are owned by the state, companies that acquire the right to use land and industrial property rights show them as intangibles. Assets are revalued when a change in ownership takes place, as when a state-owned enterprise is privatized. Certified asset assessment firms or CPA firms determine these valuations.

Research costs are expensed, but development costs are capitalized if technological feasibility and cost recovery are established. Finance leases are capitalized. Deferred taxes are provided in full for all temporary differences. Employee benefits are expensed as they are earned rather than when paid. Contingent obligations are provided for when they are both probable and their amount can be reliably estimated.

India

India occupies much of the South Asian subcontinent, with Pakistan to the west, China, Nepal, and Bhutan to the north, and Bangladesh to the east. The Himalaya Mountains, the tallest mountain system in the world, are located on India's northern border.[49] Coastal India has the Arabian Sea to the west, the Indian Ocean to the south, and the Bay of Bengal to the east. India has 15 percent of the world's population, the second most populous nation in the world after China. India is also one of the most ethnically diverse countries in the world. It is home to several hundred languages, 18 of which have official status. Hindi is the official language and the most widely spoken, but English is widely used in government, business, science, and education.

The people of India have had a continuous civilization for more than 5,000 years. Extensive urbanization based on commerce and agricultural trade appears to have begun in the Indus River Valley (in the northwest) around 3000 B.C. Since this time, numerous empires have ruled various portions of South Asia, often assimilating a rich array of peoples, each adding its own contribution to the region's increasingly diverse cultures, ideas, and technologies. The political map of ancient and medieval India was made up of myriad kingdoms with fluctuating boundaries. In the 4th and 5th centuries A.D., northern India was unified under the Gupta Dynasty. During this period, known as India's Golden Age, science, literature, and the arts flourished under Hindu culture. The south also experienced several great empires. Arab, Turkic, and Afghan Muslims ruled successively from the 8th to the 18th century A.D.[50]

European economic competition in India began soon after the Portuguese arrived in 1498. The first British outpost was established by the East India Company in 1619, and permanent trading stations were opened in other parts of the country over the rest of the 17th century. The British expanded their influence

---

[49]The country's exact size is subject to debate because some of its borders are disputed.
[50]Hinduism, Buddhism, Jainism, and Sikhism were born in India.

from these footholds until, by the 1850s, they controlled—politically, militarily and economically—most of present-day India, Pakistan, Sri Lanka, and Bangladesh. A mass campaign against British colonial rule began in the 1920s under the leadership of Mohandas Gandhi and Jawaharlal Nehru. Rising civil disobedience and World War II eventually rendered India too costly and difficult to administer, and the British government granted independence in 1947. British India was immediately partitioned into two separate states: India, with a Hindu majority; and East and West Pakistan—now Bangladesh and Pakistan—with Muslim majorities. The British legacy in India is substantial, including its common law legal system, its parliamentary system of central government, and the widespread use of the English language.

From 1947 to the late 1970s, the Indian economy was characterized by central government socialist-style planning and import-substitution industries. Economic production was transformed from primarily agriculture, forestry, fishing, and textile manufacturing to various heavy industries and transportation. However, the lack of competition contributed to poor product quality and inefficiencies in production. Facing an economic crisis, the government began opening up the economy in 1991.[51] The market-oriented economic reforms adopted since then include the privatization of some state-owned industries, liberalized foreign investment and exchange regimes, reductions in tariffs and other trade barriers, reform and modernization of the financial sector, significant adjustments in government monetary and fiscal policies, and safeguarding intellectual property rights. However, a large proportion of heavy industry is still state-owned, and high tariffs and limits on foreign direct investment are still in place.[52] The services sector has proved to be India's most dynamic sector in recent years, with telecommunications and information technology recording particularly rapid growth.[53]

Future economic growth is constrained by an inadequate infrastructure, a cumbersome bureaucracy and red tape, labor market rigidities, and corruption. The lack of reliable and affordable infrastructure, especially electricity, is viewed by many as the single most important brake on future growth. Red tape also imposes heavy costs on business in many parts of the country.[54] Finally, labor laws impose extra costs—for example, in bribes paid to inspectors.[55] The reforms that began in 1991 have cut away bureaucratic

---

[51]Community and family networks have a long tradition in India and have affected the structuring of businesses. Family-controlled businesses are very common. In general, ownership in Indian companies is concentrated, either by families or the government.

[52]U.S. Department of State, "Background Notes: India" (October 2006), www.state.gov; Library of Congress – Federal Research Division, "Country Profile: India" (December 2004), http://lcweb2.loc.gov/frd/cs/profiles/India.pdf; "Now for the Hard Part: A Survey of India," *Economist* (June 3, 2006): 1–18.

[53]The industry barely existed in India in 1991, when the economic reforms began. It is said that India's telecommunications and information technology sector is successful because it has always competed in a global marketplace. It never benefited from government favors or suffered distorted incentives of government protection. See "Now for the Hard Part: A Survey of India," *Economist* (June 3, 2006): 4.

[54]Priya Basu of the World Bank is quoted as saying, "Entrepreneurs have to spend significant time in dealing with permits, clearances and inspections, and end up paying substantial 'rents' to the inspectors." See *Economist*, "Now for the Hard Part: A Survey of India" (June 3, 2006): 14. The article goes on to say that collusion between contactors and vendors is so common that it is probably not even recognized as corrupt.

[55]Chapter 5B of the 1947 Industrial Disputes Act prohibits companies with more than 100 employees from laying off workers without the permission of the state government. This law discourages hiring and encourages the substitution of capital for labor in a country that is people rich.

controls and encouraged the creation of a more competitive marketplace. Most observers agree that further reforms and additional investment in infrastructure are needed to make India a leading economic player, but as noted at the beginning of this chapter, the same observers are optimistic about India's growth prospects.

Accounting Regulation and Enforcement

The British influence extends to accounting: Financial reporting is aimed at fair presentation, and there is an independent accounting profession that sets accounting and auditing standards. The two major sources of financial accounting standards in India are companies law and the accounting profession. The first companies act was legislated in 1857, and the first law relating to the maintenance and audit of accounting records was enacted in 1866, along with the first formal qualifications of auditors. Both were based on British law.

The current Companies Act 1956 is administered and updated by a government agency, the Ministry of Company Affairs. The act provides a broad framework for keeping so-called books of account and the requirements for an audit. According to the act, books of account

- must give a true and fair view of the state of affairs of the company
- must be kept on an accrual basis according to the double-entry system of accounting.

The act requires an audited balance sheet and profit and loss account, approved by the board of directors.[56] An accompanying directors' report must address the state of affairs of the company, its material commitments, recommended dividends, and other information necessary for understanding the nature of the company's business and subsidiaries.

The Institute of Chartered Accountants of India, established in 1949, regulates the profession of chartered accountancy and is responsible for developing both accounting and auditing standards.[57] Chartered accountants were previously known as registered accountants and the institute was preceded by other organizations of professional accountants, such as the Society of Auditors, founded in Madras in 1927. The institute prescribes the qualifications for becoming a chartered accountant, holds examinations and training programs for candidates, issues certificates to practice, and disciplines members for professional misconduct and breaches of ethical behavior. Its Accounting Standards Board issues Indian Accounting Standards (AS), and its Auditing and Assurance Standards Board issues Auditing and Assurance Standards (AAS). AS have statutory authority, and AAS are mandatory for the practice of auditing. The institute is supervised by the Ministry of Company Affairs. In 2006, the government announced that it intended to introduce comprehensive new company legislation that would include aligning AS with International Financial Reporting Standards. The institute set up a task force to study the possibility of adopting all IFRS in full, without modification, as AS.

There are 22 stock exchanges in India, the oldest of which is the Mumbai (Bombay) Stock Exchange, established in 1875 and now listing more than 6,000 stocks. The regulatory agency that oversees the functioning of stock markets is the

---

[56]As noted later, Indian accounting standards also require a cash flow statement.
[57]The Institute's Web site is www.icai.org.

Securities and Exchange Board of India (SEBI), an agency of the Ministry of Finance established in 1988 and given statutory authority in 1992. In general, the accounting and disclosure requirements for listed companies are similar to those in the AS.

Financial Reporting

Financial statements consist of two-year balance sheets, income statements, cash flow statements, and accounting policies and notes. Companies that are not listed are only required to prepare parent-only statements, but listed companies must prepare both consolidated and parent-only statements. Neither a statement of shareholders' equity nor a statement of comprehensive income is required. Financial statements must present a true and fair view, but there is no true and fair override as there is in the United Kingdom. As noted above, the Companies Act requires that a directors' report accompany the financial statements. Companies listed on a stock exchange must also provide a management discussion and analysis covering such topics as the industry structure and development, opportunities and threats faced by the company, internal controls, and risks that affect the performance of business segments or products. Listed companies must also provide interim financial results on a quarterly basis.

Accounting Measurements

Subsidiaries are consolidated when the parent owns more than half of the entity's voting power or controls the composition of its board of directors. Subsidiaries may be excluded from consolidation if control is temporary or if there are long-term restrictions on the subsidiary's ability to transfer funds to the parent. There are no standards on accounting for business combinations, but most of them are accounted for as a purchase. However, the uniting-of-interests (pooling) method is used for mergers (called amalgamations). Goodwill is the difference between the consideration given and the existing carrying amounts of the assets and liabilities acquired. Practice varies between no amortization of goodwill to amortization over no more than 10 years. Goodwill is also reviewed for impairment. Proportional consolidation is used for jointly controlled entities (joint ventures). The equity method is used to account for associates—entities over which there is significant influence but not control.

Translation of the financial statements of a foreign operation depends on whether it is integral or nonintegral to the operations of the reporting (parent) entity. For integral foreign operations, monetary assets and liabilities are translated at the closing (year-end) exchange rate, nonmonetary items carried at historical cost are translated at the exchange rate at the date of the transaction, and nonmonetary items carried at fair value are translated at the exchange rate when fair value was determined. Income statement amounts are translated at the exchange rate on the date of transaction or weighted average rate for the period. Exchange differences are reported in income. Assets and liabilities of nonintegral foreign operations are translated at the closing exchange rate, income and expense items are translated at the exchange rates at the dates of the transactions, and the resulting exchange difference is accumulated in a foreign currency exchange reserve on the balance sheet. AS have no provisions for subsidiaries in hyperinflationary economies.

Fixed assets are valued at either historical cost or revalued (fair) value. Revaluations must be applied to the entire class of fixed asset, but there is no requirement that revaluations be performed at regular intervals. Depreciation is allocated on a systematic basis over the life of the asset. If assets are revalued, depreciation is based on the revalued amount. Intangible assets are normally amortized over no more than 10 years. Internally generated goodwill or other intangibles (e.g., brand names) are not recognized as assets. Research costs are expensed as incurred, but development costs may be deferred if the technical feasibility of the product or process has been demonstrated and the recoverability of the costs is reasonably certain. Inventory is valued at the lower of cost or net realizable value. FIFO and average are acceptable cost-flow methods.

Finance leases are capitalized at fair market value and depreciated over the life of the lease. Operating leases are expensed on a straight-line basis over the lease term. The costs of employee benefits are accounted for as the employee earns them rather than when they are paid. Contingent losses are provided for when they are probable (likely) and a reasonable estimate of the amount can be made. Deferred taxes are provided for all timing differences. Deferred tax assets and liabilities are not discounted to their present values.

Exhibit 4-4 summarizes the significant accounting practices in the countries surveyed in this chapter.

EXHIBIT 4-4 Summary of Significant Accounting Practices

	United States	Mexico	Japan	China	India
1. Business combinations: purchase or pooling	Purchase	Purchase	Both	Purchase	Both
2. Goodwill	Capitalize and impairments test	Capitalize and impairments test	Capitalize and amortize; and impairments test	Capitalize and impairments test	Capitalize and amortize; and impairments test
3. Associates	Equity method	Equity method	Equity method	Equity method	Equity method
4. Asset valuation	Historical cost	Price-level adjusted	Historical cost	Historical cost	Historical cost and fair value
5. Depreciation charges	Economic based	Economic based	Tax based	Economic based	Economic based
6. LIFO inventory valuation	Permitted	Not used	Permitted	Not permitted	Not permitted
7. Probable losses	Accrued	Accrued	Accrued	Accrued	Accrued
8. Finance leases	Capitalized	Capitalized	Capitalized[a]	Capitalized	Capitalized
9. Deferred taxes	Accrued	Accrued	Accrued	Accrued	Accrued
10. Reserves for income smoothing	No	No	No	No	Some

[a] When ownership is transferred. Other finance leases may be capitalized or treated as operating leases.

SELECTED REFERENCES

Alexander, D., and E. Jermakowicz, "A True and Fair View of the Principles/Rules Debate," *Abacus* 42, no. 2 (2006): 132–164.

Benston, G. J., M. Bromwich, and Al Wagenhofer, "Principles- Versus Rules-Based Accounting Standards: The FASB's Standard Setting Strategy," *Abacus* 42, no. 2 (2006): 165–188.

Davis-Friday, P. Y., and E. A. Gordon, "Relative Valuation Roles of Equity Book Value, Net Income, and Cash Flows During a Macroeconomic Shock: The Case of Mexico and the 1994 Currency Crisis," *Journal of International Accounting Research* 4, no. 1 (2005): 1–21.

Davis-Friday, P. Y., and J. M. Rivera, "Inflation Accounting and 20-F Disclosures: Evidence from Mexico," *Accounting Horizons* (June 2000): 113–135.

Deloitte, *China's New Accounting Standards*, August 2006 (www.iasplus.com/dttpubs/ 0607prcifrsenglish.pdf).

Deloitte "Country Accounting Standards Update," IAS Plus Web site (www.iasplus.com).

Gordon, E. A., "Accounting for Changing Prices: The Value Relevance of Historical Cost, Price Level, and Replacement Cost Accounting in Mexico," *Journal of Accounting Research* 39, no. 1 (June 2001): 177–200.

Ijiri, Y., "U.S. Accounting Standards and Their Environment: A Dualistic Study of Their 75 Years of Transition," *Journal of Accounting and Public Policy* 24, no. 4 (2005): 255–279.

Kimber, D., and P. Lipton, "Corporate Governance and Business Ethics in the Asia-Pacific Region," *Business and Society* 44, no. 2 (2005): 178–210.

KPMG, *Sarbanes-Oxley: A Closer Look*, Montvale, NJ: KPMG International, January 2003.

Lin, Z. J., F. Chen, and Z. Tang, "The Perceptions of Chinese Financial Reporting Regulations by Various Stakeholders," *Journal of International Accounting Auditing & Taxation* 10, no. 1 (2001): 23–49.

Meek, G. K., *Developments in Country Studies in International Accounting*, Cheltenham, U.K.: Edward Elgar, 2004.

Nobes, C., and R. Parker, *Comparative International Accounting*, 9th ed., Harlow, U.K.: Pearson Education, 2006.

"Now for the Hard Part: A Survey of India," *Economist* (June 3, 2006): 1-18.

Ordelheide, D., and KPMG, eds., *Transnational Accounting*, 2nd ed., Hampshire and New York, Palgrave, 2001.

PricewaterhouseCoopers, *Similarities and Differences: A Comparison of IFRS, U.S. GAAP, and Indian GAAP*, November 2006 (www.pwc.com/extweb/pwcpublications.nsf/ docid/C979CF8DC0F18F77CA2571F50039012E).

PricewaterhouseCoopers, *Similarities and Differences: A Comparison of IFRS and U.S. GAAP*, October 2006 (www.pwc.com/extweb/pwcpublications.nsf/docid /C979CF8DC0F18F77CA2571F50039012E).

"Survey: Asian Business," *Economist* (April 7, 2001): 1–18.

Zeff, S. A., "How the U.S. Accounting Profession Got Where It Is Today: Part I," *Accounting Horizons* 17, no. 3 (September 2003): 189–205.

Zeff, S. A., "How the U.S. Accounting Profession Got Where It Is Today: Part II," *Accounting Horizons* 17, no. 4 (December 2003): 267–286.

DISCUSSION QUESTIONS

1. Compare and contrast the mechanisms for regulating and enforcing financial reporting in the five countries discussed in this chapter.
2. Compare and contrast the main features of financial reporting in the five countries discussed in this chapter.

3. Auditor oversight bodies have recently been established in several countries discussed in this chapter. Identify the auditor–oversight bodies discussed in the chapter. What is the reason for this recent trend?

4. What is the role of tax legislation in the financial accounting practices in each of the five countries discussed in the chapter?

5. Does the development of accounting lead or lag behind the development of a nation's economy? Cite evidence from this chapter to support your answer.

6. What is the difference between principles-based and rules-based accounting standards? What evidence indicates that U.S. GAAP is rules-based?

7. U.S. financial statements "present fairly," while U.K. financial statements are "true and fair." What is the difference between these two concepts?

8. Mexican companies that list their shares on the New York Stock Exchange are required by the U.S. Securities and Exchange Commission to reconcile net income and stockholders' equity from Mexican to U.S. GAAP. What are likely to be the most significant reconciliation items?

9. What was the reason for Japan's Big Bang, and what changes in accounting practice have resulted from it?

10. What important features of accounting and reporting are necessary to develop an efficient stock market with fair trading? How likely is it that China will develop such a stock market? Why do you say so?

11. China's aim is to develop accounting standards that are harmonized with international practices. Cite some examples indicating that Chinese accounting standards are consistent with "world-class" practices.

12. What evidence is there of British influence on accounting in India?

EXERCISES

1. This chapter provides synopses of national accounting practice systems in five countries.
   Required:
   For each country, list:
   a. The name of the national financial accounting standard-setting board or agency.
   b. The name of the agency, institute, or other organization charged with supervising and enforcing financial accounting standards.

2. The International Federation of Accountants (IFAC) is a worldwide organization of professional accounting bodies. IFAC's Web site (www.ifac.org) has links to accounting bodies around the world.
   Required: Visit IFAC's Web site. List the accounting organizations discussed in this chapter that are linked to IFAC's Web site.

3. Reread Chapter 4 and its discussion questions.
   Required:
   a. As you go through this material, prepare a list of five expressions, terms, or short phrases unfamiliar or unusual in your home country.
   b. Write a concise definition or explanation of each item.

4. Analyze the five national accounting practice systems summarized in the chapter.
   Required:
   a. For each of the five countries treated in the chapter, select the most important financial accounting practice or principle at variance with international norms.
   b. For each selection you make, briefly state your reasons for including it on your list.
   c. How does this variance affect reported earnings and the debt-to-asset ratio?
   d. How likely is it that an analyst could adjust for this variance to achieve an "apples to apples" comparison with companies from other countries?

5. The world's stock exchanges differ in terms of the number of domestic- versus foreign-listed firms.

   Required: Go to the World Federation of Stock Exchanges Web page (www.world-exchanges.org) (Statistics). For each country discussed in this chapter, identify the number of domestic and foreign listed firms. How do the countries compare, and what are the implications of the observed patterns?

6. Refer to Exhibit 4-4.

   Required: Which country's GAAP appears to be the most oriented toward equity investors? Which country's GAAP appears to be the least oriented toward equity investors? Why do you say so?

7. Several companies from Mexico, Japan, China, and India are listed on the New York Stock Exchange (NYSE).

   Required: Go to the NYSE Web site (www.nyse.com). Identify the companies listed on the NYSE from Mexico, Japan, China, and India. How do the numbers of listed companies from these countries compare to the numbers from other countries in their respective regions? What are the implications of the observed patterns?

8. The United Kingdom and the United States have a common accounting heritage and are linked by history and language. The term *Anglo-American accounting* is sometimes used to denote their accounting styles because of the similarities in orientation, purpose, and approach. Nonetheless, accounting differences still exist between these two countries.

   Required:
   a. Identify the major differences between U.K. and U.S. accounting that are discussed in Chapter 3 and this chapter.
   b. Which country is likely to be systematically more conservative in measuring reported earnings? Why do you think so?

9. The following describes Japanese accounting before the Big Bang:

   The preparation of consolidated financial statements is based on the Securities and Exchange Law. Individual-company accounts are the basis for the consolidated statements, and normally the same principles are used at both levels. Subsidiaries are consolidated if a parent directly or indirectly owns more than 50 percent of the shares. (However, Japanese regulations have materiality tests that can lead to the exclusion of significant subsidiaries in consolidation.) The purchase method of accounting for business combinations is normally used for business combinations. Goodwill is measured on the basis of the book value of the net assets acquired, not the fair market value as is common in most other countries. Goodwill is amortized over five years. The equity method is used in consolidated statements for investments in nonconsolidated subsidiaries and 20 percent- to 50 percent-owned affiliated companies, but the cost method is used in individual company statements. The equity method is also used to account for joint ventures; proportional consolidation is not allowed. Under the foreign currency translation standard, assets and liabilities of foreign subsidiaries are translated at the current (year-end) exchange rate, revenues and expenses at either the year-end or average rate, and translation adjustments are carried as an asset or liability on the balance sheet.

   Accounting measurements based on historical cost are pervasive. Inventory may be valued at cost or the lower of cost or market; cost is most often used. However, in the event of a significant and permanent decline in value, inventory must be written down to market. FIFO, LIFO, and average are all acceptable cost-flow methods, with average the most popular. Fixed assets are valued at cost and depreciated in accordance with the tax laws.

Research and development costs may be capitalized if they relate to new products or techniques, the exploitation of resources, or the development of markets. When capitalized, research and development is amortized over five years. Finance leases, those transferring the risks and rewards of ownership to the lessee, are capitalized, while lease payments on operating leases are charged to income when incurred.

Deferred taxes are not provided for (or needed) in individual company accounts. They are permitted in consolidated financial statements, but normally not provided there, either. Contingent losses are provided for when they are probable and can be reasonably estimated. Tax regulations limit the deductibility of employee retirement and severance benefits to 40 percent of the amount and so are normally only accrued up to this amount. Pension costs are expensed as paid, and unfunded obligations are not accrued. Legal reserves are required: Each year a company must allocate an amount equal to at least 10 percent of cash dividends and bonuses paid to directors and statutory auditors until the legal reserve reaches 25 percent of capital stock.

Required: Identify the major changes that have occurred in Japanese accounting since the Big Bang.

10. The following describes Chinese accounting in the late 1990s:

Financial statements consist of the balance sheet, income statement, statement of changes in financial position (or cash flow statement), notes, and supporting schedules. Consolidated financial statements are required. The purchase method must be used to account for business combinations, and goodwill is amortized over the period benefited. The equity method is used when ownership of another enterprise exceeds 25 percent. When ownership exceeds 50 percent, the accounts of the subsidiary are consolidated. For overseas subsidiaries, the balance sheet is translated at the year-end exchange rate, the income statement is translated at the average-for-the-year exchange rate, and any translation difference is shown as a reserve in equity.

Accounting measurements sometime have a tax orientation. For example, straight-line depreciation is used because tax laws specify this method. Tax law is also referred to in specifying the useful lives of assets and salvage value. Compared to international practice, historical cost is more strictly adhered to and the principle of conservatism is practiced on a more limited basis. These practices also reflect a tax law influence. For example,

1. The lower of cost or market inventory valuation method is not allowed.
2. Provisions for bad debts are allowed only up to 3 percent of the receivables balance.
3. Long-term investments are not written down for permanent declines in value.

Historical cost is the basis for valuing tangible assets. FIFO, average, and LIFO are acceptable costing methods. Acquired intangibles are also recorded at cost and amortized over the periods benefited. Since land and much of the industrial property in China is owned by the state, companies that acquire the right to use land and industrial property rights show them as intangibles.

Costs associated with research and development can be capitalized in some circumstances. No guidance is provided on accounting for capital versus operating leases, nor for deferred taxes. Contingent losses are not accrued; however, contingency funds may be set up as appropriations of retained earnings. Reserves for future expansion may also be appropriated out of retained earnings.

Required: Identify the major changes that have occurred in Chinese accounting since the 1990s.

11. Accounting standard setting in most countries involves a combination of private- and public-sector groups. The private sector includes the accounting profession and other groups affected by the financial reporting process, such as users and preparers of financial statements and organized labor. The public sector includes government agencies, such as tax authorities, ministries responsible for commercial law, and securities commissions. The stock market is another potential influence.

    Required: Complete a matrix indicating whether each of these groups significantly influences accounting standard setting in the five countries discussed in this chapter. List the groups across the top and the countries down the side; indicate the influence of each group with a yes or no.

12. The following are financial ratios used by analysts:

    - *Liquidity:* current ratio; cash flow from operations to current liabilities
    - *Solvency:* debt to equity; debt to assets
    - *Profitability:* return on assets; return on equity

    Required: Assume that you are comparing the financial ratios of companies from two countries discussed in this chapter. Discuss how the accounting practices identified in Exhibit 4-4 would affect your comparisons for each of the six ratios listed.

CASES

Case 4-1   Standing on Principles

Recent U.S. accounting scandals, such as Enron and WorldCom, have caused some to question whether current U.S. generally accepted accounting principles (GAAP) are really protecting investors. Critics, including the U.S. Securities and Exchange Commission (SEC), charge that the rules-based approach to U.S. GAAP encourages a check-the-box mentality that inhibits transparency in financial reporting. Some observers express a preference for principles-based standards, such as International Financial Reporting Standards or those found in the United Kingdom. Both the Financial Accounting Standards Board (FASB) and the SEC have released reports on the feasibility of principles-based accounting standards in the United States.[58]

The following appeared in a leading British professional accounting journal.

> Ever since the Enron debacle first hit the news, smug U.K. accountants have found a new excuse for feeling superior to their transatlantic cousins. The U.S. Financial Accounting Standards Board's massive *oeuvre* have been scoffed at as being merely a whole bunch of rules that don't hang together. Both British and International standards, by way of contrast, are asserted to be based on principles. This essential difference, it is argued, helps to explain why the U.S. profession has got itself into such deep trouble.
>
> Perhaps. But probably not. It certainly seems true that the highly detailed American standards have tended to invite legalistic interpretations and loopholing, whereas the U.K.'s paramount requirement to present a true and fair view has helped to remind us that accounting is more than a compliance activity. However, it is much too glib to characterise their accounting standards as lacking in principle compared to ours; in terms of their intellectual rigour, American accounting standards compare favourably with any others in the world.
>
> How is it that the U.K. and International Accounting Standards Boards appear to have found reliable principles on which to base their own standards, principles that have eluded FASB? After all, both bodies have themselves adopted conceptual frameworks that are largely copies of the FASB's version, and claim to follow them. The answer is that they haven't. Our standards aren't really more principled than the American ones, they are simply less detailed. And even that is changing—both the U.K. and IASB rulebooks have swollen very considerably in recent years, often inspired (if that is the word) by the content of the equivalent American standards.[59] ∎

---

[58]Financial Accounting Standards Board, "Proposal: Principles-Based Approach to U.S. Standard Setting," http://www.fasb.org/proposals/principles-based_approach.pdf (October 21, 2002); and Securities and Exchange Commission, "Study Pursuant to Section 108(d) of the Sarbanes-Oxley Act of 2002 on the Adoption by the United States Financial Reporting System of a Principles-Based Accounting System," www.sec.gov/news/studies/principlesbasedstand.htm#1f (July 25, 2003).
[59]Ron Paterson, "A Matter of Principle," *Accountancy* (February 2003): 98.

REQUIRED

1. What is the difference between rules-based and principles-based accounting standards, and what are the advantages and disadvantages of each?
2. Why has U.S. GAAP evolved into a rules-based approach? Would principles-based standards be effective in the United States? Why or why not?
3. What needs to change in the United States to make principles-based standards effective?
4. Are investors and analysts better served by rules-based or principles-based accounting standards? Why do you say so?

Case 4-2   Casino Capital

What conditions are necessary to develop an efficient stock market with fair trading? What role does accounting and financial reporting play in stock market development? Consider the case of China:

Those Chinese who think of themselves as street-smart tell a joke about three fools. The first is the boss who plays around with his secretary and ends up her husband. The second is the investor who plays the property market and ends up a homeowner. And the third is the punter who plays the stock market and finds himself a shareholder. This sums up the culture of China's fledgling capital markets. "Trading, not ownership," is the approach of China's investors, says Anthony Neoh, a former head of Hong Kong's Securities and Futures Commission who is now the chief outside adviser to Chinas' regulatory body. "That's what we need to change."

This marks a shift in China's capital market reforms. So far, Beijing has focused almost entirely on the "supply side" of the securities market. This has included listing more, and better, companies, and forcing them to adopt better standards of corporate governance and disclosure. Such efforts have a long way to go.

However, the government now realizes that it also needs to work on the "demand side." At present, China's stock market, Asia's second-largest by capitalization, consists of 60m mainly clueless retail investors, driven to trade almost entirely on rumor.[60]

[T]he balance sheets of Chinese companies are, by common consent, a joke. In January [2001] the government's official auditing body admitted that more than two-thirds of the 1,300 biggest state-owned enterprises cook their books. Johnny Chen, the Beijing head of PricewaterhouseCoopers, says that even this is an understatement. Quite simply, the SOEs' numbers are whatever the key man wants them to be. And without genuinely independent directors to chair an audit committee, that will not change.[61]

Even China's mostly hapless stock market investor (66m of them, officially) had something to cheer about this month, after the country's highest court said that shareholders could file individual or class action lawsuits against companies that lie about their

---

[60]"Fools in Need of Institutions," *Economist* (June 30, 2001), p. 65.
[61]"Survey: Asian Business," *Economist* (April 7, 2001), p. 13.

accounts. There appear to be a lot of liars about. Around 900 shareholder suits are pending, in a country with 1,200 listed companies.

It remains to be seen whether these steps amount to mere tinkering, or herald the new and bolder approach to financial reform that China badly needs. Its markets for labor, goods, and services are nowadays more liberal than those in some capitalist economies. Its capital markets, by contrast, have changed only cosmetically since the days of central planning. In effect, all capital in China is allocated, one way or the other, by the government, which wastes much of it.

The decade-old stock market is dominated by state-owned enterprises that were listed for political rather than economic reasons. Some two-thirds of the market's capitalization is not traded, so the state retains total control. There is no corporate bond market to speak of.[62]

[A]ll is not what it seems in China's capital markets. For a start, growth in the domestic stock market has outstripped the efforts—game as they are—of the regulators and the legal system to police it. The authorities say that computer matching of share transactions has allowed them pretty much to stop powerful syndicates ramping up share prices. They have even sent the biggest manipulators to jail, yet insider trading is still rife on a heroic scale. Stock exchange executives reckon that the real number of investors is around half the official number: investors use multiple accounts for dodgy share dealings.

The real issue is the quality of the listed companies themselves, says one financial official. Even some of the better-regarded ones indulge in all sorts of market abuses, such as lending money raised on the stock market to the parent company rather than investing it, or speculating in the stock market on their own account. Almost all companies allowed a listing are the beneficiaries of government favoritism. Their profitability is usually abysmal, their levels of disclosure poor, and—with the state holding roughly two-thirds of the shares of companies listed in Shanghai and Shenzhen—their treatment of minority shareholders appalling.[63]

[T]he biggest problem is the poor quality of the listed companies. All but a handful are state enterprises, which are approved for an IPO by a political committee rather than by independent underwriters. A 2002 survey by the China Securities Regulatory Commission (CSRC), the top regulator, found that one in ten listed companies had doctored its books, and the finance ministry reported in January [2004] 152 firms it had surveyed had misstated their profits by a combined 2.9 billion yuan. "The stock market has been used to support national industrial policy, to subsidize SOE restructuring, not to allow private companies to raise capital," says Stephen Green of the Royal Institute of International Affairs.[64] ■

---

[62]"Banking on Growth," *Economist* (January 18, 2003), p. 67.
[63]"A Survey of Asian Finance," *Economist* (February 8, 2003), pp. 10–11.
[64]"Behind the Mask: A Survey of Business in China," *Economist* (March 20, 2004): 19.

REQUIRED

1. Describe the conditions necessary to develop a stock market in an emerging economy.
2. How do these conditions compare to the situation in China?
3. How likely is China to develop a stock market with fair trading? Why do you say so?
4. Outline a plan of reforms necessary to achieve stock market development in China.

CHAPTER 5

Reporting and Disclosure

In this chapter we examine the communication of financial and nonfinancial information in an international setting. Much of the discussion addresses disclosure related to financial reporting for external users. We focus on selected topics and do not attempt to discuss every disclosure issue that applies to financial statement users, preparers, and financial professionals.

The relative importance of equity markets in national economies is growing and individual investors are becoming more active in those markets. As a result, public disclosure, investor protection, shareholder value, and stock market-driven forms of corporate governance are becoming increasingly important.[1] Although disclosure practices vary from country to country, they are converging. However, important differences among countries will continue to affect many firms, particularly those that are not active in international capital or product markets.

Government regulators who seek to maintain or increase the credibility of their national capital markets also influence disclosure practices around the world. Stock exchanges have concluded that their continued growth and success depends on offering a high-quality market with effective investor protection. As a result, oversight by regulators and stock exchanges is increasing and disclosure requirements are becoming more stringent. The trend toward greater investor protection and enhanced disclosure will continue as stock exchanges face growing competition from each other and from less-regulated trading systems.

DEVELOPMENT OF DISCLOSURE

The development of disclosure systems closely parallels the development of accounting systems discussed in Chapter 2.[2] Disclosure standards and practices are influenced by sources of finance, legal systems, political and economic ties, level of economic development, education level, culture, and other factors.

---

[1] For example, Schering AG, a German company, states the following on its Web site: "Open and honest communication creates transparency and trust." Its *Annual Report 2005* notes that "Schering AG is committed to making comprehensive information available simultaneously to the financial markets and all other parties interested in the development of the Company. We offer detailed company reports as well as, among other things, comprehensive information on corporate management in the internet at www.schering.de under Investor Relations, section Corporate Governance."

[2] The terms *disclosure systems* and *accounting systems* overlap considerably. Often, as in Chapter 2 of this text, "accounting development" refers to the development of accounting standards and practices. "Disclosure development" as discussed in this chapter refers to the development of financial and nonfinancial disclosures presented in financial reports. We do not discuss disclosures made in press releases, although much of the discussion in this chapter applies to this area.

National differences in disclosure are driven largely by differences in corporate governance and finance. In the United States, the United Kingdom, and other Anglo-American countries, equity markets have provided most corporate financing and have become highly developed. In these markets, ownership tends to be spread among many shareholders, and investor protection is emphasized. Institutional investors play a growing role in these countries, demanding financial returns and increased shareholder value. Public disclosure is highly developed in response to companies' accountability to the public.

In many other countries (such as France, Germany, Japan, and numerous emerging-market countries), shareholdings remain highly concentrated and banks (and/or family owners) traditionally have been the primary source of corporate financing. Structures are in place to protect incumbent management. Banks (which sometimes are both creditors and owners) and other insiders (such as corporate members of interlocking shareholder groups) provide discipline. These banks, insiders, and others are closely informed about the company's financial position and its activities. Public disclosure is less developed in these markets and large differences in the amount of information given to large shareholders and creditors vis-à-vis the public may be permitted.

Voluntary Disclosure

Managers have better information than external parties about their firm's current and future performance. Several studies show that managers have incentives to disclose such information voluntarily. The benefits of enhanced disclosure may include lower transaction costs in the trading of the firm's securities, greater interest in the company by financial analysts and investors, increased share liquidity, and lower cost of capital. One recent report supports the view that companies can achieve capital markets benefits by enhancing their voluntary disclosure.[3] The report includes guidance on how companies can describe and explain their investment potential to investors.

As investors around the world demand more detailed and timely information, voluntary disclosure levels are increasing in both highly developed and emerging-market countries. It is widely recognized, however, that financial reporting can be an imperfect mechanism for communicating with outside investors when managers' incentives are not perfectly aligned with the interests of all shareholders. In one classic paper, the authors argue that managers' communication with outside investors is imperfect when (1) managers have superior information about their firm, (2) managers' incentives are not perfectly aligned with the interests of all the shareholders, and (3) accounting rules and auditing are imperfect.[4] The authors state that contracting mechanisms (such as compensation linking managers' rewards to long-term share value) can reduce this conflict.

---

[3]Financial Accounting Standards Board, *Improving Business Reporting: Insights into Enhancing Voluntary Disclosures*, www.fasb.org/brrp/BRRP2.PDF, 2001.
[4]See P. M. Healy and K. G. Palepu, "The Effect of Firms' Financial Disclosure Strategies on Stock Prices?," *Accounting Horizons* (March 1993): 1–11.

Evidence strongly indicates that corporate managers often have strong incentives to delay the disclosure of bad news, "manage" their financial reports to convey a more positive image of the firm, and overstate their firm's financial performance and prospects. For example, executives face significant risks of being dismissed in firms whose financial or stock market performance is relatively weak. Seriously stressed firms may have a higher risk of bankruptcy, acquisition, or hostile takeover, leading to a management change. Also, the possible competitive disadvantage created when proprietary information is made public may offset the benefits of full disclosure.

Regulation (e.g., accounting and disclosure regulation) and third-party certification (e.g., auditing) can improve the functioning of markets. Accounting regulation attempts to reduce managers' ability to record economic transactions in ways that are not in shareholders' best interests. Disclosure regulation sets forth requirements to ensure that shareholders receive timely, complete, and accurate information. External auditors try to ensure that managers apply appropriate accounting policies, make reasonable accounting estimates, maintain adequate accounting records and control systems, and provide the required disclosures in a timely manner.

Although these mechanisms can strongly influence practice, managers occasionally conclude that the benefits of noncompliance with reporting requirements (e.g., a higher stock price due to inflated earnings) outweigh the costs (e.g., the risk of job loss and litigation resulting in criminal or civil penalties if the noncompliance is detected and reported). Thus, managers' disclosure choices reflect the combined effects of disclosure requirements and their incentives to disclose information voluntarily.

Regulatory Disclosure Requirements

To protect investors, most securities exchanges (together with professional or government regulatory bodies such as the U.S. Securities and Exchange Commission and the Financial Services Agency in Japan) impose reporting and disclosure requirements on domestic and foreign companies that seek access to their markets. These exchanges want to make sure that investors have enough information to allow them to evaluate a company's performance and prospects. Nowhere is this concern more evident than in the United States, whose disclosure standards generally are considered to be the most stringent in the world.

Stock exchanges and government regulators generally require foreign listed firms to furnish almost the same financial and nonfinancial information as that required of domestic companies. Foreign listed firms generally have some flexibility in regard to the accounting principles they use and the extent of disclosure. In many countries, foreign listed firms must file with the stock exchange any information made public, distributed to shareholders, or filed with regulators in the domestic market. However, many countries do not monitor or enforce this "cross-jurisdictional conformity of disclosure" requirement.

Shareholder protection varies substantially among countries. Anglo-American countries such as Canada, the United Kingdom, and the United States provide extensive and strictly enforced shareholder protection. In contrast, shareholder protection receives less emphasis in other parts of the world. For example, while China prohibits insider trading, its weak judiciary makes enforcement almost nonexistent. Shareholder protection codes in the Czech Republic, Mexico, and many other emerging-market countries also are rudimentary. Even in many developed countries, the concept of investor protection is of recent origin, and many commentators argue that it still is inadequate. For example, insider trading was not a criminal offense in Germany until the enactment of the Securities Trading Act 1994.

Frost and Lang discuss the twin objectives of investor-oriented markets: investor protection and market quality.[5]

- *Investor Protection.* Investors are provided with material information and are protected by monitoring and enforcing market rules. Fraud is inhibited in the public offering, trading, voting, and tendering of securities. Comparable financial and nonfinancial information is sought so that investors may compare companies across industries and countries.
- *Market Quality.* Markets are fair, orderly, efficient, and free from abuse and misconduct. Market fairness is promoted through equitable access to information and trading opportunities. Market efficiency is advanced by enhancing liquidity and reducing transactions costs. Quality markets are marked by investor confidence and they facilitate capital formation. Prices reflect investors' perceptions of value without being arbitrary or capricious.

Frost and Lang also outline four principles under which investor-oriented market should operate:

1. *Cost effectiveness.* The cost of market regulation should be proportionate to the benefits it secures.
2. *Market freedom and flexibility.* Regulation should not impede competition and market evolution.
3. *Transparent financial reporting and full and complete disclosure.*
4. *Equal treatment of foreign and domestic firms.*

As Frost and Lang note, investor protection requires that investors receive timely material information and are protected through effective monitoring and enforcement. Disclosure should be sufficient to allow investors to compare companies across industries and countries. Furthermore, full and credible disclosure will enhance investor confidence, which will increase liquidity, reduce transactions costs, and improve overall market quality.

The U.S. SEC Financial Reporting Debate

The SEC generally requires foreign registrants to furnish financial information substantially similar to that required of domestic companies. However, foreign registrants' financial statements need not be prepared in accordance with U.S. GAAP if they are presented in accordance with another comprehensive body of accounting principles and are accompanied by a quantitative reconciliation to U.S. GAAP of net income, shareholders' equity, and earnings per share, if materially different.

---

[5]Carol A. Frost and Mark Lang, "Foreign Companies and U.S. Securities Markets: Financial Reporting Policy Issues and Suggestions for Research," *Accounting Horizons* 10 (March 1996): 97.

Whether the reconciliation requirement helps or hinders the SEC in meeting its regulatory objectives is widely debated. The SEC's reporting requirements are generally consistent with the objectives of investor protection and market quality. However, stringent reporting requirements may achieve the goal of investor protection at the cost of reducing investment opportunities or imposing high transaction costs on investing.

Some commentators argue that the SEC's financial reporting requirements for foreign companies deter them from making their securities available in the United States.[6,7] As a result, it is claimed, U.S. investors are more likely to trade in markets such as the U.S. Over-the-Counter (OTC) market or overseas markets where liquidity may be relatively low, transaction costs relatively high, and investor protection less important than on the national exchanges in the United States. It then is argued that the SEC could provide U.S. investors with more investment opportunities within the regulated U.S. markets by relaxing its financial reporting requirements; this, in turn, would better balance the SEC's objectives of investor protection and market quality. It also is argued that the SEC's registration requirements actually may mislead U.S. investors by giving a false appearance of comparability to foreign financial statements that may require a significantly different interpretation than U.S. statements.

Others counter that the current accounting and disclosure system both protects investors and ensures the quality of U.S. capital markets.[8] Underlying this argument are the principles of full disclosure and equal treatment of foreign and domestic issuers. If investors in domestic securities require financial information based on U.S. GAAP to make informed decisions, then such information is just as necessary for making informed decisions about non-U.S. securities. Indeed, the competitive strength of U.S. capital markets, including their substantial liquidity and high level of investor confidence, is often attributed (at least in part) to the SEC's existing disclosure system and vigorous enforcement. It also has been argued that the SEC's reporting requirements are not the primary obstacles to foreign companies desiring to list securities in the United States.

The implementation of the 2002 Sarbanes-Oxley Act (SOX) has been accompanied by new complaints about its Section 404 requiring the chief executives and chief financial officers of public companies (and their external auditors) to appraise and certify the effectiveness and adequacy of internal controls. Some foreign firms have

---

[6]See J. L. Cochrane, "Are U.S. Regulatory Requirements for Foreign Firms Appropriate?" *Fordham International Law Journal* 17 (1994): S58–S67; J. L. Cochrane, J. E. Shapiro, and J. E. Tobin, "Foreign Equities and U.S. Investors: Breaking Down the Barriers Separating Supply and Demand," *Stanford Journal of Law, Business and Finance* 1997.

[7]New regulations enacted by the 2002 Sarbanes-Oxley Act are also said to deter foreign companies from a U.S. listing. See John Rossant, "Who Needs U.S. Markets?" *Business Week* (February 16, 2004): 13.

[8]See Richard C. Breeden, "Foreign Companies and U.S. Securities Markets in a Time of Economic Transformation," *Fordham International Law Journal* 17 (1994): S77–S96; Pat McConnell, "Practical Company Experience in Entering U.S. Markets: Significant Issues and Hurdles from the Advisor's Perspective," *Fordham International Law Journal* 17 (1994): S120–S128; and remarks by SEC Commissioner Isaac C. Hunt, Jr. at the Second European FASB-SEC Financial Reporting Conference, Frankfurt, Germany (March 23, 2000), www.sec.gov/news/speech/spch363.htm.

delisted from U.S. stock exchanges (such as British companies Cable and Wireless and Rank Group). Others are apparently avoiding U.S. listings and choosing to list on other markets such as the London Stock Exchange.[9] This issue raises concerns similar to those about the reconciliation requirement. Sarbanes-Oxley has imposed significant new audit costs on companies (estimates range from 35 to 150 percent of pre-SOX audit fees). But the benefits of better auditing and more trustworthy financial statements are no less real.

REPORTING AND DISCLOSURE PRACTICES

What do companies around the world actually disclose in their annual reports? Annual report disclosure practices reflect managers' responses to regulatory disclosure requirements and their incentives to provide information to financial statement users voluntarily. In many parts of the world, disclosure rules mean little, and monitoring and enforcement are largely absent. Insofar as disclosure rules are not enforced, the required disclosures are (in practice) voluntary, because corporate managers will not comply with disclosure rules if compliance is more costly than the expected costs of noncompliance. Therefore, it is important to clearly distinguish between disclosures that are "required" and disclosures that actually are made. It is misleading to focus on disclosure rules without also looking at actual disclosure practices.

For some types of disclosure (e.g., disclosures about material developments) managerial discretion plays such an important role that monitoring (and hence enforcement) is difficult. Therefore, these types of disclosure are more or less voluntary. Finally, disclosure rules vary dramatically worldwide in areas such as changes in equity statements, related party transactions, segment reporting, fair value of financial assets and liabilities, and earnings per share.

In this section we focus on (1) disclosures of forward-looking information, (2) segment disclosures, (3) social responsibility reporting, (4) special disclosures for nondomestic financial statement users, (5) corporate governance disclosures, and (6) Internet business reporting and disclosure. These disclosure and reporting items were selected because of their importance to financial statement users. For example, financial analysts and regulators have emphasized the importance of corporate disclosures of forward-looking information, such as that related to corporate goals and planned expenditures, and business-segment information. Governance disclosures have become important in recent years as a result of corporate scandals at Enron, WorldCom, Parmalot, Ahold, and other companies.

Disclosures of Forward-Looking Information

Disclosures of forward-looking information are considered highly relevant in equity markets worldwide. For example, the EU's Fourth Directive states that the annual report should include an indication of the company's likely future developments. The SEC's Regulation S-K requires companies to disclose presently known information

---

[9]See "404 Tonnes of Paper," *Economist* (December 18, 2004): 116; "Big Apple Blues," *Economist* (January 29, 2005): 73; "Escape from New York," *Accountancy Magazine* (April 2006): 52–53.

that will materially impact future liquidity, capital resources, and operating results. As a third example, the Tokyo Stock Exchange "requests" management of listed firms to provide forecasts of sales, earnings, and dividends in their annual and semiannual press releases.

As used here, the term *forward-looking information* includes (1) forecasts of revenues, income (loss), cash flows, capital expenditures, and other financial items; (2) prospective information about future economic performance or position that is less definite than forecasts in terms of projected item, fiscal period, and projected amount;[10] and (3) statements of management's plans and objectives for future operations. These three categories of forward-looking information become more general as we move from (1) forecasts to (2) prospective information to (3) plans and objectives. Given that a primary aim of investors and analysts is assessing a company's future earnings and cash flows, it is reasonable to ask whether companies provide their own internal forecasts of such financial information. The practice is not very common, particularly precise forecasts. (Range forecasts are more common than precise forecasts, and directional forecasts [increase or decrease] are more common still.) One reason is that forecasts can be unreliable because they incorporate subjective estimates of uncertain future events. In addition, there can be legal repercussions for management if forecasts are not met. In the United States, the potential for lawsuits is a major deterrent to providing financial forecasts. However, as perhaps could be expected, vaguer forms of forward-looking information are more common. A study of 200 large public companies in France, Germany, Japan, the United Kingdom, and United States found that most of them disclosed information about management's plans and objectives. Softer, prospective information was also fairly common, but forecasts were much less common.[11]

An example is the forecast disclosure of Schering AG (a German firm, now Bayer Schering Pharma AG) in its Annual Report 2005. Schering forecasts "mid to high single-digit" growth in net sales. A forecast of this kind is reasonably precise but still open to interpretation. For example, a financial statement reader might reasonably expect an increase in sales between 5 and 8 percent. Schering also expects its profitability "to grow" in the future, a vague statement that it will increase.[12]

Segment Disclosures

Investor and analyst demand for information about firms' industry and geographic-segment operations and financial results is significant and growing. For example, financial analysts in the United States consistently request financial statement data disaggregated in much greater detail than it is now. International Financial Reporting Standards (IFRS) include highly detailed segment reporting, as do accounting standards in many countries.[13] Segment disclosures help financial statement users better

---

[10]For convenience we use the term *prospective disclosure* to refer to "softer" nonforecast disclosures.

[11]Carol A. Frost and Kurt P. Ramin, "Corporate Financial Disclosure: A Global Assessment," in *International Finance and Accounting Handbook*, ed. Frederick D. S. Choi, 3rd ed. (New York: John Wiley, 2003), pp. 13–31.

[12]Refer to www.schering.de/html/en/50_media/download/_files/2005/fin_rep/annual/05GB_en.pd(pp. 80–81) for Schering's forecast disclosure.

[13]See Lee H. Radebaugh and Donna L. Street, "Segmental and Foreign Operations Disclosure," in *International Finance and Accounting Handbook*, ed. Frederick D. S. Choi, 3rd ed. (New York: John Wiley, 2003), for a detailed discussion of segment and foreign operations disclosure.

understand how the parts of a company make up the whole. After all, product lines and areas of the world vary in terms of risks, returns, and opportunities. A disaggregation by lines of business and geographic area should make for more informed judgments about the overall company.

Exhibit 5-1 presents the business segment and geographic area disclosure made in the 2005 Annual Report of Lafarge (a French firm). The business-segment disclosure reveals the most recent two years' revenue, operating income, depreciation and amortization, capital expenditures, capital employed, investments in associates, segment assets, and segment liabilities for Lafarge's four main product lines. The geographic area disclosure shows two years' revenue, capital expenditure, and capital employed by regions of the world and selected countries. Lafarge also discusses its product and geographic markets in significant detail elsewhere in the annual report.

Social Responsibility Reporting

Increasingly, companies are being called upon to answer to a wide range of "stakeholders"—employees, customers, suppliers, governments, activist groups, and the general public—who have areas of concern other than the company's ability to create economic value. Social responsibility reporting refers to the measurement and communication of information about a company's effects on employee welfare, the local community, and the environment. It reflects a belief that companies owe stakeholders an annual accounting of their social and environmental performance just like the financial information they provide shareholders. More important, as suggested by the saying "What gets measured, gets managed," social responsibility reporting is a way to demonstrate corporate citizenship. "Sustainability" reports that integrate economic, social, and environmental performance are referred to as "triple-bottom-line reporting" (profits, people, and planet). Moreover, to avoid criticism that the reporting is "green-washing" (i.e., a public relation ploys without substance), such information is increasingly being verified by independent third parties.[14]

Information on employee welfare has long been of interest to labor groups.[15] Particular areas of concern relate to working conditions, job security, equal opportunity, workforce diversity, and child labor. Employee disclosures also are of interest to investors in that they provide useful insights about a firm's labor relations, costs, and productivity.

Information disclosure regarding number of employees is of great interest to national governments. Number-of-employees disclosure by geographic area gives host governments information on the employment effect of multinational companies. Employee disclosure by line of business, in turn, helps identify those industries and activities that foreign direct investors find economically attractive. If there is a conflict between the behavior of the investors and the goals of the host government—for example, if investors invest in operations that employ low-skill workers while the government seeks to expand high-skill employment—an alert government could take steps to encourage foreign investment in the desired direction. When combined with

---

[14]Mel Wilson and Rosie Lombardi, "Globalization and Its Discontent: The Arrival of Triple-Bottom-Line Reporting, *Ivey Business Journal* 66, 1 (September/October 2001): 69–72. See also P. Engardio, "Beyond the Green Corporation," *Business Week* (January 29, 2007): 50–64.

[15]For many years, workers have been considered business partners in continental Europe, with worker participation in works councils mandatory in the large companies of many countries.

EXHIBIT 5-1   Segment Disclosures by Lafarge

Note 3 - Business Segment and Geographic Area Information

(a) Business segment information

(million euros)	2005					
	Cement	Aggregates & Concrete	Roofing	Gypsum	Other	Total
STATEMENT OF INCOME						
Gross revenue	8,314	5,392	1,514	1,479	25	16,724
Less: intersegment	(719)	(15)	-	(17)	(4)	(755)
REVENUE	**7,595**	**5,377**	**1,514**	**1,462**	**21**	**15,969**
Current operating income	1,770	398	98	151	(60)	2,357
Gains on disposals, net	10	14	(3)	3	13	37
Other operating income (expenses)	(76)	(6)	(52)	(8)	(15)	(157)
Including impairment on assets and goodwill	*(53)*	*(4)*	*(20)*	*(7)*	*(1)*	*(85)*
OPERATING INCOME	**1,704**	**406**	**43**	**146**	**(62)**	**2,237**
Finance (costs) income						(427)
Income from associates	8	8	7	15	-	38
Income taxes						(424)
NET INCOME						**1,424**
OTHER INFORMATION						
Depreciation and amortization	(519)	(233)	(123)	(71)	(27)	(973)
Other segment non cash income (expenses) of operating income	(88)	(11)	2	4	175	82
Capital expenditures	824	358	139	101	32	1,454
Capital employed	13,982	3,932	2,181	1,267	290	21,652
BALANCE SHEET						
Investments in associates	115	40	143	71	7	376
Other segment assets	16,043	5,313	2,289	1,524	1,883	27,052
Unallocated assets [a]						467
TOTAL ASSETS						**27,895**
Segment liabilities	2,023	1,138	670	321	1,744	5,896
Unallocated liabilities and equity [b]						21,999
TOTAL EQUITY AND LIABILITIES						**27,895**

(a) Deferred tax assets and derivative instruments.

(b) Deferred tax liability, financial debt including put option on minority interests and derivative instruments, equity.

(million euros)	2004					
	Cement	Aggregates & Concrete	Roofing	Gypsum	Other	Total
STATEMENT OF INCOME						
Gross revenue	7,403	4,761	1,493	1,353	51	15,061
Less: intersegment	(593)	(14)	-	(13)	(5)	(625)
REVENUE	**6,810**	**4,747**	**1,493**	**1,340**	**46**	**14,436**
Current operating income	1,597	357	149	132	(34)	2,201
Gains on disposals, net	50	18	3	-	20	91
Other operating income (expenses)	(80)	(9)	(52)	-	(77)	(218)
Including impairment on assets and goodwill	*(55)*	*(1)*	*(24)*	*-*	*(52)*	*(132)*
OPERATING INCOME	**1,567**	**366**	**100**	**132**	**(91)**	**2,074**
Finance (costs) income						(547)
Income from associates	40	5	10	13	6	74
Income taxes						(267)
NET INCOME						**1,334**
OTHER INFORMATION						
Depreciation and amortization	(507)	(187)	(114)	(65)	(25)	(898)
Other segment non cash income (expenses) of operating income	46	13	(8)	1	(8)	44
Capital expenditures	631	285	124	48	45	1,133
Capital employed	12,167	3,337	2,118	1,147	139	18,908
BALANCE SHEET						
Investments in associates	125	30	140	59	18	372
Other segment assets	13,935	4,793	2,411	1,434	1,066	23,639
Unallocated assets [a]						489
TOTAL ASSETS						**24,500**
Segment liabilities	1,657	970	656	279	1,688	5,250
Unallocated liabilities and equity [b]						19,250
TOTAL EQUITY AND LIABILITIES						**24,500**

(a) Deferred tax assets and derivative instruments.

(b) Deferred tax liability, financial debt including put option on minority interests and derivative instruments, equity.

(b) Geographic area information

(million euros)	2005			2004		
	Revenue	Capital expenditure	Capital employed	Revenue	Capital expenditure	Capital employed
WESTERN EUROPE	6,280	528	8,802	6,020	387	8,439
Of which:						
France	2,384	221	1,888	2,238	158	1,698
Germany	530	52	1,030	583	58	1,072
Spain	519	99	718	464	20	756
United Kingdom	1,453	155	2,560	1,391	74	2,434
NORTH AMERICA	4,516	440	5,273	3,938	384	4,225
Of which:						
United States	2,909	328	3,900	2,552	292	3,129
Canada	1,607	112	1,373	1,386	92	1,096
MEDITERRANEAN BASIN	671	70	926	534	39	770
CENTRAL AND EASTERN EUROPE	905	79	1,188	746	70	1,142
LATIN AMERICA	707	101	1,261	579	62	793
AFRICA	1,414	76	1,034	1,190	64	837
ASIA / PACIFIC	1,476	160	3,168	1,429	127	2,702
TOTAL	15,969	1,454	21,652	14,436	1,133	18,908

SOURCE: 2005 Lafarge Annual Report

geographical and/or line-of-business reporting, employee disclosure by function enables governments and labor groups to examine whether employment practices of multinational companies are consistent with local laws and norms.

Environmental issues include the impact of production processes, products, and services on air, water, land, biodiversity, and human health. As an example, French listed companies are now required to publish the results of their environmental activities. Among other items, information must be given on:

- Water, raw material, and energy consumption, and actions taken to improve energy efficiency
- Activities to reduce pollution in the air, water, or ground, including noise pollution, and their costs
- Amount of provision for environmental risks

Social responsibility reporting has its critics. For example:

One problem with the triple-bottom-line is quickly apparent. Measuring profits is fairly straightforward; measuring environmental protection and social justice is not. The difficulty is partly that there is no single yardstick for measuring progress in those areas. How is any given success for environmental action to be weighed against any given advance in social justice—or, for that matter, against any given change in profits? And how are the three to be traded off against each other? . . . Measuring profits—the good old single bottom line—offers a pretty clear test of business success. The triple-bottom-line does not.

The problem is not just that there is no one yardstick allowing the three measures to be compared with each other. It is also that there is no agreement on what progress on the environment, or progress in the social sphere, actually mean—not, at least, if you are trying to be precise about it. In other words, there are no yardsticks by which different aspects of environmental protection can be compared even with each other, let alone with other criteria. And the same goes for social justice. . . .

The great virtue of the single bottom line is that it holds managers to account for something. The-triple-bottom line does not. It is not so much a license to operate as a license to obfuscate.[16]

Despite such criticisms, social responsibility reporting is becoming mainstream among large multinational companies. A recent survey found the number of companies issuing environmental, social or sustainability reports, in addition to their annual financial reports, is growing. Nearly half of the world's 250 largest companies issue such reports. Reporting rates are highest in countries with large corporations, such as France, Germany, Japan, the United Kingdom, and the United States. Reporting rates are also highest in certain industries, notably chemicals and synthetics, pharmaceuticals, electronics and computers, automotive, and oil and gas.[17] Another survey of large global companies found that European companies (particularly French, German and U.K.) and Japanese companies are the most active in sustainability reporting, with U.S. companies lagging. The survey also found that about one-third of the companies surveyed had their sustainability reports audited.[18,19]

Guidelines for sustainability reports have been issued by the Global Reporting Initiative (GRI), an independent institution affiliated with the United Nations Environment Programme. The GRI framework recommends the disclosure of performance indicators in the areas of:

- Economic performance, such as payroll, taxes, and community donations
- Environmental performance, such as greenhouse gas emissions and water use
- Social performance, specifically
  - Labor practices, such as worker health and safety, training, and diversity
  - Human rights, such as policies on nondiscrimination, child labor and indigenous rights

---

[16]"The Good Company: A Survey of Corporate Social Responsibility," *Economist* (January 22, 2005): 14.
[17]*KPMG International Survey of Corporate Sustainability Reporting 2002* (June 2002), www.kpmg.com.
[18]Ans Kolk, "Sustainability, Accountability and Corporate Governance: Exploring Multinationals' Reporting Practices," *Business Strategy and the Environment* (March 22, 2006), www3.interscience.wiley.com/cgi-bin/fulltext/112535145/PDFSTART.
[19]Standards for the audit of financial information exist worldwide. However, few countries have assurance standards for sustainability reports. Among European countries Sweden has such a standard, France has issued informal guidance, and Germany and the Netherlands have issued exposure drafts of standards. For an overview of Europe, refer to the Web site of the Fédération des Experts Comptables Européens (FEE), www.fee.be.

- Society, such as community impacts, bribery, and political contributions
- Product responsibility, such as customer health and safety, advertising, and consumer privacy[20]

Exhibits 5-2, 5-3, and 5-4 present examples of social responsibility disclosures. They are taken from the 2005 Business Report of the Swiss company, Roche. Exhibit 5-2 shows employment levels and personnel costs by division and region of the world. The disclosure also discusses management development, compensation, diversity, and human rights. Exhibit 5-3 discusses Roche's safety and environmental record. Finally, Exhibit 5-4 is the auditor's report on the company's Sustainability Report.[21]

EXHIBIT 5-2   Employment Disclosure by Roche

A successful business creates new jobs

As in recent years, Roche has been expanding faster than its competitors. This has led to an increase in headcount in many business areas and regions. In 2005 the Roche Group created a total of 3,624 new jobs, an increase of 5.6%. Headcount increased by 679 in the Diagnostics Division and by 2,941 in the Pharmaceuticals Division, of which Genentech accounted for 1,917. In 2005 Roche spent 9,049 million Swiss francs on employee remuneration, an increase of 801 million Swiss francs (+9.7%) over the previous year. These figures exclude the impact of a one-off gain on the return of part of the Chugai employees' pension fund to the Japanese government.

The largest number of new positions was created in the regions, such as Europe and North America, where sales also grew faster than average. For instance, 2005 saw the founding of new companies in the Eastern European region, leading to an increase in headcount of over 12%. Overall, the increase in the number of new positions was greatest in Research and Development and in Marketing and Sales. The Roche Group hired a total of 8,180 new employees in 2005 in order to fill vacancies as well as to create new jobs. Besides retaining talented and motivated employees, it is also important—in view of our goal of increasing both sales and profit—to take an effective approach to attracting new talent (http://careers.roche.com).

Employment Policy

The Employment Policy lays down the requirements that human resources management in the Roche Group has to meet and also establishes the rights and obligations of Roche employees with regard to the company. Further information on this topic is available at www.roche.com/en/home/company/com_gov/com_gov_emp.htm.

---

[20]www.globalreporting.org/guidelines/062002guidelines.asp.
[21]See Helen Gernon and Gary K. Meek, *Accounting: An International Perspective*, 5th ed. (Boston: Irwin McGraw-Hill, 2001); Carol Adams, Geoffrey Frost, and Sidney J. Gray, "Corporate Social and Environmental Disclosures," in *International Finance and Accounting Handbook*, ed. Frederick D. S. Choi, 3rd ed.(New York: John Wiley, 2003) for further discussion and illustrations. Also see Jee Hong Kim, In Ki Joo and Frederick D. S. Choi, "The Information Content of Productivity Measures: An International Comparison," *Journal of International Financial Management and Accounting* 7 (1996): 167–190.

Number of employees and personnel costs by division

	2005	2004	Change	Personnel costs[1]		Change
				2005	2004	
Roche Group	68,218	64,594	+3,624	9,049	8,248	+801
Pharmaceuticals	48,049	45,108	+2,941	6,586	5,835	+751
Diagnostics	19,788	19,109	+679	2,329	2,256	+73
Others	381	377	+4	134	157	-23

[1] in million francs

Number of employees by region

	2005	2004	Change
Europe	29,934	28,601	+1,333
Switzerland alone	7,860	7,498	+362
North America	21,899	19,715	+2,184
Latin America	4,465	4,971	-506
Asia	10,459	9,885	+574
Japan alone	5,988	5,663	+325
Africa Australia Oceania	1,461	1,422	+39

Roche is a popular employer

The labour market for highly qualified talents in the pharmaceutical industry is extremely competitive. Since 2003, Roche has considerably improved its global presence in this market, becoming more effective in attracting outstanding employees. The approach has been two-pronged: employer branding which underscores the key advantages of Roche as a global employer in our industry, and the introduction of global e-recruiting. In 2004 we launched an Internet-based global recruitment tool which enables candidates to view current vacant positions at a glance, apply for a job online or register in the global or various local talent pools. The tool was used by over 130,000 candidates in 2005 to register or apply for employment. In the past year Roche achieved three demonstrable competitive advantages: recruiting has become faster and more efficient, a better selection from the growing number of well qualified external applicants is possible, and, lastly, transparency for internal applicants. Roche has come considerably closer to achieving its goal of 'one door into Roche' through a unique combination of systems. By the end of 2005, 65% of all known vacancies worldwide were viewable on a website. This percentage will be increased in 2006.

Once again in 2005 Roche companies won a number of prizes or topped the rankings as an attractive employer: e.g. Roche and Genentech in the USA; in Germany (best employer); in Switzerland (best employer for women), in Spain (best employer) and in Australia. Roche was also voted the 'highest climber' in popularity as an employer in Europe. We record employee satisfaction by conducting surveys and through two indirect indicators: illness rate and departures not initiated by Roche. A global illness rate of 3.7% is a clear indication that our employees enjoy good working conditions and feel comfortable working at Roche.

The total attrition rate of permanent staff was 6.7% in 2005. The number of regretted losses was only 2.2% (1,533 employees). The proportion of departures of qualified staff was highest in Sales (6.3%) and Administration (4.3%). We are pleased that the lowest numbers of departures of qualified staff in 2005 were in Research (1.7%), Production (2.7%) and Marketing (3.1%).

This demonstrates overall that Roche can count on a stable pool of motivated employees. The risk of not achieving the projected results in business-critical areas as a result of significant numbers of regretted losses can still be regarded as minimal.

	2005	2004
Fluctuation	6.7%	6.1%
	4,556 employees	
'Regretted losses', i.e. fluctuation not initiated by Roche	2.2%	2.9%
	1,533 employees	

Performance culture at Roche

Since 2002 performance management has been emphasised as a key management instrument for generating sustainable added value at Roche. The link between corporate goals and the day-to-day business carried out by management and employees is forged using goal-setting management. In this process, the performance of management staff is measured in terms of their contribution to sustainable value creation within the company. All senior managers at Roche share a common goal: sustainably increasing enterprise value, as measured against OPAC (operating profit after cost of capital).

In 2005 the target group of this standardised performance management, which had originally been senior management (approx. 1,000 managers), was extended to include a larger population in specific critical segments. In 2004 and 2005 Roche refined a Group-wide standardised database and an integrated system. This provides goal-setting agreements with greater transparency, thus facilitating comparison and control. It also provides a broader factual basis for decisions regarding development, promotions and transfers.

In 94% of the affiliates, various goal-setting models for performance management or regular feedback on performance are in place. Altogether, 85% of the workforce have defined goals or set objectives, or regularly receive feedback on their performance.

Talent management and development at Roche

Business success at Roche, today and in the future, depends on the efforts of a large number of motivated and highly qualified employees and managers. What characterises performance culture at Roche is a high degree of individual responsibility. Regular feedback and development reviews are the cornerstones of performance management and career development. Staff are promoted to higher management positions on the basis of their leadership qualities and actual performance.

The succession management process for global key positions is well established and is reviewed at regular intervals. Succession planning was carried out in 2005, as it is every year, for the Group's 1,000 top managers at Group and Divisional level. The talent situation at Roche is very encouraging on the whole. In the Group, we have an average of 2.5 succession candidates for each key position (compared with 2.6 in 2004), which is in the best-practice range of 2.5–3.0 candidates per position. We are confident that our focus on performance management not only produces a sufficient number of internal candidates but ensures that they are of a very high standard. The risk of gaps in key positions causing a negative impact on business as a result of people leaving is therefore negligible. In 2005 there were only very few cases of vacancies among the top 1,000 positions not being filled within a short time. The processes of global succession planning and talent identification have been taken over and adapted in many countries. In 2005, 69% of Roche affiliates had a systematic succession planning process in place. 83% of our affiliates have put programmes into place for the systematic identification and development of talents.

Training and management development

	2005	*2004*
Total hours invested in training/staff development	2.14 million	1.85 million
Training time per employee	3.3 days (26.7 hours)	2.9 days (23 hours)

Employee development at Roche takes many forms. The primary tool in this process is the development plan. In 2005 a training or development plan that described concrete development prospects or steps was agreed to by 62% of all Roche employees. In addition to continuing education, the plan calls for strategic postings of talented employees abroad and a growing number of project assignments and job rotation.

In an effort to deal efficiently with peaks in the work volume, we have employed 3,006 employees on a temporary basis (as per end-2005) compared with 3,745 as per end-2004. In addition, we are currently training 959 apprentices and offering them the prospect of a career with a future.

In 2005 Roche introduced the Leadership Charter, a competence model for managers in the company, which was adapted by both Divisions. This model is based on the essential competencies that managers at Roche should possess. This gives Roche managers a consistent view of what is expected from them in terms of management competencies. Another achievement in 2005 was the new Executive Development Programme for senior management at Roche which will begin in 2006. The target group for this programme are the top 350 managers in the company.

Compensation and benefits

The remuneration policy adopted in 2004 is designed to support value creation and reinforce Roche's culture of performance and innovation, while delivering remuneration to meet employees' needs both now and in the future. The first awards were made under Roche Long Term, the new incentive programme for executives and key managers which was approved at the end of 2004. Participants receive either stock-settled stock appreciation rights or options to acquire Genussscheine, depending on tax efficiency. This marks a notable change, particularly in the USA, where incentives were traditionally based on American Depositary Receipts instead of the Genussscheine. The incentives for entitled participants worldwide are all based on the growth in the value of the Genussscheine. Thus, everyone involved has an immediate financial interest in increasing our company's value.

Following on from the two awards won in 2004 for Roche Connect, the employee stock ('Genussscheine') purchase plan, Roche has again received external recognition for its employee equity programmes. The Global Equity Organization (GEO) – a leading international organisation promoting share ownership for employees—awarded Roche their 2005 award for the most creative and innovative design for companies with more than 30,000 employees. This time the award was received for the new Roche Long Term incentive programme. In making the award the judges praised the way that Roche had identified and addressed differences in prior incentive plans, and in the changing competitive, accounting and tax environments, to arrive at the new global programme. With the launch of the plan in Argentina in 2005, a further country was included, bringing the total number of countries where the plan is offered to 41. Membership of the plan also continued to grow significantly, reaching over 11,600 (+22% vs. 2004: 9,067). This is a further indication that Roche employees identify with their company.

A number of new benefit plans and changes to existing plans were approved during the past year, including some changes to the pension plan for employees in Switzerland.

Promoting diversity in the workplace

Roche places a high value on diversity and seeks to benefit from it by integrating differences in perspective into the Group's activities. Roche employs people from over 190 countries. 60% of our affiliates are headed by general managers from the local country and the trend is rising. The affiliates' management teams, too, boast a consistently high proportion of staff from the local region. Talent pools worldwide feature a growing percentage of personnel from a variety of countries and continents. The 336 employees at our Corporate Center come from 23 countries.

Roche aims to be an attractive employer for both women and men and for this reason promotes diversity in its staff. 2005 was the fourth year in a row in which Roche recruited more women than men. Women account for 43% of the entire workforce. By contrast, only about 30% of the 4,556 employees who left Roche in 2005 were women. 32% of managers at Roche are female. Among our identified global key positions (mainly global senior and middle management) 19% of all incumbents are female.

Respect for the work/life balance is also a key concern at Roche. This follows different paths depending on the country, but is based on a straightforward principle: For instance, Roche supports its employees to enable them to deliver optimal performance in accordance with their family obligations. There are a variety of working arrangements at Roche: special working-time (e.g. part-time employment, flexitime, sabbaticals, parental leave for men and women), childcare facilities or other arrangements that help to reconcile the needs of career and family. All these measures comply with local legislation and in many cases go far beyond the legal requirements. Roche offers the option of part-time employment wherever the requirements of the job permit. Approximately 6% of our current employees work on a part-time basis (over 10% of them are men).

	2005	*2004*
Women as a percentage of the total workforce	43%	42%
Percentage of women in management positions	32%	31%
Number of women in the top 80 positions	7	5
Percentage of women among candidates for top management positions	16%	12%

Respecting human rights

Roche supports and respects human rights as defined by the United Nations and applies these principles consistently. The Compliance Officer monitors this policy throughout the Roche Group, and serves as a contact person for all employees. Further information on this topic can be found at www.roche.com/en/home/sus/sus_soc_comm_hum.htm

Two violations of employment policy principles were reported to the Roche Executive Committee or the Compliance Officer in 2005. As soon as these violations became known, measures were taken to deal with them appropriately.

SOURCE: 2005 Roche Annual Report

EXHIBIT 5-3 Safety and Environmental Disclosure by Roche

Corporate policy in the field of safety, health and environmental protection

Roche gears its corporate policy in the field of safety, health and environmental protection (SHE) to ISO 14 000 'Environmental Management Systems'. This policy is based on its own experience going back many years and on the commitment to sustainable development it has entered into in the context of the Charter of the International Chamber of Commerce (ICC), the World Business Council for Sustainable Development (WBCSD) and the chemical industry's Responsible Care Programme. The Roche Guidelines for the Assurance of Safety, Health and Environmental Protection apply throughout the Group. Each division has an eco-delegate who supports the organisation with concrete SHE projects. (Further information can be found at www.roche.com/en/home/sustainability/sus_env/sus_env_pol.htm).

Thanks to the professionalism and hard work of the staff involved, no Roche company was fined any significant amount for infringements of safety, health or environmental regulations. As this can evidently be accomplished without resorting to rigid management systems that consume considerable resources, there is no intention to attain ISO and/or EMAS certification centrally. Nevertheless, approximately nine local manufacturing companies (representing 30% of total production volume and 70% of chemical production volume) have decided at their own discretion to adopt such an approach, based on existing corporate policies.

SHE key figures[1]

	2005	*2004*
Investments in SHE (in millions of CHF)	240	160
Operating costs for SHE (in millions of CHF)	356	323
Occupational accidents	563	493
Work-related fatalities	0	0
Work-related accidents per million working hours	4.66	4.78
Workdays lost due to work-related accidents	6,629	5,051
Total number of workdays	15,083,631	12,871,583
Occupational illnesses	333	208
Occupational illnesses per million working hours	2.76	2.03
Workdays lost due to occupational illnesses	1,416	996
Occupational accidents (contractor firms)	133	129
Work-related accidents per million working hours (contractor firms)	11.6	13.9
Number of transport accidents (road)	2	1
Transport accidents per metric ton transported (road)	2.7×10^{-5}	6.0×10^{-6}
Total energy consumption (TJ/year)	12,515	11,899
CO_2 (t/year)	1,059,304	1,013,860
NO_x (t/year)	363	442
SO_2 (t/year)	151	261
VOCs (t/year)	604	1,010
Particulate matter (t/year)	50	63
Water consumption (in million cubic meters per year)	3.9	4.3
TOC (t/year)	1,830	1,344
Heavy metals (t/year)	1.463	2.231
Chemical waste (t/year)	38,380	42,722
Full-time SHE personnel	559	532
Total number of employees	68,218	64,594

[1]*Based on the CEFIC Health, Safety and Environment Reporting Guidelines (November 1998)*

Auditing

Safety, health and environmental protection audits ('SHE audits') are a key element in the Roche SHE management system. Corporate Safety, Health and Environmental Protection CSE has been carrying out systematic Group-wide SHE audits at company sites since 1980—to date, nearly 800 have been completed. In the year under review, a total of 24 production facilities, distribution centres, research sites and office buildings were audited in 15 countries. Once again, the results were good.

The audits focused primarily on the safe and environmentally responsible behaviour of employees in the workplace, as well as on the technical safety of processes and plants. The risk of dust explosions in production formulation as well as hazards in the handling of biologically active compounds and potentially contaminated diagnostic instruments have become increasingly important aspects of risk assessment.

Systematic audits of strategically important suppliers manufacturing chemical intermediates, finished products or exclusive equipment parts were also performed again. Eighteen of these audits were completed in the past year.

Scope of reporting

This year SHE reporting covers the Roche Group with the Pharmaceuticals and Diagnostics Divisions as well as Chugai and Genentech. As the scope of the reporting is the same as for the previous year, the key figures are directly comparable even in absolute terms. Owing to the different system boundaries, this is not possible for earlier years. The bulk of the data was collected in November on the basis of ten months and then extrapolated for the entire year. For SHE costs, as well as for accidents and incidents, the full-year data for 2005 have been collected. For details on safety, health and environmental protection, please see www.roche.com/en/home/sustainability/sus_env/sus_env_care.htm.

Results in brief

The Group's SHE performance in 2005 is being published as part of the Sustainability Report for the third year in succession. For more than ten years previously, it was published in a separate SHE Report. The Group's performance can be described as good on the whole. The trend for achieving the goals set in 2003 for energy consumption and greenhouse gas and VOC emissions is pointing in the right direction. New targets are intended to spur the Roche Group on to further improve its SHE performance.

In 2005 there were no reports throughout the entire Group of significant damage that affected either individuals or the environment. The number of occupational accidents was kept at a low level. The number of occupational illnesses per million working hours increased as well as the number of working days lost as a result of occupational illnesses. In line with the growth of the company in terms of headcount and number of sites as well as production volume, energy consumption has increased in absolute figures, but efficiency has improved in relation to sales revenue or number of employees. The same is true for the volume of greenhouse gas emissions. Other emissions in air and water have declined, as has the volume of chemical waste.

Goals and progress in safety, health and environmental protection

In 2003 Roche set itself a target of reducing the Group's greenhouse gas emissions—i.e. CO_2 from energy generation and halogenated hydrocarbons from air conditioning equipment and chillers—by 10 percent within five years.

Over the same period, energy consumption and emissions of volatile organic compounds (VOC) were to be reduced by the same percentage. Absolute values are based on Group sales in order to allow for the changes in the corporate structure and to enable comparisons to be made from the same baseline.

Owing to various measures to reduce emissions and the positive trend of Group sales revenue, the targets set for 2008 have already been reached. Roche is determined to make further efforts to confirm and improve these good results.

In 2004 additional SHE objectives were defined within the framework of a medium to long-term programme.

- a 20% reduction in the Roche Accident Rate (RAR) by 2010
- a 10% reduction in absences overall by 2015 (the relevant indicator will be recorded this year for the first time)
- a 10% improvement in the ecobalance by 2015 (this indicator will also be recorded this year for the first time)
- a further 10% reduction in consumption per employee by 2010 in line with the energy-saving goal
- annual target: no relevant fines in the SHE area

Eco-efficiency and expenditure for safety, health and environmental protection

Eco-efficiency

Eco-efficiency is an important element in promoting sustainable development. Eco-efficient production processes conserve resources such as raw materials and energy and reduce the impact on the environment by decreasing emissions and waste volumes. There is also a positive financial impact.

Roche quantifies eco-efficiency by calculating the Eco-Efficiency Rate (EER). The EER is an indicator of the ecological effect of expenditure in the environmental area. It is determined by means of readily measurable parameters (such as quantities of substances emitted or waste produced) as well as by financial figures such as sales and spending earmarked for environmental protection. The higher the EER, the greater the degree of eco-efficiency. For further details see www.roche.com/en/home/sustainability/sus_env/sus_env_care.htm.

Expenditures for SHE 2005[1]

	Roche Group
Investments for Safety and Health	120
for Environmental Protection	120
for SHE	240
Operating costs for SHE	356
Total expenditure for SHE	596

[1]*In millions of CHF*

Eco-Efficiency Rate (EER) (including Chugai abnd Genentech as of 2004)

	2005	*2004*	*2003*	*2002*	*2001*
Sales[1]	35,511	29,561	22,428	21,438	22,757
Environmental expenditure[1]	242	192	172	144	130
Environmental damage[2]	6.02	8.40	4.38	6.37	7.38
EER	24.39	18.34	29.28	23.28	23.72

[1]*In millions of CHF*
[2]*In millions of environmental damage units*

Key figures for eco-efficiency (including Chugai and Genentech as of 2004 and including other sources such as CO_2 emissions from external energy generation – hence not comparable with previous years)

Key figures	Unit	2005	2004	1992	Δ% 92/05
Energy	TJ/1 million sales	0.352	0.403	0.649	−45.8
CO_2	t/1 million sales	29.83	34.35	26.755	11.4
VOC	t/1 million sales	0.017	0.034	0.207	−91.8
Water	m^3/1 million sales	109.8	145.65	1,776	−93.8
TOC	t/1 million sales	0.051	0.045	0.199	−74.2
Chemical waste	t/1 million sales	1.08	1.45	1.72	−37.2

Ecobalance

To achieve the target of a 10% improvement in the Group's ecobalance, a criterion must be established that can be compared over a number of years. For this purpose, Roche employs a method of the Swiss Agency for the Environment (BAFU) in which environmental impact points are given to ecologically relevant parameters such as emissions, waste or energy consumption. The points are added up and expressed as a function of the number of employees. For the past year the ratio was 6.58, a figure which serves as the baseline for measuring any improvements.

Investment and operating costs

SHE expenditure in the Roche Group totalled 596 million Swiss francs in 2005. This amount comprises investments that were made in various areas as well as to operating costs. The calculation of SHE investments takes account of the full value of construction projects solely for the purpose of SHE, e.g. fire extinguisher systems, wastewater treatment or waste incineration plants. A portion of the investment was calculated for SHE arising out of other projects such as new production facilities or plants. In 2005 investments amounted to 120 million Swiss francs for environmental protection and to 120 million Swiss francs for safety and health.

SHE operating costs for the year under review amounted to 356 million Swiss francs. This includes current spending for services and personnel costs in the area of SHE. In 2005 the total number of employees working full-time in SHE in the Roche Group was 559. SHE expenses expressed as a proportion of total sales were 1.68% in 2005 (2004 1.62%).

Safety and health protection

Roche believes it is very important that employees can work in as healthy and safe a working environment as possible. Safety and health committees that focus on technical activities (production, laboratories, workshops) have been introduced at virtually all Roche subsidiaries. They cover all employees at a given site.

We are increasingly using the workplace as a way of reaching employees not only in order to help prevent potential work-related problems, but also to enhance staff health in general. Initiatives include offering preventive medicine measures as part of health monitoring programmes, motivating staff to increase their level of physical activity and providing information on healthy nutrition. In 2005 Roche began collecting data on general absences. The aim is to discover something about the causes of such absences and to seek possible improvements.

Accident statistics 2005

	Roche Group
No. of employees in Roche Group	68,218
No. of employees recorded for statistics	65,949
No. of workdays	15,083,631
No. of lost workdays recorded	6,629

(continued)

No. of occupational accidents recorded	563
Occupational accidents/1,000 employees	8.54
Accidents/million working hours (CEFIC)	4.66
RAR (Roche Accident Rate)[1]	0.099

[1]*See Glossary/ Explanatory notes at www.roche.com/en/home/sustainability/sus_env/sus_env_care.htm*

Occupational accidents

The figures for occupational accidents at Roche deteriorated slightly, though at a low level, in the year under review. The number of accidents involving Roche employees rose by 14.2% in 2005, the severity of accidents, i.e. the number of working days lost per accident as a result of accidents, increased by 12%, the Roche Accident Rate (RAR) rose by 12.5%.

In addition to Roche employees, a total of 133 employees from contractor firms were involved in accidents, i.e. 3.1% more than the previous year. The figure parallels the number of contractors, who in the past year worked mainly in the construction sector.

Occupational illnesses

The total number of occupational illnesses reported increased by 60%, 42% more working days were lost as a result of illness in the year under review. The types of illnesses reported over the last few years have remained unchanged. Locomotor disorders continue to be the most common. Most of these are back problems and especially inflammation of the upper extremities movements. Illnesses relating to the use of chemicals are limited to allergies; there were, however, no cases of intoxication.

Incidents

In 2005 no incident or accident with a significant impact on people or the environment was reported anywhere in the Roche Group. Owing to the small number of minor incidents, statistical analysis of such events is virtually impossible. Nevertheless, human error has been identified as the main cause.

Transport

As in previous years, road transport accounted for the bulk of all goods moved (81.6%), followed by air transport (14%). Only two incidents were reported in 2005: A lorry loaded with pharmaceutical active substance was stolen, and the cargo of another lorry was destroyed as a result of an accident.

Environmental protection

Energy consumption

Sustainable development also implies responsible use of the resource energy. Roche has therefore set itself two goals for reducing energy consumption in the company: Alongside the corporate target of reducing energy consumption by 10% in relation to sales within five years (by 2008), an additional longer-term goal has been formulated: to reduce consumption by a further 10% in relation to head-count for the period 2005–2010. There is a close correlation between energy consumption and CO_2 emissions. A decrease in energy consumption will therefore lead to a reduction in the release of greenhouse gases into the atmosphere.

In the year under review, the Roche Group needed 12,515 terajoules of energy from various sources to run its operations. This figure includes the energy required to run the Group companies and the fleet of vehicles as well as the energy consumed for business travel. In absolute terms, consumption has thus risen by 5.2% year-on-year; however, use per employee has actually fallen by 0.4%.

Greenhouse gases

Roche supports the efforts of the international community, as laid down in the Kyoto Protocol, to adopt a worldwide approach to controlling global warming and the greenhouse gases which are responsible for it. The Group-wide target of a 10% decrease in these emissions in relation to sales by 2008 through its own measures has already been reached. Trading of emissions certificates is currently not an option for us and is unlikely to become so in the foreseeable future.

Greenhouse gas emissions are measured in accordance with the Greenhouse Gas Protocol, which serves as the GRI standard. This requires us to account for direct emissions (power generation from fossil fuels, waste incineration, fleet of vehicles, business travel, wastewater treatment) as well as those from imported energy (electricity).

Greenhouse gas emissions at Roche mostly consist of CO_2 from power generation. Direct emissions from the combustion of fossil fuels account for about half of CO_2 output. Approximately 45% of all emissions comes from the CO_2 resulting from imported energy, in particular electricity. Roche was responsible for CO_2 emissions that amounted to 1,059,304 metric tons in 2005.

Halogenated hydrocarbons play a smaller role in greenhouse gas emissions. They are used in cooling and air conditioning installations as well as in fire extinguishing equipment. In 2005 these emissions mounted to 7.2 metric tons. The global warming potential of halogenated hydrocarbons is converted into CO_2 equivalents, using the conversion factors stipulated by the Intergovernmental Panel on Climate Change (IPCC), and added to the total quantity of CO_2 emissions.

The Roche climate strategy prescribes measures to lower emissions in both areas: the close link between power generation and CO_2 output means that energy saving measures will automatically lead to a reduction in CO_2 emissions. Corporate guidelines exist in relation to the use of halogenated hydrocarbons in cooling systems, outlining their gradual phasing-out from use by 2015. The 5.4% fall in the inventory of these compounds compared with the previous year illustrates the progress made in implementing these guidelines.

Specific contribution to the anthropogenic greenhouse effect, Roche Group					
	2005	*2004*	*2003*	*2002*	*2001*
CO_2 emissions from combustion (t)	1,059,304	1,014,000	334,000	326,000	348,000
CO_2 equivalents from halogenated hydrocarbon emissions [1] (t)	19,141	13,567	27,497	40,289	23,281
CO_2 equivalents total	1,078,445	1,027,567	361,497	366,289	371,281
Sales (in Swiss francs millions)	35,511	29,522	28,960	26,545	25,761
CO_2 equivalents (t)/1 million francs of sales	30.37	34.80	12.48	13.80	14.41

[1] *Mean global warming potential of halogenated hydrocarbons based on recalculation using conversion factor from I PCC*

Greenhouse effect—Roche's contribution

To calculate Roche's exact contribution to the greenhouse effect—expressed in CO_2 equivalents per million francs of sales—greenhouse gas emissions and sales serve as benchmarks. In 2005 this results in a value of 30.37, representing an improvement of 12.7% over 2004.

Waste

In 2005 the volume of waste from chemical production amounted to 38,380 metric tons, of which 37,116 metric tons were incinerated. The rest, including inert substances such as the incineration residues slag and ash, but also sewage sludge, was deposited in landfills. As waste or by-products, 5,674 metric tons of residual substances were recycled. The total of general waste came to 17,604 metric tons in 2005, of which 1,732 metric tons were construction waste, the majority of which was deposited in landfills. A total of 12,597 metric tons of general waste was deposited in landfills.

General waste in 2005 (in metric tons per year)

	Roche Group
Incineration	5,007
Landfill	12,597
of which construction waste	1,732
Total	17,604
Recycling	22,183

Chemical waste in 2005 (in metric tons per year)

	Roche Group
Incineration	37,116
Landfill	1,264
Total	38,380
Valorisation	5,674

Contaminated sites are the responsibility of the originator

Industrial activities can leave traces in the subsoil at the sites in question. The substances used at installations where chemicals are manufactured or processed often leave residues in the soil. In addition, by its very nature the synthesis of pharmaceutical substances results not only in the desired substance, but also in by-products which ultimately have to be disposed of as chemical waste. In the past, a lack of know-how and the appropriate technical resources meant that landfill dumping was the disposal method of choice. This approach was governed by legislation, as a result of which various local authorities have made suitable plots of land available for a charge, often for joint use by a number of companies.

Improved knowledge of geological characteristics and negative experiences with leaking earth formations have led to the discontinuation of landfills for the disposal of chemical waste. Contaminated sites are subject to increased monitoring and thorough examination in order to evaluate the associated risks and initiate the steps required for containment or remediation of the site in question.

Since Roche has always been a pharmaceutical company with relatively low volumes of chemical production, our total quantities of chemical waste and share of deposits in common landfill sites are as a rule small. As soon as a contaminated site is brought to our attention, we authorise the studies required to evaluate the associated risks. Depending on the outcome, steps for containment or, if necessary, remediation of the site are subsequently taken. This process is conducted in close collaboration with the competent authorities and in compliance with current legislation.

Where we have been solely responsible for a contaminated site or a landfill, we have promptly conducted an investigation and taken all the necessary remediation measures. Thus, for example, a number of contaminated sites, originating with companies prior to their acquisition by Roche, have been remediated. Conversely, Roche continues to assume responsibility and the costs of any necessary remediation of contaminated sites or landfills arising in connection with the Vitamins Division, which has been sold, and to bear the costs relating to such actions. Sizeable reserves have been set aside for this purpose.

In the case of landfill sites shared with other companies, collaboration is sought with all parties concerned in order to come up with solutions that are acceptable to all.

We accept responsibility for all waste deposited by Roche at its sites or in landfills, even if the method of disposal was widespread at the time and based on the relevant legal requirements.

Air emissions

In 2005 Roche was responsible for 514 metric tons of inorganic emissions in the form of sulphur dioxide (SO_2) and nitrogen oxides (NO_x). These substances were the result of incineration processes in energy generation. Air emissions of soot particulates and dust came to 50 metric tons. Emissions of volatile organic compounds (VOCs) came to 604 metric tons, of which 6% contain halogens.

Wastewater

The organic carbon load is measured as total organic carbon (TOC) after wastewater treatment. A total of 1,830 metric tons was discharged in 2004. In addition, heavy metal discharges in wastewater amounted to 1,463 metric tons.

Water consumption

Reporting on water consumption at Roche is based on the GRI Water Protocol. In 2004, 3.9 million metric tons of water were consumed, i. e. went into a product or were vaporised in cooling or air conditioning systems. 7.1 million metric tons of wastewater from chemical production were purified in wastewater treatment plants; 9.8 million metric tons represented water from cooling systems that could be returned to receiving waters after thorough analysis without further purification.

Water consumption (in million cubic metres per year)

	Roche Group
Withdrawal from various sources	20.8
Purified in treatment plants	7.1
Returned to receiving waters	9.8
Used	3.9

Special chemicals

In the year under review, a total of 4,346 metric tons of halogenated solvents were used by Roche production facilities and laboratories. Methylene chloride accounted for the greater part of this total, at around 98%. Production of the active substance used in the AIDS drug Fuzeon accounted for more than half the total used. The higher consumption reported in 2005 reflects the increase in production volume. Chloroform is used in small quantities only in laboratories.

In compliance with a Group Directive, all Roche affiliates supply figures regarding quantities and use of substances that, as precursor substances for chemical weapons, drugs or narcotics, are subject to international regulation. The quantities reported have remained at a consistently low level for a number of years. These compounds were used for the manufacture of Roche products. No such substances were sold to third parties.

SOURCE: 2005 Roche Annual Report

EXHIBIT 5-4 Auditor's Report on Sustainability Reporting by Roche

Independent Assurance Report on the Roche Group Sustainability Reporting 2005

To the Roche Corporate Sustainability Committee

We have been engaged to provide assurance on the Sustainability Reporting of Roche and its consolidated subsidiaries excluding Chugai and Genentech (the 'Group'), all for the year ended December 31, 2005. We have performed evidence-gathering procedures on (hereafter jointly referred to as the 'subject matter'):

- The SHE key figures of the table entitled 'most important SHE key figures' on page 86;
- Some selected social dimension information ('social data'); and
- The management and reporting for the preparation of the report and figures.

We have evaluated the subject matter against the following criteria (the 'evaluation criteria') described on page 58:

- The Roche Group internal sustainability reporting guidelines with respect to the Responsible Care Health, Safety and Environmental reporting guidelines published by the European Chemical Industry Council CEFIC and the 'Sustainability Reporting Guidelines 2002' published by the Global Reporting Initiative (GRI);
- The procedures by which the SHE data and the social data are prepared, collated and aggregated internally; and
- The control environment over the accuracy and completeness of the SHE data and the social data.

Our statement should be read in conjunction with the inherent limitations of accuracy and completeness for sustainability data, as well as in connection with the Roche Group internal reporting guidelines explained on page 88 and the 'scope of reporting' on page 88.

Roche Group is responsible for both, the subject matter and the evaluation criteria.

Our responsibility is to report on the internal reporting processes, data, and key figures for Social Dimension and SHE based on our evidence-gathering procedures in accordance with International Framework Standards for Assurance Engagements, approved December 2003 by the International Auditing and Assurance Standards Board (IAASB).

We planned and performed our evidence-gathering procedures to obtain a basis for our conclusions in accordance to the International Standard on Assurance Engagements (ISAE) 3000 'Assurance Engagements other than Audits or Reviews of Historical Information,' approved December 2003 by the IAASB.

The scope of our evidence-gathering procedures was to:

- Assess how Roche staff apply the Group internal sustainability reporting guidelines at the site level using a sample of five production sites covering the Pharmaceutical and Diagnostics divisions;
- Test the effectiveness of the internal sustainability reporting system used to collect SHE data and the social data from Group sites;
- Observe compliance with the Group internal sustainability reporting guidelines at selected sites; and
- Perform specific procedures to check, on a sample basis, the SHE data and the social data.

Our evidence-gathering procedures included the following work:

- Visiting selected sites in Austria, South Africa, Turkey and the US
- Interviewing the responsible staff for data collection and sustainability reporting on the sites we visited and on Group level;

- Assessing the data consolidation process on Group level;
- Reading and performing tests of the relevant documentation on a sample basis, including Group policies, management and reporting structures, documentation and systems used to collect, analyze and aggregate reported SHE data and social data; and
- Performing tests on a sample basis on evidence supporting selected SHE data and social data with regard to the reported data aggregation from the selected sites to Group level. However, we have not performed site visits at Chugai and Genentech.

In our opinion

- the Roche Group internal sustainability reporting guidelines are applied properly at the selected sites;
- the internal SHE reporting system to collect the SHE data is functioning as designed; and
- the social dimension reporting provides an appropriate basis for the disclosure of social dimension information, in all material respects, based on the evaluation criteria.

Based on our work described in this report, nothing has come to our attention that causes us not to believe that the procedures by which the SHE data and social dimension information was prepared, collated and aggregated and the control environment at the selected sites are based on established and accepted measurement and analytical methods and give a fair picture of the SHE and social dimension performance, in all material respects, based on the evaluation.

PricewaterhouseCoopers AG
Dr Thomas Scheiwiller
Jürg Hutter
Zurich, 16 January, 2006

SOURCE: 2005 Roche Annual Report

Special Disclosures for Nondomestic Financial Statement Users and Accounting Principles Used

Annual reports can include special disclosures to accommodate nondomestic financial statement users. Such disclosures include (1) "convenience restatements" of financial information to a nondomestic currency, (2) discussion of differences between accounting principles used in the primary financial statements and some other set of accounting principles, (3) limited restatements of financial results and position to a second set of accounting standards, and (4) a complete set of financial statements prepared in conformance with a second set of accounting principles. In countries where English is not the primary language, many firms translate their entire annual reports from the home-country language into English. Also, some firms prepare financial statements that conform to accounting standards more widely accepted than domestic standards (primarily IFRS or U.S. GAAP), or that conform both to domestic standards and a second set of accounting principles.

Exhibit 5-5 presents the limited restatement between IFRS and U.S. GAAP from the 2005 annual report of Novartis, a Swiss company listed on the New York Stock Exchange. The disclosure reconciles net income and stockholders' equity to U.S. GAAP, as required by the U.S. SEC. Accompanying this disclosure are eight additional annual report pages explaining the details of the IFRS/U.S. GAAP differences.

This level of detail is comparable to the financial statement disclosures made by many non-U.S. companies that have listed equity in the United States and must comply with SEC financial reporting requirements.[22]

EXHIBIT 5-5   Limited Restatement by Novartis

34. Significant differences between IFRS and United States generally accepted accounting principles (US GAAP)

The Group's consolidated financial statements have been prepared in accordance with IFRS, which as applied by the Group, differs in certain significant respects from US GAAP. The effects of the application of US GAAP to net income and equity are set out in the tables below.

	Notes	*2005*	*2004 Restated*	*2003 Restated*
		($ millions)	*($ millions)*	*($ millions)*
Net income under IFRS		**6,141**	**5,380**	**4,787**
US GAAP adjustments:				
Available-for-sale securities	34.1	278	(183)	(240)
Inventory impairment reversal	34.2	20	(43)	0
Associated companies	34.3	(6)	179	82
Intangible assets	34.4	(1,238)	(590)	(848)
Property, plant and equipment	34.5	53	77	69
Pensions and other post-employment benefits	34.6	(181)	(82)	(98)
Deferred taxes	34.7	178	423	48
Share-based compensation	34.8	(44)	(61)	(127)
Currency translation	34.9	0	(301)	0
Minority interests	34.10	(11)	(15)	(44)
Others			9	(5)
Net income under US GAAP		**5,190**	**4,793**	**3,624**
Basic earnings per share under US GAAP ($)		2.22	2.03	1.52
Diluted earnings per share under US GAAP ($)		2.22	2.02	1.50

---

[22]The SEC has proposed eliminating the reconciliation requirement for companies using IFRS. If approved, the change would go into effect in 2009.

	Notes	December 31, 2005	December 31, 2004 Restated
		($ millions)	($ millions)
Equity under IFRS		**33,164**	**31,315**
US GAAP adjustments:			
Available-for-sale securities	34.1	(24)	(64)
Inventory impairment reversal	34.2	(23)	(43)
Associated companies	34.3	25	6
Intangible assets	34.4	4,142	6,036
Property, plant & equipment	34.5	(409)	(558)
Pensions and other post-employment benefits	34.6	3,133	3,379
Deferred taxes	34.7	(1,438)	(2,082)
Share-based compensation	34.8	(96)	(118)
Minority interests	34.10	(174)	(138)
Total US GAAP adjustments		**5,136**	**6,418**
Equity under US GAAP		**38,300**	**37,733**

SOURCE: Novartis 2005 Annual Report

Corporate Governance Disclosures

Corporate governance relates to the internal means by which a corporation is operated and controlled—the responsibilities, accountability, and relationships among shareholders, board members, and managers designed to meet corporate objectives. That is, corporate governance is the system by which companies are directed and controlled. Among corporate governance issues are the rights and treatment of shareholders, the responsibilities of the board, disclosure and transparency, and the role of stakeholders.

Dallas provides a framework for understanding and assessing corporate governance in a country.[23] The four components of his framework are the market infrastructure, legal environment, regulatory environment, and informational infrastructure.

1. *Market infrastructure* includes ownership patterns (concentrated vs. dispersed), the extent to which companies are publicly listed, ownership rights, and the market for corporate control (takeovers). The structure of the board, traditions of board independence, and whether the chairperson and CEO roles are separated are related issues.

---

[23]George S. Dallas, *Governance and Risk* (New York: McGraw-Hill, 2004).

2. *Legal environment* includes the type of legal system and whether share-holder/stakeholders' rights are clearly defined and consistently and effectively enforced. Company laws and securities laws are part of the legal environment. Company laws cover how companies are formed and managed, and the rights and responsibilities of managers, directors, and shareholders. Securities laws relate to the issuance and trading of securities, including filing and disclosure requirements. In addition, general commercial laws are important in ensuring the rights of owners (including minority shareholders), creditors, and other stakeholders.

3. *Regulatory environment* is closely linked to the legal environment. Regulatory agencies are responsible for regulating markets to conform to existing laws. They ensure orderly and efficient markets and enforce public disclosure requirements.

4. *Informational infrastructure* pertains to the accounting standards used and whether they result in accurate, complete, and timely financial reporting. It also includes the structure of the auditing profession and professional standards for auditing practice and independence. The timely disclosure of reliable, publicly available information enables stakeholders to judge a company's governance effectiveness and its operating and financial performance.

Exhibit 5-6 summarizes the relationships of Dallas's governance framework. Note that the four components are interconnected.

As implied by Exhibit 5-6, internal corporate governance structures and practices vary around the world, reflecting differences in culture, traditional sources of finance, patterns of corporate ownership concentration, and legal systems and frameworks. To

EXHIBIT 5-6 Corporate Governance Framework (Dallas 2004)

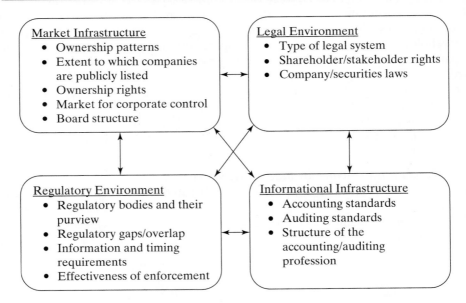

Market Infrastructure
- Ownership patterns
- Extent to which companies are publicly listed
- Ownership rights
- Market for corporate control
- Board structure

Legal Environment
- Type of legal system
- Shareholder/stakeholder rights
- Company/securities laws

Regulatory Environment
- Regulatory bodies and their purview
- Regulatory gaps/overlap
- Information and timing requirements
- Effectiveness of enforcement

Informational Infrastructure
- Accounting standards
- Auditing standards
- Structure of the accounting/auditing profession

EXHIBIT 5-7   Comparison of Germany and Japan vs. the United Kingdom and United States

Germany and Japan	*United Kingdom and United States*
• Consensus culture; cooperative relationships	• Competition; arm's-length relationships
• Network-oriented	• Market-oriented
• Bank-oriented: relatively more reliance on debt; stock exchange less important as source of finance	• Stock market-oriented: relatively more reliance on equity; stock exchange more important as source of finance
• Insider-dominated; concentrated ownership and relatively more influence of controlling shareholder(s)	• Outsider-dominated; dispersed ownership and relatively less influence of controlling shareholder(s)
• Stakeholder focused	• Shareholder focused
• Code (civil) law legal system	• Common law legal system

illustrate, Exhibit 5-7 lists some broad generalizations about Germany and Japan on the one hand, and the United Kingdom and the United States on the other. Because of these differences, governance mechanisms are historically weaker in Germany and Japan than in the United Kingdom and United States. However, corporate governance is being improved in many countries around the world, including Germany and Japan, as companies' governance practices receive increased attention from regulators, investors, and analysts.

The United States, United Kingdom, and Australia are among the growing number of countries that require listed companies to make specific corporate governance disclosures in their annual reports. The EU recently amended its Fourth and Seventh Directives (see Chapter 8) to require publicly traded European companies to provide corporate governance statements. The Organisation for Economic Cooperation and Development (OECD, also discussed in Chapter 8) issued its revised *Principles of Corporate Governance* in 2004, enunciating six basic principles of corporate governance.[24] Disclosure and transparency are covered in the fifth principle, shown in Exhibit 5-8.

EXHIBIT 5-8   OECD Fifth Principle of Corporate Governance: Disclosure and Transparency

The corporate governance framework should ensure that timely and accurate disclosure is made on all material matters regarding the corporation, including the financial situation, performance, ownership and governance of the company.

A. Disclosure should include, but not be limited to, material information on:
  1. The financial and operating results of the company.
  2. Company objectives.
  3. Major share ownership and voting rights.
  4. Remuneration policy for members of the board and key executives, and information about board members, including their qualifications, the selection process, other company directorships and whether they are regarded as independent by the board.

---

[24]Organisation for Economic Cooperation and Development, *OECD Principles of Corporate Governance* (2004), www.oecd.org/dataoecd/32/18/31557724.pdf. The six principles are (1) ensuring the basis for an effective corporate governance framework, (2) the rights of shareholders and key ownership functions, (3) equitable treatment of shareholders, (4) the role of stakeholders in corporate governance, (5) disclosure and transparency, and (6) the responsibilities of the board.

5. Related party transactions.
6. Foreseeable risk factors.
7. Issues regarding employees and other stakeholders.
8. Governance structures and policies, in particular, the content of any corporate code of policy and the process by which it is implemented.

B. Information should be prepared and disclosed in accordance with high quality standards of accounting and financial and nonfinancial disclosure.

C. An annual audit should be conducted by an independent, competent, and qualified auditor in order to provide an external and objective assurance to the board and shareholders that the financial statements fairly present the financial position and performance of the company in all material respects.

D. External auditors should be accountable to the shareholders and owe a duty to the company to exercise due professional care in the conduct of the audit.

E. Channels for disseminating information should provide for equal, timely, and cost-efficient access to relevant information by users.

F. The corporate governance framework should be complemented by an effective approach that addresses and promotes the provision of analysis or advice by analysts, brokers, rating agencies and others, that is relevant to decisions by investors, free from material conflicts of interest that might compromise the integrity of their analysis or advice.

SOURCE: *OECD Principles of Corporate Governance* (2004): 22–23
(www.oecd.org/dataoecd/32/18/31557724.pdf).

Disclosure is a key element in any system of good corporate governance. Exhibit 5-9 presents an example of a corporate governance disclosure from the annual report of the Swedish company Volvo. Included in its disclosure are statements about how governance is carried out, information about the board of directors, and a discussion of internal controls. Board of directors disclosures include the names of board members, how often the board meets, statements about independent directors, and the workings of the audit and remuneration committees. Volvo's disclosures are typical of many large multinational corporations.

EXHIBIT 5-9   Volvo Governance Disclosure

Corporate bodies in corporate governance

The governance and control of the Volvo Group is carried out through a number of corporate bodies. At General Meetings, the shareholders exercise their voting rights with regard, for example, to the composition of the Board of Directors of AB Volvo and election of external auditors. An Election Committee proposes candidates to serve as Board members, Board Chairman and external auditors. The Board is responsible for the Group's long-term development and strategy as well as controlling and evaluating the company's daily operations. In addition, the Board appoints the President of AB Volvo, who is also the Chief Executive Officer (CEO). The duties of the Board are partly exercised through its Audit Committee and its Remuneration Committee. The CEO is in charge of the daily management of the Group in accordance with guidelines and instructions provided by the Board. The presidents of the Group's eight business areas report to the CEO.

Swedish Code of Corporate Governance

Volvo applies the Swedish Code of Corporate Governance ("the Code").

Between July 1, 2005 and December 31, 2005 Volvo did not deviate from any of the Code's regulations that were applicable during this period. With reference to Swedish Corporate Governance Board's statement regarding a transition solution for the Code's rules about internal controls for financial reporting, the Board's report on internal control in accordance with Section 3.7.2 of the Code, within the scope of this corporate governance report, is limited to a description of how internal control is organized without making any statement about how well it functions and without a review by the auditors.

This corporate governance report has been examined by the company's auditors.

Election Committee

The Election Committee is the shareholders' body responsible for submitting to the Annual General Meeting the names of candidates to serve as Chairman and other members of the Board, the fees to be paid distributed among the Chairman, other members of the Board and any remuneration for work on the Board's committees. In the years in which election of auditors for Volvo shall be held, the Election Committee presents proposals for election of auditors and audit fees to be paid based on the preparations carried out by Volvo's Audit Committee.

In conjunction with the Election Committee proposing candidates for Chairman and the other members of the Board, the Election Committee shall comment on whether those persons who are proposed are to be considered as independent in relation to the company and company management as well as to large shareholders in the company. The Election Committee's proposal shall be presented to Volvo in sufficient time to be able to be included in the notice of the Annual General Meeting and at the same time on Volvo's website.

The Election Committee, which was appointed at Volvo's Annual General Meeting in 2005, comprises Volvo's Chairman Finn Johnsson, Lars Idermark, representing the Second Swedish National Pension Fund, Marianne Nilsson, representing Robur Funds, Curt Källströmer, representing Svenska Handelsbanken and Thierry Moulonguet, representing Renault SA. The Election Committee internally selected Lars Idermark as Chairman. The work of the Election Committee is governed by the instructions approved by the Volvo Annual General Meeting in 2005.

The Election Committee's proposal for the 2006 Annual General Meeting will be provided on Volvo's website.

The Board

In 2005, Volvo's Board of Directors consisted of eight members elected by the Annual General Meeting. In addition, the Board had three members and two deputy members appointed by employee organizations. The CEO, Leif Johansson, was a member of the Board.

The Board held six regular meetings and three extraordinary meetings in 2005.

The Board has adopted work procedures for its activities that contain rules pertaining to the distribution of work between the Board members, the number of Board meetings, matters to be handled at regular meetings of the Board and duties incumbent on the Chairman. In addition thereto, the work procedures contain directives concerning the tasks of the Audit Committee and the Remuneration Committee respectively. The Board has also issued written instructions specifying when and how information required to evaluate the company's and Group's financial position should be reported to the Board as well as the distribution of duties between the Board and the President and in what circumstances the Executive Vice President and Deputy CEO is to substitute for the CEO.

The Annual General Meeting decides on the fees to be paid to the Board members elected by the shareholders. The Annual General Meeting held on April 12, 2005 approved a total fee to the Board, for the time until the end of the next Annual General Meeting, of SEK 4,775,000. The fee was to be distributed among the Board Members according to the following. The Chairman of the Board receives a fee of SEK 1,350,000, the remaining members a total of SEK 2,700,000 to be distributed among the members as the Board decides. In addition, the Chairman of Audit Committee shall receive SEK 250,000 and the other two members of the Audit Committee SEK 125,000 each and the members of the Remuneration Committee SEK 75,000 each.

During the year, the Board reviewed the business plans and strategies for the various businesses in the Volvo Group. In addition thereto, the Board reviewed the financial positions of AB Volvo and the Volvo Group on a regular basis and acted in order to ascertain that there are efficient systems in order to follow-up and control the business and financial position of the Volvo Group. In connection therewith, the Audit Committee is responsible for preparing for the Board's work through quality assurance of the company's financial reporting through reviewing the interim reports and the annual report. The Board has met with the company's auditors during 2005. The Board also dealt regularly with matters involving divestments, acquisitions, the establishment of new operations, and matters related to investments in product renewal and product development in the Group's business areas.

The Board's work is mainly performed through the Board meetings and through meetings in the respective committees of the Board. In addition thereto, the chairman of the Board is in regular contact with the CEO in order to discuss the on-going business and to ensure that the decisions taken by the Board are executed.

An account of each Board member's age, education, main professional experience, other board memberships, ownership of shares in Volvo and the years of membership on the Volvo Board is presented on page 79.

During 2005, the Board performed its yearly evaluation of the Board's work. The written report has been submitted to the Election Committee.

The Board's composition and attendance at meetings 1 January 2005 - 31 December 2005

	Board	*Audit Committee*	*Remuneration Committee*
Finn Johnsson	9		4
Per-Olof Eriksson	9	4	
Patrick Faure	9		
Haruko Fukuda	9	4	
Tom Hedelius	9		4
Leif Johansson	9		
Louis Schweitzer	8		3
Ken Whipple	8	4	
Martin Linder, employee representative	9		
Olle Ludvigsson, employee representative	9		
Johnny Rönnkvist, employee representative	9		
Total number of meetings	**9**	**4**	**4**

Independence requirements

The Board of Directors of Volvo must meet independence requirements pursuant to the rules of the Stockholm Stock Exchange, the Code and NASDAQ's regulations, as well as the Sarbanes-Oxley Act. Below follows a short description of the rules of the Stockholm Stock Exchange and the Code. The independence requirements mainly mean that only one person from the company's management may be a member of the Board, that a majority of the Board shall be independent of the company and the company management and that at least two of the members that are independent from the company and the company's management shall also be independent of the company's major shareholders. In addition, the Code demands that a majority of the members in the Audit Committee shall be independent of the company and that at least one member shall be independent of the company's major shareholders. With regard to the Remuneration Committee, the Code sets the requirement that members of the Remuneration Committee, with the exception of the Board chairman if a member of the Remuneration Committee, shall be independent of the company and company management.

The Election Committee has informed the company about its proposal for Board members and the Board Chairman that it intends to present to the Volvo Annual General Meeting.

Considering the above demands regarding the Board's independence, the Election Committee has reported to the company the following understanding about the proposed

Board members independence from the company and the company management as well as the company's largest shareholders.

Finn Johnsson, Patrick Faure, Haruko Fukuda, Louis Schweitzer and Ken Whipple are all independent from the company and company management.

Leif Johansson, as Volvo's CEO, is not independent of the company and company management.

Tom Hedelius and Per-Olof Eriksson have been members of the Board of Volvo since January 19, 1994. Accordingly, they have, at the time of issuance of this corporate governance report, been members for more than 12 years and consequently in accordance with the Code are not to be considered independent of the company and company management.

Patrick Faure and Louis Schweitzer are employed by Renault SA and represent Renault SA on the company's Board. Since Renault SA controls more than 10% of the shares and votes in Volvo, these persons may not pursuant to the Code be considered as independent in relation to one of the company's major shareholders.

Audit Committee

In December 2002, the Board established an Audit Committee primarily for the purpose of overseeing the accounting and financial reporting processes and the audit of the financial statements. The Audit Committee is responsible for preparing the Board's work through quality assurance of the company's financial reporting through reviewing the interim reports and the annual report. In addition, the Audit Committee's task is to establish guidelines specifying what other services than audit the company may procure from the company's auditors and to provide guidelines for and decisions on transactions with companies and persons closely associated with Volvo. The Audit Committee is also responsible for evaluating the auditors' work as well as to provide the Election Committee with the results of the evaluation and to assist in preparing proposals for auditors.

In 2005, the Audit Committee comprised Board members Haruko Fukuda, Ken Whipple and Per-Olof Eriksson, Chairman. The Audit Committee held three ordinary meetings and one extraordinary meeting in 2005. The Audit Committee met with the external auditors and Head of Internal Audit at the ordinary meetings as well as the external auditors without the presence of the company management.

Remuneration Committee

In April 2003, the Board established a Remuneration Committee primarily for the purpose of preparing and deciding on issues relating to remuneration to senior executive in the Group. The duties of the Committee include presenting recommendations for resolution by the Board regarding terms of employment and remuneration for the President and Executive Vice President of AB Volvo, principles for remuneration, including pensions and severance payment for other members of the Group Executive Committee, and principles for variable salary systems, share-based incentive programs, pensions and severance payment for other senior executives in the Group. In addition the Remuneration Committee decides the individual terms of employment for the other members of the Group Executive Committee in accordance with the principles established by the Board.

In 2005, the Remuneration Committee comprised Board members Tom Hedelius, Louis Schweitzer and Finn Johnsson, Chairman. The Remuneration Committee held four meetings during the year.

Group Executive Committee

An account of their respective age, education, Board memberships, ownership of shares in Volvo, and year of joining Volvo for the CEO and each member of the Group Executive Committee is presented on page 77.

External auditing

Volvo's auditors are elected by the Annual General Meeting, for a period of four years. The current auditors were elected at the 2003 Annual General Meeting and the next election of auditors will be at the 2007 Annual General Meeting. Volvo's auditor is PricewaterhouseCoopers AB

("PwC"). Two PwC partners, Olof Herolf and Olov Karlsson, are responsible for the audit of Volvo. Olof Herolf has the primary responsibility.

The Auditors report their findings to the shareholders through the audit report, which they present to the Annual General Meeting of the shareholders. In addition, the auditors report the detailed findings made since the latest meeting to the Audit Committee at each of the ordinary meetings of the Audit Committee and to the full Board once a year.

PwC provides certain services to Volvo in addition to the audit. In 2005 such services included advice on the company's preparation and implementation of the testing and reporting of internal controls, which is mandatory under the provisions of the US Sarbanes-Oxley Act. PwC also advised on the transition to International Financial Reporting Standards. In addition, PwC provides tax advice and other audit related services to Volvo. When PwC is retained to provide services other than the audit, it is done in accordance with rules decided by the Audit Committee pertaining to preapproval of the nature of the services and the fees. Accordingly, Volvo believes that the provision of the additional services does not jeopardize PwC's independence.

For more detailed information concerning auditors' fees see Note 35 of the notes to the consolidated financial statements.

The organization of the internal control over financial reporting

Volvo has since long had an internal control organisation.

Going forward policies and procedures have to be adjusted so that they comply with Sarbanes-Oxley Act (SOX) requirements due to the fact that Volvo's shares are registered with the Securities & Exchange Commission (SEC) in the U.S. This adjustment shall ascertain that the work is following well-developed and documented processes. Policies and instructions shall be in accordance with internationally accepted standard and best practices, which are reassessed annually.

SOX section 404 requires an SEC registrant to include in its annual report a report on the internal control over financial reporting.

The report shall include a statement regarding the outcome of the company's evaluation of the effectiveness of the internal control over the financial reporting as at the end of the relevant financial year and shall be accompanied by an auditor's report. Volvo will make its first SOX 404 reporting in the filing of its U.S. annual report (Form 20) for the financial year ending at December 31, 2006.

During 2005, Volvo has continued the work initiated in 2004 on documenting relevant processes in order to ensure that the internal control over financial reporting is well functioning. In 2006, this work will be finalised, the relevant processes will be tested and an evaluation of the effectiveness of the internal control will be made.

In order to fulfil the requirements of SOX 404, an SEC registrant must implement a recognised internal control framework.

Volvo applies a framework introduced by the Committee of Sponsoring Organisations of the Treadway Commission (COSO). COSO consists of five interrelated components where a number of objectives have to be met in each component. The components are; control environment, risk assessment, control activities, information and communication and monitoring.

Volvo has an internal audit function (internrevision) of which the main responsibility is to ensure adherence to the internal control framework that the company applies. The internal audit function reports directly to the Group's CFO and has a dotted line to the Audit Committee of the Board of Directors.

Disclosure Committee

A Disclosure Committee was established in 2004. The Committee contributes to ensuring that Volvo fulfills its obligations according to applicable legislation as well as to listing rules to timely disclose to the financial market all material information that affects the share price.

The Committee comprises the heads of the corporate staffs, Corporate Finance, Internal Audit, Investor Relations, Corporate Legal and Financial Reporting.

Principles for remuneration and other employment terms for the Group Executive Committee

The Board has decided to propose to the 2006 Annual General Meeting principles for remuneration and other employment terms for the members of Volvo's Group Executive Committee ("Remuneration Policy") in accordance with Section 4.2.2 of the Code. The proposed principles comply with what has historically been applied within Volvo. The principles for remuneration and other employment terms can be summarized as follows.

The guiding principle is that remuneration and other employment terms for company management shall be competitive to ensure that Volvo can attract and retain skilled persons in the Group Executive Committee. The fixed salary shall be competitive and reflect the individual's area of responsibility and performance. In addition to the fixed salary a variable salary may be paid. A variable salary may amount to a maximum of 50% of the fixed annual salary and be based on the Volvo Group's and/or the executive's Group company's fulfillment of certain improvement goals. The improvement goals are decided by the Board of AB Volvo and may be related, for example, to operating income or cash flow. In addition to fixed and variable salary, normally other customary benefits, such as company car and company healthcare are provided. In individual cases, housing and other benefits are provided. In addition to pension benefits provided by law and collective agreements, the members of the Group Executive Committee domiciled in Sweden are offered a defined-contribution pension whereby the amount of the individual's pension comprises the premium paid and any return. In individual cases, other pension solutions may be considered. Members of the Group Executive Committee domiciled outside Sweden are offered pension solutions that are competitive in the country in which the person is domiciled. With regard to notice of termination of employment for members of the Group Executive Committee domiciled in Sweden, the notification period is 12 months if the company terminates the employment and six months if the individual terminates employment. In addition, the employee is entitled to a severance pay of 12 months' salary if Volvo terminates employment. In individual cases, other principles for notification periods and severance pay may be considered. Those members who are domiciled outside Sweden are offered terms in this respect that are competitive in the country in which the person is domiciled.

A more detailed account of remuneration to the President and principles for the remuneration to other senior executives is presented in Note 34 to the consolidated financial statements.

Outstanding share- and share-price-related incentive programs

An account of outstanding share- and share-price-related incentive programs is provided in Note 34 to the consolidated financial statements.

Internet Business Reporting and Disclosure

The World Wide Web is increasingly being used as an information dissemination channel, with print media often playing a secondary role. Electronic information dissemination is often less expensive than print media and offers instantaneous communication. The Web also allows interactive information dissemination in a manner not possible in print form.[25] Securities trading using the Internet has increased the demand for Web-based business and financial reporting. Individual investors are increasingly using the Web to trade and make investment decisions, and use the Web as an important information source.

One important development that will facilitate Web-based business reporting is eXtensible Business Reporting Language (XBRL). XBRL is a system for labeling

---

[25]See International Accounting Standards Committee, "Business Reporting on the Internet: A Discussion Paper Issued by the IASC Staff" (London: November 1999).

information or data. Data "tags," which work like barcodes, describe the financial information to which they are attached. Taxonomies are then developed for distributing, exchanging, and summarizing the information. This standard will be built into nearly all future releases of accounting and financial reporting software, and most users will not need to learn how to manipulate it directly in order to enjoy its benefits.[26] XBRL is on the verge of revolutionizing financial reporting. According to the Financial Executive Research Foundation, "XBRL will have as big an impact on commerce in the 21st century as double-entry bookkeeping had on the Industrial Revolution."[27]

The concept of a universal financial reporting computer language emerged in 1999. Soon after, Microsoft and IBM recognized both its potential and the need to develop a single standard cooperatively rather than each software company develop its own standard, which would undermine the very idea of making the language universal. Because it has been developed cooperatively, XBRL is free to software companies that wish to use it in their software, and extensions of XBRL developed for specific industries are free for downloading from the Internet.

Once implemented, XBRL will automatically translate any desired item of business information—words or numbers—so that the information need be entered only once. Once entered, this information can be used and worked with in many ways without being reformatted.[28] To quote one observer:

> Everyone along the information supply chain—investors, creditors, analysts, stock exchanges, auditors, regulators, policymakers and others—can quickly, accurately, easily and inexpensively access, validate, compare, analyze, slice, dice, mix, match, and manipulate information for any number of companies. It also allows the same body of data to automatically—instantly—find its proper place in spreadsheets, tax returns, business reports, annual reports, pie charts, government forms, Web sites and financial statements. No manual transcription. No mistakes along the way.[29]

XBRL taxonomies have already been developed for U.S. and German GAAP and for IFRS, enabling financial statement preparation according to these accounting standards. Taxonomies of other national GAAP are also being developed.

Stock exchanges, regulators, and public companies are increasingly using the Internet to provide financial statement users with immediate low-cost access to company information. For example, more and more stock exchanges now use electronic news services to provide immediate access to all announcements by listed companies. These services offer an important benefit to listed companies and investors: All listed company announcements, not just those deemed "newsworthy" by the financial press, are made publicly available on a single Web site. Appendix 1-2 lists Web site addresses for selected stock

---

[26]See Kurt Ramin, "Fair Values," *Business Excellence for the Intellectual Capital Investor* 1 (summer 2000): 13–16; Stanley Zarowin and Wayne E. Harding, "Finally, Business Talks the Same Language," *Journal of Accountancy* (August 2000): 24–30.
[27]Glenn Cheney, "XBRL: A Technology Whose Time Is Now," *Financial Executive* (March 2005): 45.
[28]Further information is available at www.xbrl.org.
[29]Glenn Cheney, "XBRL: A Technology Whose Time Is Now," *Financial Executive* (March 2005): 45.

exchanges around the world. Many stock exchange Web sites provide links to corporate Web addresses where examples of the disclosures discussed in this chapter can be found.

ANNUAL REPORT DISCLOSURES IN EMERGING-MARKET COUNTRIES

Disclosures in the annual reports of companies from emerging-market countries are generally less extensive and less credible than those of companies from developed countries. Insufficient and misleading disclosure and lax investor protection have been cited as factors contributing to the East Asia financial crisis of 1997.

The low disclosure levels in emerging-market countries are consistent with their systems of corporate governance and finance. Equity markets are not well developed, banks and insiders such as family groups supply most of the financing, and so in general there has been less demand for credible, timely public disclosure than in more developed economies.

However, investor demand for timely and credible information about companies in emerging-market countries has been growing. Regulators have responded to this demand by making disclosure requirements more stringent, and by stepping up their monitoring and enforcement efforts.

A recent study presents evidence supporting the view that disclosure levels and quality are lower in emerging-market countries than in developed countries.[30] The study is concerned with the "opacity" of earnings in 34 countries around the world.

EXHIBIT 5-10   Earnings Opacity Ranking of Countries from Least to Most

1. United States	13. Switzerland	25. South Africa[a]
2. Norway	14. Sweden	26. Malaysia[a]
3. Portugal	15. Germany	27. Italy
4. Brazil[a]	16. The Netherlands	28. Pakistan[a]
5. Belgium	17. Finland	29. Japan
6. Mexico[a]	18. Austria	30. Chile[a]
7. Canada	19. Thailand[a]	31. India[a]
8. France	20. Ireland	32. Indonesia[a]
9. Australia	21. Hong Kong[a]	33. South Korea[a]
10. Spain	22. Singapore[a]	34. Greece[a]
11. United Kingdom	23. Taiwan[a]	
12. Denmark	24. Turkey[a]	

[a] *Emerging market country*

SOURCE: Utpal Bhattacharya, Hazem Daouk, and Michael Welker, "The World Price of Earnings Opacity," *Accounting Review* 78, no. 3 (July 2003): 660.

---

[30]See Utpal Bhattacharya, Hazem Daouk, and Michael Welker, "The World Price of Earnings Opacity," *Accounting Review* 78, no. 3 (July 2003): 641–678.

Opacity, the opposite of transparency, may be thought of as the extent to which an earnings amount obscures real economic performance. Exhibit 5-10 ranks countries in terms of their overall earnings opacity from least to most opaque. Emerging-market countries tend to have the most opaque earnings. A further issue is having adequate numbers of accountants and auditors to monitor and enforce sound financial reporting systems. In general, there are far fewer accountants and auditors per capita in emerging-market countries than in developing countries, suggesting potential enforcement difficulties in emerging markets.[31]

Empirical evidence on disclosure practices in emerging-market countries was limited until recently. However, as these countries' stock markets and listed companies seek to increase their presence, researchers are developing more evidence on what these practices are and how they differ from those in developed countries.

IMPLICATIONS FOR FINANCIAL STATEMENT USERS AND MANAGERS

Financial statement users should expect wide variation in disclosure levels and financial reporting practices. Although managers in many firms continue to be strongly influenced by the costs of disclosing proprietary information, the levels of both mandatory and voluntary disclosure are increasing worldwide. Managers in traditionally low-disclosure countries should consider whether adopting a policy of enhanced disclosure might provide significant benefits for their firms. In addition, managers who decide to provide enhanced disclosures in areas investors and analysts consider important, such as segment and reconciliation disclosures, might obtain a competitive advantage over firms with restrictive disclosure policies. Further study of the costs and benefits of enhanced disclosure in international settings should provide important evidence in this area.

---

[31]Shahrokh M. Saudagaran and Joselito G. Diga, "Financial Reporting in Emerging Capital Markets: Characteristics and Policy Issues," *Accounting Horizons* 11 (June 1997): 41–64. Chapter 4 discusses this issue in the case of China.

SELECTED REFERENCES

ACCA, *Towards Transparency: Progress on Global Sustainability Reporting, 2004* (www.accaglobal.com/pdfs/environment/towards_trans_2004.pdf).

Adams, C., G. Frost, and S. J. Gray, "Corporate Environmental and Social Reporting," in *International Finance and Accounting Handbook*, ed. Frederick D. S. Choi, 3rd ed. (New York: John Wiley, 2003).

Bhattacharya, U., H. Daouk, and M. Welker, "The World Price of Earnings Opacity," *Accounting Review* 78, no. 3 (July 2003): 641–678.

Choi, F. D. S., and R. M. Levich, "Accounting Diversity," in *The European Equity Markets: The State of the Union and an Agenda for the Millennium,* ed.B. Steil (London: European Capital Markets Institute, 1996), pp. 259–320.

Francis, J. R., I. K. Khurana, and R. Pereira, "Disclosure Incentives and Effects on Cost of Capital Around the World," *Accounting Review* 80, no. 4 (October 2005): 1125–1162.

Frost, C. A., E. A. Gordon, and A. F. Hayes, "Stock Exchange Disclosure and Market Development: an Analysis of 50 International Exchanges," *Journal of Accounting Research* 44, no. 3 (June 2006): 437–483.

Frost, C. A., and K. P. Ramin, "Corporate Financial Disclosure: A Global Assessment," in *International Finance and Accounting Handbook*, ed. Frederick D. S. Choi, 3rd ed. (New York: John Wiley, 2003).

"The Good Company: A Survey of Corporate Social Responsibility," *Economist* (January 22, 2005): 1–22.

Gray, R., M. Javad, D. M. Power, and C. D. Sinclair, "Social and Environmental Disclosure and Corporate Characteristics: A Research Note and Extension," *Journal of Business Finance and Accounting* 28, no. 3 (April/May 2001): 327–356.

Hail, L. and C. Leuz, "International Differences in the Cost of Equity Capital: Do Legal Institutions Matter?" *Journal of Accounting Research* 44, no. 3 (June 2006): 485–531.

Khanna, T., K. G. Palepu, and S. Srinivasan, "Disclosure Practices of Foreign Companies Interacting with U.S. Markets," *Journal of Accounting Research* 42, no. 2 (May 2004): 475–508.

Kolk, A., "Sustainability, Accountability and Corporate Governance: Exploring Multinational's Reporting Practices," *Business Strategy and the Environment* (March 22, 2006), www3.interscience.wiley.com/cgi-bin/fulltext/112535145/PDFSTART.

LaPorta, R., F. Lopez-de-Silanes, A. Shleifer, and R. Vishny, "Legal Determinants of External Finance," *Journal of Finance* 52 (July 1997): 1131–1150.

Leuz, C., D. Nanda, and P. D. Wysocki, "Earnings Management and Investor Protection," *Journal of Financial Economics* 69, no. 3 (September 2003): 505–527.

Organisation for Economic Cooperation and Development, *OECD Principles of Corporate Governance* (2004),www.oecd.org/dataoecd/32/31557724.pdf.

Radebaugh, L. H., and D. L. Street, "Segmental and Foreign Operations Disclosure," in *International Finance and Accounting Handbook*, ed. Frederick D. S. Choi, 3rd ed. (New York: John Wiley, 2003).

Robb, S. W. G., L. E. Single, and M. T. Zarzeski, "Non-financial Disclosures across Anglo-American Countries," *Journal of International Accounting Auditing and Taxation* 10, no. 1 (2001): 71–83.

Saudagaran, S. M., and J. G. Diga, "Financial Reporting in Emerging Capital Markets: Characteristics and Policy Issues," *Accounting Horizons* 11 (June 1997): 41–64.

Saudagaran, S. M., and G. K. Meek, "A Review of Research on Financial Reporting in International Capital Markets," *Journal of Accounting Literature* 16 (1997): 127–159.

Stulz, R. M., and R. Williamson, "Culture, Openness, and Finance," *Journal of Financial Economics* 70, no. 3 (December 2003): 313–349.

DISCUSSION QUESTIONS

1. Briefly explain the difference between accounting measurement and accounting disclosure. Which of the two reporting processes do you think promises substantial innovative advances during the next 10 years? Why?
2. Why are multinational corporations increasingly being held accountable to constituencies other than traditional investor groups?
3. Should foreign companies seeking to issue securities in the United States be required to disclose as much as U.S. companies issuing securities in the United States? Critically evaluate the arguments presented in this chapter.
4. Accounting rules in Japan, France, and Germany now require disclosure of business-segment financial results. However, managers in these countries traditionally have been opposed to disclosing detailed segment information. Why have managers chosen to disclose relatively little information about the business segments of their companies, and why have accounting rules become more stringent despite their opposition?
5. What is the difference between voluntary disclosure and mandatory disclosure? Provide at least two explanations for the differences in managers' *voluntary* disclosure practices. Provide at least two explanations for the differences in managers' *mandatory* disclosure practices.
6. What is triple-bottom-line reporting, and why is it a growing trend among large multinational corporations? There are now few requirements for this type of reporting. Is more regulation necessary? Why or why not?
7. Do you expect to observe more or less voluntary disclosure by companies in emerging-market countries than in developed countries? Why?
8. Do you expect to observe more or less regulatory disclosure requirements in emerging-market countries than in developed countries? Why?
9. What are the two broad objectives for investor-oriented markets? Which of these do you think is more important? Present reasons for your response.
10. From the perspective of a securities market regulator, is more required disclosure always better than less? Why or why not?
11. Why are forecasts of revenues and income relatively uncommon?
12. What is corporate governance? Listed companies in some countries are required to disclose information about their corporate governance practices. Why might investors and analysts find such information useful?

EXERCISES

1. The chapter discusses the objectives of investor-oriented markets: investor protection and market quality. Transparent financial reporting is important for achieving these objectives.

   Required:
   a. What is transparent financial reporting?
   b. Explain how transparent financial reporting (a) protects investors and (b) improves market quality.
   c. The Hong Kong Exchange (HKE) is the second-largest stock market in Asia and the seventh-largest in the world. Go to the HKE Web site (www.hkex.com.hk) and learn about its financial reporting requirements.
      i. To what extent do these requirements promote transparent financial reporting?
      ii. To what extent do these requirements protect investors and promote market quality?

CHAPTER 5   Reporting and Disclosure   **193**

2. The forecast disclosures appearing in the 2005 annual report of Schering AG may be found at www.schering.de/html/en/50_media/download/_files/2005/fin_rep/annual/05GB_en.pdf (pp. 80-81).

   Required: Provide (1) a list of items forecasted (e.g., sales, profits, economic growth), (2) the forecast horizon (e.g., one year ahead, six months ahead, not stated), and (3) the amount forecasted (e.g., growth of U.S. $10 million, 10 percent growth). How might an investor or analyst use such forecast information? Overall, how useful is Schering AG's forecast disclosure? Why do you say so?

3. Exhibit 5-1 presents the business-segment and geographic-segment information of Lafarge, a French company that uses International Financial Reporting Standards (IFRS) in its consolidated financial statements.

   Required: Go to the Web site of the International Accounting Standards Board (www.iasb.org) and find the summary of IFRS 8, "Operating Segments." Compare the segment disclosures of Lafarge to the requirements of IFRS 8. Does Lafarge voluntarily report any information beyond the requirements of IFRS 8?

4. Exhibit 5-2 presents the employment disclosure of Roche.

   Required:
   a. How does the number of employees compare between the two periods presented? What are the reasons for the changes?
   b. What is the meaning of "regretted losses," and how do the statistics on regretted losses compare between the two periods presented?
   c. What is Roche's policy on diversity in the workplace, and what is the evidence that its policy is being achieved?
   d. What is the relevance of the above information for outside investors?

5. Exhibit 5-3 presents the safety and environmental disclosure of Roche.

   Required: Comparing the two years: (1) Which measures show an improved record of safety and environmental protection? (2) Which measures show a worse record of safety and environmental protection? What is your overall conclusion about Roche's safety and environmental record for the two years presented?

6. Exhibit 5-4 presents the independent assurance report on Roche's sustainability reporting. The auditor's engagement was carried out "in accordance with International Framework Standards for Assurance Engagements, approved December 2003 by the International Auditing and Assurance Standards Board (IAASB)."

   Required:
   a. Go to the World Wide Web and learn about the IAASB (www.ifac.org/IAASB).
   b. What is the difference between auditing and assurance engagements?
   c. Has Roche earned a "clean opinion" on its sustainability reporting?

7. Corporate social responsibility (CSR), as practiced by business, means many different things. Consider the following: "At one end of the broad span of CSR lie corporate policies that any well-run company ought to have in place anyway, policies that are called for on any sensible view of business ethics or good management practice. These include not lying to your employees, for instance, not paying bribes, and looking farther ahead than the next few weeks. At the other end of the range are the more ambitious and distinctive policies that differentiate between leaders and laggards in the CSR race—large expenditures of time and resources on charitable activities, for instance, or binding commitments to 'ethical investment,' or spending on environmental protection beyond what regulators demand."[32]

---

[32] "The Good Company: A Survey of Corporate Social Responsibility," *Economist* (June 22, 2005): 8.

Required:

a. Discuss the meaning of corporate social responsibility.

b. Do companies have an obligation to do more than the law requires? Why or why not?

c. Should companies report on their social responsibility activities? Why or why not?

d. What is the relevance of CSR disclosures for outside investors?

8. The Global Reporting Initiative (GRI) has developed a set of guidelines for social responsibility reporting.

Required: Go to the GRI Web site (www.globalreporting.org) and find its guidelines. The disclosure guidelines are categorized as indicators of economic, environmental, and social performance.

a. List the performance indicators recommended in the GRI guidelines.

b. Which category requires the most extensive disclosures?

c. Which areas of disclosure are likely to be the easiest and which areas are likely to be the most difficult to provide?

9. Exhibit 5-5 presents the reconciliation disclosures made by the Swiss company Novartis. As discussed in the chapter, the U.S. SEC requires foreign listed firms to present reconciliation information for material differences in net income (loss), and shareholders' equity.

Required:

a. Discuss why the SEC requires such reconciliation disclosures.

b. Specifically, how would U.S. investors use information presented in such disclosures?

c. Identify the three IFRS/U.S. GAAP accounting principles differences that have the largest impact on financial measures of Novartis for each of the periods shown.

10. Exhibit 5-9 is the corporate governance disclosure of the Volvo Group. Some of the disclosures relate to independence requirements for the board of directors and audit committee.

Required:

a. What is the independence requirement for the board of directors?

b. How many Volvo board members are independent? Does this number meet the requirement?

c. Certain board members are considered not independent. What criteria were used to determine that these board members are not independent? What rationale can you think of for viewing these board members as not independent?

d. How many members does the audit committee have? What percentage of these members is independent?

11. The Organisation for Economic Cooperation and Development (OECD) published its revised Principles of Corporate Governance in 2004.

Required: Obtain the document from the OECD Web site (www.oecd.org).

a. Outline the six sections of the OECD's corporate governance principles.

b. Discuss how these principles contribute to better corporate governance.

12. Exhibit 5-10 ranks 34 countries on earnings opacity. Which five countries have the most surprising placement? Why do you say so?

Case 5-1   Novartis

Exhibit 5-5 presents the limited restatement from Novartis Group's 2005 annual financial statement, reconciling net income and shareholders' equity from International Financial Reporting Standards (IFRS) to U.S. GAAP. Note 34 of the annual report further explains the details of the IFRS/U.S.GAAP differences in the reconciliation. ■

REQUIRED

1. Identify the three IFRS/U.S. GAAP accounting-principle differences that cause the largest differences in Novartis's 2005 net income prepared in conformance with the two sets of accounting principles.
2. Go to the Novartis Web site (www.novartis.com) and locate Note 34 in the 2005 annual report. For each of the three accounting-principle differences identified in requirement 1, discuss:
   a. treatment under IFRS
   b. treatment under U.S. GAAP
   c. effect of the accounting-principle difference on Novartis's net income in 2005 and 2004
   d. evaluation of the two treatments (IFRS vs. U.S. GAAP). Which treatment do you believe provides more useful information?
3. Does Novartis's discussion of differences between IFRS and U.S. GAAP in Note 34 provide enough information for the financial statement reader to critically compare the two sets of accounting principles? Present an explanation for your response.
4. Assume that Novartis forecasts (IFRS-based) net income of U.S. $6,300 million for the next year. Develop a forecast of Novartis's U.S. GAAP-based net income using information provided in Note 34. How reliable is your U.S. GAAP-based forecast, and how might you use the forecast?

Case 5-2   Seeing Is Believing

Greg Benson is a stock picker responsible for recommending Mexican securities for his brokerage firm's clients. He is often frustrated about the lack of credible information on companies in Mexico. "Everything is always so top secret," he says. "Any time I try to learn about a company's activities, all I hear is 'I wouldn't know what to tell you'." In Mexico, it seems, information is power. Trivial or not, information seems to be off-limits to anyone who is not an insider.

Greg knows that this secretiveness goes way back in Mexico's history. The Aztec rulers kept their subjects amazed by powerful deities who were both unpredictable and hard to understand. The Spanish followed many detailed bureaucratic rules but hardly ever shared them with ordinary Mexicans. After independence, the ruling political parties made sure that compromising information never got in the wrong hands.

Historian and novelist Hector Aguilar Camin has written, "In Mexico, powerful people have traditionally kidnapped information. Part of the process of democratization is freeing it." But "there is still a tendency to want to hold it hostage for some kind of benefit."[33]

Most economists believe that government secrecy made the 1994 currency collapse more severe because the Mexican government withheld vital macroeconomic statistics from the international banking community. Many worry now that secrecy will limit Mexico's economic growth. Yet pressure for transparency has grown along with an influx of foreign investors doing business in Mexico. The rise of opposition political parties and the growth of a free press have fueled a new debate over access to information.

"What good are all of these trends to me?" complains Greg. "I need better information now." ■

REQUIRED

1. Discuss at least five characteristics that predict relatively *low* disclosure levels in Mexico. Your response should be based on a review of the material presented in Chapters 2 and 4 and this chapter, in addition to the case information above.

2. Discuss characteristics or features that predict relatively *high* levels of disclosure in Mexico.

3. Accounting measurement and disclosure practices are improving (from an investor-protection viewpoint) in many emerging-market economies. What are some of the recent improvements in these areas in Mexico? Discuss the underlying factors that help explain why the improvements are occurring. Again, refer to the material presented in Chapters 2 and 4 in addition to the case information above.

---

[33]*Wall Street Journal*, September 10, 1998, p. 1a.

CHAPTER 6

Foreign Currency Translation

Examine the following performance data and related commentary. They are extracted from the management discussion section of the annual report of Alcan, a Canadian-based multinational company engaged in many aspects of the aluminum and packaging business. Alcan has bauxite holdings and aluminum production facilities in five countries, aluminum smelting and engineeered product operations in 11 countries, and packaging facilities in 30 countries.

NET INCOME (US$ millions)	2005	2004	2003
Included in income from continuing operations are:			
Foreign currency balance sheet translation	(86)	(153)	(326)
Other specified items:			
Synergy costs	(57)	(44)	(14)
Restructuring charges	(162)	(41)	(26)
Asset impairments	(314)	(66)	(4)
Goodwill impairment	(122)	(154)	(28)
Gains from nonroutine sales of assets, net	36	54	39
Tax adjustments	(37)	13	72
Novelis costs	(21)	(31)	—
Legal and environmental provisions	—	(7)	(17)
Pechiney financing-related gains (losses)	—	(2)	65
Purchase accounting and related adjustments	—	(122)	(32)
Other	7	(4)	(12)
Total Other Specified Items	(670)	(404)	43
Income from continuing operations	155	243	262
Income (loss) from discontinued operations	(26)	15	(159)
Cumulative effect of accounting change	—	—	(39)
Net Income	129	258	64

RESULTS OF OPERATIONS

In 2005, income from continuing operations was $155 million compared to $243 million in 2004 and $262 million in 2003.... In 2005 the company benefited from higher prices, an improved sales mix and increased volumes in the primary aluminum and engineered products businesses, as well as synergy gains associated with the Pechiney acquisition. LME prices were up on average 10% compared to 2004 reflecting further improvement in industry fundamentals. Offsetting these positive factors were substantially higher costs for key inputs across all businesses, the negative effects of the weaker U.S. dollar on operating costs and the loss of contribution from the rolled products businesses spun-off into Novelis on January 6, 2005....

Included in income from continuing operations for 2005 were foreign currency balance sheet translation losses of $86 million compared to losses of $153 million in 2004 and $326 million in 2003. Foreign currency balance sheet translation effects arise from translating monetary items (principally income taxes, operating working capital and long-term liabilities) denominated in Canadian and Australian dollars into U.S. dollars for reporting purposes. While lower than in the previous year, the translation losses in 2005 reflected the continuing weakening of the U.S. dollar against the Canadian dollar, partially offset by the appreciation of the U.S. dollar against the Australian dollar. ... Although balance sheet translation effects are primarily non-cash in nature, they can have a significant impact on the Company's net income....

In 2005, the Company recorded other income (net of other expenses) of $4 million. The most significant items included: interest revenue of $73 million of which $33 million related to income tax refunds; gains of $32 million resulting from disposal of businesses and investments; asset impairment charges of $28 million related principally to certain Bauxite and Alumina project costs in Australia and certain Engineered Products assets primarily in Germany and Brazil; losses of $49 million related to the marking-to-market of derivatives; and foreign exchange losses of $10 million.

The paragraphs in the preceding commentary suggest a variety of ways in which Alcan's reported performance, which the company chooses to report in U.S. dollars,[1] is impacted by foreign currencies. The first paragraph suggests that the company benefitted from increased sales volumes in the primary aluminum and engineered products businesses. At the same time, the company experienced higher costs for key inputs across all its businesses. To understand the effects of exchange rates on both revenues and expenses, assume that Alcan is selling engineered products, priced in Canadian dollars, to an importer in Italy. As Italy is a member of the European Union,[2] the Italian

---

[1] The dollar is the currency most used to set prices for raw materials and the currency most used to conduct trade. See, Robert J. Samuelson, "Why the Buck Is on the Edge," *Newsweek*, December 11, 2006, p. 49.
[2] At the time of this writing, members of the European Union include Austria, Belgium, Cyprus, Czech Republic, Denmark, Estonia, Finland, France, Germany, Greece, Hungary, Ireland, Italy, Latvia, Lithuania, Luxembourg, Malta, the Netherlands, Poland, Portugal, Slovakia, Slovenia, Spain, Sweden and the U.K.

importer must exchange euros for dollars to effect payment. Assume further that the value of the Canadian dollar unexpectedly falls in relation to the euro. The Italian buyer benefits from having to exchange fewer euros for dollars than would otherwise be the case, effectively lowering the price of Alcan's products. If the euro does not change in value relative to other national currencies, this would make Alcan's products cheaper relative to similar aluminum products supplied from other countries. The result would be increased demand for Alcan's products in Italy and other EU countries adopting the euro as their national currency, and hence, larger sales volume than originally anticipated. Similarly, an unexpected fall in the value of the dollar relative to the euro would have an adverse impact on Alcan's future expenses, such as planned advertising expenditures in Italy and all EU countries mentioned above. The effect of changes in foreign currency values on a firm's future sales and future costs is referred to as *economic exposure* and is a major concern of business entities engaged in global commerce and investment. Strategies to minimize the risk of loss arising from unexpected changes in the prices of foreign currencies are the subject of Chapter 11.

The negative effects of the weaker U.S. dollar on Alcan's reported operating costs as well as the currency effects reported in the remaining two paragraphs of Alcan's commentary are the principal subject of this chapter. These effects relate to a process in which accounts denominated in foreign currency are translated to Alcan's reporting currency, U.S. dollars. The currency effects on Alcan's operating costs result from translating operating expenses denominated in, say, Canadian dollars to a devalued U.S. dollar. A Canadian-dollar expense will translate to a higher U.S. dollar equivalent, other things being the same. The currency effects reported in the second paragraph occur because Alcan prepares a single set of financial statements that consolidates the results of all of its subsidiaries to afford its readers a more holistic view of Alcan's total operations, both foreign and domestic. Consolidated statements, in turn, require that financial statements expressed in foreign currency be translated to the reporting currency of the parent company. The currency effects disclosed in the third paragraph relate to foreign currency transactions, that is, sales, purchase, borrowing, or lending transactions denominated in foreign currency.

Do reported currency effects resulting from the translation process matter? Some studies suggest that they do not.[3] Recent studies suggest that they do. Bartov and Bodner, for example, provide evidence of a lagged relation between changes in currency values and stock returns but not for all translation methods employed by reporting entities.[4] Pinto initially reported that lagged values of per share foreign currency translation adjustments are useful in predicting year-to-year changes in earnings per share. More recently, she found that the currency translation adjustments, when

[3]See T.D. Garlicki, F.J. Fabozzi and R. Fonfeder, "The Impact of Earnings Under FASB 52 on Equity Returns," *Financial Management* (Autumn 1987): 36–44; B.S. Soo and L. Gilbert Soo, "Accounting for the Multinational Firm: Is the Translation Process Valued by the Stock Market?" *The Accounting Review*, Vol. 69(October 1994): 617–637; D. Dhaliwal, K. Subra and R. Trezevant, "Is Comprehensive Income Superior to Net Income as a Measure of Firm Performance?" *Journal of Accounting and Economics*, Vol. 26(1999): 43–67; Steven F. Cahan, Stephen M. Courtnay, Paul L. Gronewoller and David Upton, "Value relevance of Mandated Comprehensive IncomeDisclosures," *Journal of Business Finance and Accounting*, Vol. 27 Nos. 9&10(2000): 1273–1301.
[4]See E. Bartov, "Foreign Currency Exposure of Multinational Firms: Accounting Measures and Market Valuation," Contemporary Accounting Research, 14 (1997): 623–652.

measured properly, are value relevant in providing a measure of a firm's exchange rate exposure.[5]

> Financial executives also attach mixed importance to gains and losses associated with foreign currency translation. While some assert that accounting gains and losses generated by accounting measurements have no impact on their operational decisions,[6] others express great concern over the distortions they cause in reported corporate earnings. History is replete with instances of management expending resources to minimize the effects of balance sheet translation gains and losses on reported performance.[7] Differing opinions notwithstanding, all agree that foreign currency translation can have significant effects on reported earnings.

What are the implications of the foregoing discussion? To properly interpret the reported performance of multinational companies, statement readers must understand the nature of foreign exchange gains and losses, how these numbers are derived, and what they mean. To facilitate this understanding, we begin with an examination of why foreign currency translation is necessary.

REASONS FOR TRANSLATION

Companies with significant overseas operations prepare consolidated financial statements that give statement readers an aggregate view of the firm's global operations. To accomplish this, financial statements of foreign subsidiaries that are denominated in foreign currencies are restated to the reporting currency of the parent company. The process of restating financial information from one currency to another is called *translation*.

Many of the problems associated with currency translation stem from the fact that the relative value of foreign currencies are seldom fixed. The variability of rates of exchange, combined with the differences between translation methods and the different treatments of translation gains and losses, make it difficult to compare financial results from one company to another, or in the same company from one period to the next. In these circumstances, it becomes a challenge for multinational enterprises to make informative disclosures of operating results and financial position as per Alcan's example. Financial analysts find that interpreting such information can also be quite challenging, and these problems extend to evaluating managerial performance.

There are three additional reasons for foreign currency translation: recording foreign currency transactions, measuring a firm's exposure to the effects of currency gyrations, and communicating with foreign audiences of interest.

---

[5]Jo Ann M. Pinto, "Foreign Currency Translation Adjustments as Predictors of Earnings Changes," *Journal of International Accounting, Auditing and Taxes* (2001): 51–69 and "How Comprehensive is Comprehensive Income? The Value Relevance of Foreign Currency Translation Adjustments," *Journal of International Financial Management and Accounting*, Vol. 16 No. 2(2005): 97–122.
[6]Richard K. Goeltz, "International Accounting Harmonization: The Impossible (And Necessary?) Dream," *Accounting Horizons* (March 1991): 86.
[7]For example, see Carol O. Houston, "Translation Exposure Hedging Post SFAS No. 52," *Journal of International Financial Management and Accounting* (Summer & Autumn 1990): 145–169.

Foreign currency transactions, such as the purchase of merchandise from China by a Canadian importer, must be translated because financial statements cannot be prepared from accounts that are expressed in more than one currency. How, for example, is one to prepare cost of goods sold when purchases are denominated in Chinese renminbi, Russian rubles, and Argentine pesos?

For accounting purposes, a foreign currency asset or liability is said to be exposed to currency risk if a change in the rate at which currencies are exchanged causes a change in the parent (reporting) currency equivalent. The measurement of this exposure will vary depending on the translation method a firm chooses to employ.

Finally, the expanded scale of international investment increases the need to convey accounting information about companies domiciled in one country to users in others. This need occurs when a company wishes to list its shares on a foreign stock exchange, contemplates a foreign acquisition or joint venture, or wants to communicate its operating results and financial position to its foreign stockholders. Many Japanese companies translate their entire financial statements from Japanese yen to U.S. dollars when reporting to interested American audiences. This practice is often called a *convenience translation* and is described more fully in Chapter 9.

BACKGROUND AND TERMINOLOGY

Translation is not the same as conversion, which is the physical exchange of one currency for another. Translation is simply a change in monetary expression, as when a balance sheet expressed in British pounds is restated in U.S. dollar equivalents. No physical exchange occurs, and no accountable transaction takes place as it does in conversion.

Foreign currency balances are translated to domestic currency equivalents by the foreign exchange rate: the price of a unit of one currency expressed in terms of another. The currencies of major trading nations are bought and sold in global markets. Linked by sophisticated telecommunications networks, market participants include banks and other currency dealers, business enterprises, individuals, and professional traders. By providing a venue for buyers and sellers of currencies, the foreign exchange market facilitates the transfer of international payments (e.g., from importers to exporters), allows international purchases or sales to be made on credit (e.g., bank letters of credit that permit goods to be shipped in advance of payment to an unfamiliar buyer), and provides a means for individuals or businesses to protect themselves from the risks of unstable currency values. (Chapter 11 gives a fuller discussion of exchange risk management.)

Foreign currency transactions take place in a spot, forward, or swap market. Currency bought or sold spot must normally be delivered immediately, that is, within two business days. Thus, an American tourist departing for Geneva can purchase and immediately receive Swiss francs by paying the spot rate in dollars. Spot market rates are influenced by many factors, including different inflation rates among countries, differences in national interest rates, and expectations about the direction of future rates. Spot market exchange rates may be direct or indirect.[8] In a direct quote, the exchange rate specifies the number of domestic currency units needed to acquire a unit of foreign currency. For example, on a given day, the U.S. dollar price of an Indian rupee might be $0.02232. An indirect quote is the reciprocal of the direct quote: the

---

[8]For a daily listing of foreign exchange rates, visit www.ozforex.com.

price of a unit of the domestic currency in terms of the foreign currency. In this example, it would take approximately 44.8 rupees to acquire 1 U.S. dollar.

Translation of foreign currency balances is straightforward with either direct or indirect quotes. Domestic currency equivalents are obtained by multiplying foreign currency balances by direct exchange rate quotations or dividing foreign currency balances by indirect quotations. To illustrate, suppose that the cash balance of a U.S. subsidiary located in Bombay, India, on January 31 is INR1,000,000. The direct (spot) exchange rate on that date is $0.02232. The U.S. dollar equivalent of the rupee cash balance on January 31 is $22,320, calculated by translating INR1,000,000 in either of the following ways:

$$INR1,000,000 \times \$0.02232 = \$22,320 \text{ or}$$

$$INR1,000,000 \div INR44.8 = \$22,320$$

Transactions in the forward market are agreements to exchange a specified amount of one currency for another at a future date. Quotations in the forward market are expressed at either a discount or a premium from the spot rate, or as outright forward rates. We will illustrate the latter. Moreover, spot and forward rates may often include bid and ask quotes. The bid quote is what the foreign exchange dealer would pay you for foreign currency; the ask quote is the rate at which the dealer would sell you foreign currency. If spot Swiss francs are offered at $0.8318, while the six-month forward franc is offered at $0.8462, six-month forward Swiss francs are selling at a premium of 3.4 percent in the United States, calculated as follows: forward premium (discount) = (forward rate – spot rate)/spot rate × 12/n, where n is the number of months in the forward contract. Thus, ($0.8462 – $0.8318)/$0.8318 × 12/6 = 3.4%. Had the Swiss franc been quoted indirectly, the premium would have been determined as: forward premium (discount) = (spot rate – forward rate)/forward rate × 12/n, or (CHF1.2022 – CHF1.1818)/1.1818 × 12/6 ≈ 3.4%.

Spot and forward quotes for major foreign currencies on any business day can be found in the business section of many major newspapers. Exhibit 6-1 contains spot and

EXHIBIT 6-1   Sample of Spot and Forward Foreign Exchange Quotes

Currency	Foreign Currency in Dollars		Dollars in Foreign Currency	
	Bid	Ask	Bid	Ask
British pound	1.9585	1.9590	.5105	.5104
1 month	1.9574	1.9598	.5102	.5109
3 months	1.9578	1.9604	.5101	.5108
6 months	1.9576	1.9604	.5101	.5108
EU euro	1.3251	1.3256	.7546	.7543
1 month	1.3261	1.3279	.7540	.7530
3 months	1.3297	1.3310	.7520	.7513
6 months	1.3343	1.3361	.7494	.7484
Japanese yen	.008557	.0085535	116.86	116.91
1 month	.008590	.008600	116.41	116.27
3 months	.008660	.008660	115.47	115.47
6 months	.008760	.008760	114.15	114.15
Swiss franc	.8321	.8318	1.2017	1.2022
1 month	.8347	.8353	1.1971	1.1980
3 months	.8390	.8397	1.1909	1.1918
6 months	.8455	.8462	1.1817	1.1827

forward quotes for selected currencies. A more comprehensive listing can be found by clicking on www.federalreserve.gov.

A swap transaction involves the simultaneous spot purchase and forward sale, or spot sale and forward purchase, of a currency. Investors often use swap transactions to take advantage of higher interest rates in a foreign country while simultaneously protecting themselves against unfavorable movements in the foreign exchange rate. As an example, should interest rates in the United States exceed those in Switzerland, Swiss investors could purchase dollars in the spot market and invest them in higher-yielding U.S. dollar debt instruments, say six-month U.S. Treasury notes. In doing so, however, Swiss investors would lose this yield advantage if the U.S. dollar loses value relative to the Swiss franc in the six-month period. To protect against this possibility, Swiss investors could simultaneously sell the dollars they expect to receive in six months at the guaranteed forward rate. Such swap transactions work well when the U.S./Swiss interest rate differential is greater than the discount on forward dollars (i.e., the difference between spot and six-month forward dollars). Over time, foreign currency traders will eliminate this difference, thereby creating interest rate parity.

Exhibit 6-2 defines the foreign currency translation terms used in this chapter.

EXHIBIT 6-2   Glossary of Foreign Currency Translation Terms

attribute. The quantifiable characteristic of an item that is measured for accounting purposes. For example, historical cost and replacement cost are attributes of an asset.

conversion. The exchange of one currency for another.

current rate. The exchange rate in effect at the relevant financial statement date.

discount. When the forward exchange rate is below the current spot rate.

exposed net asset position. The excess of assets measured or denominated in foreign currency and translated at the current rate over liabilities measured or denominated in foreign currency and translated at the current rate.

foreign currency. A currency other than the currency of the country being referred to; a currency other than the reporting currency of the enterprise being referred to.

foreign currency financial statements. Financial statements that employ foreign currency as the unit of measure.

foreign currency transactions. Transactions (e.g., sales or purchases of goods or services or loans payable or receivable) whose terms are stated in a currency other than the entity's functional currency.

foreign currency translation. The process of expressing amounts denominated or measured in one currency in terms of another currency by use of the exchange rate between the two currencies.

foreign operation. An operation whose financial statements are (1) combined or consolidated with or accounted for on an equity basis in the financial statements of the reporting enterprise, and (2) prepared in a currency other than the reporting currency of the reporting enterprise.

forward exchange contract. An agreement to exchange currencies of different countries at a specified rate (forward rate) at a specified future date.

functional currency. The primary currency in which an entity does business and generates and spends cash. It is usually the currency of the country where the entity is located and the currency in which the books of record are maintained.

(continued)

EXHIBIT 6-2 Glossary of Foreign Currency Translation Terms (*Continued*)

historical rate. The foreign exchange rate that prevailed when a foreign currency asset or liability was first acquired or incurred.

local currency. Currency of the particular country being referred to; the reporting currency of a domestic or foreign operation being referred to.

monetary items. Obligations to pay or rights to receive a fixed number of currency units in the future.

reporting currency. The currency in which an enterprise prepares its financial statements.

settlement date. The date on which a payable is paid or a receivable is collected.

spot rate. The exchange rate for immediate exchange of currencies.

transaction date. The date at which a transaction (e.g., a sale or purchase of merchandise or services) is recorded in a reporting entity's accounting records.

translation adjustments. Translation adjustments result from the process of translating financial statements from the entity's functional currency into the reporting currency.

unit of measure. The currency in which assets, liabilities, revenue, and expense are measured.

THE PROBLEM

If foreign exchange rates were relatively stable, currency translation would be no more difficult than translating inches or feet to their metric equivalents. However, exchange rates are seldom stable. The currencies of most industrialized countries are free to find their own values in the currency market. For an illustration of the volatility of the exchange rates of selected countries, examine the data compiled by the Federal Reserve Bank at www.federalreserve.gov/releases/H10/hist/.

Fluctuating exchange values are particularly evident in Eastern Europe, Latin America, and certain parts of Asia. Currency fluctuations increase the number of translation rates that can be used in the translation process and create foreign exchange gains and losses. Currency movements are also closely tied to local rates of inflation, the subject of Chapter 7.

FINANCIAL STATEMENT EFFECTS OF ALTERNATIVE TRANSLATION RATES

The following three exchange rates can be used to translate foreign currency balances to domestic currency. First, the *current rate* is the exchange rate prevailing as of the financial statement date. Second, the *historical rate* is the prevailing exchange rate when a foreign currency asset is first acquired or a foreign currency liability first incurred. Finally, the *average rate* is a simple or weighted average of either current or historical exchange rates. As average rates are simply variations of current or historical rates, the following discussion focuses on the latter two.

What are the financial statement effects of using historical as opposed to current rates of exchange as foreign currency translation coefficients? Historical exchange rates generally preserve the original cost equivalent of a foreign currency item in the domestic currency statements. Suppose that a foreign subsidiary of a U.S. parent company acquires an item of inventory for 1,000 foreign currency (FC) units when the exchange rate (indirect quote) is FC2 = $1. This asset would appear in the U.S. consolidated statements at $500. Now assume that the exchange rate changes from FC2 = $1 to FC4 = $1 by the next financial statement date and that the inventory item is still on hand. Will the U.S. dollar equivalent of the inventory now change to $250? It would not. As long as we translate the original FC1,000 cost at the rate that prevailed when the asset was acquired (historical rate), it will appear in the U.S. financial statements at $500, its historical cost expressed in U.S. dollars. Use of historical exchange rates shields financial statements from foreign currency *translation gains or losses*, that is, from increases or decreases in the dollar equivalents of foreign currency balances due to fluctuations in the translation rate between reporting periods. The use of current rates causes translation gains or losses. Thus, in the previous example, translating the FC1,000 piece of inventory at the current rate (FC4 = $1) would yield a translation loss of $250 [(FC1,000 ÷ 2) − (FC1,000 ÷ 4)].

Here we must distinguish between *translation* gains and losses and *transaction* gains and losses, both of which are exchange gains and losses. Foreign currency transactions occur whenever an enterprise purchases or sells goods for which payment is made in a foreign currency or when it borrows or lends foreign currency. Translation is necessary to maintain the accounting records in the currency of the reporting enterprise.

Of the two types of transaction adjustments, the first, *gains and losses on settled transactions*, arises whenever the exchange rate used to book the original transaction differs from the rate used at settlement. Thus, if a U.S. parent company borrows FC1,000 when the exchange rate is FC2 = $1 and then converts the proceeds to dollars, it will receive $500 and record a $500 liability on its books. If the foreign exchange rate rises to FC1 = $1 when the loan is repaid, the U.S. company will have to pay out $1,000 to discharge its FC1,000 debt. The company has suffered a $500 conversion loss.

The second type of transaction adjustment, *gains or losses on unsettled transactions*, arises whenever financial statements are prepared before a transaction is settled. In the preceding example, assume that the FC1,000 is borrowed during year 1 and repaid during year 2. If the exchange rate prevailing at the financial statement date (end of year 1) is FC1.5 = $1, the dollar equivalent of the FC1,000 loan will be $667, creating an exchange loss of $167. Until the foreign currency debt is actually repaid, however, this *unrealized* exchange loss is similar in nature to a translation loss because it results from a restatement process.

Exhibit 6-3 lays out the differences between transaction and translation gains and losses. Differences in exchange rates in effect at the various dates shown cause the various types of exchange adjustments.

When considering exchange gains and losses, it is critical to distinguish between transaction gains and losses and translation gains and losses. A realized (or settled) transaction creates a real gain or loss. Accountants generally agree that such a gain or loss should be reflected immediately in income. In contrast, translation adjustments (including gains or losses on unsettled transactions) are unrealized or paper items. The appropriate accounting treatment of these gains or losses is less obvious.

An informed reader of consolidated financial statements must understand three major issues associated with fluctuating exchange rates:

1. What exchange rate was used to translate foreign currency balances to domestic currency?

EXHIBIT 6-3 Types of Exchange Adjustments

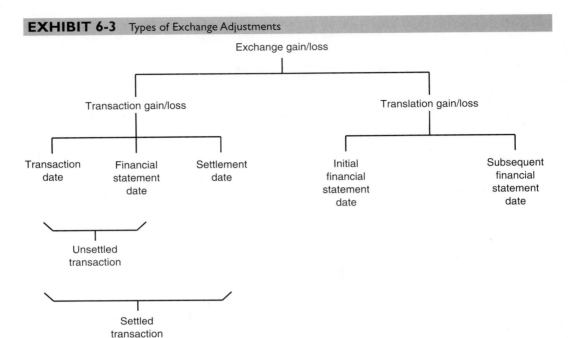

2. Which foreign currency assets and liabilities are exposed to exchange rate changes?
3. How are translation gains and losses accounted for?

These issues are examined in the balance of this chapter.

Foreign Currency Transactions

The distinguishing feature of a foreign currency transaction is that settlement is effected in a foreign currency. Thus, foreign currency transactions occur whenever an enterprise purchases or sells goods for which payment is made in a foreign currency or when it borrows or lends foreign currency. As an example, a company purchasing inventories denominated in Saudi Arabian riyals suffers an exchange loss should the riyal gain in value before settlement.

A foreign currency transaction may be *denominated* in one currency but *measured* in another. To understand why, consider first the notion of *functional currency*. The functional currency of an entity is the primary currency in which it transacts business and generates and spends cash. If a foreign subsidiary's operation is relatively self-contained and integrated within the foreign country (i.e., one that manufactures a product for local distribution), it will normally generate and spend its local (country-of-domicile's) currency. Hence, the local currency (e.g., euros for the Belgian subsidiary of a U.S. parent) is its functional currency. If a foreign entity keeps its accounts in a currency other than the functional currency (e.g., the Indian accounts of a U.S. subsidiary whose functional currency is really British pounds rather than Indian rupees), its functional currency is the third-country currency (pounds). If a foreign entity is merely an extension of its parent company (e.g., a Mexican assembly operation that receives components from its U.S. parent and ships the assembled product back to the United States), its functional currency is the U.S. dollar. Exhibit 6-4 identifies circumstances justifying use of either the local or parent currency as the functional currency.

EXHIBIT 6-4 Functional Currency Criteria

Economic Factors	Circumstances Favoring Local Currency as Functional Currency	Circumstances Favoring Parent Currency as Functional Currency
Cash flows	Primarily in the local currency and do not impact parent's cash flows	Directly impact parent's cash flows and are currently remittable to the parent
Sales price	Largely irresponsive to exchange rate changes and governed primarily by local competition	Responsive to changes in exchange rates and determined by worldwide competition
Sales market	Largely in the host country and denominated in local currency	Largely in the parent country and denominated in parent currency
Expenses	Incurred primarily in the local environment	Primarily related to productive factors imported from the parent company
Financing	Primarily denominated in local currency and serviced by local operations	Primarily from the parent or reliance on parent company to meet debt obligations
Intercompany	Infrequent, not extensive	Frequent and extensive transactions

Adapted from: Financial Accounting Standards Board, *Statement of Financial Accounting Standards No. 52* (Stamford, CT: FASB, 1981), Appendix A.

To illustrate the difference between a transaction being denominated in one currency but measured in another, assume that a U.S. subsidiary in Hong Kong purchases merchandise inventory from the People's Republic of China payable in renminbi. The subsidiary's functional currency is the U.S. dollar. In this instance, the subsidiary would measure the foreign currency transaction—denominated in renminbi—in U.S. dollars, the currency in which its books are kept. From the parent's point of view, the subsidiary's liability is denominated in renminbi but measured in U.S. dollars, its functional currency, for purposes of consolidation.

FAS No. 52, the authoritative U.S. pronouncement on accounting for foreign currency, mandates the following treatment for foreign currency transactions:[9]

1. At the date the transaction is recognized, each asset, liability, revenue, expense, gain, or loss arising from the transaction shall be measured and recorded in the functional currency of the recording entity by use of the exchange rate in effect at that date.
2. At each balance sheet date, recorded balances that are denominated in a currency other than the functional currency of the recording entity shall be adjusted to reflect the current exchange rate.

On this basis, a foreign exchange adjustment (i.e., gain or loss on a settled transaction) is necessary whenever the exchange rate changes between the transaction date and the settlement date. Should financial statements be prepared before settlement, the accounting adjustment (i.e., gain or loss on an unsettled transaction) will equal the difference between the amount originally recorded and the amount presented in the financial statements.

The FASB rejected the view that a distinction should be drawn between gains and losses on settled and unsettled transactions, because such distinctions cannot be

---

[9]Financial Accounting Standards Board, *FASB Statement No. 52*, Stamford, CT: FASB, par. 15.

applied in practice. Two accounting treatments for transactions gains and losses are possible.

Single-Transaction Perspective

Under a single-transaction perspective, exchange adjustments (both settled and unsettled) are treated as an adjustment to the original transaction accounts on the premise that a transaction and its settlement are a single event. The following example illustrates this treatment.

On September 1, 2008, a U.S. manufacturer sells, on account, goods to a Swedish importer for 1 million Swedish krona (SEK). The dollar/krona exchange rate is $0.14 = SEK 1, the krona receivable are due in 90 days, and the U.S. company operates on a calendar-year basis. The krona begins to depreciate before the receivable is collected. By the end of the month, the dollar/krona exchange rate is $0.13 = SEK 1; on December 1, 2008, it is $0.11 = SEK 1. (These transactions are posted in Exhibit 6-5.)

In this illustration, until the account is collected, the initial dollar amount recorded for both accounts receivable and sales is considered an estimate to be subsequently adjusted for changes in the dollar/krona exchange rate. Further depreciation of the krona between the financial statement date (September 1) and the settlement date (December 1) would require additional adjustments. In the Alcan example at the beginning of the chapter, the effect of exchange rate changes illustrated in Exhibit 6-5 would have impacted consolidated revenues.

Two-Transaction Perspective

Under a two-transaction perspective, collection of the krona receivable is considered a separate event from the sale that gave rise to it. In the preceding illustration, the export sale and related receivable would be recorded at the exchange rate in effect at that date. Depreciation of the krona between September 1 and December 1 would

---

EXHIBIT 6.5   U.S. Company's Record: Single-Transaction Perspective

		Foreign Currency	U.S. Dollar Equivalent
Sept. 1, 2008	Accounts receivable	SEK 1,000,000	140,000
	Sales	SEK 1,000,000	140,000
	(To record credit sale)		
Sept. 30, 2008	Sales		10,000
	Accounts receivable		10,000
	(To adjust existing accounts for initial exchange rate change: SEK 1,000,000 $0.14 − SEK 1,000,000 $0.13)		
Dec. 1, 2008	Retained earnings		20,000
	Accounts receivable		20,000
	(To adjust accounts for additional rate change: SEK 1,000,000 × $0.13 minus SEK 1,000,000 × $0.11)		
Dec. 1, 2008	Foreign currency	SEK 1,000,000	110,000
	Accounts receivable	SEK 1,000,000	110,000
	(To record settlement of outstanding foreigncurrency receivables)		

EXHIBIT 6-6 U.S. Company's Record: Two-Transaction Perspective

	Foreign Currency	*U.S. Dollar Equivalent*
Sept. 1, 2008 Accounts receivable	SEK 1,000,000	$140,000
Sales	SEK 1,000,000	$140,000
(To record credit sale at Sept. 1, 2008 exchange rate)		
Sept. 30, 2008 Foreign exchange loss		10,000
Accounts receivable		10,000
(To record effect of initial rate change)		
Dec. 1, 2008 Foreign currency	SEK 1,000,000	110,000
Foreign exchange loss		20,000
Accounts receivable	SEK 1,000,000	130,000
(To record settlement of foreign currency receivable)		

result in an exchange loss (i.e., loss on an unsettled transaction), and currency receivable on December 1, 2008, at the even lower exchange rate would result in a further exchange loss (i.e., loss on a settled transaction). See Exhibit 6-6.

In the interest of uniformity, FAS No. 52 requires the two-transaction method of accounting for foreign currency transactions. Gains and losses on settled and unsettled transactions are included in the determination of income; thus, for example, the gains and losses illustrated in Exhibit 6-6 are the foreign currency effects explained in the third paragraph of the Alcan example that began this chapter. Major exceptions to this requirement occur whenever (1) exchange adjustments relate to certain long-term intercompany transactions, and (2) transactions are intended and effective as hedges of net investments (i.e., hedges of foreign operations' exposed net asset/liability positions) and foreign currency commitments. (The notion of an exposed asset or liability position is described further on.)

FOREIGN CURRENCY TRANSLATION

Companies operating internationally use a variety of methods to express, in terms of their domestic currency, the assets, liabilities, revenues, and expenses that are stated in a foreign currency. These translation methods can be classified into two types: those that use a single translation rate to restate foreign balances to their domestic currency equivalents and those that use multiple rates. Exhibit 6-7 summarizes the treatment of specific balance sheet items under these translation methods.

Single-Rate Method
The single-rate method, also known as the current-rate method, has long been popular in Europe. It applies a single exchange rate, the current or closing rate, to all foreign currency assets and liabilities. Foreign currency revenues and expenses are generally translated at the exchange rates prevailing when these items are recognized. For convenience, however, revenues and expenses are typically translated by an appropriately weighted average of current exchange rates for the period.

EXHIBIT 6-7   Exchange Rates Employed in Different Translation Methods for Specific Balance Sheet Items

	Current	Current Noncurrent	Monetary Nonmonetary	Temporal
Cash	C	C	C	C
Accounts receivable	C	C	C	C
Inventories				
Cost	C	C	H	H
Market	C	C	H	C
Investments				
Cost	C	H	H	H
Market	C	H	H	C
Fixed assets	C	H	H	H
Other assets	C	H	H	H
Accounts payable	C	C	C	C
Long-term debt	C	H	C	C
Common stock	H	H	H	H
Retained earnings	*	*	*	*

*Note: C, current rate; H, historical rate; and *, residual, balancing figure representing a composite of successive current rates.*

Under the single-rate method, the financial statements of a foreign operation (viewed by the parent as an autonomous entity) have their own reporting domicile: the local currency environment in which the foreign affiliate does business. The consolidated statements preserve the original financial statement relationships (such as financial ratios) of the individual consolidated entities because all foreign currency financial statement items are translated by a constant. That is, consolidated results reflect the currency perspectives of each entity whose results go into the consolidated totals, not the single-currency perspective of the parent company. Some people fault this method on the grounds that using multiple currency perspectives violates the basic purpose of consolidated financial statements.

For accounting purposes, a foreign currency asset or liability is said to be *exposed* to exchange rate risk if its parent currency equivalent changes owing to a change in the exchange rate used to translate that asset or liability. Given this definition, the current-rate method presumes that all local currency assets are exposed to exchange risk as the current (vs. the historical) rate changes the parent currency equivalent of all foreign currency assets every time exchange rates change. This seldom accords with economic reality, because inventory and fixed asset values are generally supported by local inflation.

Consider the following example. Suppose that a foreign affiliate of a U.S. multinational corporation (MNC) buys a tract of land at the beginning of the period for FC1,000,000. The exchange rate (historical rate) was FC1 = $1. Thus, the historical cost of the investment in dollars is $1,000,000 (FC1,000,000 ÷ FC1). Due to changing prices, the land rises in value to FC1,500,000 (unrecognized under U.S. GAAP), while the exchange rate declines to FC1.4 = $1 by the period's end. If this foreign currency asset were translated to U.S. dollars using the current rate, its original dollar value of $1,000,000 would now be recorded as $714,286 (FC1,000,000 ÷ FC1.4), implying an exchange loss of $285,714. Yet the increase in the fair market value of the land indicates that its current value in U.S. dollars is really $1,071,285 (FC1,500,000 ÷ FC1.4). This suggests that translated asset values make little sense unless local price-level adjustments are made first. Also, translation of a historical cost number by a current market-determined exchange rate (e.g., FC1,000,000 ÷ FC1.4 = $714,286) produces a result that resembles neither historical cost ($1,000,000) nor current market value ($1,071,285).

Finally, translating all foreign currency balances by the current rate creates translation gains and losses every time exchange rates change. Reflecting such exchange adjustments in current income could significantly distort reported measures of performance. Many of these gains and losses may never be fully realized, because changes in exchange rates often reverse direction.

Multiple-Rate Methods

Multiple-rate methods combine current and historical exchange rates in the translation process.

Current-Noncurrent Method

Under the current–noncurrent method, a foreign subsidiary's current assets (i.e., assets that are usually converted to cash within a year) and current liabilities (i.e., obligations that mature within a year) are translated into their parent company's reporting currency at the current rate. Noncurrent assets and liabilities are translated at historical rates. Income statement items (except for depreciation and amortization charges) are translated at average rates applicable to each month of operation or on the basis of weighted averages covering the whole period being reported. Depreciation and amortization charges are translated at the historical rates in effect when the related assets were acquired.

Unfortunately, this method often does not square with reality. Using the year-end rate to translate current assets implies that all foreign currency cash, receivables, and inventories are equally exposed to exchange risk; in other words, will be worth more or less in the parent currency if the exchange rate changes during the year. This is simply not true. For example, if the local price of inventory can be increased after a devaluation, its value is protected from currency exchange risk. On the other hand, translation of long-term debt at the historical rate shifts the impact of fluctuating currencies to the year of settlement. Many consider this to be at odds with reality, since analysts are always assessing the current realizable values of a firm's long-run obligations. Moreover, current and noncurrent definitions are merely a classification scheme, not a conceptual justification, of which rates to use in translation.

Monetary-Nonmonetary Method

The monetary-nonmonetary method also uses a balance sheet classification scheme to determine appropriate translation rates.[10] Monetary assets and liabilities (i.e., claims to and obligations to pay a fixed amount of currency in the future) are translated at the current rate. Nonmonetary items (fixed assets, long-term investments, and inventories) are translated at historical rates. Income statement items are translated under procedures similar to those described for the current-noncurrent framework. Unlike the

---

[10]This method was originally proposed in Samuel R. Hepworth, *Reporting Foreign Operations* (Ann Arbor: University of Michigan Press, 1956).

current-noncurrent method, this method views monetary assets and liabilities as exposed to exchange rate risk. Since monetary items are settled in cash, use of the current rate to translate these items produces domestic currency equivalents that reflect their realizable or settlement values. It also reflects changes in the domestic currency equivalent of long-term debt in the period in which exchange rates change, producing a more timely indicator of exchange rate effects.

Note, however, that the monetary-nonmonetary method also relies on a classification scheme to determine appropriate translation rates. This may lead to inappropriate results. For example, this method translates all nonmonetary assets at historical rates, which is not reasonable for assets stated at current market values (e.g., investment securities and inventory and fixed assets written down to market). Multiplying the current market value of a nonmonetary asset by a historical exchange rate yields an amount in the domestic currency that is neither the item's current equivalent nor its historical cost. This method also distorts profit margins by matching sales at current prices and translation rates against cost of sales measured at historical costs and translation rates.

Temporal Method

With the temporal method,[11] currency translation does not change the *attribute* of an item being measured; it only changes the *unit of measure*. In other words, translation of foreign balances restates the currency denomination of these items, but not their actual valuation. Under U.S. GAAP, cash is measured in terms of the amount owned at the balance sheet date. Receivables and payables are stated at amounts expected to be received or paid when due. Other assets and liabilities are measured at the money prices that prevailed when the items were acquired or incurred (historical prices). Some, however, are measured at the prices prevailing as of the financial statement date (current prices), such as inventories under the lower of cost or market rule. In short, a time dimension is associated with these money values.

In the temporal method, monetary items such as cash, receivables, and payables are translated at the current rate. Nonmonetary items are translated at rates that preserve their original measurement bases. Specifically, assets carried on the foreign currency statements at historical cost are translated at the historical rate. Why? Because historical cost in foreign currency translated by a historical exchange rate yields historical cost in domestic currency. Similarly, nonmonetary items carried abroad at current values are translated at the current rate because current value in foreign currency translated by a current exchange rate produces current value in domestic currency. Revenue and expense items are translated at rates that prevailed when the underlying transactions took place, although average rates are suggested when revenue or expense transactions are voluminous.

When nonmonetary items abroad are valued at historical cost, the translation procedures resulting from the temporal method are virtually identical to those produced by the monetary-nonmonetary method. The two translation methods differ only if other asset-valuation bases are employed, such as replacement cost, market value, or discounted cash flow.

---

[11]This method was originally proposed in Leonard Lorensen, "Reporting Foreign Operations of U.S. Companies in U.S. Dollars," Accounting Research Study No. 12 (New York: American Institute of Certified Public Accountants, 1972).

Because it is similar to the monetary-nonmonetary method, the temporal method shares most of its advantages and disadvantages. In deliberately ignoring local inflation, this method shares a limitation with the other translation methods discussed. (Of course, historical cost accounting ignores inflation as well!)

All four methods just described have been used in the United States at one time or another and can be found today in various countries. In general, they produce noticeably different foreign currency translation results. The first three methods (i.e., current rate, current-noncurrent, and monetary-nonmonetary) are predicated on identifying which assets and liabilities are exposed to, or sheltered from, currency exchange risk. The translation methodology is then applied consistent with this distinction. The current-rate method presumes that the entire foreign operation is exposed to exchange rate risk since all assets and liabilities are translated at the year-end exchange rate. The current-noncurrent-rate method presumes that only the current assets and liabilities are so exposed, while the monetary-nonmonetary method presumes that monetary assets and liabilities are exposed. In contrast, the temporal method is designed to preserve the underlying theoretical basis of accounting measurement used in preparing the financial statements being translated.

Financial Statement Effects

Exhibits 6-8 and 6-9 highlight the financial statement effects of the major translation methods described. The balalce sheet of a hypothetical Mexican subsidiary of a

EXHIBIT 6-8 Mexican Subsidiary Balance Sheet

	Pesos	U.S. Dollars before Peso Devaluation ($ 0.11 = MXN1)	U.S. Dollars after Peso Depreciation ($ 0.09 = MXN1)			
			Current Rate	*Current– Noncurrent*	*Monetary– Nonmonetary*	*Temporal*
Assets						
Cash	3,000	$ 330	$ 270	$ 270	$ 270	$ 270
A/R	6,000	660	540	540	540	540
Inventories	9,000	990	810	810	990	810[a]
F/A (net)	18,000	1,980	1,620	1,980	1,980	1,980
Total	36,000	$3,960	$3,240	$3,600	$3,780	$3,600
Liabilities and Owners' Equity						
S-T payables	9,000	$990	$ 810	$ 810	$ 810	$ 810
L-T debt	12,000	1,320	1,080	1,320	1,080	1,080
O/E	15,000	1,650	1,350	1,470	1,890	1,710
Total	36,000	$3,960	$3,240	$3,600	$3,780	$3,600
Accounting exposure (MXN)			15,000	9,000	(12,000)	(3,000)
Translation gain (loss) ($)			(300)	(180)	240	60

Note: If the exchange rate remained unchanged over time, the translated statements would be the same under all translation methods.

[a] *Assume that inventories are carried at the lower of cost or market. If they were carried at historical cost, the temporal balance sheet would be identical to the monetary-nonmonetary method.*

EXHIBIT 6-9 Mexican Subsidiary Income Statement

	Pesos	($ 0.11 =MXN1)	Current Rate	Current– Noncurrent	Monetary– Nonmonetary	Temporal
		U.S. Dollars before Peso Devaluation		**U.S. Dollars after Peso Depreciation ($ 0.09 = MXN1)**		
Sales	40,000	$4,400	$3,600	$3,600	$3,600	$3,600
Cost of sales	20,000	2,200	1,800	1,800	2,200	1,800[a]
Depreciation[b]	1,800	198	162	198	198	198
Other expenses	8,000	880	720	720	720	720
Pre-tax income	10,200	1,122	918	882	482	882
Income tax (30%)	3,060	(337)	(275)	(275)	(275)	(275)
Translation g/l[c]	—	—	(300)	(180)	240	60
Net income/(loss)	7,140	$ 785	$ 343	$ 427	$ 447	$ 667

Note: This example assumes that the income statement is prepared the day after devaluation.

[a]*Assumes that inventories were written down to market at period's end.*

[b]*Estimated life of fixed assets is assumed to be 10 years.*

[c]*This example reflects what reported earnings would look like if all translation gains or losses were immediately reflected in current income.*

U.S.-based multinational enterprise appears in pesos in the first column of Exhibit 6-9. The second column depicts the U.S. dollar equivalents of the Mexican peso (MXN) balances when the exchange rate was MXN1 = $0.13. Should the peso depreciate to MXN1 = $0.10, several different accounting results are possible.

Under the current-rate method, exchange rate changes affect the dollar equivalents of the Mexican subsidiary's total foreign currency assets (TA) and liabilities (TL) in the current period. Since their dollar values are affected by changes in the current rate, they are said to be *exposed* (in an accounting sense) to foreign exchange risk. Accordingly, under the current-rate method, an exposed net asset position (TA > TL) results in a translation loss if the Mexican peso loses value, and an exchange gain if the peso gains value. An exposed peso net liability position (TA < TL) produces a translation gain if the Mexican peso loses value and a loss if the peso gains value. In our example, current rate translation yields a $300 translation loss, since the dollar equivalent of the Mexican subsidiary's net asset position *after* the peso depreciation is $1,350 (MXN15,000 × $0.09), whereas the dollar equivalent *before* the depreciation was $1,650 (MXN15,000 × $0.11).

Under the current-noncurrent method, the U.S. company's accounting exposure is measured by its peso net current asset or liability position (a positive MXN9,000 in our example). Under the monetary-nonmonetary method, exposure is measured by its net peso monetary asset or liability position (a negative MXN12,000). Accounting exposure under the temporal principle depends on whether the Mexican subsidiary's inventories or other nonmonetary assets are valued at historical cost (and therefore not exposed) or some other valuation basis (a negative MXN3,000 in our example).

To summarize, the different translation methods in our example give a wide array of accounting results, ranging from a $300 loss under the current-rate method to a $240 gain under the monetary-nonmonetary method. This difference is large, given that all the results are based on the same facts. What is more, operations reporting respectable profits before currency translation may well report losses or much lower earnings after translation (the converse is also true). To protect themselves against the financial statement effects of currency swings, financial managers may execute protective maneuvers known as *hedging* strategies. Chapter 11 covers hedging options and foreign exchange risk management in greater detail.

Which Is Best?

We begin by asking whether a single translation method is appropriate for all circumstances in which translations occur and for all purposes that translation serves. Our answer would be no. The circumstances underlying foreign exchange translation differ widely. Translating accounts from a stable to an unstable currency is not the same as translating accounts from an unstable currency to a stable one. Likewise, there is little similarity between translations involving import- or export-type transactions and those involving a permanently established affiliate or subsidiary company in another country that reinvests its local earnings and does not intend to repatriate any funds to the parent company in the near future.

Second, translations are made for different purposes. Translating the accounts of a foreign subsidiary to consolidate them with the accounts of the parent company has very little in common with translating the accounts of an independent company mainly for the convenience of various foreign audiences of interest.

We pose two additional questions:

1. What are acceptable foreign currency translation methods and under what conditions?
2. Are there situations in which currency translation may be inappropriate?

Regarding the first question, we think that there are three different translation approaches that make sense from a reader's viewpoint: (1) the historical method, (2) the current method, and (3) no translation at all. Financial accounts of foreign entities can be translated either from a parent-company perspective or from a local perspective. Under the parent-company perspective, foreign operations are extensions of parent company operations and are, in large measure, sources of domestic currency cash flows. Accordingly, the object of translation is to change the unit of measure for financial statements of foreign subsidiaries to the domestic currency, and to make the foreign statements conform to accounting principles generally accepted in the country of the parent company. We think these objectives are best achieved by translation methods that use historical rates of exchange. We prefer the temporal principle because it generally maintains the accounting principles used to measure assets and liabilities originally expressed in foreign currency units.[12] Because foreign statements under a parent-company perspective are first adjusted to reflect parent-company accounting principles (before translation), the temporal principle is appropriate, because it

---

[12]Frederick D. S. Choi and Gerhard G. Mueller, *An Introduction to Multinational Accounting* (Upper Saddle River, NJ: Prentice-Hall, 1978).

changes a measurement in foreign currency into a measurement in domestic currency without changing the basis of measurement. The temporal translation method is easily adapted to processes that make accounting adjustments during the translation. When this is so, adjustments for differences between two or more sets of accounting concepts and practices are made along with the translation of currency amounts. For example, inventories or certain liabilities may be restated according to accounting practices different from those originally used. The temporal principle can accommodate any asset-valuation framework, be it historical cost, current replacement price, or net realizable values.

The current-rate method of translation is a straightforward translation (restatement) from one currency language to another. There is no change in the nature of the accounts; only their particular form of expression is changed. The current-rate method is appropriate when the translated accounts of foreign subsidiaries keep the local currency as the unit of measure; that is, when foreign entities are viewed from a local (as opposed to a parent–company) perspective. Translation at the current rate does not change any of the initial relationships (e.g., financial ratios) in the foreign currency statements, because all account balances are simply multiplied by a constant. This approach is also useful when the accounts of an independent company are translated for the convenience of foreign stockholders or other external user groups.

The current-rate method is also appropriate when price-level-adjusted accounts are translated to another currency. If reliable price-level adjustments are made in a given set of accounts, and if domestic price-level changes for the currency are closely reflected in related foreign exchange rate movements, the current rate translation of price-level-adjusted data yields results that are comparable to translating historical cost accounts under the historical rate translation method.[13] This topic is covered in Chapter 7.

Are there situations in which currency translations can confuse rather than enlighten? We think so. No translation is appropriate between highly unstable and highly stable currencies. Translation of one into the other will not produce meaningful information using any translation method. No translation also means nonconsolidation of financial statements. We think this is reasonable. If a currency is unstable enough to put account translations out of the question, financial statement consolidation should also be out of the question. No translation is necessary when financial statements of independent companies are issued for purely informational purposes to residents in another country that is in a comparable stage of economic development and has a comparable national currency situation. Finally, certain special management reports should not be translated. Effective international managers should be able to evaluate situations and reach decisions in terms of more than one currency unit. (These and related issues are discussed in Chapter 10.) Some internal company reports may have several different columns of monetary

---

[13]Alas, empirical evidence suggests that exchange rate changes and differential inflation are seldom perfectly negatively correlated. Distortions caused by this market anomaly are discussed by David A. Ziebart and Jong-Hag Choi, "The Difficulty of Achieving Economic Reality Through Foreign Currency Translation," *International Journal of Accounting* 33, no. 4 (1998): 403–414.

amounts, each in a different currency unit. Translation may be impossible for certain other reports (such as those on a possible international acquisition) because historical foreign exchange rate information may not be available. Still other types of reports may only translate current or monetary items and leave other items untranslated.

Appropriate Current Rate

Thus far we have referred to the rates of exchange used in translation methods as either historical or current. Average rates are often used in income statements for expediency. The choice of an appropriate exchange rate is not clear-cut, because several exchange rates are in effect for any currency at any time. There are buying and selling (bid and ask) rates, spot rates and forward rates, official rates and free-market rates, and so on. An appropriate translation rate should reflect economic and business reality as closely as possible. The free-market rate quoted for spot transactions in the country where the accounts to be translated originate is a rate that appropriately measures current transaction values.

Sometimes a country applies different exchange rates to different transactions. In these situations, one must choose among several existing rates. Several possibilities have been suggested: (1) dividend remittance rates, (2) free-market rates, and (3) any applicable penalty or preference rates, such as those associated with imports or exports. The authors believe that free-market rates are preferable, with one exception: Where specific exchange controls are in effect (i.e., when certain funds are definitely ear-marked for specific transactions to which specific foreign exchange rates apply), the applicable rates should be used. For instance, if a Latin American subsidiary of a U.S. parent has received permission to import certain goods from the United States at a favorable rate and has set aside certain funds to do so, the ear-marked funds should be translated to dollars at the special preference rate. The current year-end free-market rate should then be applied to the balance of the foreign cash account. This procedure translates portions of a foreign currency cash account at two or more different translation rates. That is fine as long as it properly and fully reflects economic reality.

Translation Gains and Losses

Exhibit 6-8 illustrated four translation adjustments resulting from applying various translation methods to foreign currency financial statements. Internationally, accounting treatments of these adjustments are as diverse as the translation procedures. Approaches to accounting for translation adjustments range from deferral to no deferral with hybrid approaches in between.

Deferral

Exclusion of translation adjustments in current income is generally advocated because these adjustments merely result from a restatement process. Changes in the domestic currency equivalents of a foreign subsidiary's net assets are unrealized and have no effect on the local-currency cash flows generated by the foreign entity. Therefore, it would be misleading to include such adjustments in current income. Under these circumstances, translation adjustments are accumulated separately as a part of consolidated equity. Parkinson offers additional reasons to support deferral:

> It can be argued that the gain or loss relates to a very long-term investment—perhaps even a permanent investment—of a . . . parent in a foreign subsidiary; that the gain or loss will not become realized until the foreign operation is closed down and all the net assets are distributed to the parent; that at or before such time the change in the exchange rate may have reversed—i.e., that no gain or loss will ever be realized. It can also be argued that operating results recorded in the periods following the currency revaluation (and translated at the then current exchange rate) will indicate the increased or decreased worth of the foreign operation and that in these circumstances there is no need to record a one-time translation gain or loss in the income statement—that in fact the recording of such a gain or loss might be misleading.[14]

Some analysts oppose deferral on the grounds that exchange rates may not reverse themselves. Even if they do, deferral of exchange adjustments is premised on predicting exchange rates, a most difficult task. Some argue that deferring translation gains or losses masks the behavior of exchange rate changes; that is, rate changes are historical facts, and financial statement users are best served if the effects of exchange rate fluctuations are accounted for when they occur.

Deferral and Amortization

Some firms defer translation gains or losses and amortize these adjustments over the life of related balance sheet items. As an example, assume that the acquisition of a fixed asset is financed by issuing debt. It can be argued that principal and interest payments on the debt are covered by cash flows generated from using the fixed asset. Here, the translation gain or loss associated with the debt would be deferred and amortized over the life of the related fixed asset, that is, released to income in a manner compatible with depreciation expense. Alternatively, the translation gain or loss arising from the debt could be deferred and amortized over the remaining life of the debt as an adjustment to interest expense.

Such approaches are sometimes criticized on theoretical and practical grounds. For example, finance theory tells us that capital budgeting decisions about fixed-asset investments are independent of decisions about how to finance them. Linking the two looks more like a device to smooth income. Adjusting interest expense is also suspect. Domestic borrowing costs are not adjusted to reflect changes in market interest rates or the fair value of the debt. Thus, the argument goes, why should fluctuations in currency values have such an effect?

Partial Deferral

A third option in accounting for translation gains and losses is to recognize losses as soon as they occur, but to recognize gains only as they are realized. This was common

---

[14]MacDonald R. Parkinson, *Translation of Foreign Currencies* (Toronto: Canadian Institute of Chartered Accountants, 1972), pp. 101–102.

practice in the United States at one time. Although conservative, deferring a translation gain solely because it is a gain denies that a rate change has occurred. Moreover, it is logically inconsistent to defer translation gains but recognize translation losses. This approach lacks any explicit criteria to determine when to realize a translation gain. Also, those who favor deferral of translation gains are at a loss to determine how much to defer. In the past, companies have netted current gains against prior losses and deferred the difference. This implies that translation gains or losses are not period items and will "wash out" in the long run. If this were so, deferrals would be a questionable practice.

No Deferral

A final reporting option utilized by many firms around the world is to immediately recognize translation gains and losses in the income statement. This option views deferral of any type as artificial and misleading. Deferral criteria are often attacked as internally inconsistent and impossible to implement. However, including translation gains and losses in current income introduces a random element to earnings that could result in significant earning fluctuations whenever exchange rates change. Moreover, including such paper gains and losses in reported earnings can mislead statement readers, because these adjustments do not always provide information compatible with the expected economic effects of rate changes on an enterprise's cash flows.

Where Are We?

The objectives of translation have an important bearing on the nature of any potential translation adjustment. If a local-currency perspective is maintained (local-company perspective), reflecting a translation adjustment in current income is unwarranted. Recall that a local-company perspective requires the current-rate translation method in order to preserve relationships existing in the foreign currency statements. In our opinion, including translation gains or losses in income distorts the original financial relationships and may mislead users of the information. Management, for example, is interested in how a particular affiliate is faring in its local currency, and translation gains and losses generated from a restatement process do not shed much light on local performance. In this instance, it makes sense to treat translation gains or losses as adjustments to consolidated equity.

If the reporting currency of the parent company is the unit of measure for the translated financial statements (parent-company perspective), it is advisable to immediately recognize translation gains or losses in income. The parent-company perspective views a foreign subsidiary as an extension of the parent. Translation gains and losses reflect increases or decreases in the domestic currency equity of the foreign investment and should be recognized.

TRANSLATION ACCOUNTING DEVELOPMENT

Translation accounting practices have evolved over time in response to the increasing complexity of multinational operations and changes in the international monetary system. Since financial reporting initiatives in the United States are representative of experiences elsewhere, a brief summary will provide some historical perspective on the current state of translation accounting.

Pre-1965

Before 1965 the translation practices of many U.S. companies were guided by Chapter 12 of Accounting Research Bulletin No. 43.[15] This statement advocated the current-noncurrent method. Transaction gains or losses were taken directly to income. Translation gains or losses were netted during the period. Net translation losses were recognized in current income, while net translation gains were deferred in a balance sheet suspense account and used to offset translation losses in future periods.

1965–1975

ARB No. 43 allowed certain exceptions to the current-noncurrent method. Under special circumstances, inventory could be translated at historical rates. Long-term debt incurred to acquire long-term assets could be restated at the current rate when there was a large (presumably permanent) change in the exchange rate. Any accounting difference caused by debt restatement was treated as part of the asset's cost. Moreover, translating all foreign currency payables and receivables at the current rate was allowed after Accounting Principles Board Opinion No. 6 was issued in 1965.[16] This change to ARB No. 43 gave companies another translation option.

1975–1981

To end the variety of treatments allowed under previous translation standards, the Financial Accounting Standards Board (FASB) issued FAS No. 8 in 1975.[17] This statement significantly changed the practice of U.S. companies and of foreign companies subscribing to U.S. GAAP by requiring the temporal method of translation. Equally important, deferral of translation gains and losses was no longer permitted. Translation and transaction exchange gains and losses had to be recognized in income during the period of the rate change.

FAS NO. 8 proved controversial. While some applauded its theoretical merits, many condemned the distortions it caused in reported corporate earnings. The pronouncement was criticized for producing accounting results not in accord with economic reality. The yo-yo effect of FAS No. 8 on corporate earnings also caused concern among executives of multinational companies. They worried that their companies' reported earnings would appear more volatile than those of domestic companies, and thereby depress their stock prices.

1981–Present

In May 1978, the FASB invited public comment on its first 12 pronouncements. Most of the 200 letters received related to FAS No. 8, urging that it be changed. Responding

---

[15]American Institute of Certified Public Accountants, Committee on Accounting Procedure, "Restatement and Revision of Accounting Research Bulletins," Accounting Research Bulletin No. 43 (New York: AICPA, 1953).

[16]American Institute of Certified Public Accountants, "Status of Accounting Research Bulletins," Accounting Principles Board Opinion No. 6 (New York: AICPA, 1965).

[17]Financial Accounting Standards Board, "Accounting for the Translation of Foreign Currency Transactions and Foreign Currency Financial Statements," Statement of Financial Accounting Standards No. 8 (Stamford, CT: FASB, 1975).

to the dissatisfaction, the FASB reconsidered FAS No. 8 and, after many public meetings and two exposure drafts, issued Statement of Financial Accounting Standards No. 52 in 1981.[18]

FEATURES OF STANDARD NO. 52/INTERNATIONAL ACCOUNTING STANDARD 21

The objectives of translation under FAS No. 8 differed substantially from those of FAS No. 52. FAS No. 8 adopted a parent-company perspective by requiring that foreign currency financial statements be presented as if all transactions had taken place in parent currency. Standard No. 52 recognizes that the parent-company and local-company perspectives are both valid reporting frameworks. At the international level, the IASB issued a parallel pronouncement, IAS 21, that was recently amended to clarify its requirements and to resolve certain implementation concerns.[19] Both FAS No. 52 and the current version of IAS 21 seek to:

1. Reflect, in consolidated statements, the financial results and relationships measured in the primary currency in which each consolidated entity does business (its *functional currency*).
2. Provide information that is generally compatible with the expected economic effects of an exchange rate change on an enterprise's cash flows and equity.

These objectives are based on the concept of a functional currency. Recall that the functional currency of an entity is the currency of the primary economic environment in which it operates and generates cash flows. Moreover, the functional currency designation determines the choice of translation method employed for consolidation purposes and the disposition of exchange gains and losses.

Translation When Local Currency Is the Functional Currency

If the functional currency is the foreign currency in which the foreign entity's records are kept, its financial statements are translated to dollars using the current-rate method. Resulting translation gains or losses are disclosed in a separate component of consolidated equity. This preserves the financial statement ratios as calculated from the local currency statements. The following current rate procedures are used:

1. All foreign currency assets and liabilities are translated to dollars using the exchange rate prevailing as of the balance sheet date; capital accounts are translated at historical rates.
2. Revenues and expenses are translated using the exchange rate prevailing on the transaction date, although weighted average rates can be used for expediency.
3. Translation gains and losses are reported in a separate component of consolidated stockholders' equity. These exchange adjustments do not go into the income statement until the foreign operation is sold or the investment is judged to have permanently lost value.

---

[18]Financial Accounting Standards Board, "Foreign Currency Translation," Statement of Financial Accounting Standards No. 52 (Stamford, CT: FASB, 1981).
[19]Comments on the paper are available at www.iasb.org/news.

Translation When the Parent Currency Is the Functional Currency

When the parent currency is a foreign entity's functional currency, its foreign currency financial statements are remeasured to dollars using the temporal method. All translation gains and losses resulting from the translation process are included in determining current-period income. Specifically:

1. Monetary assets and liabilities and nonmonetary assets valued at current market prices are translated using the rate prevailing as of the financial statement date; other nonmonetary items and capital accounts are translated at historical rates.
2. Revenues and expenses are translated using average exchange rates for the period except those items related to nonmonetary items (e.g., cost of sales and depreciation expense), which are translated using historical rates.
3. Translation gains and losses are reflected in current income.

Translation When Foreign Currency Is the Functional Currency

A foreign entity may keep its records in one foreign currency when its functional currency is another foreign currency. In this situation, the financial statements are first remeasured from the local currency into the functional currency (temporal method) and then translated into U.S. dollars using the current-rate method.

Exhibit 6-10 charts the translation procedures described here, and the appendix to this chapter demonstrates the mechanics of foreign currency translation.

An exception to the current-rate method is required for subsidiaries located in places where the cumulative rate of inflation during the preceding three years exceeds 100 percent. In such hyperinflationary conditions, the dollar (the stronger currency) is considered the functional currency, requiring use of the temporal translation method. In contrast, IAS 21 requires that financial statements of the local subsidiary be restated for inflation prior to translation to the parent currency.

Where an entity has more than one distinct and separable operation (e.g., a branch or division), each operation may be considered as a separate entity with its own functional currency. Thus, a U.S. parent might have a self-contained manufacturing operation in Mexico designed to serve the Latin American market and a separate sales outlet for the parent company's exported products. Under these circumstances, the financial statements of the manufacturing operation would be translated to dollars using the current-rate method. The peso statements of the Mexican sales outlet would be remeasured in dollars using the temporal method.

Once the functional currency for a foreign entity is determined, that currency designation must be used consistently unless changes in economic circumstances clearly indicate that the functional currency has changed. If a reporting enterprise can justify the change, analysts should note that the accounting change need not be accounted for retroactively.

Recall that Alcan, introduced at the beginning of this chapter, is a Canadian-based multinational company. It has chosen, however, to report the results of its consolidated operations in U.S. dollars. Foreign accounts denominated in foreign currency that are integral to Alcan's operations are thus translated (remeasured) to its functional currency, Canadian dollars, using the temporal method. The results of this remeasurement process are then translated to U.S. dollars using the current-rate method. The translation gains or losses generated by the remeasurement process

EXHIBIT 6-10   Translation Procedure Flowchart

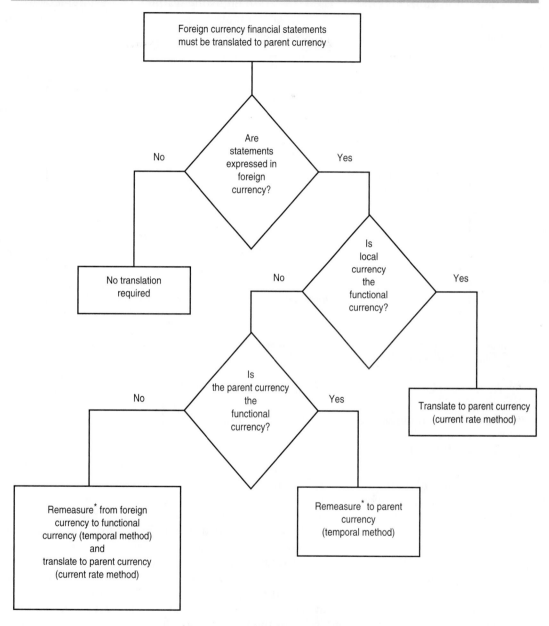

*The term *remeasure* means to translate so as to change the unit of measure from a foreign currency to the functional currency.

appear in Alcan's consolidated earnings numbers as foreign currency balance sheet translation gains and losses. The translation adjustment following restatement from Canadian to U.S. dollars appears in consolidated equity as a deferred translation adjustment, as follows:

Alcan Inc.	
Consolidated Balance Sheet	
December 31	
(in millions of U.S.$)	
Shareholders' equity:	
Redeemable nonretractable preference shares	160
Common shareholders' equity:	
Common shares	6,181
Additional paid-in capital	683
Retained earnings	3,048
Accumulated other comprehensive income	(397))*
	9,706

Comprises deferred translation adjustments of $264, unrealized gain on "available-for-sale" securities of $4, minimum pension liability of ($450), and unreleased loss on derivatives of ($215).

MEASUREMENT ISSUES

Readers of consolidated accounts must address several issues if they are to properly interpret the financial statement effects of foreign currency translation. Several of these issues are discussed in the following sections.

Reporting Perspective

In adopting the notion of functional currency, FAS No. 52 and IAS 21 accommodate both local- and parent-company reporting perspectives in the consolidated financial statements. But are financial statement readers better served by incorporating two different reporting perspectives and, therefore, two different currency frameworks in a single set of consolidated financial statements? Is a translation adjustment produced under the temporal method any different in substance from one produced under the current-rate method? If not, is any useful purpose served by disclosing some translation adjustments in income and others in stockholders' equity? Is FAS No. 8's concept of a single unit of measure (the parent company's reporting currency) the lesser of two evils? Should we stop translating foreign currency financial statements altogether? Doing so would avoid many of the pitfalls associated with current translation methods, including the problem of incorporating more than one perspective in the translated results.

It has also been suggested that FAS No. 52 is inconsistent with the theory of consolidation, which is to show the statements of a parent company and its subsidiaries as if the group were operating as a single company. Yet subsidiaries whose functional currency is the local currency operate relatively independently of the parent. If the multinational doesn't operate as a single company, then why consolidate those parts of it that are independent?[20]

What Happened to Historical Cost?

As noted earlier in the chapter, translating a balance measured under historical cost at the current exchange rate produces an amount in U.S. dollars that is neither the item's historical cost nor its current-value equivalent. Such a translated amount defies theoretical description. Historical cost is the basis of U.S. GAAP, and most overseas assets of most multinationals will have historical cost measurements. Yet the current-rate method is used for translation whenever a local currency is deemed to be the functional currency. Even if financial statement users can still make sense of the consolidated amounts, the theoretical incoherence remains.

Concept of Income

Under the currency translation pronouncements described above, adjustments arising from the translation of foreign currency financial statements and certain transactions are made directly to shareholders' equity, thus bypassing the income statement. The apparent intention of this was to give statement readers more accurate and less confusing income numbers. Some, however, dislike the idea of burying translation adjustments that were previously disclosed. They fear that readers may be confused about the effects of fluctuating exchange rates on a company's worth.

Managed Earnings

Currency translation pronouncements such as those just described provide opportunities to manage earnings. Consider the choice of functional currencies. An examination of the functional currency criteria shown in Exhibit 6-4 suggests that the choice of a functional currency is not straightforward. A foreign subsidiary's operations could satisfy opposing criteria. For example, a foreign subsidiary may incur its expenses primarily in the local country and make its sales primarily in the local environment and denominated in local currency. These circumstances would favor selection of the local currency as the functional currency. Yet the same operation may be financed entirely by the parent company, with cash flows remitted to the parent. Therefore, the parent currency could be selected as the functional currency. The different possible outcomes involved in selecting functional currencies may be one reason why Exxon–Mobil Oil chooses the local currency as the functional currency for most of its foreign operations, while Chevron-Texaco and Unocal choose the dollar. When choice criteria conflict and the choice can significantly affect reporting outcomes, there are opportunities for earnings management.

---

[20]C. W. Nobes, "An Analysis of the Use of 'Theory' in the UK and US Currency Translation Standards," reprinted in C. W. Nobes, *Issues in International Accounting* (New York: Garland, 1986), pp. 129–130.

Research to date is inconclusive as to whether managers manipulate income (and other financial statement amounts) by the choice of functional currency.[21] Some evidence of earnings management appears when one looks at when companies choose to adopt a new currency translation pronouncement. For example, evidence regarding adoption dates for the U.K.'s currency translation pronouncement, SSAP 20, shows that companies chose to defer adoption of the standard to influence their financial performance and, achieve certain corporate financial objectives.[22] Such motives as these reduce the credibility of multinationals' consolidated financial statements.

FOREIGN CURRENCY TRANSLATION AND INFLATION

An inverse relationship between a country's rate of inflation and its currency's external value has been empirically demonstrated.[23] Consequently, use of the current rate to translate the cost of nonmonetary assets located in inflationary environments will eventually produce domestic currency equivalents far below their original measurement bases. At the same time, translated earnings would be greater because of correspondingly lower depreciation charges. Such translated results could easily mislead rather than inform. Lower dollar valuations would usually understate the actual earning power of foreign assets supported by local inflation, and inflated return on investment ratios of foreign operations could create false expectations of future profitability.

The FASB decided against inflation adjustments before translation, believing such adjustments to be inconsistent with the historical cost-valuation framework used in basic U.S. statements. As a solution, FAS No. 52 requires use of the U.S. dollar as the functional currency for foreign operations domiciled in hyperinflationary environments (i.e., countries where the cumulative rate of inflation exceeds 100 percent over a three-year period). This procedure would hold constant the dollar equivalents of foreign currency assets, because they would be translated at the historical rate (by the temporal method). This method has its limitations. First, translation at the historical

---

[21]For example, see J. H. Amernic and B. J. B. Galvin, "Implementing the New Foreign Currency Rules in Canada and the United States: A Challenge to Professional Judgement," *International Journal of Accounting* (spring 1984): 165–180; Thomas G. Evans and Timothy S. Doupnik, *Determining the Functional Currency Under Statement 52* (Stamford, CT: FASB, 1986), pp. 11–12; Dileep R. Mehta and Samanta B. Thapa, "FAS 52, Functional Currency, and the Non-comparability of Financial Reports," *International Journal of Accounting* 26, no. 2 (1991): 71–84; Robert J. Kirsch and Thomas G. Evans, "The Implementation of FAS 52: Did the Foreign Currency Approach Prevail?" *International Journal of Accounting* 29, no. 1 (1994): 20–33; M. Aiken and D. Ardern, "Choice of Translation Methods in Financial Disclosure: A Test of Compliance with Environmental Hypotheses," *British Accounting Review* 35 (2003): 327–348.
[22]George Emmanuel Iatrides and Nathan Lael Joseph, "Characteristics of UK Firms Related to Timing of Adoption of Statement of Standard Accounting Practice No. 20," *Accounting and Finance* 46 (2006): 429–455. For evidence of earnings motivation for switching currency translation methods, see Dahli Gray, "Corporate Preferences for Foreign Currency Accounting Standards," *Journal of Accounting Research* (autumn 1984): 760–764; James J. Benjamin, Steven Grossman, and Casper Wiggins, "The Impact of Foreign Currency Translation on Reporting During the Phase-in of SFAS No. 52," *Journal of Accounting, Auditing, and Finance* 1, no. 3 (1996): 174–184; Frances L. Ayres, "Characteristics of Firms Electing Early Adoption of SFAS 52," *Journal of Accounting and Economics* (June 1986): 143–158; Robert W. Rutledge, "Does Management Engage in the Manipulation of Earnings?" *Journal of International Accounting, Auditing, and Taxation* 4, no. 1 (1995): 69–86.
[23]B. Balassa, "The Purchasing Power Parity Doctrine: A Reappraisal," *Journal of Political Economy* (1964): 145–154; R. Z. Aliber and C. P. Stickney, "Accounting Measures of Foreign Exchange Exposure: The Long and Short of It," *Accounting Review* (January 1975): 44–57; W. Beaver and M. Wolfson, "Foreign Currency Translation in Perfect and Complete Markets," *Journal of Accounting Research* (autumn 1982): 528–560.

rate is meaningful only if differential rates of inflation between the subsidiary's host country and parent country are perfectly negatively correlated with exchange rates. If not, the dollar equivalents of foreign currency assets in inflationary environments will be misleading. Should inflation rates in the hyperinflationary economy fall below 100 percent in a future three-year period, switching to the current-rate method (because the local currency would be the functional currency) could produce a significant translation adjustment to consolidated equity, since exchange rates may change significantly during the interim. Under these circumstances, charging stockholders' equity with translation losses on foreign currency fixed assets could have a significant effect on financial ratios with stockholders' equity in the denominator. The issue of foreign currency translation cannot be separated from the issue of accounting for foreign inflation, which is treated at greater length in the next chapter.[24]

FOREIGN CURRENCY TRANSLATION ELSEWHERE

We now look briefly at foreign currency translation in other parts of the world. The Canadian Institute of Chartered Accountants (CICA), the U.K.'s Accounting Standards Board, and the International Accounting Standards Board all participated in the deliberations that led to FAS No. 52. It is not surprising, therefore, to find that their corresponding standards are largely compatible with FAS No. 52.[25]

A distinctive feature of Canada's standard (CICA 1650) concerns foreign long-term debt. In Canada, gains and losses from translation are deferred and amortized, as opposed to being recognized in income immediately. Canada has issued a second exposure draft proposing to eliminate its defer and amortize approach.

A major difference between the United Kingdom and the United States relates to self-contained subsidiaries in hyperinflationary countries and whose functional currency is the local currency. In the U.K., financial statements must first be adjusted to current price levels and then translated using the current rate; in the United States, the temporal method is used.

Finally, there is an important distinction between IAS 21 (as revised) and FAS No. 52. Under IAS 21, the financial statements of subsidiaries in highly inflationary environments must be adjusted to reflect changes in the general price level before translation, a treatment like that in the U.K. standard.

Japan recently changed its standard to require the current-rate method in all circumstances, with translation adjustments shown on the balance sheet in stockholders' equity. The EU's Fourth and Seventh Directives (see Chapter 8) have no provisions on foreign currency translation. As a result, currency translation practices vary considerably. However, foreign currency translation practices in Europe have narrowed as International Financial Reporting Standards have become the reporting norm for listed EU companies. Observation suggests that foreign currency translation standards globally are converging on FAS No. 52 and IAS 21.

---

[24]For a recent examination of this relationship, see John Hughes, Jing Liu, and Mingshan Zhang, "Valuation and Accounting for Inflation and Foreign Exchange," *Journal of Accounting Research* 42, no. 4(2004): 731–754.

[25]All three standards were issued in 1983, roughly 18 months after FAS No. 52. The Canadian standard is Accounting Recommendation 1650 and the British standard is Statement of Standard Accounting Practice 20; both are titled "Foreign Currency Translation." The original International Accounting Standard 21 was modified in 1993 and is now called, "The Effects of Changes in Foreign Exchange Rates."

APPENDIX 6-1

Translation And Remeasurement Under FAS No. 52

Exhibit 6-11 presents comparative foreign currency balance sheets at December 31, 20X7 and 20X8, and a statement of income for the year ended December 31, 20X8, for CM Corporation, a wholly-owned foreign subsidiary of a U.S. company. The statements conform to U.S. generally accepted accounting principles before translation to U.S. dollars.

Capital stock was issued and fixed assets acquired when the exchange rate was FC1 = $0.17. Inventories at January 1, 20X8, were acquired during the fourth quarter of 20X7. Purchases (FC6,250), sales, other expenses, and dividends (FC690) occurred evenly during 20X8. Retained earnings in U.S. dollars at December 31, 20X7, under the temporal method were $316. Exchange rates for calendar 20X8 were as follows:

January 1, 20X8	FC1 = $0.23
December 31, 20X8	FC1 = $0.18
Average during 20X8	FC1 = $0.22
Average during fourth quarter, 20X7	FC1 = $0.23
Average during fourth quarter, 20X8	FC1 = $0.19

EXHIBIT 6-11 Financial Statements of CM Corporation

Balance Sheet	12/31/X7	12/31/X8
Cash	FC 300	FC 500
Accounts receivable (net)	1,300	1,000
Inventories (lower of FIFO cost or market)	1,200	1,500
Fixed assets (net)	9,000	8,000
Total assets	FC 11,800	FC 11,000
Accounts payable	FC 2,200	FC 2,400
Long-term debt	4,400	3,000
Capital stock	2,000	2,000
Retained earnings	3,200	3,600
Total liabilities and owners' equity	FC 11,800	FC 11,000

Income Statement		Year ended 12/31/X8
Sales		FC 10,000
Expenses		
Cost of sales	5,950	
Depreciation (straight-line)	1,000	
Other	1,493	8,443
Operating income		FC 1,557
Income taxes		467
Net income		FC 1,090

CURRENT-RATE METHOD

Translation adjustments under the current-rate method arise whenever (1) year-end foreign currency balances are translated at a current rate that differs from the one used to translate the ending balances of the previous period, and (2) foreign currency financial statements are translated at a current rate that differs from the exchange rates used during the period. The translation adjustment is calculated by (1) multiplying the beginning foreign currency net asset balance by the change in the current rate during the period, and (2) multiplying the increase or decrease in net assets during the period by the difference between the average exchange rate and the end-of-period exchange rate. Exhibit 6-12 depicts how the FAS No. 52 translation process applies to these figures.

EXHIBIT 6-12   Current-Rate Method of Translation (Local Currency Is Functional Currency)

	Foreign Currency	Exchange Rate	Dollar Equivalents
Balance Sheet Accounts			
Assets			
Cash	FC 500	$.18	$ 90
Accounts receivable	1,000	.18	180
Inventories	1,500	.18	270
Fixed assets	8,000	.18	1,440
Total	FC 11,000		$1,980
Liabilities and Stockholders' Equity			
Accounts payable	FC 2,400	.18	$ 432
Long-term debt	3,000	.18	540
Capital stock	2,000	.17	340
Retained earnings	3,600	*a*	404
Translation adjustment (cumulative)		*b*	264
Total	FC 11,000		$1,980
Income Statement Accounts			
Sales	FC 10,000	.22	$2,200
Cost of sales	(5,950)	.22	(1,309)
Depreciation	(1,000)	.22	(220)
Other expenses	(1,493)	.22	(328)
Income before income taxes	FC 1,557		$ 343
Income taxes	(467)	.22	(103)
Net income	FC 1,090		$ 240
Retained earnings, 12/31/X7	3,200		316
Less: dividends	(690)	.22	(152)
Retained earnings, 12/31/X8	FC 3,600		$ 404

a See statement of income and retained earnings.

b The cumulative translation adjustment of $264 is comprised of two parts: (1) the cumulative translation adjustment at the beginning of the year and (2) the translation adjustment for the current year and would be disclosed as a component of other comprehensive income.

As can be seen, translation procedures under the current-rate method are straightforward. However, the derivation of the beginning cumulative translation adjustment merits some explanation. Assume that calendar 20X8 is the first year in which the current-rate method is adopted (e.g., the previous translation method was the temporal method, as the U.S. dollar was considered functional before 20X8). Under this scenario, a one-time translation adjustment would be calculated as of January 1, 20X8. This figure approximates the amount by which beginning stockholders' equity would differ in light of the switch from the temporal to the current-rate method. It is calculated by translating CM Corporation's January 1, 20X8, foreign currency net asset position at the current rate prevailing on that date. (This result simulates what CM's beginning net asset position would be had it used the current-rate method all along.) The difference between this amount and the amount of net assets under the temporal method constitutes CM Corporation's beginning-of-period cumulative translation adjustment, as illustrated here.

Net assets, 12/31/X7		FC 5,200
Multiplied by exchange rate as of 1/1/X8 (FC1 = $0.23)		X$0.23
Less: As reported stockholders' equity, 12/31/X7:		1,196
Capital stock	$340	
Retained earnings (per temporal method)	316	656
Cumulative translation adjustment, 1/1/X7		$540

Given this information, the following steps yield a translation adjustment of $(276) for calendar 20X8.

1. Net assets, 12/31/X7		FC 5,200	
Multiplied by change in current rate:			
Rate, 12/31/X7	FC1 = $0.23		
Rate, 12/31/X8	FC1 = $0.18	X$(0.05)	$(260)
2. Change in net assets during year (net income less dividends)		FC 400	
Multiplied by difference between average and year-end rate:			
Average rate	FC1 = $0.22		
Year-end rate	FC1 = $0.18	X$(0.04)	$ (16)
Total			$(276)

The final cumulative translation adjustment for 20X8 of $264 is reached by adding the $(276) translation adjustment for 20X8 to the beginning balance of $540.

TEMPORAL METHOD

Exhibit 6-13 illustrates the FAS No. 52 remeasurement process when the dollar is the functional currency.

EXHIBIT 6-13   Temporal Method of Translation (U.S. Dollar is Functional Currency)

	Foreign Currency	Exchange Rate	Dollar Equivalents
Balance Sheet Accounts			
Assets			
Cash	FC 500	$.18	$ 90
Accounts receivable	1,000	.18	180
Inventories	1,500	.19	285
Fixed assets	8,000	.17	1,360
Total	FC 11,000		$1,915
Liabilities and Stockholders' Equity			
Accounts payable	FC 2,400	.18	$ 432
Long-term debt	3,000	.18	540
Capital stock	2,000	.17	340
Retained earnings	3,600	a	603
Translation adjustment	—	b	—
Total	FC 11,000		$1,915
Income Statement Accounts			
Sales	FC 10,000	.22	$2,200
Cost of sales	(5,950)	c	(1,366)
Depreciation	(1,000)	.17	(170)
Other expenses	(1,493)	.22	(328)
Aggregate exchange gain (loss)	—	d	206
Income taxes	467	.22	(103)
Net income	FC 1,090		$ 439
Retained earnings, 12/31/X7	3,200		316
Dividends	(690)	.22	(152)
Retained earnings, 12/31/X8	FC 3,600		$ 603

[a]See statement of income and retained earnings.

[b]Under the temporal method, translation adjustments ("gains and losses") appear directly in consolidated income as opposed to stockholders' equity.

[c]The dollar equivalent of cost of sales is derived by translating the components of cost of sales— namely, purchases or cost of production plus beginning and ending inventories by appropriate exchange rates as follows:

Beginning inventories	FC 1,200 at $.23 =	$ 276
Purchases	FC 6,250 at $.22 =	$1,375
Cost of goods available for sale		$1,651
Ending inventories	FC 1,500 at $.19 =	$ 285
Cost of sales		$1,366

[d]The aggregate exchange gain or loss figure combines both transaction and translation gains and losses.

In contrast to the current-rate method, the temporal method translates foreign currency balances using historical as well as current exchange rates. Calculation of the exchange adjustment, which aggregates both transaction and translation gains and losses, also differs. In this example, the first component of the translation adjustment is found by multiplying the beginning net monetary asset position by the change in the current rate during the year. Thus:

$$\begin{aligned}
&(12/31/X7 \text{ Monetary assets} \\
&\quad - \text{monetary liabilities}) \\
&\quad \times \text{change in current rate} \\
&= (FC1,600 - FC6,600) \\
&\quad \times (\$0.18 - \$0.23) \\
&= \$250
\end{aligned}$$

The second component is found by first identifying the variables (i.e., sources and uses of monetary items) that caused the foreign subsidiary's net monetary asset position (exposure) to change, and then multiplying these items by the difference between the year-end exchange rate and the rates that pertain to them. This is illustrated here.

Change in net monetary asset position:

12/31/X7	FC (5,000)
12/31/X8	FC (3,900)
	FC 1,100

Composition of change:

Sources of monetary items multiplied by difference between year-end and average rate:

Net income	FC 1,090
Depreciation	FC 1,000
	$2,090 \times (0.18 - 0.22) = \$ (84)$

Uses of monetary items multiplied by the difference between the year-end and average rate:

Increase in inventories	FC 300
Dividends	FC 690
	$990 \times (0.18 - 0.22) = \$40$

The aggregate exchange adjustment is the sum of any transaction gain or loss together with the individual translation components derived, that is, $\$250 + (\$84) + \$40 = \$206$.

SELECTED REFERENCES

Aiken, M., and D. Ardern, "Choice of Translation Methods in Financial Disclosure: A Test of Compliance with Environmental Hypotheses," *British Accounting Review* 35 (2003): 327–348.

Ayres, Frances L., and Jacci L. Rodgers, "Further Evidence on the Impact of SFAS 52 on Analysts' Earnings Forecasts," *Journal of International Financial Management and Accounting* 5, no. 2(1994): 120–141.

Bartov, Eli, "Foreign Currency Exposure of Multinational Firms: Accounting Measures and Market Valuation," *Contemporary Accounting Research* 14, no. 4 (1997): 623–652.

Cohen, Benjamin J., "Global Currency Rivalry: Can the Euro Ever Challenge the Dollar?" *Journal of Common Market Studies* 41, no. 4 (2003): 575–595.

Collins, Daniel W., and William K. Salatka, "Noisy Accounting Earnings Signals and Earnings Response Coefficients: The Case of Foreign Currency Accounting," *Contemporary Accounting Research* 10, no. 1(1993): 119–159.

Financial Accounting Standards Board, *Foreign Currency Translation: Statement of Financial Accounting Standards No. 52* (Stamford, CT: FASB, December 1981).

Hegelin, Niclas, and Bengt Pramborg, "Hedging Foreign Exchange Exposure: Risk Reduction from Transaction and Translation Hedging," *Journal of International Financial Management and Accounting* 15, no. 1 (2004): 1–20.

Houston, Carol Olson, "Foreign Currency Translation Research: A Review and Synthesis," *Journal of Accounting Literature* 8 (1989): 25–48.

Hughes, John, Jing Liu, and Mingshan Zhang, "Valuation and Accounting for Inflation and Foreign Exchange," *Journal of Accounting Research* 42, no. 4 (2004): 731–754.

Iatradis, George Emmanuel, and Nathan Lael Joseph, "Characteristics of UK Firms Related to Timing of Adoption of Statement of Standard Accounting Practice No. 20," *Accounting and Finance* 46 (2006): 429–455.

International Accounting Standards Committee, *The Effects of Changes in Foreign Exchange Rates: International Accounting Standard 21 (revised)* (London: IASC, 1993).

Lane, Philip R., and GianMaria Milesi-Ferretti, "Financial Globalization and Exchange Rates," IMF Working Paper No. 05/3 (January 1, 2005).

Lewis, Henock. "The Value Relevance of the Foreign Translation Adjustment," *Accounting Review* 78, no. 4 (2003): 1027–1047.

Liu, J., "Foreign Currency Translation Gains and Losses, and the Valuation of Multinational Firms," Working Paper (University of California at Los Angeles, 2003).

Louis, H., "The Value Relevance of the Foreign Translation Adjustment," *Accounting Review* 78 (2003): 1027–1047.

Pinto, Jo Ann M. "Foreign Currency Translation Adjustments as Predictors of Earnings Changes," *Journal of International Accounting, Auditing and Taxation* 10, no. 1(2001): 51–69.

Pinto, Jo Ann M. , "How Comprehensive Is Comprehensive Income? The Value Relevance of Foreign Currency Translation Adjustments," *Journal of International Financial Management and Accounting* 16, no. 2 (2005): 97–122.

Rees, William, and Sanjay Unni, "Exchange Rate Exposure Among European Firms: Evidence from France, Germany and the UK," *Accounting and Finance* 45, no. 3 (2005): 479–497.

Soo, Billy S., and Lisa Gilbert Soo, "Accounting for the Multinational Firm: Is the Translation Process Valued by the Stock Market?" *Accounting Review* (October 1994): 617–637.

Ziebart, David A., and Jong-Hag Choi, "The Difficulty of Achieving Economic Reality Through Foreign Currency Translation," *International Journal of Accounting* 33, no. 4 (1998): 403–414.

DISCUSSION QUESTIONS

1. Distinguish between a foreign currency translation process and a foreign currency conversion process.

2. What is the difference between the spot, forward, and swap markets? Illustrate each description with an example.

3. What do current, historical, and average exchange rates mean in the context of foreign currency translation? Which of these rates give rise to translation gains and losses? Which do not?

4. A foreign currency transaction can be denominated in one currency but measured in another. Explain the difference between these two terms using the case of a Canadian dollar borrowing on the part of a Mexican affiliate of a U.S. parent company that designates the U.S. dollar as the functional currency.

5. What is the difference between a transaction gain or loss and a translation gain or loss?
6. Briefly explain the nature of foreign currency translation as (a) a restatement process and (b) a remeasurement process.
7. Compare and contrast features of the major foreign currency translation methods introduced in this chapter. Which method do you think is best? Why?
8. Under what set of conditions would the temporal method of currency translation be appropriate. Under what set of conditions would the current rate method be appropriate?
9. What lessons, if any, can be learned from examining the history of foreign currency translation in the United States?
10. In what way is foreign currency translation tied to foreign inflation?
11. In what way does the currency translation methodology prescribed by FAS No. 52 differ from the foreign currency translation method in the U.K.? In your country?
12. How does the treatment of translation gains and losses differ between the current and temporal translation methods under FAS No. 52, and what is the rationale for each accounting treatment?

EXERCISES

1. Assume that your Japanese affiliate reports sales revenue of 250 million yen. Referring to Exhibit 6-1, translate this revenue figure to U.S. dollars using the direct bid spot rate. Do the same using the indirect spot quote.
2. Refer to Exhibit 6-1 and using the information provided, can you determine the cross spot rate (i.e., a rate computed from two other exchange rates) between the euro and the British pound?
3. On April 1, A. C. Corporation, a calendar-year U.S. electronics manufacturer, buys 32.5 million yen worth of computer chips from the Hidachi Company paying 10 percent down, the balance to be paid in three months. Interest at 8 percent per annum is payable on the unpaid foreign currency balance. The U.S. dollar/Japanese yen exchange rate on April 1 was $1.00 = ¥116.91; on July 1 it was $1.00 = ¥115.47.

   Required:

   Prepare dated journal entries in U.S. dollars to record the incurrence and settlement of this foreign currency transaction assuming:
   a. A. C. Corporation adopts a single-transaction perspective, and
   b. it employs a two-transactions perspective.
4. On January 20X7, the wholly-owned Mexican affiliate of a Canadian parent company acquired an inventory of computer hard drives for its assembly operation. The cost incurred was 15,000,000 pesos when the exchange rate was MXN9.3 = C$1. By year-end, the Mexican affiliate had used three-fourths of the acquired hard drives. Due to advances in hardware technology, the remaining inventory was marked down to its net realizable value of MXN1,750,000. The year-end exchange rate was MXN10.3. = C$1. The average rate during the year was MXN9.8 = C$1.

   Required:

   a. Translate the ending inventory to Canadian dollars. Assume that the Mexican affiliate's functional currency is the Mexican peso.
   b. Would your answer change if the functional currency were the Canadian dollar? Please explain.
5. A U.S. multinational corporation's subsidiary in Bangkok has on its books fixed assets valued at 7,500,000 baht. One-third of the assets were acquired two years ago when the exchange rate was THB40 = $1. The other fixed assets were acquired last year when the

exchange rate was THB38 = $1. Each layer of fixed assets is being depreciated straight-line with an estimated useful life of 20 years. Relevant exchange rates for the current year are:

$$\text{Year-end rate: THB36} = \$1$$

$$\text{Average rate: THB37} = \$1$$

Required:

a. Calculate the Thai subsidiary's depreciation expense for the current year, assuming the baht is the functional currency.

b. Repeat requirement (a), assuming instead that the U.S. dollar is the functional currency.

6. Sydney Corporation, an Australian-based multinational, borrowed **10 million** euros from a German lender at the beginning of the calendar year when the exchange rate was EUR.60 = AUD1. Before repaying this one-year loan, Sydney Corporation learns that the Australian dollar has depreciated to EUR.55 = AUD1. It also discovers that its Frankfurt subsidiary has an exposed net asset position of EUR30,000,000, which will produce a translation gain upon consolidation. What is the exchange gain or loss that will be reported in consolidated income if

a. The euro is the foreign operation's functional currency?

b. The Australian dollar is the foreign operation's functional currency?

7. Shanghai Corporation, the Chinese affiliate of a U.S. manufacturer, has the balance sheet shown below. The current exchange rate is $0.12 = CNY1.

Balance Sheet of Shanghai Corporation(000's)

Assets		Liabilities and OE	
Cash	CNY 5,000	Accounts payable	CNY 21,000
Accounts receivable	14,000	Long-term debt	27,000
Inventories[a] (cost = 24,000)	22,000		
Fixed assets, net	39,000	Stockholders' equity	32,000
Total assets	CNY80,000	Total liabilty & SE	CNY80,000

[a]Inventories are carried at the lower of cost or market.

Required:

a. Translate the Chinese dollar balance sheet of Shanghai Corporation into U.S. dollars at the current exchange rate of $0.12 = CNY1. All monetary accounts in Shanhai's balance sheet are denominated in Chinese yuan.

b. Assume that the Chinese yuan revalues from $0.12 = CNY1 to $0.15 = CNY1. What would be the translation effect if Shanghai's balance sheet is translated by the current-noncurrent method? By the monetary-nonmonetary method?

c. Assume instead that the Chinese yuan weakens from $0.12 = CNY1 to $0.09 = CNY1. What would be the translation effect under each of the two translation methods?

8. Use the information provided in Exercise 7.

Required:

a. What would be the translation effect if Shanghai Corporation's balance sheet were translated by the temporal method assuming that the Chinese yuan appreciates by 25 percent? By the current rate method?

b. If the Chinese yuan depreciates by 25 percent, what would be the translation effects under each of the two methods in requirement (a)?

c. Based on your previous calculations and in Exercise 7, which translation method—current-noncurrent, monetary-nonmonetary, temporal, or current—gives statement readers the most meaningful information?

9. Company A is headquartered in Country A and reports in the currency unit of Country A, the apeso. Company B is headquartered in Country B and reports in the currency unit of Country B, the bol. Company A and B hold identical assets, apeso100 and bol100, at the beginning and end of the year. At the beginning of the year, the exchange rate is apeso1 = bol1.25. At the end of the year, the exchange rate is apeso1 = bol 2. No transactions occur during the year.

Required:

a. Calculate the total assets reported by Company A and Company B at the beginning and end of the year. Which company has a gain and which has a loss for the year?

b. Does your answer to part (a) make sense? Would it matter if Companies A and B intended to repatriate their respective foreign assets rather than keep them invested permanently abroad?

c. What is the lesson for statement readers from all of this? Is it all a shell game?

10. A 100 percent–owned foreign subsidiary's trial balance consists of the accounts listed as follows: Which exchange rate—current, historical, or average—would be used to translate these accounts to parent currency assuming that the foreign currency is the functional currency? Which rates would be used if the parent currency were the functional currency?

Trial Balance Accounts	
Cash	Common stock
Marketable securities (cost)	Premium on common stock
Accounts receivable	Retained earnings
Inventory (market)	Sales
Equipment	Purchases
Accumulated depreciation	Cost of sales
Prepaid expenses	General and administrative expenses
Goodwill	Selling expenses
Accounts payable	Depreciation
Due to parent (denominated in dollars)	Amortization of goodwill
Bonds payable	Income tax expense
Income taxes payable	Intercompany interest expense
Deferred income taxes	

11. On December 15, MSC Corporation acquires its first foreign affiliate by acquiring 100 percent of the net assets of the Armaselah Oil Company based in Saudi Arabia for 930 million Saudi Arabian riyals (SAR). At the time, the exchange rate was $1.00 = SAR3.750. The acquisition price is traceable to the following identifiable assets:

Cash	SAR60,000,000
Inventory	120,000,000
Fixed assets	750,000,000

As a calendar-year company, MSC Corporation prepares consolidated financial statements every December 31. However, by the consolidation date, the Saudi Arabian riyal has depreciated such that the new spot rate is $1.00 = SAR4.125.

Required:

a. Assuming that no transactions took place before consolidation, what would be the translation gain or loss if Armaselah's balance sheet were translated to dollars by the temporal-rate method?

b. How does the translation adjustment affect MSC's cash flows?

c. What adjustments to Armaselah's accounts would be necessary to enable you to compare its financial statements to another company of comparable size in the same industry that is employing the current rate translation method per IAS 21?

12. Revisit Alcan's income statement on the first page of this chapter together with the accompanying notes, and answer the following questions.

a. Which currency effects described in the three explanatory paragraphs affect Alcan's cash flows and in what manner?

b. What currency translation method is Alcan employing?

c. Now that you understand the nature of foreign currency translation adjustments, what adjustments would you make to Alcan's earnings numbers and how would that affect the patterns of Alan's disclosed earnings?

Case 6-1   Regents Corporation

Regents Corporation is a recently acquired U.S. manufacturing subsidiary located on the outskirts of London. Its products are marketed principally in the United Kingdom, with sales invoiced in pounds and prices determined by local competitive conditions. Expenses (labor, materials, and other production costs) are mostly local, although a significant quantity of components is now imported from the U.S. parent. Financing is primarily in U.S. dollars provided by the parent.

Headquarters management must decide on the functional currency for its London operation: Should it be the U.S. dollar or the British pound? You are asked to advise management on the appropriate currency designation and its relative financial statement effects. Prepare a report that supports your recommendations and identify any policy issues your analysis uncovers.

Exhibit 6-14 presents comparative balance sheets for Regents Corporation at December 31, 20X7 and 20X8, and a statement of income for the year ended December 31, 20X8. The statements conform with U.S. generally accepted accounting principles prior to translation to dollars. ■

EXHIBIT 6-14   Regents Corporation Financial Statements

Balance Sheet	12/31/X7	12/31/X8
Assets		
Cash	£ 1,060	£ 1,150
Accounts receivable	2,890	3,100
Inventory (FIFO)	3,040	3,430
Fixed assets	4,400	4,900
Accumulated depreciation	(420)	(720)
Intangible asset (patent)		70
Total	£10,970	£11,930
Liabilities and Stockholders' Equity		
Accounts payable	£ 1,610	£ 1,385
Due to parent	1,800	1,310
Long-term debt	4,500	4,000
Deferred taxes	80	120
Common stock	1,500	1,500
Retained earnings	1,480	3,615
Total	£10,970	£11,930
Income Statement Year Ended 12/31/X8		
Sales		£16,700
Expenses		
Cost of sales	£11,300	
General and administrative	1,600	
Depreciation	300	
Interest	480	13,680
Operating income		£ 3,020
Transaction gain (loss)		125
Income before taxes		£ 3,145

(continued)

		12/31/X8
Income taxes Current	£ 670	
Deferred	40	710
Net income		£ 2,435
Retained earnings at 12/31/X7 (residual)		1,480
		3,915
Dividends		300
Retained earnings at 12/31/X8		£ 3,615

Exchange rate information and additional data:

1. Exchange rates:

December 31, 20X7	$1.80 = £1
December 31, 20X8	$1.90 = £1
Average during 20X8	$1.86 = £1
Average during fourth quarter 20X7	$1.78 = £1
Average during fourth quarter 20X8	$1.88 = £1

2. Common stock was acquired, long-term debt issued, and original fixed assets purchased when the exchange rate was $1.70 = £1.

3. Due to parent account is denominated in U.S. dollars.

4. Exchange rate prevailing when the intangible asset (patent) was acquired and additional fixed assets purchased was $1.82 = £1.

5. Purchases and dividends occurred evenly during 20X8.

6. Of the £300 depreciation expense for 20X8, £20 relates to fixed assets purchased during 20X8.

7. Deferred taxes are translated at the current rate.

8. Inventory represents approximately 3 months of production.

Case 6-2   Managing Offshore Investments: Whose Currency?

The Offshore Investment Fund (OIF) was incorporated in Fairfield, Connecticut, for the sole purpose of allowing U.S. shareholders to invest in Spanish securities. The fund is listed on the New York Stock Exchange. The fund custodian is the Shady Rest Bank and Trust Company of Connecticut ("Shady Rest"), which keeps the fund's accounts. The question of which currency to use in keeping the fund's books arose at once. Shady Rest prepared the fund's books in euros, since the fund was a country fund that invested solely in securities listed on the Madrid Stock Exchange. Subsequently, the fund's auditors stated that in their opinion,

the functional currency should be the U.S. dollar. This case is based on an actual occurrence. Names and country of origin have been changed to ensure anonymity.

EFFECTS OF THE DECISION

The decision to possibly adopt the U.S. dollar as the functional currency for the fund created considerable managerial headaches. For one thing, the work of rewriting and reworking the accounting transactions was a monumental task that delayed the publication of the annual accounts. The concept of the functional currency was a foreign concept in Spain, and the effects of the functional currency choice were not made clear to the managers. Consequently, it was not until late in November that they began to appreciate the impact the currency choice had on the fund's results.

Additional difficulties caused by the functional currency choice were:

a. Shady Rest, with some $300 billion in various funds under management, still had not developed an adequate multi-currency accounting system. Whereas accounting for a security acquisition would normally be recorded in a simple bookkeeping entry, three entries were now required. In addition, payment for the purchase could itself impact the income statement in the current period.

b. More serious problems related to day-to-day operations. When a transaction was initiated, the fund manager had no idea of its ultimate financial effect. As an example, during the first year of operations, the fund manager was certain that portfolio sales had generated a profit of more than $1 million. When the sales finally showed up in the accounts, the transaction gain was offset by currency losses of some $7 million!

REASONS GIVEN FOR CHOOSING THE DOLLAR AS FUNCTIONAL

The auditors gave the following reasons for choosing the dollar as the fund's functional currency:

a. Incorporation in the United States
b. Funded with U.S. shareholder capital
c. Dividends determined and paid in U.S. dollars
d. Financial reporting under U.S. GAAP and in U.S. dollars

e. Administration and advisory fees calculated on U.S. net assets and paid in U.S. dollars
f. Most expenses incurred and paid in U.S. dollars
g. Accounting records kept in U.S. dollars
h. Subject to U.S. tax, SEC, and 1940 Exchange Act regulations

Since the fund was set up to invest in Spain, it is assumed that the U.S. shareholders are interested in the impact of an exchange rate change on the fund's cash flows and equity; that is, the shareholders did not invest in Spanish securities only because of attractive yields, but also were making a currency play that directly would directly affect the measurement of cash flow and equity.

MANAGEMENT'S VIEWPOINT

Management disagreed with the auditors. Following is its rebuttal:

a. Incorporation in the United States with U.S. shareholders. FAS 52 clearly states that the functional currency should be determined by "the primary economic environment in which that entity operates rather than by the technical detail of incorporation." Similarly, nowhere does FAS 52 state that the facts that the company has U.S. shareholders and pays dividends in U.S. dollars are relevant. In fact, FAS 52 concerns itself throughout with the firm and its management rather than its shareholders.

b. Financial reporting in U.S. dollars under U.S. GAAP. The auditors fail to differentiate between reporting currency and functional currency. It is clear that the U.S. dollar should be the reporting currency, but that alone does not mean that the U.S. dollar is the functional currency.

c. Payment of certain expenses in dollars. The payment of expenses in U.S. dollars is no reason to make the dollar the functional currency. While expenses of some $8 million for calendar year 20X7 were incurred in U.S. dollars, income of over $100 million was earned in euros.

d. U.S. tax and SEC regulations. These considerations are relevant for the reporting currency, not the functional currency.

The decisive argument against identifying the dollar as the functional currency is that doing so does not provide information that is, in the words of FAS 52, "generally compatible with the expected economic effect of a rate change on an enterprise's cash flow and equity." Specifically, the operating cash flow of the fund is located entirely in Spain once the initial transfer of funds raised by the issue of capital is made. The fund buys and sells investments in Spain, and receives all its income from Spain. If the functional currency is euros, then realized currency fluctuations are recognized only when money is repatriated to the United States. The present practice of "realizing" an exchange profit or loss when, for example, cash in Spain is exchanged for an investment purchased in Spain is wrong and misleading.

Consider an example. Suppose that the fund deposits EUR100,000,000 in a Spanish bank when the exchange rate is EUR1 = $0.8496. One week later, when the exchange rate is EUR1 = $0.8393, the fund purchases and pays for an investment of EUR100,000,000, which it sells for cash on the same day, having decided that the investment was unwise. Ignoring transaction costs, the fund has EUR100,000,000 in cash in Madrid at both the beginning and the end of the week. If the functional currency is euros, there is no realized gain or loss. However, translation to dollars generates an unrealized currency loss of $1,030,000, which would be realized only when the amount in question is repatriated to the United States. This is analogous to the purchase of a stock whose price later falls. If the U.S. dollar is the functional currency, the transaction in question would result in a realized loss on exchange of $1,030,000. This result is absurd in terms of any common-sense view of cash flow; indeed, it highlights that, given the fund's purpose, the effect on the reported income of adopting the U.S. dollar as the functional currency is equally absurd.

The net asset value of the fund is determined each week in U.S. dollars, and reported to stockholders in U.S. dollars. This is entirely consistent with having the U.S. dollar as the appropriate reporting currency. Using the dollar as the functional currency implies that there is a realistic and practical option on each transaction of moving between the dollar and the euro. This assumption is patently wrong; the fund will only repatriate its base capital under two circumstances: (1) liquidation or (2) as a temporary expedient if Spanish yields fall below U.S. yields.

GENERAL THRUST OF FAS 52

The language of FAS 52 indicates that its authors did not write it with direct reference to a situation like that of the Offshore Investment Fund, that is, a company that raises money for the single purpose of investing it in a foreign country. FAS 52 seems rather to be written from the viewpoint of an operating holding company owning a separate, distinct foreign operating subsidiary.

FAS 52 defines the functional currency of an entity as the currency of the primary economic environment in which that entity operates. Had the fund been incorporated in Malta and, as a separate entity, borrowed the funds from its U.S. parent, use of the local currency would have been automatic. If substance is to prevail over form, one must conclude that the euro should still be used.

Paragraph 6 of FAS 52 states, "for an entity with operations that are relatively self-contained and integrated within a particular country, the functional currency generally would be the currency of that country." This statement reinforces the operational aspect that governs the choice of the functional currency; it is surely wrong to argue that the operations of the fund are conducted anywhere but in Spain.

Paragraph 8 reinforces the contention that "management's judgment will be required to determine the functional currency in which financial results and relationships are measured with the greatest degree of relevance and reliability."

Finally, paragraphs 80 and 81 draw a very clear distinction that reinforces our (management's) contention. Paragraph 80 reads:

> In the first class are foreign operations that are relatively self-contained and integrated within a particular country or economic environment. The day-to-day operations are not dependent upon the economic environment of the parent's functional currency; the foreign operation primarily generates and expends foreign currency. The foreign currency net cash flows that it generates may be reinvested and converted and distributed to the parent. For this class, the foreign currency is the functional currency.

This definition should be contrasted with paragraph 81, which states:

> In the second class ... the day-to-day operations are dependent on the economic environment of the parent's currency, and the changes in the foreign entity's individual assets and liabilities impact directly on the cash flows of the parent company in the parent's currency. For this class, the U.S. dollar is the functional currency.

Since the purpose of single-country funds is to create entities of the first rather than the second class, paragraph 80 precisely describes the operations of the Overseas Investment Fund. ■

REQUIRED

1. Based on the arguments presented, what do you think should be the functional currency in this case?

CHAPTER 7

Financial Reporting and Changing Prices

Fluctuating currencies and changes in money prices of goods and services are integral features of international business. Chapter 6 focused on the former. This chapter dwells on the financial statement effects of changing prices.

Grupo Modello S.A., the largest beer manufacturer in Mexico, operates in an environment where changing prices have been nontrivial. To see whether these price changes are reflected in the company's published accounts, examine Exhibit 7-1, which contains selected excerpts from Grupo Modello S.A.'s financial statements and related notes.

EXHIBIT 7-1 Selected Excerpts from Grupo Modelo's Financial Accounts

Grupo Modelo S.A. De C.V. and Subsidiaries

Consolidated Income Statements for the years ended December 31, 2005 and 2004 (Amounts in thousands of constant Mexican pesos as of December 2005)

	2005	*2004*
Operating profit	MXP13,773,025	MXP13,587,835
Other (expenses) and income, net	253,528	298,354
Comprehensive financing income:		
Interest earned and paid, net	1,337,842	893,938
Foreign exchange profit(loss), net	(98,159)	(3,032)
Loss from monetary position	(619,672)	(790,977)
	620,011	99,929
Profit before provisions		
Provisions for: (Note 12)	14,646,564	13,986,118
Income and asset tax	4,317,213	4,065,951
Employees' profit-sharing	826,356	1,543,549
	5,143,569	5,609,500
Consolidated net income for the year	MXP9,502,995	MXP8,376,618

Consolidated Balance Sheets

As of December 31, 2005 and 2004 (Notes 1, 2, and 15) (Amounts in thousands of constant Mexican pesos as of December 31, 2005)

Assets	*2005*	*2004*
Current		
Cash and marketable securities	MXP17,633,734	MXP16,377,740
Accounts and notes receivable (Note 3)	3,146,273	1,993,655
Inventories (Note 4)	5,762,102	5,697,891
Prepaid expenses and other current items	2,213,752	1,953,400
Total current assets	28,755,861	26,022,686
Long-term accounts and notes receivable (Note 3)	1,156,582	1,092,766
Investment in shares of associated companies (Note 5)	2,748,219	2,799,294
Property, plant, and equipment (Note 6)	67,351,012	64,599,590
Accumulated depreciation	(21,550,741)	(20,381,482)
	45,800,271	44,218,108
Other assets (Note 7)	1,820,326	1,781,260
Total assets	MXP80,281,259	MXP75,914,114
Total liabilities	MXP12,169,265	MXP13,075,293
Stockholders' equity:		
Common stock (Note 10)	15,169,230	15,169,230
Premium on share subscription	1,010,236	1,010,236
Earned surplus (Notes 11 and 12):		
Legal reserve	2,202,843	1,887,020
Reserve for acquisition of own shares	638,100	638,100
Retained earnings	32,310,677	29,725,630
Net income	7,291,275	6,388,968
	26,797,597	23,690,042
Initial effect of deferred tax	(5,069,105)	(5,069,105)
Adjustment to capital for retirement obligations	(493,335)	(771,580)
Deficit in the restatement of stockholders' equity	(694,678)	(695,458)
Total majority stockholders' equity	MXP52,365,243	MXP48,283,041

Notes to the Consolidated Financial Statements

As of December 31, 2005 and 2004 (Amounts in thousands of constant Mexican pesos as of December 31, 2005)

2. Accounting policies—The main accounting policies applied by the Group in the preparation of these consolidated financial statements are in accord with generally accepted accounting principles in Mexico.

b) Basis for Preparation—The consolidated financial statements of the Group include the effects of inflation on the financial information, as required by Statement B-10, issued by the Mexican Institute of Public Accountants(MIPA).

c) Comparability—The figures shown in the consolidated financial statements and its notes are stated consistently in Mexican pesos of December 31, 2005 purchasing power by applying factors derived from the National Consumer Price Index (NCPI).

d) Translation of the Financial Information of Subsidiaries Located Abroad—Translation of the financial information of foreign subsidiaries to Mexican pesos, required for consolidation, was carried out in accordance with the guidelines of Statement B-15 "Transactions in Foreign Currency and Translation of the Financial Statements of Foreign Operations," issued by the MIPA, by the integrated foreign operation method. The purchase exchange rate of MXP10.63(MXP11.00 in 2004) per U.S. dollar was used in translating monetary items; nonmonetary items and the income statement were translated into Mexican pesos at the exchange rates prevailing on the dates on which the underlying transactions were carried out. The effects of this translation are included in comprehensive financing income.

6. Property, Plant, and Equipment — Net

a) The balance of this account is made up as follows:

Item		2005		2004
	Net historical cost	*Net restatement*	*Net total value*	*Net total value*
Land	MXP 1,502,140	MXP 3,106,019	MXP 4,608,159	MXP 4,452,500
Machinery and equipment	13,631,210	7,362,791	20,994,001	18,380,073
Transportation equipment	2,287,791	438,824	2,726,615	2,432,491
Building and other structures	6,438,810	6,480,152	12,918,962	11,474,653
Computer equipment	507,772	30,434	538,206	352,015
Furniture and other equipment	396,640	109,008	505,648	548,458
Antipollution equipment	594,346	285,061	879,407	701,640
Construction in progress	2,490,191	139,082	2,629,273	5,876,278
	MXP27,848,900	MXP17,951,371	MXP45,800,271	MXP44,218,108

Depreciation for the year amounted to MXP2,394,064 (MXP,122,584 in 2004).

A quick scan of Modello's income statement reveals an account labeled "Comprehensive Financing Income." Two of its components should be familiar to you. The first relates to interest on the firm's receivables and payables. The second, discussed in Chapter 6, is the translation gains or losses resulting from the currency translation process (examine footnote 2d in Exhibit 7-1). The third component, "Loss from monetary position," is probably new to you and stems from Modello's attempts to reflect the effects of changing prices on its financial accounts. But what does this figure mean, and how is it derived?

Grupo Modello's balance sheet also introduces financial statement items that are unfamiliar to most statement readers. The first relates to its fixed assets. Footnote 6 suggests that the 2005 balance of P45,800,271 for Property, Plant, and Equipment, net of accumulated depreciation, consists of two components: one labeled "Net historical cost," the other, "Net restatement." While the former may be a familiar term, the latter probably is not. Another novel balance sheet account appears in Stockholders' Equity, labeled "Deficit in the Restatement of Stockholders' Equity."

Finally, footnote 2c states that all figures disclosed in Modello's comparative statements, and the notes thereto, are expressed in December 2005 purchasing power. What does "December 2002 purchasing power" mean, and what is its rationale? And, more important, do statement readers actually impound the foregoing information in their security pricing and managerial decisions?

Subsequent sections of this chapter are devoted to answering these and related questions. The managerial implications of changing prices are covered in Chapter 10. To make informed decisions, financial analysts must understand the contents of financial accounts that have been adjusted for changing prices. Moreover, they must have some facility for adjusting accounts for changing prices in those instances where companies choose not to account for inflation so as to facilitate apple-to-apple comparisons over time and/or with companies that do.

CHANGING PRICES DEFINED

To understand what *changing prices* means, we must distinguish between general and specific price movements, both of which are embraced by the term. A *general price level* change occurs when, on average, the prices of all goods and services in an economy change. The monetary unit gains or loses purchasing power. An overall increase in prices is called *inflation*; a decrease, *deflation*. What causes inflation? Evidence suggests that aggressive monetary and fiscal policies designed to achieve high economic growth targets, excessive spending associated with national elections, and the international transmission of inflation are causal explanations.[1] The issue, however, is complex.

A *specific price* change, on the other hand, refers to a change in the price of a specific good or service caused by changes in demand and supply. Thus, the annual rate of inflation in a country may average 5 percent, while the specific price of one-bedroom apartments may rise by 50 percent during the same period. Exhibit 7-2 defines additional terminology used in this chapter.

As consumers, we are well aware of inflation's effects on our material standard of living. We immediately feel its impact in our pocketbooks when the price of oil or a Big Mac increases. The social and political devastation resulting from bouts of *hyperinflation* (e.g., when the inflation rate soars by more than 50 percent per month) can be extreme. Consider the following commentary offered by Steve H. Hanke, former economic adviser to the president and state counselor of the Republic of Montenegro.

> Voters in Montenegro recently turned out in record numbers to denounce their republic's loose union with Serbia. This action followed a bizarre history of monetary policy that wreaked havoc with people's lives. Following a 20-year period of double-digit inflation (annualized rates averaging 75%), the Serbian Parliament, controlled by Slobodan Milosevic, secretely ordered the Serbian National Bank (a regional central bank) to issue $1.4 billion in credits to Milosevic's friends and political allies. This illegal move doubled the quantity of money the National Bank of Yugoslavia had planned to create and fanned the flames of inflation. Beginning in 1992, Yugoslavia experienced one of the highest and longest periods of hyperinflation in history. When it peaked in 1994, prices had increased by 313,000,000% in one month! There were a total of 14 maxi-devaluations during the hyperinflation, completely wiping out the Yugoslav dinar's value. To appreciate the impact of this hyperinflation on the local population, first, assume you had the equivalent of $10,000 in the bank, next, move the decimal point of the dollar 22 places to the left, and finally, try to buy something to eat. Little wonder why stable prices are a national priority for much of the world. Businesses also feel inflation's effects when the prices of their factor inputs rise.[2]

---

[1]John F. Boschen and Charles L. Weise, "What Starts Inflation: Evidence from the OECD Countries," *Journal of Money, Credit and Banking* (June 2003): 323.
[2]Steve H. Hanke, "Inflation Nation," *Wall Street Journal*, May 24, 2006, p. A14.

EXHIBIT 7-2   Glossary of Inflation Accounting Terms

attribute. The quantifiable characteristic of an item that is measured for accounting purposes. For example, historical cost and replacement cost are attributes of an asset.

current-cost adjustments. Adjusting asset values for changes in specific prices.

disposable wealth. The amount of a firm's net assets that could be withdrawn without reducing its beginning level of net assets.

gearing adjustment. The benefit to shareholders' purchasing power gain from debt financing and signals that the firm need not recognize the additional replacement cost of operating assets to the extent they are financed by debt. The U.S. expression for gearing is *leverage*.

general purchasing power equivalents. Currency amounts that have been adjusted for changes in the general level of prices.

general purchasing gains and losses. See **monetary gains and losses.**

historical cost-constant currency. See **general purchasing power equivalents.**

holding gain. Increase in the current cost of a nonmonetary asset.

hyperinflation. An excessive rate of inflation, as when the general level of prices in an economy increases by more than 25 percent per annum.

inflation. Increase in the general level of prices of all goods and services in an economy.

monetary asset. A claim to a fixed amount of currency in the future, like cash or accounts receivable.

monetary gains. Increases in general purchasing power that occur when monetary liabilities are held during a period of inflation.

monetary liability. An obligation to pay a fixed amount of currency in the future, such as an account payable or debt that bears a fixed rate of interest.

monetary losses. Decreases in general purchasing power that occur when monetary assets are held during a period of inflation.

monetary working capital adjustment. The effect of specific price changes on the total amount of working capital used by the business in its operations.

nominal amounts. Currency amounts that have not been adjusted for changing prices.

nonmonetary asset. An asset that does not represent a fixed claim to cash, such as inventory or plant and equipment.

nonmonetary liability. A debt that does not require the payment of a fixed sum of cash in the future, such as a customer advance. Here the obligation is to provide the customer a good or service whose value may change because of inflation.

parity adjustment. An adjustment that reflects the difference in inflation between the parent and host countries.

permanent assets. A Brazilian term for fixed assets, buildings, investments, deferred charges and their respective depreciation, and depletion or amortization amounts.

price index. A cost ratio where the numerator is the cost of a representative "basket" of goods and services in the current year and the denominator is the cost of the same basket of goods and services in a benchmark year.

purchasing power. The general ability of a monetary unit to command goods and services.

real profit. Net income that has been adjusted for changing prices.

replacement cost. The current cost of replacing the service potential of an asset in the normal course of business.

reporting currency. The currency in which an entity prepares its financial statements.

restate-translate method. Used when a parent company consolidates the accounts of a foreign subsidiary located in an inflationary environment. With this method, the subsidiary's accounts are first restated for local inflation and then translated to the parent currency.

specific price change. The change in the price of a specific commodity, such as inventory or equipment.

translate-restate method. A consolidation method that first translates a foreign subsidiary's accounts to parent currency and then restates the translated amounts for parent-country inflation.

While changing prices occur worldwide, their business and financial reporting effects vary from country to country. Europe and North America, for instance, have enjoyed relatively modest general price-level increases, averaging less than 3 percent per year during the last decade. By contrast, Eastern Europe, Latin America, and Africa have experienced much higher inflation rates. Annual rates of inflation have been as high as 106 percent in Turkey, 2,076 percent in Brazil, and, most recently, 1,042 percent in Zimbabwe.[3]

Local inflation affects the exchange rates used to translate foreign currency balances to their domestic currency equivalents. As we shall see, it is hard to separate foreign currency translation from inflation when accounting for foreign operations.

WHY ARE FINANCIAL STATEMENTS POTENTIALLY MISLEADING DURING PERIODS OF CHANGING PRICES?

During a period of inflation, asset values recorded at their original acquisition costs seldom reflect the assets' current (higher) value. Understated asset values result in understated expenses and overstated income. From a managerial perspective, these measurement inaccuracies distort (1) financial projections based on unadjusted historical time series data, (2) budgets against which results are measured, and (3) performance data that fail to isolate the uncontrollable effects of inflation. Overstated earnings may, in turn, lead to:

- Increases in proportionate taxation
- Requests by shareholders for more dividends
- Demands for higher wages by workers
- Disadvantageous actions by host governments (e.g., imposition of excess profit taxes)

Should a firm distribute all of its overstated earnings (in the form of higher taxes, dividends, wages, and the like), it may not keep enough resources to replace specific assets whose prices have risen, such as inventories and plant and equipment.

Failure to adjust corporate financial data for changes in the purchasing power of the monetary unit also makes it hard for financial statement readers to interpret and compare reported operating performances of companies. In an inflationary period,

---

[3]"Zimbabwe's Inflation Tops 1,000%," *BBC News*, May 12, 2006.

revenues are typically expressed in currency with a lower general purchasing power (i.e., purchasing power of the current period) than applies to the related expenses. Expenses are expressed in currency with a higher general purchasing power because typically they reflect the consumption of resources that were acquired a while back (e.g., depreciating a factory purchased ten years ago) when the monetary unit had more purchasing power. Subtracting expenses based on historical purchasing power from revenues based on current purchasing power results in an inaccurate measure of income.

Conventional accounting procedures also ignore purchasing power gains and losses that arise from holding cash (or equivalents) during an inflationary period. If you held cash during a year in which the inflation rate was 100 percent, it would take twice as much cash at the end of the year to have the same purchasing power as your original cash balance. This further distorts business-performance comparisons for financial statement readers.

Therefore, it is useful to recognize inflation's effects explicitly for several reasons:

1. The effects of changing prices depend partially on the transactions and circumstances of the enterprise. Users do not have detailed information about these factors.
2. Managing the problems caused by changing prices depends on an accurate understanding of the problems. An accurate understanding requires that business performance be reported in terms that allow for the effects of changing prices.
3. Statements by managers about the problems caused by changing prices are easier to believe when businesses publish financial information that addresses the problems.[4]

Even when inflation rates slow, accounting for changing prices is useful because the cumulative effect of low inflation over time can be significant. As examples, the cumulative inflation rate during the last ten years was approximately 22 percent in highly industrialized countries like the Eurozone, Japan, the U.K., and the United States, approximately 61 percent for emerging economies in Asia, 575 percent for Latin America, and 804 percent for Central and Eastern Europe.[5] The distorting effects of prior inflation can persist for many years, given the long lives of many assets. And, as mentioned earlier, specific price changes may be significant even when the general price level does not change much.

TYPES OF INFLATION ADJUSTMENTS

Statistical series that measure changes in both general and specific prices do not generally move in parallel.[6] Each type of price change has a different effect on measures of a firm's financial position and operating performance and is accounted for with

---

[4]Financial Accounting Standards Board, *Financial Reporting and Changing Prices: Statement of Financial Accounting Standards No. 33* (Stamford, CT: FASB, September 1979).
[5]Bank for International Settlements 76th Annual Report (June 2006).
[6]Carlos Dabus, "Inflationary Regimes and Relative Price Variability: Evidence from Argentina," *Journal of Development Economics* 62 (2000): 535–547.

different objectives in mind. Hereinafter, accounting for the financial statement effects of general price-level changes is called the *historical cost-constant purchasing power* model. Accounting for specific price changes is referred to as the *current-cost* model.

GENERAL PRICE-LEVEL ADJUSTMENTS

Currency amounts adjusted for general price-level (purchasing power) changes are called *historical cost-constant currency* or *general purchasing power equivalents*. Currency amounts that have not been so adjusted are called *nominal* amounts. For example, during a period of rising prices, a long-lived asset that is on the balance sheet at its original acquisition cost is expressed in nominal currency. When its historical cost is allocated to the current period's income (in the form of depreciation expense), revenues, which reflect current purchasing power, are matched with costs that reflect the (higher) purchasing power of the earlier period when the asset was bought. Therefore, nominal amounts must be adjusted for changes in the general purchasing power of money to match them appropriately with current transactions.

Price Indexes

General price-level changes are measured by a price-level index of the form $\sum p_1 q_1 / \sum p_0 q_0$, where p = the price of a given commodity and q = quantity consumed. A price index is a cost ratio. For example, if a family of four spends $20,000 to buy a representative basket of goods and services at the end of year 1 (the base year = start of year 2) and $22,000 to buy the same basket a year later (start of year 3), the year-end price index for year 2 is $22,000/$20,000, or 1.100. This figure implies a 10 percent rate of inflation during year 2. Similarly, if the basket in question costs our family of four $23,500 two years later (end of year 3), the general price-level index would be $23,500/$20,000, or 1.175, implying 17.5 percent inflation since the base year. The index for the base year is $20,000/$20,000, or 1.000.

Use of Price Indexes

Price index numbers are used to translate sums of money paid in past periods to their end-of-period purchasing power equivalents (i.e., historical cost-constant purchasing power). The method used is as follows:

$$\text{GPL}_c / \text{GPL}_{td} \times \text{Nominal amount}_{td} = \text{PPE}_c$$

where

GPL = general price index
c = current period
td = transaction date
PPE = general purchasing power equivalent

For example, suppose that $500 is spent at the end of the base year, and $700 one year later. To restate these expenditures at their year 3 purchasing power equivalents, using price index numbers from our example, we would do the following:

End of:	Nominal Expenditure	Year 3 Adjustment Factor	Purchasing Power Equivalent
Year 1	$500	1.175/1.000	$587.50
Year 2	$700	1.175/1.100	$747.73

It would take $587.50 at the end of year 3 to buy (in general) what $500 would have bought at the end of year 1. Similarly, it would take $747.73 at the end of year 3 to buy (in general) what $700 would have bought a year earlier. Alternatively, during a period of inflation, the nominal expenditures of $500 at the end of year 1, and $700 a year later, are not comparable unless they are expressed in terms of a common denominator, which is year 3 general purchasing power equivalents. This is why Grupo Modello, cited earlier in the chapter, restates all of its trend data to December 31, 2005, purchasing power.

Price-level adjusted figures do not represent the current cost of the items in question; they are still historical cost numbers. The historical cost numbers are merely restated in a new unit of measure: general purchasing power at the end of the period. When transactions occur uniformly throughout a period (such as revenues from the sale of goods or services), a shortcut price-level adjustment can be used. In expressing revenues as end-of-period purchasing power equivalents rather than price-level adjusting each day's revenues (365 calculations!), one could multiply total annual revenues by the ratio of the year-end index to the average general price-level index (such as a monthly weighted average) for the year. Thus:

$$GPL_c \ / \ GPL_{avg} \times \text{Total revenues} = PPE_c$$

Object of General Price-Level Adjustments

Let us briefly review the conventional notion of enterprise income. Traditionally, income (disposable wealth) is that portion of a firm's wealth (i.e., net assets) that the firm can withdraw during an accounting period without reducing its wealth beneath its original level. Assuming no additional owner investments or withdrawals during the period, if a firm's beginning net assets were £10,000 and its ending net assets increased to £25,000 due to profitable operations, its income would be £15,000. If it paid a dividend of £15,000, the firm's end-of-period wealth would be exactly what it was at the beginning. Hence, conventional accounting measures income as the maximum amount that can be withdrawn from the firm without reducing its original money capital.

If we cannot assume stable prices, the conventional measure of income may not accurately measure a firm's disposable wealth. Assume that the general price level rises by 21 percent during a year. To keep up with inflation, a firm that begins the year with £10,000 would want its original investment to grow to at least £12,100, because it would take that much at year's end to buy what £10,000 would have bought at the beginning. Suppose that, using conventional accounting, the firm earns £15,000 (after tax). Withdrawing £15,000 would reduce the firm's nominal end-of-period wealth to the original £10,000. But this is less than it needs to keep up with inflation (£12,100). The historical cost-constant purchasing power model takes this discrepancy into account by measuring income so that the firm could pay out its entire income as dividends while having as much purchasing power at the end of the period as at the beginning.

To illustrate, suppose that an Argentine merchandiser begins the calendar year with ARS100,000 in cash (no debt), which is immediately converted into salable inventory (e.g., 10,000 compact discs of an Argentinian rock star at a unit cost of 10 pesos). The firm sells the entire inventory uniformly during the year at a 50 percent markup. Assuming no inflation, enterprise income would be ARS50,000, the difference between ending and beginning net assets ($150,000 – $100,000), or as revenue minus expenses (cost of CDs sold). Withdrawal of ARS50,000 would leave the firm with ARS100,000, as much money capital as at the start of the year, maintaining its original investment.

Suppose instead that the period had a 21 percent inflation rate, with the general price level (1.21 at year-end) averaging 1.10 during the year. Inflation-adjusted income would be measured (in thousands) as follows:

	Nominal Pesos	Adjustment Factor	Constant Pesos
Revenues	ARS150,000	1.21/1.10	ARS165,000
– Expenses	100,000	1.21/1.00	121,000
Operating income	ARS 50,000		ARS 44,000
– Monetary loss	=		15,000
Net income	ARS 50,000		ARS 29,000

In these calculations, sales took place at the same rate throughout the year, so they are adjusted by the ratio of the end-of-year index to the year's average price index. Because the inventory sold during the year was bought at the beginning of the year, cost of sales is adjusted by the ratio of the year-end index to the beginning-of-year index.

Where did the monetary loss come from? During inflation, firms will have changes in wealth that are unrelated to operating activities. These arise from monetary assets or liabilities—claims to, or obligations to pay, a fixed amount of currency in the future. Monetary assets include cash and accounts receivable, which generally lose purchasing power during periods of inflation. Monetary liabilities include most payables, which generally create purchasing power gains during inflation. In our example, the firm received and held cash during a period when cash lost purchasing power. As inventory was sold for cash, cash was received uniformly throughout the year. The firm's cash balance at the end of the year, if expressed in terms of year-end purchasing power, should be ARS165,000. It is actually only ARS150,000, resulting in an ARS15,000 loss in general purchasing power (a monetary loss). This explains the loss from monetary position figure in Grupo Modelo's income statement cited earlier. During 2004 and 2005, Modelo had more monetary assets on its books than monetary liabilities, giving rise to a purchasing power loss each year.

In contrast to conventional accounting, income using the historical cost-constant purchasing power model is only $29,000. However, withdrawing ARS29,000 makes the firm's end-of-period wealth ARS121,000 (ARS150,000 – AP 29,000), giving it as much purchasing power at the end of the period as at the beginning.

The International Accounting Standards Board's pronouncement IAS29 is consistent with this approach to accounting for changing prices. Reproduced in Exhibit 7-3 is the inflation-adjusted income statement of VESTEL, one of the world's largest original-equipment manufacturers (OEM), headquartered in Turkey.

EXHIBIT 7-3   Inflation-Adjusted Financial Statements of VESTEL ELEKTRONIK SANAYIVE TICARET A.S.

(Currency shown in thousands of new Turkish lira (YTL) in equivalent purchasing power at 31.12.2005 unless otherwise indicated)

	01.01-31.12.2005	*01.01-31.12.2004*
Net sales	4.456.229	4.604.903
Cost of sales	(3.798.115)	(3.854.366)
Gross profit	658.114	750.537
Selling expenses	(337.763)	(318.197)
General and administrative expenses	(141.642)	(138.197)
Warranty expenses	(30.085)	(30.327)
Other income/(expense), net	22.265	5.224
Income from operations	170.002	269.148
Financing income/(expense), net	(36.085)	(74.057)
Income before taxation	133.917	195.091
Taxation charge:		
Current	(54.699)	(41.036)
Deferred	43.592	(2.428)
Taxation on income	(11.107)	(43.464)
Income before minority interest	122.810	151.627
Minority interest	(30.168)	(45.979)
Monetary loss	(9.296)	(18.710)
Net income for the year	83.346	86.938
Basic and fully diluted earnings per share (in full TL)	524	546

Notes:

2.a. Measurement Currency, Reporting Currency

In accordance with Law No. 5083 in respect of "The Currency of the Turkish Republic" published in the Legal Gazette dated January 31, 2004, numbered 25363, which came into force from January 1, 2005, a new local measurement and reporting currency unit has been introduced. Turkish Lira (TL) currency units formerly used have been converted to New Turkish Lira (YTL) at the rate of 1.000.000 TL = 1 YTL. Both notes and coins of the former (TL) as well as the new currency units (YTL) were in circulation during 2005.

IAS29—Financial Reporting in Hyperinflationary Economies ("IAS29") requires that financial statements prepared in the currency of a hyperinflationary economy be stated in terms of the measuring unit current at the most recent balance sheet date and the corresponding figures for previous periods be restated in the same terms. One characteristic (but not limited to) that necessitates the application of IAS29 is a cumulative three-year inflation rate approaching or exceeding 100 percent. The restatement of previous periods in the accompanying financial statements has been based on the conversion factors obtained from the Wholesale Price Indices ("WPI") published by the State Institute of Statistics of Turkey. As of 31 December 2005, the three-year cumulative rate has been 36 percent (December 2004): 70 percent based on the Turkish countrywide wholesale price index published by the State Institute of Statistics. These indices and the conversion factors are shown below:

Year	2005	2004	2003
Index	8.785,7	8.403,8	7.382,1
Conversion factor	1.000	1.045	1.190

VESTEL has price-level adjusted all revenues and expenses to December 31, 2005 purchasing power equivalents, using the year-end WPI over the relevant index that prevailed when each revenue and expense transaction occurred. The monetary loss of YTL 9,296,000 occurs because VESTEL held an excess of monetary assets over monetary liabilities during 2005. The company calculated this loss by multiplying the change in a general price-level index by the weighted average of the difference between monetary assets and liabilities for the year. The company wisely cautions the reader that its price-level-adjusted amounts do not reflect current costs. To quote VESTEL:

> Restatement of balance sheet and income statement items through the use of a general price index and relevant conversion factors does not necessarily mean that the company could realize or settle the same values of assets and liabilities as indicated in the balance sheets. Similarly, it does not necessarily mean that the company could return or settle the same values of equity to its shareholders.

CURRENT-COST ADJUSTMENTS

The current-cost model differs from conventional accounting in two major respects. First, assets are valued at their current cost rather than their historical cost. As an asset is conceptually equal to the discounted present value of its future cash flows, current-cost advocates argue that current values provide statement readers with a better measure of a firm's future earnings and cash-flow potential. Second, income is defined as a firm's *disposable wealth*—the amount of resources the firm could distribute during a period (not counting tax considerations) while maintaining its productive capacity or physical capital. One way to maintain capital is to adjust the firm's original net asset position (using appropriate specific price indexes or direct pricing, such as current invoice prices, supplier price lists, etc.) to reflect changes in the asset's current-cost equivalent during the period. Continuing our previous example, the transactions of our hypothetical merchandiser under the current-costing framework can be illustrated using the accounting equation as our analytical framework (figures given in thousands):

	Assets = Liabilities + Owners' Equity		
	Cash	Inventory	Capital
1.	100,000		100,000
2.	(100,000)	100,000	
3.	150,000		150,000 (revenue)
4.		40,000	40,000 OE reval.
5.		(140,000)	(140,000) exp.

Line 1 depicts the financial statement effects of the initial ARS100,000 investment into the firm. Line 2 depicts the exchange of cash for inventory. Assuming a 50 percent markup, line 3 shows the sale of inventory for cash, which increases owners' equity by the same amount. To reflect the current cost of the sale, the merchandiser increases the carrying value of inventories by 40 percent, as depicted in line 4. The offset to the 40 percent writeup of inventory is an ARS40,000 increase in the owners' equity revaluation account. This adjustment does two things. The owners' equity revaluation amount tells statement readers that the firm must keep an additional ARS40,000 in the business to enable it to replace inventories whose replacement costs have risen. The inventory revaluation, in turn, increases the cost of resources consumed (cost of sales), line 5. Thus, current revenues are matched against the current economic cost (not the historical cost) incurred to generate those revenues. In our example, current-cost-based net income is measured as ARS150,000 − (ARS100,000 × 140/100) = ARS10,000. The current-cost profit of ARS10,000 is the amount the firm could spend without reducing its business operations. Thus, the current-cost model attempts to preserve a firm's physical capital or productive capacity.

An example of current-cost reporting is provided by Infosys, whose current-cost financial statements are presented on pages 143 and 144 of its annual report referenced in Chapter 1. In the commentary that precedes the financial statements, Infosys explains that the purpose of its current-cost information is to present the assets and liabilities of the firm at their current values and to disclose the current sacrifices that are being incurred to generate the current period's revenues. The company explains that to maintain its operating capability, it is important to take into account the rising cost of assets consumed in generating period revenues. It also emphasizes that its current-cost disclosures account for the changes in specific prices as they affect the enterprise. This last statement provides the rationale for the "gearing adjustment" that Infosys includes in its income statement. The gearing adjustment is explained in more detail on page 260 of this chapter.

GENERAL PRICE-LEVEL ADJUSTED CURRENT COSTS

This third reporting option to account for changing prices combines features of the general price-level model and the current-cost framework discussed in the preceding paragraphs.[7] This measurement construct, referred to here as the *price-level-adjusted current-cost model*, employs both general and specific price indexes. Consistent with the general price-level model, one of its objectives is to express a firm's earnings and net assets in terms of their end-of-period purchasing-power equivalents. The income statement would also include information on purchasing-power gains or losses on holding net monetary items. In keeping with the current-cost framework, another set of objectives is to report the firm's net assets in terms of their current cost and to report an earnings number that represents the firm's disposable wealth.

---

[7]For detailed guidance see, Financial Accounting Standards Board, "Financial Reporting and Changing Prices," *Statement of Financial Accounting Standards No. 89*, Stamford, CT: FASB, December 1986.

A distinctive feature of the price-level-adjusted current-cost framework is that it discloses the changes in the current costs of a firm's nonmonetary assets, net of inflation. The idea here is to show that portion of the change in a nonmonetary asset's value that exceeds or falls short of a change in the general purchasing power of money. To illustrate, assume that the current cost of a piece of machinery was $1,000 at the beginning of the year. Its current replacement cost at the end of the year rises to $1,250. The general price level over that same period rises from a level of 100 to 110; that is, it would take $110 dollars at the end of the year to command what $100 would at the beginning. In this example, the current cost of the machinery increased by $250 ($1,250 − $1,000). The portion of the increase that was due merely to a change in the purchasing power of money is determined by first restating the beginning current cost to end-of-period purchasing-power equivalents, $1,000 × 110/100 = $1,100. Thus the change in the machinery's replacement cost that was simply due to a change in the purchasing power of money was $100 ($1,100 − $1,000), and the real change in the machinery's current cost was $250 − $100, or $150. As asset values are used by analysts to estimate a firm's future earnings and cash flows (e.g., multiplying asset values by past return on asset ratios), isolating the changes in asset values that are real as opposed to illusionary is important. These two disclosures that usually appear in stockholders' equity are usually interpreted as follows: The increase in nonmonetary assets due to general inflation is the amount that must be retained in the firm just to enable it to keep up with general inflation. The second component—for example, the increase in current costs that exceeds general inflation—is viewed by some as the unrealized real holding gain on nonmonetary assets. We argue that the latter is not a gain but an increase in the cost of doing business that should be retained in the business to allow the firm to preserve its productive capacity.

The financial statements of Grupo Modello, highlighted at the beginning of this chapter, provide a good example of the price-level-adjusted current-cost model. Selected subparagraphs of Modello's footnote describing its accounting policies are instructive.

2. Accounting policies:

b) Basis for preparation—The consolidated financial statements of the Group include the effects of inflation on the financial information, as required by Statement B-10, issued by the Mexican Institute of Public Accountants (MIPA).

c) Comparability—The figures shown in the consolidated financial statements and its notes are stated consistently in Mexican pesos of December 31, 2005 purchasing power by applying factors derived from the National Consumer Price Index (NCPI).

g) Inventories—These items revalued by the replacement cost method, not exceeding their net realizable value.

h) Cost of sales—This item is determined based on the restated value of inventories sold.

i) Property, plant, and equipment—These items are recorded at acquisition cost, restated by applying the inflation factors derived from the NCPI to the net replacement value determined by independent expert appraisers at December 31, 1996, and to their acquisition cost in the case of purchase subsequent to that date.

j) Depreciation—This item is calculated based on the restated values of property, plant, and equipment, based on the probable useful life as determined by independent appraisers and the technical department of the Group.

t) Restatement of stockholders' equity—The components of stockholders' equity are restated by applying factors derived from the NCPI, and are presented in the consolidated financial statements at the restated amounts.

u) Deficit in the restatement of stockholders' equity—The balance of this account represents the sum of the items "Cumulative gain or loss from holding nonmonetary assets" and "Cumulative monetary gain or loss," which are described below:

Cumulative gains or loss from holding nonmonetary assets—This item represents the cumulative change in the value of nonmonetary assets due to causes other than general inflation.

It is determined only when the specific-cost method is used, since these costs are compared with restatements determined using the NCPI. If the specific costs are higher than the indexes, there will be a gain from holding nonmonetary assets; otherwise, a loss will occur. The gain or loss from holding nonmonetary assets, generated until 1996, due to restatement of fixed assets, is restated in the same way as the other stockholders' equity accounts.

Cumulative monetary gain or loss—This item is the net effect arising on the initial restatement of the financial statement figures.

v) Gains or loss from monetary position—This account represents the effect of inflation on monetary assets and liabilities, even though they continue having the same nominal value. When monetary assets exceed monetary liabilities, a monetary loss is generated; although the assets maintain their nominal value, they lose purchasing power. When liabilities are greater, a gain will be obtained, since they are settled with money of lower purchasing power. These effects are charged or credited to income, forming part of comprehensive financial income.

The account *"Loss from monetary position"* appearing in the income statement section entitled "Comprehensive Financing Income" is the general purchasing loss from holding an excess of monetary assets over monetary losses during the year. The property, plant, and equipment schedule appearing in footnote 6 of Exhibit 7-1 and related expenses have been adjusted to their end-of-period general-price-level adjusted current costs. Ditto for inventories and cost of sales. Finally, the account "Deficit in the restatement of stockholders' equity" appearing in shareholders' equity consists of two parts: the gain in current costs that exceed or fall short of general inflation, and the change in the nonmonetary asset's carrying value that is due to general inflation. In this case, the change in the general price level exceeded the increase in the current costs of Modello's nonmonetary assets. The portion of the change in current costs that fall short of the change in the general price level is viewed as an unrealized holding loss.

NATIONAL PERSPECTIVES ON INFLATION ACCOUNTING

Other countries have experimented with different inflation accounting approaches. Actual practices also reflect pragmatic considerations, such as the severity of national inflation and the views of those directly affected by inflation accounting numbers. Examining additional national approaches to inflation accounting is helpful in understanding current practice.

United States

In 1979 the FASB issued Statement of Financial Accounting Standards (SFAS) No. 33. Entitled "Financial Reporting and Changing Prices," this statement required U.S. enterprises with inventories and property, plant, and equipment (before deducting accumulated depreciation) of more than $125 million, or total assets of more than $1 billion (after deducting accumulated depreciation), to experiment for five years with disclosing both historical cost-constant purchasing power and current cost-constant purchasing power. These disclosures were to supplement rather than replace historical cost as the basic measurement framework for primary financial statements.[8]

Many users and preparers of financial information that complied with SFAS No. 33 found that (1) the dual disclosures required by the FASB were confusing, (2) the cost of preparing the dual disclosures was excessive, and (3) historical cost-constant purchasing power disclosures were less useful than current cost data. Since then, the FASB has decided to encourage but no longer require U.S. reporting entities to disclose either historical cost-constant purchasing power or current cost-constant purchasing power information. The FASB published guidelines (SFAS 89) to assist enterprises that report the statement effects of changing prices and to be a starting point for any future inflation accounting standard.[9]

Reporting enterprises are encouraged to disclose the following information for each of the five most recent years:

- Net sales and other operating revenues
- Income from continuing operations on a current-cost basis
- Purchasing power (monetary) gains or losses on net monetary items
- Increases or decreases in the current cost or lower recoverable amount (i.e., the net amount of cash expected to be recoverable from use or sale) of inventory or property, plant, and equipment, net of inflation (general price-level changes)
- Any aggregate foreign currency translation adjustment, on a current-cost basis, that arises from the consolidation process
- Net assets at year-end on a current-cost basis
- Earnings per share (from continuing operations) on a current-cost basis
- Dividends per share of common stock
- Year-end market price per share of common stock
- Level of the Consumer Price Index (CPI) used to measure income from continuing operations

To increase the comparability of these data, information may be presented either in (1) average (or year-end) purchasing-power equivalents, or (2) base period (1967) dollars used in calculating the CPI. Whenever income on a current-cost constant purchasing-power basis differs significantly from historical-cost income, firms are asked to provide more data.

---

[8]Financial Accounting Standards Board, "Financial Reporting and Changing Prices," Statement of Financial Accounting Standards No. 33, Stamford, CT: FASB, 1979.
[9]Financial Accounting Standards Board, "Financial Reporting and Changing Prices," Statement of Financial Accounting Standards No. 89, Stamford, CT: FASB, December 1986.

   The SFAS No. 89 disclosure guidelines also cover foreign operations included in the consolidated statements of U.S. parent companies. Enterprises that adopt the dollar as the functional currency for measuring their foreign operations view these operations from a parent-currency perspective. Accordingly, their accounts should be translated to dollars, then adjusted for U.S. inflation (the translate-restate method). Multinational enterprises adopting the local currency as functional for most of their foreign operations adopt a local-currency perspective. The FASB allows companies to either use the translate-restate method or adjust for foreign inflation and then translate to U.S. dollars (the restate-translate method). Accordingly, adjustments to current-cost data to reflect inflation may be based on either the U.S. or the foreign general-price-level index. Exhibit 7-4 summarizes these provisions.

EXHIBIT 7-4   Restatement Methodology for Foreign Operations

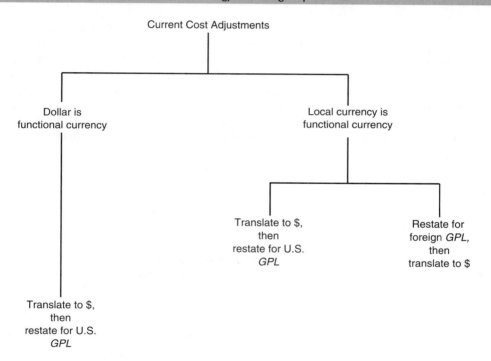

United Kingdom

The U.K. Accounting Standards Committee (ASC) issued Statement of Standard Accounting Practice No. 16 (SSAP No. 16), "Current-Cost Accounting," on a three-year experimental basis in March 1980. Although SSAP No. 16 was withdrawn in 1988, its methodology is recommended for companies that voluntarily produce inflation adjusted accounts.[10]

---

[10]Accounting Standards Committee, *Handbook on Accounting for the Effects of Changing Prices* (London: Chartac Books, 1986).

SSAP No. 16 differs from SFAS No. 33 in two major respects. First, whereas the U.S. standard required both constant dollar and current-cost accounting, SSAP No. 16 adopted only the current-cost method for external reporting. Second, whereas the U.S. inflation adjustment focused on the income statement, the U.K. current-cost statement required both a current-cost income statement and a balance sheet, with explanatory notes. The U.K. standard allowed three reporting options:

1. Presenting current-cost accounts as the basic statements with supplementary historical-cost accounts.
2. Presenting historical-cost accounts as the basic statements with supplementary current-cost accounts.
3. Presenting current-cost accounts as the only accounts accompanied by adequate historical-cost information.

In its treatment of gains and losses related to monetary items, FAS No. 33 required separate disclosure of a single figure. SSAP No. 16 required two figures, both reflecting the effects of specific price changes. The first, called a monetary working capital adjustment (MWCA), recognized the effect of specific price changes on the total amount of working capital used by businesses in their operations. Similar in nature to the monetary gain or loss figure required under the general price-level model, this adjustment acknowledges the fact that the baskets of goods and services that companies acquire are much more firm-specific in regard to supplies, inventories, and the like than those consumed by the general public. The second, called the gearing adjustment, allowed for the impact of specific price changes on a firm's nonmonetary assets (e.g., depreciation, cost of sales, and monetary working capital). As a formula, the gearing adjustment equals:

$$[(TL - CA) / (FA + I + MWC)] \ (CC \ Dep. \ Adj. + CC \ Sales \ Adj. + MWCA)$$

where

TL	=	total liabilities other than trade payables
CA	=	current assets other than trade receivables
FA	=	fixed assets including investments
I	=	inventory
MWC	=	monetary working capital
CC Dep. Adj.	=	current-cost depreciation adjustment
CC Sales Adj.	=	current cost of sales adjustment
MWCA	=	monetary working capital adjustment

The gearing adjustment acknowledges that such expenses as cost of goods sold and depreciation need not be inflated to recognize the higher replacement cost of these assets to the extent that they are financed by debt. The latter normally gives rise to "monetary gains" computed using specifics as opposed to general price indexes.

Brazil

Inflation is often an accepted part of the business scene in Latin America, Eastern Europe, and Southeast Asia. Brazil's past experience with hyperinflation makes its inflation accounting initiatives informative.

Although no longer required, recommended inflation accounting in Brazil today reflects two sets of reporting options—Brazilian Corporate Law and the Brazil Securities and Exchange Commission.[11] Inflation adjustments complying with corporate law restate permanent assets and stockholders' equity accounts using a price index recognized by the federal government for measuring devaluation of the local currency. Permanent assets include fixed assets, buildings, investments, deferred charges and their respective depreciation, and amortization or depletion accounts (including any related provisions for losses).[12] Stockholders' equity accounts comprise capital, revenue reserves, revaluation reserves, retained earnings, and a capital reserves account used to record the price-level adjustment to capital. The latter results from revaluing fixed assets to their current replacement costs less a provision for technical and physical depreciation.

Inflation adjustments to permanent assets and stockholders' equity are netted, with the excess being disclosed separately in current earnings as a monetary correction gain or loss. Exhibit 7-5 and related commentary provide an illustration of this inflation accounting methodology and the rationale for the monetary correction account.

The price-level adjustment to stockholders' equity (BRL275) is the amount by which the shareholders' beginning-of-period investment must grow to keep up with inflation. A permanent asset adjustment that is less than the equity adjustment causes a purchasing power loss reflecting the firm's exposure on its net monetary assets (i.e., working capital). To illustrate, let:

M = monetary assets
N = nonmonetary assets
L = liabilities
E = equity
i = inflation rate

Then

$$M + N = L + E \qquad (7.1)$$

Multiplying both sides of Equation (7.1) by $(1 + i)$ quantifies the impact of inflation on the firm's financial position. Thus

$$M(1 + i) + N(1 + i) = L(1 + i) + E(1 + i) \qquad (7.2)$$

Equation (7.2) can be reexpressed as

$$M + Mi + N + Ni = L + Li + E + Ei \qquad (7.3)$$

---

[11]Financial analysts and Brazilian financial executives we have interviewed continue to adjust Brazilian accounts for changing prices to facilitate their analyses. Should significant inflation recur in Brazil, the inflation adjustments we describe will likely be reinstated.

[12]Permanent assets do not include inventories, which is a conceptual shortcoming of this inflation accounting model.

EXHIBIT 7-5 Inflation Adjustments, Brazilian Style

Inflation-Corrected Amounts

Historical Amounts			*Assuming a 25% Rate of Inflation*		
Balance Sheet	1/1/X7	12/31/X7			12/31/X7
Current assets	BRL150	BRL450	Current assets		BRL450
Permanent assets	1,600	1,600	Permanent assets		2,000[a]
Provision for depreciation	(200)	(300)	Provision for depreciation		(300)
			Monetary correction	(75)[b]	
			Correction of historical charge to P&L	(25)[c]	(400)
Total	BRL1,550	BRL1,750	Total		BRL2,050
Current liabilities	BRL50	BRL50	Current liabilities		BRL50
Long-term debt	400	400	Long-term debt		400
Equity:			Equity:		
Capital	800	800	Capital		800
			Capital reserve		200[d]
Reserves	300	300	Reserves		375[e]
Profit of period		200	Profit of period		225
Total	BRL1,550	BRL1,750	Total		BRL2,050

Income Statement Year Ended 2/31/X7			Year Ended 12/31/X7		
Operating profit		BRL500	Operating profit		BRL500
Depreciation of period (historical)		100	Depreciation of period	100	
			Correction of depreciation	25	125
Trading profit		400	Trading profit		375
			Inflationary loss:		
Exchange loss on foreign debt		(100)	Exchange loss on foreign debt	(100)	
Monetary correction on local debt		(100)	Monetary correction on local debt	(100)	
			Gain on correction of balance sheet	50[f]	(150)
Net profit		BRL200	Net profit		BRL225

[a]*Represents the original BRL1,600 plus a 25 percent (BRL400) adjustment.*
[b]*25 percent of the original BRL300.*
[c]*25 percent of the period's depreciation expense (typically based on the average value of fixed assets).*
[d]*25 percent of the original capital balance of BRL800.*
[e]*Represents the original R$300 plus a 25 percent (BRL75) adjustment.*
[f]*Gain on correction of the balance sheet:*

Correction of permanent assets	BRL400	
Correction of depreciation allowance	75	325
Correction of capital	200	
Correction of reserves	75	275
		50

Regrouping Equation (7.3) as:

$$M + \underbrace{N + Ni}_{\substack{\text{permanent} \\ \text{asset} \\ \text{adjustment}}} = L + \underbrace{E + Ei}_{\substack{\text{owner's} \\ \text{equity} \\ \text{adjustment}}} + \underbrace{(L - M)i}_{\substack{\text{monetary} \\ \text{gain or loss}}} \qquad (7.4)$$

Since $M + N = L + E$:

$$Ni = Ei + (L - M)\, i \qquad (7.5)$$

Or

$$\underset{\substack{\text{inflation} \\ \text{adjustment} \\ \text{to nonmonetary} \\ \text{(permanent)} \\ \text{assets}}}{Ni} \quad - \quad \underset{\substack{\text{inflation} \\ \text{adjustment} \\ \text{to owners'} \\ \text{equity}}}{Ei} \quad = \quad \underset{\substack{\text{monetary} \\ \text{gain or loss}}}{(L - M)i} \qquad (7.6)$$

Conversely, a permanent asset adjustment greater than the equity adjustment produces a purchasing power gain, suggesting that some of the assets have been financed by borrowing. For example, suppose that a firm's financial position before monetary correction is

Permanent assets	1,000	Liabilities	500
		Owners' equity	500

With an annual inflation rate of 30 percent, a price-level adjusted balance sheet would show:

Permanent assets	1,300	Liabilities	500
		Capital	500
		Capital reserve	150
		Monetary gain	150[13]

---

[13]This analysis (monetary gain) assumes that liabilities are of the fixed-rate variety or are floating-rate obligations where the actual rate of inflation exceeds the expected rate that is incorporated into the terms of the original borrowing.

The Brazilian Securities Exchange Commission requires another inflation accounting method for publicly traded companies.[14] Listed companies must remeasure all transactions during the period using their functional currency. At the end of the period, the prevailing general price-level index converts units of general purchasing power into units of nominal local currency. Also:

- Inventory is included as a nonmonetary asset and is remeasured with the functional currency.
- Noninterest-bearing monetary items with maturities exceeding 90 days are discounted to their present values to allocate resulting inflationary gains and losses to appropriate accounting periods (the discount on trade receivables is treated as a reduction of sales, the discount on accounts payable reduces purchases, etc.).
- Balance sheet adjustments are similarly reclassified to appropriate line items in the income statement (e.g., the balance sheet adjustment to accounts receivable is reclassified as a reduction of sales).

To relieve Brazilian firms from having to present two sets of financial statements in their annual reports, the Securities Exchange Commission blended features of the corporate law methodology into its price-level accounting methodology.

INTERNATIONAL ACCOUNTING STANDARDS BOARD

The IASB has concluded that reports of financial position and operating performance in local currency are not meaningful in a hyperinflationary environment. IAS 29,[15] mentioned in conjunction with VESTEL's inflation-adjusted financial statements (see Exhibit 7-3) requires (rather than recommends) the restatement of primary financial statement information. Specifically, financial statements of an enterprise that reports in the currency of a hyperinflationary economy, whether based on a historical or current-cost valuation framework, should be reexpressed in terms of constant purchasing power as of the balance sheet date. This rule also applies to corresponding figures for the preceding period. Purchasing-power gains or losses related to a net monetary liability or asset position are to be included in current income. Reporting enterprises should also disclose

1. The fact that restatement for changes in the general purchasing power of the measuring unit has been made
2. The asset-valuation framework employed in the primary statements (i.e., historical or current-cost valuation)
3. The identity and level of the price index at the balance sheet date, together with its movement during the reporting period
4. The net monetary gain or loss during the period

---

[14]Coopers & Lybrand, *1993 International Accounting Summaries* (New York: John Wiley, 1993), B32–B33
[15]International Accounting Standards Committee, "Financial Reporting in Hyperinflationary Economies," International Accounting Standard No. 29, London: IASC, 1989.

INFLATION ISSUES

Analysts must address the following issues when reading inflation-adjusted accounts: (1) whether constant dollars or current costs better measure the effects of inflation, (2) the accounting treatment of inflation gains and losses, (3) accounting for foreign inflation, and (4) the combined effects of inflation and foreign exchange rates. We discuss the first and third issues together.

Inflation Gains and Losses

Treatment of gains and losses on monetary items (i.e., cash, receivables, and payables) is controversial. Our survey of practices in various countries reveals important variations in this respect.

Gains or losses on monetary items in the United States are determined by restating, in constant dollars, the beginning and ending balances of, and transactions in, all monetary assets and liabilities (including long-term debt). The resulting figure is disclosed as a separate item. This treatment views gains and losses in monetary items as different in nature from other types of earnings.

In the United Kingdom, gains and losses on monetary items are partitioned into monetary working capital and a gearing adjustment. Both figures are determined in relation to specific (not general) price changes. The gearing adjustment indicates the benefit (or cost) to shareholders from debt financing during a period of changing prices. This figure is added (deducted) to (from) current-cost operating profit to yield a disposable wealth measure called "current-cost profit attributable to shareholders."

The Brazilian approach, no longer required, does not adjust current assets and liabilities explicitly, as these amounts are expressed in terms of realizable values. However, as Exhibit 7-5 shows, the adjustment from netting price-level adjusted permanent assets and owners' equity represents the general purchasing-power gain or loss in financing working capital from debt or equity. A permanent asset adjustment that exceeds an equity adjustment represents that portion of permanent assets being financed by debt, creating a purchasing-power gain. Conversely, an equity adjustment greater than the permanent asset adjustment denotes the portion of working capital financed by equity. A purchasing-power loss is recognized for this portion during an inflationary period.

SSAP No. 16 has great merit in dealing with the effects of inflation. Along with inventories and plant and equipment, an enterprise needs to increase its net nominal monetary working capital to maintain its operating capability with increasing prices. It also benefits from using debt during inflation. However, the magnitude of these phenomena should not be measured in general purchasing power terms because a firm rarely, if ever, invests in an economy's market basket. We believe that the purpose of inflation accounting is to measure the performance of an enterprise and enable anyone interested to assess the amounts, timing, and likelihood of future cash flows.

A firm can measure its command over specific goods and services by using an index to calculate its monetary gains and losses.[16] Because not all enterprises can

---

[16]Frederick D. S. Choi, "Foreign Inflation and Management Decisions," *Management Accounting* (June 1977): 21–27.

construct firm-specific purchasing-power indexes, the British approach is a good practical alternative. However, rather than disclose the gearing adjustment (or some equivalent), we prefer to treat it as a reduction of the current-cost adjustments for depreciation, cost of sales, and monetary working capital. We think that current-cost charges from restating historical-cost income during inflation are offset by the reduced burden of servicing debt used to finance these operating items.

Holding Gains and Losses

Current value accounting divides total earnings into two parts: (1) operating income (the difference between current revenues and the current cost of resources consumed) and (2) unrealized gains that result from the possession of nonmonetary assets whose replacement value rises with inflation. The measurement of holding gains is straightforward, but their accounting treatment is not. Should portions of raw materials inventory gains be realized in periods when the respective inventories are turned into finished goods and sold? Are there ever unrealized adjustment gains or losses that should be deferred? Or should all such gains or losses be lumped together and disclosed in a special new section within stockholders' equity?

We think that increases in the replacement cost of operating assets (e.g., higher projected cash outflows to replace equipment) are not gains, realized or not. Whereas current-cost-based income measures a firm's approximate disposable wealth, changes in the current cost of inventory, plant, equipment, and other operating assets are revaluations of owners' equity, which is the portion of earnings that the business must keep to preserve its physical capital (or productive capacity). Assets held for speculation, such as vacant land or marketable securities, do not need to be replaced to maintain productive capacity. Hence, if current-cost adjustments include these items, increases or decreases in their current-cost (value) equivalents (up to their realizable values) should be stated directly in income.

Foreign Inflation

When consolidating the accounts of subsidiaries located in inflationary environments, should management first restate these accounts for foreign inflation, then translate to parent currency? Or should it first translate the unadjusted accounts to the parent currency, then restate them for parent-country inflation? In the United States, the FASB tried to cope with inflation by requiring large reporting entities to experiment with both historical cost-constant purchasing power and current-cost disclosures. FAS No. 89, which encourages (but no longer requires) companies to account for changing prices, leaves the issue unresolved at two levels. First, companies may continue to maintain the value of their nonmonetary assets at historical cost (restated for general price-level changes) or may restate them to their current-cost equivalents. Second, companies that elect to provide supplementary current-cost data for foreign operations have a choice of two methods for translating and restating foreign accounts in U.S. dollars. They can either restate for foreign inflation, then translate to the parent currency (the restate-translate method), or they can translate to the parent currency, then restate for inflation (translate-restate). How do we choose between these two methods? We can choose with a decision-oriented framework.

Investors care about a firm's dividend-generating potential, because their investment's value ultimately depends on future dividends. A firm's dividend-generating potential is directly related to its capacity to produce goods and services. Only when a firm preserves its productive capacity (and thus its earning power) will there be future dividends to consider.

Therefore, investors need specific, not general, price-level-adjusted statements. Why? Because specific price-level adjustments (our current-cost model) determine the maximum amount that the firm can pay as dividends (disposable wealth) without reducing its productive capacity.

This conclusion implies that the restate-translate and translate-restate methods are both deficient. They are both based on a valuation framework that has little to recommend it—historical cost. Neither method changes that framework. No matter how it is adjusted, the historical-cost model is still the historical-cost model!

We favor the following price-level adjustment procedure:

1. Restate the financial statements of all subsidiaries, both domestic and foreign, and the statements of the parent to reflect changes in specific prices (e.g., current costs).
2. Translate the accounts of all foreign subsidiaries into domestic currency equivalents using a constant (e.g., the current or a base-year foreign exchange rate).
3. Use specific price indexes that are relevant to what the firm consumes in calculating monetary gains or losses. A parent-company perspective requires domestic price indexes; a local-company perspective requires local price indexes.

Restating both foreign and domestic accounts to their specific current-price equivalents produces decision-relevant information. This information provides investors the greatest possible amount of information concerning future dividends. It would be much easier to compare and evaluate the consolidated results of all firms than it is now. This reporting philosophy was stated by Dewey R. Borst, comptroller of Inland Steel Company:

> Management seeks the best current information to monitor how they have done in the past, and to guide them in their current decision making. Outsiders value financial statements for the same general purpose of determining how the firm has done in the past and how it is likely to perform in the future. Therefore, there is no legitimate need to have two distinct sets of data and methods of presentation of financial information. The same data now available through the development of managerial accounting is also suitable for outsiders.[17]

Avoiding the Double-Dip

When restating foreign accounts for foreign inflation, firms sometimes double-count for the effects of inflation, the *double-dip*. This problem exists because local inflation directly affects the exchange rates used in translation. While economic theory assumes an inverse relationship between a country's internal rate of inflation and the external

---

[17]Dewey R. Borst, "Accounting vs. Reality: How Wide Is the 'GAAP'?" *Week in Review* (July 13, 1982): 1.

value of its currency, evidence suggests that this relationship seldom holds (at least in the short run).[18] Accordingly, the size of the resulting adjustment to eliminate the double-dip will vary depending on the degree to which exchange rates and differential inflation are negatively correlated.

As noted before, inflation adjustments to cost of sale or depreciation expense are designed to reduce "as reported" earnings to avoid overstating income. However, due to the inverse relationship between local inflation and currency values, changes in the exchange rate between successive financial statements, generally caused by inflation (at least over a period of time), will make at least part of the impact of inflation (i.e., currency translation adjustments) affect a company's "as reported" results. Thus, to avoid adjusting for the effects of inflation twice, the inflation adjustment should take into account the translation loss already reflected in a firm's "as reported" results.

This adjustment is relevant to U.S.-based multinational corporations (MNCs) that have adopted the dollar as the functional currency for their foreign operations under FAS No. 52 and that translate inventories using the current exchange rate. It is also germane to non-U.S.-based MNCs that recognize translation gains and losses in current income. Absent any offsetting adjustments, such companies could reduce or increase earnings twice when accounting for foreign inflation.

The following inventory accounting example shows the relationship between inflation and foreign currency translation. The company in question uses the FIFO inventory costing method and translates inventory to dollars at the current exchange rate. We assume the following:

- Local country inflation was 20 percent in the year just ended. U.S. inflation was 6 percent during the year.
- The opening exchange rate on January 1 was LC1 = $1.00.
- The closing exchange rate on December 31 was LC1 = $0.88.
- Currency devaluation during the year to maintain purchasing power parity was 12 percent.
- Local currency inventory was LC200 on January 1 and LC240 on December 31.
- No change occurred in the physical quantity of inventory during the year.

The dollar equivalent of beginning and ending inventory is calculated as follows:

	LC Amount	Exchange Rate	$ Amount
Jan. 1 FIFO inventory	200	LC = $1.00	$200
Dec. 31 FIFO inventory	240	LC = $0.88	$211

"As reported" income will reflect a translation loss of $29 (assuming that the currency was devalued at year-end), the difference between translating LC240 inventory on December 31 at $0.88 versus $1.00.

During the next inventory turnover period, "as reported" cost of sales will, therefore, be LC240 in local currency, $211 in dollars.

---

[18]Michael Adler and Bernard Dumans, "International Portfolio and Corporation Finance: A Synthesis," *Journal of Finance* (June 1983): 925–984.

If cost of sales was adjusted for inflation by the restate-translate method, the company might do as follows:

- Remove the year's 20 percent inflation from the December 31 local currency inventory (240/1.20), reducing it to LC200—the same as it was on January 1 (before inflation).
- The local currency cost of sales adjustment would then be LC40, the amount required to change the December 31 inventory from LC240 to LC200.
- Translate the local currency cost of sales adjustment (LC40) to dollars at $1.00, making a $40 cost of sales adjustment (LC40 × $1.00 = $40).

Note that on an inflation-adjusted basis, the company has reduced earnings by a $29 translation loss and a $40 cost of sales inflation adjustment—a total of $69, or 34 percent of what began as $200 of inventory on January 1. Yet inflation was only 20 percent! Double-dipping caused this difference. The dollar calculations include a partial overlap between the currency devaluation loss, which results from inflation, and the cost of sales adjustment for inflation, which is a root cause of the currency devaluation. The restate-translate cost of sales inflation adjustment alone was enough. It would offset not only the U.S. inflation rate (6 percent in this example) but also the 12 percent inflation differential between the country's 20 percent rate and the U.S. 6 percent rate—which led to the 12 percent devaluation. We conclude that if cost of sales is adjusted to remove local country inflation, it is necessary to reverse any inventory translation loss that was reflected in "as reported" earnings. Appendix 7-1 provides a case analysis.

APPENDIX 7-1

Accounting For Foreign Inflation: A Case Analysis

The following case study highlights how a leading U.S.-based MNE, the General Electric Company (GE), accounts for foreign inflation. Most of our discussion will be limited to inventory and cost of sales, as well as monetary gains and losses. The procedures for inventories and cost of sales also apply to fixed assets and their related cost expirations when these accounts are translated using the current rate.[19]

GE uses the temporal method of foreign currency translation because the U.S. dollar is its functional currency for most of its foreign operations. Inventories are generally translated at the current rate to signal that they are exposed to exchange-rate risk. GE management believes that it needs the restate-translate method of accounting for inflation, using specific local price indexes for fixed assets and inventory, to properly measure its foreign operations on an inflation-adjusted basis. Accordingly, GE adjusts the local currency cost of foreign fixed assets and inventory for local specific price changes and then translates at the current exchange rate. Restatement of fixed assets, from which restated depreciation expense is derived, uses generally understood practices (i.e., restate for current cost and then translate to dollars) and is not repeated here. For inventory, however, the cost of sales inflation adjustment cannot be derived from the restated balance sheet inventory value. Therefore, we will explain these two inflation adjustments separately.

CURRENT-COST INVENTORY ADJUSTMENT

For FIFO inventories that are not material in amount or that turn over very frequently, GE assumes that current cost and FIFO book cost are essentially equivalent. Accordingly, the historical book cost is reported as current cost.

With LIFO inventories, and FIFO inventories not excluded by the previous criteria, GE restates ending inventories to their current-cost equivalents using local specific price indexes before translation to dollars at the current rate. If the inventory input rate is relatively constant, the current-cost inventory adjustment is approximated by applying one-half of the local inflation rate during the inventory accumulation period. Thus, assuming a four-month accumulation period, an annual inflation rate of 30 percent, an ending inventory balance of LC1,000,000, and an ending exchange rate of LC1 = $0.40, the dollar FIFO inventory value restated to a current-cost basis would be:

$$[(2.5\% \text{ per mo.} \times 4 \text{ mos.})/2] \times \text{LC1,000,000} = \text{LC50,000}$$

$$\text{LC1,000,000} + \text{LC50,000} = \text{LC1,050,000} \times \$0.40 = \$420,000$$

If the foreign subsidiary carries its inventories on a LIFO basis, its restated FIFO value is calculated in the same manner, using its LIFO cost index as the inflation rate.

---

[19]The following discussion is excerpted from Frederick D. S. Choi, "Resolving the Inflation/Currency Translation Dilemma," *Management International Review* 27, no. 2 (1987): 28–33.

CURRENT COST OF SALES ADJUSTMENT: SIMULATED LIFO

When a foreign operation uses LIFO accounting for its "as reported" results, the cost of sales is close to market. Therefore, no cost of sales inflation adjustment is made. For foreign operations that use FIFO accounting, GE's inflation adjustment simulates what would have been charged to cost of sales under LIFO accounting. However, to avoid the double-dip effect, the company also takes into account any inventory translation loss that is already reflected in "as reported" results. To illustrate, suppose that the December 31 FIFO inventory balance is LC5,000, that the year's inflation rate was 30 percent (January 1 = index 100, December 31 index = 130), and that the currency devalued by 20 percent from LC1 = $0.50 at January 1 to LC1 = $0.40 at December 31.

The following sequential analysis shows how the double-counting phenomenon is minimized. Steps 1 through 3 illustrate how the current cost of sales adjustment is derived in local currency. Step 4 expresses this inflation adjustment in the parent currency (i.e., U.S. dollars). Step 5 identifies the translation loss that has already been booked as a result of having translated inventories to dollars at a current rate that fell during the year. Finally, step 6 subtracts the translation loss already reflected in "as reported" results from the current cost of sales adjustment.

Usually, when inflation outpaces devaluation, the dollar current cost of sales adjustment will be positive (i.e., a deduction from "as reported" earnings). However, if devaluation outpaces inflation, the adjustment will be negative (i.e., the dollar cost of sales adjustment would be subtracted from, rather than added to, "as reported" dollar cost of sales).

1. December 31 FIFO inventory subject to simulated LIFO charge	LC5,000
2. Restate line 1 to January 1 cost level (LC5,000 × 100/130)	LC3,846
3. The difference between line 1 and line 2 inventory values represents current year local currency FIFO inventory inflation	LC1,154
4. Translate line 3 to dollars at the January 1 exchange rate (LC1 = $0.50). The result is simulated dollar LIFO expense for the current year	$ 577
5. Calculate the translation loss on FIFO inventory (line 1) that was already reflected in "as reported" results:	
a. Translate line 1 to January 1 exchange rate (LC5,000 × $0.50)	$2,500
b. Translate line 1 at December 31 exchange rate (LC5,000 × $0.40)	$2,000
c. The difference is the inventory translation loss already reflected in "as reported" results	$(500)
6. The net of lines 4 and 5c is the cost of sales adjustment in dollars:	
a. Simulated dollar LIFO expense from line 4	$ 577
b. Less: Inventory translation loss already reflected in "as reported" results (from line 5c)	$(500)
c. The difference is the net dollar current cost of sales adjustment	$ 77

CURRENT-COST MONETARY ADJUSTMENT

The final inflation adjustment described here relates to the fact that debtors typically gain during inflation because typically they repay fixed monetary obligations in currencies of reduced purchasing power. Accordingly, if a foreign affiliate has used debt to finance part of its fixed assets and inventory, its inflation-adjusted data include a monetary adjustment (i.e., a purchasing power gain). However, because GE limits its inflation adjustments to inventories, fixed assets, and their related cost expirations, it limits the monetary adjustment to that portion of liabilities used to finance fixed assets and inventories—hereinafter known as applied liabilities. As a debtor's gain, the monetary adjustment recognizes that the interest expense being paid on applied liabilities includes compensation to the lender for the eroding purchasing power of the funds loaned. It also partly offsets the income-reducing inflation adjustments for depreciation expense and cost of sales due to the impact of inflation on fixed assets and inventory replacement costs.

Calculation of the monetary adjustment involves two steps, because local inflation impacts exchange rates used to translate local currency liabilities to their dollar equivalents. Thus, the purchasing power gain on local currency liabilities used to finance fixed assets and inventories during an inflationary period is partly or fully offset by a reversal of any translation gains (or losses) on these liabilities already reflected in "as reported" results. These gains result from having translated monetary liabilities by an exchange rate that fell during the period.

In the following illustration, assume that a foreign subsidiary's local currency cost of fixed assets and FIFO inventory add up to LC10,600, that its net worth is LC7,500, that differential inflation between the parent and host country is 30 percent, and that the local currency devalued by 20 percent from LC1 = $0.50 at January 1 to LC1 = $0.40 at December 31. The current cost monetary adjustment is calculated as follows.

Steps 1 through 5 identify the portion of monetary liabilities employed to finance assets whose values have been adjusted for inflation. Steps 6 and 7 calculate the monetary gains on these applied liabilities in local currency. Step 8 reexpresses this gain in U.S. dollars. Step 9 identifies the translation gain resulting from having translated monetary liabilities to dollars by an exchange rate (the current rate) that depreciated during the year. Finally, step 10 subtracts the translation gain on the monetary liabilities from the purchasing power gain on the same accounts to yield (in this example) a net monetary gain from changing prices.

1. Local currency cost fixed assets at December 31	LC5,600
2. FIFO inventory at December 31	LC<u>5,000</u>
3. Total of lines 1 and 2	LC10,600
4. Subtract net worth at December 31	LC(<u>7,500</u>)
5. The balance represents "applied liabilities"	LC3,100
6. Restate December 31 applied liabilities to their January 1 purchasing power equivalent (i.e., multiply LC3,100 by 100/130)	LC<u>2,385</u>
7. The difference between lines 5 and 6 is the purchasing power gain on applied liabilities	LC715
8. Translate line 7 to dollars at the January 1 exchange rate. The result is the debtor's gain from inflation in dollars (LC715 × $0.50)	$ 358
9. Calculate the year's translation gain (loss) on applied LC liabilities already reflected in "as reported" results:	
a. Line 5 times January 1 exchange rate (LC3,100 × $0.50)	$1,550
b. Line 5 times December 31 exchange rate (LC3,100) × $0.40)	$<u>1,240</u>
c. The difference is the translation gain	$ 310
d. The difference between line 8 and line 9c. is the dollar current cost monetary adjustment:	
10.	
a. Line 8 (debtor's gain from inflation)	$358 cr.
b. If line 9(c) is a translation gain, show it as a debit to reverse it, and vice versa	$(310) dr.
c. Add lines 10(a) and 10(b). If the sum is a credit, treat it as an addition to "as reported" income, and vice versa	$ <u>48</u>

SELECTED REFERENCES

Aboody, D., M. E. Barth, and R. Kasnik, "Revaluation of Fixed Assets and Future Firm Performance: Evidence from the UK," *Journal of Accounting and Economics* 26 (1999): 149–178.

Accounting Standards Committee, *Handbook on Accounting for the Effects of Changing Prices* (London: ASC, 1986).

Barniv, Ran, "The Value Relevance of Inflation-Adjusted and Historical Cost Earnings During Hyperinflation," *Journal of International Accounting, Auditing and Taxation* 8, no. 2 (1999): 269–287.

Boschen, John F., and Charles L. Weise, "What Starts Inflation: Evidence from the OECD Countries," *Journal of Money, Credit and Banking* 35 (June 2003): 323–337.

Choi, Frederick D. S., "Financial Reporting in Hyperinflationary Environments: A Transaction Analysis Framework for Management," in *International Finance and Accounting Handbook*, ed. Frederick D. S. Choi, 3rd ed. (New York: John Wiley, 2003), p. 27.

Crowe, Christopher W., "Inflation, Inequality and Social Conflict," IMF Working Paper No. 06/158 (June 1, 2006).

Davis, Nicole, and Ali M. Kutan, " Inflation and Output as Predictors of Stock Returns and Volatility: International Evidence," *Applied Financial Economics* 13 (September 2003): 693.

Davis-Friday, Paquita, "Equity Valuation and Current Cost Disclosures: The Case of Mexico," *Journal of International Financial Management and Accounting* 12, no. 3 (2001): 260–285.

Fanizza, Domenico, and Ludwig Soderling, "Fiscal Determinants of Inflation: A Primer for the Middle East and North Africa," IMF Working Paper No. 06/216 (October 1, 2006).

Financial Accounting Standards Board, "Financial Reporting and Changing Prices," Statement of Financial Accounting Standards No. 33, (Stamford, CT: FASB, September 1979).

Financial Accounting Standards Board, "Financial Reporting and Changing Prices," Statement of Financial Accounting Standards No. 89 (Stamford, CT: FASB, December 1986).

Gordon, Elizabeth A., "Accounting for Changing Prices: The Value Relevance of Historical Cost, Price Level, and Replacement Cost Accounting in Mexico," *Journal of Accounting Research* 39, no. 1 (2001): 177–200.

Hughes, John, Jing Liu, and Mingshan Zhang, "Valuation and Accounting for Inflation and Foreign Exchange," *Journal of Accounting Research* 42, no. 4 (2004): 731–754.

Ihrig, Jane, and Jaime Marquez, "An Empirical Analysis of Inflation in OECD Countries," *International Finance* 7, no. 1 (2004): 61–84.

International Accounting Standards Committee, "Information Reflecting the Effects of Changing Prices," International Accounting Standard 15 (London: IASC, November 1981).

International Accounting Standards Committee, "Financial Reporting in Hyperinflationary Economies," International Accounting Standard 29 (London: IASC, 1989).

O'Hanlon, John, and Ken Peasnell, "Residual Income Valuation: Are Inflation Adjustments Necessary?" *Review of Accounting Studies* 9, no. 4 (2004).

Sharpe, Steven A., "Reexamining Stock Valuation and Inflation: The Implications of Analysts' Earnings Forecasts," *Review of Economics and Statistics*, forthcoming.

Silver, Mick, "Core Inflation Measures and Statistical Issues in Choosing Among Them," IMF Working Paper No. 06/97 (April 1, 2006).

Wyman, H. E. "Accounting for the Effects of Inflation," in *International Finance and Accounting Handbook*, ed. Frederick D. S. Choi, 3rd ed. (New York: John Wiley, 2003), p. 20.

DISCUSSION QUESTIONS

1. From a user's perspective, what is the inherent problem in attempting to analyze historical cost-based financial statements of a company domiciled in an inflationary, devaluation-prone country?

2. What is a general price-level index, and of what use is it for financial statement readers?

3. Consider the statement: "The object of accounting for changing prices is to ensure that a company is able to maintain its operating capability." How accurate is it?

4. Following are the remarks of a prominent member of the U.S. Congress. Explain why you agree or disagree.

   The plain fact of the matter is that inflation accounting is a premature, imprecise, and underdeveloped method of recording basic business facts. To insist that any system of inflation accounting can afford the accuracy and fairness needed for the efficient operation of our tax system is simply foolish. My years on the Ways and Means Committee have exposed me to the many appeals of business—from corporate tax "reform" to the need for capital formation—which have served as a guise for reducing the tax contributions of American business. In this respect, I see inflation accounting as another in a long line of attempts to minimize corporate taxation through backdoor gimmickry.

5. Professional accountancy bodies the world over generally agree that inflation may become so great that conventional financial statements lose much of their significance and price-level adjusted statements become more meaningful. Since domestic rates of inflation vary significantly from country to country, at what point do price-level adjusted financial statements become more meaningful? How does one determine whether the benefits of price-level adjusted accounting information exceed its costs?

6. Briefly describe how adjustments for changing prices differ between the United States and the U.K.

7. As more and more companies span the globe in terms of their operating, financing, and investing activities, they will increasingly turn to international financial reporting standards when communicating with domestic and non-domestic financial statement readers. What approaches to inflation accounting does IAS29 sanction when a firm is domiciled or has major operations in a hyperinflationary environment? Why should analysts understand the requirements of this pronouncement?

8. Briefly describe the historical-cost constant purchasing power and current-cost models. How are they similar? How do they differ?

9. As a potential investor in the shares of multinational enterprises, which inflation method, restate-translate or translate-restate, would give you consolidated information most relevant to your decision needs? Which information set is best from the viewpoint of the foreign subsidiary's shareholders?

10. What is a gearing adjustment, and on what ideas is it based?

11. How does accounting for foreign inflation differ from accounting for domestic inflation?

12. What does double-dipping mean in accounting for foreign inflation?

EXERCISES

1. Examine the income statements of Modello (Exhibit 7-1), VESTEL (Exhibit 7-3), and Infosys (referenced on page 255). Which earnings number do you feel provides the better earnings metric for an investment analyst, and why?

2. Sobrero Corporation, a Mexican affiliate of a major U.S.-based hotel chain, starts the calendar year with 1 billion pesos (MXP) cash equity investment. It immediately acquires a refurbished hotel in Acapulco for MXP 900 million. Owing to a favorable tourist season, Sobrero Corporation's rental revenues were MXP 144 million for the year. Operating expenses of MXP 86,400,000 together with rental revenues were incurred uniformly throughout the year. The building, comprising 80 percent of the original purchase price (balance attributed to land), has an estimated useful life of 20 years and is being depreciated in straight-line fashion. By year-end, the Mexican consumer price index rose to 420 from an initial level of 263, averaging 340 during the year.

   Required:
   a. Prepare financial statements for Sobrero Corporation's first year of operations in terms of the historical-cost model and the historical-cost constant dollar model.
   b. Compare and evaluate the information content of rate-of-return statistics computed using each of these models.

3. The comparative historical-cost balance sheets of Majikstan Enterprises for 20X7 and 20X8 are reproduced below. The accounts are expressed in 000's of renges (MJR's).

Balance Sheet	20X7	20X8
Cash	MJR 2,500	MJR 5,100
Equipment, net	4,000	3,500
Total assets	MJR 6,500	MJR 8,600
Current liabilities	MJR 1,000	MJR 1,200
Long-term debt	3,000	4,000
Owners' equity	2,500	3,400
Total	MJR 6,500	MJR 8,600

Required: What was the change in Majikstan's net monetary asset or liability position?

4. Using the information provided in item (3), calculate Majikstan Enterprises' net monetary gain or loss in local currency for 20X6 based on the following general price-level information.

12/31/X7	30,000
Average	32,900
12/31/X8	36,000

5. Revisit Sobrero Corporation in Exercise 2. In addition to the information provided there, assume that Mexico's construction cost index increased by 80 percent during the year, while the price of vacant land adjacent to Sobrero Corporation's hotel increased in value by 90 percent.

   Required: Use the new information to restate the value of Sobrero's nonmonetary assets. What would Sobrero Corporation's financial statements look like under the current-cost model?

6. Majikstan Enterprises has equipment on its books that it acquired at the start of 20X6. The equipment is being depreciated in straight-line fashion over a 10-year period and has no salvage value. The current cost of this equipment at the end of 20X7 was MJR8,000,000,000. During 20X8, the specific price index for equipment increased from 100 to 137.5.

   Required: Based on this information, calculate the equipment's net current cost (i.e., current cost less accumulated depreciation) at the end of 20X8.

7. General price-level index information for the country of Majikstan is as follows:

12/31/X7	30,000
Average	32,900
12/31/X8	36,000

   Required: Using this information and the information in Exercise 6, calculate the increase in the current cost of Majikstan Enterprise's equipment, net of inflation.

8. Now assume that Majikstan Enterprises is a foreign subsidiary of a U.S.-based multinational corporation and that its financial statements are consolidated with those of its U.S. parent. Relevant exchange rate and general price-level information for the year are given here:

Exchange rate:		General Price Level Index:	
		Majikstan	U.S.
12/31/X7	MJR 4.400 = $1	30,000	281.5
Average 20X8	MJR 4,800 = $1	32,900	292.5
12/31/X8	MJR 5,290 = $1	36,000	303.5

   Required: What would be the increase in the current cost of Majikstan Enterprise's equipment, net of inflation, when expressed in U.S. dollars under the restate-translate methodology? Under the translate-restate method?

9. The balance sheet of Rackett & Ball plc., a U.K.-based sporting goods manufacturer, is presented here. Figures are stated in millions of pounds (£m). During the year, the producers' price index increased from 100 to 120, averaging 110. The aggregate current cost of sales, depreciation, and monetary working capital adjustment is assumed to be £216m.

   Required: Assuming that changes in the producer's price index are a satisfactory measure of the change in R&B's purchasing power, calculate, as best as you can, R&B's monetary working capital adjustment and its gearing adjustment.

	£20X7m	£20X8 m
Fixed Assets:		
Intangible assets	56	150
Tangible assets	260	318
Investments	4	5
	320	473
Current Assets:		
Inventory	175	220
Trade receivable	242	270
Marketable securities	30	50
Cash	25	25
	472	565
Current Liabilities:		
Trade payables	(170)	(160)
Net current assets	302	405
Total assets less current liabilities	622	878
Long-term liabilities	385	422
Total net assets	237	456
Owner's Equity:		
Common stock	42	42
Premium on common stock	87	87
Retained earnings	108	327
Total owner's equity	237	456

10. Ninsuvaan Corporation, a U.S. subsidiary in Bangkok, Thailand, begins and ends its calendar year with an inventory balance of BHT500 million. The dollar/baht exchange rate on January 1 was $0.02 = BHT1. During the year, the U.S. general price level advances from 180 to 198, while the Thai general price level doubles. The exchange rate on December 31 was $0.015 = BHT1.

    Required:
    a. Using the temporal method of translation, calculate the dollar equivalent of the inventory balance by first restating for Thai inflation, then translating to U.S. dollars.
    b. Repeat part (a), but translate the nominal baht balances to dollars before restating for U.S. inflation.
    c. Which dollar figure do you think provides the more useful information?
    d. If you are dissatisfied with either result, suggest a method that would provide more useful information than those in parts (a) and (b).

11. Doosan Enterprises, a U.S. subsidiary domiciled in South Korea, accounts for its inventories on a FIFO basis. The company translates its inventories to dollars at the current rate. Year-end inventories are recorded at 10,920,000 won. During the year, the replacement cost of inventories increases by 20 percent. Inflation and exchange rate information are as follows:

    Required: Based on this information, calculate the dollar current-cost adjustment for cost of sales while avoiding a double-charge for inflation.

12. The year-end balance sheet of Helsinki Corporation, a wholly owned British affiliate in Finland, is reproduced here. Relevant exchange rate and inflation information is also provided.

Balance Sheet Year Ended 20X8			
Cash	EUR2,000	Short-term debt	EUR8,000
Inventory	8,000	Long-term debt	25,000
Plant & equipment, net	20,000		
Other assets	5,000	Owners' equity	2,000
Total	EUR35,000		EUR35,000

Exchange rate and price information:

January 1:	General price index = 300
	EUR1.5 = £1
December 31:	General price index = 390
	EUR1.95 = £1

Required: Using this information, calculate the monetary adjustment without double-counting for the effects of foreign inflation (assume that the U.K inflation rate is negligible).

CASES

Case 7-1   Kashmir Enterprises

Kashmir Enterprises, an Indian carpet manufacturer, begins the calendar year with the following Indian rupee (INR) balances:

Cash	920,000	Accounts payable	420,000
Inventory	640,000	Owners' equity	1,140,000
	$1,560,000		$1,560,000

During the first week in January, the company acquires additional manufacturing inventories costing INR2,400,000 on account and a warehouse for INR3,200,000 paying INR800,000 down and signing a 20-year, 10 percent note for the balance. The warehouse (assume no salvage value) is depreciated straight-line over the period of the note. Cash sales were INR6,000,000 for the year; selling and administrative expenses, including office rent, were INR1,200,000. Payments on account totaled INR2,200,000, while inventory on hand at year-end was INR480,000. Except for interest expense paid on December 31, all other cash receipts and payments took place uniformly throughout the year.

On January 1, the U.S. dollar/rupee exchange rate was $.025 = INR1; at year-end it was $.02 = INR1. The average exchange rate during the year was $.022. The Indian consumer price index rose from 128 to 160 by December 31, averaging 144 during the year. At the new financial statement date, the cost to replace inventories had increased by 30 percent; the cost to rebuild a comparable warehouse (based on the construction cost index) was approximately INR4,480,000. ■

REQUIRED

1. Assuming beginning inventories were acquired when the general price index level was 128, prepare Kashmir Enterprises' financial statements (i.e., income statement and balance sheet) under the (a) conventional original transactions cost model, (b) historical-cost constant rupee model, and (c) current-cost model.

2. Comment on which financial statement set gives financial analysts the most useful performance and wealth measures.

3. Now assume that management at Kashmir Enterprises' U.S. headquarters wants to see the Indian rupee statements in U.S. dollars. Two price-level foreign currency translation procedures are requested. The first is to translate Kashmir's unadjusted rupee statements to dollars (use the current-rate method) and then restate the resulting dollar amounts accounting for U.S. inflation (the U.S. general price level at the financial statement date was 108, up 8 percent from the previous year). The second is to restate the Indian rupee statements accounting for inflation (using the historical-cost constant rupee model), then translate the adjusted amounts to dollars using the current rate. Comment on which of the two resulting sets of dollar statements you prefer for use by American readers. (The U.S. general price level averaged 104 during the year.)

Case 7-2 Icelandic Enterprises, Inc.

In 1993 Icelandic Enterprises was incorporated in Reykjavik to manufacture and distribute women's cosmetics in Iceland. All of its outstanding stock was acquired at the beginning of 2001 by International Cosmetics, Ltd. (IC), a U.S.-based MNE headquartered in Shelton, Connecticut.

Competition with major cosmetics manufacturers both within and outside Iceland was very keen. As a result, Icelandic Enterprises (now a wholly-owned subsidiary of International Cosmetics) was under constant pressure to expand its product offerings. This required frequent investment in new equipment. Competition also affected the company's pricing flexibility. As the demand for cosmetics was price elastic, Icelandic lost market share every time it raised its prices. Accordingly, when Icelandic increased selling prices, it did so in small increments while increasing its advertising and promotional efforts to minimize the adverse effects of the price increase on sales volume.

International Cosmetics' financial policies with respect to Icelandic were dictated by two major considerations: the continued inflation and devaluation of the Icelandic krona (ISK). To counter these, headquarters management was eager to recoup its dollar investment in Icelandic Enterprises through dollar dividends. If dividends were not possible, subsidiary managers were instructed to preserve IC's original equity investment in Icelandic krona. Due to the unstable krona, all financial management analyses were made in dollars. International Cosmetics designated the dollar as Icelandic Enterprise's functional currency. Accordingly, it adopted the temporal method when translating Icelandic's krona accounts to their dollar equivalents. All monetary assets and liabilities were translated to dollars using the current exchange rate. All nonmonetary items, except those assets that were carried at current values, were translated using historical rates. Income and expense accounts were translated at the average exchange rates prevailing during the year, except depreciation and amortization charges related to assets translated at historical exchange rates. Translation gains and losses were taken directly to consolidated earnings.

Adjusting Icelandic's accounts for inflation was not attempted. Management believed that such restatements were too costly and subjective. IC's management also claimed that translating Icelandic's accounts to dollars automatically approximated the impact of inflation. The following is a comparative balance sheet and income statement for Icelandic Enterprises, along with relevant foreign exchange and general price-level indexes. ■

REQUIRED

1. Comment on International Cosmetics' policies on the basis of "as reported" earnings.
2. Is management correct in stating that by translating their financial reports into dollars they "automatically approximate the impact of inflation"?
3. What revised actions/policies would you recommend based on inflation-adjusted figures?

Balance Sheet	2001		2002	
(000's)	Dollars	Krona	Dollars	Krona
Cash	7,715	221,176	9,086	368,414
Accounts receivable	18,000	516,078	21,202	859,633
Inventory	118,706	2,949,017	154,988	4,912,187
PP&E, net[a]	283,252	1,221,237	265,706	3,057,000
Other assets	22,022	272,013	28,838	1,024,950
Total	449,695	5,179,521	479,820	8,172,284
Current liabilities	94,748	2,716,438	82,673	3,351,980
Due to parent	50,000	1,433,500	50,000	2,027,250
Capital stock[b]	98,758	713,430	98,758	713,430
Retained earnings	206,189	316,153	248,389	2,079,624
Total	449,695	5,179,521	479,820	8,172,284

Income Statement	2001		2002	
	Dollars	Krona	Dollars	Krona
Net sales	328,805	8,168,500	462,248	14,650,500
Cost of sales	150,012	3,726,750	199,874	6,334,800
Gross margin	178,793	4,441,750	262,354	8,315,700
Selling expenses	78,493	1,950,000	110,841	3,513,000
General and administrative expenses	28,680	712,500	49,647	1,573,500
Depreciation	44,056	122,124	47,002	305,700
Operating income	27,564	1,657,126	54,864	2,923,500
Interest expense	7,064	175,500	11,453	363,000
Income before taxes[c]	20,500	1,481,626	43,411	2,560,500

	1997	1998	1999	2000	2001	2002
National Inflation and Exchange Rates[d]						
Consumer price index:						
Iceland	63.1	100.0	150.6	224.7	418.2	547.0
United States	88.1	100.0	110.4	117.1	120.9	126.1
Krona per dollar:						
Year-end	3.949	6.239	8.173	16.625	28.670	40.545
Average	3.526	4.798	7.224	12.352	24.843	31.694

[a]Plant and equipment were acquired at the beginning of each period as follows: 1998, ISK 1,250,000; 1999, ISK 427,500; 2000, ISK 375,000; 2001, ISK 160,000; 2002, ISK 844,500. Depreciation is calculated at 10 percent per annum. A full year's depreciation is charged in the year of acquisition. Assume there were no disposals during any of the years.

[b]Common stock was acquired when the exchange rate was ISK 7.224 = $1.

[c]Inclusive of translation gains and losses.

[d]The inflation and exchange rate relationships used here are based on actual data for an earlier period.

CHAPTER 8

Global Accounting and Auditing Standards

Efforts to "harmonize" accounting around the world began even before the creation of the International Accounting Standards Committee (IASC) in 1973.[1] Companies seeking capital outside of their home markets and investors attempting to diversify their investments internationally faced increasing problems resulting from national differences in accounting measurement, disclosure, and auditing. International accounting harmonization efforts accelerated during the 1990s, matching the growing globalization of international business and securities markets, and the increased cross-listings by companies.[2] The harmonization efforts involved accounting standard setters, securities market regulators, stock exchanges, and those who prepare or use financial statements. The substantial differences in financial reporting requirements and practices around the world, and the increasing need of financial statement users to compare information of companies from different countries, were, and continue to be, the driving forces behind the movement to harmonize accounting.

Harmonized standards are compatible, that is, they do not contain conflicts. The term *convergence* is associated with the International Accounting Standards Board (IASB), discussed later in this chapter. As envisioned by the IASB, the convergence of international and national accounting standards involves the gradual elimination of differences through the cooperative efforts of the IASB, national standard setters, and other groups seeking best solutions to accounting and reporting issues. Thus, the notions behind harmonization and convergence are closely aligned. However, harmonization was generally taken to mean the elimination of differences between existing accounting standards, while convergence might also involve coming up with a new accounting treatment not in any current standard. *Convergence* is now the term most commonly used, and *harmonization* is used much less. It is important to note that neither process necessarily implies replacing national standards with international ones; national and international accounting standards can coexist.[3]

Accounting convergence includes the convergence of (1) accounting standards (which deal with measurement and disclosure), (2) disclosures made by publicly traded companies in connection with securities offerings and stock exchange listings, and (3) auditing standards.[4]

---

[1]The IASC was the predecessor body to the International Accounting Standards Board (IASB).
[2]See Chapter 1 for data on these phenomena.
[3]Some people use the term *standardization* interchangeably with *harmonization* and *convergence*. However, standardization generally means imposing a rigid and narrow set of rules—a one-size-fits-all approach. Harmonization and convergence are more flexible approaches to achieving compatibility.
[4]This is just a partial listing. For example, efforts are also under way to converge auditor education and requirements for offering and listing securities on stock markets.

A SURVEY OF INTERNATIONAL CONVERGENCE

Advantages of International Convergence

Proponents of international convergence claim that it has many advantages. Donald T. Nicolaisen, former chief accountant of the U.S. Securities and Exchange Commission, said the following in September 2004:

> At a conceptual level, supporting convergence is easy. An accounting treatment that transparently reflects the economics of a transaction to readers of financial statements in the U.K., will also do so for readers in France, Japan, the U.S. or most any other country. Similarly, the auditing requirements and procedures that are the most effective are likely to be the same in the U.S., Canada, China, or Germany. Disclosures relevant to investors in Italy, Greece or the Middle East, are likely to be just as useful to investors in the U.S. and elsewhere. Having high-quality standards for accounting, auditing, and disclosure benefits investors and reduces the cost of accessing the capital markets around the world. In short, convergence is good business and good for investors.[5]

In April 2005, Nicolaisen wrote the following:

> Key forces favoring a single set of globally accepted accounting standards are the continued strong expansion of the capital markets across national borders and the desire by countries to achieve strong, stable and liquid capital markets to fuel economic growth. A thriving capital market requires a high degree of investor understanding and confidence. Converging with or embracing a common set of high quality accounting standards contributes immensely to this investor understanding and confidence.
>
>   If a company's financial statements are prepared using accounting standards which are not viewed as being of high quality or with which the investor is unfamiliar, then investors may not be able to fully understand a company's prospects and thus may insist on a risk premium for an investment in that company. The relative cost of obtaining capital will thereby increase for those companies. And, at the extreme, if as a result of companies using weak or incomplete accounting standards it becomes excessively time-consuming or difficult for investors to distinguish good investment opportunities from bad, investors may choose instead to invest in what they consider to be safer opportunities rather than in particular securities which may actually offer greater reward.
>
>   Financial statements prepared using a common set of accounting standards help investors better understand investment opportunities as opposed to financial statements prepared under differing sets of national accounting standards. Without common standards, global investors must incur the time and effort to understand and convert the financial statements so that they can confidently

---

[5]D. T. Nicolaisen, "Remarks Before the IASB Meeting with World Standard-Setters" (September 28, 2004), www.sec.gov/news/speech/spch092804dtn.htm.

compare opportunities. This process is time-consuming and can be difficult, sometimes causing investors to resort to educated guesses as to content and comparability. Additionally, if investors are presented with financial information that varies substantially depending on which accounting standards are employed, that can cause investors to have doubt about the actual financial results of a company, resulting in a correspondingly adverse effect on investor confidence....

Embracing a common set of accounting standards can also lower costs for issuers. When companies access capital markets beyond their home jurisdiction, they incur additional costs of preparing financial statements using different sets of accounting standards. These include the costs for company personnel and auditors to learn, keep current with and comply with the requirements of multiple jurisdictions. Similarly, use of resources dedicated to standards writing could potentially be optimized if fewer separate accounting models are pursued.[6]

Finally, a recent paper argued for "global GAAP." Among the benefits cited are:

- High-quality financial reporting standards that are used consistently around the world improve the efficiency with which capital is allocated. The cost of capital will be reduced.
- Investors can make better investment decisions. Portfolios are more diverse and financial risk is reduced. There is more transparency and comparability between competitors in the global markets.
- Companies can improve their strategic decision-making in the merger and acquisition area.
- Accounting knowledge and skills can be transferred seamlessly around the world.
- The best ideas arising from national standard setting activities can be leveraged in developing global standards of the highest quality.[7]

To summarize, most arguments for accounting convergence relate in one way or another to increasing the operational and allocational efficiency of capital markets.

Criticisms of International Standards

The internationalization of accounting standards has also had critics. As early as 1971 (before the IASC was formed), some said that international standards were too simple a solution for a complex problem. Arguing that accounting, as a social science, has built-in flexibility, critics maintained that the ability to adapt to widely different situations is one of its most important values. They doubted that international standards could be flexible enough to handle differences in national backgrounds, traditions, and economic environments, and some thought that internationalization would be a politically unacceptable challenge to national sovereignty.

Other observers claim that large international accounting service firms are using international accounting standards as a tool with which to expand their markets. Multinational accounting firms, they say, are indispensable to apply international

---

[6]D. T. Nicolaisen, "A Securities Regulator Looks at Convergence," *Northwestern University Journal of International Law and Business* (April 2005), www.sec.gov/news/speech/spch040605dtn.htm.
[7]PricewaterhouseCoopers, *Global GAAP: The Future of Corporate Reporting* (2003), www.pwcglobal.com.

standards in national environments where such standards might seem distant and complex. As international financial institutions and international markets insist on the use of international standards, only large international accounting firms will be able to meet the demand.

There are also fears that adoption of international standards may create "standards overload." Corporations responding to an ever-growing array of national, social, political, and economic pressures will be hard put to comply with additional complex and costly international requirements. A related argument holds that national political concerns frequently intrude on accounting standards, and that international political influences would compromise accounting standards unacceptably.

Finally, some critics maintain that international standards are not suitable for small and medium-sized companies, particularly unlisted ones with no public accountability. Standards written to meet the needs of users in the world's capital markets are unnecessarily complex and require too much detailed disclosure for these types of companies. In such firms, there is often no separation between ownership and management, and shares change hands infrequently—perhaps only on succession in a family business. To counteract this problem, a version of "big GAAP/little GAAP" has been proposed with international standards for global companies and simplified standards for the others.[8]

Reconciliation and Mutual Recognition

As international equity issuance and trading grow, problems related to distributing financial statements in nondomestic jurisdictions become more important. As noted above, supporters argue that international convergence will help resolve problems associated with filings of cross-border financial statements.

Two other approaches have been advanced as possible solutions to the problems related to cross-border financial statement filings: (1) reconciliation, and (2) mutual recognition (also known as "reciprocity"). With reconciliation, foreign firms can prepare financial statements using home-country accounting standards, but also must provide a reconciliation between critical accounting measures (such as net income and shareholders' equity) of the home country and the country where the financial statements are being filed. For example, the U.S. Securities and Exchange Commission (SEC) permits foreign registrants to use accounting principles other than U.S. GAAP as the basis for the financial statements they file. However, the SEC also requires reconciliation disclosures (see Chapter 5). Reconciliations are less costly than preparing a full set of financial statements under a different set of accounting principles. However, they only provide a summary, not the full picture of the enterprise.

Mutual recognition exists when regulators outside the home country accept a foreign firm's financial statements based on home-country principles. For example, the London Stock Exchange accepts U.S. GAAP-based financial statements in filings made by foreign companies. Reciprocity does not improve the cross-country comparability of financial statements and can create an "unlevel playing field" in that it may allow foreign companies to apply standards less rigorous than those that apply to domestic companies.

---

[8]For example, see B. Shearer, "In Support of a GAAP Gap," *Accountancy Magazine* (September 2005): 96–97.

Evaluation

The harmonization/convergence debate may never be completely settled. Some arguments against harmonization have merit. However, increasing evidence shows that the goal of international harmonization of accounting, disclosure, and auditing has been so widely accepted that the trend toward international convergence will continue or even accelerate. Debates aside, all dimensions of accounting *are* becoming harmonized worldwide. Many companies are voluntarily adopting International Financial Reporting Standards (IFRS). Growing numbers of countries have adopted IFRS in their entirety, base their national standards on IFRS, or allow the use of IFRS. Leading international organizations and standard-setting bodies throughout the world (the European Commission, World Trade Organization, and Organization for Economic Cooperation and Development, among others) endorse the goals of the International Accounting Standards Board (IASB). Progress in harmonizing disclosure and auditing has been impressive.

Finally, national differences in the underlying factors that lead to variation in accounting, disclosure, and auditing practice are narrowing as capital and product markets become more international. As noted above, many companies have voluntarily adopted IFRS. They have done so because they see economic benefit in adopting accounting and disclosure standards that are credible internationally. Moreover, as discussed in Chapter 5, companies are voluntarily expanding their disclosures in line with IFRS in response to demand from institutional investors and other financial statement users. The success of recent convergence efforts by international organizations may indicate that convergence is happening as a natural response to economic forces.

SOME SIGNIFICANT EVENTS IN THE HISTORY OF INTERNATIONAL ACCOUNTING STANDARD SETTING

1959—Jacob Kraayenhof, founding partner of a major European firm of independent accountants, urges that work on international accounting standards begin.

1961—Groupe d'Etudes, consisting of practicing accounting professionals, is established in Europe to advise European Union authorities on matters concerning accounting.

1966—Accountants International Study Group is formed by professional institutes in Canada, United Kingdom, and United States.

1973—International Accounting Standards Committee (IASC) is created.

1976—Organization for Economic Cooperation and Development (OECD) issues Declaration on Investment in Multinational Enterprises containing guidelines on "Disclosure of Information."

1977—International Federation of Accountants (IFAC) is founded.

1977—Group of Experts appointed by United Nations Economic and Social Council issues four-part report on *International Standards of Accounting and Reporting for Transnational Corporations*.

1978—Commission of European Community issues Fourth Directive as first move toward European accounting harmonization.

1981—IASC establishes consultative group of nonmember organizations to widen input to international standard setting.

1984—London Stock Exchange states that listed companies not incorporated in United Kingdom or Ireland are to comply with international accounting standards.

1987—International Organization of Securities Commissions (IOSCO) resolves at annual conference to promote use of common standards in accounting and auditing practices.

1989—IASC issues Exposure Draft 32 on comparability of financial statements and publishes *Framework for the Preparation and Presentation of Financial Statements*.

1995—IASC Board and IOSCO Technical Committee agree on work plan whose successful completion will result in IAS forming a comprehensive core set of standards. Successful completion of these standards will allow IOSCO Technical Committee to recommend endorsement of IAS for cross-border capital raising and listing purposes in all global markets.

1995—European Commission adopts new approach to accounting harmonization that allows use of IAS by companies listing on international capital markets.

1996—U.S. Securities and Exchange Commission (SEC) announces that it "supports the IASC's objective to develop, as expeditiously as possible, accounting standards that could be used for preparing financial statements that could be used in cross-border offerings."

1998—IOSCO publishes "International Disclosure Standards for Cross Border Offerings and Initial Listings by Foreign Issuers."

2000—IOSCO accepts all 40 core standards prepared by IASC in response to IOSCO's 1993 wish list.

2001—European Commission proposes regulation requiring all EU companies listed on regulated markets to prepare consolidated accounts in accordance with IAS by 2005.

2001—International Accounting Standards Board (IASB) succeeds IASC and assumes its responsibilities. IASB standards, designated International Financial Reporting Standards (IFRS), include IAS issued by the IASC.

2002 – European Parliament endorses Commission proposal that virtually all EU listed companies must follow IASB standards starting no later than 2005 in their consolidated financial statements. Member states may extend requirement to nonlisted companies and to individual company statements. European Council later adopts enabling regulation.

2002 –IASB and FASB sign the "Norwalk Agreement" committing them to convergence of international and U.S. accounting standards.

2003 – European Council approves amended EU Fourth and Seventh Directives removing inconsistencies between old directives and IFRS.

2004 – Australian Accounting Standards Board announces intent to adopt IFRS as Australian accounting standards.

2005 – SEC proposes "roadmap" to eliminate requirement for reconciliation between IFRS and U.S. GAAP. SEC and EU Commission later agree on roadmap to eliminate requirement no later than 2009.

2005 – Chinese Ministry of Finance commits to converging Chinese accounting standards to IFRS by 2007. Canadian Accounting Standards Board proposes eliminating Canadian GAAP in favor of IFRS by 2011. IASB and Accounting Standards Board of Japan launch convergence project.

2006 – FASB and IASB sign Memorandum of Understanding setting out milestones the two boards must reach in order to demonstrate acceptable level of convergence between U.S. GAAP and IFRS to SEC and EU Commission.

2006 – IASB publishes statement on its working relationships with other accounting standard setters.

2006 – EU issues Statutory Audit Directive, replacing Eighth Directive.

2007 – SEC proposes eliminating reconciliation requirement for companies using IFRS.

OVERVIEW OF MAJOR INTERNATIONAL ORGANIZATIONS PROMOTING ACCOUNTING CONVERGENCE

Six organizations have been key players in setting international accounting standards and in promoting international accounting harmonization:

1. International Accounting Standards Board (IASB)
2. Commission of the European Union (EU)
3. International Organization of Securities Commissions (IOSCO)
4. International Federation of Accountants (IFAC)
5. United Nations Intergovernmental Working Group of Experts on International Standards of Accounting and Reporting (ISAR), part of United Nations Conference on Trade and Development (UNCTAD)
6. Organization for Economic Cooperation and Development Working Group on Accounting Standards (OECD Working Group)

The IASB represents private-sector interests and organizations. The EU Commission, referred to as the European Commission (EC), the OECD Working Group, and the ISAR are political entities that derive their powers from international agreements. IFAC's main activities include issuing technical and professional guidance and promoting the adoption of IFAC and IASB pronouncements. IOSCO promotes high standards of regulation, including harmonized accounting and disclosure standards for cross-border capital raising and trading.

Also important is the World Federation of Exchanges (WFE), the trade organization for regulated securities and derivative markets worldwide. The WFE promotes the professional business development of financial markets. One of the WFE's goals is to establish harmonized standards for business processes (including financial reporting and disclosure) in cross-border trading in securities, including cross-border public offerings.

Many regional accounting organizations (e.g., the ASEAN Federation of Accountants, the Nordic Federation of Accountants) participate in cross-country standard setting within their respective regions. The Fédération des Experts Comptables Européens (FEE: Federation of European Accountants) represents national accounting bodies in Europe. Other regional organizations include the Fédération des Bourses Européennes (FESE: Federation of European Securities Exchanges) and the Committee of European Securities Regulators (CESR), consisting of securities market regulators from EU member nations.

Refer to Exhibit 8-1 for Web sites offering information about major international organizations. Exhibit 8-2 presents the Web site addresses of national regulatory and accountancy organizations, many of which are actively involved in accounting convergence activities.

EXHIBIT 8-1   Web Sites Offering Information about Major International Organizations and International Convergence Activities

Organization	Web Site Address
Bank for International Settlements	www.bis.org
Committee of European Securities Regulators	www.cesr-eu.org
Confederation of Asian & Pacific Accountants (CAPA)	capa.com.my
Deloitte IAS Plus Web site	www.iasplus.com
European Union (EU)	europa.eu
European Commission—Internal Market and Financial Services	europa.eu.int/comm/internal_market/en/index.htm
Fédération des Experts Comptables Européens (FEE) a/k/a European Federation of Accountants	www.fee.be
Federation of European Securities Exchanges a/k/a Fédération des Bourses Européennes (FESE)	www.fese.be/en/
International Accounting Standards Board (IASB)	www.iasb.org.
International Federation of Accountants (IFAC)	www.ifac.org
International Monetary Fund (IMF)	www.imf.org
International Organization of Securities Commissions (IOSCO)	www.iosco.org
Organization for Economic Cooperation and Development (OECD)	www.oecd.org
United Nations Conference on Trade and Development (UNCTAD)	www.unctad.org
World Bank	www.worldbank.org
World Federation of Exchanges (WFE)	www.world-exchanges.org
World Trade Organization (WTO)	www.wto.org

Note: These listings were correct when this book went to press.

EXHIBIT 8-2   Web Site Addresses of Selected Regulatory and Accountancy Organizations

Organization	Web Site Address
Government and Regulatory Organizations	
U.K. Financial Services Authority (FSA)	www.fsa.gov.uk
U.S. Public Company Accounting Oversight Board	www.pcaobus.org
U.S. Securities and Exchange Commission (SEC)	www.sec.gov
U.S. Securities and Exchange Commission (SEC) Edgar Database	www.sec.gov/edgar.shtml
French Autorité des Marché Financiers (AMF)	www.amf-france.org
National Professional Accountancy Organizations	
Argentina—Federación Argentina de Consejos Profesionales de Ciencias Económicas	www.facpce.org.ar

(continued)

Organization	*Web Site Address*
Barbados—Institute of Chartered Accountants of Barbados	www.icab.bb
Belgium—Institut des Experts Comptables	www.accountancy.be
Belgium—Institut des Réviseurs d'Entreprises	www.accountancy.be
Canada—Society of Management Accountants of Canada	www.cma-canada.org
Canada—Chartered Accountants of Canada	www.cica.ca
Canada—Certified General Accountants Association of Canada	www.cga-canada.org
China—Chinese Institute of Certified Public Accountants	www.cicpa.org.cn
Cyprus—Institute of Certified Public Accountants of Cyprus	www.icpac.org.cy
Czech Republic—Union of Accountants of the Czech Republic	www.svaz-ucetnich.cz
France—Conseil Supérieur de l'Ordre des Experts-Comptables	www.experts-comptables.com
Georgia—Georgian Federation of Professional Accountants and Auditors	www.gfpaaa.ge
Germany—Institut der Wirtschaftsprüfer in Deutschland	www.idw.de
Hong Kong—Hong Kong Institute of Certified Public Accountants	www.hksa.org.hk
Hong Kong—Hong Kong Association of Accredited Accounting Technicians	www.hkaat.org.hk
India—Institute of Chartered Accountants of India	www.icai.org
Ireland—Institute of Chartered Accountants in Ireland	www.icai.ie
Japan—Japanese Institute of Certified Public Accountants	www.jicpa.or.jp
Jordan—Arab Society of Certified Accountants	www.ascasociety.org
Kenya—Institute of Certified Public Accountants of Kenya	www.icpak.com
Korea—Korean Institute of Certified Public Accountants	www.kicpa.or.kr
Malaysia—Malaysian Institute of Accountants	www.mia.org.my
Malta—Malta Institute of Accountants	www.miamalta.org
Mexico—Instituto Mexicano de Contadores Públicos	www.imcp.org.mx
Nepal—Institute of Chartered Accountants of Nepal	www.ican.org.np
Netherlands—Koninklijk Nederlands Instituut van Registeraccountants	www.nivra.nl
New Zealand—Institute of Chartered Accountants of New Zealand	www.nzica.com
Nigeria—Institute of Chartered Accountants of Nigeria	www.ican-ngr.org
Norway—Den norske Revisorforening (DnR)	www.revisornett.no
Pakistan—Institute of Cost and Management Accountants of Pakistan	www.icmap.com.pk
Pakistan—Institute of Chartered Accountants of Pakistan	www.icap.org.pk
Philippines—Philippine Institute of Certified Public Accountants	www.picpa.com.ph
Romania—Corpul Expertilor Contabili si Contabililor Autorizati din Romania	www.ceccar.ro
Singapore—Institute of Certified Public Accountants of Singapore	www.accountants.org.sg
South Africa—South African Institute of Chartered Accountants (SAICA)	www.saica.co.za
South Africa—South African Institute of Professional Accountants	www.cfa-sa.co.za
Sri Lanka—Institute of Chartered Accountants of Sri Lanka	www.icasrilanka.com
Sweden—Branchorganisationen för revisorer och rådgivare	www.farsrs.se
U.K.—Institute of Chartered Accountants in England & Wales	www.icaew.co.uk
U.K.—Chartered Institute of Management Accountants	www.cimaglobal.com

(continued)

Organization	*Web Site Address*
U.K.— Association of Chartered Certified Accountants	www.acca.org.uk
U.K.— Chartered Institute of Public Finance and Accountancy	www.cipfa.org.uk
U.K.— Institute of Chartered Accountants of Scotland	www.icas.org.uk
U.K.—Association of Accounting Technicians	www.aat.co.uk
U.S.—American Institute of CPAs	www.aicpa.org
U.S.—National Association of State Boards of Accountancy	www.nasba.org
U.S.—Institute of Management Accountants	www.imanet.org
U.S.— Institute of Internal Auditors	www.theiia.org
Zimbabwe—Institute of Chartered Accountants of Zimbabwe	www.icaz.org.zw
Accounting Standard Setting Bodies	
Australia—Accounting Standards Board (AASB)	www.aasb.com.au
Canada—Accounting Standards Board (ASB)	www.acsbcanada.org
France—Conseil National de la Comptabilité (CNC)	www.finances.gouv.fr
Germany—German Accounting Standards Committee (GASC)	www.standardsetter.de
Japan—Accounting Standards Board (ASBJ)	www.asb.or.jp
Netherlands— Dutch Accounting Standards Board	www.rjnet.nl
New Zealand—Accounting Standards Review Board	www.asrb.co.nz
United Kingdom—Accounting Standards Board (ASB)	www.frc.org.uk
United States—Financial Accounting Standards Board (FASB)	www.fasb.org

Note: These listings were correct when this book went to press.

INTERNATIONAL ACCOUNTING STANDARDS BOARD

The International Accounting Standards Board (IASB), formerly the IASC, is an independent private-sector standard-setting body founded in 1973 by professional accounting organizations in nine countries and restructured in 2001. (The restructuring made IASC into an umbrella organization under which the IASB carries out its work.) Before the restructuring, the IASC issued 41 International Accounting Standards (IAS) and a Framework for the Preparation and Presentation of Financial Statements. The IASB's objectives are:

1. To develop, in the public interest, a single set of high-quality, understandable, and enforceable global accounting standards that require high-quality, transparent, and comparable information in financial statements and other financial reporting to help participants in the world's capital markets and other users make economic decisions.
2. To promote the use and rigorous application of those standards.
3. In fulfilling the objectives associated with (1) and (2), to take account of, as appropriate, the special needs of small and medium-sized entities and emerging economies.
4. To bring about convergence of national accounting standards, and International Accounting Standards and International Financial Reporting Standards to high-quality solutions.[9]

---

[9]See the IASB Web site (www.iasb.org).

The IASB represents accounting organizations from approximately 100 countries. With a remarkably broad base of support, the IASB is the driving force in international accounting standard setting. Exhibit 8-3 lists the current IASB standards (as of January 2007).[10] The IASB Web site (www.iasb.org) presents a summary of current IASB standards. IASB standards follow the principles of fair presentation and full disclosure (see Chapter 2). Financial reporting and accounting measurement principles are described in Chapter 3.

During the first decade of the IASC, international accounting standards were more descriptive than prescriptive. These early standards codified similar national practices and excluded outlier practices. The IASC began to address more difficult issues during its second 10 years and responded to concerns that its standards included too many alternative accounting treatments and were not rigorous enough.

IASC's Core Standards and the IOSCO Agreement

The IASB (like the former IASC) has been striving to develop accounting standards that will be accepted by securities regulators around the world. As part of this effort, the IASC adopted a work plan to produce a comprehensive core set of high-quality standards. In July 1995 the IOSCO Technical Committee stated its agreement with the work plan. The Core Standards were completed with the approval of IAS 39 in December 1998. IOSCO's review of the Core Standards began in 1999, and in 2000 it endorsed the use of IASC Standards for cross-border offerings and listings.

EXHIBIT 8-3   Current IASB Standards

Standard	*Description*
IAS 1	Presentation of Financial Statements
IAS 2	Inventories
IAS 3	No longer effective. Replaced by IAS 27 and IAS 28.
IAS 4	No longer effective. Replaced by IAS 16, 22, and IAS 38.
IAS 5	No longer effective. Replaced by IAS 1.
IAS 6	No longer effective. Replaced by IAS 15.
IAS 7	Cash Flow Statements
IAS 8	Accounting Policies, Changes in Accounting Estimates and Errors
IAS 9	No longer effective. Replaced by IAS 38.
IAS 10	Events Occurring after the Balance Sheet Date
IAS 11	Construction Contracts
IAS 12	Income Taxes
IAS 13	No longer effective. Replaced by IAS 1.
IAS 14	No longer effective. Replaced by IFRS 8.
IAS 15	No longer effective. Withdrawn December 2003.
IAS 16	Property, Plant, and Equipment
IAS 17	Leases
IAS 18	Revenue

(continued)

---

[10]Standards issued by the IASB are referred to as International Financial Reporting Standards (IFRS); those issued by the IASC are called International Accounting Standards (IAS). The IASB has adopted all previously issued IAS. All references to IFRS include IAS.

Standard	Description
IAS 19	Employee Benefits
IAS 20	Accounting for Government Grants and Disclosure of Government Assistance
IAS 21	The Effects of Changes in Foreign Exchange Rates
IAS 22	No longer effective. Replaced by IFRS 3.
IAS 23	Borrowing Costs
IAS 24	Related Party Disclosures
IAS 25	No longer effective. Replaced by IAS 39 and IAS 40.
IAS 26	Accounting and Reporting by Retirement Benefit Plans
IAS 27	Consolidated and Separate Financial Statements
IAS 28	Investments in Associates
IAS 29	Financial Reporting in Hyperinflationary Economies
IAS 30	No longer effective. Replaced by IFRS 7.
IAS 31	Interests in Joint Ventures
IAS 32	Financial Instruments: Disclosures and Presentation
IAS 33	Earnings Per Share
IAS 34	Interim Financial Reporting
IAS 35	No longer effective. Replaced by IFRS 5.
IAS 36	Impairment of Assets
IAS 37	Provisions, Contingent Liabilities, and Contingent Assets
IAS 38	Intangible Assets
IAS 39	Financial Instruments: Recognition and Measurement
IAS 40	Investment Property
IAS 41	Agriculture
IFRS 1	First-time Adoption of International Financial Reporting Standards
IFRS 2	Share-based Payment
IFRS 3	Business Combinations
IFRS 4	Insurance Contracts
IFRS 5	Non-current Assets Held for Sale and Discontinued Operations
IFRS 6	Exploration for and Evaluation of Mineral Resources
IFRS 7	Financial Instruments: Disclosure
IFRS 8	Operating Segments

Note: As of January 30, 2007. Consult IASB Web site, www.iasb.org, for current list.

The New IASB Structure

The IASC board formed a Strategy Working Party (SWP) to consider what the IASC's strategy and structure should be after completion of the core standards work program. In 1998, the SWP approved a discussion paper, "Shaping IASC for the Future," to encourage and focus discussion. In 1999 the IASC board unanimously approved a resolution supporting a proposed new structure with the following main features: (1) IASC would be established as an independent organization; (2) the organization would have two main bodies, the trustees and the board, as well as a Standing Interpretations Committee (now called the International Financial Reporting Interpretations Committee) and a Standards Advisory Council; (3) the trustees would appoint the board members, exercise oversight, and raise the funds needed, whereas the board would have sole responsibility for setting accounting standards.

The restructured IASB met for the first time in 2001. The IASB, as reorganized, includes the following bodies.[11]

1. **Trustees.**   The IASB has 22 trustees: six from North America, six from Europe, six from the Asia/Pacific region, and four from any area ("subject to establishing overall geographic balance").[12] The trustees appoint the members of the board, the International Financial Reporting Interpretations Committee, and the Standards Advisory Council. The trustees are responsible for raising funds, and supervise and review the priorities and operations of the IASB.

2. **IASB Board.**   The board establishes and improves standards of financial accounting and reporting for businesses. Its responsibilities include "complete responsibility for all IASB technical matters including the preparation and issuing of International Accounting Standards, International Financial Reporting Standards, and Exposure Drafts . . . and final approval of Interpretations by the International Financial Reporting Interpretations Committee," and approving the technical agenda and the conduct of its work. The board consists of 14 members, appointed by the trustees to provide "the best available combination of technical expertise and diversity of international business experience." All board members are paid IASB employees; 12 must be full-time and two may be part-time. The board maintains liaison with national standard setters and other official bodies concerned with standard setting. (The purpose is to partner with these national bodies to achieve the convergence of national and international accounting standards.)[13] Members are appointed for a five-year term, renewable once.

3. **Standards Advisory Council.**   The Standards Advisory Council, appointed by the trustees, is made up of "thirty or more members, having a diversity of geographic and professional backgrounds, appointed for renewable terms of three years." The Standards Advisory Council normally meets three times each year. Its responsibilities are to give the board advice on its agenda and priorities, inform the board of the views "of the organizations and individuals on the council on major standard setting projects," and give "other advice" to the board or the trustees.

4. **International Financial Reporting Interpretations Committee (IFRIC).**   The IFRIC consists of 12 members appointed by the trustees. The IFRIC interprets "the application of International Accounting Standards and International Financial Reporting Standards and provides timely guidance on financial reporting issues not specifically addressed in IAS and IFRS, in the context of IASB's Framework," publishes draft interpretations and reviews public comments on them, and obtains board approval for final interpretations.

The IASB follows due process in setting accounting standards. For each standard, the board normally publishes a discussion paper that sets out the possible requirements for the standard and the arguments for and against each one. Subsequently, the

---

[11]Much of this section is based on information published on the IASB Web site (www.iasb.org). The new IASB structure is modeled after the U.S. accounting standard setting structure, as described in Chapter 4.
[12]All direct quotations in this section are from the IASB constitution (revised July 2002), found on its Web site (www.iasb.org).
[13]The IASB has formal liaison relationships with standard setters in Australia and New Zealand, Canada, France, Germany, Japan, the United Kingdom, the United States, and the Technical Expert Group of the European Financial Reporting Advisory Group (EFRAG, discussed later in this chapter).

board publishes an exposure draft for public comment, and it then examines the arguments put forward in the comment process before deciding on the final form of the standard. An exposure draft and final standard can be issued only when nine members of the board have voted in favor of doing so.[14]

Recognition and Support for the IASB

International Financial Reporting Standards are now widely accepted around the world. They are (1) used by many countries as the basis for national accounting requirements or are adopted entirely; (2) accepted by many stock exchanges and regulators that allow foreign or domestic companies to file financial statements prepared in conformance with IFRS; and (3) recognized by the EC and other supranational bodies. In 1995, the EC endorsed IFRS. Rather than amend existing directives, the EC determined that the EU should associate with IASC/IASB and IOSCO efforts toward a broader international harmonization of accounting standards. EU companies listed on recognized stock exchanges now use IFRS in preparing consolidated financial statements.

The signing of the 2002 "Norwalk Agreement" by the IASB and U.S. Financial Accounting Standards Board symbolized the commitment of national standard setters to converge toward a single set of international accounting standards worldwide. In 2004, the Australian Accounting Standards Board adopted IFRS as Australia's accounting standards. In 2005, China and Japan committed to converging their respective national accounting standards to IFRS. Also in 2005, the Canadian Accounting Standards Board proposed replacing Canadian accounting standards with IFRS by 2011. Standard setters from Australia/New Zealand, Canada, France, Germany, Japan, the United Kingdom, and the United States actively partner with the IASB in their standard-setting activities.

U.S. Securities and Exchange Commission Response to IFRS

During the 1990s, the SEC came under increasing pressure to make U.S. capital markets more accessible to non-U.S. issuers. At the time, the SEC expressed support for the IASB's objective to develop accounting standards for use in financial statements used in cross-border offerings. However, the SEC also stated that three conditions must be met for it to accept IASB standards.[15]

1. The standards must include a core set of accounting pronouncements that constitutes a comprehensive, generally accepted basis of accounting.
2. The standards must be of high quality—they must result in comparability and transparency, and they must provide for full disclosure.
3. The standards must be rigorously interpreted and applied.

Later, senior officials of the SEC indicated that if the IASB and FASB make sufficient progress in converging their standards, and if sufficient progress is made in creating an infrastructure for interpreting and enforcing accounting standards, the SEC would consider allowing foreign registrants to file in the United States using IFRS without reconciling to U.S. GAAP.

---

[14]Source: IASB, *Due Process Handbook for the IASB* (March 2006).
[15]U.S. Securities and Exchange Commission, "News Release—SEC Statement Regarding International Accounting Standards" (Washington, DC: U.S. Securities and Exchange Commission, April 11, 1996).

In 2005, the SEC issued a "roadmap" setting out the steps for eliminating the requirement to reconcile IFRS to U.S. GAAP by 2009. The SEC roadmap reaffirmed that sufficient convergence must have been achieved between the two sets of standards and that the SEC has confidence in auditing and enforcement practices. The SEC and the EU Commission (discussed next) signed an agreement on the roadmap later that same year. In 2006, the FASB and IASB signed a memorandum of understanding on how they will achieve convergence between U.S. GAAP and IFRS in order for the SEC to eliminate the reconciliation requirement. This memorandum of understanding is essentially their own roadmap containing a "to do" list and milestones for achieving equivalence between the two sets of standards. These efforts resulted in an SEC proposal in 2007 to eliminate the reconciliation requirement for companies using IFRS. If approved, the change would go into effect in 2009. The SEC's proposal implies confidence in the quality and application of IFRS and in the convergence process between the FASB and IASB.

EUROPEAN UNION (EU)

The Treaty of Rome established the EU in 1957, with the goal of harmonizing the legal and economic systems of its member states. The EU now comprises 27 member countries (Austria, Belgium, Bulgaria, Cyprus, Czech Republic, Denmark, Estonia, Finland, France, Germany, Greece, Hungary, Ireland, Italy, Latvia, Lithuania, Luxembourg, Malta, the Netherlands, Poland, Portugal, Romania, Slovakia, Slovenia, Spain, Sweden, and the United Kingdom). In contrast to the IASB, which has no authority to require implementation of its accounting standards, the European Commission (EC, the governing body of the EU) has full enforcement powers for its accounting directives throughout the member states.

One of the EU's goals is to achieve integration of European financial markets. Toward this end, the EC has introduced directives and undertaken major initiatives to achieve a single market for:

- raising capital on an EU-wide basis
- establishing a common legal framework for integrated securities and derivatives markets
- achieving a single set of accounting standards for listed companies

The EC embarked on a major program of company law harmonization soon after it was formed.[16] EC directives now cover all aspects of company law. Several have a direct bearing on accounting. Many observers consider the Fourth, Seventh, and Eighth Directives to be historically and substantively the most important.

---

[16]EU directives become the law of member states through a complex, lengthy process. Preliminary work leads to the issuance of a draft directive (i.e., exposure draft) by the EU. When a draft directive is broadly acceptable (after hearings and other evaluation procedures), it is submitted to the member states for ratification after approval from the European Council. After the EU adopts a directive, each member state adopts and implements it. Directives are binding on member states, but the method of implementation is left to the discretion of national authorities.

Fourth, Seventh, and Eighth Directives

The EU's Fourth Directive, issued in 1978, is the broadest and most comprehensive set of accounting rules within the EU framework. Both public and private companies above certain minimum size criteria must comply. Fourth Directive requirements apply to individual company accounts and include format rules for financial statements, disclosure requirements, and valuation rules. The true and fair view is the overriding requirement and holds for footnote disclosures just as it does for financial statements. The Fourth Directive also requires that financial statements be audited. It aims to ensure that European companies disclose comparable and equivalent information in their financial statements.

The Seventh Directive, issued in 1983, addresses the issue of consolidated financial statements. At the time, consolidated financial statements were the exception rather than the rule. They were the norm in Ireland, the Netherlands, and the United Kingdom, and Germany required consolidation of German subsidiaries (only). Elsewhere in Europe consolidated statements were rare. The Seventh Directive requires consolidation for groups of companies above a certain size, specifies disclosures in notes and the directors' report, and requires an audit. Because of the newness of consolidations as a legal requirement, member states were given wide latitude and many options for incorporating the Seventh Directive into their individual national company laws.

The Eighth Directive, issued in 1984, addresses various aspects of the qualifications of professionals authorized to carry out legally required (statutory) audits. Essentially, this directive lays down minimum qualifications for auditors. It covers requirements for the education and training of auditors and independence. The Eighth Directive was substantially amended in 2006 and is now referred to as the Statutory Audit Directive. The new directive is a response to accounting scandals involving European companies such as Parmalat, the Italian dairy company, and Ahold, the Dutch grocery chain, as well to as American accounting scandals involving WorldCom, Global Crossing, and Enron, and others. It includes requirements for the appointment and removal of auditors, audit standards, continuing professional education, auditor rotation, and public oversight. It requires that all statutory audits in the EU observe International Standards on Auditing (discussed later). Among its more important provisions is one requiring each member state to establish a public oversight body for the audit profession and the establishment of the European Group of Auditors' Oversight Bodies (EGAOB) to coordinate their activities. Exhibit 8-4 compares certain features of the Statutory Audit Directive to the U.S. Sarbanes-Oxley Act (see Chapter 4).

Have EU Harmonization Efforts Been Successful?

The Fourth and Seventh Directives had a dramatic impact on financial reporting throughout the EU, bringing accounting in all the member states up to a good and reasonably uniform level. It harmonized the presentation of the profit and loss account (income statement) and balance sheet and added minimum supplementary information in the notes, in particular a disclosure of the impact of tax regulations on reported results. It accelerated accounting development in many EU countries and also influenced accounting in neighboring, non-EU countries.

However, the success of EU harmonization efforts has been debated. For example, member states generally did not scrap their existing accounting rules when adopting

EXHIBIT 8-4 Comparison of EU Statutory Audit Directive and U.S. Sarbanes-Oxley Act

Issue	EU Statutory Audit Directive	U.S. Sarbanes-Oxley Act
Audit committees	Required for listed companies. Appoints or dismisses the auditor. At least one member must be independent. At least one member must have financial expertise.	Required for listed companies. Appoints or dismisses the auditor. Committee must be independent. At least one member must have financial expertise. Also requires procedures for complaints from whistleblowers.
Internal controls	Audit firm must report on key matters that arise from the audit, especially weaknesses in internal controls.	Same. Requirements are more detailed.
Public oversight of auditors	Each member state must appoint an oversight body for auditors.	Public Company Accounting Oversight Board (PCAOB) oversees audit of public companies, establishes standards for auditing, quality control, ethics, and independence of audit firms.
Firm vs. partner rotation	Key audit partner rotation every seven years, with member-state option of rotation of audit firm.	Lead audit partner must rotate every five years.
Auditing standards	International Standards on Auditing.	PCAOB standards.

EU directives. Instead, they adapted the new rules to their existing ones. Another issue is the extent to which member states enforced compliance with the directives. Thus, some question whether the directives harmonized accounting as much as had been intended when they were issued.[17]

Karel van Hulle, former head of the accounting and audit unit at the European Commission, described some of the difficulties.

It must be admitted that the comparability achieved through the harmonisation process is far from perfect. First of all, the Accounting Directives contain primarily minimum rules. They are *not* dealing with a number of important accounting issues. Secondly, the provisions of the Directives are not always interpreted in the same way by Member States. A number of questions relating to the interpretation of the Directives have been dealt with by the Contact Committee on the Accounting Directives.[18] Other questions have remained on the table. It has been difficult to arrive at an agreed position on these questions because the text of the Directives often leaves much scope for interpretation

---

[17]Peter Walton, "European Harmonization," in *International Finance and Accounting Handbook*, ed. Frederick D. S. Choi, 3rd ed. (New York: John Wiley, 2003).
[18]European Commission Contact Committee on the Accounting Directives, *The Accounting Harmonisation in the European Community: Problems of Applying the Fourth Directive on the Annual Accounts of Limited Companies* (Luxembourg: Office for Official Publications of the European Communities, 1990).

and Member States were not prepared to compromise on the interpretation. The general wording of some of the provisions in the Accounting Directives has been an important reason why the Commission has not brought some of these questions before the European Court of Justice for a final ruling.[19]

The EU's New Approach and the Integration of European Financial Markets

In 1995 the EC adopted a new approach to accounting harmonization, referred to as the New Accounting Strategy. The commission announced that the EU needs to move promptly in order to give a clear signal that companies seeking listings in the United States and other world markets will be able to remain within the EU accounting framework.[20] The EC also stressed that the EU needs to strengthen its commitment to the international standard-setting process that offers the most efficient and rapid solution for the problems of companies operating on an international scale.

In 2000, the EC adopted a new financial reporting strategy. The cornerstone of this strategy was a proposed regulation that all EU companies listed on regulated markets, including banks, insurance companies, and SMEs (small and medium-sized companies), prepare consolidated accounts in accordance with IFRS. (Unlisted SMEs are not covered, but may find it in their interest to adopt IFRS voluntarily, especially if they seek international capital.) The EU Parliament endorsed this proposal, and the EU Council adopted the necessary enabling legislation in 2002.[21]

This regulation affects some 7,000 listed EU companies (compared with nearly 300 listed EU companies that used IFRS in 2001). It is designed "to encourage cross-border trade in financial services and so create a fully-integrated market, by helping to make financial information more transparent and easily comparable."[22]

To become legally binding, IFRS must be adopted by the EC. Included in the above regulation is a two-tiered "endorsement mechanism" and the establishment of the Accounting Regulatory Committee (ARC), an EU body with representatives from member states. An IFRS is first given a technical review and opinion by the European Financial Reporting Advisory Group (EFRAG), a private-sector organization of auditors, preparers, national standard setters, and others.[23] The Standards Advice Review Group, an EU body of independent experts and representatives of national standard setters, next assesses whether EFRAG's endorsement advice is well balanced and objective. Then the ARC recommends that the IFRS be endorsed (or not) based on whether it is compatible with European directives and conducive to the European public good. EC endorsement completes the process. The entire endorsement process normally takes around 10 months. To date, all IFRS have been endorsed, with the

---

[19]Karel van Hulle, "International Harmonisation of Accounting Principles: A European Perspective," *Wirtschaftsprüferkammer—Mitteilungen,* special edition (June 1997): 44–50.
[20]See the EC's communication "Accounting Harmonisation: A New Strategy vis-à-vis International Harmonisation," COM 95 (508) final of November 14, 1995.
[21]Regulation (EC) No. 1606/2002. Member states may defer application until 2007 for companies listed in the EU and elsewhere that use U.S. GAAP (or other GAAP) as their primary basis of accounting, as well as for companies that only have publicly traded debt. Member states may extend this requirement to all companies, not just listed ones, including individual company accounts.
[22]"International Accounting Standards: Mandatory for Listed Companies by 2005," *Single Market News,* no. 25 (March 2001): 18–19.
[23]The EFRAG Web site is www.efrag.org.

exception of one "carve-out" to IAS 39.[24] The Fourth and Seventh Directives were also amended in 2003 to remove inconsistencies between the old directives and IFRS.

Finally, there have been developments designed to strengthen enforcement of IRFS in Europe. In 2003, the Committee of European Securities Regulators adopted Standard 1 on Financial Information. This standard contains 21 principles aimed at developing and implementing a common approach to the enforcement of IFRS throughout the EU.[25] Standard 2 on Financial Information Coordination and Enforcement Activities was issued in 2004 to provide a framework for coordinating enforcement in the EU.[26]

INTERNATIONAL ORGANIZATION OF SECURITIES COMMISSIONS (IOSCO)

The International Organization of Securities Commissions (IOSCO) consists of securities regulators from more than 100 countries. The objectives of IOSCO's member agencies are:

- To cooperate together to promote high standards of regulation in order to maintain just, efficient, and sound markets
- To exchange information on their respective experiences in order to promote the development of domestic markets
- To unite their efforts to establish standards and an effective surveillance of international securities transactions
- To provide mutual assistance to promote the integrity of the markets by a rigorous application of the standards and by effective enforcement against offenses

Together, IOSCO members are responsible for regulating more than 90 percent of global securities markets. As financial markets have become increasingly global, so cross-border cooperation among securities regulators has become an increasingly important objective for the organization.

IOSCO has worked extensively on international disclosure and accounting standards to facilitate the ability of companies to raise capital efficiently in global securities markets. In 1998 IOSCO published a set of nonfinancial disclosure standards that may eventually enable companies to use a single prospectus to offer or list shares on any of the world's major capital markets. Securities regulators worldwide are increasingly adopting these standards.

An IOSCO technical committee focuses on multinational disclosure and accounting. Its main objective is to facilitate the process whereby world-class issuers can raise capital in the most effective and efficient way on all capital markets where investor demand

---

[24]A carve-out is an exception to one or more provisions of a particular standard. The EC has endorsed IAS 39 with the exception of its provisions on hedge accounting. This carve-out allows entities to use hedge accounting in circumstances that are not permitted by IAS 39.

[25]*Standard No. 1 on Financial Information: Enforcement of Standards on Financial Information in* Europe, CESR 03-073 (March 12, 2003). CESR was established in 2001 as an EC advisory group on securities market regulation.

[26]*Standard No. 2 on Financial Information Coordination and Enforcement Activities* CESR 03-317c (April 2004).

exists. It cooperates with the IASB by, among other activities, providing input on IASB projects. It has endorsed IFRS for cross-border securities offerings. A working-party study completed in 1998 presented recommendations for facilitating multinational equity offerings. The report recommended "that regulators be encouraged, where consistent with their legal mandate and the goal of investor protection, to facilitate the use of single disclosure documents, whether by harmonisation of standards, reciprocity or otherwise."[27]

Exhibit 8-5 presents a brief summary of the 10 disclosure standards. The summary is important because it indicates the comprehensiveness proposed by the working party. The disclosure standards proposed are also highly detailed.

In 2002, a companion disclosure document for ongoing disclosures was published. Excerpts from this document are reproduced in Exhibit 8-6.

EXHIBIT 8-5   Summary of International Disclosure Standards for Cross-Border Offerings and Initial Listings by Foreign Issuers

1. **Identity of Directors, Senior Management, and Advisers and Responsibility Statement**

   This standard identifies the company representatives and other individuals involved in the company's listing or registration, and indicates the persons responsible. The definition of the persons covered by this standard may vary in each country and would be determined by host country law.

2. **Offer Statistics and Expected Timetable**

   This standard provides key information regarding the conduct of any offering and the identification of important dates relating to the offering. It is understood that listings do not always involve offerings.

3. **Key Information**

   This standard summarizes key information about the company's financial condition, capitalization, and risk factors.

4. **Information on the Company**

   This standard provides information about the company's business operations, the products it makes or the services it provides, and the factors that affect the business.

5. **Operating and Financial Review and Prospects**

   This standard provides management's explanation of factors that have affected the company's financial condition and results of operations, and management's assessment of factors and trends that are anticipated to have a material effect on the company's financial condition and results of operations in future periods. In some countries a forecast or statement of the company's prospects for the current year and/or other future periods may be required.

6. **Directors and Officers**

   This standard provides information concerning the company's directors and managers that will allow investors to assess their experience, qualifications, and levels of compensation, as well as their relationship with the company. The definition of the persons covered by this disclosure standard may vary in each country and would be determined by host country law. Information is also required concerning the company's employees.

   (continued)

---

[27]International Organization of Securities Commissions, *International Disclosure Standards for Cross Border Offerings and Initial Listings by Foreign Firms*, 1998.

7. **Major Shareholders and Related-Party Transactions**

This standard provides information regarding the major shareholders and others that control or may control the company. The standard also provides information regarding transactions the company has entered into with persons affiliated with the company and whether the terms of such transactions are fair to the company.

8. **Financial Information**

This standard specifies which financial statements must be included in the document, as well as the periods to be covered, the age of the financial statements, and other information of a financial nature. The country in which the company is listed (or is applying for listing) will determine the comprehensive bodies of accounting and auditing principles that will be accepted for use in preparation and audit of the financial statements.

9. **The Offer**

This standard provides information regarding the offer of securities, the plan for distribution of the securities, and related matters.

10. **Additional Information**

This standard provides information, most of it of a statutory nature, that is not covered elsewhere in the document.

SOURCE: International Organization of Securities Commissions (IOSCO), *International Disclosure Standards for Cross Border Offerings and Initial Listings by Foreign Issuers,* 1998 (public document).

EXHIBIT 8-6 Principles for Ongoing Disclosure and Reporting of Material Developments

1. **The Key Elements of an Ongoing Disclosure Obligation**

Listed entities should have an ongoing disclosure obligation requiring disclosure of all information that would be material to an investor's investment decision.

2. **Timeliness**

The listed entity shall disclose ongoing information on a timely basis, which could require disclosure on an:

   a. immediate basis for disclosure of material developments, where such a term could be defined as "as soon as possible" or prescribed as a maximum of specified days; and

   b. periodic basis, prescribed by law or listing rules, such as quarterly or annual reports. Such information would also include management discussion and analysis (MD&A), where required, which can be disclosed in a separate report or included in a periodic report. The disclosure obligation may require disclosure of relevant information on an immediate basis even when it belongs to periodic reporting.

3. **Simultaneous and Identical Disclosure**

If the entity is listed in more than one jurisdiction, the information released under the ongoing disclosure obligation of one jurisdiction where it is listed should be released on an identical basis and simultaneously in all the other jurisdictions where it is listed. This obligation should not be dependent on where the listed entity is principally listed.

4. **Dissemination of Information**

Under the ongoing disclosure obligation, listed entities should ensure that full information is promptly made available to the market by using efficient, effective, and timely means of dissemination.

(continued)

5. **Disclosure Criteria**

   Ongoing disclosure of information should be fairly presented, not be misleading or deceptive, and contain no material omission of information.

6. **Equal Treatment of Disclosure**

   The information to be disclosed in compliance with the ongoing disclosure obligation should not be disclosed to selected investors or other interested parties before it is released to the public. Certain narrow exceptions may be permitted to this principle to allow communications with advisers and rating agencies or, in the ordinary course of business, communications with persons with whom the listed entity is negotiating, or intends to negotiate, a commercial, financial or investment transaction or representatives of its employees or trade unions acting on their behalf. In all these cases, the recipients have a duty to keep the information confidential.

SOURCE: International Organization of Securities Commissions, *Principles for Ongoing Disclosure and Material Development Reporting by Listed Entities: A Statement of the Technical Committee*, October 2002 (public document).

INTERNATIONAL FEDERATION OF ACCOUNTANTS (IFAC)

High-quality auditing standards are necessary to ensure that accounting standards are rigorously interpreted and applied. Auditors validate and add credibility to external financial reports. Credible financial reporting is at the core of the efficient functioning of capital markets. International accounting and auditing standards are interrelated. Accounting standards define what is useful accounting information. Auditing standards guide the auditor in determining whether the information is reliable. Useful and reliable accounting information puts investors, creditors, and others in a position to make better decisions. It therefore makes sense that the development of international accounting and auditing standards should be aligned.

External auditing in 10 countries of Europe, the Americas, and Asia was discussed in Chapters 3 and 4. From this discussion, the following points about (independent, external) auditing may be discerned:

1. The main purpose of an external audit varies around the world. For example,
   a. In the United States, auditors attest to whether financial statements "present fairly" a company's financial position and results. The test of fair presentation is compliance with (U.S.) GAAP.
   b. In the United Kingdom, auditors attest to whether financial statements present a "true and fair view" of a company's financial position and results. There is a "true and fair override" of U.K. GAAP.
   c. In Germany, auditors primarily attest to whether financial statements comply with the law.
2. Auditor responsibility varies around the world. For example,
   a. In France, auditors must report criminal acts they become aware of to the state prosecutor, in addition to their other responsibilities.
   b. In Germany, auditors must provide a private report to the company's managing board of directors and supervisory board on the company's future prospects, in addition to their other responsibilities.

3. Who can conduct an audit varies around the world. For example,
   a. In the United States, only certified public accountants may do so.
   b. In the United Kingdom, members of four professional associations are allowed to do so: chartered accountants in England and Wales, chartered accountants in Ireland, chartered accountants in Scotland, and chartered certified accountants.
   c. In the Netherlands, administrative accountants may audit smaller companies, while *registeraccountants* may audit all companies.
   d. In Germany, sworn book examiners audit small and medium-sized companies, while *wirtschaftsprüfer* may audit all companies.
4. Nations have recently taken steps to tighten control over the auditing profession. For example,
   a. In the United States, the 2002 Sarbanes-Oxley Act established the Public Company Accounting Oversight Board, a government agency.
   b. In France, the Haut Counseil du Commissariat aux Comptes (High Council of External Auditors) was established in 2003. The Ministry of Justice oversees it.
   c. In the United Kingdom, the Professional Oversight Board was established in 2003. The Financial Reporting Council, an independent private-sector body, is sanctioned by law to oversee it.
   d. In Japan, the Certified Public Accountant and Auditing Oversight Board was established in 2004. It is overseen by the Financial Services Agency, a government agency.
5. Auditors are facing increasing responsibility for improving corporate governance. For example,
   a. In the United States, auditors express an opinion on internal controls (for listed companies).
   b. In Japan, starting in 2008, auditors will express an opinion on management's assessment of the internal controls (for listed companies).

The rationale for converging accounting standards was made earlier in this chapter: Comparability is necessary so that investors can make "apples to apples" comparisons. The reason for converging auditing standards is subtler. Fundamentally, an audit assures users that they can trust the information communicated by the financial statements. However, if auditors around the world are not comparably trained or do not observe comparable standards, then their work varies in quality. As a result, the inherent reliability of financial statements also varies. (See Chapter 9 for further discussion of international auditing issues, both internal and external.)

IFAC is a worldwide organization with over 160 member organizations in 120 countries, representing more than 2.5 million accountants. Organized in 1977, its mission is "to strengthen the accountancy profession worldwide and contribute to the development of strong international economies by establishing and promoting adherence to high-quality professional standards, furthering the international convergence of such standards, and speaking out on public interest issues where the profession's expertise is most relevant."[28]

IFAC is governed by the IFAC Council, which is made up of one representative from each member organization. The council elects the IFAC board, which is responsible for

---

[28]IFAC 2005 Annual Report (www.ifac.org), p. 1.

setting policy and overseeing IFAC operations, the implementation of programs, and the work of IFAC's standard-setting groups and committees. The Public Interest Oversight Board (PIOB), an independent board established in 2005, provides additional oversight. Day-to-day administration is provided by the IFAC chief executive located in New York, which is staffed by accounting professionals from around the world.

IFAC's professional work is done through its standard-setting boards and standing committees. The IFAC standard-setting boards are:

- International Accounting Education Standards Board
- International Auditing and Assurance Standards Board
- International Ethics Standards Board for Accountants
- International Public Sector Accounting Standards Board

The IFAC standing committees are the following:

- Compliance Advisory Panel
- Developing Nations Committee
- Nominating Committee
- Professional Accountants in Business Committee
- Small and Medium Practices Committee
- Transnational Auditors Committee

IFAC's International Auditing and Assurance Standards Board issues International Standards on Auditing (ISA), which are organized into the following groups:

- Introductory Matters
- General Principles and Responsibilities
- Risk Assessment and Response to Assessed Risk
- Audit Evidence
- Using Work of Others
- Audit Conclusions and Reporting
- Specialized Areas[29]

IFAC has close ties with other international organizations, such as IASB and IOSCO. The financial statements of an increasing number of companies are being audited in conformity with IFAC's International Standards on Auditing. As noted earlier, all financial statement audits in the EU must follow ISA.

UNITED NATIONS INTERGOVERNMENTAL WORKING GROUP OF EXPERTS ON INTERNATIONAL STANDARDS OF ACCOUNTING AND REPORTING (ISAR)

ISAR was created in 1982 and is the only intergovernmental working group devoted to accounting and auditing at the corporate level. Its objective "is to promote the transparency, reliability and comparability of corporate accounting and reporting as

---

[29]The *Handbook of International Auditing, Assurance, and Ethics Pronouncements* is available at the IFAC Web site (www.ifac.org).

well as to improve disclosures on corporate governance by enterprises in developing countries and countries with economies in transition. ISAR achieves this through an integrated process of research, intergovernmental consensus building, information dissemination and technical cooperation."[30] ISAR discusses and publishes best practices, including those recommended by the IASB.

ISAR was an early proponent of environmental reporting, and recent initiatives have focused on corporate governance and accounting by small and medium-sized enterprises. It has also conducted technical assistance projects in a number of areas, such as accounting reform and retraining in the Russian Federation, Azerbaijan, and Uzbekistan, and designing and developing a long-distance learning program in accountancy for French-speaking Africa. Its *ISAR Update* is published twice a year.

ORGANIZATION FOR ECONOMIC COOPERATION AND DEVELOPMENT (OECD)

The OECD is the international organization of 30 (mostly industrialized) market-economy countries. It functions through its governing body, the OECD Council, and its network of about 200 committees and working groups. Its publication *Financial Market Trends,* issued twice a year, assesses trends and prospects in the international and major domestic financial markets of the OECD area. Descriptions and analyses of the structure and regulation of securities markets are often published either as OECD publications or as special features in *Financial Market Trends.* An important activity is promoting good governance in the public and private sectors. (See Chapter 5 for a discussion of *OECD Principles of Corporate Governance.*) With its membership consisting of larger, industrialized countries, the OECD is often a counterweight to other bodies (such as the United Nations and the International Confederation of Free Trade Unions) that have built-in tendencies to act contrary to the interests of its members.[31]

CONCLUSION

Most people now believe that international convergence is necessary to reduce the regulatory barriers to cross-border capital-raising efforts. The debate is no longer *whether* to converge, nor even *how* to converge. Although national differences in environmental factors that affect accounting development (such as systems of corporate governance and finance) will persist for some time, financial reporting systems are converging as international capital markets become more investor oriented. The International Accounting Standards Board is at the center of this movement. These days it is impossible to address capital market and stock exchange regulatory issues without considering international convergence of accounting principles, disclosure, and/or auditing.

---

[30]ISAR Web site (www.unctad.org/Templates/Startpage.asp?intItemID=2531), January 2007.
[31]From the OECD Web site (www.oecd.org), April 1, 1998.

SELECTED REFERENCES

Ali, M. J., "A Synthesis of Empirical Research on International Accounting Harmonization and Compliance with International Financial Reporting Standards," *Journal of Accounting Literature* 24 (2005): 1–52.

Cuijpers, R., and W. Buijink, "Voluntary Adoption of Non-Local GAAP in the European Union: A Study of Determinants and Consequences," *European Accounting Review* 14, no. 3 (2005): 487–524.

Fédération des Experts Comptables Européens, *Financial Reporting: Convergence, Equivalence and Mutual Recognition* (March 2006), www.fee.be/fileupload/upload/PP%20Financial%20Reporting%20Converge nce%2C%20Equivalence%20and%20Mutual %20Recognition%2006032732006241139.pdf.

Gannon, D. J., and A. Ashwal, "Financial Reporting Goes Global," *Journal of Accountancy* (September 2004): 43–47.

Haller, A., "Financial Accounting Developments in the European Union: Past Events and Future Prospects," *European Accounting Review* 11, no. 1 (2002): 153–190.

International Accounting Standards Board (IASB). *International Financial Reporting Standards 2007*, London: IASC, 2007.

International Federation of Accountants (IFAC), *Handbook of International Auditing, Assurance, and Ethics Pronouncements*, New York: IFAC, 2007.

Land, J., and M. H. Lang, "Empirical Evidence on the Evolution of International Earnings," *Accounting Review* 77 (Supplement 2002): 115–138.

Larson, R. K., and D. L. Street, "Convergence with IFRS in an Expanding Europe: Progress and Obstacles Identified by Large Accounting Firms' Survey," *Journal of International Accounting, Auditing, and Taxation* 13, no. 2 (2004): 89–119.

Needles, B. E., Jr., "Taxonomy of Auditing Standards," in *International Finance and Accounting Handbook,* ed. Frederick D. S. Choi, 3rd ed., New York: John Wiley, 2003.

Nobes, C. W., *Developments in the International Harmonization of Accounting*, Cheltenham, U.K.: Edward Elgar, 2004.

Pacter, P., "What Exactly Is Convergence?" *International Journal of Accounting, Auditing and Performance Evaluation* 2, nos. 1/2 (2005): 67–83.

PricewaterhouseCoopers, "A Global Approach to Corporate Governance, Accountability, Auditing and Capital Market Regulation" (August 2003), www.pwc.com.

PricewaterhouseCoopers, "Global GAAP: The Future of Corporate Reporting," (2003), www.cfodirect.com/cfopublic.nsf/0/a0a5f4b91d 752bb885256d4f004fb8ad/$FILE/Global%20 GAAP_V_7.pdf.

Schipper, K., "The Introduction of International Accounting Standards in Europe: Implications for International Convergence," *European Accounting Review* 14, no. 1 (2005): 101–126.

Street, D. L., "Large Firms Envision Worldwide Convergence of Standards," *Accounting Horizons* 16, no. 3 (September 2002): 215–218.

Street, D. L., and S. J. Gray, *Observance of International Accounting Standards: Factors Explaining Noncompliance, ACCA Research Report No. 74*, London: Association of Chartered Certified Accountants, 2001.

Walton, P., "European Harmonization," in *International Finance and Accounting Handbook*, ed. Frederick D. S. Choi, 3rd ed., New York: John Wiley, 2003.

Whittington, G., "The Adoption of International Accounting Standards in the European Union," *European Accounting Review* 13, no 1 (2005): 127–153.

Wong, P., *Challenges and Successes in Implementing International Standards: Achieving Convergence to IFRSs and ISAs* (September 2004), www.ifac.org/Members/Source_Files/Other_Publications/Wong_Report_Final.pdf.

DISCUSSION QUESTIONS

1. From a financial statement user's viewpoint, what is the most important source of accounting difference: measurement or disclosure? For which area is it most important to achieve international accounting convergence?
2. Distinguish between the terms "harmonization" and "convergence" as they apply to accounting standards.
3. Compare and contrast the following proposed approaches for dealing with international differences in accounting, disclosure, and auditing standards: (1) reciprocity, (2) reconciliation, (3) international standards.
4. What are the key rationales that support the development and widespread application of International Financial Reporting Standards?
5. What are the key rationales *against* the development and widespread application of International Financial Reporting Standards?
6. What evidence is there that International Financial Reporting Standards are becoming widely accepted around the world?
7. Describe the structure of the International Accounting Standards Board and how it sets International Financial Reporting Standards.
8. What is the purpose of accounting harmonization in the European Union (EU)? Why did the EU abandon its approach to harmonization via directives to one favoring the IASB?
9. Do you believe that international accounting harmonization/convergence will end investor concerns about cross-national differences in accounting practices?
10. Why is the concept of auditing convergence important? Will international harmonization of auditing standards be more or less difficult to achieve than international harmonization of accounting principles? Describe IFAC's work on converging auditing standards.
11. Describe IOSCO's work on harmonizing disclosure standards for cross-border offerings and initial listings by foreign issuers. Why is this work important to securities regulators around the world?
12. What role do the United Nations and the Organization for Economic Cooperation and Development play in harmonizing accounting and auditing standards?

EXERCISES

1. Three solutions have been proposed for resolving the problems associated with filing financial statements across national borders: (1) reciprocity (also known as mutual recognition), (2) reconciliation, and (3) use of international standards.
   Required: Present a complete but concise evaluation of each of the three approaches. What do you expect would be the preferred approach from the perspective of each of the following: (1) investors, (2) company management, (3) regulatory authorities, (4) stock exchanges, (5) professional associations? Discuss your reasons for each response. Which approach do you predict will eventually prevail?
2. Exhibit 8-1 presents the Web site addresses of many major international organizations involved in international accounting harmonization. Consider the following three: the International Federation of Accountants (IFAC), the United Nations Intergovernmental Working Group of Experts on International Standards of Accounting and Reporting (ISAR), and the Organization for Economic Cooperation and Development (OECD).
   Required: For each of these three organizations, describe its membership, its organizational focus, and why it is concerned with international financial accounting standard setting.

3. Exhibit 8-2 presents the Web site addresses of national accountancy organizations, many of which are involved in international accounting standard-setting and convergence activities. **Required:** Select one of the accounting organizations and search its Web site for information about its involvement in international accounting standard setting and convergence. Prepare a detailed description of the organization's activities in these areas.

4. The text discusses the many organizations involved with international convergence activities, including the IASB, EU, and IFAC.
   Required:
   a. Compare and contrast these three organizations in terms of their standard-setting procedures.
   b. At what types and sizes of enterprises are their standards *primarily* directed?
   c. Briefly critique the following statement: "Acceptance of international accounting standards (accounting principles, disclosures, and auditing), as far as it has come and is likely to come in the near future, is significantly centered in companies operating in multiple countries."

5. The chapter contains a chronology of some significant events in the history of international accounting standard setting.
   Required: Consider the 1995 European Commission adoption of a new approach to accounting harmonization. Consult some literature references about this event; prepare a short essay describing it and indicating why it is deemed significant.

6. Exhibit 8-3 identifies current IASB standards and their respective titles.
   Required: Using information on the IASB Web site (www.iasb.org) or other available information, prepare an updated list of IASB standards.

7. The biographies of current IASB board members are on the IASB Web site (www.iasb.org).
   Required: Identify the current board members (including the chair and vice-chair). Note each member's home country and prior affiliation(s). Which board members have previously served on national accounting standard setting bodies?

8. The IASB published 13 revised standards in December 2003. A summary is available at www.iasplus.com/iasplus/improve0401.pdf.
   Required: Prepare a list of the major differences between these revised standards and the GAAP of your home country.

9. Refer to Exercise 8.
   Required: How would each difference affect the balance sheet and income statement? How would each difference affect the following financial ratios used by analysts?
   a. *Liquidity*: current ratio
   b. *Solvency*: debt to equity; debt to assets
   c. *Profitability*: return on assets; return on equity

10. The IASB Web site (www.iasb.org) summarizes each of the current International Financial Reporting Standards.
    Required: Identify the standards that permit the use of alternative accounting treatments. For each, briefly describe the benchmark treatment and the allowed alternative treatment. To what extent might companies' use of these different treatments reduce the comparability of the resulting financial statements?

11. Consider the following restatement of net profit and shareholders' equity from IFRS to U.S. GAAP by the Swiss company Novartis.
    Required: Calculate return on equity (ROE) under IFRS and U.S. GAAP for 2005 and 2004. What important measurement differences between IFRS and U.S. GAAP are revealed by this restatement? Are the differences consistent between the two years? How would the adherence of IFRS versus U.S. GAAP affect a loan covenant requirement for a minimum ROE?

	2005 ($ millions)	2004 Restated ($ millions)	2003 Restated ($ millions)
Net income under IFRS	**6,141**	**5,380**	**4,787**
US GAAP adjustments:			
Available-for-sale securities	278	(183)	(240)
Inventory impairment reversal	20	(43)	0
Associated companies	(6)	179	82
Intangible assets	(1,238)	(590)	(848)
Property, plant, and equipment	53	77	69
Pensions and other post-employment benefits	(181)	(82)	(98)
Deferred taxes	178	423	48
Share-based compensation	(44)	(61)	(127)
Currency translation	0	(301)	0
Minority interests	(11)	(15)	(44)
Others		9	(5)
Net income under US GAAP	**5,190**	**4,793**	**3,624**
Basic earnings per share under US GAAP ($)	2.22	2.03	1.52
Diluted earnings per share under US GAAP ($)	2.22	2.02	1.50

	December 31, 2005 ($ millions)	December 31, 2004 Restated ($ millions)
Equity under IFRS	**33,164**	**31,315**
US GAAP adjustments:		
Available-for-sale securities	(24)	(64)
Inventory impairment reversal	(23)	(43)
Associated companies	25	6
Intangible assets	4,142	6,036
Property, plant, and equipment	(409)	(558)
Pensions and other post-employment benefits	3,133	3,379
Deferred taxes	(1,438)	(2,082)
Share-based compensation	(96)	(118)
Minority interests	(174)	(138)
Total US GAAP adjustments	**5,136**	**6,418**
Equity under US GAAP	**38,300**	**37,733**

12. The IASB Web site (www.iasb.org) summarizes each of the current International Financial Reporting Standards.

    Required:

    Answer each of the following questions.

    a. In measuring inventories at the lower of cost or net realizable value, does net realizable value mean:
       i. estimated replacement cost, or
       ii. estimated selling price less estimated costs to complete and sell the inventory?

    b. Under International Financial Reporting Standards, which of the following methods is (or are) acceptable to account for an investment in a joint venture?
       i. cost method
       ii. equity method
       iii. proportionate consolidation
       iv. consolidation

    c. Which of the following would be classified as an extraordinary item?
       i. loss from settlement of a product liability lawsuit
       ii. claims paid by an airline as a result of a plane crash
       iii. destruction of a communications satellite during launch
       iv. none of the above

    d. In Year 1, an enterprise accrued its warranty obligation based on its best estimate of the expected cost to repair defective products during the three-year warranty coverage period. During Year 2, warranty claims were significantly more than expected due to unrecognized quality-control problems in Year 1. Is it appropriate to restate the financial statements for Year 1 to reflect the revised estimate of the warranty obligation?

    e. True or false: An enterprise with a December 31 year-end declares a dividend on its common shares on January 5. The dividend is recognized as a liability at year-end.

    f. After initial recognition, which of the following financial assets is (are) not remeasured at fair value?
       i. options on unquoted equity securities
       ii. marketable securities (equities)
       iii. derivative financial instruments that are financial assets
       iv. fixed maturity instruments the enterprise intends to hold to maturity

    g. Which of the following is true? An enterprise that follows the policy of revaluing its property, plant, and equipment may apply that policy:
       i. to all assets within a single country on a country-by-country basis
       ii. to all assets within a single broad class, such as to land and buildings
       iii. to all assets of a certain age, such as all assets 10 years old or older.

    h. True or false: Interest costs on funds borrowed by an enterprise to finance the construction of a new building must be capitalized as part of the cost of the building.

CASES

Case 8-1   PetroChina Company Limited

PetroChina Company Limited (PetroChina) was established as a joint stock company under the company law of the People's Republic of China in 1999 as part of the restructuring of China National Petroleum Corporation. PetroChina is an integrated oil and gas company with operations in virtually every aspect of China's oil and gas industry, including exploration and production, refining and marketing, natural gas transmission, and petrochemicals. PetroChina manages some 70 percent of China's oil and gas reserves and 45 percent of its oil-refining capacity. Its shares were listed on the Hong Kong and New York Stock Exchanges in 2000.

You are an equity research analyst and have been asked to prepare a research report on PetroChina. Your business strategy analysis indicates that PetroChina's sales growth and financial performance can probably be sustained. However, although your qualitative analysis has yielded promising results, you are concerned that your financial analysis will be difficult due to accounting and audit-quality issues.

You start your analysis by becoming familiar with the accounting principles used to prepare PetroChina's financial statements. You are encouraged that the company states that its financial statements conform to IASB standards, but realize that how accounting standards are applied is as important as the standards themselves.■

REQUIRED

PetroChina's financial statements may be found at www.petrochina.com.cn/english/tzzgx/2005nb.htm. Examine PetroChina's Note 3, "Summary of Principal Accounting Policies," and read about the IASB Standards on the IASB Web site (www.iasb.org) and the IAS Plus Web site (www.iasplus.com).

1. As much as possible, assess the extent to which PetroChina's accounting principles conform to IASB standards.
2. How reliable is your assessment?
3. What further information would help your assessment?
4. Does the auditor's report provide information useful in your assessment? Explain.

Case 8-2   Whither The Withering Standard Setters?

Sir David Tweedie, chairman of the International Accounting Standards Board, is quoted as saying that the IASB and the FASB will eventually merge. "U.S. standards and ours will become so close that it will be senseless having two boards, and they will merge eventually.... Ultimately, it doesn't make sense having two standard setters producing the same standards."[32] ■

---

[32]L. Bolton, "IASB and FASB Will Eventually Merge, Says Tweedie," *Accountancy Magazine* (October 2005): 6.

REQUIRED

1. Go to the Web sites of the International Accounting Standards Board (www .iasb.org) and the U.S. Financial Accounting Standards Board (www .fasb.org). Compare and contrast the two boards in terms of their composition and standard-setting processes.

2. Why is so much attention paid to convergence between International Financial Reporting Standards (IFRS) and U.S. GAAP and not to convergence between IFRS and other national accounting standards? What evidence is there of the direction of convergence: Is U.S. GAAP converging to IFRS, are IFRS converging to U.S. GAAP, or are they converging toward each other?

3. U.S. companies must use U.S. GAAP in their financial statements, not IFRS. Why should U.S. accountants, analysts, and others involved in financial reporting need to know about IFRS?

4. Will the IASB and FASB eventually merge, or will they remain separate accounting standard-setting bodies? Why do you say so?

CHAPTER 9

International Financial Statement Analysis

INTRODUCTION

Trends in global trade, investment and external finance, documented in Chapter 1, imply that financial managers, vendors, investors, equity research analysts, bankers, and other financial statement users have a growing need to read and analyze nondomestic financial statements. Cross-border financial comparisons are vital when assessing the financial promise and soundness of a foreign direct or portfolio investment. There has been tremendous growth in international capital issuance and trading in recent years due to privatizations, economic growth, relaxation of capital controls, and continued advances in information technology.

The need to use, and therefore understand, nondomestic financial statements has also increased as merger and acquisition activities have become more international. The value of cross-border mergers grew steadily during the 1990s, and this growth shows no signs of abatement.

Finally, as business becomes more global, financial statements become more important than ever as a basis for competitive analysis, credit decisions, business negotiations, and corporate control. Continued reduction in national trade barriers, the emergence of Europe as a unified market, convergence of consumer tastes and preferences, and a growing sophistication of business firms in penetrating nondomestic markets have significantly intensified multinational business competition. All this creates a further need for international financial statement analysis and valuation.

This chapter synthesizes information presented in Chapters 1 through 8. It examines opportunities and challenges encountered in analyzing foreign financial statements, and provides suggestions for the analyst.

CHALLENGES AND OPPORTUNITIES IN CROSS-BORDER ANALYSIS

Cross-border financial analysis involves multiple jurisdictions. An analyst, for example, may have occasion to study a company outside her home country or to compare companies from two or more countries. Unique challenges face those doing international analysis.

Nations vary dramatically in their accounting and auditing practices, disclosure quality, legal and regulatory systems, nature and extent of business risk, and modes of conducting business. This variation means that analytical tools that are effective in one jurisdiction may be less so in another. The analyst often faces daunting challenges in obtaining credible information. In many emerging market economies, financial analyses often have limited reliability.

International financial analysis and valuation are characterized by many contradictions. On the one hand, the rapid pace of harmonization of accounting standards is leading to enhanced comparability of financial information worldwide. However, vast differences in financial reporting practices remain. An examination of international financial reporting standards (IFRS's) issued by the IASB to date suggest that definitions of corporate transparency are not necessarily consistent with the notion of transparency that analysts are accustomed to. To wit, IASB pronouncements focus on the extent of disclosure as opposed to disclosures that help reveal the economics of underlying transactions. Restatement of prior year financial statements for first-time adopters of IFRS's are limited to one year thereby complicating trend analysis. And, some standards continue to permit reporting options. As one example, in adjusting their accounts for changing prices, reporting entities are allowed the option of accounting for general price level changes or specific price changes. As Chapters 7 illustrates, the information content of both measurement options are very different. Some analysts question the extent to which greater uniformity in accounting standards will actually result in the provision of comparable information by leading companies in an industry.[1]

As discussed in Chapter 5, companies around the world are disclosing more information voluntarily, and more credible information. At the national level, many countries are striving to improve the availability and quality of information about public companies. Empirical research has validated the benefits of doing so. Specifically, the strength of a country's disclosure system, including disclosure requirements, monitoring and enforcement, is positively associated with market development.[2] Moreover, access to freely available information relevant for financial analysis is growing dramatically with dissemination of company information on the Internet. However, in many countries there continues to be a great gulf between expectations based on these advances and reality. Financial analysts are often frustrated in their attempts to gather information. Also, many governments continue to publish highly suspect information.

Despite the foregoing contradictions, the environment of international financial analysis and valuation are improving, and the overall outlook for the analyst is positive. Globalization of capital markets, advances in information technology, and increasing competition among national governments, stock exchanges, and companies for investors and trading activity continue. Together these forces are creating incentives for companies to voluntarily improve their external financial reporting practices.

With the implementation of the euro, together with continued advances in European corporate disclosure practices, distinctions between cross-border and within-border financial analysis are blurring. Portfolio diversification strategies in Europe are increasingly based on industry sectors rather than countries. Rather than balancing stock picks among strong and weak currency countries, portfolio managers

---

[1]For example, see Hope, Ole-Kristan, "Variations in the Financial Reporting Environment and Earnings Forecasting," Journal of International Financial Management and Accounting 15, No. 1 (2004): 22.
[2]Carol Ann Frost, Elizabeth A. Gordon and Andrew F. Hayes, "Stock Exchange Disclosure and Market Development: An Analysis of 50 International Exchanges," *Journal of Accounting Research*, Vol. 44 No. 3(2006): 437-483.

are increasingly focusing on picking the best companies in an industry regardless of country of origin. Globalization also means that strictly domestic analyses are becoming less relevant. Interdependencies are growing and no company is insulated from events happening worldwide.

BUSINESS ANALYSIS FRAMEWORK

Palepu, Bernard, and Healy provide a useful framework for business analysis and valuation using financial statement data.[3] The framework's four stages of analysis (discussed in more detail in the following pages) are: (1) business strategy analysis, (2) accounting analysis, (3) financial analysis (ratio analysis and cash flow analysis), and (4) prospective analysis (forecasting and valuation). The relative importance of each stage depends on the purpose of the analysis. The business analysis framework can be applied to many decision contexts including securities analysis, credit analysis, and merger and acquisition analysis.

INTERNATIONAL BUSINESS STRATEGY ANALYSIS

Business strategy analysis is an important first step in financial statement analysis. It provides a qualitative understanding of a company and its competitors in relation to its economic environment. This ensures that quantitative analysis is performed using a holistic perspective. By identifying key profit drivers and business risks, business strategy analysis helps the analyst make realistic forecasts.[4] Standard procedures for gathering information for business strategy analysis include examining annual reports and other company publications, and speaking with company staff, analysts, and other financial professionals. The use of additional information sources, such as the World Wide Web, trade groups, competitors, customers, reporters, lobbyists, regulators, and the trade press is becoming more common. The accuracy, reliability, and relevance of each type of information gathered also needs to be evaluated.[5]

Business strategy analysis is often complex and difficult in an international setting. As noted previously, key profit drivers and types of business risk vary among countries. Understanding them can be daunting. Business and legal environments and corporate objectives vary around the world. Many risks (such as regulatory risk, foreign exchange risk, and credit risk, among others) need to be evaluated and brought together coherently. In some countries, sources of information are limited and may not be accurate.

Information Availability

Business strategy analysis is especially difficult in some countries due to a lack of reliable information about macroeconomic developments. Governments in developed countries are sometimes accused of publishing faulty or misleading economic statistics. The situation is much worse in many emerging economies. For example, one reason the

---

[3]Krishna G. Palepu, Victor L. Bernard, and Paul M. Healy, Business Analysis and Valuation Using Financial Statements, Cincinnati, Ohio: South-Western College Publishing, 1996.
[4]Profit drivers are principal financial and operating elements that affect a firm's profitability.
[5]Financial analysts are increasingly using techniques developed in the fast-growing business discipline of competitive intelligence (CI).

1994/95 Mexican currency crisis was a surprise was that the government concealed information about its shrinking foreign reserves and exploding money supply. Some countries delay publishing statistics when the numbers are unfavorable, or even falsify their economic figures.

Obtaining industry information is also difficult in many countries and the quantity and quality of company information varies greatly. The availability of company-specific information has been strikingly low in many developing economies.[6] Recently, many large companies that list and raise capital in overseas markets have been expanding their disclosures and have voluntarily switched to globally recognized accounting principles such as International Financial Reporting Standards.

Recommendations for Analysis

Data constraints make it difficult to perform business strategy analyses using traditional research methods. Very often, travel is necessary to learn about local business climates and how industries and companies actually operate, especially in emerging market countries. The World Wide Web also offers quick access to information that recently was unavailable or difficult to obtain. Exhibit 9-1 presents a sampling of freely available Web resources that can be used to learn about country risks and travel conditions.

EXHIBIT 9-1   Country Information Freely Available on the Internet

Organization	Web Site Address	Description
Canada Department of Foreign Affairs and International Trade	http://www. dfait-maeci.gc.ca/ english/menu.htm	Market information
China's Official Gateway to News and Information	www.china.org.cn	Country information on a variety of fronts.
CRUISE	www.cranfield.ac. uk/ cils/Library/ subjects/country.htm	Country reports including economic and market data.
CIA-The World Factbook	www.cia.gov/cia/ publications/ Factbook/geos/ fm.html	Information on government, economy, communications, transnational issues.
Financial Times	http://ft.com	Country reports (also industry reports, company news and financial information)
Political and Economic Risk Consultancy, Ltd. (PERC)	http://www.asiarisk. com/	Country outlooks; connection to other WWW sites
UNCTAD	www.unctad.org	Data for analysis of international trade, foreign direct investment commodities and development
U.S. Federal Reserve	www.federalreserve. gov	Foreign exchange rates
U.S. State Department	http://travel.state. gov/	Travel warnings
World Bank	www.dev.data. worldbank.org	Country development data
World Tourism Organization	http://www. world-tourism.org	Newsletters, press releases

[6]See Chapter 5 for further discussion. Also see S. M. Saudagaran, and J. G. Diga, "Financial Reporting in Emerging Capital Markets: Characteristics and Policy Issues," Accounting Horizons (June 1997): 41–64.

Country information can also be found in "international briefings" publications distributed by large accounting firms, banks, and brokerages.[7] The International Federation of Stock Exchanges (FIBV, http://www.fibv.com) and the Federation of European Stock Exchanges (FESE, http://www.fese.be) publish highly informative international newsletters, and Accountancy, The Economist, Financial Analysts Journal, and Euromoney magazines provide many articles highly relevant for international financial analysis.

Enormous risks may follow an inadequate business strategy analysis. Consider the Parmalat affair, representing the largest fraud in European financial history. In this case, at least $13 billion in missing assets of Italy's fastest growing dairy group could not be accounted for, resulting in huge losses for the company's investors and creditors alike. Commentators attribute this financial debacle to several causes. Foreign investors reportedly invested in a company that did not provide complete or credible disclosures. They did not know much about the business environment in which they were investing and participated in a market in which financial reporting rules were not strictly enforced.[8]

ACCOUNTING ANALYSIS

The purpose of accounting analysis is to assess the extent to which a firm's reported results reflect economic reality. The analyst needs to evaluate the firm's accounting policies and estimates, and assess the nature and extent of a firm's accounting flexibility. The latter refers to management's discretion in choosing which accounting policies and estimates to apply to a particular accounting event. To reach reliable conclusions, the analyst must adjust reported accounting amounts to remove distortions caused by the use of accounting methods the analyst deems inappropriate. Examples might include marking trading assets to market and not recording the gains or losses in income but in an allowance account, prematurely recognizing revenues, or reversing estimated liability accruals to smooth earnings.

Corporate managers are allowed to make many accounting-related judgments because they know the most about their firm's operations and financial condition. Flexibility in financial reporting is important because it allows managers to use accounting measurements that best reflect the company's particular operating circumstances. However, managers have incentives to distort operating reality by using their accounting discretion to distort reported profits. One reason is that reported earnings are often used to evaluate their managerial performance.[9]

---

[7]For example, PricewaterhouseCoopers LLC publishes International Briefings every month, which reports on notable business, political, and economic developments worldwide.

[8]Gail Edmondson, David Fairlamb, and Nanette Byrnes, "The Milk Just Keeps on Spilling," BusinessWeek (January 26, 2004): 54, 55, 58.

[9]Additional influences on corporate managers' accounting decisions include: (1) accounting-based debt covenants; (2) management compensation; (3) corporate control contests; (4) tax considerations; (5) regulatory considerations; (6) capital market considerations; (7) stakeholder considerations; and (8) competitive considerations. Palepu, Bernard, and Healy, op. cit.

Healy and colleagues suggest the following process for evaluating a firm's accounting quality:

1. Identify key accounting policies
2. Assess accounting flexibility
3. Evaluate accounting strategy
4. Evaluate the quality of disclosure
5. Identify potential red flags (e.g., unusually large asset write-offs, unexplained transactions that boost profits, or an increasing gap between a company's reported income and its cash flow from operations)
6. Adjust for accounting distortions

To illustrate this process, consider the accounting quality of WorldCom, a large U.S. company whose accounting policies resulted in a major Wall Street scandal. In formally indicting the company on its faulty accounting practices, the following questions might be asked: (1) How did WorldCom account for its major operating expenditures? (2) What options does U.S. GAAP allow for such expenditures? (3) Did WorldCom adopt an overly aggressive or conservative approach to accounting for these expenditures? (4) Did WorldCom capitalize an expenditure that should have been expensed to manage its earnings? (5) Did WorldCom disclose sufficient information for investors to undo the company's aggressive accounting treatment? (6) Would reversal of WorldCom's selected accounting posture have a significant depressing effect on reported earnings?

In this case, WorldCom chose to capitalize what were in effect operating expenses. While this practice is in clear violation of U.S. GAAP, management chose to conceal this information from investors by disguising operating expenses as capital expenditures. The financial statement effects of capitalizing versus expensing its major expenditures had a significant effect on reported earnings as the amounts involved approached $2 billion!

Two major issues confront those doing accounting analysis in an international setting. The first is cross-country variation in accounting measurement quality, disclosure quality, and audit quality; the second concerns the difficulty in obtaining information needed to conduct accounting analysis.

Cross-country variation in quality of accounting measurement, disclosure, and auditing is dramatic. National characteristics that cause this variation include required and generally accepted practices, monitoring and enforcement, and extent of managerial discretion in financial reporting.[10] Chapters 3 and 4 of this text present summaries of significant accounting practices in six highly developed and four emerging countries, respectively. These chapters, which summarize only a subset of major accounting topics, show that significant managerial discretion may be used in many countries, including France, Germany, China, and Taiwan.

Consider accounting practices in Germany. As discussed in Chapter 3, German financial accounting is closely aligned with tax reporting. Creditor protection is a second goal of financial reporting. As a result, financial reports are prepared with a creditor focus rather than an investor focus. The resulting conservative reporting bias may

---

[10]While faulty application of accounting principles is frequently touted as the leading cause of low accounting quality, some argue that the application of faulty accounting principles is the root cause. See Paul Rosenfield, "What Drives Earnings Management?" Journal of Accountancy [October 2000]: 5.

generate accounting amounts that do not reflect actual operating performance. German managers have great discretion in their use of reserves and in implementing many accounting policies. Even where specific procedures are mandated, monitoring and enforcement of compliance with reporting requirements is far short of what investors can expect in the United States.

Disclosure quality and the level of audit assurances must also be closely scrutinized when analyzing a German company's financial statements. Footnote disclosure of accounting policies is quite limited in some German annual reports. Identifying the components of large financial statement items (such as reserve accounts) can be difficult. Auditing issues are so important that we discuss international auditing in a separate section of this chapter.

Financial reporting in China provides a second example of how accounting measurement, disclosure, and audit quality can vary dramatically from accounting practices in Anglo-American countries. Although China is implementing major accounting reform as part of its transition from a planned economy to a controlled market economy, until recently it did not have financial reporting and external auditing in forms that would be familiar to Westerners.[11] Private investors and creditors were virtually nonexistent for three decades after the People's Republic was founded in 1948, and The Accounting Law, which sets forth accounting and reporting requirements, was adopted only in 1985. Accounting Standards for Business Enterprises, which specifies that such basic accounting practices as double-entry bookkeeping and the accrual basis should be used, became effective in 1993. The auditing profession is also very new in China.

[Also, the German auditing environment is dramatically different from countries such as the United Kingdom and the United States. Auditor independence rules in Germany are much less comprehensive and intricate than in the United Kingdom and the United States, and German managers might consider it inappropriate for auditors to question their oral statements. German auditors are also more hesitant to accept responsibility for detecting irregularities than their U.K. or U.S. counterparts.

External auditors play a key role in ensuring that accounting standards are followed. Legal systems provide enforcement mechanisms for ensuring that auditors remain as independent as practicable. However, audit environments are not uniform around the world. For example, while auditor litigation is relatively common in the United States, they have been rare in Germany.

Suggestions for the Analyst

Especially when analyzing companies in emerging market countries, the analyst should meet often with management to evaluate their financial reporting incentives and accounting policies. Many companies in emerging market countries are closely held, and managers may not have strong incentives for full and credible disclosure. Accounting policies in some countries may be similar or identical to IAS (or other widely accepted standards), but managers often have great discretion in how those policies are applied.

---

[11]For further discussion, see Chapter 4; Ajay Adhikari and Shawn Z. Wang, "Accounting for China," Management Accounting (April 1995): 27-32.

Finally, as noted earlier, new communications technology (including the World Wide Web) is having a great impact on all stages of financial research. Many companies and countries now have Web sites that make it much easier for anyone interested to gather information. Refer to the section entitled "Information Access" later in this chapter for a discussion of useful information sources for accounting analysis.

INTERNATIONAL FINANCIAL ANALYSIS

The goal of financial analysis is to evaluate a firm's current and past performance, and to judge whether its performance can be sustained. Ratio analysis and cash flow analysis are important tools in financial analysis. Ratio analysis involves comparison of ratios between the firm and other firms in the same industry, comparison of a firm's ratios across years or other fiscal periods, and/or comparison of ratios to some absolute benchmark. It provides insights on the comparative and relative significance of financial statement items and can help evaluate the effectiveness of managements' operating, investing, financing and earnings retention policies. A summary of commonly used financial ratios appears in Exhibit 9-2.

Cash flow analysis focuses on the cash flow statement, which provides information about a firm's cash inflows and outflows, classified among operating, investing, and financing activities, and disclosures about periodic noncash investing and financing activities. Analysts can use cash flow analysis to address many questions about the firm's performance and management. For example, has the firm generated positive cash flows from operations? How have cash flow components changed across time in relation to changes in income statement components, sales, and cost of sales in particular? What have been the cash flow consequences of management decisions about financial policy, dividend policy, and investment? When used in conjunction with the income statement, cash flow information also informs analysts about the validity of the going concern assumption, a firm's liquidity and management's use of measurement options to manage earnings.

Ratio Analysis

Two issues must be addressed in analyzing ratios in an international setting. First, do cross-country differences in accounting principles cause significant variation in financial statement amounts of companies from different countries? Second, how do differences in local culture and economic and competitive conditions affect the interpretation of accounting measures and financial ratios, even if accounting measurements from different countries are restated to achieve "accounting comparability"?

Extensive evidence reveals substantial cross-country differences in profitability, leverage, and other financial statement ratios and amounts that result from both accounting and nonaccounting factors. (The next section discusses cross-country differences in two valuation ratios, the price-to-earnings and price-to-book ratios.) In one study, sales revenue, net income, and leverage (total debt/shareholders' equity) was compared among firms domiciled in France, Germany, Japan, the

EXHIBIT 9-2 Summary of Financial Ratios

Ratio	Formula for Computation

I. Liquidity

1. Current ratio

$$\frac{\text{Current assets}}{\text{Current liabilities}}$$

2. Quick or acid-test ratio

$$\frac{\text{Cash, marketable securities, and receivables}}{\text{Current Liabilities}}$$

3. Current cash debt ratio

$$\frac{\text{Net cash provided by operating activities}}{\text{Average current liabilities}}$$

II. Efficiency

4. Receivables turnover

$$\frac{\text{Net sales}}{\text{Average trade receivables (net)}}$$

5. Inventory turnover

$$\frac{\text{Cost of goods sold}}{\text{Average inventory}}$$

6. Asset turnover

$$\frac{\text{Net sales}}{\text{Average total assets}}$$

III. Profitability

7. Profit margin on sales

$$\frac{\text{Net income}}{\text{Net sales}}$$

8. Rate of return on assets

$$\frac{\text{EBIT}[12]}{\text{Average total assets}}$$

9. Rate of return on common stock equity

$$\frac{\text{Net income minus preferred dividends}}{\text{Average common stockholders' equity}}$$

10. Earnings per share

$$\frac{\text{Net income minus preferred dividends}}{\text{Weighted common shares outstanding}}$$

11. Payout ratio

$$\frac{\text{Cash dividends}}{\text{Net income}}$$

IV. Coverage

12. Debt to total assets ratio

$$\frac{\text{Debt}}{\text{Total assets or equities}}$$

13. Times interest earned

$$\frac{\text{Income before interest charges and taxes}}{\text{Interest charges}}$$

14. Cash debt coverage ratio

$$\frac{\text{Net cash provided by operating activities}}{\text{Average total liabilities}}$$

15. Book value per share

$$\frac{\text{Common stockholders' equity}}{\text{Outstanding common shares}}$$

---

[12]EBIT = earnings before interest and taxes. Some analysts prefer to use EBITDA which also includes depreciation and amortization charges in the numerator.

United Kingdom, and the United States.[13] The five 80-firm country samples were matched according to size (market value of equity), with all firms belonging to the manufacturing industry group (SIC codes 20 through 39). All three financial measures varied substantially among the country samples. For example, median net income was much greater in the United Kingdom and the United States than in Germany and Japan. Variation in net income was partially explained by accounting principle differences because financial reporting is generally less conservative in the United Kingdom and the United States than in Germany and Japan. Nonaccounting factors also affected reported net income. For example, the creditor focus in France, Germany, and Japan accounted for lower net income than in the United States and the United Kingdom as there is less pressure on managers in those countries to report steadily increasing net income.

In the foregoing study, Frost found median leverage in the United Kingdom and the United States to be lower than in Germany and Japan. This is partially attributed to the fact that conservative accounting in Germany and Japan results in lower reported shareholders' equity than in the United Kingdom and the United States. Higher leverage in Germany, Japan, and France is also attributed to higher debt in capital structures, reflecting the heavy dependence on bank financing in those countries.

How large are the differences in financial statement items caused by differences among national accounting principles? Hundreds of non-U.S. companies listed on U.S. stock exchanges give footnote reconciliation disclosures that provide evidence on this question, at least in the context of differences between U.S. GAAP-based and non-U.S. GAAP-based accounting amounts.

An earlier survey of financial statement reconciliations by foreign registrants prepared by the U.S. SEC is informative.[14] Approximately one-half of the 528 non-U.S. registrants surveyed disclosed material differences between net income as reported in their financial statements and U.S. GAAP-based net income. The five types of financial statement differences disclosed by the largest number of registrants were (in descending order): (1) depreciation and amortization, (2) deferred or capitalized costs, (3) deferred taxes, (4) pensions, and (5) foreign currency translation.

The study also shows that more than two-thirds of the registrants that disclosed material differences in net income reported that income under U.S. GAAP was lower than under non-U.S. GAAP. Nearly half of them reported income differences greater than 25 percent. Twenty-five of the 87 registrants that reported that income under U.S. GAAP was greater than under non-U.S. GAAP reported differences greater than 25 percent. Similar results were found for reconciliations of shareholders' equity. Overall, the evidence in the SEC study shows that financial statement differences under U.S. versus non-U.S. GAAP are highly material for many companies.

Evidence from SEC registrants' reconciliation disclosures therefore indicates that GAAP differences can cause significant variation in financial statement numbers. The analyst will often choose to make financial statements more comparable by making accounting principle adjustments to the financial statements being analyzed.

---

[13]Carol A. Frost, "Characteristics and Information Value of Corporate Disclosures of Forward-Looking Information in Global Equity Markets," Dartmouth College Working Paper, July 2002.
[14]U.S. Securities and Exchange Commission, Division of Corporation Finance, Survey of Financial Statement Reconciliations by Foreign Registrants, May 1, 1993.

Appendix 9-1 illustrates the restatement of an income and balance sheet from Japanese GAAP to U.S. GAAP. Even after financial statement amounts are made reasonably comparable (by adjusting for accounting principle differences), interpretation of those amounts must consider cross-country differences in economic, competitive, and other institutional differences. Analysis of Japanese companies provides a good illustration. Brown and Stickney argue that the relation between financial and tax reporting, the importance in Japan of operating through corporate groups (keiretsu), and the tolerance in Japan for heavy use of short-term financial leverage must all be considered when analyzing the profitability and risk of Japanese companies.[15] For example, Japanese reported earnings tend to be lower than earnings reported in Anglo-American countries, even after adjusting for GAAP differences. The close linkage between tax and financial reporting gives Japanese companies an incentive to be conservative in determining their income. Also, because high intercorporate stock holdings reduce the percentage of shares held by outsiders, Japanese companies are under less pressure to report ever-increasing earnings than are companies in the United States and other Anglo-American countries.[16] Refer to Appendix 9-2 for further detailed discussion of international ratio analysis. The appendix focuses on comparison of Japanese and U.S. financial ratios and their interpretation.

Cash Flow Analysis

As discussed earlier, cash flow analysis provides insights about a company's cash flows and management. Highly detailed cash flow statements are required under U.S. GAAP, U.K. GAAP, IFRS, and accounting standards in a growing number of other countries. Cash flow–related measures are especially useful in international analysis because they are less affected by accounting principle differences than are earnings-based measures. When cash flow statements are not presented, it is often difficult to compute cash flows from operations and other cash flow measures by adjusting accrual-based earnings. Many companies simply do not disclose the information needed to make the adjustments. As one example, German balance sheets often contain surprisingly large reserve accounts that reflect many different types of accrual. Few (if any) details are presented that might allow the financial statement user to assess the implications for operating, investment, and financing cash flows.

Coping Mechanisms

How do financial statement users cope with cross-country accounting principle differences? Several approaches are used. Some analysts restate foreign accounting measures to an internationally recognized set of principles, or to some other common basis.

---

[15]Paul R. Brown and Clyde P. Stickney, "Instructional Case: Tanaguchi Corporation," Issues in Accounting Education 7 (Spring 1992): 57–68.

[16]Jill L. McKinnon, "Application of Anglo-American Principles of Consolidation to Corporate Financial Disclosure in Japan," ABACUS 20 (1984): 16–33 provides further detail on corporate groups in Japan versus those in Anglo-American countries. She argues that the Anglo-American consolidation methods adopted by Japan in 1977 may reflect international pressure for accounting conformity more than the inherent desirability of those methods. She implies that as a result, Japanese consolidated financial statements are less useful than they might be. The McKinnon study provides an important illustration that knowing what accounting principles are used is only the first step in interpreting financial statements from different countries

Others develop a detailed understanding of accounting practices in a limited set of countries and restrict their analysis to firms located in those countries.

Brown, Soybel, and Stickney illustrate the use of a restatement algorithm to enhance cross-border comparisons of financial performance.[17] They restate the operating performance of U.S. and Japanese companies to a similar reporting basis. Rather than convert U.S. data to a Japanese financial reporting basis, or Japanese data to a U.S. financial reporting basis, they adjust (as necessary) both U.S. and Japanese data to achieve uniform accounting principles.

Appendix 9-1 illustrates another approach, in which the financial statements of a hypothetical Japanese business (Toyoza Enterprises) are restated from a Japanese GAAP basis to a U.S. GAAP basis. The restatement algorithm used in Appendix 9-1 involves a detailed analysis of numerous financial statement items.

Relatively simple restatement algorithms can be effective. One approach is to focus on a few of the most material financial statement differences for which enough information is available to make reliable adjustments. For example Brown and colleagues, mentioned above, summarize many differences between Japan and U.S. GAAP, but their restatement algorithm focuses on only four accounting principle differences: (1) inventory cost assumptions, (2) depreciation method, (3) bonuses to directors and statutory auditors, and (4) deferred taxes and special tax reserves.

INTERNATIONAL PROSPECTIVE ANALYSIS

Prospective analysis involves two steps: forecasting and valuation. In forecasting, analysts make explicit forecasts of a firm's prospects based on its business strategy, accounting, and financial analysis. It addresses questions such as, How will a company's change in business strategy affect future sales volume and profits? Has the company recently adopted new accounting policies that will make current earnings appear stronger, perhaps at the cost of lower earnings next year? Will financial relationships evidenced in an analyst's ratio analysis continue?

In valuation, analysts convert quantitative forecasts into an estimate of a firm's value. Valuation is used implicitly or explicitly in many business decisions. For example, valuation is the basis of equity analysts' investment recommendations. In analyzing a possible merger, the potential acquirer will estimate the value of the target firm. Many different valuation approaches are used in practice, ranging from discounted cash flow analysis to simpler techniques based on price-based multiples.[18]

Experts in international valuation give this warning to those doing international prospective analysis: "Any rules you've learned in your home country will fall apart overseas." Exchange rate fluctuations, accounting differences, different business practices and customs, capital market differences, and many other factors will have major effects on international forecasting and valuation.

---

[17]See Paul R. Brown, Virginia E. Soybel, and Clyde P. Stickney, "Achieving Comparability of U.S. and Japanese Price-Earnings Ratios," in Frederick D. S., Choi, ed., International Accounting and Finance Handbook, 2nd ed., New York: John Wiley & Sons, 1997, pp. 7.1–7.18.

[18]See Aswath Damodaran, Investment Valuation, 2nd ed., New York: John Wiley & Sons, 2000.

For example, discounted cash flow analysis values a business as the present value of its expected cash flows, discounted at a rate that reflects the riskiness of those cash flows. While this valuation principle is no different for developed and emerging markets alike, many of the inputs taken for granted in the former may not be as accessible in emerging economies.[19] For example, the government bond rate, often used as a surrogate for the risk-free rate, assumes that governments do not default, at least on local borrowing. This is often not the case internationally. Other inputs including risk parameters and premiums are typically more difficult to estimate owing to the paucity of historical data. And earnings forecasts, as a basis for estimating future cash flows, are less reliable. Hope attributes this to several factors.[20] One factor is the greater choice that managers have in choosing among accounting methods. Greater choice makes it more difficult to do cross-section analyses and makes it easier for managers to distort economic reality in reporting firm performance. Forecast accuracy is also positively related to the extent to which accrual accounting is prescribed in a country. Accruals provide a better measure of a firm's future cash generating ability than cash receipts and disbursements and irons out discontinuities in reported revenues and expenses. Finally, the accuracy of analysts' earnings forecasts are positively related to the strength of a country's enforcement standards. This is attributed to the notion that enforcement narrows the range of permitted accounting choices. This, in turn, reduces analysts' uncertainty about the degree of firms' reporting discretion.[21]

Consider next the use of price-based (valuation) multiples in an international setting. Valuation multiples such as price-to-earnings (P/E) and price-to-book (P/B) ratios are often used to estimate a firm's value. One common approach is to calculate the desired multiple for a group of comparable firms (such as other firms in the same industry), and then apply that multiple to the firm being valued to get a reasonable price. For example, if the price-to-earnings ratio of the industry group is 15, and the firm's earnings are forecast to be $1.80/share, then $27.00 per share is a reasonable price for the firm being analyzed. One might use the valuation multiples approach to determine the bid price for an acquisition candidate. If the candidate is a European company, comparable firms might be chosen from selected European countries.

Reliance on valuation multiples assumes that market prices reflect future prospects and that pricing of firms with similar operating and financial characteristics (such as firms in the same industry) is applicable to the firm being analyzed because of its similarity to those firms. Application of price multiples in a cross-border setting is challenging because it requires that the determinants of each multiple, and reasons why multiples vary across firms, be thoroughly understood.

Exhibit 9-3 displays mean price to earnings ratios for stock indexes in 17 countries at the end of 2006.

Exhibit 9-3 shows that P/E ratios vary across countries. At the end of 2006 P/E multiples ranged from 7.3 in Russia to 33.6 for firms listed on the stock exchange in Japan. But what accounts for these variations across national boundaries?

National differences in accounting principles are one potential source of cross-country ratio variations. Such differences, for example, cause P/E ratios in Japan to

---

[19]Aswath Damodaran, "Valuation in Emerging Markets," in Frederick D. S. Choi, ed., *International Finance and Accounting Handbook*, 3rd ed., New York: John Wiley & Sons, 2003, p. 9.3.
[20]Hope, op. cit., pp. 21–39.
[21]Hope op. cit., p. 23.

EXHIBIT 9-3   International Price/Earnings Ratios

Country	Index	P/E
Canada	SPTSX	18.5
China (PRC)	SHCOMP	23.3
France	CAC	12.5
Hong Kong	HIS	11.8
India	SENSEX	17.7
Italy	MIB30	12.8
Japan	NKY	33.6
Mexico	MEXBOL	9.6
Netherlands	AEX	10.6
Russia	RTSI$	7.3
Singapore	STI	12.2
South Africa	TOP40	8.9
Spain	IBEX	12.7
Sweden	OMX	11.8
Switzerland	SMI	16.1
UK	UKX	15.8
US	SPX	16.6

SOURCE: "Global P/E Ratios, Ticker Sense Blogger,"
Birinyi Associates, Inc., December 29, 2006.

generally be higher than those in the United States (recall that reported earnings in Japan are lower than in the United States for comparable companies with similar financial performance). However, even after adjusting for accounting differences, P/E ratios in Japan are still much higher than in the United States.

French and Poterba examined disparities between Japanese and U.S. P/E ratios and the steep increase in Japanese P/E ratios during the late 1980s.[22] They made several accounting adjustments to the Japanese data and found that their adjustments reduced but did not eliminate the difference between Japanese and U.S. P/E ratios. French and Poterba concluded that accounting differences explain about half of the long-term differences between U.S. and Japanese P/E ratios.

Brown, Soybel, and Stickney also investigated why Japanese P/E ratios are higher than U.S. P/E ratios.[23] They found that adjusting for different accounting principles explains only a small part of the difference. A comparison of their study with French and Poterba's shows how different approaches and assumptions can lead to very different conclusions about valuation ratios.

---

[22]Kenneth R., French and James M. Poterba, "Were Japanese Stock Prices Too High?" Journal of Financial Economics 29 (1991): 337–362.

[23]See Paul R. Brown, Virginia E. Soybel, and Clyde P. Stickney, "Achieving Comparability of U.S. and Japanese Price-Earnings Ratios," op. cit., for a review of comparative analyses of Japanese and U.S. P/E ratios. For further comparative evidence on cross-country differences in P/E and P/B ratios, see Peter Joos and Mark Lang, "The Effects of Accounting Diversity: Evidence from the European Union," Journal of Accounting Research 32 (Suppl., 1994): 141–175.

The substantial variation in valuation ratios shown in Exhibit 9-3 reflects changes in financial performance and in market prices across time and countries. As discussed previously, even French and Poterba's rigorous analysis of the changes in P/E ratios in Japan during the late 1980s yielded only partial answers. Thus, accounting offers only a partial explanation for differences among P/E ratios in different countries and over time. An understanding of additional environmental considerations (see Appendix 9-2) is necessary for meaningful analysis and interpretation.

FURTHER ISSUES

All four stages of business analysis (business strategy, accounting, financial and prospective analysis) may be affected by the following factors: (1) information access, (2) timeliness of information, (3) language and terminology barriers, (4) foreign currency issues, and (5) differences in types and formats of financial statements.

Information Access

Information about thousands of companies from around the world has become more widely available in recent years. Countless information sources are appearing on the World Wide Web. Companies around the world now have Web sites, and their annual reports are available free of charge from various Internet and other sources. Refer to Exhibit 9-4 for Web sites that provide information highly relevant for company research.

EXHIBIT 9-4   Freely Available Web Sites for Company Research (all Web sites begin with the prefix http://www)

Name of Web Site	*Web Site Address*	*What It Provides*
Annual Reports Library	zpub.com/sf/arl/	Alphabetical listing of U.S. corporations with links to home pages and annual reports that can be downloaded free of charge with Adobe Acrobat Reader.
Annual Report Gallery	reportgallery.com/bigaz .htm	Access to annual reports.
Asian Business Watch	asianbusinesswatch.com	Company and stock market news for Japan and Asia.
Babel	babel.altavista.com	Translates text files; only does first few pages of long documents.
Bank of England	bank of england.co.uk/	United Kingdom monetary and financial statistics, working papers, and other publications, information on the bank's structure and functions, and much more.
BFA-NET: Bureau of Financial Analysis Network	bfanet.com	South African company and stock market information; check out "Little Facts."
Bloomberg News Service	bloomberg.com/	Highlights from the Bloomberg news service.
Businessjeeves.com	businessjeeves.com	Good starting place; many links.

(Continued)

EXHIBIT 9-4   Freely Available Web Sites for Company Research (all Web sites begin with the prefix http://www) *(Continued)*

Name of Web Site	Web Site Address	What It Provides
Business Week Online	businessweek.com	Current issue, archives, and an assortment of worthwhile data.
CAROL: Company Annual Reports Online	carolworld.com	Online annual reports for some European companies.
Cross Border Capital	liquidity.com/	Reports on equity, fixed income, and currency markets in over 70 developed and emerging markets. Reports over 6 months old available for free (with registration).
Daiwa Securities	dir.co.jp/Reception/ research.html	Research reports and forecasts on the Japanese economy.
Edgar—U.S. Securities & Exchange Commission	sec.gov/edgar.shtml	Most SEC filings since 1996.
Emerging Markets Companion	emgmkts.com/	Many useful links and resources on Asia, Latin America, Africa, and Europe.
EnterWeb: The Enterprise Development Web site	enterweb.org/welcome .htm	Meta-index to business and finance globalization, and more. "The focus is on micro, small, and medium-sized enterprise development both in developed and developing countries."
Europages—European Business Directory	europages.com/	Lists 500,000 companies in 30 countries; includes some manufacturers' catalogs.
FEE Euro Information Service	euro.fee.be	Information on the transition to the euro in the European Union; requires registration (free).
Financial Times of London	ft.com/	Online edition of the Financial Times; current articles, market information, and more.
FT Interactive Data	turboguide.com/data2/ cdprod1/doc/cdrom frame/002/686.pub.FT .Excel.html	Good sampling from FT Excel databases; must register.
Hong Kong Securities and Futures Commission	hksfc.org.hk	Information on Hong Kong securities markets.
Hoover's Online	hoovers.com	Some information, such as press releases, is free. Links to company home pages and other information. Includes more than 800 of the most important non-U.S. companies.
INO Global Market	ino.com/	Information for traders in futures and options markets worldwide.
International Business (Michigan State University Center for International Business Education and Research)	ciber.bus.msu.edu/ busres.htm	Links to good investment and macro sites.
International Monetary Fund	imf.org/	IMF news, publications, and more.

(Continued)

EXHIBIT 9-4   Freely Available Web Sites for Company Research (all Web sites begin with the prefix http://www) (*Continued*)

Name of Web Site	*Web Site Address*	*What It Provides*
Internet Corruption Rankings	gwdg.de/~uwvw/ icr_serv.htm	Provides the TI-Corruption Perception Index, a comparative assessment of the integrity of many countries, along with many other links and services.
National Corporate Services, Inc. International Investing	natcorp.com/	Excellent start point; many links to sites providing free information.
NIRI Useful Investor Relations Sites	niri.org	Links to interesting Web sites.
Public Register's Annual Report, The	prars.com	Annual reports, prospectuses, or 10-Ks on over 32,000 U.S. companies.
Rutgers Accounting Network (RAW)	rutgers.edu/Accounting/ raw.html	Excellent starting place.
Stewart Mayhew's Directory of Worldwide Securities Exchanges	voltaire.is.tcu.edu/ ~vmihov/exchanges/ xlinks.Htm	Links to official home pages of stock markets and derivatives exchanges around the world.
Stock City	stockcity.com	ADR profiles, organized by sector, region, and country. Profiles require Adobe Acrobat Reader.
Streetlink Investor Information Center	streetlink.com	Financial reports available online; U.S. companies only.
United Nations System	unsystem.org	Spotty coverage of companies and accounting information; good information on communications and country background.
USA Today Money	usatoday.com/money/ mfront.htm	Comprehensive assortment of news and data.
VIBES: Virtual International Business and Economic Sources	uncc.edu/lis/library/ reference/intbus/ vibehome.htm	Great for linking to regional sites; excellent starting place, especially good for macro data.
Wright Investor' Service	profiles.wisi.com	Can search alphabetically by country or by industry.
Yahoo! Finance	quote.yahoo.com	Extensive data, news, and stock quotes.

Many companies also respond to written and telephone requests for their annual reports and other financial documents. However, the amount of company information available varies considerably from country to country.

Many commercial databases provide access to financial and stock market data for tens of thousands of companies around the world. Companies covered by commercial databases tend to be large companies that are of most interest to financial statement users and investors. It is striking that even in emerging market countries such as China and the Czech Republic, data for many firms are now available.

Other valuable information sources include (1) government publications, (2) economic research organizations, (3) international organizations such as the United Nations, and (4) accounting, auditing, and securities market organizations. Web site addresses appear throughout this text and are only a starting point for gathering information.

Timeliness of Information

The timeliness of financial statements, annual reports, regulatory filings, and accounting-related press releases varies dramatically by country. Whereas quarterly financial reporting is a generally accepted practice in the United States, this is seldom the case elsewhere.[24] Financial reporting lags can also be estimated by comparing a company's fiscal year-end with its audit report date. The latter is often considered a reasonable indication of when corporate financial information first becomes publicly available. For Brazil, Canada, Chile, Colombia, Mexico, the Philippines, South Korea, Taiwan, Thailand, and the United States, this reporting lag reportedly averaged between 30–60 days. It averaged 61–90 days in Argentina, Australia, Denmark, Finland, Ireland, Israel, Japan, the Netherlands, New Zealand, Norway, Portugal, Singapore, South Africa, Spain, Sweden, Switzerland, the United Kingdom, and Zimbabwe. In Austria, Belgium, France, Germany, Greece, Hong Kong, India, Italy, Malaysia, Nigeria, and Sri Lanka, information lags averaged 91–120 days. And for Pakistan, the average lag exceeded 120 days.[25]

Frost documents further international variations in the timeliness of earnings-related press releases.[26] She defined disclosure lags as the average number of days between a company's fiscal year-end and the date of the press release. These lags were 73 days for companies domiciled in France, 82 days for Germany, 46 days for Japan, 72 days for the United Kingdom, and 26 days for the United States.

Variability in the timeliness of accounting information places additional burdens on readers of foreign financial statements. This burden is especially pronounced for firms whose operating circumstances are changing over time. Meaningful valuations require constant updates of reported numbers using both conventional and unconventional means.

Foreign Currency Considerations

Accounts denominated in foreign currency present financial analysts with two types of problems. The first relates to reader convenience, the second to information content.

The vast majority of companies around the world denominate their financial accounts in the currency of their national domicile. To a U.S. reader accustomed to dealing in dollars, analysis of accounts expressed in euros may be discomforting. A normal inclination is to translate foreign currency balances to domestic currency. However, foreign currency reports are, for the most part, troublesome in appearance only. Financial ratios that transform nominal (interval) measurements to percentage relationships are independent of currency. A current ratio computed from a Dutch balance sheet expressed in euros is the same as one computed from the same financial

---

[24]An informal survey of many world-class company Web sites suggests that more and more are voluntarily choosing to provide quarterly reports owing to capital market pressures to do so.
[25]See International Accounting and Auditing Trends, 4th ed., Center for International Financial Analysis & Research, Princeton, NJ: CIFAR Publications, Inc., 1995.
[26]Carol A. Frost, "Characteristics and Information Value of Corporate Disclosures of Forward-Looking Information in Global Equity Markets," Dartmouth College Working Paper, February 1998.

statement translated into dollars. Consider the following year-end balance sheet accounts of a British company.

	20X6	20X7	20X8
Current assets	£12,500	£12,200	£12,800
Current liabilities	£8,333	£7,625	£8,000

Assuming year-end dollar/pound exchanges rates of $2.10, $2.20, and $1.60 for 20X6, 20X7, and 20X8, respectively, the current ratio will be 1.5 to 1 for 20X6, 1.6 to 1 for 20X7, and 1.6 to 1 for 20X8, whether expressed in British pounds or U.S. dollars. Local currency (e.g., pound) balances are especially appropriate when analyzing financial trends.

Readers who prefer a domestic currency framework when analyzing foreign currency accounts may apply a convenience translation using year-end exchange rates. One must be careful, however, when analyzing translated trend data. Use of convenience rates to translate foreign currency accounts can distort underlying financial patterns in local currency. To illustrate, assume the following 3-year sales revenue patterns for our British concern.

	20X6	20X7	20X8
Sales revenue	£23,500	£28,650	£33,160

Convenience translations using the year-end exchange rates employed earlier (i.e., $2.10 for 20X6, $2.20 for 20X7, and $1.60 for 20X8) yield a U.S. dollar sales increase of 7.5 percent [($53,056–$49,350) / $49,350] over the 3-year period. The sales gain in pounds, however, is 41 percent [(£33,160–£23,500) / £23,500].

An alternative approach is to translate foreign currency data to domestic currency using a single base year's exchange rate. But which base-year exchange rate should be used? In our example, should the sales figures be translated using the 20X6 exchange rate, the 20X7 exchange rate, or the 20X8 exchange rate?

Although we prefer to analyze foreign statements in local currency, we favor the use of the most recent year's exchange rate as a convenience translator for readers who prefer domestic currency statistics. An exception is warranted, however, if the foreign currency financial statements have been adjusted for changes in the general purchasing power of the foreign currency unit (see Chapter 7 for a discussion of this treatment). If foreign currency balances are expressed in base-year purchasing power equivalents, year-end exchange rates associated with the given base year should be employed. In our example, if sales revenues were expressed in pounds of 20X6 general purchasing power, the 20X6 exchange rate would have been an appropriate translation rate.

While translated statements give readers the convenience of viewing foreign currency accounts in a familiar currency, they may give a distorted picture. Specifically, exchange rate changes and accounting procedures together often produce domestic currency equivalents that conflict with underlying events. We illustrate this problem using the statement of cash flows as an example.

Recall from Chapter 6 that consolidated financial statements allow a multinational company to report the results of its worldwide operations in a single currency. Also recall that a variety of currency translation methods are in use internationally. Regardless of the currency translation method employed, it is not always clear to readers of consolidated funds flow statements, whether reported fund sources or uses reflect the results of an operational decision or simply an exchange rate change.

To illustrate, the translated statements of earnings, financial position, and cash flows for the Norwegian affiliate of a U.S.-based multinational company appear in Exhibit 9-5. The parent company employs the current rate method and defines the krone as its functional currency for consolidation purposes.

A cursory examination of the translated statement of cash flows shows that major sources of cash were operations (net income plus depreciation), the issuance of long-term debt, and a translation adjustment. In turn, cash was used to increase the company's investment in fixed assets.

The pattern of cash flow shown in Exhibit 9-5 differs from that experienced by a purely domestic company due to the presence of an aggregate translation adjustment. However, examination of this component of the translated funds statement reveals

EXHIBIT 9-5   Translated Financial Statements of Norwegian Subsidiary

Translated Balance Sheets as of 12/31/X6 and 12/31/X7

	December 31	
	20X6	**20X7**
Assets (000's)		
Cash	$ 2,400	$ 3,990
Net fixed assets	8,500	10,640
Total assets	$10,900	$14,630
Liabilities and owners' equity		
U.S. $500 payable	$ 500	$ 500
Long-term franc debt	4,800	6,384
Capital stock	3,818	3,818
Retained earnings	1,782	2,030
Translation adjustment	—	1,898
Total liabilities and stockholders' equity	$10,900	$14,630
Translated Statement of Income for the Year 20X7 (000's)		
Sales		$ 1,332
Expenses		
Operating costs	$ 666	
Depreciation	555	
Foreign exchange gain	(139)	1,082
Net income		$ 250
Translated Statement of Cash Flows (000's)		
Sources		
Net income	$ 250	
Depreciation	555	
Increase in long-term debt	1,584	
Translation adjustment	1,898	$ 4,287
Uses		
Increase in fixed assets		2,695
Net increase in cash (approximate due to rounding)		$ 1,590

that it does not really constitute a source or use of cash. The translation adjustment is calculated by multiplying the beginning foreign currency net asset balance by the change in the current rate during the period and, second, by multiplying the increase or decrease in net assets during the period by the difference between the average exchange rate and end-of-period exchange rate. This procedure, together with the dual nature of the accounting equation, suggests that most components of the translated funds statement are a mix of translation effects and actual cash flows. In our current example, a statement reader needs to figure out whether the increase of long-term debt in the amount of $1,584,000 is an indication of the Norwegian affiliate's financing activities or is largely an accounting adjustment. Similar considerations apply to the purported $2,695,000 investment in fixed assets.

Assume that the translated statements appearing in Exhibit 9-5 are based on the Norwegian krone balances appearing in Exhibit 9-6 and that the relevant exchange rate information is as stated.

A cash flow comparison between the functional currency (krone) and the reporting currency (dollars) yields some striking contrasts. While the cash flow statement generated from the translated balance sheet and income statement (Exhibit 9-5) shows long-term debt as a source of funds, the krone statement (Exhibit 9-6) suggests that this was not the case. Likewise, what appears to be an investment in fixed assets from a dollar perspective turns out to be a pure translation phenomenon.

EXHIBIT 9-6   Financial Statements for Wholly-Owned Norwegian Subsidiary

Local Currency Balance Sheet as of 12/31/X6 and 12/31/X7

	December 31	
	20X6	**20X7**
Assets		
Cash	NOK 24,000	NOK 30,000
Net fixed assets	85,000	80,000
Total assets	NOK 109,000	NOK 110,000
Liabilities and owners' equity		
U.S. $500 payable	NOK 5,000	NOK 3,750
Long-term krona debt	48,000	48,000
Capital stock	46,000	46,000
Retained earnings	10,000	12,250
Total liabilities and owners' equity	NOK 109,000	NOK 110,000
Statement of Cash Flows		
Sources		
Net income		NOK 2,250
Depreciation		5,000
Less: Krona foreign-exchange gain		1,250
Uses:		
None		—
Net increase in cash		NOK 6,000
Relevant Exchange Rates		
December 31, 20X6		NOK1 = $.100
Average during 20X7		NOK1 = $.111
December 31, 20X6		NOK1 = $.133

Closer analysis provides insight into the magnitude of the translation effects. An analysis of the fixed asset account reveals that there was no purchase, sale, or retirement of fixed assets during the year. Thus, the year-end balance should have been the beginning book value, $8,500,000 (NOK85,000,000), less depreciation of $555,000 (NOK5,000,000), or $7,945,000. The actual ending balance was $10,640,000, suggesting that the entire increase in fixed assets ($10,640,000–$7,945,000) was due to an exchange rate effect. Similarly, there was no change in Norwegian krone long-term debt during the year. Because this monetary liability was translated by an exchange rate that revalued during the year, the entire increase in long-term debt ($6,384,000–$4,800,000) also arose from a translation adjustment. Similar transactional analyses account for additional translation effects related to the Norwegian subsidiary's working capital accounts. These effects are summarized in Exhibit 9-7.

Note that the sum of all the translation effects appearing in Exhibit 9-6 equals the aggregate translation adjustment appearing in the shareholders' equity section of the translated balance sheet. An informed reader can better determine the influence of exchange rate changes from a firm's financing and investing activities using the foregoing analysis.

Differences in Statement Format

Balance sheet and income statement formats vary from country to country. For example, in contrast to the United States, where most companies adopt the balance sheet account format with assets appearing on the left and equity claims on the right, the format is often the reverse in the United Kingdom. As a second example, in contrast to U.S. balance sheets, which display assets in decreasing order of liquidity and liabilities in increasing order of maturity, in many countries the most liquid assets and the shortest-term liabilities appear at the foot of the balance sheet.

Classification differences also abound internationally. For example, accumulated depreciation is reported as a contra-asset account in the United States. In Germany, depreciable assets are usually reported net of accumulated depreciation, but all current period changes in long-term asset accounts are shown directly in the balance sheet. In most countries, the distinction between a current and noncurrent liability is 1 year. In Germany it is often 4 years. Handbooks like Transactional Accounting[27] may be consulted for a detailed treatment of other classification differences prevailing in individual countries.

EXHIBIT 9-7   Analysis of Exchange Rate Effects

	Debit	Credit
Cash	$ 924	
Fixed assets	2,695	
Intercompany payable		$ 138
Long-term debt		1,584
	$3,619	$1,722
Aggregate translation adjustment		1,897
	$3,619	$3,619

---

[27]Dieter Ordelheide and KPMG, Transactional Accounting, 2nd ed., Hampshire, U.K.: Palgrave, 2001.

Financial statement format differences, while troublesome, are seldom critical because the underlying structure of financial statements is quite similar around the world. Accordingly, most format differences can usually be reconciled with a little effort.

Language and Terminology Barriers

Language differences among countries can present information barriers to financial statement users. Most companies domiciled in non-English-speaking countries publish their annual reports in the home country language. However, growing numbers of the relatively large companies in developed economies provide English-language versions of their annual reports.

Accounting terminology differences can also cause difficulty.[28] For example, U.S. readers associate the term stock with certificates of corporate ownership. Readers in the United Kingdom, on the other hand, associate the term with a firm's inventory of unsold goods. Other examples of terminology differences between the United Kingdom and the United States include turnover (sales revenue), and debtors and creditors (accounts receivable and payable).

In summary, many substantial issues confront the user of international financial statements. Perhaps the most difficult issues concern foreign currency and the availability and credibility of financial information. Difficulties with foreign currency will probably have a pervasive influence on international accounting for some time. In contrast, problems related to information availability and credibility are gradually decreasing as more and more companies, regulatory authorities, and stock exchanges recognize the importance of improving investors' access to timely and credible information.

FINANCIAL STATEMENT ANALYSIS AND AUDITING

In our earlier section on accounting analysis, we noted the importance of assessing the quality of the information contained in a firm's published accounts. Thoughtful readers must judge the adequacy of accounting measurements employed and remove distortions caused by the use of accounting methods deemed inappropriate. A corollary of this quality assessment is an assessment of the credibility of the information provided, irrespective of the measurement rules employed. In addition to questions of information quality and quantity, financial analysts must be relatively free from undue risk due to fraud or deception on the part of those making the financial representations. We now discuss the attest or audit function and the role it plays in international financial statement analysis.

The Attest Function

Independent auditors perform the attest function in financial reporting. As competent outside experts they review financial information provided by a firm's management and then attest to its reliability, fairness and other aspects of quality. This process establishes and maintains the integrity of financial information.

---

[28]Lisa Evans, "Language, Translation and the Problem of International Accounting Communication," *Accounting, Auditing and Accountability Journal*, Vol. 17 No. 2(2004): 248.

While auditing processes are rooted in antiquity, the growth of auditing as a separate and distinct profession during the nineteenth century was encouraged by the enactment in the United Kingdom, circa 1845, of a requirement that companies keep accounts which had to be audited by persons other than directors. The earliest accounting body was the Society of Accountants in Edinburgh.

Investors and other readers of financial statements have a big stake the attestation of professional auditors. They can make decisions with better expected outcomes if they have relatively better information available. The public is also better served. Incomplete, unreliable or even misleading financial information may well have a negative effect on capital formation processes within an economy. Moreover, scarce resources may be misdirected to socially less desirable channels or wasted through excessive rates of bankruptcy. Sensitivity to the importance of the attest function is probably higher in multinational settings than it is in single-country situations.

Aside from decision and public interest effects, independent audits introduce efficiency into the financial reporting process. If users of financial information had to obtain firm information on their own and verify this information item by item and user by user, an immensely costly process would ensue. In this regard, division of responsibilities produces net benefits. Management has a comparative advantage in preparing and offering financial information needed by outsiders. Auditors , in turn, have a comparative advantage in ensuring that management's financial representations are relatively free of bias. Their independent attestations enable statement readers around the world to discriminate among generally acceptable and unacceptable accounting practices and to assess the overall quality of financial reports at a lower cost than would otherwise be the case.

The Audit Report

The auditors' attestation is typically communicated to financial statement readers by way of an audit report. This report either follows, or in some cases, precedes the firm's principal financial statements appearing in its annual report. But, what is included in such a report? Do auditors in all countries employ identical reporting formats? Exhibit 9-8 contains a taxonomy of audit reporting requirements in a sample of countries. [29]

EXHIBIT 9-8   Selected Reporting Requirements for Audit Reports

United Kingdom

The auditor's report discloses the responsibilities of company directors and the scope of the audit; basis of opinion and statement of opinion. The balance sheet, income statement and related notes must be covered by statute; auditing standards extend this coverage to the cash flow statement. The auditors' opinion must state whether the financial statements give a true and fair view and that the statements comply with statutory requirements. Auditors must state that they have read other information contained in the audit report, including the corporate governance statement, and describe implications for the audit report if the auditors become aware of any inconsistencies.

---

[29]Exhibit 9-8 and subsequent exhibits on various facets of international auditing practice draw on an excellent survey conducted by Belverd Needles. For greater detail, see his chapter "Taxonomy of Auditing Standards," in Frederick D.S. Choi, *International Finance and Accounting Handbook, 3rd ed.*, New York: John Wiley & Sons, 2003.

EXHIBIT 9-8 Selected Reporting Requirements for Audit Reports (*Continued*)

The scope section also explains the auditor's responsibilities in relation to the separate directors' report, the accounting records, information and explanations required, and rules regarding the disclosure of directors' remuneration.

United States

A standard three paragraph report identifies the company and the principal financial statements being audited (scope) and states the responsibilities of management and the auditor. The auditor must indicate whether or not the audit complied with generally accepted auditing standards. The auditor must express an opinion as to whether the financial statements are presented fairly in accordance with GAAP and whether GAAP has been consistently observed in relation to reports in previous years. If an opinion cannot be expressed this must be stated.

Sweden

The Swedish Companies Act requires the auditor statements about:

1. The preparation of the annual report is in accordance with the Act.

2. The adoption of the balance sheet and income statement.

3. The proposal included in the administration report for disposition of the unappropriated earnings or deficit.

4. The discharge from the liability of members of the board of directors and the managing director.

Germany

The German Commercial Code specifies that the auditor's report contain a description of the process and result of the audit, including management's report, a forecast of future developments, a statement of compliance with legal regulation and a statement describing the company's risk management system. The auditor must provide a summary of the content, type and volume of the audit in the Bestaetigungsvmerk, an evaluation of the audit results, and statements as to whether or not the financial statements and managemnt's report present a true and fair view.

Based on the sample data provided in Exhibit 9-8, it should be evident that auditors reports vary internationally in terms of the information they contain. Both the U.K. and U.S. audit reports identify the scope of the audit, identify the auditing and accounting standards adhered to and set forth the auditor's opinion. The German report expands the information set to include information on future developments as well as description of the company's risk management system, both useful pieces of information for statement readers. The reports differ most markedly in terms of the opinions that are expressed. Exhibit 9-9 focuses on the wording of auditor opinions selected randomly from company annual reports in the U.K., U.S., Sweden, Switzerland and Norway.

Exhibit 9-9 suggests that actual audit opinions very often exceed reporting minima prescribed by statute. In documenting the diversity of audit opinions internationally, Exhibit 9-9 also raises information issues for analysts. U.K. auditors state that the financial statements they audit give a true and fair view of a company's affairs. In this instance, does the term *true* mean "the truth, the whole truth and nothing but the truth?" Does inclusion of the term "fair" imply that the truth has somehow been compromised? U.S. auditors take a less absolute stance and state that the audited statements

EXHIBIT 9-9   Diversity of Audit Opinions

U.K

In our opinion, the financial statements give a **true** and **fair** view of the state of affairs of the company and of the group as at 31 December 20X8 and of the profit and cash flows of the group for the year then ended and have been properly prepared in accordance with the Companies Act 1985.

U.S.

In our opinion, the financial statements referred to above present **fairly**, in all material respects, the consolidated financial position of Time Warner at December 31, 20X7 and 20X8, and the consolidated results of its operations and its cash flows for each of the three years in the period ended December 31, 20X8 in conformity with U.S. GAAP.

Sweden

The annual accounts and the consolidated accounts have been prepared in accordance with the Annual Accounts Act and, thereby, give a true and fair view of the Company's and the Group's financial position and results of operations in accordance with generally accepted accounting principles in Sweden.

Switzerland

In our opinion, the accounting records and financial statements and the proposed appropriation of available earnings comply with **Swiss law** and the company's **articles of incorporation**.

Norway

The financial statements of Norsk Hydro are prepared in accordance with the law and regulations and present fairly ... the financial position of the Company ... in accordance with accounting principles generally accepted in Norway.

In our opinion, such consolidated financial statements ... present fairly ... in conformity with U.S. GAAP.

present fairly and in accordance with a set of U.S. measurement rules. Does this wording connote the same meaning as true and fair? The Swedish opinion is more informative than the requirements set forth in Exhibit 9-8 where Swedish auditors are allowed to opine to nothing. However, is Swedish GAAP and the Annual Accounts Act synonymous? The wording in Exhibit 9-9 seems to suggest this. If so, does this imply that imply that Swedish GAAP is legally-based which normally differs from standards promulgated by private professional groups. Or, does it mean that the Companies Act prescribes adherence to generally accepted auditing standards promulgated by the Swedish accounting profession? If it means the former, does compliance with the law (also read the Swiss opinion) assure that the statements provide a true and fair view of a company's affairs? Finally, observe that Norsk Hydro provides two audit reports. This is related to the fact that the company reconciles it accounts to U.S. GAAP in the notes section of the annual report. In catering to the information needs of U.S. investors, is the firm suggesting that U.S. GAAP provides more decision-relevant information than Norwegian GAAP? Which set of financial statements should international analysts rely on?

Auditing and Credibility

The credibility of the audit report rests on several platforms. These include, but are not limited to, the source of auditing standards, their enforcement, and the professionalism of the individual or individuals performing the audit.

Exhibit 9-7 suggests that auditing standards emanate from national legislation such as Companies Acts and/or private professional accounting associations. In many cases it is a matter of degree. Auditing standards are primarily promulgated by private professional groups in most countries. Notable exceptions are Austria, Germany and Switzerland, where auditing standards are largely influenced by legislation. Countries such as France, Japan, Korea, Kenya, Sweden and the U.K. rely on a combination of legal and professional standards.[30] In some cases standards promulgated by private professional groups are much more rigorous than those crafted by the government; in other cases, just the opposite may be true. Accordingly, credibility of the attest function is also a function of enforcement mechanisms and the extent of auditor liability.

Enforcement of auditing standards and auditing lapses has proved difficult at the international level. Professionally-developed standards generally lack the force of law, the possibility of of economic sanction, and, more generally, international political and diplomatic recognition. Hence, enforcement of standards is by and large left to the profession itself. Insistence upon strict or tightening auditing standards invariably produces adverse economic consequences for clients (i.e., increased audit service fees) which, in turn, leads to competitive pressures among independent auditors. At the national level, the effectiveness of enforcing auditing and ethical standards varies from country to country. In most of the countries he surveyed, Needles finds that an auditor who violates auditing standards may be disciplined either by law or by professional sanctions. Penalties include reprimands, fines and in some cases expulsion from the professional bodies of which the auditor or audit firm is a member. Professional bodies in the U.K. have experienced difficulty in obtaining evidence of wrong doing as they lack subpeona power. In the U.S. an expelled member from a state society of accountants or the American Institute of CPA's does not necessarily prevent the expelled member from conducting audits. Only individual states, operating through their state boards of accounting, have the authority to revoke a license to practice. Press coverage often reveals that boards often fail to impose sanctions or to follow up on imposed sanctions. Governments in countries such as France, Japan, Germany Kenya and the Netherlands often take a formal role in enforcement actions. Hence, enforcement at the national level has proved uneven.

Auditor liability to third parties for wrongful acts represents a form of market enforcement. Here too, market practices vary. At one end of the spectrum, in countries such as Germany and the United States, simple negligence on the part of the auditor is usually insufficient for aggrieved third parties to prevail in their litigation claims. In countries such as Hong Kong, Japan, Kenya, Saudi Arabia, Sweden and the United Kingdom, just the opposite may be the case. In most countries, auditors can be held liable for gross negligence or fraud.

In the final analysis, the credibility of auditing is a function of who is doing the audit. Here, statement readers must distinguish between two classes of accountants. Assume you are examining the annual report of a French firm as a basis for an investment decision. Being removed from the local scene, one of the first things you would now do would be to look to see if the annual report contains an audit report by an independent account. You find the report and it is signed by the Commisaires aux Comptes. Can you conclude that managements' financial representations have been

---

[30]Needles, ibid.

subjected to a rigorous independent audit? Not necessarily. The Commisaires is a statutory auditor, whose appointment is mandatory under French commercial law. Statutory auditors in France are required to oversee in very general terms a company's bookkeeping and accounting and then to report annually to the stockholders' meeting. The law does not specify any professional qualifications for the Commisaires which may range from very minimal to substantial. Often one or several stockholders serve in this capacity. Consequently, a statement of an opinion by a Commisaire has a completely different meaning and premise from a possibly similar statement or opinion by an Expert des Comptable. The latter is a well-trained professional accountant who is comparable in stature to a U.K. chartered accountant or an American certified public accountant. Exhibit 9-10 contains examples of auditor distinctions in selected countries.

Then there is the issue of auditor qualifications and licensure. Educational requirements for professional qualification are modest in the United Kingdom and fairly substantial in the United States. Indeed, most countries require academic training and candidates applying for auditor certification must must meet various licensing requirements, including passing comprehensive professional exams. On the other hand, practical experience requirements for professional qualification are substantial in Germany and the Netherlands but are no longer required at all in some jurisdictions of the United States. Once certified as a professional auditor, continuing education to keep an auditor abreast of current business and professional developments are required in Australia, Japan, Korea, Mexico, the Netherlands , U.K. and U.S. This is seldom the case elsewhere.

Ultimately, the value of an auditor lies in his or her independence from the firm he or she is auditing. Most would agree that CPA's in the United States are subject to the most stringent independence standards that exist internationally. In some countries, such as Hong Kong, auditors may sit on corporate boards of directors, or as is the

---

EXHIBIT 9-10   Differing Auditor Status in Selected Countries

France
    Commisaires aux Compte
    Expert des Comptable

Japan
    Statutory Auditor
    Accounting Auditor

United Kingdom
    Certified Accountant
    Chartered Accountant

United States
    Public Accountant
    Certified Public Accountant

Mexico
    Comisario
    Contador Publico

case in South Korea, may own small financial interests in companies their firms audit. On the Continent, many large audit firms are owned, at least in part, by large banks that they may very well audit. This does not mean that European auditors are necessarily dependent in fact or in appearance. Rather, it means that a thoroughly different organization of the independent auditing profession prevails. While a non-U.S. person may hold that an audit firm performing management advisory services and tax advocacy for a client cannot possibly be independent, U.S. auditors whose activities in these areas have recently been constrained would argue that bank equity ownership of an audit firm (although separated from audit operations) impairs independence. Who is right?

The auditor independence question often raises some operational problems in multinational engagements. Auditor independence is a concept not only entrenched in professional ethics codes in the United States but anchored in administrative SEC regulations such as their basic Regulation SX and Accounting Series Release No. 126. Therefore international affiliates of publicly-held U.S. parent companies are all audited by persons who meet U.S. definitions of auditor independence. This is not always a simple matter when audits abroad are conducted by associated or correspondent firms rather than by an audit firm's own branch offices. The situation may be even more vexing in those countries where local rules require that independent audits be performed only by local nationals.

Coping Mechanisms

We have now seen that audit reports internationally are varied in their information content. We have also documented variations in the platforms that help to give the attest function credibility. These differences support the case for strong international harmonization efforts in auditing. A leading organization that has as its mission the harmonization of global auditing standards is the International Federation of Accountants(IFAC).[31] A description of this organization and its activities are described in Chapter 8. Assisting IFAC in its mission is IFAD, which is the acronym for International Forum on Accountancy Development.[32] Established in 1999, this organization is a consortium of international groups that have joined together in a collaborative effort to achieve a worldwide financial reporting framework based on common measurement, disclosure and audit standards. Member organizations of IFAD include such heavy weights as IFAC, IASB, IOSCO, the World Bank, the OECD, and the IMF. At the same time, differences in audit conditions described in the previous sections, especially in the area of independence standards and audit standards that are anchored to legal systems, suggest that global harmonization efforts will not be easy.

The European Community is also pursuing harmonization of audit standards at the regional level. This effort, however, is complicated by the diversity that characterizes organizational structures of the accounting profession in various EU countries. For example, the U.K. currently has six accounting bodies four of which have ministerial approval to serve as statutory auditors. France has two accountancy bodies while

---

[31]Additional information on IFAC is available at www.ifac.org. Also see, Anne Loft, Christopher Humphrey and Stuart Turley, "In Pursuit of Global Regulation: Changing Governance and Accountability Structures at the International Federation of Accountants(IFAC)," *Accounting, Auditing and Accountability Journal*, Vol. 19 No. 3(2006), p. 451.
[32]Additional information on IFAD is available at www.ifad.net.

Germany has three. This diverse range of acounting structures makes it very difficult to secure agreement in the audit area. Suffice it to say that tangible progress towards harmonized auditing standards in Europe has been slow.[33]

In the absence of harmonized audit standards, financial analysts must make it a point to understand the audit conditions that exist in the country that hosts the business entity whose financial statements are under scrutiny. Failing this, restricting financial analyses to those companies whose statements have been audited by reputable audit firms known for their professional expertise and integrity is one coping option. If the stakes are sufficiently high, as they are for institutional investors, insisting on or paying for a second audit opinion by a world-class international audit firm is another.

Internal Auditing

A sound external audit of a reporting entity's financial statements is a *necessary* condition to assure the credibility of managements communications with external parties. However, it is not *sufficient*. The effectiveness of a firm's internal control system is equally important as it provides a more timely system of "checks and balances" than can be provided by a firm's outside auditors. The service activity that crafts and monitors a firm's internal control system is the internal audit function.

Many explanations have been advanced concerning the recent rise of internal auditing. One is the phenomenal growth of audit committees of corporate boards of directors. These audit committees, which play an active role in corporate governance, often rely on internal audit functions as their direct instrumentality. This has enhanced the stature of internal auditors as well as given them direct access to top management.

Another contributing factor to the growing importance of internal auditing is the unprecedented growth in corporate control needs. Security problems inherent in today's computerized information systems make effective internal auditing a "must" activity. The question of illicit payments by MNC's has ushered in yet another generation of specific tasks for internal auditing. In the United States, for instance, the Foreign Corrupt Practicers Act triggered major expansions of internal audit departments of most larger U.S. corporations.

The importance of internal auditing was recently highlighted in the U.S. by the spate of corporate scandals which began during the late 1990's. The roots of these scandals are directly attributed to lax corporate governance systems in which management placed their personal interests above the interests of their shareholders.[34] To bolster investor confidence, the U.S. Congress enacted the Sarbanes-Oxley Act(SOX). This act puts the onus on both management and their auditors to create an operating environment that (1) minimizes conflicts of interest, (2)fosters greater corporate transparency, reliability and accuracy in financial reporting, and (3) increases the independence among management, the board of directors and the auditors, key players in any system of corporate governance. It also increases the enforcment tools available to market regulators and attempts to minimize conflict of interest inherent in securities

---

[33]See Pater Walton, "European Harmonization," in Frederick D.S. Choi, *International Finance and Accounting Handbook, 3rd. ed.*, New York: John Wiley & Sons, 2003.
[34]This is known in agency theory as asymmetric behavior whereby the agent (management) maximizes its own personal interest at the expense of the principal (shareholders) to whom they owe their primary fiduciary responsibility.

market transactions (i.e., putting investor interests ahead of transactions-driven behavior of investment advisors and investment banks).[35]

Two sections of SOX that merit special note are sections 303 and 404. Section 303 states that both the CFO and CEO must personally sign off on all required financial statements, attesting that the statements are complete and accurate and comply with all relevant regulations and accounting standards. Section 404 mandates that management include a written statement assuring the reader that they have designed and tested adequate internal controls and that these controls are working. These controls must be audited by the company's outside auditors , thus formalizing the relationship between a firm's external and internal auditors. SOX also created the Public Company Accounting Oversight Board(PCAOB) which, among other things, provides guidance for auditing a company's internal controls and establishes the content of the auditor's report.

To show how the Sarbanes-Oxley Act has been operationalized we provide language from U.S. annual reports. Exhibit 9-11 reproduces the additional paragraph that is now included in U.S. audit reports. This paragraph follows the paragraphs describing audit scope, audit standards, and the opinion that the statements present fairly and in accordance with GAAP.

Exhibit 9-11 contains management's responsibility report for the firm's internal controls and Exhibit 9-12 illustrates the new internal control responsibilities of the

---

EXHIBIT 9-11   Report of [Coca-Cola's] Management on Internal Control

Report of Management on Internal Control over Financial Reporting

[The Coca-Cola Company and Subsidiaries]

Management of the Company is responsible for the preparation and integrity of the Consolidated Financial Statements appearing in our Annual Report on Form 10-K. The financial statements were prepared in conformity with generally accepted accounting principles appropriate in the circumstances and, accordingly, include certain amounts based on our best judgements and estimates. Financial information in this Annual Report on Form 10-K is consistent with that in the financial statements.

Management of the Company is responsible for establishing and maintaining adequate internal control over financial reporting as such term is defined in Rules 13a-15(f) under the Securities and Exchange Act of 1934 ("Exchange Act"). The Company's internal control over financial reporting is designed to provide reasonable assurance regarding the reliability of financial reporting and the preparation of the Consolidated Financial Statements. Our internal control over financial reporting is supported by a program of internal audits and appropriate reviews by management, written policies and guidelines, careful selection and training of qualified personnel and a written Code of Business Conduct adopted by our Company's Board of Directors, applicable to all Company Directors and all officers and employees of our Company and subsidiaries.

Because of its inherent limitations, internal control over financial reporting may not prevent or detect misstatements and even when determined to be effective, can only provide reasonable assurance with respect to financial statement preparation and presentation. Also, projections of any evaluation of effectiveness to future periods are subject to the risk that controls may become

(Continued)

---

[35]Jorge E. Guerra, "The Sarbanes-Oxley Act and Evolution of Corporate Governance," *The CPA Journal*, March 2004, pp. 4.

EXHIBIT 9-11   Report of [Coca-Cola's] Management on Internal Control (*Continued*)

inadequate because of changes in conditions, or that the degree of compliance with the policies or procedures may deteriorate.

The Audit Committee of our Board of Directors, composed solely of Directors who are independent in accordance with the requirements of the New York Stock Exchange listing standards, the Exchange Act and the Company's Corporate Governance Guidelines, meets with the independent auditors, management and internal auditors periodically to discuss internal control over financial reporting and auditing and financial reporting matters. The Committee reviews with the independent auditors the scope and results of the audit effort. The Committee also meets periodically with the independent auditors and the chief internal auditor without management present to ensure that the independent auditors and the chief internal auditor have free asccess to the Committee. Our Audit Committee's Report can be found in the Company's 20X6 Proxy statement.

Management assessed the effectiveness of the Company's internal control over financial reporting as of December 31, 20X5. In making this assessment, management used the criteria set forth by the Committee of Sponsoring Organizations of the Treadway Commission (COSO) in *Internal Control-Integrated Framework*. Based on our assessment, management believes that the Company maintained effective internal control over financial reporting as of December 31, 20X5.

The Company's independent auditors, Ernst & Young LLP, a registered public accounting firm, are appointed by the Audit Committee of the Company's Board of Directors, subject to ratification by our Company's shareholders. Ernst & Young LLP have audited and reported on the Consolidated Financial Statements of the Coca-Cola Company and subsidiaries, management's assessment of the effectiveness of the Company's internal control over financial reporting and the effectiveness of the Company's internal control over financial reporting. The reports of the independent auditors are contained in this Annual Report.

Signed,

> Chairman, Board of Directors,
> and Chief Executive Officer
> Date [February 24, 2006]
> [Conine D. McDaniel]
> Vice Presdent and Controller
> Date [February 24, 20X6]
> [Gary P. Fayard]
> Executive Vice President
> and Chief Financial Officer
> Date[February 24, 20X6]

EXHIBIT 9-12   Report of the Independent Auditors on Internal Control

Report of Independent Registered Public Accounting Firm on Internal Control Over Financial Reporting

Board of Directors and Shareholders

[The Coca-Cola Company]

[We have audited management's assessment, included in the accompanying Report of Management on Internal Control Over Financial Reporting, that The Coca-Cola Company and subsidiaries maintained effective internal control over financial reporting as of December 31, 20X5, based on criteria established in Internal Control-Integrated Framework issued by the Committee of Sponsoring Organizations of the Treadway Commission (the COSO criteria). The Coca-Cola Company's management is responsible for maintaining effective internal control over financial reporting and

(Continued)

EXHIBIT 9-12 Report of the Independent Auditors on Internal Control (*Continued*)

for its assessment of the effectiveness of internal control over financial reporting. Our responsibility is to express an opinion on management's assessment and an opinion on the effectiveness of the Company's internal control over financial reporting based on our audit.]

We conducted our audit in accordance with the standards of the Public Company Accounting Oversight Board (United States). Those standards require that we plan and perform the audit to obtain reasonable assurance about whether effective internal control over financial reporting was maintained in all material respects. Our audit included obtaining an understanding of internal control over financial reporting, evaluating management's assessment, testing and evaluating the design and operating effectiveness of internal control, and performing such other procedures as we considered necessary in the circumstances. We believe that our audit provides a reasonable basis for our opinion.

A company's internal control over financial reporting is a process designed to provide reasonable assurance regarding the reliability of financial reporting and the preparation of financial statements for external purposes in accordance with generally accepted accounting principles. A company's internal control over financial reporting includes those policies and procedures that (1) pertain to the maintenance of records that, in reasonable detail, accurately and fairly reflect the transactions and dispositions of the assets of the company; (2) provide reasonable assurance that transactions are recorded as necessary to permit preparation of financial statements in accordance with generally accepted accounting principles, and that receipts and expenditures of the company are being made only in accordance with authorizations of management and directors of the company; and (3) provide reasonable assurance regarding prevention or timely detection of unauthorized acquisition, use, or disposition of the company's assets that could have a material effect on the financial statements.

Because of its inherent limitations, internal control over financial reporting may not prevent or detect misstatements. Also projections of any evaluation of effectiveness to future periods are subject to the risk that controls may become inadequate because of changes in conditions, or that the degree of compliance with the policies or procedures may deteriorate.

In our opinion, management's assessment that The Coca-Cola Company and its subsidiaries maintained effective control over financial reporting as of December 31, 20X5, is fairly stated, in all material respects, based on the COSO criteria. Also, in our opinion, the [Coca-Cola] Company and subsidiaries maintained, in all material respects, effective internal control over financial reporting as of December 31, 20X5, based on the COSO criteria.

We also have audited, in accordance with the standards of the Public Company Accounting Oversight Board (United States), the consolidated balance sheets of The Coca-Cola Company and subsidiaries as of December 31, 20X5 and 20X4, and the related consolidated statements of income, shareholders' equity, and cash flows for each of the three years in the period ended December 31, 20X5, and our report dated February 24, 20X6, expressed an unqualified opinion thereon.

Name of Audit Firm
Date

[Atlanta, Georgia
February 24, 20X6]

company's external auditors. Infosys also provides an excellent example of voluntary corporate governance disclosures. See Appendix 1-3 in Chapter 1.

Additional factors that help to explain the growth and recognition and importance of internal auditing include:

1. Ever-increasing corporate management accountability
2. Increasing organizatinal complexities, especially in multinational enterprises

3. Growth of corporate mergers, acquisitions, and restructurings
4. Growing use of electronic funds remittances and other transfers for illicit purposes(i.e., money laundering)
5. Increased reliance on internal auditing by external auditors(i.e., greater reliance on the work of an internal auditor improves the economics of the attest function.),
6. Increase of regulatory requirements for the performance of internal audits the likes of Sarbanes-Oxley(SOX)

Evidence from Asia(e.g., Japan recently enacted its own version of SOX) and Europe also points to expansion of internal auditing within larger corporations worldwide.

Still another explanation is probably found in the world economic environment. The phenomenon of global competition, described in Chapter 1, has resulted in thinning corporate profit margins highlighting the importance of cost and expense controls. Internal auditing plays an important role in monitoring such controls.

Professional Organization

Professional focus for internal auditing is provided by the Institute of Internal Auditors (IIA), which is headquartered in the United States and has an international membership. Established in 1941, IIA is committed to:

- Providing, on an international scale, comprehensive professional development activities, standards for the practice of internal auditing, and certification
- Researching, disseminating, and promoting to its members and to the public throughout the world, knowledge and information concerning internal auditing, including internal control and related subjects
- Establishing meetings worldwide in order to educate members and others as to the practice of internal auditing as it exists in various countries throughout the world
- Bringing together internal auditors and promoting education in the field of internal auditing

The professional examination and certification activites of IIA leads to qualification as a Certified Internal Auditor (CIA). The CIA designation is the only globally-accepted certification for internal auditors. At present, the IIA boasts a membership approaching 130,000 from 165 countries.

Evolving Role of Internal Auditing

The role of internal auditors has evolved over time. Initial growth of internal auditing was initially evidenced in Europe where many countries enacted regulations specifically referring to internal audit functions and requirements. Early auditors adopted a "traffic cop" mentality in their work. They were largely concerned with ascertaining the extent of compliance with established policies, plans and procedures, verifying a firm's assets, and reconciling inventory and cash to accounting records. It is not suprising that management views of internal auditing were generally guarded with internal auditors being regarded as necessary evils. Your authors have personally observed instances where managers were loathe to communicate with auditors. In turn, internal auditors were always trying to catch managers doing something wrong.

This type of situation is wasteful and detrimental to the health of the organization and its stakeholders, including financial statement users.

In an environment of global competition, managers today are looking to internal auditors for expertise that transcends traditional control functions. The major international public accounting firm of PricewaterhouseCoopers offers ten imperatives to internal auditors to improve their value to companies operating in a post-Enron world.[36] They are:

1. Sharpen dialog with top management and directors in order to clearly establish the value-added objectives of internal audit(i.e., strategic issues, risk management and protection of company assets).
2. Realign to meet key stakeholders' expectations(stockholders, executive management, external auditors and market regulators).
3. Think and act strategically.
4. Expand audit coverage to include "tone set at the top," the conduct of executive management in protecting the company.
5. Assess and strengthen expertise for complex business auditing.
6. Leverage technology in high-risk areas.
7. Focus on enterprise risk management capabilities.
8. Make the audit process dynamic.
9. Strengthen quality assurance processes.
10. Measure the enhanced performance against expectations of shareholders.

The idea here is that if the internal audit function is considered a mere policing function, management support will continue to be lukewarm as manifested by their continual questioning of internal audit costs. This will not serve the organization nor its major constituents well. If auditors are viewed as contributing members of the management team and provide helpful managerial advice, for example, on how to control a firm's risk exposures, they will be valued and their costs deemed more than acceptable.

Being a valued advisor to management need not and should not compromise an auditor's independence. Compromising ones integrity does not earn management's respect. Doing so would increase the risk that management would violate their fiduciary responsibility to maintain a sound system of internal controls which is now mandated by law. Rather management would value and embrace auditors who (1) fulfill their responsibilitiies to their key constuents, i.e., readers of the firm's financial reports and (2) are talented enough to offer advice that helps a firm to maintain its international competitiveness.

---

[36]Seymour Jones, "Internal Auditing," in Frederick D.S. Choi, *International Finance and Accounting Handbook, 3rd. ed.,* New York: John Wiley & Sons, 2003, p. 32.13.

APPENDICES

APPENDIX 9-1

Illustration of Restatement of Japanese GAAP Financial Statements to a U.S. GAAP Basis

In this appendix we show how GAAP restatements might be used to reduce the effects of accounting diversity. Exhibit 9-13 contains the year-end financial statements of Toyoza Enterprises (Japan) and Lincoln Enterprises (United States), with relevant notes.

EXHIBIT 9-13 Year-End Unadjusted Financial Statements and Related Notes

	Toyoza Enterprises *(¥Thousands)*	*Lincoln Enterprises* *($Thousands)*
Income Statements		
Sales	¥1,400,000	$12,000
Operating expenses:		
Cost of sales	1,120,000	10,044
Selling and administrative	100,000	575
Other operating	114,200	319
Goodwill amortization		10
Operating income	¥ 65,800	$ 1,052
Gains (losses)		
Interest expenses	28,000	130
Income before taxes	37,800	922
Income taxes	23,800	258
Income after taxes	14,000	664
Equity in earnings of unconsolidated subsidiaries		116
Net income	¥ 14,000	$ 780
Balance Sheets		
Cash	¥ 124,500	$ 1,920
Accounts receivable, net	510,000	1,660
Marketable securities	45,000	500
Inventory	390,000	1,680
Investments	150,000	1,000
Plant and equipment, net	280,500	5,160
Goodwill	—	80
Total assets	¥1,500,000	$12,000
Short-term payables	¥ 165,000	$ 1,800
Short-term debt	525,000	2,160
Deferred taxes	—	—

(Continued)

EXHIBIT 9-13   Year-End Unadjusted Financial Statements and Related
Notes (*Continued*)

	Toyoza *Enterprises* *(¥Thousands)*	*Lincoln* *Enterprises* *($Thousands)*
Other current liabilities	90,000	—
Long-term debt	520,000	2,400
Reserves	90,000	—
Capital stock	75,000	960
Retained earnings	35,000	4,680
Total liabilities and owners' equity	¥1,500,000	$12,000

Notes to Toyoza's Financial Statements:

1. The balance sheet and income statement were prepared in accordance with the Japanese Commercial Code and related regulations.

2. Investments in subsidiaries and affiliated companies are accounted for using the equity method.

3. Inventories are stated at average cost. Ending inventories restated to a FIFO basis would have been ¥198 million higher.

4. Plant and equipment are carried at cost. Depreciation, with minor exceptions, is computed by the sum-of-the-years-digits method. Plant and equipment, purchased 2 years ago, have an estimated life of 4 years.

5. Operating expenses include lease rental payments of ¥40 million. The average term of the lease contracts is 4 years. All leases transfer ownership to the lessor at the end of the lease term. Lincoln Enterprises' cost of capital is estimated to be 8 percent.

6. A translation gain of ¥20 million relating to consolidation of foreign operations with a net monetary liability position is being deferred under long-term debt.

7. Purchased goodwill is amortized over 20 years. The current period's amortization expense is ¥12 million for the year and is included under other operating expenses. Under a U.S. GAAP impairments test, it would have been 10% of that amount.

8. Toyoza Enterprises is allowed to set up special-purpose reserves (i.e., government-sanctioned charges against earnings) equal to a certain percentage of total export revenues. This year's charge (including other operating expenses) was ¥26,400,000. Similarly, this year's addition to Toyoza's general-purpose reserves was ¥30,800,000.

9. The ¥/$ exchange rate at year-end was ¥110 = $1.

10. Toyoza Enterprise's marginal income tax rate is 35 percent.

Notes to Lincoln Enterprises' financial statements:

1. The balance sheet and income statement are based on U.S. GAAP.

2. Inventories are carried at FIFO cost.

3. Plant and equipment are depreciated in straight-line fashion.

4. Foreign operations are consolidated with those of the parent using the temporal method of currency translation as Lincoln adopts the U.S. dollar as its functional currency.

Comparative financial ratios for Toyoza and Lincoln Enterprises are provided in Exhibit 9-14.

Based on this preliminary analysis, Toyoza appears less liquid, less efficient, less profitable, and financially less solvent than Lincoln Enterprises. But is it? A good analyst will attempt to ascertain to what extent these observed differences are due to real economic differences versus differences in accounting measurements and other environmental influences.

EXHIBIT 9-14   Comparative Financial Ratios Based on Unadjusted Data

	Toyoza	Lincoln
Liquidity		
Current ratio	1.37x	1.45x
Acid-test ratio	.87x	1.03x
Efficiency		
Receivables turnover	2.75x	7.23x
Inventory turnover	2.87x	5.98x
Asset turnover	.93x	1.00x
Profitability		
Profit margin	1.0%	6.5%
Return on assets	4.4%	9.7%
Return on equity	12.7%	13.8%
Coverage		
Debt to total assets	92.7%	53.0%
Times interest earned	2.4x	8.9x

To aid comparison with Lincoln, we restate Toyoza's statements to a U.S. GAAP basis. Based on the information provided and examining the notes in sequence, the following adjustments are required:

1. Inventories are adjusted to reflect differences in costing methods. Adjustments would increase inventories and decrease cost of sales by ¥198,000.
2. The difference between straight-line and sum-of-the-year's-digits depreciation for the current year yields an adjustment to cost of sales and net plant and equipment of ¥46,750. The difference in depreciation for the preceding year is ¥140,250. Based on a marginal tax rate of 35 percent, the ¥140,250 increase in reported pre-tax earnings would create ¥49,088 in deferred taxes with the balance credited to retained earnings.
3. Under U.S. GAAP the lease transaction would be capitalized. Discounting the stream of ¥40,000,000 rental payments for 5 years at 8 percent yields a present value of ¥159,600,000 attributed to both a leased asset and a lease obligation. Based on this amount,

we can break down the ¥40,000,000 lease payment into an interest payment of ¥12,768,000 and a ¥27,232,000 reduction of the lease obligation. Straight-line depreciation would yield an expense of ¥31,920,000.

4. Under SFAS No. 52 the translation gain would be removed from long-term debt and included in income.
5. Compared to U.S. GAAP, the goodwill amortization expense is ¥10,800,000 larger. We would make an adjusting entry to recognize an asset and reduce operating expenses.
6. As the United States does not permit discretionary reserves, these reserves would be removed and included in income. Moreover, they would be reclassified as equity as opposed to debt.
7. These adjustments, which Exhibit 9-15 summarizes in spreadsheet form, increase Toyoza's restated earnings by ¥220,240,000. Of this, ¥20,000,000 relating to the translation gain is not recognized for tax purposes. This yields a tax expense of ¥107,822,000 and a balance of ¥107,822,000 currently payable.

EXHIBIT 9-15 Adjustment Spreadsheet

	Unadjusted	*Adjustments*	*Adjusted*	*Dollars*
Sales	¥1,400,000		¥1,400,000	$12,727
-Operating expenses:				
Cost of sales	1,120,000	1) (198,000)		
		2a) (46,750)		
		3) 31,920	907,170	8,247
Selling and administrative	100,000		100,000	909
Other operating	114,200	3) (40,000)		
		5) (10,800)		
		6) (26,400)		
		7) (30,800)	6,200	56
Losses (gains)	—	4) (20,000)	(20,000)	(182)
Interest	28,000	3) 12,768	40,768	371
Taxes	23,800	7) 107,822	131,622	1,197
Net income	¥ 14,000	8) 220,240	¥ 234,240	$ 2,129
Cash	¥ 124,500		¥ 124,500	$ 1,132
Accounts receivable	510,000		510,000	4,636
Marketable securities	45,000		45,000	409
Inventory	390,000	3) 198,000	588,000	5,345
Investments	150,000		150,000	1,364
Plant and equipment, net	280,500	2a) 46,750		
		2b) 140,250		
		3) 127,680	595,180	5,411
Goodwill		7) 10,800	10,800	98
Total assets	¥1,500,000		¥2,023,480	$18,395
Short-term payables	¥ 165,000		¥ 165,000	$ 1,500
Short-term debt	525,000		525,000	4,773
Deferred taxes	—			
Other current liabilities	90,000	2b) 49,088		
		7) 107,822	246,910	2,244
Long-term debt	520,000	4) (20,000)		
		3) 132,368	632,368	5,749
Reserves	90,000	6) 26,400		
		6) 30,800	32,800	298
Capital stock	75,000		75,000	682
Retained earnings	35,000	2b) 91,162		
		8) 220,240	346,402	3,149
Total liabilities and owners' equity	¥1,500,000		¥2,023,480	$18,395

Exhibit 9-16 shows a ratio comparison of Toyoza and Lincoln Enterprises based on data adjusted for accounting differences. As can be seen, adjusted ratios show a much improved profitability picture for Toyoza. However, liquidity and efficiency ratios have worsened. While solvency (coverage) ratios have improved, the debt to total assets ratio remains exceedingly high by U.S. standards.

If accounting principle differences were the only differences among countries, adjustments such as those illustrated above would be sufficient to enable anyone to analyze and interpret foreign financial statements without ambiguity. Unfortunately, institutional and cultural differences among countries are not constant. If these differences are major, further analysis is necessary to ensure proper analysis and understanding. Appendix 9-2 amplifies this important point.

EXHIBIT 9-16 Comparative Financial Ratios Based on Adjusted Data		
	Toyoza	*Lincoln*
Liquidity		
Current ratio	1.35x	1.45x
Acid-test ratio	.73x	1.03x
Efficiency		
Receivables turnover	2.75x	7.23x
Inventory turnover	1.54x	5.98x
Asset turnover	.69x	1.00x
Profitability		
Profit margin	16.7%	6.5%
Return on assets	20.1%	9.7%
Return on equity	51.5%	13.8%
Coverage		
Debt to total assets	77.6%	53.0%
Times interest earned	9.9x	8.9x

APPENDIX 9-2

International Ratio Analysis[37]

Financial ratio analysis is a well-established tool for financial performance evaluation, credit analysis, and security analysis. While financial ratios may correctly measure liquidity, efficiency, and profitability in within-country comparisons, they are often misused when applied to cross-border financial comparisons, due in part to accounting principle differences. A more serious problem is that investors may misinterpret these ratios because they do not understand a foreign environment, even when financial statements have been restated to a common set of accounting principles.

---

[37]The following discussion is taken from a three-nation study by collaborators in Japan, Korea, and the United States. Participants in that study were Messers. Hisaaki Hino of Morgan Guaranty Trust Company, Junichi Ujiie of Nomura Securities Company, Ltd., Professors Sang Kee Min and Sang Oh Nam of Seoul National University, and Professor Arthur I. Stonehill of Oregon State University and Frederick D.S. Choi of New York University.

Consider Japan. An initial comparison of aggregate financial ratios for Japanese and U.S. firms reveals striking differences. Japanese companies generally appear less liquid, less solvent, less efficient, and less profitable than their U.S. counterparts. However, after Japanese ratios are adjusted for differences between Japanese and U.S. GAAP, they are still very different from ratios found in comparable U.S. companies.

ENVIRONMENTAL CONSIDERATIONS

Japanese companies appear to have very high leverage. For example, an earlier study conducted by the SEC found that mean leverage (total debt/shareholders' equity) in their Japan sample was 2.032, compared with 0.514 in the U.S. sample. However, high debt ratios traditionally have not been major sources of concern in Japan. Part of the reason is historical.

When the Japanese government (under pressure from the United States) ended 200 years of isolation in the mid-19th century, it made rapid economic growth and development a major national goal. To achieve this goal, the government established an extensive banking infrastructure to supply industry with most of its financing. The dependence of industrial companies on the banking system increased after World War II. Large, new industrial groupings called keiretsu evolved with major commercial banks at their core. Linked through business and personal ties, banks and their associated companies are very close. When loans become delinquent, banks (often) extend the terms of repayment or (occasionally) refinance the loan. A bank might even install a key bank official as president or board member of a troubled company to help it out.

Other companies in the keiretsu can prepay receivables owed to the distressed firm and allow longer periods for that firm to repay its receivables. With this ability to manipulate and postpone interest and principal payments, long-term debt in Japan works more like equity in the United States.[38]

Because long-term debt in Japan has many of the characteristics of preferred stock, interest payments in Japan can be likened to dividends.

Accordingly, interest coverage ratios, which are generally much lower in Japan than in the United States, are not viewed with much concern. Earnings in Japan beyond those needed to make loan payments benefit the bank little. When loans are negotiated, the borrower makes (and seldom discloses) a general agreement to give the bank collateral or guarantees upon the bank's request. Also at the bank's request, borrowing companies must submit their year-end proposed appropriation of revenue (including dividends) to the bank before it can be submitted to shareholders for approval. Banks customarily insist on compensating balances even though they are illegal, with 20 to 50 percent of company borrowings reportedly kept with the bank as time (or other) deposits. Under these conditions, low interest coverage usually does not mean a high risk of default.

Institutional and cultural factors also affect liquidity ratios without necessarily changing the financial risk that the ratios are designed to measure. For example, an American reader who sees the relatively low current ratios of Japanese companies (resulting from relatively high short-term debt) might conclude that Japanese companies have a relatively lower ability to cover their short-term debt. In Japan, however, high short-term debt seldom indicates a lack of liquidity. Short-term debt is attractive

---

[38]The gradual liberalization of Japan's financial system is increasing the exceptions to this practice.

to companies because short-term obligations typically have lower interest rates than long-term obligations. Moreover, short-term borrowings in Japan are seldom repaid but normally are renewed or rolled over. Banks are happy to renew these loans as this allows them to adjust their interest rates to changing market conditions. Thus, short-term debt in Japan works like long-term debt elsewhere. In fact, the use of short-term debt to finance long-term assets appears to be the rule, not the exception, in Japan.

Longer average collection periods also reflect differences in business customs. Purchases in Japan are rarely made in cash. Postdated checks with maturities ranging between 60 and 90 days are common. The Japanese tradition of lifetime employment has some influence on collection policies. Companies often go to great lengths to accommodate their commercial customers. During business downturns, companies extend repayment terms to avoid placing their customers in a financial bind that might force them to discharge employees. In return, continued patronage ensures stability in employment (and other respects) for the selling company. Inventory turnover numbers are similarly affected.

During slack periods, manufacturing companies prefer to continue production and build inventories rather than idle workers. Japanese managers are not as concerned with short-term profits as their U.S. counterparts. They have more job security than prevails in the United States. Equity shares in Japanese companies are largely held by related commercial banks, suppliers, and customers. These shareholders are more interested in maintaining their close business ties than in stock market gains, and will hold shares on a long-term basis regardless of short-term market performance.

Corporate managers in Japan believe that increased market share will ensure long-run profits. For this reason, sales growth is a main objective. Growing sales contribute to higher employment and greater job security, and as such are consistent with the tradition of lifetime employment. Because all Japanese enterprises seek sales growth, price competition is intense, resulting in low profit margin and profitability statistics. This is especially so for large companies that usually sell heavily in extremely competitive export markets.

So, are Japanese companies truly more risky, less efficient, and less profitable than their U.S. counterparts? Not necessarily.

In Europe, national characteristics also appear to strongly influence profit measurement. Large companies in France and Germany tend to be more conservative in measuring profits than large companies in the United Kingdom. Also important are tax laws and reliance on lenders rather than investors for capital.

Thus, when analyzing foreign financial statements, readers must be careful to determine whether observed differences in firm performance result from: (a) accounting measurement differences; (b) economic, cultural, or institutional differences; or (c) real differences in the attributes being measured.

SELECTED REFERENCES

Ashbaugh, H., and M. Pincus, "Domestic Accounting Standards, International Accounting Standards and the Predictability of Earnings," Journal of Accounting Research 39 No. 3 (2001): 417–434.

Basu, S., L. Hwang, and C.L. Jain, "International Variation in Accounting Measurement Rules and Analysts' Earning Forecast Errors," Journal of Business Finance and Accounting 25, Nos. 9&10 (1998): 1207–1247.

Bradshaw, Mark T. Brian Bushee, and Gregory S. Miller, "Accounting Choice, Home Bias, and U.S. Investment in Non-U.S. Firms," *Journal of Accounting Research*, Vol. 42 No. 5(2004): 795–841.

Capstaff, J., K. Paudyal, and W. Rees, "A Comparative Analysis of Earnings Forecasts in Europe," Journal of Business Finance and Accounting 28, Nos. 5&6 (2001): 531–562.

Damodaran, Aswath, "Valuation in Emerging Markets," in International Finance and Accounting Handbook, 3rd ed., F.D.S. Choi, ed., New York: John Wiley & Sons, 2003, pp. 9.1–9.38.

Davidson, Ryan, Jenny Goodwin Stewart, and Pamela Kent, "Internal Governance Structures and Earnings Management," *Accounting and Finance*, Vol. 45 No. 2(2005): 241–267.

Demirakos, Efthimios G., Norman C. Strong and Martin Walker, "What Valuation Models Do Analysts Use?" *Accounting Horizons*, Vol. 18 No. 4(2004): 221–240.

Erb, Claude B., Campbell R. Harvey, and Tadas E. Viskanta, Country Risk in Global Financial Management, Charlottesville, VA: Association for Investment Management and Research, 1998.

Evans, Lisa, "Language, Translation and the Problem of International Accounting Communication," *Accounting, Auditing and Accountability Journal*, Vol. 17 No. 2(2004): 248.

Farber, David B. "Restoring Trust After Fraud: Does Corporate Governance Matter?" *Accounting Review*, Vol. 80 No. 2(2005): 539–561.

Frost, Carol Ann, Elizabeth Gordon, and Andrew F. Hayes,"Stock Exchange Disclosure and Market Development: An Analysis of 50 International Exchanges," Journal of Accounting Research, Vol. 44 No. 3(2006): 437–483.

Hope, Ole-Kristian, "Variations in the Financial Reporting Environment and Earnings Forecasting," Journal of International Financial Management and Accounting 15, No. 1 (2004): 21–43.

Hung, M., "Accounting Standards and Value Relevance of Earnings: An International Analysis," Journal of Accounting and Economics 30, No. 3 (2000): 401–420.

Jiang, Li and Jeong-Bon Kim, "Foreign Equity Ownership and Information Asymmetry: Evidence from Japan," *Journal of International Financial Management and Accounting*, Vol. 15 No. 3(2004): 185–211.

Jones, Seymour, "Internal Auditing," in Frederick D.S. Choi, *International Finance and Accounting Handbook, 3rd ed.,* New York: John Wiley & Sons, 2003, Chapter 32.

Land, J. and M. Lang, "Empirical Evidence on the Evolution of International Earnings," *The Accounting Review*, Vol. 77(2001): 115–133.

Lang, M., J. Raedy, and W. Wilson, "Earnings Management and Cross Listing: Are Reconciled Earnings Comparable to U.S. Earnings?" Working paper, University of North Carolina.

Loft, Anne, Christopher Humphrey, and Stuart Turley, "In Pursuit of Global Regulation: Changing Governance and Accountability Structures at the International Federation of Accountants(IFAC)," *Accounting, Auditing and Accountability Journal*, Vol. 19 No. 3(2006), p. 451.

Murdock, Herman, "Global Auditing: Challenges and Opportunities for Internal Auditors," *Internal Auditing*, Vol. 21 No. 6(2006).

Palepu, Krishna G., Victor L. Bernard, and Paul M. Healy, Business Analysis and Valuation Using Financial Statements, Cincinnati, OH: South-Western College Publishing, 1996.

DISCUSSION QUESTIONS

1. What are the four main steps in doing a business strategy analysis using financial statements? Why, at each step, is analysis in a cross-border context more difficult than a single-country analysis?

2. What are the information needs of four user groups that rely on foreign financial statements for their financial decisions? Are the four main steps in financial statement analysis equally important to your four groups? If not, what are the differences?

3. One interpretation of the popular efficient markets hypothesis is that the market fully impounds all public information as soon as it becomes available. Thus, it is supposedly not possible to beat the market if fundamental financial analysis techniques are applied to publicly available information such as a firm's published accounts. Why might this hypothesis be more tenable in the United States than in other international capital markets?

4. Describe the impact on accounting analysis of cross-country variations in accounting measurement and disclosure practices.

5. Choi and Levich found that investors cope with accounting principles differences in two fundamentally different ways. What are these coping mechanisms and which of the two do you favor?

6. What are common pitfalls to avoid in conducting an international prospective analysis?

7. How does the translation of foreign currency financial statements differ from the foreign currency translation process described in Chapter 6?

8. The quick (or acid test) ratio is frequently used to assess the short-term debt-paying ability of a business enterprise. As a rule of thumb, U.S. commercial lenders often consider a ratio of at least 1 to 1 to be satisfactory. Why might it be inappropriate to apply this standard when evaluating the liquidity of a non-U.S. company?

9. If you were asked to provide the five most important recommendations you could think of to others analyzing nondomestic financial statements, what would they be?

10. ABC Company, a U.S.-based MNC, uses the temporal translation method (see Chapter 6) in consolidating the results of its foreign operations. Translation gains or losses incurred upon consolidation are reflected immediately in reported earnings. Company XYZ, a Dutch MNC, employs the current rate method with translation gains and losses going into owners' equity. What financial ratios are most likely to be affected by these different accounting principles, and what are the implications for security analysts?

11. What role does the attest function play in international financial statement analysis?

12. What is internal control, how do internal auditors relate to it, and how does this process relate to the analysis of financial statements?

EXERCISES

1. Condensed comparative income statements of Señorina Panchos, a Mexican restaurant chain, for the years 20X5 through 20X7 are presented in Exhibit 9-17 (000,000's pesos). You are interested in gauging the past trend in dividends paid by Señorina Panchos from a dollar perspective. The company's payout ratio (ratio of dividends paid to reported earnings) has averaged 30 percent. Foreign exchange rates during the 3-year period are found in Exhibit 9-18.

EXHIBIT 9-17   Comparative Income Statements: Señorina Panchos

	20X6	20X7	20X8
Sales	91,600	114,300	138,900
Gross margin	15,500	20,500	27,700
Net income	8,500	10,800	15,900

EXHIBIT 9-18   Foreign Exchange Rates

	20X6	20X7	20X8
Year-end rates	$1 = P 12.112	$1 = P 12.640	$1 = P 13.000

Required: Prepare a trend analysis of dividends paid by Señorina Panchos from a U.S. perspective assuming (a) there are no restrictions on the payment of dividends to U.S. investors and (b) Señorina Panchos' accounting practices are similar to those in the United States.

2. Based on the balance sheet and income statement data contained in Exhibit 9-5, and using the suggested worksheet format shown in Exhibit 9-19 or one of your own choosing, show how the statement of cash flows appearing in Exhibit 9-5 was derived.

3. Refer again to Exhibits 9-5 and 9-6. Show how you would modify the consolidated funds statement appearing in Exhibit 9-5 to enable an investor to get a better feel for the actual investing and financing activities of the Norwegian subsidiary.

4. Infosys Technologies, introduced in Chapter 1, regularly provides investors with a performance measure called *economic value-added*(EVA). Pioneered by GE, EVA measures the profitability of a company after deducting not just the cost of borrowing, but also the firm's cost of equity capital as well. So EVA is the after-tax return *on* capital employed (adjusted for the tax shield on debt) less the cost *of* capital employed. Companies that earn a higher return on capital employed than its cost of capital create value for its shareholders. Those that do not destroy shareholder value.

Reproduced below is EVA calculations for Infosys for 2006.

Required:

1. Did Infosys create value for its shareholders?
2. Is EVA a useful performance metric relative to net income?(Compare PAT or profit after tax, and EVA to average capital employed.)

Cost of capital:	
Cost of risk-free debt(%)	7.50
Market premium	7.00
Beta variant	0.78
Cost of equity(%)	12.96
Average debt/Total capital(%)	—
Cost of debt – net of tax(%)	NA
Weighted average cost of capital(%)	12.96
Average capital employed	6,177
PAT as % of average capital employed(%)	40.14
Economic Value Added:	
Operating profit(excluding extraordinary income)	2,654
Less: Taxes	313
Less: Cost of capital	801
EVA	1,540
Ratios:	
EVA as a percentage of average capital employed(%)	24.93

EXHIBIT 9-19   Statement of Cash Flow Worksheet

	Beginning Balance	Debit	Credit	Ending Balance
Balance sheet items (detailed)		Sources of Funds	Uses of Funds	
Net change in Cash				

5. Read Appendix 9-1. Referring to Exhibit 9-14 and related notes, assume instead that Toyoza's inventories were costed using the FIFO method and that Lincoln Enterprises employed the LIFO method. Provide the adjusting journal entries to restate Toyoza's inventories to a LIFO basis, assuming that ending inventories would have been ¥250 million lower under the LIFO method.

6. The following sales revenue pattern for a British trading concern was cited earlier in the chapter:

	20X6	20X7	20X8
Sales revenue	£23,500	£28,650	£33,160

Required:

a. Perform a convenience translation into U.S. dollars for each year given the following year-end exchange rates:

20X6	£1 = $2.10
20X7	£1 = $2.20
20X8	£1 = $1.60

b. Compare the year-to-year percentage changes in sales revenues in pounds and in U.S. dollars. Do the two time series move in parallel fashion? Why or why not?

c. Suggest a method for minimizing the effect of exchange rate changes on foreign currency trend data.

7. Exhibit 9-20 provides a recent summary of the Volvo Group's net income and shareholders' equity determined in accordance with Swedish GAAP and U.S. GAAP.

EXHIBIT 9-20 Volvo Group's Restated Net Income and Shareholders' Equity Numbers

Net income	*20X5*
Net income in accordance with Swedish GAAP	4,709
Items increasing (decreasing) reported net income:	
Foreign currency derivatives	(654)
Income taxes	—
Business combinations	(91)
Shares and participations	24
Interest costs	(3)
Leasing	16
Investments in debt and equity securities	(548)
Items affecting comparability	(281)
Pensions and other post-employment benefits	(170)
SPP surplus funds	(523)
Software development	384
Entrance fees, aircraft engine programs	(336)
Tax effect of above U.S. GAAP adjustments	600
Net increase (decrease) in net income	(1,582)
Approximate net income in accordance with U.S. GAAP	3,127
Shareholders' equity	20X5

(Continued)

EXHIBIT 9-20 Volvo Group's Restated Net Income and Shareholders' Equity Numbers *(Continued)*

Shareholders' equity in accordance with Swedish GAAP	88,338
Items increasing (decreasing) reported shareholders' equity:	
Foreign currency derivatives	(1,286)
Income taxes	—
Business combinations	1,317
Shares and participations	36
Interest costs	112
Leasing	(163)
Investments in debt and equity securities	(6,066)
Items affecting comparability	579
Pensions and other post-employment benefits	109
SPP surplus funds	(523)
Software development	754
Entrance fees, aircraft engine programs	(387)
Other	—
Tax effect of above U.S. GAAP adjustments	1,941
Net increase (decrease) in shareholders' equity	(3,577)
Approximate shareholders' equity based on U.S. GAAP	84,761

Required:

 a. Compute the return on shareholders' equity for the year based first on Swedish GAAP, and then on U.S. GAAP.

 b. Which return statistic is the better measure of performance and why?

If you were comparing your preferred statistic in b. with a comparable statistic for a U.S. firm in a comparable industry as Volvo, what factors would you take into account in making your assessment?

 8. Refer to Exhibit 9-3. This Exhibit presents P/E ratios for public companies in various countries. What factors might explain the differences in P/E ratios that you observe?

 9. Assume you are a member of an international policy setting committee and are responsible for harmonizing audit report requirements internationally. Examine Exhibit 9-9. Based on the varying requirements you observe, what minimum set of requirements would you advocate for on behalf of the international investing community? Your committee also includes delegates from Austria, Bahrain, France, Finland, Malaysia, Nigeria, Scotland and Chile.

 10. Exhibit 9-21 presents cross-country differences in auditor liability by country and audit firm.

Required: Does the incidence of liability cases vary more by country or by auditor? In what countries is auditor litigation most frequent? Less frequent? Why? What are the implications for doing financial analysis in the 12 countries presented? Are relatively high levels of auditor litigation good or bad for financial statement users? Present reasons for your answer.

 11. Examine Exhibit 9-10. On the basis of the information provided there, which opinion gives you the most comfort as an investor in non-domestic securities?

 12. Identify three to four criteria that you would personally use to judge the merits of any corporate database. Use these criteria to rate the information content of any Web site appearing in Exhibit 9-4 as excellent, fair, or poor.

EXHIBIT 9-21   Auditor's Liability Cases by Country and Audit Firm

Country	Arthur Andersen	Coopers & Lybrand	Deloitte Touche	Ernst and Young	KPMG	Price Waterhouse Coopers	Others
Australia	1	1	4	–	3	3	2
Canada	–	3	1	2	1	–	3
Germany	–	–	–	1	–	1	–
Hong Kong	–	–	1	–	–	1	–
Ireland	–	–	–	1	–	–	1
Italy	1	–	–	1	2	2	1
Netherlands	–	–	–	1	–	–	–
New Zealand	–	–	–	1	1	–	1
Spain	1	1	–	1	–	2	–
Sweden	–	–	–	–	1	1	–
United Kingdom	1	3	3	2	5	1	2
United States	7	8	7	3	5	1	4
Total	11	16	16	13	18	12	14

SOURCE: Center for International Financial Analysis & Research, International Accounting and Auditing Trends, 4th ed., 1995, Vol. II, Princeton, N.J.: CIFAR Publications, Inc., 1995.

Case 9-1   Sandvik

One of the accounting development patterns that was introduced in Chapter 2 was the macroeconomic development model. Under this framework accounting practices are designed to enhance national macroeconomic goals. A national policy advocating stable employment by avoiding major swings in business cycles would sanction accounting practices that smooth income. Similarly, national policies supporting growth in certain industries would sanction rapid write-offs of fixed assets to encourage capital formation. Sweden is a good example of this reporting pattern. Assets may be revalued upwards if they are deemed to have "enduring value," the tax law permits shorter asset lives, and ceiling tests for depreciation charges include the higher of 130 percent declining balance method or 20 percent straight line. Companies are also permitted to allocate a portion of pre-tax earnings to special tax equalization reserves which are not available for dividends until reversed.

Reproduced below are the parent company financial statements of Sandvik for the years 2004 and 2005 and selected notes. Sandvik is a global high technology company headquartered in Sweden, with advanced products and well-known brands. Its core areas of competence include high speed tools for metal working, machinery, tools and service for rock excavation and specialty steels. Examine the data presented and answer the following questions.

1. What advantages and disadvantages arise for firms that chose to employ the Swedish system of special reserves?
2. What are the potential benefits of the system of special reserves to the Swedish government?
3. In what way does the existence of the Swedish reserve system affect the ability of a financial analyst to evaluate a Swedish firm vis-à-vis a non-Swedish firm?
4. In what way does the use of "reserves" affect Sandvik's financial statements for the year 2005?
5. Show the accounting entry used to create the 2005 *Appropriations* figure.
6. If you were to unwind the effect of reserves, how would Sandvik's key profitability ratios, such as return on sales and return on assets change? ∎

PARENT COMPANY INCOME STATEMENT

Amounts in SEK M		2005	2004
Revenue	Note 2	15,242	12,984
Cost of sales and service		−11,427	−9,646
Gross profit		3,815	3,338
Selling expenses		−488	−553
Administrative expenses		−1,646	−1,620
Research and development costs	Note 4	−837	−700
Other operating income	Note 5	390	419
Other operating expenses	Note 6	−801	−25
Operating profit	Notes 3, 7, 8	433	859
Income from shares in group companies	Note 9	3,880	6,362
Income from shares in associated companies	Note 9	2	6

Income from LT investments	Note 9	0	–1
Interest income and similar items	Note 9	235	162
Interest expense and similar items	Note 9	–633	–366
Profit after financial items		3,917	7,022
Appropriations	Note 10	–185	85
Income tax expense	Note 11	–1	–193
Profit for the year		3,731	6,914

PARENT COMPANY BALANCE SHEET

Amounts in SEK M		2005	2004
Assets			
Non-current assets			
Intangible assets			
Patents and similar rights	Note 14	50	27
Property, plant & equipment:			
Land and buildings	Note 14	478	474
Plant and machinery	Note 14	3,543	3,391
Equipment, tools and installations	Note 14	312	310
CIP and advance payments	Note 14	567	624
		4,900	4,799
Financial assets:			
Shares in group companies	Note 15	10,521	6,815
Advances to group companies		94	207
Investments in associated companies	Note 16	8	8
Advances to associated companies		1	1
Other investments		0	0
Non-current receivables	Note 18	22	22
		10,646	7,053
Total non-current assets		15,596	11,879
Current assets			
Inventories	Note 19	3,857	3,385
Current receivables			
Trade receivables		828	637
Due from group companies		16,873	5,282
Due from associated companies		82	146
Income tax receivables	Note 11	169	260
Other receivables	Note 18	287	275
Prepaid expenses and accrued income		440	422
		18,679	7,022
Cash and cash equivalents		10	—
Total current assets		22,546	10,407
Total assets		38,142	22,286

EQUITY AND LIABILITIES

Equity			
Nondistributable equity			
Share capital		1,424	1,581
Share premium reserve		—	1,057
Legal reserve		1,611	297
		3,035	2,935
Distributable equity			
Profit brought forward		1,008	802
Profit for the year		3,731	6,914
		4,739	7,716
Total equity	Note 20	7,774	10,651

Untaxed reserves			
Accelerated depreciation	Note 21	2,287	2,115
Tax allocation reserves	Note 22	1,076	1,076
Other untaxed reserves	Note 22	26	13
		3,389	3,204
Provisions			
Provisions for pensions	Note 23	103	97
Provision for taxes	Note 11	133	117
Other provisions	Note 24	143	74
		379	288
Non-current interest bearing liabilities			
Loans from financial institutions	Note 25	894	378
Loans from group companies	Note 25	39	138
Other liabilities	Note 25	3,075	3,808
Non-current noninterest-bearing liabilities			
Deferred tax liabilities	Note 11	5	7
Other liabilities		9	9
		14	16
Current interest-bearing liabilities			
Loans from financial institutions(overdraft facility)		—	13
Loans from group companies		18,343	220
Other liabilities		1,016	29
		19,359	262
Current noninterest-bearing liabilities			
Advances from customers		19	75
Accounts payable		1,110	822
Due to group companies		158	1,418
Due to associated companies		79	36
Other liabilities		78	70
Accrued expenses and deferred income	Note 28	1,775	1,120
		3,219	3,541
Total equity and liabilities		38,142	22,286
Contingent liabilities	Note 29	11,171	7,195

Notes:

NOTE 10 APPROPRIATIONS

Parent Company	2005	2004
Accelerated depreciation	−172	−168
Change in tax allocation reserves	—	254
Change in other untaxed revenues	−13	−1
Total	−185	85

The Parent Company's effective tax rate of 0.03% is less than the nominal tax rate in Sweden, mainly due to tax-exempt dividend income from subsidiaries and associated companies.

NOTE 11 INCOME TAX

Current tax	4	−157
Adjustment of taxes attributable to prior years	−7	−43
Total current tax expense	−3	−200
Deferred tax relating to temporary differences and unused tax losses	2	7
Share of taxes of associated companies	—	—
Total tax expense	−1	−193

The Group's tax expense for the year was SEK2,427 M (1,766) or 27.5% of the profit after financial items.

NOTE 21 PARENT COMPANY'S ACCELERATED DEPRECIATION

	Land and Buildings	Plant and Machinery	Equipment Tools and Installations	Patents and Similar Rights	Total
Balance at 1 January 2004	11	1,730	205	—	1,946
Accelerated Depreciation for the yr	-7	190	-29	15	169
Balance at 31 December 2004	4	1,920	176	15	2,115
Balance at 1 January 2005	4	1,920	176	15	2,115
Accelerated depreciation for the yr	-3	155	6	14	172
Balance at 31 December 2005	1	2,075	182	29	2,287

NOTE 22 PARENT COMPANY'S OTHER UNTAXED RESERVES

	2005	2004
Tax allocation reserves		
Appropriated at 2001 tax assessment	437	437
Appropriated at 2002 tax assessment	435	435
Appropriated at 2004 tax assessment	204	204
Balance at 31 December 2005	1,076	1,076
Other untaxed reserves	26	13
Total untaxed reserves	1,102	1,089

Case 9-2   Continental A.G.

Dietrich Becker and Marisa Skye, tire analysts for a global investment fund located in Manhattan, are examining the 20X0 earnings performance of two potential investment candidates. Reflecting the company's investment philosophy of picking the best stocks wherever they are located in the world, both junior analysts have adopted an approach of undertaking matched comparisons of leading firms in the tire industry. For starters, Dietrich and Marisa focused on Goodyear Tire & Rubber Company (United States) and Continental A.G. (Germany) as their first screen.

DIETRICH: Well, what do you think, Marisa?

MARISA: Looking at the income trends (see Exhibit 9-22), I sort of like Continental.

DIETRICH: Yes, I agree. Goodyear's results are much more volatile.

MARISA: I always look to see how a company has done in an off year. Owing to the continued consolidation of the tire industry, excess capacity created by reduced demand for autos and trucks, as well as reduced consumer spending for replacement tires in light of economic and political uncertainties, 20X0 was a disastrous year for every major company in the industry. Given that environment, Continental's performance was stellar!

DIETRICH: Maybe we'd better check with Prawit, our accountant, to see if we're reading the tea leaves correctly.

MARISA: I'll give him a call.

(After a 5-minute conversation)

DIETRICH: Well, what did he say?

MARISA: He said, we're probably correct in our overall assessment (I think he's just being polite), but that we'd better check the company's accounting policies. He says German accounting principles tend to impart a conservative bias to corporate earnings. He'll send us an e-mail attachment summarizing some major GAAP differences between the United States and Germany very soon.

(The e-mail attachment is reproduced as Exhibit 9-23.)

EXHIBIT 9-22 Comparative Performance Data

Goodyear ($ millions)

	19X6	19X7	19X8	19X9	20X0
Sales	9,040	9,905	10,810	10,869	11,273
Net income(loss)	124	771	350	207	(38)

Continental (DM millions)

	19X6	19X7	19X8	19X9	20X0
Sales	4,969	5,098	7,906	8,382	8,551
Net income(loss)	115	139	195	228	93

EXHIBIT 9-23 Major Accounting Differences between Germany and the United States

	Germany	*United States*
Goodwill	Written off against reserves or amortized; commercial law prescribes 4 years; most companies amortize over 15 years for tax purposes.	Capitalized and amortized subject to an impairments test.
Long-term leases	Generally no lease capitalization.	Capitalization required when specific criteria met.
Depreciation	Highest rates allowable for tax purposes.	Generally straight-line over estimated useful lives.
Inventory	Costing must mirror physical flow of goods. Average costing is common.	LIFO costing method is common.
Reserves	Use of discretionary reserves to smooth earnings are not uncommon.	Use of discretionary reserves to smooth earnings are discouraged.

MARISA: (Having examined the attachment) Looks like there are some major differences in reporting rules between Germany and the United States.

DIETRICH: Do you think we should attempt to restate Continental's accounts to a U.S. GAAP basis?

MARISA: Why don't we try.

DIETRICH: Where should we start?

MARISA: Let's examine Continental's financial statements (see Exhibit 9-24) to see if we can detect any unusual accounting practices that may have a distorting effect on the company's reported performance. I notice that Continental follows the European practice of including both parent company (Consolidated A.G.) and consolidated numbers. Let's just focus on the consolidated figures for now.

DIETRICH: Right. And if we find some disparities, maybe we should just attempt one or two adjustments, particularly those for which we have sufficient information. If these adjustments have a significant earnings impact, then let's press the right buttons and see if we can't get the company to give us some additional information so that we can do a more comprehensive analysis.

MARISA: Sounds good. Let's get started.■

EXHIBIT 9-24   Continental's Financial Statements and Related Notes

Continental Aktiengesellschaft
Consolidated Balance Sheet at December 31, 20X0

Assets	See Note No.	12/31/20X0 euro 000	12/31/19X9 euro 000
Fixed assets and investments			
Intangible assets	(1)	430,920	11,944
Property, plant, and equipment	(2)	2,196,724	1,797,125
Investments	(3)	225,729	189,428
		2,853,373	1,998,497
Current assets			
Inventories	(4)	1,611,566	1,506,771
Receivables and other assets	(5)	1,475,557	1,386,212
Marketable securities	(6)	51,426	339,219
Liquid assets	(7)	144,625	134,079
		3,283,174	3,366,281
Prepaid expenses	(8)	31,070	41,092
		6,167,617	5,405,870

Shareholders' equity and liabilities	See Note No.	12/31/20X0 euro 000	12/31/19X9 euro 000
Shareholders' equity			
Subscribed capital	(9)	439,097	435,022
Capital reserves	(10)	962,275	956,240

(Continued)

EXHIBIT 9-24 Continental's Financial Statements and Related Notes *(Continued)*

Retained earnings	(11)	137,788	133,770
Minority interests	(12)	94,286	46,692
Reserve for retirement benefits	(13)	2,861	3,691
Net income available for distribution		36,383	70,984
		1,672,690	
Special reserves	(14)	80,552	118,103
Provisions	(15)	1,733,440	1,386,799
Liabilities	(16)	2,680,935	2,254,569
		6,167,617	5,405,570

Continental Aktiengesellschaft
Consolidated Statement of Income for the period
from January 1 to December 31, 20X0

	See Note No	*20X0*	*19X9*
		euro 000	*euro 000*
Sales	(17)	8,551,015	8,381,880
Cost of sales	(18)	6,490,128	6,256,858
Gross profit on sales		2,060,887	2,125,002
Selling expenses	(19)	1,255,474	1,174,268
Administrative expenses	(20)	504,277	474,932
Other operating income	(21)	194,266	164,076
Other operating expenses	(22)	140,218	91,351
Net income from investments and financial activities	(23)	2138,777	2116,536

Continental Aktiengesellschaft
Consolidated Statement of Income for the period
from January 1 to December 31, 20X0

	See Note No	*20X0*	*19X9*
		euro 000	*euro 000*
Net income from regular business activities		216,407	431,991
Taxes	(24)	122,972	204,153
Net income for the year		93,435	227,838
Balance brought forward from previous year		1,380	1,199
Minority interests in earning	(25)	288	258
Withdrawal from the reserve for retirement benefits		+ 830	+ 544
Change in reserves		259,174	2158,539
Net income available for distribution		36,383	70,984

Based on an audit performed in accordance with our professional duties, the consolidated financial statements comply with the legal regulations. The consolidated financial statements present, in compliance with required accounting principles, a true and fair view of the net worth, financial position, and results of the corporation. The management report for the corporation is in agreement with the consolidated financial statements.
Berlin/Hanover, April 8, 20X0

EXHIBIT 9-24   Continental's Financial Statements and Related Notes *(Continued)*

Accounting policies:

Assets

Acquired intangible assets are carried at acquisition cost and amortized by the straight-line method over their anticipated useful life. Capitalized goodwill resulting from the acquisition of companies is deducted in installments from retained earnings on the balance sheet, over periods estimated individually at from 10 to 20 years.

Property, plant, and equipment is valued at acquisition or manufacturing costs, less scheduled depreciation.

Continental Aktiengesellschaft uses the declining balance method to depreciate movable fixed assets, while the straight-line method is used for all other fixed assets. We change over from the declining balance method to the straight-line method as soon as this leads to higher depreciation. In the financial statements of Continental Aktiengesellschaft, the special depreciation permitted by the tax laws is taken insofar as necessary in view of the fact that the commercial balance sheet is the basis for the balance sheet prepared in accordance with the tax regulations.

Since 1989, pursuant to internationally accepted accounting principles, additions have been depreciated exclusively by the straight-line method in the consolidated financial statements.

The following table shows the useful life taken as a basis for depreciating the major categories of property, plant, and equipment:

Buildings up to 33 years
Additions from 1990 on, up to 25 years
Technical facilities and machinery, 10 years
Plant and office equipment, 4 to 7 years
Molds up to 4 years

Additions to movable assets made during the first 6 months of the year are depreciated at the full annual rate, and those made during the last 6 months at half the annual rate. Minor fixed assets are written off completely in the year of acquisition.

These depreciation rules are applied by each of the domestic and foreign companies as of the date it became part of the Corporation.

Interests in affiliates and other companies held as investments are valued at acquisition cost, less the necessary write-downs.

Interest-bearing loans granted are shown at face value; loans that bear little or not interest are discounted to their cash value.

Inventories are carried at the lower acquisition/manufacturing cost or market.

Manufacturing cost includes direct costs, as well as a proportional part of material and production overhead and depreciation. Appropriate adjustment are made for declines in value due to reduced usability or prolonged storage.

In valuing receivables and miscellaneous assets, we make reasonable allowances to cover all perceivable risks, as well as lump-sum deductions to cover the general credit risk.

Marketable securities are valued at the lower of cost or market.

Insofar as permissible, we have continued to take all the extraordinary depreciation and write-downs, as well as the depreciation and write-downs for tax purposes, which were taken in previous years on fixed assets, investments, and current assets.

Discounts and issue costs of loans and bonds are shown as prepaid expenses and amortized over the term of the individual loans and bonds.

Shareholders' Equity and Liabilities

Provisions based on sound business judgment are set up for all perceivable risks, undetermined obligations, and impending losses.

At our German companies, the provisions for pension plans and similar obligations are set up at a 6% interest rate, on the basis of actuarial computations in accordance with the statutory method.

Pension commitments and similar obligations of foreign companies are also computed according to actuarial principles, discounted to the present value at the interest rates prevailing in the respective countries, and covered by appropriate provisions for pension plans or by pension funds. Employee claims for severance benefits under national laws have also been taken into account.

The pension obligations of American companies are valued according to the stricter valuation rules that have been in force in the U.S.A. since 1987. The provision made for this purpose in the balance sheet is slightly higher than if the corresponding German method of computation had been applied.

The obligations of General Tire Inc., Akron, Ohio, for post-retirement medical benefits are fully covered by provisions computed according to actuarial principles. New U.S. regulations (FASB No. 106) require that by no later than 1993, a provision must be established for not only the retirees and vested workforce, but also for the nonvested employees. Although this regulation allows a build-up of the provision over a 20-year period, we have already transferred the full additional amount required (DM270.7 million) to the provisions shown on the consolidated balance sheet. To balance this item, goodwill deducted from consolidated retained earnings at the time of the acquisition of General Tire has been capitalized in the same amount.

As a rule, provisions for repairs that have been postponed to the subsequent year are established in the amount of the probable cost.

When there are temporary differences between the values of the individual companies' assets and liabilities as determined according to the tax laws and those appearing in their balance sheets, which are prepared according to valuation principles that are uniform throughout the Corporation, deferred taxes may result. We show the latter only when they are reflected in provisions for future tax expenses. Liabilities are stated at the redemption amount.

Selected Notes:

(10) Capital reserves. This item includes amounts received upon the issuance of shares in excess of their par value totaling euro 724 .9 million, as well as the premium of euro 237.4 million paid upon the exercise of warrants attached to the bonds issued in 19X4, 19X6 and 19X7 and to the 19X8 convertible debentures. Capital reserves increased by euro 6.0 million due to the exercise of the conversion and option rights in 20X0.

(11) Retained earnings

euro 000	Continental AG	Consolidated
As of 12/31/19X9	141,699	133,770
Differences from translation	—	55,009
Other	—	147
Allocation from net income	8,000	59,174
As of 12/31/20X0	149,699	137,788

(14) Special reserves

euro 000	12/31/20X0 Continental AG	12/31/20X0 Consolidated	12/31/19X9 Continental AG	12/31/19X9 Consolidated
Reserve per/3. Foreign Investment Act	59,766	15,000	84,312	38,265
Reserve per/6b, Income Tax Act	—	448	—	289
Reserve per/52 Par.8 Income Tax Act	705	1,069	940	1,425
Governmental capital investment Subsidies	—	57,664	—	60,988
Other	2,533	6,371	4,137	17,136
	63,004	80,552	89,389	118,103

The decrease in special reserves is due, in particular, to the elimination of the special reserve pursuant to /3. Foreign Investment Act, following the write-down made in connection with Semperit (Ireland) Ltd., Dublin, Ireland. The special reserves are divided into an equity portion of euro 69.5 million and a debt portion of euro 11.1 million, representing deferred taxes, which will be paid in due course, when the reserves are eliminated. Including the shareholders equity of euro 1,672.7 million shown on the balance sheet, the actual shareholders equity amounts to euro 1,742.2 million and the equity ratio to 28.2%.

(15) Provisions

euro 000	12/31/20X0		12/31/19X9	
	Continental AG	*Consolidated*	*Continental AG*	*Consolidated*
Provision for pensions	220,977	972,173	206,374	636,626
Provision for taxes	31,937	72,210	53,144	92,265
Miscellaneous provisions	191,465	689,057	188,817	657,908
	444,379	1,733,440	448,335	1,386,799

The Corporation's provisions for pensions and similar obligations rose considerably. Apart from normal allocations, this increase was due, in particular, to an addition to cover claims for medical benefits which may be made by employees of General Tire Inc., Akron, Ohio, U.S.A., after their retirement.

At two of our retirement benefit organizations, there is a shortfall of euro 22.0 million in the coverage of pension obligations. The provisions at four other German companies have been funded only to the maximum amount permitted for tax purposes.

Lower tax liabilities permitted a reduction in provisions for taxes, which include amounts relating both to the current fiscal year and to previous years.

Provisions for deferred taxes in the individual financial statements, after deduction of the net prepaid taxes arising from consolidation procedures, amounted to euro 7.4 million.

Miscellaneous provisions cover all perceivable risks and other undetermined obligations. In addition to provisions for warranties, bonuses and miscellaneous risks, they consist mainly of provisions for personnel and social welfare payments, deferred repairs and service anniversaries.

(21) Other operating income

euro 000	12/31/20X0		12/31/19X9	
	Continental AG	*Consolidated*	*Continental AG*	*Consolidated*
Gains on the disposal of fixed assets and investments	6,179	33,423	2,435	10,733
Credit to income from the reversal of provisions	1,418	17,312	7,400	33,559
Credit to income from the reduction of the general bad debt reserve	—	1,101	—	2,014
Credit to income from the reversal of special reserves	26,385	38,824	12,645	32,456
Miscellaneous income	120,143	103,606	106,843	85,294
	154,125	194,266	129,323	164,056

In addition to current income from rentals, leasing and miscellaneous sideline operations, other operating income includes indemnification paid by insurance companies and income attributable to other fiscal years.

For the parent company, this item consists mainly of cost apportionments received from other companies belonging to the Corporation.

(22) Other operating expenses

euro 000	12/31/20X0		12/31/19X9	
	Continental AG	Consolidated	Continental AG	Consolidated
Losses on the disposal of fixed assets and investments	2,015	6,694	306	4,315
Losses on the disposal of current assets	1,414	19,197	257	22,818
Allocation to special reserves	—	168	46,995	1,278
Miscellaneous expenses	111,504	114,161	89,374	62,940
	114,933	140,220	136,932	91,351

The miscellaneous expenses relate primarily to sideline operations and the establishment of necessary provisions; at the parent company, they include cost apportionments paid to other companies belonging to the Corporation.

(24) Taxes

euro 000	12/31/20X0		12/31/19X9	
	Continental AG	Consolidated	Continental AG	Consolidated
On income	45,747	59,884	75,612	141,476
Other taxes	14,186	63,088	17,527	62,877
	59,933	122,972	93,139	204,353

CHAPTER 10

Managerial Planning and Control

The preceding chapters have largely had an external reporting orientation. This chapter focuses on internal reporting and control issues. Admittedly, the distinction between the two is increasingly blurred.

Global competition together with continued advances in technology is significantly altering the landscape of business and its internal reporting requirements. Continued reductions in national trade barriers, floating currencies, sovereign risk, restrictions on fund remittances across national borders, differences in national tax systems, interest rate differentials, and the effects of changing commodity and equity prices on enterprise assets, earnings, and capital costs are variables that complicate management decisions. At the same time, such developments as the Internet, video conferencing, and electronic transfer are changing the economics of production, distribution, and financing. Production is increasingly awarded to the company, no matter where located, that does it, or parts of it, best. Globally coordinated value chains based on strategic alliances are replacing arm's-length relationships among manufacturers, suppliers, and customers. Understandably, greater emphasis is being placed on information providers who understand the strategic information needs of management and possess strong analytic skills and intellectual capital.[1]

Global competition and the speed of knowledge dissemination support the narrowing of national variations in management accounting practices.[2] Additional pressures include market and technology changes, the growth of privatization, cost and performance incentives, the coordination of global operations through joint venturing and other strategic linkages, and continual shareholder demands for value-added initiatives. These pressures are common to business organizations everywhere. They are driving the managers of multinational companies not only to adopt comparable internal accounting techniques, but to use these techniques in similar fashion.[3] The managerial accounting issues discussed in this book fall into three broad areas: financial planning and control (this chapter), international risk management (Chapter 11), and international taxation and transfer pricing (Chapter 12). The planning topics in this chapter include business modeling, capital budgeting, and profitability management, together with the information systems needed to implement them. The balance of the chapter focuses on financial control.

---

[1]Robert A. Howell, "The 1CFO: From Controller to Global Strategic Partner," *Financial Executive,* (April 2006): 20–25.
[2]Chris Guilding, Karen S. Cravens, and Mike Tayles, "An International Comparison of Strategic Management Accounting Practices," *Management Accounting Research* 9 (2000): 113–135.
[3]Ramona Dzinkowski, "Global Economic Impacts on Strategic Financial Management," *Strategic Finance* 87, no. 6 (2005): 36–41.

BUSINESS MODELING

A recent survey finds that management accountants are spending more time on strategic planning issues than ever before. This reflects the fact that financial managers, major consumers of internal accounting data, are increasingly becoming strategic advisers to the chief executive. As Charles Noski, former CFO and vice chairman of AT&T, stated:

> I think the CFO will continue to evolve, with more emphasis on the strategic issues facing the company and a requirement that the CFO be the business partner to the CEO. . . . Compliance and internal controls will likely always be a part of the job, but the expectation for value-added contributions by the CFO to the growth, competitiveness and performance of the company will gain momentum.[4]

Business modeling is big picture, and it consists of formulating, implementing, and evaluating a firm's long-range business plan. It involves four critical dimensions:

1. Identifying key factors relevant to the future progress of the company
2. Formulating appropriate techniques to forecast future developments and assess the company's ability to adapt to or exploit these developments
3. Developing information systems to support strategic choices
4. Translating selected options into specific courses of action[5]

PLANNING TOOLS

In identifying factors relevant to its future, it is helpful for a company to scan its external and internal environments to identify threats and opportunities. Systems can be set in place to gather information on competitors and market conditions. Both competitors and market conditions are analyzed for their impact on the company's competitive status and profitability. Insights gleaned from this analysis are used to plan measures to maintain or enlarge market share, or to identify and exploit new product and market opportunities.

One such tool is the WOTS-UP analysis. It is concerned with corporate strengths and weaknesses in relation to a firm's operating environment. This technique helps management generate a set of feasible strategies.[6] Exhibit 10-1 shows a WOTS-UP analysis done by the German automaker Daimler. For example, extending Daimler's distribution and service network in Eastern Europe is a promising strategy, given the company's strengths in product quality, truck sales, lower breakeven point, and synergistic

---

[4]Jeffrey Marshall and Ellen M. Heffes, "What Does the Future Hold for Finance and CFO's?" *Financial Executive* (December 2006): 16–20.
[5]Kiyohiko Ito and Klaus R. Macharzina, "Strategic Planning Systems," in *International Accounting and Finance Handbook*, ed. Frederick D. S. Choi , 2nd ed. (New York: John Wiley, 1997), chap. 25.
[6]WOTS-UP analysis is a modified version of SWOT analysis, which is constantly being improved upon as a strategic planning tool. See George Panagiotou, "Bringing SWOT into Focus," *Business Strategy Review* 14, no. 2 (2003): 8–10.

EXHIBIT 10-1 WOTS-UP Analysis of Daimler-Benz AG

	Strengths (S)	Weaknesses (W)
	1. Product quality improved 20% from previous year 2. R & D potential higher than other automobile producers 3. 50% share of comfort limousine market 4. Daimler Benz trucks lead industry 5. Breakeven point decreased from 1.0 to 0.7 million vehicles 6. Several acquisitions (e.g., AEG, Dornier, MBB) improved the synergistic potential of Daimler Benz 7. Excellent financial situation of Daimler Benz 8. High economies of scope	1. Acquisition of high-tech firms leads to coordination problems 2. wage level (most of the production is located in Germany) 3. Fewer joint ventures (international alliances) than Japanese automobile producers
Opportunities (O)	**SO-Strategies**	**WO-Strategies**
1. High-tech industries (micro electronics, aerospace) growing 20% per year 2. Consumers' disposable income increasing 6% per year 3. Liberalization of Eastern European countries 4. Image and service problems of Japanese automobile firms	1. Acquire automobile producers in Eastern Germany (03/S7) 2. Extend the distribution and service net in Eastern Europe (03/S7) 3. Develop several versions of the Baby Benz (02, 03/S5, S7) 4. Use production capacity for civil products (03/S6, S8)	1. Expand transfer of managers between headquarters and subsidiaries (03/W1) 2. Produce cars in the eastern part of Germany (03/W2) 3. Intensify HR development on each level (01/W2) 4. Form international aerospace joint venture company (01/W3)
Threats (T)	**Short-Term Strategies**	**Long-Term Strategies**
1. Low value of the dollar 2. Rising interest rate 3. Foreign imports, esp. luxury cars, gaining market share 4. Gulf crisis leads to increasing gas prices 5. BMW has an excellent new line of cars 6. Rising ecological problems throughout the world 7. Military (defense) markets may break off due to peace movement	1. Place selective advertising; boost advertising expenditures 30% (T3, T5/S1, S3) 2. Strengthen basic research in new fields of technology (solar energy, biotechnology, computing and robotics, electrical car engines) (T4, T6/S7, S8)	1. Build strategic alliances (strategic networks) to reduce cost of R & D investment and to solve ecological problems (T6/W3) 2. Improve productivity and quality (in production, administration, distribution, and services) (T1, T3/W2)

SOURCE: K. Ito and K. R. Macharzina, "Strategic Planning Systems," in F. D. S. Choi, ed., *International Accounting and Finance Handbook*, 2nd ed., New York: John Wiley & Sons, 1997, p. 25.9.

potential. The low value of the U.S. dollar, rising foreign competition in Germany, and the perceived advantages of strengthening basic research in new technologies by building strategic alliances may explain Daimler's former acquisition of the Chrysler Corporation in the United States.

Decision tools currently used in strategic planning systems all depend on the quality of information regarding a firm's internal and external environment. Accountants can help corporate planners obtain data useful in strategic planning decisions. Much of the required information comes from sources other than accounting records.

CAPITAL BUDGETING

As Exhibit 10-1 reveals, one of Daimler's strategies to capitalize on its strength/opportunity set was to initially acquire automobile producers in eastern Germany. This strategy subsequently embraced the acquisition of an auto manufacturer in the United States. This decision to invest abroad is a critical element in the global strategy of a multinational company.[7] Direct foreign investment typically involves large sums of capital and uncertain prospects. Investment risk is compounded by an unfamiliar, complex, constantly changing international environment. Formal planning is imperative and normally is done within a capital budgeting framework that compares the benefits and costs of the proposed investment.[8] As an example of the second dimension of corporate modeling described earlier, capital budgeting analysis helps ensure that strategic plans are financially feasible and advantageous.

Sophisticated approaches to investment decisions are available. Procedures exist to determine a firm's optimum capital structure, measure its cost of capital, and evaluate investment alternatives under conditions of uncertainty. Decision rules for investment choice typically call for discounting an investment's risk-adjusted cash flows at an appropriate interest rate: the firm's weighted average cost of capital. Normally, a firm increases the wealth of its owners by making investments that promise positive net present values. When considering mutually exclusive options, a rational company will select the option that promises the maximum net present value.[9] In the international arena, investment planning is not straightforward. Different tax laws, accounting systems, rates of inflation, risks of expropriation, currency frameworks, market segmentation, restrictions on the transferability of foreign earnings, and language and intercultural differences introduce elements of complexity seldom encountered domestically. The difficulty of quantifying such data makes the problem that much worse.

Multinational adaptations of traditional investment planning models have been made in three areas of measurement: (1) determining the relevant return from a multinational investment, (2) measuring expected cash flows, and (3) calculating the multinational cost of capital. These adaptations provide data that support strategic choices, step 3 in the corporate modeling process.

---

[7]Cristiano Busco, Mark L. Frigo, Elena Giovannoni, Angelo Riccaboni, and Robert W. Scapens, "Integrating Global Organizations Through Performance Measurement Systems," *Strategic Finance* (January 2006): 31–35.

[8]For a state-of-the art piece on capital budgeting in Sweden, see Gert Sandahl and Stefan Sjogren, "Capital Budgeting Methods Among Sweden's Largest Groups: The State of the Art and a Comparison with Earlier Studies," *International Journal of Production Economics* 84 (2003): 51–69.

[9]The performance metric Economic Value Added (EVA) is derived from this construct.

FINANCIAL RETURN PERSPECTIVES

A manager must determine the relevant return to assess a foreign investment opportunity. But relevant return is a matter of perspective. Should the international financial manager evaluate expected investment returns from the perspective of the foreign project or of the parent company?[10] Returns from the two perspectives could differ significantly due to (1) government restrictions on repatriation of earnings and capital, (2) license fees, royalties, and other payments that provide income to the parent but are expenses to the subsidiary, (3) differential rates of national inflation, (4) changing foreign currency values, and (5) differential taxes, to name a few.

One might argue that the return and risk of a foreign investment should be evaluated from the point of view of the parent company's domestic stockholders. However, it also can be argued that such an approach is no longer appropriate. First, investors in the parent company increasingly come from a worldwide community. Investment objectives should reflect the interests of all shareholders, not just the domestic ones. Observation also suggests that many multinational companies have long-run (as opposed to short-run) investment horizons. Funds generated abroad tend to be reinvested abroad rather than repatriated to the parent company. Under these circumstances, it may be appropriate to evaluate returns from a host country perspective. Emphasis on local project returns is consistent with the goal of maximizing consolidated group value.[11]

An appealing solution is to recognize that financial managers must meet many goals, responding to investor and noninvestor groups in the organization and its environment.[12] The host country government is one such group for a foreign investment. Compatibility between the goals of the multinational investor and the host government can be gauged through two financial return calculations: one from the host country perspective, the other from the parent country perspective. The host country perspective assumes that a profitable foreign investment (including the local opportunity cost of capital) does not misallocate the host country's scarce resources.[13] Evaluating an investment opportunity from a local perspective also gives the parent company useful information. If a foreign investment does not promise a risk-adjusted return higher than the returns of local competitors, parent company shareholders would be better off investing directly in the local companies.

At first glance, the accounting implications of multiple rate-of-return calculations seem straightforward. Nothing could be less true. In an earlier discussion, we assumed that project rate-of-return calculations were a proxy for host-country evaluation of a foreign investment. In practice, the analysis is much more complicated. Do projected rate of return calculations really reflect a host country's opportunity costs? Are the expected returns from a foreign investment limited to projected cash flows, or must

---

[10]This issue parallels, in many respects, the problem of currency perspectives associated with foreign currency translation discussed in Chapter 6.

[11]John C. Edmunds and David M. Ellis, "A Stock Market–Driven Reformulation of Multinational Capital Budgeting," *European Management Journal* 17, no. 3 (1999): 310–317.

[12]David K. Eiteman, Arthur I. Stonehill, and Michael Moffett, *Multinational Business Finance*, 11th ed. (Reading, MA: Addison-Wesley, 2007).

[13]For example, a country would probably look favorably on a proposed investment promising a 21 percent return on assets employed when investments of comparable risk elsewhere in the country yield 18 percent.

other externalities be considered? How are any additional benefits measured? Does a foreign investment require any special overhead spending by the host government? What is the risk from a host-country viewpoint, and how can it be measured? Questions such as these call for a massive increase in the amount and complexity of the information needed to calculate rates of return.

MEASURING EXPECTED RETURNS

It is challenging to measure the expected cash flows of a foreign investment. Assume, for purposes of discussion, that Samsung Electronics' U.S. manufacturing operation is considering purchasing 100 percent ownership of a manufacturing facility in Russia. The U.S. parent will finance one-half of the investment in the form of cash and equipment; the balance will be financed by local bank borrowing at market rates. The Russian facility will import one-half of its raw materials and components from the U.S. parent and export one-half of its output to Hungary. To repatriate funds to the parent company, the Russian facility will pay the U.S. parent a licensing fee, royalties for use of parent company patents, and technical service fees for management services rendered. Earnings of the Russian facility will be remitted to the parent as dividends. Exhibit 10-2 provides a diagram of prospective cash flows that need to be measured.[14]

The methods for estimating projected cash flows associated with the Russian facility are similar to those used for a domestic company. Expected receipts are based on sales projections and anticipated collection experience. Operating expenses (converted to their cash equivalents) and local taxes are similarly forecast. Additional complexities must be considered, however. They include:

1. Project vs. parent cash flows
2. Parent cash flows tied to financing
3. Subsidized financing
4. Political risk

The process also must consider the impact of changing prices and fluctuating currency values on expected foreign currency returns. If local currency cash flows were fixed (e.g., if the Russian venture was in the form of a bond investment), it would be straightforward to measure exchange rate effects. Here, depreciation of the Russian ruble relative to the U.S. dollar reduces the dollar equivalent of future interest income. When an ongoing manufacturing enterprise generates foreign currency income, the analysis is more complicated. Exchange rate changes influence net operating cash flows. Accordingly, accounting measurements of exchange rate effects become necessary for each type of activity (e.g., domestic vs. export sales, domestic vs. imported costs, and their cumulative effects on projected cash flows).

---

[14]For an extended discussion of this subject, see David K. Eiteman, "Foreign Investment Analysis," in *International Finance and Accounting Handbook*, ed. Frederick D. S. Choi, 3rd ed. (New York: John Wiley, 2003), pp. 4.1–4.19.

EXHIBIT 10-2 Cash Flow Components

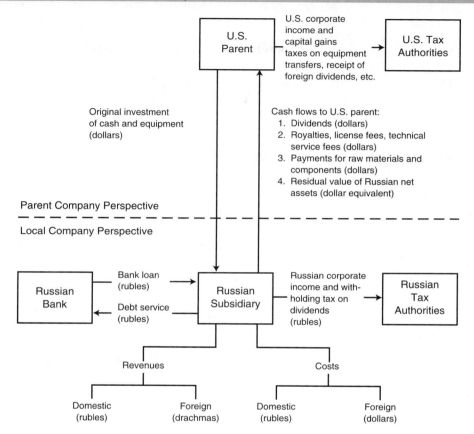

The following example illustrates the effects of changing prices and currency values on expected returns for the first two years of a six year investment project. The Russian facility's cash flows, as shown in Exhibit 10-3, are determined under the following assumptions.

1. The Russian facility is expected to sell 100,000 units of its manufactured product in the local market at an initial unit price of 2,020 Russian rubles (RUB). Another 100,000 units will be exported to Hungary and priced in forints (HUF) reflecting the ruble base price.

2. Changes in local selling prices are tied to annual rates of inflation in Russia and Hungary, which are expected to average 20 percent and 10 percent, respectively.

3. Domestic and foreign unit sales are expected to increase each year by 10 percent.

4. The ruble is forecast to depreciate relative to the forint by 10 percent per year.

5. Variable costs of production (raw materials and labor) also reflect local inflation rates.

6. Because 50 percent of the Russian manufacturer's raw materials are imported from the United States, imported raw material prices are expected to increase by 10 percent each year in line with anticipated U.S. and Russian inflation.

7. Anticipated depreciation of the ruble relative to the U.S. dollar is 5 percent.
8. Licensing and other fees are expected to average 10 percent of gross revenues.
9. Selling and administrative expenses are expected to increase by 15 percent each year from an initial level of RUB48,000,000.
10. Depreciation expense is RUB60,000,000 a year.
11. The Russian corporate tax rate is 40 percent.
12. Projected annual cash flows will increase from RUB93,360,000 to RUB124,016,000 in local currency. Measured in U.S. dollars, net cash flows will increase from $4,668,000 to $5,905,000.

EXHIBIT 10-3 Cash Flows from Russian Subsidiary

	Year 1	Year 2
Sales (units)		
Domestic	100,000	110,000
Foreign	100,000	110,000
Price (per unit)		
Domestic	RUB2,020	RUB2,424
Foreign	RUB2,020	RUB2,444
Gross revenues		
Domestic	RUB202,000,000	RUB266,640,000
Foreign	RUB202,000,000	RUB268,640,000
	(HUF2,020,000,000)	(HUF2,444,000,000)
Total	RUB404,000,000	RUB535,480,000
Raw materials (cost per unit)		
Domestic	RUB400	RUB480
Foreign	RUB400	RUB462
	($20)	($22)
LABOR (COST PER UNIT)	RUB200	RUB240
Variable cost (per unit)	RUB1,000	RUB1,182
Total variable costs	RUB200,000,000	RUB260,040,000
Licensing fees, royalties, etc.	RUB40,400,000	RUB53,548,000
Depreciation expense	RUB60,000,000	RUB60,000,000
Selling and administrative expenses	RUB48,000,000	RUB55,200,000
Total	RUB348,400,000	RUB428,788,000
Net operating income	RUB33,360,000	RUB64,016,000
Corporate income tax (40%)	RUB22,240,000	RUB42,676,000
Net income	RUB33,360,000	RUB64,016,000
+Depreciation	RUB60,000,000	RUB60,000,000
Net cash flow (rubles)	RUB93,360,000	RUB124,016,000
Net cash flow (dollars)	$ 4,668,000	$ 5,905,000
Exchange rates:		
	RUB0.1 = HUF1	RUB0.11 = HUF1
	RUB20 = $1	RUB21 = $1

In this example, a depreciating local currency had increased projected local cash flows due to the structure of the foreign operation's product and factor markets.

When a parent company perspective is used, cash flows to the parent company seldom mirror those of its overseas affiliate. The only relevant cash flows are those with direct consequences for the parent.

Major sources of parent cash flows include debt service on loans by the parent, dividends, licensing fees, overhead charges, royalties, transfer prices on purchases from or sales to the parent (see Chapter 12 for a further discussion of this managerial topic), and the estimated terminal value of the project. Measurement of these cash flows requires an understanding of national accounting differences, governmental repatriation policies, potential future inflation and exchange rates, and differential taxes.

Differences in accounting principles are relevant if financial managers rely on locally based pro forma financial statements in estimating future cash flows. When the measurement rules used in preparing these accounts differ from those of the parent country, differences in cash flow estimates could arise. One example is depreciation based on replacement values rather than historical costs (as practiced by certain large multinationals in the Netherlands and Italy). This difference could affect corporate income taxes and, consequently, cash flow. As another example, differences in inventory costing methods could influence both the measurement and the timing of total cash flow. Balance of payment concerns may prompt host governments to limit the repatriation of dividends or other cash payments to the parent company. For example, dividend remittances may be limited to a certain proportion of a company's capital base that has been formally registered with the host government. Some countries disallow repatriation of cash flows made possible by tax-deductible expenses, because these are not part of the accrual-based earnings from which dividends are declared. This consideration alone would reduce the cash flows that could be repatriated in our previous Russian example by 66 and 50 percent, respectively, for the two years examined. A parent company naturally cares about the value of foreign cash flows measured in parent currency.

Accordingly, it needs estimates of future inflation and its impact on future exchange rates used to convert foreign cash flows to the parent currency. Finally, provisions relating to the taxation of foreign source income must be considered. For instance, in the United States the receipt of a royalty payment on which a foreign withholding tax has been assessed gives rise to a foreign tax credit designed to minimize the double taxation of foreign source income. (International tax considerations are detailed in Chapter 12.)

MULTINATIONAL COST OF CAPITAL

If foreign investments are evaluated with this discounted cash flow model, an appropriate discount rate must be developed. Capital budgeting theory typically uses a firm's cost of capital as its discount rate; that is, a project must yield a return at least equal to the firm's capital costs to be accepted. This hurdle rate is related to the proportions of debt and equity in a firm's financial structure as follows:

$$k_a = k_e \ (E/S) + k_i \ (1 - t) \ (D/S)$$

where:

ka = weighted average (after tax) cost of capital
ke = cost of equity
ki = cost of debt before tax
E = value of firm's equity
D = value of firm's debt
S = value of firm's capital structure (E + D)
t = marginal tax rate

It is not easy to measure a multinational company's cost of capital. The cost of equity capital may be calculated in several ways. One popular method combines the expected dividend yield with the expected dividend growth rate. Letting DV_i = expected dividends per share at period's end, P_0 = the current market price of the stock at the beginning of the period, and g = expected growth rate in dividends, the cost of equity, ke, is calculated as ke = DV_i/P_0 + g. Even though it is easy to measure current stock prices, in most countries where a multinational firm's shares are listed, it is often trublesome to measure DV_i and g. First, DV_i is an expectation. Expected dividends depend on the operating cash flows of the company as a whole. Measuring these cash flows is complicated by environmental considerations such as those mentioned in our Russian example. Moreover, measurement of the dividend growth rate, a function of expected future cash flows, is complicated by exchange controls and other government restrictions on cross-border funds transfers.

Similar problems relate to the measurement of the debt component of the average cost of capital.[15] In a single nation, the cost of debt is the effective interest rate multiplied by (1 – t) because interest is generally a tax-deductible expense. When a multinational company borrows foreign currencies, however, additional factors enter the picture. The effective after-tax interest cost now includes foreign exchange gains or losses that arise whenever foreign exchange rates fluctuate between the transaction and settlement dates (see Chapter 6). Suppose that a U.S. multinational borrows 100,000 Israeli shekels (ILS) for one year at 8 percent interest when the dollar/shekel exchange rate is $0.24 = ILS1. Should the shekel appreciate to $0.264 = ILS1 before repayment, the borrowing company will incur a transaction loss of ILS108,000 × ($ 0.264 – $0.240) = $2,592. This additional cost of debt financing would be tax deductible. Assuming a corporate tax rate of 40 percent, the after-tax cost of debt would be 0.18 (1 – 0.40), or 10.8 percent, as opposed to 4 percent in a purely domestic transaction.

Additional tax considerations apply when a multinational borrows funds in several foreign capital markets. Current and prospective tax rates in each foreign market over the life of the loan must be considered. The tax-deductible status of interest payments must be checked, because not all national taxing authorities recognize interest deductions (particularly if the associated loan is between related entities). Moreover, recognition of deferred taxes, which arise whenever income for tax purposes differs from income for external reporting purposes, is becoming a generally accepted practice in many industrialized countries where MNCs operate. Because deferred taxes are considered a liability on which no interest is paid, one can ask whether they are

---

[15]In countries with underdeveloped capital markets, internal borrowing is a common substitute. Mihir A. Desai, C. Fritz Foley, and James R. Hines, "A Multinational Perspective on Capital Structure Choice and Internal Capital Markets," *Journal of Finance* 59, no. 6 (2004): 2451–2478.

really an interest-free source of financing and should be included in determining the cost of capital. Although this idea merits consideration, we do not believe that the cost of capital calculation should include deferred taxes.[16]

It is not always straightforward to implement international capital budgeting theory in practice. All of the capital budgeting approaches we have examined assume that the required information is readily available. Unfortunately, in actual practice, the most difficult and critical aspect of the entire capital budgeting process is obtaining accurate and timely information, especially in the international sphere, where different climates, culture, languages, and information technologies complicate matters.

MANAGEMENT INFORMATION SYSTEMS

Organization of a firm's worldwide information systems is crucial in supporting corporate strategies, including the planning processes described above. This task is challenging, as a multinational framework is inherently more complex than a single-country framework. Exhibit 10-4 sets forth some environmental factors that complicate the flow of business information.

EXHIBIT 10-4   Framework for Systems Design

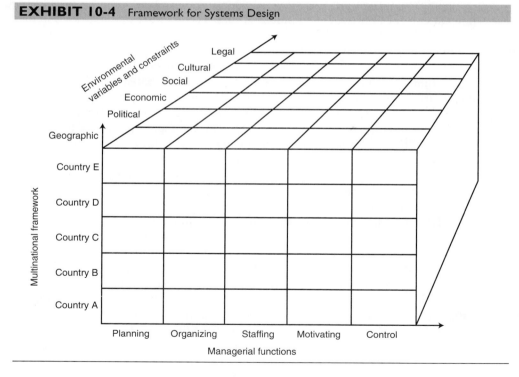

Systems Issues

Distance is an obvious complication. Due to geographic circumstances, formal information communications generally substitute for personal contacts between local operating managers and headquarters management. Developments in information technology should reduce this complication, but will not entirely eliminate it.

As another example, the information requirements of regional or corporate financial planners concern both operating and environmental data. Information demanded from managerial accountants in the field depends on how much decision-making power local managers have. The greater the authority of local managers, the less information is passed on to headquarters.

In "Patterns in the Organization of Transnational Information Systems," Vikram Sethi and Joseph Katz identify three global IT strategies, each related to a specific type of multinational organization. Success hinges on matching systems design to corporate strategies.[17]

Low dispersal with high centralization is employed by smaller organizations with limited international business operations, domestic IS needs dominate. A standard platform of data and applications dominates the worldwide IT system.

High dispersion with low centralization is the strategy favored by multinational companies with geographically diverse operations. Local subsidiaries are afforded significant control over the development of their IT strategies and related systems.

High dispersal with high centralization is a "glocal" IT strategy employed by truly global companies with strategic alliances worldwide. Information systems are designed that reflect both corporate requirements tailored to local circumstances.

Perhaps the biggest challenge facing systems specialists is designing corporate information systems that allow financial managers to respond appropriately to the phenomenon of global competition. Conditions are changing. Owing to deregulation of markets and reduction of tariff barriers, firms are increasingly able to access foreign markets either directly or indirectly through joint ventures, strategic alliances, and other cooperative arrangements. This more open access has led to competitive intensities where firms adopt strategies to (1) protect market share at home, (2) penetrate competitors' home markets to deny them market share and revenues, and (3) generate significant market share in key third-country markets.

CEOs need information systems that enable them to plan, coordinate, and control effective worldwide production, marketing, and financial strategies. To facilitate this objective, software information developers in the United States have created XBRL, a new computer language. XBRL stands for "extensible business reporting language" and is a standard computer programming enhancement that is now included in all accounting and financial reporting software in the United States. Once added to the software, XBRL automatically translates all numbers and words so that each data segment is identified in a standard way when viewed by a Web browser or sent to a particular spreadsheet application. Specifically, XBRL tags each segment of computerized business information with an identification marker that remains with the data when moved or changed. No matter how an application software formats or rearranges the information, the markers remain with the data. Links are created that identify the

---

[17]Peter Gwynne, "Information Systems Go Global," *MIT Sloan Management Review* (summer 2001): 14.

location on a financial statement where the data elements reside, instruct users as to how the data elements should be calculated in relation to other elements in the financial statements, detail descriptive labels that should be applied to the data elements, including the national language in which they should be reported, and specify other information, such as currency of denomination, time period covered, and the like. Useful for all enterprises regardless of industry or size, XBRL reduces information processing, calculating, and formatting costs because financial data only need to be created and formatted once regardless of intended use. It will also improve a firm's investor relations because it facilitates automated interfirm comparisons along many dimensions, including financial accounts, accounting policies, and related footnotes.[18] This systems effort is being led in the United States by a consortium of accounting firms, financial service providers, and technology companies, including software giants Microsoft and IBM. Not only is this system making the distribution of financial information fast and easy, it is also eliminating the need for rewriting financial reports to accommodate incompatible accounting systems. Parallel efforts are reportedly under way in other countries along with involvement of the International Accounting Standards Board.

Information Issues

Management accountants prepare many kinds of information for corporate management, ranging from collections data to liquidity reports to operational forecasts of various types to expense disbursements. For each set of data transmitted, corporate management must determine the relevant time period of the reports, the level of accuracy required, the frequency of reporting, and the costs and benefits of timely preparation and transmission.

Here too, environmental factors affect the usage of information generated internally. Consider the influence of culture: Culture shapes the values of a given society. Citizens of these societies bring these values with them when employed by business organizations. These values, in turn, frame employees' organizational behavior and how they use information technology within the organization. Although organizations around the world are becoming more similar in their conduct of business, the people who comprise these organizations tend to maintain their cultural behavior patterns. As one example, Johns, Smith, and Strand examine the impact of uncertainty avoidance on database usage.[19] They find that cultures that are less uncomfortable with uncertainty and ambiguity tend to embrace information technology more readily than those that are very uncomfortable in such situations. A major implication of their study for managerial accountants is that culture is a major impediment to the international flow of data and must be explicitly dealt with in information systems design.[20]

---

[18]Neal J. Hannon and Robert J. Gold, "XBRL Revisited," *Journal of Accountancy* (February 2005): 4 pp.
[19]The term *uncertainty avoidance* was coined by Gerte Hofstede in his oft-cited study on values as determinants of behavior. Uncertainty avoidance is a value construct that describes the degree to which one is more or less comfortable with task uncertainty and ambiguity. See the discussion of Hofstede's work in Chapter 2.
[20]Sharon K. Johns, L. Murphy Smith, and Carolyn A. Strand, "How Culture Affects the Use of Information Technology," *Accounting Forum* 27, no. 1 (March 2002): 84–109.

Managers in different environments have different ways of analyzing and resolving problems, different decision time frames, and compete under different operating conditions. Different information needs are a direct consequence. Hence, we have a fundamental problem for the multinational enterprise. Local managers are likely to require different decision information than headquarters management. For example, a special feature of the U.S. consolidation process is that financial statements prepared according to foreign accounting principles are first restated to U.S. GAAP prior to being consolidated. Does this restatement somehow alter the information content of the accounts that go into a group consolidation? We provide an illustration of this reporting conundrum in the following section.

Another major information problem is the question of translation. In evaluating operations, U.S. managers generally prefer reports stated in U.S. dollars. Accordingly, reports from foreign operations of U.S. multinationals are typically translated to their U.S. dollar equivalents in order for U.S. headquarters managers to evaluate their dollar investments. However, does translating foreign currency amounts for managerial review purposes preserve the data without distortions? We address this issue empirically in Case 10-1 at the end of this chapter.

MANAGEMENT INFORMATION AND HYPERINFLATION

FAS No. 52 mandates the use of the temporal translation method, described in Chapter 6, in consolidating the accounts of foreign affiliates domiciled in high-inflation environments. Even though FAS No. 52 and similar national pronouncements provide useful guidelines on preparing hard currency statements, they do not meet the information needs of firms operating in high-inflation countries. In high-inflation environments, financial reports prepared in conformity with FAS No. 52 tend to distort reality by

- Overstating or understating revenues and expenses
- Reporting large translation gains or losses that are difficult to interpret
- Distorting performance comparisons over time

Our reporting framework overcomes these limitations and is based on the following assumptions:[21]

1. Management's objective of maximizing the value of the firm is framed in terms of a currency that holds its value (i.e., a hard currency). Accordingly, the best way to measure the performance of an affiliate located in a high-inflation environment is in terms of hard currency.[22]
2. Our model also implicitly assumes that inflation rates, exchange rates, and interest rates are interrelated. (This assumption is not critical to the proposal.)

---

[21]Frederick D. S. Choi, "Financial Reporting in Hyperinflationary Environments: A Transactions Analysis Framework for Management," in *International Finance and Accounting Handbook*, ed. Frederick D. S. Choi, 3rd ed. (New York: John Wiley, 2003), pp. 27.1–27.13.

[22]Interviews with financial executives of U.S.-based multinationals as well as with subsidiary managers suggest that this assumption is consistent with corporate practices at the micro-level. It also appears consistent with practices at the macro-level, because more and more Latin American countries have pegged their currencies to the U.S. dollar.

A common reporting convention in accounting for foreign currency transactions is to record revenues and expenses at the exchange rates prevailing on the financial statement date. (Use of average rates is also common.) A better option is to report local currency transactions at the exchange rate prevailing on the payment date. Recording a transaction at any other date muddles the measurement process by introducing gains or losses in the purchasing power of money or, alternatively, implicit interest into the exchange transaction.

In a perfectly competitive market, all local currency transactions would be in cash. With inflation, it is advantageous for buyers to delay payment for as long as possible and for sellers to accelerate collections. The payment date is determined by the competitive strengths of the contracting parties. Our recommended reporting treatment produces reported numbers that are reliable, economically interpretable, and symmetric in the sense that economically similar transactions produce similar financial statement numbers when translated into a common currency. One could say that the model uses accrual accounting with a cash accounting mentality.

An example will highlight the translation gains and losses generated by FAS No. 52 reporting. While many would attribute the gains or losses in our example to foreign exchange risk, they are really due to improper accounting for events that occurred above the line.

Following are our working assumptions:

- Inflation and Turkish lira (YTL) devaluation is 30 percent per month, or 1.2 percent per workday.
- The exchange rates at selected intervals for months 1 and 2 are:

1/1	100.0
1/10	109.6
1/20	119.6
1/30	130.0
2/10	141.6
2/20	154.5
2/30	169.0

The real rate of interest is 1.5 percent per month, or 20 percent per year.
- Cash balances are kept in hard currency (U.S. dollars).
- Month-end rates are used to record expense transactions.

Sales Revenue

Suppose that the firm sells YTL 2,000,000 worth of merchandise in month 1, with varying invoice dates and payment terms. Assuming that financial statements are prepared monthly, the conventional practice is to record the sales transaction at the month-end exchange rate regardless of when the sale is invoiced or when payment is received. Sales reported using the month-end exchange rate are YTL 2,000,000/YTL 130 = $15,385.

First assume that the sale is invoiced on day 1 of month 1, with payment received immediately in cash = YTL 2,000,000/YTL 100 = $20,000. Conventional treatment measures the transaction at month's end rather than when cash is received, but the economic basis of the transaction is the cash that is actually received on the invoice date. Here revenues are understated by 30 percent, or $4,615, determined as follows:

Cash received	$20,000
Reported sales	15,385
Variance	$ 4,615

In keeping with the temporal translation method, this $4,615 understatement of sales is offset by an equivalent nonoperating translation gain appearing below the line.[23] Next, assume instead that the sale is invoiced on day 5, and that the client receives 25 days payment terms. In our model, the transaction is booked on the same day that payment is received. From an economic point of view, there is no variance and no nonoperating translation gain or loss.

Cash received	$15,385
Reported sales	15,385
Variance	$ -0-

From a control perspective, management should be able to learn from the salesperson what the expected profit margin is on the day of sale. The salesperson does not have to wait until the books are closed to have this information, which is already at hand because invoices in hyperinflationary environments clearly state the payment due date.

In the following example, assume that the client is invoiced on day 30, with payment required a month later. From an economic point of view, the firm collects $11,834 (= YTL2,000,000/YTL169). The accounting system reports $15,385, resulting in a variance of $3,551.

Cash received	$11,834
Reported sales	15,385
Variance	$ 3,551

Here, the conventional reporting system overstates sales by 23.1 percent, with the positive variance offset by an equivalent nonoperating translation loss below the line.

Exhibit 10-5 shows the magnitude of the distortions associated with differing invoicing and payment terms. Depending on sales terms, sales can be overstated or understated by significant amounts.

Why do we care about these distortions? The traditional reporting system has a bad effect on the behavior of the sales force. For example, it gives the company's sales force no motivation to improve payment terms. If sales are recorded at the end-of-month rate, sales personnel do not care whether they are paid in cash or in 30 or 60 days. It is important to have a system that encourages the sales force to act in the company's best interests.

---

[23]Assume that the firm in question begins the period with a $10,000 equity investment and immediately converts this cash balance to saleable inventories. The goods are marked up 100 percent over cost and sold for cash the next day. In this case, the aggregate exchange adjustment would be $4,615, determined either as a plug when preparing the end-of-period translated balance sheet, or as a positive aggregate translation adjustment comprising the gain on the hard currency cash balance.

EXHIBIT 10-5 Distortions in Invoice and Payment Due Dates (YTL2,000,000 Sales in Month 1)

Invoice Day	Payment Terms	Today's Number	Proposed Number	Diff.	%
1	Cash	15,385	20,000	4,615	30.0%
5	5 days	15,385	18,248	2,863	18.6%
5	15 days	15,385	16,722	1,337	8.7%
5	25 days	15,385	15,385	0.000	0.0%
10	30 days	15,385	14,124	–1,261	8.2%
20	30 days	15,385	12,945	–2,440	–15.9%
30	30 days	15,385	11,834	3,551	–23.1%

In addition, traditional reporting systems do not motivate the sales force to invoice and ship earlier in the month. When sales are recorded at end-of-month rates, the sales force does not care about the time of delivery. But even one day's delay in shipment could be costly: 1.5 percent in lost interest in our example. Another glance at Exhibit 10-5 shows that bonuses and commission payments are based on inflated sales values whenever payment terms carry over to the following period.

Perhaps the most serious shortcoming of traditional reporting systems is that they encourage manipulation of results. Assume now that exchange rates at the end of each of the next three months are as follows:

End-of-month 1	130 = $1
End-of-month 2	169 = $1
End-of-month 3	220 = $1

Suppose that a salesperson arranges the following with a favorite customer: deliver and invoice YTL2,000,000 of a product on day 30 of month 1 at YTL2,500,000 with 60-day payment terms instead of invoicing at YTL2,000,000 on the same date with 30-day payment terms. The attractiveness of this arrangement is easy to figure out. Under conventional reporting methods, the revised sales value is YTL2,500,000/ YTL130 = $19,231 versus YTL2,000,000/YTL130 = $15,385 under traditional measurements. This represents an additional sales gain of almost $4,000, or 25 percent. From the customer's point of view, the actual cost of the purchase is only YTL2,500,000/YTL220 = $11,364 versus YTL2,000,000/YTL169 = $11,834, a savings that is hard to resist. Under these circumstances, the customer is likely to initiate such a proposal.

Under our proposed reporting system, the incentives for such arrangements are reduced. When the sales transaction is reported at the exchange rate prevailing on the payment date, the transaction is recorded at $11,364 rather than $11,834. From the selling firm's perspective, it would be better to invoice the sale at YTL2,000,000 with 30-day payment terms. Our proposed reporting system gives the salesperson an incentive to do so. Our model thus uses the actual or forecasted exchange rate prevailing on the day of payment to record local currency transactions. Because these dates are generally in the accounts receivable system (i.e., on sales invoices), this system is readily implemented. The idea is to use *accrual* accounting but maintain a *cash* accounting mentality. Some have correctly argued that sales and expenses in hyperinflationary environments have a built-in implicit interest rate. (Hence the need to discount local currency transactions to their present values before translation.) Our model emphasizes the difference in the exchange rate between the invoice date and the collection date, and thereby automatically incorporates the implicit interest differential (i.e., the International Fisher Effect).[24] Under our reporting framework, there is no need for management to think about what the interest rate is or worry about how to calculate an appropriate discount. After all, operating management cares about the exchange rate difference.

What happens if the customer delays payment beyond the promised date? In our reporting framework, normal payment conditions are shown in reported sales and gross margins. Thus, if a customer agrees to pay on a certain date, the transaction is booked at the exchange rate prevailing on the agreed payment date. If payment takes place after the promised date, the loss in dollars is reported below the line as a translation loss attributed to the applicable line of business or sales segment. That loss is offset by interest income because the original sales terms include an explicit interest cost for delayed payments, which would appear as additional interest income below the line.

To summarize, our transactions-based reporting model

- Allocates translation gains and losses to specific revenues and expenses to which they are related
- Provides both headquarters and subsidiary management with numbers that will support better decisions
- Eliminates the need for parallel controls
- Facilitates performance comparisons over time
- Can be implemented on a cost-effective basis

ISSUES IN FINANCIAL CONTROL

Once questions of strategy and information support systems have been decided, attention shifts to the equally important area of financial control and performance evaluation.[25] These considerations are especially important because they enable financial managers to

1. Implement the global financial strategy of the MNE
2. Evaluate the degree to which the chosen strategies contribute to achieving enterprise goals
3. Motivate management and employees to achieve the enterprise's financial goals as effectively and efficiently as possible

---

[24]Under a freely floating system of exchange rates, spot rates of exchange are theoretically determined by the interrelationships between national rates of inflation, interest rates, and forward rates of exchange, usually expressed as premiums or discounts from the spot rate. If the forecasted rate of inflation in Brazil one month ahead is 30 percent higher than in the United States, the real can be forecast to decline in value by 30 percent relative to the dollar. By the same token, interest rates for maturities of comparable risk can be expected to be 30 percent higher on Brazilian securities than on comparable U.S. securities. For an extended discussion of these relationships, see David K. Eiteman, Arthur I. Stonehill, and Michael H. Moffett, *Multinational Business Finance*, 11 ed. (Reading, MA.: Addison-Wesley, 2007).

[25]Corporate governance is also concerned with corporate control. However, governance issues rely on externally reported information, which is the subject of earlier chapters. For an excellent state-of-the-art piece on corporate governance, see Robert M. Bushman and Abbie J. Smith, "Financial Accounting Information and Corporate Governance," *Journal of Accounting and Economics* 32 (2001): 237–333.

Management control systems aim at accomplishing enterprise objectives in the most effective and efficient manner. Financial control systems, in turn, are quantitative measurement and communication systems that facilitate control through (1) communicating financial goals as appropriate within the organization, (2) specifying criteria and standards for evaluating performance, (3) monitoring performance, and (4) communicating deviations between actual and planned performance to those responsible.

A sound financial control system enables top management to focus the activities of its subsidiaries toward common objectives. A control system consists of operational and financial policies, internal reporting structures, operating budgets, and procedure manuals consistent with top management's goals. Thus, suboptimal behavior, which occurs when a subunit strives to achieve its own ends at the expense of the whole organization, is minimized. A timely reporting system that constantly monitors each unit is a good motivator. An efficient control system also enables headquarters management to evaluate the strategic plans of the company and to revise them when needed. Management's strategic planning tasks are aided by an information system that informs management of environmental changes that might significantly impact on the company. Finally, a good control system enables top management to properly evaluate the performance of subordinates by ensuring that subordinates are held accountable only for events they can control.

If a well-designed control system is useful to a uninational company, it is invaluable to multinational counterparts. As we have repeatedly observed, conditions that impact on management decisions abroad are not only different but are constantly changing.

Domestic Versus Multinational Control System

How should a well-functioning control system be designed in a multinational company? Should a parent company use its domestic control system, unaltered, in its foreign operations? Studies show that the systems used by many multinational enterprises to control their foreign operations are identical in many respects to those used domestically. System items commonly exported include financial and budgetary control and the tendency to apply the same standards developed to evaluate domestic operations. In a now classic paper, David Hawkins offers four basic reasons for this:

1. Financial control considerations are seldom critical in the early stages of establishing a foreign operation.
2. It is normally cheaper to transplant the domestic system than to create from scratch an entire system designed for the foreign operation.
3. To simplify preparing and analyzing consolidated financial statements, the corporate controller's office insists that all operating subsidiaries use similar forms and schedules to record and transmit financial and operating data.
4. Former domestic executives working in the foreign operation and their corporate superiors are more comfortable if they can continue to use as much of the domestic control system as possible, largely because they have reached the highest levels of management by mastering the domestic system.[26]

We feel that exporting domestic control systems abroad is fraught with pitfalls. Given that the multinational operating environment is so diverse, it is difficult to

[26]David F. Hawkins, "Controlling Foreign Operations," *Financial Executive* (February 1965): 25–32.

believe that a central controller's staff could design a single worldwide control system that would be effective everywhere. A look back at the many elements in Exhibit 10-4 will illustrate this point.

Environmental diversity has an unlimited potential impact on the financial control process. Earlier, we observed that geographical distance often impedes traditional methods of communicating between affiliates and company headquarters. Although better technology might overcome geographical distance, cultural distance is harder to overcome. Culture and the business environment interact to create unique sets of managerial values in a country. Language difficulties, cross-cultural differences in attitude toward risk and authority, differences in need-achievement levels, and other cultural attributes often result in unforseen consequences, including (1) misunderstood directives, (2) lower tolerance of criticism, (3) unwillingness to discuss business problems openly or to seek assistance, (4) loss of confidence among foreign managers, (5) unwillingness to delegate authority, and (6) reluctance to assume responsibility. Managers of multinational companies face many tough issues. This is especially the case for managers and employees of acquired companies in cross-border mergers and acquisitions.[27] Frequently, managers and employees steeped in one culture must often operate under management control systems designed in the context of another. Based on the cultural behaviors documented by Hofstede (see Chapter 2), Lere and Portz offer several caveats for those designing management control systems in an international context.[28] Systems designed for highly decentralized operations are less likely to be effective in countries characterized by high certainty avoidance, described earlier, and the high power-distance structures characteristic of socially stratified societies. Delegation of authority may be less acceptable in collectivistic societies, which tend to emphasize the authority of the group as opposed to the individual. In societies that have a longer-term orientation, performance measures that reflect sales growth and market share may be more meaningful than ROI and budget variances that focus on the shorter term. Hopper and Rathnasiri document the consequences of ignoring cultural mores in financial control. In their case analysis, Indian employees, accustomed to a formal bureaucratic rule-bound control system, resisted a new merit-based reward system imposed by the new Japanese owners of their company. Employees reportedly formed alliances with local politicians who were frustrated with their exclusion from organizational affairs. In the end, the Japanese managers were removed and the control system reverted back to its original bureaucratic state characterized by political interventions into operational issues.[29]

Distribution channels, credit terms, industrial policies, financial institutions, and business practices all vary from country to country. International financial managers have to adapt to all of these diverse business practices. In examining reward preferences in Finland and China, Chiang and Birch found that a fuller appreciation of

---

[27]Yaakov Weber and Ehud Menipaz, "Measuring Cultural Fit in Mergers and Acquisitions," *International Journal of Business* Performance *Management* 5, no. 1 (2003): 54.

[28]John C. Lere and Kris Portz, "Management Control Systems in a Global Economy," *CPA Journal* (September 2005): 62–70.

[29]Trevor Hopper and Chandra Rathnasiri, "Japanese Cost Management Meets Sri Lankan Politics: Disappearance and Reappearance of Bureaucratic Management Controls in a Privatized Utility," *Accounting, Auditing and Accountability* 17, no. 1 (2004): 120.

reward preferences entails consideration of employee characteristics and other contextual factors that transcend culture.[30]

Companies with foreign operations must also adapt to unfamiliar governmental regulations and restrictions. Exchange controls, restrictions on capital flows à la Thailand in 2007, joint ownership requirements, and many other specific business regulations are examples. Of all the matters shown in Exhibit 10-4, environmental considerations related to the strength of a nation's currency may be the most important for the design of overseas control systems. Internal rates of inflation and fluctuating currency values are critical, and corporate control systems must allow for them. Applying financial controls designed for a stable environment to one that is less stable is a recipe for failure.

Operational Budgeting

Once strategic goals and capital budgets are in place, management next focuses on short-range planning. Short-range planning involves creating operational budgets or profit plans where needed in the organization. Profit plans are the basis for cash-management forecasts, operating decisions, and management compensation schemes. Budgeted income statements of foreign affiliates are first converted to parent country accounting principles and translated from the local currency (LC) to the parent currency (PC). Periodic comparisons of actual and budgeted profit performance in parent currency require appropriate variance analyses to ensure that deviations from budget are correctly diagnosed for managerial action. While variance analysis is, in principle, the same internationally as domestically, currency fluctuations make it more complex.

The financial performance of a foreign operation can be measured in local currency, home country currency, or both. The currency used can have a significant impact in judging the performance of a foreign unit and its manager. Fluctuating currency values can turn profits (measured in local currency) into losses (expressed in home country currency).

Some favor a local currency perspective because foreign transactions take place in a foreign environment and are done in foreign currency. Foreign currency translation gains and losses are not considered when operations are evaluated in local currency. Those who favor a parent currency perspective argue that home country shareholders ultimately care about domestic currency returns. Because they judge headquarters management by domestic currency returns, foreign managers should be judged by the same standard.

Problems remain even if the parent currency is considered a better measure of performance than the local currency. In theory, the exchange rate between two countries should move in proportion to changes in their differential inflation rates. Thus, if the rate of inflation is 10 percent in Italy and 30 percent in Turkey, the Turkish lira should lose approximately 20 percent of its value relative to the euro. In practice, changes in currency exchange values that lag behind foreign rates of inflation can distort performance measures. Local currency earnings and their dollar equivalents increase during excessive inflation. In the following period, when the foreign currency loses value, the dollar value of local earnings falls even if local currency earnings increase. Under these circumstances, measuring with parent currency introduces random elements in measuring the performance of foreign operations if changes in foreign exchange rates do not track differences in inflation rates.

---

[30]Flora F. T. Chiang and Thomas A. Birtch, "An Empirical Examination of Reward Preferences Within and Across National Settings," *Management International Review* 46, no. 5 (2006): 573–596.

In the long run, one must judge a foreign unit's value as an investment in terms of home-country currency. A parent-currency perspective is appropriate for strategic planning and long-term investment decisions. However, the currency framework used in evaluating managerial performance must depend on who is held accountable for exchange risk. (This issue is separate from who is responsible for exchange risks.) If the corporate treasury manages exchange risks, then it is logical to measure foreign performance in local currency. Parent currency measures are just as valid if exchange gains and losses are removed in evaluating foreign managers. If local managers have the necessary tools to manage exchange gains and losses, measuring their performance in parent currency is justifiable.

Consider some aspects of the budgetary process. Control over a network of domestic and foreign operations requires that foreign currency budgets be expressed in parent currency for comparison. When parent currency figures are used, a change in exchange rates used to establish the budget and monitor performance causes a variance beyond that due to other changes. Three possible rates can be used in drafting the beginning-of-period operating budget:

1. The spot rate in effect when the budget is established
2. The rate expected to prevail at the end of the budget period (projected rate)
3. The rate at the end of the period if the budget is updated whenever exchange rates change (ending rate).[31]

Comparable rates can be used to track performance relative to budget. If different exchange-rate combinations are used to set the budget and track performance, this creates different allocations of responsibility for exchange-rate changes and leads to different possible managerial responses. Let us consider some possibilities.

1. Budget and track performance at initial spot rate. Exchange rate changes have no effect on the evaluation of the foreign manager's performance. Local managers have little incentive to incorporate anticipated exchange rate changes into their operating decisions.
2. Budget at ending (updated) rate and track at ending rate. This combination produces similar results. Local management need not consider exchange rates because the same rate is used for budgeting and evaluation.
3. Budgeting at initial rate and track at ending rate. Local managers have full responsibility for exchange rate changes. Potential negative consequences include padding of budgets by local managers and hedging that may not be optimal for the corporation.
4. Budget and track performance using projected exchange rates. This system reflects a local-currency perspective. Local managers are encouraged to incorporate expected exchange rate changes into their operating plans but are not held responsible for unexpected rate changes, which the parent company absorbs.
5. Budget at projected rate and track at ending rate. This exchange rate combination does not hold the local manager accountable for expected rate changes. Managers are responsible for (and thereby encouraged to hedge) unanticipated exchange rate changes.

---

[31]Donald R. Lessard and Peter Lorange, "Currency Changes and Management Control: Resolving the Centralization/Decentralization Dilemma," *Accounting Review* (July 1977): 628–637.

Which option is best for evaluating managerial performance? All five are found in practice. We focus on the last two, the most common. As an illustration, assume the following (LC = local currency):

Projected rate of exchange:	$0.50 = LC 1	Actual end-of-period rate:	$0.25 = LC 1
Budgeted earnings in LC:	800,000	Actual earnings in LC:	1,000,000
Budget earnings in $:	$400,000	Actual earnings in $:	250,000

If the projected rate is used in monitoring performance, the dollar result is $500,000 (LC 1,000,000 × $0.50), or $100,000 above budget. The manager appears to have done well. But if the actual end-of-period rate is used, the result is $250,000 (LC 1,000,000 × $0.25), or $150,000 below budget. The manager appears to have done poorly. Which rate should be used?

Most discussions of this problem favor option 4. Using the projected exchange rate in budgeting encourages managers to include expected exchange rate movements in their operating decisions. Use of the projected rate to monitor performance, in turn, shields local managers from unanticipated exchange rate changes they cannot control. Also, protection against exchange risk can be coordinated on a company-wide basis.

We think that use of a projected exchange rate for budgeting and the actual ending rate for tracking performance (option 5) also has merit. Like option 4, this approach encourages managers to include anticipated exchange rate changes in their plans for the budget period. Unlike option 4, holding local and corporate managers accountable for unexpected rate changes encourages them to respond to exchange rate movements. Imagine what would happen if a foreign manager, projecting a 30 percent local currency devaluation, actually experiences a 70 percent devaluation and does nothing to offset the larger than expected devaluation because managerial performance is measured using the projected rate.

Option 5 is especially useful when local operating plans can be changed to accommodate unanticipated currency developments. Where any remaining variances between actual and projected rates are ignored when evaluating local managers (i.e., the remaining variance is regarded as a forecasting error, which is the responsibility of corporate headquarters), this system offers additional benefits over option 4.

When responsibility for exchange variances is divided between various levels in management, budget variances need to be analyzed by responsibility level. In our previous example, the foreign subsidiary's operating variance and exchange rate variance would be analyzed as shown in Exhibit 10-6.

EXHIBIT 10-6   Analysis of Exchange Rate Variances

Responsibility	Operating Item	Exchange Rate		Variance
		Computation		
Local currency operations	LC Budget	× Budget		Local-currency
(Foreign management)	− LC Actual	× Budget	=	operating variance
Parent currency operations	LC Actual	× Budget		Parent-currency
(Headquarters'	− LC Actual	× Actual	=	exchange variance
management)				

The total budget variance of –$150,000 (LC 800,000 × $0.50 – LC 1,000,000 × $0.25) would consist of a positive variance of $100,000 attributed to the foreign manager (LC 800,000 × $0.50 – LC 1,000,000 × $0.50) and a negative variance of –$250,000 attributed to corporate headquarters (LC 1,000,000 × $0.50 – LC 1,000,000 × $0.25). Exhibit 10-7 illustrates a framework for analyzing budget variances when the responsibility for exchange variances is divided between local management, an international division's operating management (parent-currency variation), and corporate treasury (variance from budget rates). Here the international division is responsible for hedging unexpected exchange rate changes, while the corporate treasury is responsible for accurate rate forecasts.

Analysis of Exchange Rate Changes

We now provide a more comprehensive example of an exchange rate variance analysis.[32] Exhibit 10-8 shows the budgeted and actual condensed income statements for FC Company at the start and end of the 20X8 budget year. The profit plan for the year (expressed in parent company GAAP) is translated to parent currency at the beginning-of-period exchange rate of FC 1 = PC1. The foreign currency devalues by 20 percent by year-end.

A performance report breaking out price-, volume-, and exchange-rate-induced variances appears in Exhibit 10-9.

EXHIBIT 10-7 Three-Way Analysis of Exchange Rate Variance

		Computation		
Responsibility	**Operating Item**	**Exchange Rate**		**Variance**
Local currency operations (Local management)	LC Budget − LC Actual	× Budget × Budget	=	Local-currency operating variance
Parent-currency operations (International division)	LC Actual − LC Actual	× Budget × Actual	=	Parent-currency operating variance
Foreign exchange variance from budget (Treasury)	LC Budget − LC Budget	× Budget × Actual	=	Exchange rate variance from budget

EXHIBIT 10-8 Income Statement for Exchange Rate Variance Analysis

		Budget		**Actual**
Revenues		FC 5,000		FC 5,700[b]
Cost of goods sold		3,000[a]		2,880
Gross margin		FC 2,000		FC 2,820
Operating expenses	750		825	
Depreciation	500		500	
Interest	250	1,500	300	1,625
Operating income		FC 500		FC 1,195

[a]*The company employs the FIFO costing method and production equaled sales during the year. Unit production costs dropped from a planned FC 3.00 to FC 2.40 per unit.*

[b]*Actual sales increased by 200 units during the year at a price of FC 4.75, FC .25 lower than expected.*

[32]Frederick D. S. Choi and Gerald F. Lewis, "Multinational Budgeting and Control Systems," in *International Finance and Accounting Handbook,* ed. Frederick D. S. Choi, 3rd ed. (New York: John Wiley, 2003), pp. 25.1–25.22.

EXHIBIT 10-9 Performance Report FC Company (for the budget period ending 12/31/X8)

	(1)	(2)	(3)	(4)	(5)	(6)	(7)	(8)	(9)	(10)	(11)	(12)
	Budget			Actual			Variance Analysis					
							Total					
	FC	FX	PC	FC	FX	PC	FC	PC	Vol.	Price/(Cost)	Reported	Exch. Rate
Revenue	5,000	1.0	5,000	5700	.8	4,560	700	(440)	1,000	(300)		(1,140)
Beg. inventory	(3,000)	1.0	(3,000)	(2,800)	1.0	(2,800)	200	200				
Production	(3,000)	1.0	(3,000)	(2,880)	.8	(2,304)	120	696				
Goods available	(6,000)		(6,000)	(5,680)		(5,104)	320	896				
End. inventory	3,000	1.0	3,000	2,800	.8	2,240	(200)	(1,760)				
Cost of sales	(3,000)		(3,000)	(2,880)		(2,864)	120	136	(600)	720		16
Gross margin	2,000		2,000	2,820		1,696	820	(304)	400	420		(1,124)
Operating exp.	(750)	1.0	(750)	(825)	.8	(660)	(75)	90			(75)	165
Depreciation	(500)	1.0	(500)	(500)	1.0	(500)	–	–			–	–
Interest	(250)	1.0	(250)	(300)	.8	(240)	(50)	10			(50)	60
Operating income	500		500	1,195		296	695	(204)	400	420	(125)	(899)

From the perspective of the foreign affiliate, performance variances are measured in local currency and reflect the difference between budget and actual figures for each item in the income statement. These performance variances are detailed in column (7) of Exhibit 10-9. Variances for sales revenues and cost of sales can be broken down into price (cost) and volume variances. The sale volume variance of FC 1,000 is determined by multiplying the change in unit sales volume, 200 units, by the budgeted selling price of FC 5. Applying a similar methodology to cost of sales produces a volume variance of 200 units × FC 3 = FC 600. Thus, the net volume variance affecting gross margin and operating income column (9) is FC 1,000 – FC 600 = FC 400. Variances in sales revenues and cost of sales attributed to price (cost) changes during the budget period are found by multiplying the actual number of units sold by the change in selling price (production cost). This calculation yields a negative price variance of 1,200 units × –FC 0.25 = –FC 300 for sales revenue, and a positive cost variance of 1,200 units × –FC 0.60 = FC 720 for cost of sales, in column (10). Differences between budgeted and actual expenses are shown as nominal variances in column (11).

Based on this analysis, we can see that the improvement in FC Company's operating income of FC 695 (column 7) is attributable to the following factors:

Higher volume (column 9)	FC 400
Lower selling price (column 10)	(300)
Lower production cost (column 10)	720
Higher expenses (column 11)	(125)
Increase in operating income (column 7)	FC 695

When FC Company's performance is evaluated from the parent company perspective, first its local currency results are translated to parent currency. Let us assume that Parent Company designates the parent currency as its functional currency. Accordingly, FC Company's budgeted income statement is translated to parent currency using the temporal translation method. Had the local currency been designated as functional, the current rate translation method would have been used. (See Chapter 6 for a detailed description of these methods.)

To simplify our analysis, Parent Company will analyze FC Company's budget variances using the exchange rate prevailing at the budget date (FC 1.00 = PC 1.00).[33]

With this approach, price and volume variances for sales and cost of sales will mirror those calculated under a local company perspective. The effect of exchange rate changes is calculated by multiplying actual results reported in parent currency by the change in the exchange rate during the budget period. The total variance for sales revenues in parent currency, PC 5,000 – PC 4,560 = PC 440, would be broken down into the following volume, price, and exchange rate variances:

$$\text{Volume variance in col. (9)} = 200 \text{ units} \times FC\ 5 = FC\ 1{,}000 \times 1.0 = PC\ 1{,}000$$

$$\text{Price variance in col. (10)} = 1{,}200 \text{ units} \times –FC\ 0.25$$
$$= FC\ (300) \times 1.0 = PC\ (300)$$

$$\text{Exchange rate variance in col. (12)} = FC\ 5{,}700 \times –PC\ 0.2 = PC\ (1{,}140).$$

---

[33]Alternative exchange rate benchmarks and their implications for performance evaluation of foreign operations are considered in a later section of this chapter.

Similarly, the total variance for cost of sales can be broken down as follows:

$$\text{Volume variance} = 200 \text{ units} \times \text{FC } 3 = \text{FC } 600 \times 1.0 = \text{PC } (600)$$
$$\text{Cost variance} = 1,200 \text{ units} \times -\text{FC } 0.60 = \text{FC } (720) \times 1.0 = \text{PC } 720$$

Exchange rate variance is computed by multiplying each component of cost of goods sold by the exchange rate change in column (12):

Beginning inventory	FC 2,800	×	-0-	=	0
Production	FC 2,880	×	−PC .2	=	576
Ending inventory	FC 2,800	×	−PC .2	=	(560)
					16

Exchange rate variances for operating expenses and depreciation are computed by multiplying the actual figures in local currency by the exchange rate change during the period. This yields an exchange variance for operating expenses FC 825 × −PC 0.2 = PC165 and an exchange variance of FC (300) × −PC 0.2 = PC 60 for interest.

In evaluating FC Company's performance in parent currency, the shortfall of −PC 204 in operating earnings can be attributed to the following factors:

Higher sales volume	PC +400
Lower selling price	(300)
Lower production cost	+720
Higher operating expenses	(75)
Higher interest expenses	(50)
Exchange rate changes (column 12)	(899)
Decrease in parent currency operating earnings (column 8)	PC (204)

A currency translation phenomenon caused by a weakening of the local currency relative to the reporting currency is a major cause of the poor operating result. We discuss the proper evaluation of this currency effect in the section of this chapter on performance evaluation of foreign operations.

STRATEGIC COSTING

While product and standard costing systems have traditionally played a major role in cost control, certain Japanese companies have introduced cost concepts that reinforce their global manufacturing strategies.[34] In doing so they have enhanced the cost control process and, more important, have established a direct link between management accounting practices and corporate goals.[35]

---

[34]These manufacturing strategies embrace continuous improvement in productivity and quality. Specific practices include just-in-time (JIT) manufacturing, total quality control, and other lean production techniques.
[35]Antonio Davila and Marc Wouters, "Designing Cost-Competitive Technology Products Through Cost Management," *Accounting Horizons* 18, no. 1 (2004): 13–26.

In controlling costs at the manufacturing stage, many companies around the world employ standard costing systems that basically estimate what the costs of producing a product should be as a basis for arriving at a reasonable selling price. Actual costs of production are then compared with estimated costs. The resulting variances between standard and actual costs are examined as a basis for corrective action in the production or procurement process. This process can be thought of as a cost-based pricing model.

In contrast, many Japanese companies employ a price-based costing model. Also known as target costing, this strategic costing methodology is premised on designing and building products at prices intended to ensure market success.[36] Consider the Daihatsu Motor Company. Its product development cycle (which normally lasts three years) begins with the production manager instructing Daihatsu's departments to submit the design and performance specifications they believe the car should meet. This is followed by a cost estimate based not on what it will cost to build the car, but on an allowable cost per car. The allowable cost is based on subtracting a target profit margin that reflects the company's strategic plans and financial projections from a target sales price it believes the market will accept.

While used as a target, the allowable cost is not static. During production, allowable cost is reduced every month by a cost reduction rate based on short-term profit objectives. In later years, actual costs of the previous year are the starting point for further reductions, thus ensuring ongoing cost cutting for as long as the car is in production. This market-driven system, known as kaizen costing, significantly reduces the reliance on traditional standard costing systems. Standard costing systems seek to minimize the variances between budgeted and actual costs. Kaizen costing emphasizes doing what is necessary to achieve a desired performance level under competitive market conditions. Exhibit 10-10 summarizes the major differences between standard and kaizen costing concepts.

EXHIBIT 10-10   Standard versus Kaizen Costing Concepts

Standard Cost Concepts	*Kaizen Cost Concepts*
Cost Control	Cost Reduction
Predicated on existing manufacturing conditions	Predicated on continuous manufacturing improvement
Objective: Compliance with performance standards	Objective: Achieve cost reduction targets
Standards set annually	Cost reduction targets set monthly
	Continuous improvement in manufacturing methods to attain target costs
Variance analysis based on actual vs. standard	Variance analysis based on constant cost reduction
Investigate when standards not met	Investigate when target costs not achieved

SOURCE: Reprinted with permission from Yasuhiro Monden and John Y. Lee, "How a Japanese Auto Maker Reduces Costs," *Management Accounting* (Now *Strategic Finance*) August 1993. pp. 22–26, published by the IMA, Montvale, New Jersey, www.ima.org.

---

[36]Ibid.

Another strategic costing concept introduced by the Japanese is behavioral costing.[37] In a process costing system, overhead is applied to goods or routine services using an overhead application rate. From a traditional cost accounting perspective, manufacturing overhead is allocated to products on a cause-and-effect basis. Despite the capital intensity of many Japanese manufacturers, the use of direct labor as an allocation base for assigning overhead costs has continued. This practice encourages production managers to reduce rather than just accumulate costs (i.e., encourage automation). A production manager who wishes to reduce the overhead burden is motivated to substitute capital for labor.

PERFORMANCE EVALUATION OF FOREIGN OPERATIONS

Evaluating performance is central to an effective control system. A properly designed performance evaluation system allows top management to (1) ensure managerial behavior is consistent with strategic priorities, (2) judge the profitability of existing operations, (3) spot areas that are not performing as planned, (4) allocate limited corporate resources productively, and (5) evaluate managerial performance. Developing an effective performance evaluation system is as much an art as a science. Its complexity increases with overseas operations. Performance evaluation of foreign operations must deal with such complications as exchange rate volatility, foreign inflation, transfer pricing, distinctive national cultures, and a host of other environmental effects. If these factors are ignored, headquarters risks receiving distorted measures of operating results. Inappropriate standards of performance may motivate overseas managers to take actions not in line with corporate goals. Direct consequences are reduced corporate efficiency and (possibly) reduced competitiveness.

To date, management accountants have had mixed success in creating comparable financial controls for multinational companies and their foreign operations. In addition to the many contextual variables that complicate the design of global performance evaluation systems is the more recent challenge of developing dynamic performance measurement and financial controls. The behavioral model that continues to describe extant practices is that organizations establish goals, or aspiration levels, and compare their actual performance to these goals.[38] Performance relative to aspiration tends to elicit an array of corporate responses associated with success, performance that exceeds aspirations, and failure, performance that falls short of aspirations.[39]

The remaining sections of this chapter examine some major issues associated with the performance evaluation of foreign operations, describe how leading MNCs evaluate performance, and offer some general policy guidelines.

---

[37]T. Hiromoto, "Japanese Management Accounting," *Harvard Business Review* (July/August 1988): 22–26.

[38]R.M. Cyert and J. G. March, *A Behavioral Theory of the Firm* (Englewood Cliffs, NJ: Prentice-Hall, 1963).

[39]Stephen J. Mezias, Patrice Murphy, Yaru Chen, and Mikelle A. Calhoun, "Dynamic Performance Measurement Systems for a Global World: The Complexities to Come," in *International Finance and Accounting Handbook*, ed. Frederick D. S. Choi, 3rd ed. (New York: John Wiley, 2003), chap. 26.

Consistency

Survey results show that a principal goal of performance evaluation is to ensure profitability.[40] There is a potential conflict, however, when the performance evaluation system does not suit the specific nature of a foreign operation that may have purposes other than short-run profit. MNCs establish foreign operations for many reasons. Companies that depend on a steady supply of raw materials generally expand overseas to secure their supplies. Others invest abroad to lower production costs. Other reasons for expanding abroad include the need to (1) avoid losing a foreign market to major competitors, (2) create markets for components and related products, (3) diversify business risks, (4) search for new markets, (5) satisfy government regulations, and (6) spread overhead costs among more producing units. Many of these objectives are strategic rather than tactical. Emphasis on short-term profitability and efficiency can divert attention from critical manufacturing and corporate strategy and alienate corporate personnel.

Given the uniqueness of each foreign subsidiary's mission, performance evaluation systems must allow for how the subsidiary's objectives fit in with overall corporate goals. For example, if a foreign subsidiary's purpose is to produce components for other units in the system, it should be evaluated in terms of how its prices, production, quality, and delivery timetables compare to other sources of supply. This use of nonfinancial performance measures to complement traditional financial meaures of performance is consistent with the contemporary notion of employing a *balanced scorecard*. Subsidiary managers should participate fully in establishing their objectives. Their participation helps to ensure that they will be evaluated within a framework that is sensitive to local operating conditions and consistent with overall corporate goals. Companies should be sure not to sacrifice long-term objectives because subsidiary managers are preoccupied with short-term results. Adherence to long-term goals can be accomplished by making sure that short-term performance goals and management incentives are met within the company's strategic plans.

Unit vs. Managerial Performance

CONTROLLER A: I think generally we would look upon the manager's and unit's performance as about one and the same. The operation of the foreign unit is the responsibility of the manager, and how the unit does is pretty much tied in with his evaluation.[41]

CONTROLLER B: In terms of evaluating the manager, it is very much related to how he is doing against his budget because he did present his budget, which was approved by the executive office, and this was his plan of action for the coming year. Now in terms of evaluating whether his unit is one that we want to continue or invest in or whether we should be looking at other alternatives, the return on investment becomes the significant factor.[42] These are direct quotes.

---

[40]Survey results suggest that the one measure believed to provide reliable information for comparing operations in multiple countries is profitability, measured by the ratio of selling, general, and administrative expenses to sales. See Wanda A. Wallace and John Walsh, "Apples-to-Apples Profits Abroad," *Financial Executive* 2 (1995): 28–31.
[41]Paul A. Samuelson, "Economic and Cultural Aspects of Tomorrow's Multinational Firms," *Japan and the World Economy* (December 2000): 393–394.
[42]Ibid., p. 26.

Should we distinguish between the performance of the unit and the performance of its manager in evaluating a foreign operation? Although some may believe there is no distinction, this position can be held only under limited conditions.

The actions of several parties, each with a different stake in the outcome, may affect the performance of a foreign operation. These parties include (but are not limited to) local management, headquarters management, the host government, and the parent company's government.

Local managers obviously influence reported earnings through their operating decisions. Decisions made at corporate headquarters also affect foreign earnings. For example, to protect the value of assets located in devaluation-prone countries, corporate treasury will often instruct foreign units to transfer funds to subsidiaries located in strong-currency countries.

Host government actions and policies also directly affect the reported results of a foreign subsidiary. Required minimum capitalization ratios in some countries often enlarge the investment base against which earnings are compared. Foreign exchange controls that limit the availability of foreign currency to pay for needed imports will often depress a subsidiary's performance. Wage and price controls can also damage the reported performance of local managers.

These considerations make it clear that a distinction must be made between managerial and unit performance.[43] Evidence suggests that this is seldom the case in practice.[44] Local managers should be evaluated only on those balance sheet and income statement items they can influence. This specific evaluation can be done in practice by dividing each balance sheet and income statement item into controllable and noncontrollable components, as illustrated in Exhibit 10-11.

Under this framework, the manager of a U.S. affiliate in Bogota would not be held accountable for effective interest charges incurred in connection with a Canadian dollar

EXHIBIT 10-11	Financial Statement Format for Control (Local Currency)	
	Locally Controllable	*Locally Noncontrollable*
Balance Sheet		
Assets (detailed)	xx	xx
Liabilities (detailed)	xx	xx
Owners' equity (detailed)	xx	xx
Income Statement		
Revenues	xx	xx
Operating expenses	xx	xx
Interest	xx	xx
"Other"	xx	xx
Taxes	xx	xx
Net Income	xx	xx

[43]Business International Corporation, *Assessing Foreign Subsidiary Performance: Systems and Practices of Leading Multinational Companies* (New York: BIC, 1982), p. 10.
[44]Wagdy M. Abdallah, Nadeem M. Firoz, and Ikechi Ekeledo, "Performance Evaluation of Foreign Subsidiary Managers Using Intra Company Pricing," *International Tax Journal* 31, no. 4 (2005): 5–12.

borrowing mandated by corporate treasury. Because the borrowing decision was made at headquarters, headquarters management is responsible for the interest cost (i.e., the nominal interest rate in Canada plus the exchange risk). Because the affiliate derives some benefit from the loan proceeds, it should pay an equitable interest charge. This related charge is called a capital charge and is based on the cost that would have been incurred had the Colombian manager borrowed locally or from the parent.

Performance Criteria

A single criterion is unlikely to capture every factor of performance of interest to headquarters management.[45] Two of the more widely used financial performance criteria used by MNCs for evaluating their foreign operations are return on investment (ROI) and budgeted performance. ROI relates enterprise income to a specified investment base; budgeted performance compares operating performance to a budget. Budgetary control means that any difference between budget and actual performance can be traced to the manager or unit responsible. One classic study demonstrated that budgetary control is better than ROI comparisons for evaluating managerial performance. ROI measures may be more appropriate for measuring unit performance, while budget comparisons may be more useful in evaluating managers.

In an earlier performance evaluation study by Business International, U.S. and non-U.S. MNCs surveyed stated that the most important financial criterion used to evaluate the performance of overseas units is budgeted versus actual profit, followed by ROI. Also considered somewhat important were budget versus actual sales, return on sales, return on assets, budget versus actual return on investment, and operating cash flows. As for cash flows, however, U.S.-based multinationals tended to stress cash flows to the parent, whereas non-U.S. multinationals preferred cash flows to the foreign subsidiary. Interestingly, both groups gave little importance to the notion of residual income recommended in the literature. Fast-growth private companies tend to favor operating income and revenue growth.[46]

Many companies do not confine their performance criteria to financial considerations. Nonfinancial criteria reinforce financial measures by focusing on actions that may significantly affect long-term performance. These criteria are especially important in distinguishing between managerial and unit performance.

Important nonfinancial measures include market share, product and process innovation, on-time performance, product reliability, customer response time, personnel development (gauged in terms of number of people promoted in relation to the number of promotable employees), employee morale (ascertained by in-house opinion surveys), and productivity measurements. No less significant is performance in social responsibility and host government relations. Such nonfinancial factors are vital to ensure continued success abroad.[47]

---

[45]For example, see Rajiv D. Banker, Hsihui Chang, and Mina J. Pizzini, "Balanced Scorecard: Performance Measures Linked to Strategy," *Accounting Review* 79, no. 1(2004): 1–23.

[46]Trendsetter Barometer, www.barometersurveys.com

[47]Said, HassabElnaby, and Wier find that inclusion of nonfinancial performance measures in compensation contracts improves both current and future firm performance. See Amal A. Said, Hassan R. HassabElnaby, and Benson Wier, "An Empirical Investigation of the Performance Consequences of Nonfinancial Measures," *Journal of Management Accounting Research* 15, no. 1(2003): 193–223.

Despite difficulties in measurement, nonfinancial criteria are considered important in practice. Earlier surveys suggest that market share is important, followed by productivity improvement, relationships with host governments, quality control, and employee development and safety. Fullerton and Walters report that firms implementing a higher degree of just-in-time (JIT) practices, such as lean manufacturing strategies and continuous quality enhancements, are more likely to use nonfinancial criteria.[48] These often include such measures as quality results, competitive benchmarking, waste and vendor quality, setup times, scrap, and downtime.[49]

Additional issues concern identifying and measuring relevant components of ROI and budget indicators. Variations in ROI and budget comparisons relate to appropriate elements of income and the investment base. Thus, should income be the difference between revenues and expenses as they appear in a subsidiary's conventional income statement, or should it incorporate other dimensions? While conventional income measures may reflect a firm's results better than a strictly cash flow measure, they can be misleading in an international setting. To begin, net income may include allocated corporate expenses that the unit manager cannot control. It may not reflect the strategic nature of the foreign unit's mission. A subsidiary's reported results rarely reflect its total contribution.

To remedy these shortcomings, corporate accountants need to specify, as accurately as they can, the returns specifically attributable to the foreign subsidiary's existence. To report profits, therefore, they should add back such things as (1) royalty payments, service fees, and corporate allocations charged to the foreign subsidiary and (2) profits on intracorporate sales to the subsidiary. If sales to the subsidiary are not made at arm's-length prices, the foreign subsidiary's profits should be adjusted for transfer pricing subsidies (transfer prices are discussed more fully in Chapter 12). Income amounts used for managerial evaluations should preferably include only those elements of revenues and expenses that unit managers can control.

What about the ROI denominator? Should it consist of shareholders' equity? Should it incorporate shareholders' equity plus total interest-bearing debt (alternatively, fixed assets plus net working capital)? Should it be total assets? If so, should assets include nonproductive resources that are carried because of local environmental constraints? Should it include assets that are allocated by corporate headquarters, such as those corporate treasury controls?

As with income, we believe that a distinction should be made. For managers, the investment base should consist of the resources they can control. Thus, excess inventories (stockpiled because of host-government exchange control policies), should be eliminated, as should intracorporate receivables and cash balances over whose levels the local managers have little influence. For the subsidiary, the investment base should include all capital employed in accomplishing its stated objectives.

Assume, as an example, that a foreign unit ends the year with the following foreign currency (FC) financial position. (Current liabilities exclude any interest-paying debt, including the current portion of long-term debt.)

[48]Rosemary R. Fullerton and Cheryl S. McWatters, "The Role of Performance Measures and Incentive Systems in Relation to the Degree of JIT Implementation," *Accounting, Organizations and Society* 27 (2002): 711–735.

[49]S. J. Daniel and W. D. Reitsperger, "Linking JIT Strategies and Control Systems: A Comparison of the United States and Japan," *International Executive* 38 (1996): 95–121.

Cash	FC	500	Current liabilities	FC	300
Accounts receivable		200	Long-term debt		800
Inventory		300			
Fixed assets		1,000	Owners' equity		900
	FC	2,000		FC	2,000

Assume further that earnings before interest and taxes (EBIT) are FC 200. Local interest rates average 12 percent.

Many companies in the United Kingdom and the United States compute ROI by relating EBIT to fixed assets plus net working capital. In our example, this investment base yields an ROI statistic of 11.7 percent (FC 200/FC 1,700). The comparable figure for many Netherlands-based MNCs, however, is closer to 16.7 percent, because Dutch companies typically remove the ending cash balance from the definition of capital employed. (Cash on hand is considered a nonearning asset in the Netherlands.)[50]

Measurement Issues and Changing Prices in Evaluation

The designer of an evaluation system for foreign operations must also face the issue of accounting measurements. Should local currency asset values be adjusted for changing prices where inflation is a significant force?[51] Such restatements directly affect measures of various ROI components and performance statistics for budgeting and performance evaluation. For example, failure to account for inflation generally overstates return-on-investment measures. As a result, corporate resources may not be directed to their most promising use within the corporation.

In Chapter 7 we said that an internal information system, sensitive to the effects of changing prices, provides a foundation for an inflation management strategy. For a closer look at such issues, we describe a case study examining the performance evaluation practices of ICI, the U.K. chemical giant.

PERFORMANCE EVALUATION PRACTICES: ICI

During the oil embargo of the early 1970s, the price of oil, one of ICI's major raw materials, shot up by a factor of 5 in one year. As a result, top management was informed that even a 50 percent rate of return was inadequate! An examination of the impact of inflation on historical accounts disclosed six adverse consequences: (1) cost of goods sold was understated compared with current sales, (2) capital employed was understated in relation to its current value, (3) as a result of (1) and (2), returns on capital were doubly overstated, (4) comparisons of divisional performance based on similar assets of different ages were spurious, (5) intercountry comparisons of subsidiary performance were meaningless, and (6) performance comparisons over time were invalid.[52]

---

[50]On the other hand, Dutch companies use cash on hand as a standard of comparison. Return on assets employed should at least exceed the return that would have been earned had cash been invested in the local capital market, 12 percent in our example.

[51]Even in countries where rates of inflation are low, the cumulative effect of changing prices on long-lived assets can be significant. This is especially true of a capital-intensive multibusiness with older fixed assets.

[52]Business International Corporation, *Assessing Foreign Subsidiary Performance: Systems and Practices of Leading Multinational Companies* (New York: BIC, 1982), p. 124.

To eliminate these distortions, ICI incorporated current-cost adjustments (CCA) in its internal reporting system. ICI divided its performance measures into two categories: long term (at least one year) and short term. Cash flow generation by product and ROI are the principal long-term measures. With its cash flow measure, ICI sought to determine whether a product would earn enough money to pay for replacing its plant, its share of corporate costs, and return enough profit to finance realistic growth. In modeling its operations, ICI discovered that the required rate of CCA return differed by country. For example, its operations in Germany needed twice the U.K. rate of return to finance the same rate of growth, primarily due to tax factors.

ICI employed as its measure of ROI the ratio of current-cost operating profit (before interest, taxes, and dividends) to current-cost fixed assets plus net working capital. Assets were valued at replacement cost net of depreciation for large businesses, and at gross for smaller product lines to eliminate distortions due to the age of the assets (i.e., the denominator would decrease over time simply due to depreciation, thus raising the rate of return).

In Western Europe, profit was measured before interest and taxes because these expenses were the responsibility of headquarters, and it was difficult to relate a loan to a particular project or determine the actual tax paid when a product was made in one country and sold in several others. Where performance was evaluated on a subsidiary basis (e.g., Brazil and Australia), profit was measured after interest and tax. The reason ICI chose to do this was because these subsidiaries did their own borrowing, and investment decisions there were influenced by local taxes and tax incentives. By using a current-cost ROI as opposed to a historical-cost return, ICI largely insulated its measure of return from local taxes, tax incentives, and inflation. As a result, ICI could compare businesses in different countries and at different times.

While ICI mainly used cash flow generation and ROI to assess long-term performance, its principal short-term performance measure was to compare actual results against budget, with particular interest in financial ratios, such as gross profit margin (i.e., profit before corporate costs). The company employed a three-year plan: The plan's first year became that period's operating budget. Performance was tracked monthly and quarterly. Quarterly results were considered more significant.

Like many MNCs, ICI incorporated inflationary expectations when budgeting local selling prices and operating costs, such as expected labor expense. ICI preferred to incorporate current values in its budgeting system and forecasted a replacement value for cost of goods sold and depreciation. The stated reason for this approach was to force management's attention to the fact that if a company is in a volatile cost setup, as when the price of oil and derivatives rises or falls very fast, it has to use the cost it will incur to replace raw materials and factor that into its selling price. If it uses historical cost, profits may not be adequate to continue purchasing oil at current prices.

Thus performance was tracked using the actual cost of goods incurred each month. The unit's manager was held accountable for the variance (if any), because unexpected (i.e., greater than forecasted) increases in cost could be countered by raising prices.[53]

The budget also included a forecasted depreciation expense based on local indexes reflecting the asset's replacement cost. The local manager was not responsible for any variance (calculated quarterly) between forecasted and actual depreciation. It

---

[53]This assumed that competitors suffered the same cost increases, which might not always be true due to exchange rate factors.

was not considered feasible for a local manager to discern and react to a change in forecasted depreciation. However, the product manager was expected to achieve his budgeted profit after actual depreciation.

ICI also included a forecasted monetary working capital adjustment (MWCA) in its budget. (See Chapter 7 for a discussion of this concept.) ICI did not consider the difference between forecasted and actual MWCA to be very meaningful, because this variance was considered to be caused by changes in costs and selling prices and would show up elsewhere in the profit and loss account.[54]

ICI's solution to inflation reporting largely focused on aggregate balance sheets and income statements. We next offer an internal reporting system that allows management to examine reported numbers in more disaggregated fashion.

Foreign Currency Effects

The foreign exchange variance analysis earlier in the chapter assumes that local managers are responsible for domestic operating results. Ideally, the local manager's responsibility for exchange variances should be in line with the ability to react to exchange rate changes.

The economic impact of changes in exchange rates on performance may be more profound than can be seen through accounting measures alone. To more fully assess the impact of inflation and currency volatility, and gauge their own ability to react, companies need to analyze their competitive market position and the impact of currency changes on their costs and revenues and those of their competition. To shed more light on this issue, we return to ICI's handling of exchange rates and budgetary control. Like many MNCs, ICI uses a forecasted rate of exchange to set budgets and the actual end-of-period rate to measure performance. Unlike many MNCs, ICI believes that the variance that results when the actual exchange rate differs from the budget rate is not meaningful by itself. For example, the company may have budgeted a rate for the euro for its subsidiary in France, and the end-of-the-month exchange rate turns out to be identical to the forecasted rate. There is no arithmetic variance, but ICI may have lost some sales volume in France. The reason may be that its competitors are exporters from Canada and the Canadian dollar has weakened against the euro. As a result the Canadians may have a margin advantage against ICI and can lower their prices in euros to maintain the same level of profits when converting to Canadian dollars.

Thus, ICI believes that exchange rate changes have more impact than accounting measures convey. It finds that further analysis is necessary to determine the real impact of currency fluctuations on performance, arrive at effective reactions, and determine how far the local manager is to be held accountable for protecting the budgeted profit in pounds sterling.

To achieve these objectives, ICI looks at the currencies in which its costs and revenues arise in relation to those of its competitors. Here is a view from within the company:

> We buy oil and oil-related products, which are basically dollar denominated, and we are not a price-maker but are in competition with other producers in

---

[54]The gearing adjustment on net, nontraded monetary liabilities (a form of purchasing power gain) was not incorporated into budgeting because raising funds was a headquarters responsibility.

Europe. Our oil costs are dollar denominated and our revenues are denominated in other European currencies. If the pound appreciates against all other currencies, then revenues arising from foreign sales, and even those from U.K. sales subject to competitive pressures, will be reduced. As partial compensation, raw material costs (dollar-denominated oil) will be lower, but on balance ICI is worse off because the decrease in raw material costs is less than the decrease in sales revenue in absolute terms. The figure can be significant because ICI is the U.K.'s largest single exporter. Currency movements in the opposite direction are, of course, possible and in fact have recently occurred. An appreciation of the U.S. dollar against all other currencies puts the same raw material cost pressures on our European competitors as on U.K. manufacturing operations so we will not suffer a comparative disadvantage. The comparative disadvantage would arise if there was a depreciation of the pound versus the dollar coupled with a depreciation of other European currencies against the pound. This would both reduce our income and increase our costs.[55]

This approach to analyzing the economic impact of currency movements affects ICI's evaluation of its managers, whose freedom to react to such external circumstances is limited. In measuring the performance of managers, the company takes into account the extent to which they have been affected by factors beyond their control and also their reactions to these factors.

PERFORMANCE STANDARDS

Once questions of measurement are resolved, companies must develop meaningful standards with which to evaluate performance. But what standards are appropriate for a company with operations all over the world? Let's look at some possibilities.

A company may have certain corporate-wide standards, such as a minimum required ROI, that it applies to individual subsidiaries or product lines; or it may set different ROI levels or other benchmarks (such as gross margin) for different subsidiaries or product lines. These standards may be incorporated into budgets and can later be compared with results. Performance can also be measured over time. Companies may require stated improvement in specific ratios or income. Past performance is usually significant in developing the next period's budget. Finally, firms can compare their own overseas performance with that of competitors or compare its own units with one another.

Comparing the performance of foreign units against that of their competitors can be useful. At the same time, comparisons have many pitfalls. (See Chapter 9 for a more extensive discussion of the problems involved in analyzing foreign financial statements.) For example, when competitors are local firms, the problem of data availability and adequacy may be considerable, especially if the competitors are privately held. When data are available, comparisons might be difficult. Competitors' transfer pricing policies and accounting principles may be impossible to determine. Cross-border comparisons compound these problems.

---

[55]Ibid., p. 127.

Comparing subsidiaries with other units of the parent company, either at home or abroad, must also be done cautiously, because questions of comparability again arise. Differences in subsidiary objectives will automatically bias performance comparisons unless directly accounted for. Even if subsidiary objectives are the same, differences in country risk profiles must be considered. If higher levels of risk are to be offset by higher levels of return, it is reasonable to expect higher profitability from operations in riskier countries. To date, however, no single agreed-upon formula guides how to incorporate country risks in assessing subsidiary performance.

Many firms require a shorter payback period, adjust cash flow projections for risk, or raise the required rate of return when considering investments in riskier countries.[56] ROI is readily adjusted for political risk because one can set a desired ROI to include a premium in line with risk in a given country (offset to some extent by the lower risk that results from geographical diversification of a firm's portfolio of foreign operations).

Applying risk premiums to an ROI goal is unavoidably subjective, but the process can be made systematic. One approach is to adjust the corporate-wide ROI by a numerical risk index developed for each country. For example, assume that a country-by-country risk-assessment service, such as Business International, assigns a total score of 65 out of 100 possible points to Country Y. (A higher number indicates a lower country risk.) If a company's worldwide target ROI is 15 percent, Country Y's risk-adjusted target ROI is about 23 percent (15 divided by 65 percent). If Country Z's risk index is 75, its target ROI will be 20 percent (15 divided by 75 percent). Under this system, the differences between a subsidiary's actual ROI and its budgeted ROI are calculated and used to compare the performance of subsidiaries in different countries. In this example, if one subsidiary's actual ROI in Country Y was 23.5 percent, and the ROI of another subsidiary in Country Z was 21 percent, the subsidiary in Country Z will have performed better, because its variance from budgeted ROI was a positive 1 percent versus 0.5 percent for the subsidiary in Country Y. An overall risk index may not reflect the risk to which a particular foreign subsidiary is exposed. For example, the risk exposure of an oil company's subsidiary may differ from that of a consumer goods manufacturer in the same country. Thus, the risk index should be modified to reflect the specific risk to each unit. A more critical issue, however, is whether a company-wide ROI standard should be applied at all.

Performance evaluations based on a single company-wide standard are generally unsatisfactory. A performance budget is a more useful standard of comparison for multinational operations. Realistic budgets enable performance targets to incorporate considerations that are unique to a particular unit. Comparisons of actual performance to a budget also enable headquarters management to distinguish results for which subsidiary managers can be held responsible from those that are beyond their control.

---

[56]For an analysis of the impact of political risk on the cost of capital, see Kirt C. Butler and Domingo Castelo Joaquin, "A Note on Political Risk and the Required Return on Foreign Direct Investment," *Journal of International Business Studies* 29, no. 3 (1998): 599–608.

Following are seven caveats that may be useful guidelines in evaluating the results of foreign operations:

1. Foreign subsidiaries should not be evaluated as independent profit centers when they are really strategic components of a multinational system.
2. Company-wide return on investment criteria should be supplemented by performance measures tailored to the specific objectives and environments of each foreign unit.
3. Specific goals that consider each subsidiary's internal and external environment should be incorporated in performance budgets.
4. A subsidiary's performance should be evaluated in terms of departures from these objectives, the reasons for the departures, and managerial responses to unforeseen developments.
5. Subsidiary managers should not be held responsible for results that are beyond their control (at home and abroad).
6. Subsidiary managers whose performance is being measured should participate fully in setting the goals by which they will be judged.
7. Multiple measures of performance, financial and nonfinancial, should be used in evaluating foreign operations.

Value Reporting

We end this chapter with a recent management accounting development that attempts to bridge the gap between internal and external users of accounting information. It acknowledges that financial managers have a responsibility not only to assure compliance with stated objectives but to engage in value creation. It entails reporting both financial and nonfinancial measures and processes that provide company managers and their shareholders with historical and predictive indicators of shareholder value. It also recognizes that information useful to management is also of interest to investors seeking to assess future enterprise value.[57]

A company that embraces value reporting is Infosys Technologies, alluded to in earlier chapters. What follows is a case description of the company's value reporting platform. To increase its transparency with the investing community, Infosys provides investors with data that are used internally to manage its affairs. The conceptual framework that guides its disclosures is mapped below:

$$\text{Value creation} \rightarrow \text{Value Preservation} \rightarrow \text{Value Realization}$$

Value is created by developing and executing operating strategies that generate positive net present values of expected future cash flows. Value is preserved by implementing sound financial controls and engaging in the effective management of enterprise risks. By consistently delivering on its promises, management helps to assure investors that they will reap the benefits the business has created. As the firm's traditional financial statements have a historical orientation, Infosys provides a range of nonfinancial information that is related to creating long-term shareholder value. These reports are organized among four themes diagrammed in Exhibit 10-12.

---

[57]Robert Eccles, Robert Herz, Mary Keegan, and David Phillips, *The Value Reporting Revolution: Moving Beyond the Earnings Game* (New York: John Wiley, 2001).

EXHIBIT 10-12 ValueReporting™ Disclosure Model	
External Market Overview • Competitive environment • Regulatory environment • Macroeconomic environment	**Internal Value Strategy** • Goals • Objectives • Governance • Organization
Value Platform • Innovation • Brands • Customers • Supply chain • People	**Managing for Value** • Financial information • Financial position • Risk management • Segment performance

Specific information provided to investors that is consistent with the disclosure framework in Exhibit 10-12 includes information on brand valuation, economic value-added, intangible assets, financial position statement including intangible assets, current-cost financial statements (see Chapter 7), human resource accounting, and a value-added statement. The company adopts similar measures for its internal measurement of business performance. This enures congruence between the financial and nonfinancial measures used internally and those used by the market. This information model was used by Infosys before it went public in 1993. Infosys is a good example of a company that has excelled by constantly adapting to the ever-changing environment of international business.

SELECTED REFERENCES

Abdallah, Wagdy M., Nadeem M. Firoz, and Ikechi Ekeledo, "Performance Evaluation of Foreign Subsidiary Managers Using Intra Company Pricing," *International Tax Journal* 31, no. 4 (2005): 5–12, 50–51.

Awasthi, Vidya N., Chee W. Chow, and Anne Wu, "Cross-Cultural Differences in the Behavioral Consequences of Imposing Performance Evaluation and Reward Systems: An Experimental Investigation," *International Journal of Accounting* 36, no. 3 (2001): 291–309.

Banker, Rajiv, Hsihui Chang, and Mina J. Pizinni, "Balance Scorecard: Performance Measures Linked to Strategy," *Accounting Review* 79, no. 1 (2004): 1–23.

Burnett, Royce D., Mark Friedman, and Uday Murthy, "Financial Reports: Why You Need XBRL," *Journal of Corporate Accounting and Finance* 17, no. 5 (2006): 33–40.

Chiang, Flora F. T., and Thomas A. Birtch, "An Empirical Examination of Reward Preferences Within and Across National Settings," *Management International Review* 46, no. 5 (2006): 573–596.

Choi, Frederick D. S., "Financial Reporting in Hyperinflationary Environments: A Transactions Analysis Framework for Management," in *International Finance and Accounting Handbook*, ed. Frederick D. S. Choi, 3rd ed., New York: John Wiley, 2003, pp. 27.1–27.13.

Cooper, Ian A., and Evi Kaplanis, "Partially Segmented International Capital Markets and International Capital Budgeting," *Journal of*

International Money and Finance 19 (2000): 309–329.

Davila, Antonio, and Marc Wouters, "Designing Cost-Competitive Technology Products Through Cost Management," *Accounting Horizons* 18, no. 1 (2004): 13–26.

Desai, Mihir A., C. Fritz Foley, and James R. Hines, "A Multinational Perspective on Capital Structure Choice and Internal Capital Markets," *Journal of Finance* 59, no. 6 (2004): 2451–2487.

Eccles, Robert, Robert Herz, Mary Keegan, and David Phillips, *The Value Reporting Revolution: Moving Beyond the Earnings Game,* New York: John Wiley, 2001.

Eiteman, D. K., Arthur I. Stonehill, and Michael H. Moffett, *Multinational Business Finance,* Reading, MA.: Addison-Wesley, 2007.

Gapen, Michael T., Dale F. Gray, Cheng Hoom Lim, and Yingbin Xiao," Measuring and Analyzing Sovereign Risk with Contingent Claims," IMF Working paper No. 05/155, August 1, 2005.

Haka, Susan F., and Dan L. Heitger, "International Managerial Accounting Research: A Contracting Framework and Opportunities," *International Journal of Accounting* 39, no. 1 (2004): 21–69.

Howell, Robert A., "The CFO: From Controller to Global Strategic Partner," *Financial Executive* (April 2006): 20–25.

Jaruga, Alicja, and Simon S. M. Ho, "Management Accounting in Transitional Economies," *Management Accounting Research* 13 (2002): 375–378.

Lere, John C., and Kris Portz, "Management Control Systems in a Global Economy," *CPA Journal* (September 2005): 62-70.

Marshall, Jeffrey, and Ellen M. Heffes, "What Does the Future Hold for Finance and CFO's?" *Financial Executive* (December 2006): 16–20.

Mezias, Stephen J., Patrice Murphy, Ya-Ru Chen, and Mikelle A. Calhoun, "Dynamic Performance Measurement Systems for a Global World: The Complexities to Come," in *International Finance and Accounting Handbook,* ed. Fredrick D. S. Choi, 3rd ed., New York: John Wiley, 2003, pp. 26.1–26.14.

Panagiotou, George, "Bringing SWOT into Focus," *Business Strategy Review* 14, no. 2 (2003): 8–10.

Weber, Yaakov, and Ehud Menipaz, "Measuring Cultural Fit in Mergers and Acquisitions," *International Journal of Business Performance Management* 5, no. 1 (2003): 54.

DISCUSSION QUESTIONS

1. This chapter identifies four dimensions of the strategic planning process. How does Daihatsu's management accounting system conform with this process?

2. Explain the difference between a standard costing system and the kaizen costing system popularized in Japan.

3. Companies must decide whose rate of return to use (i.e., local vs. parent-currency returns) when evaluating foreign direct investment opportunities. Discuss the internal reporting dimensions of this decision in a paragraph or two.

4. As an employee on the financial staff of Multinational Enterprises, you are assigned to a three-person team that is assigned to examine the financial feasibility of establishing a wholly-owned manufacturing subsidiary in the Czech Republic. You are to compute an appropriate hurdle (discount) rate with which to conduct a discounted cash flow analysis. List all the parameters you would consider in measuring your company's cost of capital (discount rate).

5. What are some of the issues involved in designing multinational information/control systems?

6. Refer to Exhibit 10-7, which presents the methodology for analyzing exchange rate variances. Describe in your own words what this methodology accomplishes.

7. State the unique difficulties involved in designing and implementing performance evaluation systems in multinational companies.
8. Why is it better to record sales transacted in a high-inflation country and denominated in foreign currency at the expected spot rate on the date the transaction is settled, instead of the average or month-end spot rate prescribed by conventional accounting?
9. Foreign exchange rates are used to establish budgets and track actual performance. Of the various exchange rate combinations mentioned in this chapter, which do you favor? Why? Is your view the same when you add local inflation to the budgeting process?
10. WOTS-UP analysis fails to identify a best strategy. Refer to Exhibit 10-1 and examine the strategies Daimler Benz identified in its two-by-two matrix. What other strategies would you have considered?
11. List six arguments that support a parent company's use of its domestic control systems for its foreign operations, and six arguments against this practice.
12. How does value reporting differ from the financial reporting model you learned in your basic accounting course? Do you think this is a good reporting innovation?

EXERCISES

1. Slovenia Corporation manufactures a product that is marketed in North America, Europe, and Asia. Its total manufacturing cost to produce 100 units of product X is €2,250, detailed as follows:

Raw materials	€ 500
Direct labor	1,000
Overhead	750
Total	€ 2,250

The company bases its selling price on a cost-plus formula.

Required: What would be Slovenia Corporation's selling price per unit if it wants a gross profit of 10 percent above cost?

2. Slovenia Corporation (in Exercise 1) wants to be price competitive on an international basis. To accomplish this it must be able to price its product no higher than $21.50. Using the target costing methodology described in this chapter, what would be Slovenia Corporation's allowable costs? Assume that the company still wants a profit margin of 10 percent of its allowable costs. What does your calculation imply about its manufacturing costs?

3. Review the operating data incorporated in Exhibit 10-3 for the Russian subsidiary of the U.S. parent company.

Required: Using Exhibit 10-3 as a guide, prepare a cash flow report from a parent currency perspective identifying the components of the expected returns from the Russian investment for the first two years of its operations. The U.S. parent company is only allowed to receive as dividends 70 percent of its affiliate's reported net income, after Russian corporate income taxes. However, U.S. tax law provides a credit against U.S. taxes for any foreign income taxes paid.

4. Assume that management is considering whether to make the foreign direct investment described in Exercise 3. Investment will require $8,000,000 in equity capital. Cash flows to the parent are expected to increase by 5 percent over the previous year for each year after year 2 (through year 6). Exchange rate forecasts are as follows:

Year	Rate
1	RUB 20 = $1
2	RUB 21 = $1
3	RUB 23 = $1
4–6	RUB 25 = $1

Management insists on a risk premium of 10 percent when evaluating foreign projects.

Required: Assuming a weighted average cost of capital of 10 percent and no expected changes in differential tax rates, evaluate the desirability of the Russian investment using a traditional discounted cash flow analysis.

5. Do a WOTS-UP analysis for your school or firm relative to its major competitor. Based on your analysis, suggest several countermeasures your dean or CEO might consider to maintain or improve your organization's competitive standing.

6. Assume the following:

- Inflation and Turkish lira (YTL) devaluation is 30 percent per month, or 1.2 percent per workday.

- Foreign exchange rates at selected intervals for the current month are:

1/1	100.0
1/10	109.6
1/20	119.6
1/30	130.0

- The real rate of interest is 1.5 percent per month, or 20 percent per year.
- Cash balances are kept in hard currency (dollars).
- Month-end rates are used to record expense transactions.

Required: Based on these assumptions, prepare a table showing the distortions that can occur when expense transactions totaling YTL 1,000,000 are recorded using conventional measurement rules (i.e., month-end rates in this example) instead of the internal reporting structure recommended in this chapter.

Transactions:	
Invoice Date	Payment Terms
1	Cash
5	15 days
5	25 days

7. Exhibit 10-4, "Framework for Systems Design," provides a way of thinking about the financial control process in a multinational setting. Assume that a parent company domiciled in your country is comparing the performance statistics (e.g., return on equity) of two wholly-owned affiliates: one in Mexico City, the other in Singapore. Try to identify how each of the variables and constraints identified in the matrix might affect the numerator and/or denominator of the ROI statistic and its interpretation.

8. Global Enterprises, Inc., uses a number of performance criteria to evaluate its overseas operations, including return on investment. Compagnie de Calais, its Belgian subsidiary,

EXHIBIT 10-13   Compagnie de Calais Performance Report

Sales		$4,200,000
Other income		120,000
		$4,320,000
Costs and expenses:		
Cost of sales	$3,200,000	
Selling and administrative	330,000	
Depreciation	160,000	
Interest	162,000	
Exchange losses	368,000	4,220,000
Income before taxes		$ 100,000
Income taxes		42,000
Net income		$ 58,000

submits the performance report shown in Exhibit 10-12 for the current fiscal year (translated to U.S. dollar equivalents). Included in sales are $500,000 worth of components sold by Compagnie de Calais to its sister subsidiary in Brussels at a transfer price set by corporate headquarters at 40 percent above an arm's-length price. Cost of goods sold includes excess labor costs of $150,000 owing to local labor laws. Administrative expenses include $50,000 of headquarters expenses, which are allocated by Global Enterprises to its Belgian affiliate.

The parent company holds all of its subsidiaries responsible for their fair share of corporate expenses. Local financing decisions are centralized at corporate treasury, as are all matters related to tax planning. At the same time, Global Enterprises thinks that all subsidiaries should be able to cover reasonable financing costs. Moreover, it thinks that foreign managers should be motivated to use local resources as efficiently as possible. Hence, Compagnie de Calais is assessed a capital charge based on its net assets and the parent company's average cost of capital. This figure, which amounts to $120,000, is included in the $162,000 interest expense figure. One-half of the exchange gains and losses figure is attributed to transactions losses resulting from the Belgian subsidiary's export activities. The balance is due to translating the Belgian accounts to U.S. dollars for consolidation purposes. Exchange risk management is also centralized at corporate treasury.

Required: Based on the foregoing information, prepare a performance report that isolates the elements that should be included in performance appraisals of the foreign unit.

9. In evaluating the performance of a foreign manager, a parent company should never penalize the manager for things the manager cannot control. Given the information provided in Exercise 8, prepare a performance report identifying the relevant elements for evaluating the manager of Compagnie de Calais.

10. To encourage its foreign managers to incorporate expected exchange rate changes into their operating decisions, Vancouver Enterprises requires that all foreign currency budgets be set in Canadian dollars using exchange rates projected for the end of the budget period. To further motivate its local managers to react to unexpected rate changes, operating results at period's end are translated to dollars at the actual spot rate prevailing at that time. Deviations between actual and budgeted exchange rates are discarded in judging the manager's performance.

At the start of the 20X7 fiscal year, budgeted results for a Mexican affiliate, the Cuernavaca Corporation, were as follows (amounts in thousands):

Sales	MXP 8,000,000	CAD2,560
Expenses	6,400,000	2,048
Income	MXP 1,600,000	CAD512

Actual results for the year in dollars were: sales, CAD2,160,000; expenses, CAD1,680,000; net income, CAD480,000. Relevant exchange rates for the peso during the year were as follows:

Jan. 1, 20X7 spot rate:	CAD.00040
Global Enterprises one-year forecast	CAD.00032
Dec. 31, 20X7 spot rate	CAD.00024

Required: Based on the foregoing information, did the Mexican manager perform well? Support your answer using the variance analysis suggested in the chapter. (Refer to Exhibit 10-6.)

11. Exhibit 10-9 contains a performance report that breaks out various operating variances of a foreign affiliate, assuming the parent currency is the functional currency under FAS No. 52. Using the information in Exhibit 10-9, repeat the variance analysis, assuming instead that the parent company defines the local currency as its functional currency.

12. Parent Company establishes three wholly-owned affiliates in countries X, Y, and Z. Its total investment in each of the respective affiliates at the beginning of the year, together with year-end returns in parent currency (PC), appear here:

Subsidiary	Total Assets	Returns
X	PC 1,000,000	PC 250,000
Y	PC 3,000,000	PC 900,000
Z	PC 1,500,000	PC 600,000

Parent Company requires a return on its domestic investments of 10 percent and is evaluating the annual performance of its three foreign affiliates. To establish an appropriate performance benchmark, Parent Company subscribes to a country-risk evaluation service that compiles an unweighted risk index for various countries around the world. The risk scores for each of the n countries are:

Country-Risk Score (out of 60)	
X	30
Y	21
Z	15

Other things being equal, the higher the score, the lower the country's risk.

Required: Prepare an analysis for Parent Company's management indicating which affiliate performed best.

CASES

Case 10-1   Foreign Investment Analysis: A Tangled Affair

You are the CFO of Alexa Corporation, a major electronics manufacturer headquartered in Shelton, Connecticut. To date, your company's operations have been confined to the United States, but you are interested in diversifying your operations abroad. One option would be to begin establishing wholly-owned subsidiaries in Europe, Latin America, and Asia. Another option is to acquire a multinational company that

<table>
<tr><th colspan="4">EXHIBIT 10-14   MBI Data on Non-U.S. Operations</th></tr>
<tr><th>Non-U.S. Operations
(Dollars in millions)</th><th>2008</th><th>2007</th><th>2006</th></tr>
<tr><td>At year-end:</td><td></td><td></td><td></td></tr>
<tr><td>Net assets employed:</td><td></td><td></td><td></td></tr>
<tr><td>Current assets</td><td>$24,337</td><td>$20,361</td><td>$20,005</td></tr>
<tr><td>Current liabilities</td><td>15,917</td><td>12,124</td><td>11,481</td></tr>
<tr><td>Working capital</td><td>$ 8,420</td><td>$ 8,237</td><td>$ 8,524</td></tr>
<tr><td>Plant and equipment, net</td><td>11,628</td><td>9,879</td><td>9,354</td></tr>
<tr><td>Investments and other assets</td><td>9,077</td><td>6,822</td><td>5,251</td></tr>
<tr><td></td><td>$29,125</td><td>$24,938</td><td>$23,129</td></tr>
<tr><td>Long-term debt</td><td>$ 5,060</td><td>$ 3,358</td><td>$ 2,340</td></tr>
<tr><td>Other liabilities</td><td>2,699</td><td>2,607</td><td>2,505</td></tr>
<tr><td>Deferred taxes</td><td>2,381</td><td>1,184</td><td>1,580</td></tr>
<tr><td></td><td>$10,140</td><td>$ 7,779</td><td>$ 6,425</td></tr>
<tr><td>Net assets employed</td><td>$18,985</td><td>$17,159</td><td>$16,704</td></tr>
<tr><td>Number of employees</td><td>168,283</td><td>167,291</td><td>163,904</td></tr>
<tr><td>For the year:</td><td></td><td></td><td></td></tr>
<tr><td>Revenue</td><td>$41,886</td><td>$36,965</td><td>$34,361</td></tr>
<tr><td>Earnings before income taxes</td><td>$ 7,844</td><td>$ 7,496</td><td>$ 7,088</td></tr>
<tr><td>Provision for income taxes</td><td>3,270</td><td>3,388</td><td>3,009</td></tr>
<tr><td>Net earnings</td><td>$ 4,574</td><td>$ 4,108</td><td>$ 4,079</td></tr>
</table>

Notes: Non-U.S. subsidiaries that operate in a local currency environment account for approximately 90 percent of the company's non-U.S. revenue. The remaining 10 percent of the company's non-U.S. revenue is from subsidiaries and branches that operate in U.S. dollars or whose economic environments are highly inflationary.

As the value of the dollar weakens, net assets recorded in local currencies translate into more U.S. dollars than they would have at the previous year's rates. Conversely, as the dollar becomes stronger, net assets recorded in local currencies translate into fewer U.S. dollars than they would have at the previous year's rates. The translation adjustments, resulting from the translation of net assets, amounted to $3,266 million at December 31, 2008, $1,698 million at December 31, 2007, and $1,917 million at December 31, 2006. The changes in translation adjustments since the end of 2006 are a reflection of the strengthening of the dollar in 2007 and the weakening of the dollar in 2008.

already has a major international presence. You are leaning toward the latter course of action because you are interested in diversifying your company's operating risk and enhancing its bottom line as soon as possible. You also have a significant stock option package and will benefit greatly if the price of Marissa Corporation's common stock were to rise over the next year.

You are particularly interested in MBI International, a U.S.-based multinational with operations in a significant number of countries. You estimate that approximately 60 percent of the company's earnings are from abroad. Foreign operations performance statistics, provided in MBI Corporation's consolidated

financial statements, are included in Exhibit 10-14 for the years 2008, 2007, and 2006. Relevant notes are also appended.

Unfortunately, MBI does not disclose data explaining the movement of the major currencies in which it conducts its businesses. You do a Google search and uncover a trade-weighted index supplied by the U.S. government. Given MBI's large-scale operations, you decide to use the trade-weighted index as a proxy for MBI's currency experience (see Exhibit 10-15). (In using such a proxy, you are assuming that the currency mix of MBI's activities parallels the currency mix in the trade-weighted index.) ∎

REQUIRED

1. On the basis of the information provided, together with what you have learned in Chapter 6, does MBI represent an attractive acquisition candidate?

EXHIBIT 10-15	Dollar's Trade-Weighted Exchange Index, 2002–2004 (1990 = 100)
December 31	**Index**
2002	92.8
2003	93.7
2004	83.7
Average Rates for Years, 1994–2004	
1994	87.4
1995	103.4
1996	116.6
1997	125.3
1998	138.2
1999	143.0
2000	112.2
2001	96.9
2002	92.7
2003	98.6
2004	89.1

Case 10-2   Assessing Foreign Subsidiary Performance In A World Of Floating Exchange Rates

General Electric Company's worldwide performance-evaluation system is based on a policy of decentralization. The policy reflects its conviction that managers will become more responsible and their businesses will be better managed if they are given the authority and necessary tools to budget and achieve a targeted net income in dollar terms. Moreover, decentralization permits the company to overcome the difficulty of centrally exercising detailed control over its large and diverse operations. Foreign affiliate managers, like their domestic counterparts, are accountable for dollar income, a practice not followed by many MNCs.

In the words of one financial executive, "Although many U.S. corporations are decentralized in their U.S. operations, they seem to be less so with regard to their foreign operations. One reason may be the concern as to whether foreign managers are sufficiently trained in some aspects of international finance, such as foreign exchange exposure management. We feel this is essential training, and our people get that training."

General Electric does not have any rigid standards for comparing the performance of its affiliates. Strategic and operating plans are agreed upon for each business, including financial targets. Like most other companies, GE generally requires a higher rate of return from investment proposals in riskier countries and has a system of ranking countries according to relative risk. A proposed investment in a high-risk area will have more difficulty being approved and will generally require a higher ROI, but approval depends on both the forecasted ROI and the company's total strategic objectives in each country.

The system of budgeting and forecasting extends five years into the future. The first year of the long-range forecast becomes a preliminary budget for the year ahead. A year later the budget is revised, a comparison is made between it and the original forecast, and changes are accounted for.

Measurement of an affiliated company's performance is related to the objectives of its strategic plan and the annual budgets that are derived from the plan. The primary financial measure is success in achieving the affiliates' committed dollar net income. Other measurements include ROI (calculated as the sum of reported net income plus after-tax interest expense, divided by the sum of net worth plus borrowings), net income to sales ratios, market share, inventory and receivable turnover rates, and currency exposure.

While the performance of both an affiliate and its manager are measured primarily on bottom-line results, the review of the manager includes other measurements. Assessments include how well the manager has dealt with government relations, progress made toward achieving certain targets, such as increasing market share, and success in maintaining good employee relationships. These measurements are based on the strategic plan and targets established between the manager and the parent-company supervisor at the start of the period.

GE conducts periodic operating reviews where each manager is reviewed by the level above. The focus is on planning, results, and the most recent estimates. This evaluation process provides corporate management with an opportunity to determine whether short-term actions are being taken at the expense of long-range goals.

To minimize currency exposure, GE finances fixed assets with equity and holds the affiliate responsible for maintaining a balanced position on working capital. The policy is modified as necessary for varying circumstances.

Unlike MNCs that have centralized the financing and exposure management functions at the head office, GE makes exposure management a responsibility of its local managers, overseen by sector and corporate personnel. To avoid the transaction costs of having, for example, a French affiliate hedge its position by buying French francs forward, GE has provisions for internal hedging arrangements. Corporate treasury obtains currency exposure data from all affiliates and provides needed information on offsets. Therefore, units can execute a hedging agreement between themselves without going to outside sources.

In setting their budgets, affiliate managers use the exchange rate they expect to prevail. General Electric believes that, although predicting rates of exchange is not an exact science, the managers of its foreign businesses have the necessary authority and tools to take actions that will enable them to achieve their budgeted income. These tools include hedging and pricing decisions. Managers can not only raise prices, cut costs, lead payments, lag receivables, borrow locally, and remit dividends quickly, but they can also take out forward contracts if available.

The affiliate manager has the responsibility and authority to protect the unit against currency fluctuations and, therefore, is accountable for dollar profits regardless of exchange rate changes. According to a company spokesperson: "If an unexpected devaluation occurs, the affiliate's performance is still measured in terms of dollar income vis-à-vis budget. GE considers changes in the rate of exchange in the same way as other risks that occur in a country. For example, if an affiliate's sales are less than those budgeted for because of a recession in that economy, countermeasures are available to the affiliate. If one contends that these things are not controllable, how does one manage a company? We're not saying it's controllable in the sense that it can be prevented from happening, but it is susceptible to countermeasures before and after the event occurs." ∎

REQUIRED

1. Compare GE's approach to performance evaluation with that of ICI (mentioned in the chapter).
2. Critically evaluate the strengths and weaknesses of each company's approach to the performance evaluation of its foreign managers as related to the problem of fluctuating currency values.
3. Which approach to performance evaluation do you support, and why?

CHAPTER 11

Financial Risk Management

While business is normally associated with the production and distribution of goods and services, the real contribution of business to society is the assumption and management of risk. Business managers assume the risk of contracting human, physical, and financial capital to fabricate a product or service that may or may not prove acceptable to society. If their enterprise proves unsuccessful, the firm ceases to exist; if successful, the firm earns a profit. Risk management is especially challenging at the international level owing to the larger number of variables that must be considered.

The management of risk at the enterprise level, ERM, views individual risks in the context of a firm's business strategy. Risks today are increasingly viewed from a portfolio perspective, with the risks of various business functions coordinated by a senior financial manager who keeps the CEO and board of directors apprised of critical risks and devises risk optimization strategies.[1] The variables that management accountants must track to supply risk managers with relevant and timely data span a range of dimensions that varies from company to company. Exhibit 11-1 provides a corporate example of actual practice. Infosys Technologies, introduced in Chapter 1, begins by identifying its stragegic objectives and then identifying the external and internal risk factors that could affect the achievement of these objectives. These risk factors are measured by managerial accountants and formally reported to responsible managers by way of operating reviews, subsidiary reviews, disclosure committee meetings, and regular updates to its corporate risk council. Information contained in risk-management performance reports then cycles back and reaffirms or alters strategic objectives and risk-identification processes.[2] The Infosys Risk Management Report provides an excellent example of the kinds of information that make up an enterprise risk-management system. External risk factors encompass data on macroeconomic factors, exchange rate fluctuations, political intelligence, competitive environment, revenue concentration, inflation and cost structure, immigration regulations for countries where company personnel are employed, physical security, data security and business continuity, and the risk of technology obsolescence. Internal risk factors that are formally monitored include financial reporting risks, including compliance with Sarbanes-Oxley (see Chapter 9), liquidity and leverage, contractual compliance, legal compliance, intellectual property rights, engagement execution to assure high-quality

---

[1] Russ Banham, "Enterprising Views of Risk Management," *Journal of Accountancy* (online issue), June 2004.
[2] Infosys Annual Report.

EXHIBIT 11-1   Risk-Management Cycle Employed by Infosys

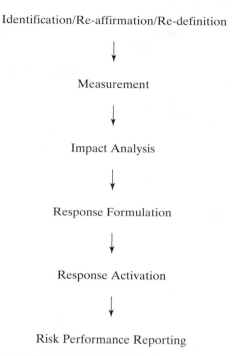

Identification/Re-affirmation/Re-definition

↓

Measurement

↓

Impact Analysis

↓

Response Formulation

↓

Response Activation

↓

Risk Performance Reporting

and timely product and service deliveries, integration and collaboration to ensure that acquistions and joint ventures are good organizational fits, human resource management, and perhaps most important, culture, values, and leadership. The latter includes building a culture of ethical core values and leadership training.

While the management of individual risks is increasingly a coordinated affair, this does not in any way minimize the importance of managing individual risks. At the individual risk level, corporate treasurers around the world value new and imaginative ways to minimize their exposures to market risks, such as the volatility of foreign exchange rates, commodity prices, interest rates, and equity prices.[3] The financial services industry now offers many financial hedge products, including currency swaps, interest rate swaps, and options. Accounting standard setters around the world over are working on appropriate measurement and reporting principles for these financial products. Many of these financial instruments are treated as off-balance-sheet items by international financial reporting entities. Accordingly, the risks inherent in their use are often masked.

---

[3]The terms *market risk* is sometimes used synonymously with *value-at-risk*. In this chapter, the latter refers to the chance of loss on a firm's trading portfolio, which could include hedging instruments, caused by changes in asset prices, interest rates, market volatility, or market liquidity.

Exhibit 11-2 is a glossary of risk-management terms used in this chapter. We now examine internal reporting and control issues associated with the management of individual risks.

EXHIBIT 11-2 Glossary of Risk-Management Terms

accounting risk. The risk that the preferred accounting treatment for a transaction is not available.

balance sheet hedge. Reducing foreign exchange (FX) exposure by varying the mix of a firm's foreign currency assets and liabilities.

counterparty. The individual or institution with whom an exchange is effected.

credit risk. The risk that a counterparty will default on its obligations.

derivative. Contractual arrangements creating special rights or obligations that derive their value from another financial instrument or commodity.

economic exposure. The effect of FX rate changes on a firm's future costs and revenues.

exposure management. Structuring a company's affairs to minimize the adverse effects of exchange rate changes on earnings.

foreign currency commitments. Firm sales or purchase commitments that are denominated in foreign currency.

inflation differential. Difference in the inflation rate between two or more countries.

liquidity risk. The inability to trade a financial instrument in a timely fashion.

market discontinuities. Sudden and significant changes in market value.

market risk. Risk of loss owing to unexpected changes in the prices of foreign exchange, credit, commodities, and equities.

net exposed asset position. An excess of exposed assets over exposed liabilities (also called a positive exposure).

net exposed liability position. An excess of exposed liabilities over exposed assets (also called a negative exposure).

net investment. A firm's net exposed asset or liability position.

notional amount. The principal amount specified in a contract to determine settlement.

operational hedge. FX risk protection that focuses on variables that impact a firm's foreign currency revenues and expenses.

option. The right but not the obligation to buy or sell a financial contract at a specified price on or before a specified date in the future.

regulatory risk. The risk that a public law will constrain the intended use of a financial product.

risk mapping. Examining the temporal relationship of various market risks to financial statement variables that affect a firm's value and assessing the likelihood of their occurrence.

structural hedges. Selecting or relocating operations to reduce a firm's overall FX exposure.

tax risk. The risk that a desired tax treatment is not available.

translation exposure. Measuring the parent-currency effects of FX changes on foreign currency assets, liabilities, revenues, and expenses.

transaction exposure. Exchange gains and losses that arise from the settlement (conversion) of foreign currency transactions.

value at risk. Risk of loss on an entity's trading portfolio caused by changes in market conditions.

value driver. Balance sheet and income statement accounts that impact firm value.

ESSENTIALS

The main goal of financial risk management at the individual risk level is to minimize the chance of loss arising from unexpected changes in the prices of currencies, credit, commodities, and equities. Exposure to price volatility is known as *market risk*. For example, a corporation in Sweden that issues new stock to domestic investors might view market risk as exposure to rising share prices. An unexpected rise in stock prices is undesirable if the issuer could have issued fewer shares for the same amount of cash by waiting. A Swedish investor, on the other hand, would view risk as the possibility of a fall in equity prices. If stock prices were to fall significantly in the near term, the investor would rather wait before buying.

Market participants tend to be risk averse. Thus, many will trade some potential profits for protection from adverse price changes. Financial intermediaries and market makers have responded by creating financial products that enable a market participant to transfer the risk of unexpected price changes to someone else — a counterparty. For example, a financial intermediary might sell a corporate issuer an option (i.e., the right but not the obligation) to buy stock and the investor (the counterparty) an option to sell the stock short.

Market risk has many dimensions. Although we will focus on price or rate volatility, management accountants consider other risks enumerated under ERM above. Liquidity risk exists because not all financial risk management products can be freely traded. Highly illiquid markets include real estate and small capitalization stocks.[4] Market discontinuities refer to the risk that markets may not always produce gradual price changes. The stock market plunge at the start of this decade is a case in point. Credit risk is the likelihood that a counterparty to a risk-management contract will not meet its obligations. For example, a counterparty agreeing to exchange euros for Canadian dollars may fail to deliver euros on the promised date. Regulatory risk is the risk that a public authority may prevent a financial product from being used for its intended purpose. For example, the Kuala Lumpur stock exchange does not permit the use of short sales as a hedge against declines in equity prices. Tax risk is the risk that certain hedge transactions will not receive the desired tax treatment. An example is the treatment of foreign exchange losses as capital gains when ordinary income is preferred. Accounting risk is the chance that a hedge transaction will not be accounted for as part of the transaction it is intended to hedge. An example of this is when the gain on the hedge of a purchase commitment is treated as "other income" instead of a reduction of the cost of the purchase.

WHY MANAGE FINANCIAL RISKS?

The rapid growth of risk-management services suggests that management can increase firm value by controlling financial risks.[5] Moreover, investors and other stakeholders increasingly expect financial managers to identify and actively manage market risk

---

[4]Recent financial innovations such as real estate investment trusts have improved liquidity in many of these previously illiquid markets.

[5]For empirical evidence on this, see James M. Nelson, Jacquelyn Sue Moffitt, and John Affleck-Graves, "The Impact of Hedging on the Market Value of Equity," *Journal of Corporate Finance* 11, no. 5 (2005): 851–881.

exposures.[6] If the value of the firm equals the present value of its future cash flows, active exposure management is justified on several grounds.

First, exposure management helps stabilize a firm's expected cash flows. A more stable cash-flow stream helps minimize earnings surprises, thereby increasing the present value of expected cash flows. Stable earnings also reduce the likelihood of default and bankruptcy risk, or the risk that earnings may not cover contractual debt-service payments. Second, active exposure management enables firms to concentrate on their primary business risks. Thus, a manufacturer can hedge its interest rate and currency risks and concentrate on production and marketing. Similar benefits are available to financial institutions. Third, debt holders, employees, and customers also gain from exposure management. As debt holders generally have a lower risk tolerance than shareholders, limiting the firm's risk exposure helps align the interests of shareholders and bondholders. Fourth, derivative products allow employer-administered pension funds to enjoy higher returns by permitting them to invest in certain instruments without having to actually buy or sell the underlying instruments. Fifth, because losses caused by certain price and rate risks are passed on to customers in the form of higher prices, exposure management limits customers' exposure to these risks.[7]

ROLE OF ACCOUNTING

Management accountants play an important role in the risk-management process. They help identify potential market risks, quantify tradeoffs associated with alternative risk-response strategies, measure a firm's exposure to specific risks, account for specific hedge products, and evaluate the effectiveness of hedging programs.

Identifying Market Risks

Risk mapping is a useful framework for identifying various types of potential market risks. This framework begins with an examination of the relationship of various market risks to the value drivers of a firm and its competitors. Exhibit 11-3 illustrates a framework developed by J. P. MorganChase. We call it the *risk-mapping cube*.[8]

The term *value drivers* in Exhibit 11-3 refers to major financial condition and operating-performance items that impact a firm's value. Market risk encompasses foreign exchange and interest rate risk, as well as commodity and equity price risk. The third dimension of the risk-mapping cube examines the relationship of market risks and value drivers for each of the firm's principal competitors.

To illustrate, let us examine the first row of the exposure-management cube. Interest rate risk may affect the revenue of the firm in the following manner. Credit sales are normally collected after a certain period, depending on the credit terms offered the client (e.g., thirty, sixty, or ninety days). The firm usually relies on short-term loans to finance current operations, such as wages and other operating expenses.

[6]Peter Coy, "Perils of the Hedge Highwire," *BusinessWeek* (October 26, 1998): 74, 76–77.
[7]J. P. Morgan & Co., Arthur Andersen & Co., and Financial Engineering Ltd., "The J. P. Morgan/Arthur Andersen Guide to Corporate Exposure Management," *Risk Magazine* (1994).
[8]J. P. Morgan et al., "The J. P. Morgan/Arthur Andersen Guide to Corporate Exposure Management." *Risk Magazine*, (1994): 19.

EXHIBIT 11-3 Risk-Mapping Cube

		Market risks				
Value drivers		Foreign exchange	Interest rates	Commodity prices	Equity prices	Other
Revenue						
Cost of sales						
Operating expenses						
Taxes						
Current assets						
Current liabilities						
Fixed assets						
Other						

(Labels above table: Competitor Z, Competitor Y, Your company)

Source: J. P. Morgan et al., "The J. P. Mohan/Arthur Andersen Guide to Corporate Exposure Management." *Risk Magazine,* 1994, 19.

Rising interest rates before the receivables are collected would reduce the firm's return from sales. Credit sales denominated in foreign currency would yield less than the expected parent currency should the foreign currency lose value before collection. Fluctuating commodity prices can have a significant impact on revenues as well as cost of sales. Finally, as managers of investment funds know all too well, falling equity prices immediately worsen fund performance statistics.

How does the third dimension of the exposure-management cube work? This dimension examines how a competitor's exposure to market risk might impact the firm. Suppose you decide to sell baseball caps of the team you expect to win the next World Series. You decide to buy and sell the caps locally. Are you exposed to foreign exchange risk? You might not think so, but if a competitor buys baseball caps from abroad and the currency of its source country loses value relative to your home currency, this change may allow your competitor to sell at a lower price than you. This is called *competitive currency exposure.*

As the object of this exercise is to identify potential risks, we add two other dimensions to the risk-management construct in Exhibit 11-3. For each cell of the cube, management accountants should incorporate a probability density function associated with a range of possible outcomes for each value driver. To illustrate, unexpected foreign exchange rate changes could have a range of effects on a firm's revenues. Each of these outcomes would, in turn, be associated with a certain likelihood based on objective or, more likely, subjective probability assessments. These probability scenarios, in turn, would be estimated over various time frames. Intervals such as three months, six months, and so forth add a temporal dimension to risk mapping. Accountants are well positioned to provide such data.[9]

Quantify Tradeoffs

Another role that accountants play in the risk-management process involves quantifying tradeoffs associated with alternative risk-response strategies. Management may prefer to keep some risk exposures rather than hedge whenever the costs of risk protection are deemed higher than the benefits. As an example, an importer that has a firm purchase commitment denominated in foreign currency may prefer not to hedge if it believes the foreign currency will weaken before the delivery date. Accountants would measure the benefits from hedging against these costs plus the opportunity costs of forgone gains from speculating in market movements.

Risk Management in a World of Floating Exchange Rates

Many of the market price movements we have been discussing are interrelated. In this chapter, we confine our analysis to a specific price exposure: foreign exchange rate changes. We do this for three reasons. First, exchange rate, or FX risk, is one of the most common forms of risk that multinational firms encounter. Second, influential financial executives state that foreign exchange risk is "one of the most difficult external risks that financial managers must cope with."[10] Third, the risk-management concepts and associated accounting treatments for foreign exchange risk parallel those for interest rate, commodity, and equity price risks.

In a world of floating exchange rates, risk management includes (1) anticipating exchange rate movements, (2) measuring a firm's exposure to exchange risk, (3) designing appropriate protection strategies, and (4) establishing internal risk-management controls. These are discussed below in turn.

Forecasting Exchange Rate Changes

In developing an exchange risk management program, financial managers must have information on the direction, timing, and magnitude of exchange rate changes. Forewarned of exchange rate prospects, financial managers can more efficiently and effectively arrange appropriate defensive measures. Whether it is possible to accurately predict currency movements, however, remains an issue.

Information frequently used in making exchange rate forecasts (e.g., currency depreciation) relates to changes in the following factors:

Inflation differentials. Evidence suggests that a higher rate of inflation in a given country tends, over time, to be offset by an equal and opposite movement in the value of its currency.

---

[9]A booklet on this subject prepared by the American Institute of Certified Public Accountants can be found at www.aicpa.org/assurance/index.htm.
[10]Quote from John Connors, former CFO of Microsoft, *Treasury and Risk*, p.mailzeen.com, December 2006.

Monetary policy. An increase in a country's money supply that exceeds the real growth rate of national output fosters inflation, which affects exchange rates.

Balance of trade. Governments often use currency devaluations to cure an unfavorable trade balance (i.e., when exports < imports).

Balance of payments. A country that spends (imports) and invests more abroad than it earns (exports) or receives in investments from abroad experiences downward pressure on its currency's value.

International monetary reserves and debt capacity. A country with a persistent balance-of-payments deficit can forestall a currency devaluation by drawing down its savings (i.e., level of international monetary reserves) or drawing on its foreign borrowing capacity. As these resources decrease, the probability of devaluation increases.

National budget. Deficits caused by excessive government spending also worsen inflation.

Forward exchange quotations. A foreign currency that can be acquired for future delivery at a significant discount signals reduced confidence in that currency.

Unofficial rates. Increases in the spread between official and unofficial or black market exchange rates suggest increased pressure on governments to align their official rates with more realistic market rates.

Behavior of related currencies. A country's currency will normally behave in a fashion similar to the currencies of countries with close economic ties to it.

Interest rate differentials. Interest rate differentials between any two countries predict future change in the spot exchange rate.

Foreign equity option prices. Since arbitrage links a foreign equity's price in its home market with its domestic currency value, changes in the domestic currency option price of a foreign equity signal a change in the market's expectations of future FX rates.[11]

These items help predict the direction of currency movements. However, they are usually not enough to predict the timing and magnitude of currency changes. Politics strongly influences currency values in many countries. Political responses to devaluation or revaluation pressures frequently result in temporary measures rather than exchange rate adjustments. These temporary measures include selective taxes, import controls, export incentives, and exchange controls. Awareness of the politics of a country whose currency is under pressure is important. It helps financial managers discern whether the government will lean toward market intervention or rely on free-market solutions.

Some claim that exchange rate forecasting is a futile exercise. In a world where exchange rates are free to fluctuate, FX markets are said to be efficient.[12] Current market rates (i.e., forward exchange rates) represent the consensus of all market participants about future FX rates. Information that is generally available is immediately

---

[11]Chu and Swidler confirm this using the case of Telmex options around the 1994 Mexican peso devaluation. Ting-Heng Chu and Steve Swidler, "Forecasting Emerging Market Exchange Rates from Foreign Equity Options," *Journal of Financial Research*, no. 3 (2002): 353–366.

[12]Gunter Dufey and Ian H. Giddy, "Management of Corporate Foreign Exchange Risk," in *International Finance and Accounting Handbook*, ed. Frederick D. S. Choi, 3rd ed. (New York: John Wiley, 2003), pp. 6.1–6.31.

impounded in current FX rates. Thus, such information has little value in predicting future exchange rates. Under these conditions, FX rate changes are random responses to new information or unforeseen events. Forward exchange rates are the best available estimates of future rates. The randomness of FX rate changes reflects the diversity of opinions on exchange values by participants.

What do all of these factors imply for management accountants? For one thing, accountants must develop systems that gather and process comprehensive and accurate information on variables correlated with exchange rate movements. These systems can incorporate information provided by external forecasting services, financial publications that track currency movements, and daily contacts with foreign currency dealers. They should be online and computer-based to ensure managers a superior source of information on which to base their currency forecasts. Financial managers must also understand the consequences of not using other forecasting methods.

If exchange rate forecasting is not possible or too expensive to undertake, then financial managers and accountants should arrange their company's affairs to minimize the detrimental effects of rate changes. This process is known as *exposure management*.

Exposure Measurement

Structuring a company's affairs to minimize the adverse effects of exchange rate changes requires information on its exposure to FX rate risk. FX exposure exists whenever a change in FX rates changes the value of a firm's net assets, earnings, and cash flows.[13] Traditional accounting measures of FX exposure center on two major types of exposure: translation and transaction.

Translation Exposure

Translation exposure measures the impact of FX rate changes on the domestic currency equivalents of a firm's foreign currency assets and liabilities. For example, a U.S. parent company operating a wholly-owned subsidiary in Ecuador (whose functional currency is the U.S. dollar) experiences a change in the dollar value of its Ecuadorean net monetary assets whenever the exchange value of the Ecuadorean sucre changes relative to the dollar. Because foreign currency amounts are typically translated to their domestic currency equivalents for either management review or external financial reporting purposes (see Chapter 6), translation effects have a direct impact on reported profits. A foreign currency asset or liability is exposed to exchange rate risk if a change in the exchange rate causes its parent-currency equivalent to change. Based on this definition, foreign currency balance sheet items exposed to exchange rate risks are those items that are translated at current (as opposed to historical) exchange rates. Accordingly, translation exposure is measured by taking the difference between a firm's exposed foreign currency assets and liabilities. This process is depicted in Exhibit 11-4.

An excess of exposed assets over exposed liabilities (i.e., those foreign currency items translated at current exchange rates) causes a net exposed asset position. This is sometimes referred to as a positive exposure. Devaluation of the foreign currency

---

[13]Abe de Jong, Jeroen Ligterrink, and Victor Macrae find that firms in open economies, such as the Netherlands, exhibit significant exchange rate exposure. See their "A Firm-Specific Analysis of the Exchange-Rate Exposure of Dutch Firms," *Journal of International Financial Management and Accounting* 17 , no. 1 (2006).

EXHIBIT 11-4 Translation Exposure

Exposed assets > Exposed liabilities = Positive exposure

Foreign currency devalues → Translation loss

Foreign currency revalues → Translation gain

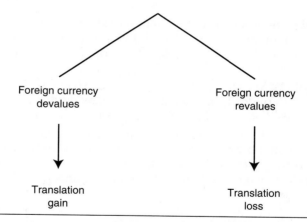

Exposed assets < Exposed liabilities = Negative exposure

Foreign currency devalues → Translation gain

Foreign currency revalues → Translation loss

relative to the reporting currency produces a translation loss. Revaluation of the foreign currency produces a translation gain. Conversely, a firm has a net exposed liability position, or negative exposure, whenever exposed liabilities exceed exposed assets. In this instance, devaluation of the foreign currency causes a translation gain. Revaluation of the foreign currency causes a translation loss.

Accounting measures of exposure vary depending on the translation method adopted. (The discussion in Chapter 6 distinguished four major translation options.) Exhibit 11-5 illustrates the major translation options described in Chapter 6. The year-end balance sheet is that of a hypothetical Philippine subsidiary of a U.S. parent company. The second column depicts the U.S. dollar equivalents of the Philippine peso (PHP) amounts at an exchange rate of $0.03 = PHP1. The peso is expected to devalue by 33⅓ percent during the coming period. As inventories are stated at market values

EXHIBIT 11-5   Accounting Exposure Illustrated (in thousands)

	Peso	*U.S. Dollars Before Peso Devaluation ($0.03 = PHP1)*	*U.S. Dollars After Philippine Peso Devaluation ($0.02 = PHP1)*			
			Current Rate	*Current-Noncurrent*	*Monetary-Nonmonetary*	*Temporal*
Assets						
Cash	PHP 500,000	$15,000	$10,000	$10,000	$10,000	$10,000
Accounts Receivable	1,000,000	30,000	20,000	20,000	20,000	20,000
Inventories	900,000	27,000	18,000	18,000	27,000	18,000
Fixed assets (net)	1,100,000	33,000	22,000	33,000	33,000	33,000
Total	PHP 3,500,000	$105,000	$70,000	$81,000	$90,000	$81,000
Liabilities and Owners' Equity						
Short-term payables	PHP 400,000	$ 12,000	$ 8,000	$ 8,000	$ 8,000	$ 8,000
Long-term debt	800,000	24,000	16,000	24,000	16,000	16,000
Stockholders' equity	2,300,000	69,000	46,000	49,000	66,000	57,000
Total	PHP 3,500,000	$105,000	$70,000	$81,000	$90,000	$81,000
Accounting exposure (PHP)			2,300,000	2,000,000	300,000	1,200,000
Translation gain (loss) ($)			(23,000)	(20,000)	(3,000)	(12,000)

under the lower-of-cost-or-market rule, the monetary-nonmonetary and temporal-translation methods produce different exposure measures and are treated separately. Assuming the U.S. parent designates the U.S. dollar as the subsidiary's functional currency, its potential foreign exchange loss on a positive exposure of PHP1,200 million would be $12 million, determined as shown in Exhibit 11-6.

Alternatively, if the parent company designates the Philippine peso as the subsidiary's functional currency, the potential exchange loss is $23 million. This is based on a positive exposure of PHP2,300 million using the current rate method mandated by FASB No. 52. An exposure report format for the income statement based on similar concepts (suggested by the Management Accounting Practices Committee of the International Federation of Accountants) appears in Exhibit 11-7.

EXHIBIT 11-6   Calculation of Potential Foreign Exchange Loss (in millions)

Exposed Assets		
Cash	PHP500	
Accounts receivable	1,000	
Inventories	900	PHP2,400
Exposed Liabilities		
Short-term payables	PHP400	
Long-term debt	800	1,200
Positive exposure		PHP1,200
Pre-depreciation rate ($0.03 = PHP1)	PHP1,200 =	$ 36
Post-depreciation rate ($0.02 = PHP1)	PHP1,200 =	24
Potential foreign exchange loss		($12)

EXHIBIT 11-7 Format for an Income Statement Exposure Forecast

Income Statement Category	Items Translated at Current Exchange Rates				Items Translated at Historic Exchange Rates				Total Exposure
	Local Currency (amount)	Foreign Currency (amount)	Conversion Rate	Local Equivalent Rate	Local Currency (amount)	Foreign Currency (amount)	Conversion Rate	Local Equivalent Rate	
Revenues (By Category) Less: Cost of Sales (By Category)									
Gross Profit									
Less: Expenses (By Category) Earnings Before Interest and Tax Expense									
Earnings Before Tax									
Tax									
Net Income									
Net Exposed Position									
Net Covered Position									
Net Uncovered Position									

Exhibit 11-6 assumed that the Philippine subsidiary's transactions were denominated solely in pesos. In most foreign operations, however, transactions are done in more than one currency. FX risk is a multidimensional issue: For example, a receivable denominated in New Zealand dollars is unlikely to have the same future value as a receivable in Singapore dollars, even if both have the same face value at the time of sale. To account for these situations, management accountants prepare a variety of exposure reports that distinguish among foreign currency assets and liabilities according to the currencies in which they are denominated. Exhibit 11-8 illustrates a multicurrency exposure report for the Philippine subsidiary, which manufactures a durable good for sale in local, Australian, and American markets. Supplies are imported from Indonesia.

The format of the exposure report in Exhibit 11-8 resembles the one in Exhibit 11-5 except that Exhibit 11-8 segregates exposed assets and liabilities by currency of denomination. Balance sheet items are typically expressed in U.S. dollars to facilitate an assessment of the relative magnitudes of the various items.

A multicurrency exposure reporting format offers many advantages over its single-currency counterpart. For one thing, the information provided is more complete.

EXHIBIT 11-8 Multicurrency Translation Exposure (in thousands)

	Philippine Pesos	Australian Dollars	Indonesian Rupiahs	U.S. Dollars	Total[1]
Exposed Assets					
Cash	$ 50,000	–	–	–	$ 50,000
Receivables	45,000	$15,000	–	$40,000	100,000
Inventories	90,000			–	90,000
Total	185,000	$14,000		$40,000	$240,000
Exposed Liabilities					
Short-term payables	$ 20,000	$ 2,500	$ 12,500	$ 5,000	$40,000
Long-term debt	50,000			30,000	80,000
Total	$ 70,000	$ 2,500	$ 12,500	$35,000	120,000
Net exposure	$115,000	$12,500	$(12,500)		

[1] *Stated in U.S. dollars at the spot rate effective on the date of the report.*

Rather than disclosing a single net positive exposure figure of $120 million, the report in Exhibit 11-8 shows that this figure comprises several different currency exposures.

Each connotes different exchange risk consequences for the U.S. parent. Also, under a single-currency perspective, the positive exposure of $12,500,000 in Australian dollars is combined with the negative exposure of $12,500,000 in Indonesian rupiahs, suggesting a natural offset. This offset is true only if the Australian dollar and the Indonesian rupiah move in tandem relative to the U.S. dollar. If they do not, the translation effects could be significantly different.

A multicurrency report also enables the parent company to aggregate similar exposure reports from all of its foreign subsidiaries and analyze, on a continual basis, its worldwide translation exposure by national currency. This type of analysis is particularly helpful when local managers are responsible for protection against translation exposure. One can easily imagine a situation where local managers in two foreign subsidiaries may face opposite exposures in the same currency. Multicurrency exposure reports enable a parent company to make sure that its local managers avoid hedging activities that are disadvantageous to the company as a whole.

Transaction exposure concerns exchange gains and losses that arise from the settlement of transactions denominated in foreign currencies. Unlike translation gains and losses, transaction gains and losses have a direct effect on cash flows as they result from a currency conversion process.

A multicurrency transaction exposure report for our Philippine subsidiary appears in Exhibit 11-9. It includes items that normally do not appear in conventional financial statements but cause transaction gains and losses, such as forward exchange contracts, future purchase and sales commitments, and long-term leases.[14] The exposure report excludes items that do not directly relate to foreign currency transactions (such as cash on hand). A transaction exposure report also has a different perspective than a translation exposure report. A translation exposure report takes the perspective of the parent company. A transaction exposure report takes the perspective of the foreign operation. Exhibit 11-9 focuses on what happens on the books of the

---

[14] These items are normally disclosed in footnotes to the financial statements.

EXHIBIT 11-9 Multicurrency Transaction Exposure ($ thousands)

	Philippine Pesos	Australian Dollars	Indonesian Rupiahs	U.S. Dollars	Total
Exposed Assets					
Receivables	$ 45,000	$15,000	—	$40,000	$100,000
Inventories	90,000	—	—	—	$ 90,000
Future sales commitments	—	10,000	—	—	10,000
Total	$135,000	$25,000		$40,000	$ 200,000
Exposed Liabilities					
Short-term payables	$ 20,000	$ 2,500	$ 12,500	5,000	$ 40,000
Long-term debt commitments	50,000	—	—	30,000	80,000
Future purchase	—	—	10,000	—	10,000
Leases	—	$ 5,000	—	—	5,000
Total	$ 70,000	$ 7,500	$ 22,500	$35,000	$135,000
Net exposure		$17,500	$(22,500)	$ 5,000	

Philippine affiliate if the peso changes value relative to the Australian dollar, the Indonesian rupiah, and the U.S. dollar. The peso column is of no concern, because peso transactions are recorded and settled in pesos. A devaluation of the peso relative to the Australian and U.S. dollars will produce transaction gains owing to positive exposures in both currencies. A devaluation of the peso relative to the rupiah would produce a transaction loss, because more pesos would be required to settle the Philippine subsidiary's foreign currency obligations. These transaction gains or losses (net of tax effects) directly impact U.S. dollar earnings upon consolidation.

Centralized control of a firm's overall exchange exposures is possible. This entails having each foreign affiliate send its multicurrency exposure reports to corporate headquarters continually. Once exposures are aggregated by currency and by country, the company can implement centrally coordinated hedging policies to offset potential losses.

Accounting vs. Economic Exposure

The reporting frameworks previously described highlight a firm's exposure to FX risk at a given time. Translation and transaction exposure reports, however, do not measure a firm's economic exposure. This is the effect of currency value changes on the future operating performance and cash flows of the firm.

Exhibit 11-9 indicates that the Philippine subsidiary is long on Australian dollars. That is to say, exposed Australian dollar assets exceed exposed Australian dollar liabilities. Based on this report, a financial manager might decide to hedge this position by selling 17.5 million Australian dollars in the forward exchange market. Would this be the right decision? Probably not. Although the Philippine subsidiary is long on Australian dollars, not all the items in the exposure report require an immediate inflow or outflow of Australian dollars. The future sales commitment of $10 million will probably not bring in cash until a later accounting period. Also, the exposure report does not include all Australian dollar receipts or disbursements because future sales denominated in Australian dollars are not considered. Although Australian dollar receivables currently total $15 million, this figure will not stay the same for long. From an external reporting perspective, future cash flows should not be considered. From an internal reporting perspective, they cannot be ignored.

More and more companies differentiate between exposures that are static and those that are fluid in nature. They prepare multicurrency cash-flow statements that enable them to monitor monthly cash receipts and disbursements for each currency in which they do business (see Exhibit 11-10). A traditional exposure report considers the effects of exchange rate changes on account balances as of the financial statement date. A multicurrency cash-flow statement emphasizes exposures generated by exchange rate changes during the forthcoming budget period. Cash receipts for each national currency include the collection of current and anticipated credit sales, asset disposals, and other cash-generating activities. Multicurrency cash disbursements incorporate those required for current and anticipated obligations, debt service, and other cash purchases.

The notion of economic exposure recognizes that exchange rate changes affect the competitive position of firms by altering the prices of their inputs and outputs relative to those of their foreign competitors. For example, assume that our hypothetical Philippine subsidiary obtains its labor and material locally. Devaluation of the Philippine peso relative to all other foreign currencies could improve rather than worsen the subsidiary's position. It could increase its exports to Australia and the United States, since the devalued peso would make its goods cheaper in terms of the Australian and U.S. dollar. Domestic sales could also rise, because the peso devaluation would make imported goods more expensive in local currency. The devaluation would have no appreciable effect on the cost of local-source inputs. Thus, the future profitability of the Philippine subsidiary might increase because of the currency

EXHIBIT 11-10   Budgeted Cash Flows by Country

Unit/Country: _____   Date: _____

Currency		Budget Periods					
		January	*February*	*March*	*April*	*May*	*June*
Philippine pesos	Receipts						
	Payments						
	Net						
Australian dollars	Receipts						
	Payments						
	Net						
Indonesian rupiahs	Receipts						
	Payments						
	Net						
Other	Receipts						
	Payments						
	Net						

depreciation. Under these circumstances, booking a transaction loss on a positive translation exposure would distort the economic implications of the peso devaluation.

Alternatively, a German manufacturing affiliate of a U.K. parent, organized to serve the German market, may have a positive translation exposure. Appreciation of the euro relative to the pound would produce a translation gain upon consolidation. If the German affiliate were to source all of its inputs in Germany, its economic exposure would appear to be shielded from exchange risk. Yet a major German competitor that obtained some of its manufacturing components from Russia might enjoy a cost advantage if the ruble were undervalued relative to the Euro.

These examples suggest that economic or operating exposure bears little or no relation to translation and transaction exposure. Accordingly, the management of such exposure will require hedging technologies that are more strategic than tactical in nature. These newer technologies include the following hedging options.[15]

Companies may opt for structural hedges that involve selecting or relocating manufacturing sites to reduce the operating exposure of the business as a whole. Such actions, however, may require forgoing economies of scale, which could reduce the expected rate of return of the business.

Alternatively, parent companies could take a portfolio approach to risk reduction by selecting businesses that have offsetting exposures.[16] In so doing, the operating exposure of the firm as a whole is minimized. This strategy will necessitate careful review of individual business units' operating results after correcting for the effects of operating exposure. A company may opt to exploit exchange rate volatility by reconfiguring its businesses. The object is to preserve maximum flexibility by being able to increase production and sourcing in countries where currencies become strongly undervalued in real terms. This entails additional costs of relocating production facilities and building excess capacity. On the other hand, these strategic moves reduce average operating costs across a range of exchange rates.

The notion of economic or operating exposure places new burdens on management accountants. Traditional sources will not contain much of the required information. The proper measurement of operating exposure will require an understanding of the structure of the market in which a company and its competitors do business, as well as the effects of real (as opposed to nominal) exchange rates. These effects are hard to measure. As operating exposures tend to be long in duration, uncertain in terms of measurables, and not based on explicit commitments, accountants will have to provide information that spans multiple operating functions and time periods.

Protection Strategies

Once foreign exchange exposures are quantified, the next step is to design hedging strategies that minimize or eliminate such exposures. These strategies include balance sheet, operational, and contractual hedges.

Balance Sheet Hedges   A balance sheet hedge reduces a firm's exposure by adjusting the levels and monetary denomination of a firm's exposed assets and liabilities. For example, increasing cash balances in foreign currency can offset declines in interest

---

[15]D. R. Lessard and J. B. Lightstone, "Volatile Exchange Rates Can Put Operations at Risk," *Harvard Business Review* (July/August 1986): 107–114.

[16]This portfolio approach is a subset of the portfolio strategy associated with the enterprise risk-management systems described at the start of this chapter.

rates and income on domestic fixed-income instruments. In Exhibit 11-8, a natural hedge against the $115 million positive exposure would be to increase the Philippine subsidiary's peso borrowings by $115 million.[17] In this case the borrowed cash must be remitted to the parent or invested in nonexposed assets, for otherwise the net exposed asset position would not change. Other methods of hedging a firm's positive exposure in a subsidiary located in a devaluation-prone country include:

1. Keeping local currency cash balances at the minimum level required to support current operations
2. Remitting profits above those needed for capital expansions back to the parent company
3. Speeding up (leading) the collection of outstanding local currency receivables
4. Deferring (lagging) payments of local currency payables
5. Speeding up the payment of foreign currency payables
6. Investing excess cash in local currency inventories and other assets less subject to devaluation loss
7. Investing in strong-currency foreign assets

Operational Hedges   This form of risk protection focuses on variables that impact foreign-currency revenues and expenses. Raising selling prices (for sales invoiced in a devaluation-prone currency) in proportion to the anticipated currency depreciation helps protect targeted gross margins. One variation of this theme is invoicing sales in hard currencies. Tighter control of costs affords a larger margin of safety against potential currency losses. A final example includes structural hedges. These entail relocating manufacturing sites to reduce operating exposures of the firm or changing the country in which raw materials or manufacturing components are sourced.

Balance sheet and operational hedging are not costless. Foreign subsidiaries in devaluation-prone countries are frequently urged to minimize their local currency working capital balances (cash and receivables in particular), simultaneously increasing holdings of local currency debt. Such actions, unfortunately, are often disadvantageous. Increased export potential resulting from a devaluation might call for more working capital rather than less. The opportunity cost in lost sales could far exceed any translation loss. Also, local currency borrowing before a devaluation can be extremely expensive. Other foreign subsidiaries usually have similar ideas at the same time, and consequently, the local banking system may accommodate such credit demands only at an excessive cost. Furthermore, bank credit during such periods is usually scarce because most countries impose severe credit restraints to counter the problems that cause devaluation pressures in the first place. The cost of borrowing under these circumstances often exceeds any protection provided.

Strategic hedges also have their limits. One strategy, for example, is to vertically integrate operations to minimize a firm's exposure to exchange rate–sensitive resources. This course of action, however, exposes the firm to additional costs connected with setting up a new foreign affiliate and the potential loss of scale economies. Vertical integration also takes a long time to carry out.

---

[17]The use of foreign currency borrowing as a means of reducing both transaction and translation exposure is documented in Niclas Hegelin and Bengt Pramborg, "Hedging Foreign Exchange Exposure: Risk Reduction from Transaction and Translation Hedging," *Journal of International Financial Management and Accounting* 15 , no. 1 (2004): 1–20.

Contractual Hedges A variety of contractual hedge instruments have been developed to afford managers greater flexibility in managing foreign exchange exposures. Exhibit 11-11 shows some foreign exchange hedge products that have recently appeared. As you can see, managers have plenty of choices to consider.

Most of these financial instruments are derivative, as opposed to basic, in nature. Basic financial instruments, such as repurchase agreements (receivables), bonds, and capital stock, meet conventional accounting definitions of assets, liabilities, and owners' equity. Derivative instruments are contractual arrangements giving rise to special rights or obligations and deriving their value from another financial instrument or commodity. Many are based on contingent events. Accordingly, they do not have the same characteristics as the instrument on which they are based. An example would be a cross-currency basis swap on a principal amount of $100 million. Here the derivative product is the promise to exchange interest payment differentials based upon, but independent of, the underlying principle or notional amount of the respective borrowings. If floating rates were higher than fixed rates, one counterparty would owe the other counterparty the difference. Any amounts owing would depend upon the movement in interest rates. The market for derivatives is a 24-hour global trading market consisting largely of banks. Derivatives traders around the world are interconnected through highly sophisticated electronic and telecommunications systems.

At the turn of this decade, numerous surprises occurred in the market for derivatives that dominated the financial headlines. Names such as Baring Brothers, Long-Term Capital Management, and Orange County gained instant notoriety because of the magnitude of the losses they sustained. Prestigious financial institutions such as

---

EXHIBIT 11-11 Exchange-Related Financial Instruments

alternative currency option. A currency option that, if exercised, can be settled in one of several alternative currencies at the choice of the option holder.

basket hedging. The use of a basket of currencies (comprising fewer currencies than the hedged portfolio) to offset the risk of all the nonbase currencies in a portfolio.

break forward. An option that allows the buyer to fully participate in the movement of a currency beyond a specified level without having to pay an explicit option premium.

combined interest rate and currency swap (CIRCUS). A transaction in which two counterparties exchange interest payment streams denominated in two different currencies (i.e., exchanging fixed interest payments in one currency for floating rate interest in another).

contingent hedge with an agreement for rebate at maturity (CHARM). A currency option that (1) is exercisable if a bidding company wins the contract or (2) is void if the company loses the contract, where the issuer of the option rebates a portion of the premium. The value of the payoff depends on (1) the buyer's ability to obtain business requiring currency protection, and (2) the movement of the underlying currency.

convertible option contract. An option to purchase or sell foreign currency that converts to a forward contract if the forward exchange rate falls below a certain price.

covered option securities (COPS). Short-term obligations that give the issuer the option to repay principal and interest in the original, or a mutually acceptable, currency.

covered interest arbitrage. An agreement in which two counterparties exchange currencies at both the spot and forward rates simultaneously.

cross-currency basis swap. A floating interest rate swap in two currencies.

(continued)

> **EXHIBIT 11-11** Exchange-Related Financial Instruments (*Continued*)

cross-currency cap. An option in which the holder is paid the positive difference between the spread on two different currency base rates and a strike spread.

currency coupon swap. A fixed to floating coupon swap in two different currencies.

currency option. The right but not the obligation to buy or sell another currency at an agreed-upon strike price within a specified time period.

currency swap. The initial exchange of two currencies and subsequent reexchange of the same currencies at the end of a certain time period.

currency swap option. (swaption). An option to buy or sell a currency swap at a specified exchange rate.

dual option bonds. A bond giving the investor the choice of currencies in which to receive interest and principal repayments.

exchange rate agreement (ERA). A synthetic agreement for forward exchange whose value is correlated with the spread between two forward currency exchange rates.

forward exchange contract. A contractual agreement between two parties to exchange a specified amount of currency for another at a fixed date in the future.

futures contract. An exchange-traded contract calling for delivery of a specified amount of currency at a fixed date in the future.

foreign equity option. The right but not the obligation to buy or sell a foreign equity at a specified price on or before a specified date in the future.

indexed currency option notes (ICONS). Bonds that are denominated and pay interest in one currency with redemption value linked to the exchange rate of another currency.

look-back option. The retroactive right to buy a currency at its low point or sell a currency at its high point within the option period.

principal exchange-rate-linked securities (PERLS). Debt instruments paying interest and principal in U.S. dollars where the principal is pegged to the exchange rate between the dollar and another currency.

range forwards. A forward exchange contract specifying a range of exchange rates at which currencies will be exchanged at maturity.

synthetic position. A combined transaction to produce a security with features that could not be obtained directly (e.g., combining a fixed rate debt with a currency swap).

tailored swap. A currency swap in which the notional principle can be adjusted to meet the changing risk exposure of a business.

SOURCE: Adapted from Gary L. Gastineau, *Swiss Bank Corporation Dictionary of Financial Risk Management,* Chicago: Probus, 1992.

Citigroup, J. P. Morgan Chase, Daiwa Bank, Merrill Lynch, and Sumitomo Corp. also made the front page. Reported losses ranged from hundreds of millions of dollars to the billions. The reasons for such losses included inadequate controls over trader behavior, pricing models that did not incorporate the risks of extreme market movements (discontinuities), market illiquidity, and ultimately the naiveté of directors and senior management as to the nature and risks of these instruments.[18]

Despite these debacles, the derivatives market, currently in excess of $100 trillion in size, continues to grow in sophistication and use. Financial managers of multinational

---

[18]Buckley and Vand Der Nat document disturbing levels of ignorance among independent directors in terms of understanding and monitoring of derivatives. Adrian Buckley and Mattheus Vand Der Nat, "Derivatives and the Non-Executive Director," *European Management Journal* 21, no. 3 (June 2003): 388.

enterprises use these instruments to manage their exposures to exchange risk, especially transactions and economic exposures as these exposures directly impact a firm's current and future cash flows. Allayannis and Ofek find a strong negative association between a firm's use of foreign currency derivatives and its exchange rate exposure. This suggests that firms use derivatives primarily to hedge rather than speculate in foreign currencies. It also implies that usage of foreign currency derivatives does indeed reduce foreign exchange rate risk.[19] Although we express a preference for hedging transactions and economic exposures, executives seem interested in managing translation exposure as well. They voice concern about reporting lower earnings to shareholders. In a comparative study of derivative usage by German and U.S. companies, minimizing the variability of reported earnings was rated most important by German companies. While U.S. companies tend to use financial derivatives to minimize the variability of cash flow, minimizing the variability of reported earnings was a close second.[20] In a related study, Swedish companies' use of derivatives to hedge the balance sheet (translation exposure) was as prevalent as their use of derivatives for committed and anticipated transactions.[21]

Accounting for Hedge Products

Contractual hedge products are financial contracts or instruments that enable users to minimize, eliminate, or otherwise transfer market risks to someone else's shoulders. They include, but are not limited to, forward contracts, futures, swaps, options, and combinations of these. While many derivative instruments have grown in complexity, user surveys document management's preference for the most basic, or vanilla, varieties.[22]

Knowledge of accounting measurement rules for derivatives is especially important when designing an effective hedge strategy for the firm. To understand the importance of hedge accounting, we illustrate some basic hedge accounting practices.

First, review the basic components of an income statement (absent taxes).

Operating revenues	XXX
– Operating expenses	XXX
= Operating income	XXX
+ Other income	XXX
– Other expense	XXX
= Net income	XXX

Analysts usually focus on operating income in evaluating how well management has operated its core business. Net income includes the confounding effects of extraordinary or nonrecurring events.

---

[19]George Allayannis and Eli Ofek, "Echange Rate Exposure, Hedging and the Use of Foreign Currency Derivatives," *Journal of International Money and Finance* 20 (2001): 273–296.

[20]Reasons for the U.S. emphasis on reported earnings relate to analysts' perceptions and prediction of future earnings and management compensation. In Germany, reported earnings play an important role in taxation and dividend distribution. Gordon M. Bodner and Gunther Gebhardt, "Derivative Usage in Risk Management by US and German Non-Financial Firms: A Comparative Study," *Journal of International Financial Management and Accounting* 10, no. 3 (1999): 153–187.

[21]Niclas Hagelin and Bengt Pramborg, "Hedging Foreign Exchange Exposure: Risk Reduction from Transaction and Translation Hedging," *Journal of International Financial Management and Accounting* 15, no. 1(2004): 1–20.

[22]Ed McCarthy, "Derivatives Revisited," *Journal of Accountancy* (May 2000) Also available at www.aicpa.org/pubs/jofa/may 2000/mccarthy.htm.

The accounting treatment for financial derivatives that is gaining acceptance internationally is to mark the product to market with any gains or losses recognized as a component of nonoperating income. In the United States at least, an exception is permitted in certain instances if the transaction meets appropriate hedge criteria, including the following:

1. The item being hedged exposes the firm to a market risk.
2. The firm describes its hedging strategy.
3. The firm designates the instrument to be employed as a hedge.
4. The firm documents its rationale as to why the hedge is likely to be effective.

If the appropriate criteria are met, the firm can use the gains or losses recognized on marking the hedge product to market to offset the gains or losses on the transaction that is being hedged (e.g., sales or purchases). To illustrate, assume that an Irish manufacturer of stout (a dark malt beverage) has a sales commitment to deliver X barrels to a buyer in the United States in two months. Fearing that the U.S. dollar will devalue before delivery, the Irish manufacturer buys a forward exchange contract that will allow it to sell U.S. dollars in two months' time at a price close to the current price. If the dollar devalues before delivery, the gain on the foreign exchange contract will offset the loss on the sales contract. If the hedging requirements listed above are met, operating income will meet its target. If the criteria are not met, the gain on the forward contract will appear as other income and operating income will come in below target.

Accounting issues associated with FX hedging products relate to recognition, measurement, and disclosure. Recognition centers on whether hedging instruments should be recognized as assets or liabilities in the body of financial statements. There is also the question of whether the hedge product should receive the same accounting treatment as the item being hedged.

Closely related to the recognition issue is the question of measurement. How, for example, should an FX derivative be valued? Should it take on the same measurement basis as the hedged instrument or transaction, or should it reflect an independent valuation? If an independent valuation, which valuation model—historical cost, market value, lower of cost or market, net realizable value, or discounted present value—is preferable? How should gains or losses related to the FX instrument be reflected in the income statement? Should they be reflected in income at all? Can and should risks associated with financial instruments be recognized and measured? The last question is especially important because the risks attaching to many of the newer financial instruments, such as options and futures, are symmetric. Someone's gain is another's loss. Finally, to what extent should buyers and sellers of financial instruments detail the nature and amounts of financial instruments to which they are a party? What attributes of financial instruments should be disclosed in general-purpose financial statements? How much disclosure is necessary to sufficiently inform readers of the nature and magnitude of off-balance-sheet risks associated with corporate financial instruments? We now examine some basic FX risk-management products. This is followed by a discussion of appropriate accounting treatments.

FX Forward Contracts

Importers and exporters generally use forward exchange contracts when goods invoiced in foreign currencies are purchased from or sold to foreign parties. The forward contract offsets the risk of transaction gains or losses as exchange rates fluctuate

between the transaction and settlement dates. Forward contracts also hedge anticipated foreign currency payables or receivables (foreign currency commitments) and
can be used to speculate in foreign currencies. These contracts are not traded on any
organized exchange and are consequently less liquid than other contracts. On the
other hand, they are flexible in contract amount and duration.

A forward exchange contract is an agreement to deliver or receive a specified
amount of foreign currency in exchange for domestic currency, on a future date, at a
fixed rate called the *forward rate*. Differences between the forward rate and the spot
rate prevailing at the date of the forward contract give rise to a premium (forward
rate > spot rate) or a discount (forward rate < spot rate). The premium or discount
rate multiplied by the amount of the foreign currency to be received or delivered, the
notional amount of the contract, produces a recognizable premium or discount on the
forward contract. The forward contract will also give rise to transaction gains or losses
whenever the exchange rate prevailing at the transaction date differs from those prevailing at interim financial statement or settlement dates.

The accounting issue here is whether premiums, discounts, gains, or losses on foreign exchange contracts should receive similar or differing treatment for each use
identified. Exhibit 11-12 summarizes how these accounting adjustments should be
reported under FAS No. 52, now amended by FAS No. 133.

Financial Futures

A financial futures contract is similar in nature to a forward contract. Like a forward,
it is a commitment to purchase or deliver a specified quantity of foreign currency at a
future date at a set price. Alternatively, it may provide for cash settlement instead of
delivery and can be cancelled before delivery by entering into an offsetting contract
for the same financial instrument. In contrast to a forward contract, a futures

---

EXHIBIT 11-12   Accounting Treatment of Forward Contracts

	Gains/Losses	Discount/Premium[a]
Unsettled foreign currency transaction	Recognize in current income	Recognize in current income
Identifiable foreign currency commitment	Recognize in current income	Recognize in current income
Exposed net asset (liability) position		
a. Foreign currency is functional currency	Disclose in separate component of consolidated equity	Same treatment as related gains/losses, or current income
b. Parent currency is functional currency	Recognize in current income	Recognize in current income
Speculation	Recognize in current income[b]	N/A[c] 1

[a]Normally amortized over the life of the underlying instrument/activity.

[b]Gains/losses in this category are a function of the difference between the forward rate available for the remaining
period of the contract and the contracted forward rate (or the forward rate last used to measure a gain or loss on
that contract for an earlier period).

[c]Not applicable.

agreement is a standardized contract, involves standardized provisions with respect to size and delivery date, is traded on an organized exchange,[23] is marked to market at the end of each day, and must meet periodic margin requirements. Losses on a futures contract give rise to a margin call; gains normally give rise to a cash payment. Exhibit 11-13 documents the growing size of this market, which nearly doubled between 2004 and 2005.[24]

Corporate treasurers generally use futures contracts to shift the risk of price changes to someone else. They can also be used to speculate in anticipated price movements and to exploit short-term anomalies in the pricing of futures contracts.

How does a financial futures contract work? If Alpha Corporation borrows yen for three months and wants to protect itself against an appreciation of the yen before maturity, it could buy a futures contract to receive an equal amount of yen in 90 days. Appreciation of the yen causes a gain on the futures contract, offsetting the loss on the yen borrowing.

Currency Options

A currency option gives the buyer the right to buy (call) or sell (put) a currency from the seller (writer) at a specified (strike) price on or before a specified expiration (strike) date. A European-type option may be exercised only at the expiration date. An American-type option may be exercised any time up to and including the expiration

EXHIBIT 11-13 Currency Futures Market

Exchange	Volume Traded (No. of contracts)		Notional Value (US$ millions)	
	2005	**2004**	**2005**	**2004**
Americas				
Buenos Aires SE	2,416	31,372	2	31
Chicago Mercantile				
Exchange (CME)	81,105,391	48,772,627	9,798,906	5,849,779
MexDer	2,934,783	1,400,448	323,969	223,331
New York Board of Trade (NYBOT)	3,604,877	2,362,615	NA	NA
Asia-Pacific				
Korea Exchange	2, 667,005	2,090,291	133,679	105,044
SFE Corp.	4,422	41,862	3,368	30,920
Tokyo Financial Exchange	600	200	5	2
Europe–Africa–Middle East				
Budapest SE	7,742,408	2,695,818	10,698	3,966
Euronext	7,435	3,985	176	90
Warsaw SE	6,216	3,455	65	38
Total	98,075,553	57,672,673	—	—

---

[23]Examples include the International Monetary Market in Chicago and newer exchanges, such as the New York Futures Exchange, the London International Financial Futures Exchange, the Singapore Money Exchange (SIMEX), the Sydney Futures Exchange, and the MATIF in Paris.
[24]Source: World Federation of Exchanges.

EXHIBIT 11-14   Market for Current Options

Exchange	Volume Traded (Number of contracts)		Notional Value (US$ millions)	
	2005	**2004**	**2005**	**2004**
Americas				
Bourse de Montréal	7,264	NA	70	NA
Chicago Mercantile Exchange (CME)	3,182,525	2,435,337	440,565	332,982
New York Board of Trade (NYBOT)	35,970	58,219	NA	NA
Philadelphia SE	159,748	230,779	NA	NA
Europe-Africa-Middle East				
Budapest SE	258,000	49,000	251	61
Euronext	403,957	239,080	4,728	2,727
Tel Aviv SE	6,937,575	6,445,397	69,802	65,936
Total	10,985,039	9,457,812	—	—

SOURCE: World Federation of Exchanges.

date. The buyer of a call pays a premium for the option and benefits if the price of the underlying asset exceeds the strike price at maturity; the buyer of a put benefits if the price falls below the strike price at the expiration date. Exhibit 11-14 illustrates the growing size of this market.

To illustrate, suppose a U.S. contractor bids for a CAD100 million construction project in Canada. The outcome of the bid will not be known for three months. Should the Canadian dollar lose value during that time, the contractor will suffer a loss if it wins the fixed-price contract. The U.S. contractor therefore buys an option to receive the difference between the future US$/CAD spot rate in 90 days at a strike price of $0.70 per Canadian dollar. The contract details are as follows:

Contract Type	FX CAD Put/US$ Call Option
Maturity	90 days
Strike rate	$0.70/CAD
Contract amount	$100 million
Option premium	$0.03

If, at maturity, the foreign exchange rate falls to $0.60, the contract holder gains 10 cents per CAD face value of the put contract. In this example, the change in value of the Canadian dollar yields an option payoff of $10,000,000 [($0.60 – $0.70) × CAD100 million]. The option premium, which can be viewed as the cost of insuring against a falling Canadian dollar, is $3 million ($0.03 × CAD100 million). By buying the put option, the contractor makes a gain in the value of the option that offsets the potential currency loss (minus the option premium). If the value of the Canadian dollar is unchanged at the strike date, the contractor would simply let the option expire, treating the option premium as a cost of insurance.

Currency options can also be used to manage earnings. Assume that an option trader believes the euro will gain in value in the near term. The trader would buy a naked call. Should the euro appreciate in value by the exercise date, the buyer would exercise the option and pocket the difference between the current and strike price, less the call premium. To limit downside risk, the buyer would obtain a bull call spread. This trading strategy involves buying a call and simultaneously selling an identical call with a higher strike price. The premium paid for the lower strike call will be partly offset by the amount received from the sale of the higher priced call. The maximum profit here is the difference between strike prices less the net premium. The net premium is, in effect, the maximum potential loss on the spread, ignoring transaction costs.

Straddles involve the sale of a call and a put with identical terms. Here the writer of the options bets that exchange rates will not change much during the life of the options. The writer gains revenue from premiums received for writing the options. It is a high-risk strategy, however. If exchange rates change enough to cause one or both of the options to be exercised, the writer's potential loss is unlimited.

Currency Swaps

A currency swap involves a current and future exchange of two different currencies at predetermined rates. Currency swaps enable companies to access an otherwise inaccessible capital market at a reasonable cost. They also allow a firm to hedge against exchange rate risks arising from international business. Suppose, for example, that Alpha Corporation (a U.S.-based multinational) wishes to raise $10,000,000 of fixed-rate debt in British pounds to fund a newly formed London affiliate. Alpha is relatively unknown to British investors. Similarly, Beta Company, Ltd., domiciled in the United Kingdom, would like to fund a New York subsidiary with a similar amount of dollar financing. It is relatively unknown in the United States. Under these circumstances, Gamma Bank may accommodate both companies by arranging a U.S. dollar/U.K pound currency swap. Assume the following: The swap exchange rate is $1.00 = £0.66 (both at inception and maturity); the swap term is five years; and the swap specifies interest rates of 10 percent in pounds and 8 percent in dollars. The following cash-flow pattern would take place. At inception, Alpha Corporation exchanges $10,000,000 for £6,600,000 from Beta Company, Ltd. Assuming interest is paid annually, Alpha pays £660,000 to Beta each year, and Beta pays $800,000 to Alpha. At the end of the five-year term, each company would re-exchange the principal amounts of $10,000,000 and £6,600,000.

As a result of this swap transaction, both Alpha Corporation and Beta Company, Ltd. have been able to access funds in a relatively inaccessible market. They have done so without incurring exchange rate risk. And, owing to their comparative advantages in borrowing in their home markets, they have achieved their foreign currency borrowings at a lower cost than they could otherwise have obtained.

Accounting Treatments

The Financial Accounting Standards Board issued FAS No. 133, as amended by FAS 138 and clarified by FAS 149, to provide a single comprehensive approach to accounting for derivative and hedge transactions.[25] IAS 39, recently revised, contains similar guidelines providing, for the first time, universal guidance on accounting for financial

---

[25]FAS No. 133 superseded FAS No. 80 and amended FAS No. 52. Financial Accounting Standards Board, *"Accounting for Derivative Instruments and Hedging Activities," Statement of Financial Accounting Standards 133* (Stamford, CT: FASB, October 1994). FAS No 149 amended and clarified FAS 133, resulting in more consistent reporting of contracts as either derivatives or hybrid instruments. Financial Accounting Standards Board, *"Amendment of Statement 133 on Derivative Instruments and Hedging Activities," Statement of Financial Accounting Standards No. 149* (Stamford, CT: FASB, April 2003). Also see the FASB's Web site at www.fasb.org.

derivatives.[26] While these two pronouncements are similar in tenor, they differ in terms of the degree of detail in implementation guidance (see Chapter 8 on accounting harmonization).

Before these pronouncements, global accounting standards for derivative products were incomplete, inconsistent, and developed in piecemeal fashion. Most derivative instruments, being executory in nature, were treated as off-balance-sheet items. An atmosphere of caveat emptor prevailed for statement readers attempting to gauge the volume and risks of derivative usage.

The basic provisions of these standards are:

- All derivative instruments are to be recorded on the balance sheet as assets and liabilities. They are to be recorded at fair value, including those embedded in host contracts that are themselves not carried at fair value.

- Gains and losses from changes in the fair value of derivative instruments are not assets or liabilities. They are automatically recognized in earnings if they are not designated as hedges. There are three types of hedging relationships to be recognized, measured, and disclosed: fair value (FV) hedges that include recognized foreign currency assets and liabilities and firm foreign currency commitments, hedges of a net investment in a foreign operation (NI), and cash-flow (CF) hedges that include FX-denominated forecasted transactions.

- Hedges must be highly effective to qualify for special accounting treatment; that is, gains or losses on hedging instruments should exactly offset gains or losses on the item being hedged.

- Hedging relationships must be fully documented for the benefit of statement readers. For hedges of recognized foreign currency assets or liabilities and unrecognized firm foreign currency commitments, gains or losses stemming from changes in the fair value of a derivative instrument (and nonderivative financial instruments) are included immediately in earnings. Changes in the value of the foreign currency asset, liability, or firm commitment being hedged are also recognized in current income.

- Gains or losses on hedges of a foreign currency net investment (an exposed net asset or liability position) are initially reported in other comprehensive income. They are subsequently reclassified into current earnings when the subsidiary is sold or liquidated.

- Gains or losses on hedges of uncertain future cash flows, such as forecasted export sales, are initially recognized as an element of comprehensive income. Gains or losses are recognized in earnings when the forecasted transaction affects earnings.

Practice Issues

While the authoritative guidelines issued by the FASB and IASB have done much to clarify the recognition and measurement of derivatives, issues remain. The first relates to the determination of fair value. Wallace estimates that there are 64 possible calculations for measuring change in the fair values of the risk being hedged and of the hedging

---

[26]International Accounting Standards Committee, "*Financial Instruments: Recognition and Measurement,*" *International Accounting Standard 39* (London: IASC, December 1998). Also see their Web site at http://iasc.org.

instrument. He identifies four ways to measure changes in the fair value of the risks being hedged: fair market value, use of spot-to-spot exchange rates, use of forward-to-forward exchange rates, and use of an option pricing model. There are as many ways of calculating the change in value of the hedging instrument. Finally, these calculations can be done either before or after taxes.[27]

Financial reporting complexities also arise if hedges are not deemed highly effective in offsetting FX risk. However, "highly effective" is a subjective notion. In theory, highly effective means a perfect negative correlation between changes in the value or cash flow of a derivative and changes in the value or cash flow of the item being hedged. This implies a range of acceptable value changes for the derivative. The FASB recommends an 80–120 percent range. If these bounds are violated, the hedge is terminated, and deferred gains or losses on the derivative are recognized in current earnings. This, in turn, reintroduces undesired volatility into a firm's reported earnings stream.

Actually, a highly effective hedge may not entirely eliminate the earnings effect of FX changes. To illustrate, assume that the dollar equivalent of a Japanese yen denominated receivable falls by $10,000,000. The forward contract used to offset this FX risk experiences a gain of $10,800,000. Since the gain on the forward falls within the bounds of 80–120 percent , the forward has been an effective hedge. However, the $800,000 excess gain would be recognized in current income.[28]

Next we illustrate selected accounting treatments for forward contracts used as hedging instruments.

HEDGE OF A RECOGNIZED ASSET OR LIABILITY OR AN UNRECOGNIZED FIRM COMMITMENT

On September 1, a Canadian manufacturer sells, on account, goods to a Mexican importer for 1 million Mexican pesos (MXP). The Canadian dollar/peso exchange rate is CAD0.14 = MXP1. The peso receivable is due in 90 days. The peso begins to depreciate before the receivable is collected. By the end of the month, the Canadian dollar/peso exchange rate is CAD0.13 = MXP1; on December 1 it is CAD0.11 = MXP1. The Canadian exporter expects to receive CAD140,000 for the MXP1,000,000 owed if the spot rate remains unchanged through December 1. To avoid the risk of receiving less than CAD140,000 should the peso lose value before December 1, the Canadian exporter acquires a forward contract on September 1 to deliver MXP1,000,000 for Canadian dollars on December 1 at a forward rate of CAD0.13 = MXP 1. In this example, pesos can be sold only at a discount, because the spot rate is greater than the forward rate. The total discount on the forward contract is CAD10,000 [(CAD0.14 spot rate – CAD0.13 forward rate) × MXP1,000,000 notional amount] and is the price of reducing uncertainty. In effect, the Canadian exporter turns an uncertain receipt of C$140,000 to a certain receipt of CAD130,000. At later financial statement dates before maturity, the forward contract

---

[27]Jeffrey B. Wallace, "FAS 133: Accounting for Derivative Instruments," in *Handbook of International Finance and Accounting*, ed. Frederick D. S. Choi, 3rd ed. (New York: John Wiley, 2003), pp. 19.1–19.24.
[28]There are several ways of testing for hedging effectiveness. Details of the dollar offset, variability reduction, and regression methods are described in John D. Finnerty and Dwight Grant, "Testing Hedging Effectiveness Under SFAS 133," www.nysscpa.org/cpajournal/2003/0403/features/f044033.htm.

amount (peso liability) is multiplied by the spot rate in effect on those dates. Changes in spot rates cause transaction gains or losses on the forward contract. Thus, if the exchange rate prevailing on December 1 is CAD0.11 = MXP1, the Canadian exporter realizes a gain of CAD30,000 (CAD0.14 spot rate – CAD0.11 future spot rate × MXP1,000,000 liability). Had the forward contract not been purchased, the exporter would have received only CAD110,000 upon conversion of the MXP1,000,000 account receivable. Thus, the forward contract offsets a transaction loss on the foreign currency receivable with a transaction gain on the foreign currency payable.

Exhibit 11-15 provides accounting entries for the forward exchange contract just described, assuming that financial statements are prepared on September 30 prior to settlement of the peso transaction. The exchange rate on September 30 is C$0.13 = Mp1.

EXHIBIT 11-15 Hedge of a Foreign Currency Transaction		
Sept. 1	(CAD) Contract receivable	C$130,000	
	Deferred discount	10,000	
	MXP Contract payable		140,000
	(To record agreement with foreign currency dealer to exchange MXP1,000,000 worth CAD140,000 for CAD130,000 in three months.)		
Sept. 30	MXP Contract payable	10,000	
	Transaction (hedge) gain		10,000
	(To record transaction gain from reduced dollar equivalent of forward contract payable CAD0.14 – CAD0.13 × MXP1,000,000)		
Sept. 30	Discount expense	3,333	
	Deferred discount		3,333
	(Amortize deferred discount for one month.)		
Dec. 1	MXP Contract payable	20,000	
	Transaction (hedge) gain		20,000
	(To record additional transaction gain by adjusting contract to new current rate CAD0.13 – CAD0.11 × MXP1,000,000.)		
Dec. 1	Discount expense	6,667	
	Deferred discount		6,667
	(Amortize deferred discount balance)		
Dec. 1	MXP Contract payable	110,000	
	Mexican pesos		110,000
	(To record delivery of MXP1,000,000 to foreign currency dealer; this MXP1,000,000 is obtained from collecting the amount owed by the Mexican importer.)		
Dec. 1	Cash	130,000	
	(CAD) Contract receivable		130,000
	(To record receipt of CAD130,000 cash per forward contract.)		

Assuming that the discount is treated as an element of operating expense, the net effect of the hedge transaction on operating income (ignoring any foreign exchange commissions) is determined as follows:

Dollar equivalent of receivable collected from Mexican importer	CAD110,000
Transaction gains on forward contract	30,000
Proceeds from sales commitment	140,000
Discount on forward contract	(10,000)
Operating income	CAD130,000

Gains on the forward contract have effectively offset the devaluation of the peso. Expected gross margins and operating income are attained. The discount on the forward contract represents the cost of hedging the FX risk.

A similar accounting treatment would prevail if our Canadian exporter were to make a sales agreement on September 1 to deliver goods and receive payment of MXP1,000,000 from the Mexican importer three months in the future rather than immediately delivering goods and waiting for payment. This type of executory contract is known as a *foreign currency commitment*.

Alternatively, the preceding illustration might have taken the form of a forecasted export sale. This expectation is not the result of a past transaction, nor is it the result of a firm sales commitment. It represents an uncertain future cash flow (an anticipated transaction). Hence, the gains or losses on the forward contract to hedge the forecasted peso receipts would initially be recorded in equity as a part of comprehensive income. These amounts would be reclassified into current earnings in the period in which the export sales are actually recognized.

HEDGE OF A NET INVESTMENT IN A FOREIGN OPERATION

As discussed in Chapter 6, whenever a foreign subsidiary with an exposed net asset position is consolidated with its parent, a translation loss results if the foreign currency loses value relative to the parent currency. A translation loss also occurs if the foreign subsidiary has an exposed net liability position and the foreign currency appreciates relative to the parent currency. One way to minimize such losses is to buy a forward contract. The strategy here is to have transaction gains realized on the forward contract offset translation losses.

To illustrate, suppose that a U.S. calendar-year foreign affiliate in Japan has a net exposed liability position of JPY135,000,000 on September 30. Its functional currency is the dollar. To minimize any translation loss triggered by an unexpected appreciation of the yen, the U.S. parent buys a forward contract to receive 135,000,000 yen in 90 days at the forward rate of $0.008570. Exchange rates to the end of the year are as follows:

September 30 spot =	$0.008505
September 30 90-day forward =	$0.008570
December 31 spot =	$0.008640

EXHIBIT 11-16 Hedge of a Net Exposed Liability Position

September 30	JPY Contract receivable	$1,148,175	
	Deferred premium	8,775	
	$ Contract payable		$1,156,950
	(To record contract with foreign currency dealer to exchange $1,021,950 for JPY135,000,000 in 90 days)		
December 31	JPY Contract receivable	18,225	
	Transaction hedge gain		18,225
	(To record transaction gain from increased dollar equivalent of forward contract receivable; $0.008640 − $.008505 × JPY135,000,000.)		
December 31	Premium expense	8,775	
	Deferred premium		8,775
	(Amortization of deferred premium.)		
December 31	$ Contract payable	1,156,950	
	Cash		1,156,950
	(To record purchase of JPY135,000,000.)		
December 31	Foreign currency	1,116,400	
	JPY Contract receivable		1,116,400
	Cash	1,116,400	
	Foreign currency		1,116,400
	(To record receipt of JPY135,000,000 from foreign currency dealer and its conversion.)		

A transactions analysis of this hedge appears in Exhibit 11-16.

This example abstracts from tax effects. The expected translation loss of $18,225 (net exposed liabilities of [JPY135,000,000 × ($0.008640 − $0.008505)]) is offset by a transaction gain on the forward contract of $18,225 minus the premium expense of $2,025. If the foreign currency had been the functional currency, any exchange adjustment arising from consolidation would bypass income and appear in other comprehensive income. Under these circumstances, transaction gains and losses on forward hedges and related premiums/discounts would also be reflected in other comprehensive income.

SPECULATING IN FOREIGN CURRENCY

Opportunities exist for enhancing reported earnings using forward and option contracts in FX markets.[29] The forward contract in the preceding example would not qualify for hedge accounting treatment had it been purchased solely to profit from an expected appreciation of the yen. Forward contracts bought as speculations are

[29]Dilip K. Ghosh and Augustine C. Arize, "Profit Possibilities in Currency Markets: Arbitrage, Hedging and Speculation," *Financial Review* 38 (2003): 473–496.

initially recorded at the forward rate. (The forward rate is the best indicator of the spot rate that will apply when the contract matures.) Transaction gains or losses recognized prior to settlement depend on the difference between the initial forward rate and the rate available for the remaining period of the contract.

Suppose that our speculator in yen (Exhibit 11-16) prepares monthly and year-end financial statements. All facts remain the same except that the 60-day forward rate for yen is $0.008525 at the end of October. The Contract receivable would be initially recorded at the 90-day forward rate, or $1,156,950. At the end of October, the transaction gain on the forward contract would be $6,075 or JPY135,000,000 × [$0.008570 (90-day forward rate on September 30) − $.008525 (60-day forward rate on October 31)]. It is recognized in current income. As the foreign currency contract is recorded at the forward rate, no discounts or premiums are recognized.

Accounting treatments for the other foreign currency instruments discussed are similar to that for forward contracts. The accounting treatment prescribed is based on the nature of the hedging activity; that is, whether the derivative hedges a firm commitment, a forecasted transaction, a net investment in a foreign operation, and so on.

A measurement complication arises in measuring the fair value and changes in the fair values of hedging instruments when financial derivatives are not actively traded. For example, measurement of the gains or losses associated with an option contract depends on whether the option is traded on or off a major exchange. Valuation of an option is readily done when the option is quoted on a major exchange. Valuation is more difficult when the option is traded over the counter. Here, one must generally rely on mathematical pricing formulas. The so-called Black-Scholes options pricing model makes it possible to value an option at any time.

DISCLOSURE

Prior to pronouncements such as FAS 133 and IAS 39, corporate financial disclosures did not tell statement readers whether, or the extent to which, management had employed derivative contracts. Assessing their potential impact on reported performance and a firm's risk complexion was difficult. Required disclosures under FAS 133 and IAS 39 remedy this to a large extent. They include the following:

- Risk-management objective and strategy for undertaking hedge transactions
- Description of the item being hedged
- Identification of the hedged item's market risk
- Description of the hedge instrument
- Amounts excluded from the assessment of a hedge's effectiveness
- A priori justification that a hedging relationship will be highly effective in minimizing market risk
- Ongoing assessment of the actual hedging effectives of all derivatives used during the period

The selected excerpts from Coca-Cola's recent annual report in Exhibit 11-17 illustrate corporate disclosure practices with respect to hedge instruments.

EXHIBIT II-17   Coca-Cola's Risk-Management Disclosures

Financial Risk Management

Our company uses derivative financial instruments primarily to reduce our exposure to adverse fluctuations in interest rates and foreign exchange rates and, to a lesser extent, adverse fluctuations in commodity prices and other market risks. We do not enter into derivative financial instruments for trading purposes. As a matter of policy, all our derivative positions are used to reduce risk by hedging an underlying economic exposure. Because of the high correlation between the hedging instrument and the underlying exposure, fluctuations in the value of the instruments are generally offset by reciprocal changes in the value of the underlying exposure. Virtually all of our derivatives are straightforward, over-the-counter instruments with liquid markets.

Foreign Currency

We manage most of our foreign currency exposures on a consolidated basis, which allows us to net certain exposures and take advantage of any natural offsets. With approximately 77 percent of this year's Operating Income, excluding Corporate, generated outside the United States, weakness in one particular currency is often offset by strengths in others over time. We use derivative financial instruments to further reduce our net exposure to currency fluctuations.

Our company enters into forward exchange contracts and collars and purchases currency options (principally euro and Japanese yen) to hedge certain portions of forecasted cash flows denominated in foreign currencies. Additionally, the Company enters into forward exchange contracts to offset the earnings impact relating to exchange rate fluctuations on certain monetary assets and liabilities. The Company also enters into forward exchange contracts as hedges of net investments in international operations.

Value at Risk

Our Company monitors our exposure to financial market risks using several objective measurement systems, including value-at-risk models. Our value-at-risk calculations use a historical simulation model to estimate potential future losses in the fair value of our derivatives and other financial instruments that could occur as a result of adverse movements in foreign currency and interest rates. We have not considered the potential impact of favorable movements in foreign currency and interest rates on our calculations. We examined historical weekly returns over the previous 10 years to calculate our value at risk. The average value at risk represents the simple average of quarterly amounts over the past year. As a result of our foreign currency value-at-risk calculations, we estimate with 95 percent confidence that the fair values of our foreign currency derivatives and other financial instruments, over a one-week period, would decline by less than $34 million, $43 million, and $37 million, respectively, using this year and the previous two years' average fair values and by less than $31 million and $37 million, respectively, using the current year-end and the previous year-end fair values. According to our interest rate value-at-risk calculations, we estimate with 95 percent confidence that any increase in our net interest expense due to an adverse move in our current year's average, or in our year-end interest rates over a one-week period, would not have a material impact on our financial statements. Year-end estimates for the prior two years also were not material to our financial statements.

The following are extracted from the notes to the financial statements.

Hedging Transactions and Derivative Financial Instruments

Our Company uses derivative financial instruments primarily to reduce our exposure to adverse fluctuations in interest rates and foreign exchange rates and, to a lesser extent, in commodity prices and other market risks. When entered into, the Company formally designates and documents the financial instrument as a hedge of a specific underlying exposure, as well as the risk management objectives and strategies for undertaking the hedge transactions. The Company formally assesses, both at the inception and at least quarterly thereafter, whether the financial instruments that are used in hedging transactions are effective at offsetting changes in either the fair value or cash flows of the related underlying exposure. Because of the high degree of effectiveness between the hedging instrument and the underlying exposure being hedged, fluctuations in the value of the derivative instruments are generally offset by changes in the fair value or cash flows of the underlying exposures being hedged. Any ineffective portion of a financial instrument's change in fair value is immediately recognized in earnings. Virtually all of our derivatives are straightforward over-the-counter instruments with liquid markets. Our Company does not enter into derivative financial instruments for trading purposes.

The fair values of derivatives used to modify our risks fluctuate over time. We do not view these fair value amounts in isolation, but rather in relation to the fair values or cash flows of the underlying hedged transactions or other exposures. The notional amounts of the derivative financial instruments do not necessarily represent amounts exchanged by the parties and, therefore, are not a direct measure of our exposure to the financial risks described above. The amounts exchanged are calculated by reference to the notional amounts and by other terms of the derivatives, such as interest rates, exchange rates or other financial indices.

Our Company recognizes all derivative instruments as either assets or liabilities in our consolidated balance sheets at fair value. The accounting for changes in the fair value of a derivative instrument depends on whether it has been designated and qualifies as part of a hedging relationship and, further, on the type of hedging relationship. At the inception of the hedge relationship, the Company must designate the derivative instrument as either a fair value hedge, a cash flow hedge or a hedge of a net investment in a foreign operation. This designation is based upon the exposure being hedged.

We have established strict counterparty credit guidelines and enter into transactions only with financial institutions of investment grade or better. We monitor counterparty exposures daily and review any downgrade in credit rating immediately. If a downgrade in a credit rating of a counterparty were to occur, we have provisions requiring collateral in the form of U.S. government securities for substantially all of our transactions. To mitigate presettlement risk, minimum credit standards become more stringent as the duration of the derivative financial instrument increases. To minimize the concentration of credit risk, we enter into derivative transactions with a portfolio of financial institutions. The Company has master netting agreements with most of the financial institutions that are counterparties to the derivative instruments. These agreements allow for the net settlement of assets and liabilities arising from different transactions with the same counterparty. Based on these factors, we consider the risk of counterparty default to be minimal. . . .

Foreign Currency Management

The purpose of our foreign currency hedging activities is to reduce the risk that our eventual U.S. dollar net cash inflows resulting from sales outside the United States will be adversely affected by changes in exchange rates.

We enter into forward exchange contracts and collars and purchase currency options (principally euro and Japanese yen) to hedge certain portions of forecasted cash flows denominated in foreign currencies. The effective portion of the changes in fair value for these contracts, which have been designated as cash flow hedges, are reported in AOCI and reclassified into earnings in the same financial statement line item and in the same period or periods during which the hedged transaction affects earnings. Any ineffective portion (which was not significant in 2005, 2004 or 2003) of the change in fair value of these instruments is immediately recognized in earnings. These contracts had maturities up to one year as of December 31, 2005.

Additionally, the Company enters into forward exchange contracts that are not designated as hedging instruments under SFAS No. 133. These instruments are used to offset the earnings impact relating in the variability in exchange rates on certain monetary assets and liabilities denominated in nonfunctional currencies. Changes in the fair value of these instruments are recognized in earnings in the line item other loss—net of our consolidated statements of income to offset the effect of remeasurement of the monetary assets and liabilities.

The Company also enters into forward exchange contracts to hedge its net investment position in certain major currencies. Under SFAS No. 133, changes in the fair value of these instruments are recognized in foreign currency translation adjustment, a component of AOCI, to offset the change in the value of the net investment being hedged. For the years ended December 31, 2005, 2004 and 2003, approximately $40 million, $8 million and $29 million, respectively, of losses relating to derivative financial instruments were recorded in foreign currency translation adjustment.

The following table presents the fair values, carrying values and maturities of the Company's foreign currency derivative instruments outstanding as of December 31, 2005 and 2004 (in millions):

2005	Carrying Values	Fair Values	Maturity
Forward contracts	$28	$28	2006
Options and collars	11	11	2006
	$39	$39	
2004	**Carrying Values**	**Fair Values**	**Maturity**
Forward contracts	$ 27	$ 27	2005
Options and collars	12	12	2005
	$39	$39	

The Company estimates the fair value of its foreign currency derivatives based on quoted market prices or pricing models using current market rates. This amount is primarily reflected in prepaid expenses and other assets in our consolidated balance sheets.

The following table summarizes activity in AOCI related to derivatives designated as cash flow hedges held by the Company during the applicable periods (in millions):

	Before-tax Amount	Income Tax	After-Tax Amount
2005			
Accumulated derivative net losses as of January 1, 2005	$(56)	$ 22	$ (34)
Net changes in fair value of derivatives	135	(53)	82
Net gains reclassified from AOCI into earnings	(44)	17	(27)
Accumulated derivative net gains as of December 31, 2005	$ 35	$(14)	$ 21
	Before-tax Amount	**Income Tax**	**After-Tax Amount**
2004			
Accumulated derivative net losses as of January 1, 2004	$ (66)	$ 26	$ (40)
Net changes in fair value of derivatives	(76)	30	(46)
Net losses reclassified from AOCI into earnings	86	(34)	52
Accumulated derivative net losses as of December 31, 2004	$ (56)	$ 22	$ (34)

(Continued)

	Before-tax Amount	Income Tax	After-Tax Amount
2003			
Accumulated derivative net losses as of January 1, 2003	$ (15)	$ 6	$ (9)
Net changes in fair value of derivatives	(165)	65	(100)
Net losses reclassified from AOCI into earnings	114	(45)	69
Accumulated derivative net losses as of December 31, 2003	$ (66)	$ 26	$ (40)

The Company did not discontinue any cash flow hedge relationships during the years ended December 31, 2005, 2004 and 2003.

Financial Control

Any financial risk-management strategy must evaluate the effectiveness of hedging programs. Feedback from a thoughtful evaluation system helps to build institutional experience in risk management practices. Performance assessment of risk-management programs also provides information on when existing strategies are no longer appropriate.

Financial Control Points

There are several areas where performance evaluation systems are fruitful. These include, but are not limited to, corporate treasury, purchasing, and foreign subsidiaries. Control of corporate treasury includes assessing the performance of the total exchange risk management program. This assessment includes quantifying all exposures that were managed, identifying the hedges that were applied, and reporting on the hedging results. Such an evaluation system also includes documentation of how and to what extent corporate treasury assisted other business units in the organization.

To illustrate, suppose the sales manager for the consumer markets division of Worldwide Company wishes to grant customer X a line of credit. Corporate treasury, which secures the needed funds, would quote the sales manager an internal transfer price. This price is based on current market rates for loans of comparable risk. Assume this rate is 8 percent. The sales manager can then quote customer X a borrowing rate of 8 percent plus a markup as compensation for assessing the client's credit risk. In the meantime, corporate treasury will enter the money markets and try to obtain a more favorable rate than it quoted the sales manager. The total return on this transaction includes the profit margin on the sale plus the financing spread. Management accountants need to set up a responsibility accounting system that credits the sales manager and corporate treasury for their fair share of the total profit on the sales transaction.[30]

Similar considerations apply to the purchasing function. Here, exchange risk-management services are just one piece of the total risk-management program. Controls

---

[30]If, for example, corporate treasury tries to beat the 8 percent benchmark rate but instead pays 9 percent, the sales manager should not be charged for the reduced spread.

are also necessary to monitor the performance of programs designed to hedge commodity price risk and mix.

In many organizations, foreign exchange risk-management is centralized at corporate headquarters. This allows subsidiary managers to concentrate on their core business. However, when comparing actual to expected results, evaluation systems must have benchmarks against which to compare the success of corporate risk protection. (See Chapter 10 for more on multinational performance evaluation systems.)

APPROPRIATE BENCHMARKS

The object of risk management is to achieve an optimal balance between risk reduction and costs. Hence, appropriate standards against which to judge actual performance are necessary ingredients in any performance-appraisal system. These benchmarks need to be specified in advance of any protection program and should be based on the concept of opportunity cost. In foreign exchange risk management, the following questions should be considered when selecting a benchmark:[31]

- Does the benchmark represent a policy that could have been followed?
- Can the benchmark be specified in advance?
- Does the benchmark provide a lower-cost strategy than some other alternative?

When FX risk-management programs are centralized, appropriate benchmarks against which to compare the success of corporate risk protection would be programs that local managers could have implemented. In other cases, firms that are averse to foreign exchange risk might automatically hedge any foreign exposure in the forward market or borrow local currency. These strategies would also be natural benchmarks against which to appraise financial risk management. The performance of a certain hedge product (e.g., a currency swap), or of a risk manager, would be judged by comparing the economic return earned on the actively hedged transaction against the economic return that would have been earned had the benchmark treatment been used.

Reporting Systems

Financial risk reporting systems must be able to reconcile both internal reporting and external reporting systems. Risk-management activities (typically managed by corporate treasury) have a future orientation. However, they must eventually reconcile with exposure measurements and financial accounts for external reporting purposes. These normally fall under the jurisdiction of the corporate controller's department. A team approach is most effective in formulating financial risk objectives, performance standards, and monitoring and reporting systems. Financial risk management is a prime example of where corporate finance and accounting are closely connected.

---

[31]Ian Cooper and Julian Franks, "Treasury Performance Measurement," *Treasurer* (February 1988): 56.

SELECTED REFERENCES

Ahlgrim, Kevin C., "An Introduction to Derivatives and Risk Management," *Journal of Risk and Insurance* 50, no. 1 (March 2003): 177.

Allayannis, L., and Eli Ofek, "Exchange Rate Exposure, Hedging and the Use of Foreign Currency Derivatives," *Journal of International Money and Finance* 20 (2001): 273–296.

Axson, David, and Greg Hackett, "Identifying Business Risks," *Financial Executive* (May 2006): 55–57.

Banham, Russ. "Enterprising Views of Risk Management," *Journal of Accountancy,* online issue (June 2004).

Barton, Jan, "Does the Use of Financial Derivatives Affect Earnings Management Decisions?" *Accounting Review* 76, no. 1 (January 2001): 1–26.

Brennan, Michael J., and Yihong Xia, "International Capital Markets and Foreign Exchange Risk," *Review of Financial Studies* 19, no. 3 (2006): 753.

Buckley, Adrian, and Mattheus Vand Der Nat, "Derivatives for the Non-Executive Director," *European Management Journal* 21, no. 3 (June 2003): 388.

Chan-Lau, Jorge A., "Hedging Foreign Exchange Risk in Chile: Markets and Instruments," IMF Working Paper No. 05/37, February 1, 2005.

De Jong, Abe, Joroen Ligterink, and Victor Macrae, "A Firm-Specific Analysis of the Exchange-Rate Exposure of Dutch Firms," *Journal of International Financial Management and Accounting* 17, no. 1 (2006): 1–28.

Dhanani, Alpa, "Foreign Exchange Risk Management: A Case in the Mining Industry," *British Accounting Review* 35, no. 1 (March 2003): 35.

Dufey, Gunter, and Ian H. Giddy, "Management of Corporate Foreign Exchange Risk," in *International Finance and Accounting Handbook*, ed. Frederick D. S. Choi, 3rd ed., New York: John Wiley, 2003, pp. 6.1–6.31.

Financial Accounting Standards Board, "Accounting for Derivative Instruments and Hedging Activities," Statement of Financial Accounting Standards 133 (Norwalk, CT: FASB, October 1994).

Financial Accounting Standards Board, "Amendment of Statement 133 on Derivative Instruments and Hedging Activities," Statement of Financial Accounting Standards No. 149 (Stamford, CT: FASB, April 2003).

Finnerty, John D., and Dwight Grant, "Testing Hedging Effectiveness Under SFAS 133," *CPA Journal* (April 2003), www.nysscpa.org/cpajournal/2003/0403/features/f044033.htm.

Gautier, Antoine, Frieda Granot, and Maurice Levy, "Alternative Foreign Exchange Management Protocols: An Application of Sensitivity Analysis," *Journal of Multinational Financial Management* 12 (2002): 1–19.

Hagelin, Niclas, and Bengt Pramborg, "Hedging Foreign Exchange Exposure: Risk Reduction from Transaction and Translation Hedging," *Journal of International Financial Management and Accounting* 15, no. 1 (2004): 1–20.

International Accounting Standards Committee, "Financial Instruments: Recognition and Measurement," International Accounting Standard 39 (London: IASC, December 1998).

Nelson, James M., Jacquelyn Sue Moffitt, and John Affleck-Graves, "The Impact of Hedging on the Market Value of Equity," *Journal of Corporate Finance* 11, no. 5 (2005): 851–881.

Papaioannou, Michael G., "Exchange Rate Risk Measurement and Management: Issues and Approaches for Firms," IMF Working Paper No. 06/255, November 1, 2006.

Wallace, Jeffrey B., "FAS 133: Accounting for Derivative Instruments," in *Handbook of International Finance and Accounting*, ed. Frederick D. S. Choi, 3rd ed., New York: John Wiley, 2003, pp. 19.1–19.24.

DISCUSSION QUESTIONS

1. Describe what ERM (Enterprise Risk Management) entails.
2. What is market risk? Illustrate this risk with a foreign exchange example.
3. Your company has just decided to purchase 50 percent of its inventory from China. Purchases will be invoiced in Chinese yuan. What four processes do you need to consider in designing a foreign exchange risk-protection system?
4. Compare and contrast the terms *translation*, *transaction*, and *economic exposure*. Does FAS No. 52 resolve the issue of accounting versus economic exposure?
5. List 10 ways to reduce a firm's foreign exchange exposure for a foreign affiliate located in a devaluation-prone country. In each instance, identify the cost–benefit tradeoffs that need to be measured.
6. Explain the difference between a multicurrency translation exposure report and a multi-currency transactions exposure report.
7. What is a financial derivative, and what are some of the accounting issues associated with it?
8. Explain how a company might use a currency swap to hedge its foreign exchange risk on a foreign currency borrowing.
9. What is a financial futures contract? How does it differ from a forward exchange contract?
10. Identify three major types of hedges recognized by IAS 39 and FAS 133 and describe their accounting treatments.
11. All hedging relationships must be "highly effective" to qualify for special accounting treatment. What is meant by highly effective, and why is measuring it important for financial managers?
12. The notion of opportunity cost was probably introduced in your first course in microeconomics. Explain how it can be applied in evaluating the effectiveness of FX risk hedging programs.

EXERCISES

1. Refer to Exhibit 11-1, which discloses the risk-management paradigm for Infosys Technologies. Explain what each step of the cycle entails, including the feedback loop from the last to the first step.
2. Reexamine the risk-mapping cube in Exhibit 11-3. Provide examples of how the various market risks—foreign exchange, interest rate, commodity price and equity price—might affect the value driver: current assets.
3. As one of your first assignments as a new hire on the corporate treasurer's staff of Global Enterprises, Ltd., you are asked to prepare an exchange rate forecast for the Zonolian ecru (ZOE). Specifically, you are expected to forecast what the spot rate for the ecru is likely to be at the end of 20X8. Selected information on which to base your forecast follows. Be sure to identify any additional bases underlying your forecast and any assumptions.

	20X3	20X4	20X5	20X6	20X7	20X8
Visible trade balance (ZOEbn)	7.1	6.5	0.6	27.7	25.4	–
Current account balance (ZOE bn)	21.6	21.9	27.3	215.8	213.8	–
Foreign direct investment (ZOEbn)	9.5	9.2	12.8	11.3	11.6	–
Portfolio flows (ZOEbn)	29.7	13.4	5.0	20.6	9.6	–

(Continued)

Foreign exchange reserves (ZOEbn)	15.25	19.18	28.14	31.46	30.99	–
Real GDP growth (% change yoy)	26.20	5.09	6.80	4.80	3.70	–
Consumer prices (% changes yoy)	51.97	27.70	15.72	18.60	12.32	–
Nominal GDP (ZOEbn)	266.0	335.0	412.0	415.0	479.0	–
Nominal exchange rate to US$	6.42	7.60	7.92	9.15	9.55	–

4. Exhibit 11-5 contains a hypothetical balance sheet of a foreign subsidiary of a U.S. MNC. Exhibit 11-6 shows how the foreign exchange loss is determined, assuming that the parent company employs the temporal method of currency translation.

    Required: Demonstrate how the exchange gains or losses would be computed under each of the other translation methodologies.

5. Following is the consolidated balance sheet (000s omitted) of Worberg Bank, a U.S. financial institution with wholly-owned corporate affiliates in London and Jerusalem. Cash and due from banks includes ILS100,000 and a £ (40,000) bank overdraft. Loans consist entirely of Israeli shekel receivables, while consolidated deposits include ILS40,000 and £15,000. Worberg Bank adopts the local currency as the functional currency for its foreign affiliates and so translates all assets and liabilities (including owners' equity) using the current rate. The exchange rate prevailing as of the balance sheet date was (£/$/ILS= 1/2/4).

    Required: Prepare a multicurrency exposure report for Worberg Bank.

Worberg Bank Consolidated Balance Sheet as of Year-End (000)			
Cash and due from banks	$ 20,000	Deposits	$ 50,000
Loans	100,000		
Fixed assets	30,000	Owners' equity	100,000
Total	150,000		150,000

6. Refer to Exercise 4. Assume that the shekel is forecast to devalue such that the new exchange relationship after the devaluation is (£ /$/ILS = 1/2/8).

    Required: Calculate the consolidated gain or loss that would result from this exchange rate movement.

7. Based on Worberg Bank's exposure to exchange risk identified in Exercise 3, corporate management decides to shield reported earnings from FX losses by actively managing its exposure in Israeli shekels.

    Required: Prepare a brief report containing suggested hedging strategies to do this, together with any tradeoffs that need to be considered.

8. Trojan Corporation USA borrowed 1,000,000 New Zealand dollars (NZ$) at the beginning of the calendar year when the exchange rate was $0.60 = NZ$1. Before repaying this one-year loan, Trojan learns that the NZ dollar has appreciated to $0.70 = NZ$1. It discovers, also, that its New Zealand subsidiary has an exposed net asset position of NZ$ 3,000,000, which will produce a translation gain upon consolidation. What is the amount of the exchange gain or loss that will be reported in consolidated income if:
    a. the U.S. dollar is the foreign operation's functional currency?
    b. the New Zealand dollar is the foreign operation's functional currency and Trojan Corp. designates the New Zealand dollar borrowing as a hedge of the New Zealand affiliate's positive exposure?

9. On April 1, Alexa Corporation, a calendar-year U.S. electronics manufacturer, invests 30 million yen in a three-month yen-denominated CD with a fixed coupon of 8 percent. To hedge against the depreciation of the yen prior to maturity, Alexa designates its accounts payable due to the Sando Company as a hedge. Alexa purchased 32.5 million yen worth of computer chips on account, paying 10 percent down, the balance to be paid in three months. Interest at 8 percent per annum is payable on the unpaid foreign currency balance. The U.S. dollar/Japanese yen exchange rate on April 1 was $1.00 = ¥ 120; on July 1 it was $ 1.00 = ¥ 110.

Required: Prepare dated journal entries in U.S. dollars to record the incurrence and settlement of this foreign currency transaction, assuming that the hedge is deemed highly effective in reducing Alexa's FX risk.

10. On June 1, ACL International, a U.S. confectionery products manufacturer, purchases on account bulk chocolate from a Swiss supplier for 166,667 Swiss francs (CHF) when the spot rate is $0.80 = CHF 1. The Swiss franc payable is due on September 1. To minimize its exposure to an exchange loss should the franc appreciate relative to the dollar prior to payment, ACL International acquires a forward contract to exchange $103,334 for francs on September 1 at a forward rate of $0.82 = CHF 1.

Required: Given the following exchange rate information, provide journal entries to account for the forward exchange contract on June 1, June 30, and September 1. The company closes its books quarterly.

| June 30 spot rate $0.81 | = | CHF 1 |
| September 1 spot rate $0.83 = | | CHF 1 |

11. What is the effective dollar cost of the Swiss chocolate purchase in Exercise 7? Show your calculations.

12. In June, Mu Corporation, a U.S. manufacturer of specialty confectionery products, submits a bid to supply a prestigious retail merchandiser with boxed chocolates for Valentine's Day. If it secures the contract, it will sign a contract with a large Swiss chocolate manufacturer to buy the necessary raw material. The outcome of the bidding will not be known for two months, and the treasurer of Mu Corporation is concerned that the franc may rise in value during the interim, thus reducing (or possibly even eliminating) its planned profit on the fixed-price bid.

To protect the company against an appreciation of the franc, the treasurer buys 25 CHF September 30 option calls at 1.80 (i.e., a premium of 1.8 cents per franc) on a standard contract amount of CHF 62,500. The treasurer's prediction proves accurate, because the franc rises in value to 41.6 cents by the end of August. Rather than await the outcome of the bid, Mu Corporation exercises its call options at the end of August.

Required: Provide the necessary journal entries to record the acquisition and exercise of the options.

Case 11-1   Exposure Identification

You are working for a consulting firm that provides risk-management products for clients. Your task is to provide your company's sales force with information on prospective clients. Assume that Infosys Technologies, whose financial statements and notes are referred to in Appendix 1-3, is a prospective client. ■

REQUIRED

1. Using Infosys' 2006 financial statements and accompanying notes as a starting point, identify as many exposures as you can that impact the company. Be sure to cross-reference your findings with the page numbers of the financial statements you are referring to.

2. Identify any exposures that the company is currently hedging.

Case 11-2   Value At Risk: What Are Our Options?

The scene is a conference room on the 10th floor of an office building on Wall Street, occupied by Anthes Enterprises, a small, rapidly growing manufacturer of electronic trading systems for equities, commodities, and currencies.

The agenda for the 8:00 A.M. meeting concerns reporting issues associated with a potential sales contract for the stock exchange in the Slovak Republic, which wants to upgrade its technology to effectively participate in the globalization of financial markets. In attendance are Shevon Estwick, the COO of Anthes Enterprises, Controller Sy Jones, Treasurer Bebi Karimbaksh, and Vice President of Marketing Autherine Allison.

SHEVON: Thank you for agreeing to meet on such short notice. Autherine, are you ready to give us an update on Slovakia?

AUTHERINE: You mean the Slovak Republic.

SHEVON: Yes.

AUTHERINE: I think there is a 90 percent chance we'll land the contract. Things move a little slowly over there, and they're still concerned about some of the legal details of our sales contract. I think they find the legalese a bit intimidating, and I can't say I blame them. I've scheduled another trip next month to go over contract details. This time I'm taking our legal counsel and have asked him to prepare another draft expressed in terms that are easier to understand. They're also waiting for approvals from their Central Bank, which has to approve major transactions like this one.

SHEVON: Good. Are we prepared to deliver on the contract?

AUTHERINE: Yes, we've lined up the financing, have done our credit checks, and the equipment and installation teams are ready to proceed on two weeks' notice.

SHEVON: Given the size of the contract, are we hedged against the possibility of a devaluation?

BEBI: Yes, we've written a put option on the koruna for ninety days.

SHEVON: Do we think we'll close on the deal before then?

BEBI: Autherine doesn't think so, but you never know. The problem is, no one will write an option for a longer term. We'll renew the option because we have other transactions of this extended duration.

SHEVON: Sy, are we all right on the reporting front?

SY: Not really.

SHEVON: How's that?

SY: It looks like we're up against a reporting standard that requires that gains or losses on cash-flow hedges whose maturities do not match those of the underlying be recognized in current earnings.

SHEVON: Come again?

SY: The bottom line is that we won't be able to treat gains or losses on our put options as a part of comprehensive income, but we'll have to recognize them in current earnings.

SHEVON: Won't that mess up our bottom line?

SY: I'm afraid so. There would be no offsetting gain or loss from our anticipated sale.

BEBI: It's taken me a whole year to get to know the right people and win their trust and friendship. I now have that. There's no doubt in my mind that this sale is a done deal, and I anticipate closing the transaction within the next six to nine months.

SY: That may be, but we just can't find anyone who's willing to write an option for more than ninety days at a time.

SHEVON: I don't want to think about what the accounting will do to our stock price! I mean, we're about to float our first euro-equity issue. A lower offering price would be disastrous at this stage of our development, not to mention the effect on our shareholders.

AUTHERINE: Given the nature of our business, I don't think the transactions side of our business will change much.

SHEVON: Do you think it would be worthwhile having a consultant advise us on this one?

SY,
AUTHERINE,
AND BEBI: (*in unison*) Why not?

SHEVON: When you do, would you show that individual the following pages that I ripped out from an annual report I just received as a shareholder and see if it has any information value? (*see attachment*) ■

REQUIRED

As a consultant for Anthes Enterprises, identify what you believe are promising hedge accounting options.

ATTACHMENT: TORN PAGES FROM THE ANNUAL REPORT OF A MAJOR U.S. MANUFACTURER

First page: Note 10:

We are exposed to the risk of loss arising from adverse changes in:

- commodity prices, affecting the cost of our raw materials and energy,
- foreign exchange risks,
- interest rates,
- stock prices, and
- discount rates affecting the measurement of our pension and retiree medical liabilities.

In the normal course of business, we manage these risks through a variety of strategies, including the use of derivatives. Certain derivatives are designated as either cash-flow or fair value hedges and qualify for hedge accounting treatment, while others do not qualify and are marked to market through earnings.

For cash-flow hedges, changes in fair value are deferred in accumulated other comprehensive loss within shareholders' equity until the underlying hedged item is recognized in net income. For fair value hedges, changes in fair value are recognized immediately in earnings, consistent with the underlying hedged item. Hedging transactions are limited to an underlying exposure. As a result, any change in the value of our derivative financial instruments would be substantially offset by an opposite change in the value of the underlying hedged items. Hedging ineffectiveness and a net earnings impact occur when the change in the value of the hedge does not offset the change in the value of the underlying hedged item. If the derivative instrument is terminated, we continue to defer the related gain or loss and include it as a component of the cost of the underlying hedged item. Upon determintation that the hedged item will not be part of an actual transaction, we recognize the related gain or loss in net income in that period. We also use derivatives that do not qualify for hedge accounting treatment. We account for such derivatives at market value with the resulting gains and losses reflected in our income statement. We do not use derivative instruments for trading or speculative purposes and we limit our exposure to individual counterparties to manage credit risk.

Commodity Prices. We are subject to commodity price risk because our ability to recover increased costs through higher pricing may be limited in the competitive environment in which we operate. This risk is managed through the use of fixed-price purchase orders, pricing agreements, geographic diversity and derivatives. We use derivatives, with terms of no more than two years, to economically hedge price fluctuations related to a portion of our anticipated commodity purchases, primarily for natural gas and diesel fuel. For those derivatives that are designated as cash-flow hedges, any ineffectiveness is recorded immediately. However our commodity cash-flow hedges have not had any significant ineffectiveness for all periods presented. We classify both the earnings and cash-flow impact from these derivatives consistent with the underlying hedged item. During the next 12 months, we expect to reclassify gains of $24 million related to cash flow hedges from accumulated other comprehensive loss into net income.

Foreign Exchange   Our operations outside of the U.S. generate over a third of our net revenue, of which Mexico, the United Kingdom and Canada comprise nearly 20 percent. As a result, we are exposed to foreign currency risks from unforeseen economic changes and political unrest. On occasion, we enter into hedges, primarily forward contracts with terms of no more than two years, to reduce the effect of foreign exchange rates. Ineffectiveness on these hedges has not been material. *(rest of page torn off)*

Partial Second Page:

Our Divisions   We manufacture or use contract manufacturers, market and sell a variety of salty, sweet, and grain-based snacks, carbonated and noncarbonated beverages, and foods through our North American and international business divisions. Our North American divisions include the United States and Canada. The accounting policies for the divisions are the same as those described in Note 2, except for certain allocation methodologies for stock-based compensation expense and pension and retiree medical expense, as described in the unaudited information in "Our Critical Accounting Policies." Additionally, beginning in the fourth quarter of 2005, we began

centrally managing commodity derivatives on behalf of our divisions. Certain of the commodity derivatives, primarily those related to the purchase of energy for use by our divisions, do not qualify for hedge accounting treatment. These derivatives hedge underlying commodity price risk and were not entered into for speculative purposes. Such derivatives are marked to market with the resulting gains and losses recognized as a component of corporate unallocated expense. These gains and losses are reflected in division results when the divisions take delivery of the underlying commodity. Therefore, division results reflect the contract purchase price of the energy or other commodities.

Division results are based on how our Chairman and Chief Executive Officer evaluates our divisions. Division results exclude certain Corporate-initiated restructuring and impairment charges, merger related costs and divested businesses. For additional unaudited information on our divisions, see "Our Operations" in Management's Discussion and Analysis.

CHAPTER 12

International Taxation and Transfer Pricing

Of all the environmental variables that financial managers must contend with in multinational operations, only foreign exchange is as influential as taxation. Tax considerations strongly influence decisions on where to invest, what form of business organization to employ, how to finance, when and where to recognize elements of revenues and expense, and what transfer prices to charge.[1]

With the possible exception of cost of goods sold, taxation is the largest expense of most businesses. Thus, it makes sense for management to minimize international taxes whenever possible. Financial managers must also contend with special rules regarding the taxation of foreign-source income. Moreover, international tax agreements, laws, and regulations are constantly changing. Changes in one country's tax provisions have complex and wide-ranging effects in a multinational tax-planning system, and computer-based simulation systems are essential aids to management.

Because it is not possible in a single chapter to provide a working knowledge of the major tax provisions in all of the world's economically important countries, we limit our discussion here to some of the major variables that financial managers need to consider in tax planning for multinational operations. These variables include major differences in national tax systems (i.e., how countries tax businesses operating in their jurisdictions), national attempts to address the issue of double taxation (i.e., how countries tax the foreign-source income of their business entities), and arbitrage opportunities between national tax jurisdictions for multinational firms. Transfer pricing, in addition to its role in minimizing multinational corporate taxes, should be considered in the broader context of strategic planning and control.

INITIAL CONCEPTS

The maze of laws and regulations that govern the taxation of foreign corporations and profits earned abroad rests on a few basic concepts. These include notions of tax neutrality and tax equity. *Tax neutrality* means that taxes have no effect (are neutral) on resource-allocation decisions. That is, business decisions are driven by economic fundamentals, such as rate of return, rather than tax considerations. Such decisions should

---

[1]For a review of empirical research on the effects of international tax on business decisions, see J. F. Hines, Jr., "Lessons from Behavioral Responses to International Taxation," *National Tax Journal* (June 1999): 305–322.

result in an optimal allocation of resources: When taxes influence the allocation of resources, the result will probably be less than optimal. In reality, taxes are seldom neutral.[2]

Tax equity means that taxpayers who are similarly situated should pay the same tax, but there is much disagreement over how to interpret this concept. For example, is a foreign subsidiary simply a domestic company that happens to operate abroad? If so, then foreign- and domestic-source income should be taxed at the same parent-country rate. Or is a foreign subsidiary a foreign company that happens to be owned by a domestic one? In this case, foreign-source income should be taxed the same as other companies in that country, that is, at the foreign country's tax rate. We shall find that actual international tax practices waver between these two extremes.

DIVERSITY OF NATIONAL TAX SYSTEMS

A firm can conduct international business by exporting goods and services or by making direct or indirect foreign investments. Exports seldom trigger a tax exposure in the importing country, because it is difficult for importing countries to enforce taxes levied on foreign exporters. On the other hand, a company that operates in another country through a branch or an incorporated affiliate subjects itself to that country's taxes. The effective management of this tax exposure requires an understanding of national tax systems, which differ greatly among countries. Differences range from types of taxes and tax burdens to differences in tax assessment and collection philosophies.

Types of Taxes

A company operating abroad encounters a variety of taxes. *Direct taxes*, such as income taxes, are easy to recognize and normally are disclosed on companies' financial statements. *Indirect taxes*, such as consumption taxes, are not so clearly recognized or as frequently disclosed. Typically they are buried in "other costs and expenses." Exhibit 12-1 illustrates the differential impact of direct and indirect taxes on pretax and after-tax income. In comparing investment performance between countries, the focus should be on after-tax returns.

EXHIBIT 12-1   Earnings Effects of Direct vs. Indirect Taxes

	Direct	*Indirect*
Revenues	250	250
Expenses	150	190
Pretax income	100	60
Direct taxes (40%)	40	-0-
After-tax income	60	60

[2]For example, there is a considerable amount of evidence showing that investment-location decisions are significantly influenced by corporate taxation. See D. Hartman, "Tax Policy and Foreign Direct Investment in the United States," *National Tax Journal* (December 1984): 42–52; and H. Grubert and J. Mutti, "Do Taxes Influence Where U.S. Corporations Invest?" *National Tax Journal* (December 2000): 825–839.

The *corporate income tax* is probably more widely used to generate government revenue than any other major tax, with the possible exception of customs duties. Since the mid-1980s, however, the international trend has been a lowering and converging of income tax rates. Fueling this trend is the recognition that reduced tax rates increase the global competitiveness of a country's business enterprises and create an attractive environment for international business. Indeed, the integration of the world economy and the increasing ability of businesses to move from high-tax environments to low-tax ones constrain a country's ability to set higher rates than elsewhere.[3] Exhibit 12-2 shows national income tax rates for selected countries.

Withholding taxes are taxes imposed by governments on dividend, interest, and royalty payments to foreign investors. For example, assume that a country has a 10 percent withholding tax on interest paid to foreign investors. The investors would receive only 90 percent of the interest paid by the bonds. While legally imposed on the foreign recipient, these taxes are typically withheld at the source by the paying corporation, which remits the proceeds to tax collectors in the host country. Because withholding taxes may hinder the international flow of long-term investment capital, they are often modified by bilateral tax treaties.

The *value-added tax* is a consumption tax found in Europe and Canada. This tax is typically levied on the value added at each stage of production or distribution. It applies to total sales less purchases from any intermediate sales unit. Thus, if a Norwegian merchant buys 500,000 krone of merchandise from a Norwegian wholesaler and then sells it for 600,000 krone, the value added is 100,000 krone, and a tax is assessed on this amount. Companies that pay the tax in their own costs can reclaim them later from the tax authorities. Consumers ultimately bear the cost of the value-added tax. Exhibit 12-3 shows how the value-added tax works.

Border taxes, such as customs or import duties, generally aim at keeping domestic goods price competitive with imports. Accordingly, taxes assessed on imports typically parallel excise and other indirect taxes paid by domestic producers of similar goods.

The *transfer tax* is another indirect tax. It is imposed on transfers of items between taxpayers and can have important effects on such business decisions as the structure of acquisitions. For example, business acquisitions in Europe are often made through the purchase of shares rather than the underlying net assets. More variations in structure are found in U.S. acquisitions because transfer taxes are less important in the United States.

Tax Burdens

Differences in overall tax burdens are important in international business. Various statutory rates of income taxation are an important source of these differences, as can be seen in Exhibit 12-2. However, differences in tax rates tell only part of the story. Many other considerations may significantly affect the *effective tax burdens* for multinational enterprises. Differences in national definitions of taxable income are important.

---

[3]"Disappearing Taxes: The Tap Runs Dry," *Economist* (May 31, 1997): 21.

EXHIBIT 12-2   Corporate Income Tax Rates

Country	(%)	Country	(%)	Country	(%)
Argentina	35	Honduras	30	Philippines	35
Australia	30	Hong Kong	17.5	Poland	19
Austria	25	Hungary	16	Portugal	27.5[g]
Bangladesh	30	Iceland	18	Romania	16
Belgium	33.99	India	33.66	Russia	24
Bolivia	25	Indonesia	30	Singapore	20
Brazil	34[a]	Ireland	12.5	Slovak Republic	19
Bulgaria	15	Israel	31	South Africa	36.9[h]
Canada	36.1[b]	Italy	37.25[e]	Spain	35
Cayman Islands	0	Japan	40.69[f]	Sri Lanka	32.5
Chile	17	Korea, Republic of	27.5	Sweden	28
China	33[c]	Latvia	15	Switzerland	21.3[i]
Colombia	35	Lithuania	15	Taiwan	25
Costa Rica	30	Luxembourg	29.63	Thailand	30
Croatia	20.32	Malaysia	28	Tunisia	35
Cyprus	10	Malta	35	Turkey	30
Czech Republic	24	Mexico	29	Ukraine	25
Denmark	28	Netherlands	29.6	United Kingdom	30
Dominican Republic	30	New Zealand	33	United States	35/40[j]
Ecuador	25	Norway	28	Uruguay	30
Fiji	31	Oman	12	Venezuela	34
Finland	26	Pakistan	35	Vietnam	28
France	33.33	Panama	30	Zambia	35
Germany	38.34	Papua New Guinea	30		
Greece	22/29[d]	Peru	30		

Note:

A simple comparison of tax rates is not sufficient for assessing the relative tax burdens imposed by different governments. The method of computing the profits to which the tax rates will be applied (the tax base) should also be taken into account.

These rates do not reflect payroll taxes, social security taxes, net wealth taxes, turnover taxes, and other taxes not levied on income.

[a]*The sum of income tax and social contribution tax.*

[b]*Includes provincial income taxes. Depending on the province, the effective overall rate ranges from 32.0% to 39.1%.*

[c] *Includes state tax rate (30%) and local tax (3%).*

[d]*Various rates based on type of company.*

[e]*The sum of corporate income tax rate (33%) and regional tax (4.25%).*

[f]*Includes corporate income tax (30%) and business, perfectural, and municipal taxes.*

[g]*Includes municipal tax of 2.5%.*

[h]*Includes corporate income tax rate (29%) and effect of tax on dividends declared.*

[i]*Includes federal, cantonal, and municipal taxes.*

[j]*Federal tax rate is 35%. State and local income tax rates range from less than 1% to 12%. State and local income taxes are deductible in determining federal income taxes, making the average effective tax rate 40%.*

SOURCE: KPMG's Corporate Tax Rate Survey—January 2006, www.kpmg.co.uk/pubs/corporate_tax_rates.pdf. ©KPMG International, a Swiss operating association. Used by permission.

EXHIBIT 12-3　Value-Added Tax

	Producer	*Wholesaler*	*Merchant*	*Consumer*
Cost	Assume 0	€12.00	€15.60	€21.60
Recoverable VAT	–	2.00	2.60	
Net cost	0	€10.00	€13.00	
Sales price before VAT	€10.00	13.00	18.00	
Value added	€10.00	€ 3.00	€ 5.00	
Value-added tax (20%)	2.00	0.60	1.00	
Sales price after VAT	€12.00	€15.60	21.60	
VAT paid	€ 2.00	€ 2.60	€ 3.60	
Recoverable VAT	0	2.00	2.60	
VAT due	€ 2.00	€ 0.60	€ 1.00	
VAT borne				€ 3.60

Consider depreciation. In theory, a portion of the cost of an asset is said to expire as the asset is used up to produce revenue. In keeping with the matching principle, this expired cost is recognized as an expense and deducted from its related revenue. Where the asset is consumed equally in each reporting period, an equal portion of its cost is commonly expensed each period for external financial reporting purposes. In the United States, however, a distinction is generally made between depreciation for external reporting and depreciation for tax purposes. As an incentive to invest in capital assets, including commercial buildings, companies in the United States are allowed to use accelerated depreciation methods. In Germany, tax law specifies depreciation rates, and buildings are depreciated in straight-line fashion. Tax law also determines depreciation rates in France, with most assets depreciated on a straight-line basis. However, anti-pollution and energy-saving assets may be depreciated on an accelerated basis. In Latin American countries where inflation rates have been high (e.g., Mexico and Uruguay), firms are required to adjust their assets for changing price levels, and the higher depreciation charges are deductible for tax purposes (see Chapter 7).

Another item that accounts for intercountry differences in effective tax burdens relates to the host country's social overhead. To attract foreign investments, less-industrialized countries often assess lower corporate income tax rates than their more industrialized counterparts. However, countries with low direct taxes need to fund government and other social services just like any other country. Therefore, lower direct corporate tax rates usually result in higher indirect taxes or in fewer and lower-quality public services. Indirect taxes reduce purchasing power in the local market. Fewer and lower-quality public services may impose a higher cost structure on multinational operations. Examples include poor transportation networks, inadequate postal services, ineffective telephone and telecommunications systems, and power shortages.

While more and more governments are reducing marginal corporate tax rates, many also are broadening corporate tax bases. In the real world, effective tax rates seldom equal nominal tax rates. Thus, it is improper to base intercountry comparisons on statutory tax rates alone. Furthermore, a low tax rate does not necessarily mean a low tax burden. Internationally, tax burdens should always be determined by examining *effective* tax rates.

Tax Administration Systems

National tax assessment systems also affect relative tax burdens. Several major systems are currently in use. For simplicity, we will only consider the classical and integrated systems.

Under the *classical system*, corporate income taxes on taxable income are levied at the corporate level and the shareholder level. Shareholders are taxed either when the corporate income is paid as a dividend or when they liquidate their investment. When a corporation is taxed on income measured before dividends are paid, and shareholders are then taxed on their dividends, the shareholders' dividend income is effectively taxed twice. To illustrate, assume that a parent corporation in Zonolia (fictitious), subject to a 33 percent corporate income tax, earns 100 zonos (Z) and distributes a 100 percent dividend to its sole shareholder, who is in the 30 percent tax bracket. Effective taxes paid on the corporate income are determined as follows:

Corporate income	Z100.00
– Income tax at 33%	33.00
= Net income (and dividend paid)	Z 67.00
Dividend	Z 67.00
– Personal income tax at 30%	20.10
= Net amount to shareholder	Z 46.90

Total tax paid on the Z100 of corporate income:

Corporate tax	Z33.00
Individual income tax	20.10
Total	Z53.10

Countries associated with this system include Belgium, Luxembourg, the Netherlands, and Sweden. The recent trend in most developed countries has been to move away from the double taxation of dividend income by adopting either an integrated or an imputation system.

Under an *integrated* system, corporate and shareholder taxes are integrated so as to reduce or eliminate the double taxation of corporate income. The *tax credit,* or *imputation,* system is a common variant of the integrated tax system. In this system, a tax is levied on corporate income, but part of the tax paid can be treated as a credit against personal income taxes when dividends are distributed to shareholders. This tax system is advocated by the European Union and is found in Australia, Canada, Mexico, and many European countries, including France, Italy, and the United Kingdom.

To see how this tax system works, assume facts similar to that of our Zonolian parent company in the preceding illustration. Further assume that shareholders receive a tax credit equal to 25 percent of dividends received. Based on these assumptions, the total taxes paid is determined as follows:

Corporate income	Z100.00
– Income tax at 33%	33.00
= Net income and dividend paid	Z 67.00
Dividend income to shareholder	Z 67.00
+ Tax credit at 25%	16.75
= Grossed-up dividend	Z 83.75
Income tax liability at 30%	Z 25.12
– Tax credit	16.75
= Tax due from shareholder	Z 8.37

Total tax paid on the Z100 of corporate income:

Corporate tax	Z 33.00
Individual income tax	8.37
Total	Z 41.37

This example illustrates a partial imputation system in which double taxation is reduced but not eliminated. Full imputation eliminates double taxation.

The *split-rate* system is another variant of the integrated tax system, where a lower tax is levied on distributed earnings (i.e., dividends) than on retained earnings. Germany once had a split-rate system. Other ways to reduce double taxation are to exempt a percentage of dividends from personal taxation, as Germany does now, or to tax dividends at a lower rate than the personal rate, as in the United States.

Foreign Tax Incentives

Countries eager to accelerate their economic development are keenly aware of the benefits of international business. Many countries offer tax incentives to attract foreign investment. Incentives may include tax-free cash grants applied toward the cost of fixed assets of new industrial undertakings or relief from paying taxes for certain time periods (*tax holidays*). Other forms of temporary tax relief include reduced income tax rates, tax deferrals, and reduction or elimination of various indirect taxes. More-industrialized countries offer targeted incentives, such as Ireland's reduced corporate tax rate for manufacturing operations (10 percent) through the year 2010.[4] Some countries, particularly those with few natural resources, offer permanent tax inducements. These so-called *tax havens* include

1. the Bahamas, Bermuda, and the Cayman Islands, which have no income taxes at all
2. Barbados, which has very low income tax rates
3. Hong Kong and Panama, which tax locally generated income but exempt income from foreign sources

Countries that allow special privileges are suitable as tax havens for very limited purposes.

---

[4]The Irish corporate tax rate is 12.5 percent. The 10 percent preferential tax rate for manufacturing companies will be eliminated after 2010.

Harmful Tax Competition

The Organization for Economic Cooperation and Development (OECD) is trying to halt tax competition by certain tax-haven countries. The worldwide trend toward both lowering and converging corporate income tax rates is a direct result of tax competition. So is tax competition harmful? Certainly it is beneficial if it makes governments more efficient. On the other hand, it is harmful when it shifts tax revenues away from governments that need them to provide services on which businesses rely. The OECD is mainly concerned about tax havens that allow businesses to avoid or evade another country's taxes. So-called *brass plate* subsidiaries have no real work or employment attached to them: They lack *substantial activities* and merely funnel financial transactions through the tax-haven country to avoid another country's taxes. The OECD especially suspects tax havens that are unwilling to share information with tax authorities elsewhere and that apply or enforce tax laws unevenly or in secret. These tax havens are being pressured to adopt practices on the effective exchange of information and transparency.[5]

International Harmonization

Given the diversity of tax systems around the world, the global harmonization of tax policies would seem to be worthwhile. Multinational companies, burdened by the disparities of national taxes, are fueling the pressure for international tax reform. The European Union is expending much energy in this direction as it works to create a single market. The EU's introduction of a single currency, the euro, highlights the tax disparities among its members.[6]

TAXATION OF FOREIGN-SOURCE INCOME AND DOUBLE TAXATION

Every nation claims the right to tax income originating within its borders. National philosophies regarding the taxation of foreign-source earnings differ, however, and this is important from a tax-planning perspective. A few countries, such as France, Hong Kong, Panama, and Venezuela, adopt the *territorial* principle of taxation and exempt from taxation the income of resident corporations generated outside their borders. This reflects the idea that tax burdens of foreign affiliates should equal those of their local competitors. In this view, foreign affiliates of local companies are viewed as foreign companies that happen to be owned by local residents.

---

[5]The OECD refers to these as uncooperative tax havens. See J. M. Weiner and H. J. Ault, "The OECD's Report on Harmful Tax Competition," *National Tax Journal* (spring 1998): 601–608; F. M. Horner, "The OECD, Tax Competition, and the Future of Tax Reform" (January 2000), www.oecd.com; "The Mystery of the Vanishing Taxpayer: A Survey of Globalisation and Tax," *Economist* (January 29, 2000): 16–17; "The OECD's Project on Harmful Tax Practices: The 2001 Progress Report" (November 2001), www.oecd.org.

[6]The EU focus is on harmonizing the corporate tax base rather than corporate tax rates. Under current proposals, companies would calculate one single, EU-wide income that would be divided among jurisdictions according to some rough measure of a firm's activities in each country. See "Discord Over Harmony," *Economist* (November 12, 2005): 81.

Most countries (e.g., Australia, Brazil, China, the Czech Republic, Germany, Japan, Mexico, the Netherlands, the United Kingdom, and the United States) adopt the *worldwide* principle and tax resident corporations and citizens on income regardless of national boundaries. The underlying idea here is that a foreign subsidiary of a local company is simply a local company that happens to operate abroad.

Foreign Tax Credit

Under the worldwide principle of taxation, the foreign earnings of a domestic company are subject to the full tax levies of its host and home countries. To avoid discouraging businesses from expanding abroad, and in keeping with the concept of foreign neutrality, a parent company's domicile (country of residence) can elect to treat foreign taxes paid as a credit against the parent's domestic tax liability or as a deduction from taxable income. Companies generally choose the credit, because it yields a one-for-one reduction of domestic taxes payable (limited to the amount of income taxes actually paid),[7] whereas a deduction is only worth the product of the foreign tax expense multiplied by the domestic marginal tax rate.

Foreign tax credits may be calculated as a straightforward credit against income taxes paid on branch or subsidiary earnings and any taxes withheld at the source, such as dividends, interest, and royalties remitted to a domestic investor. The tax credit can also be estimated when the amount of foreign income tax paid is not clearly evident (e.g., when a foreign subsidiary remits a fraction of its foreign-source earnings to its domestic parent). Here, reported dividends on the parent company's tax return would be grossed up to include the amount of the tax (deemed paid) plus any applicable foreign withholding taxes. It is as if the domestic parent received a dividend including the tax due the foreign government and then paid the tax.

The allowable foreign indirect tax credit (foreign income tax deemed paid) is determined as follows:

$$\frac{\text{Dividend payout (including any withholding tax)}}{\text{Earnings net of foreign income tax}} \times \text{Creditable foreign taxes}$$

To illustrate how foreign tax credits apply in a variety of situations, assume that a U.S. parent company receives royalties from Country A, foreign-branch earnings from Country B, and dividends from subsidiaries in Countries C and D. Withholding taxes on royalty and dividend payments are assumed to be 15 percent in Countries A, C, and D; income tax rates are assumed to be 30 percent in Country B and 40 percent in Country C. Country D assesses a 40 percent indirect sales tax as opposed to a direct tax on earnings within its jurisdiction.[8]

The key variables in this illustration, as shown in Exhibit 12-4, are the organizational form of the foreign activity (e.g., branch vs. subsidiary) and relative corporate income and withholding tax rates. In the first column, the royalty payment of $20.00 is subject to a 15 percent withholding tax in the host country. For U.S. tax purposes, the net royalty is grossed up to include the withholding tax, which then forms the base for the U.S. domestic tax of 35 percent. The U.S. tax of $7.00 is offset by the credit for the foreign tax paid to yield a net U.S. tax liability of $4.00.

---

[7]Indirect levies, such as foreign sales taxes, are generally not creditable.
[8]Note that royalty income and branch/subsidiary earnings are grossed up (i.e., included in U.S. income) before deducting foreign taxes paid.

EXHIBIT 12-4   U.S. Taxation of Foreign-Source Income

	Royalties from Operation in Country A	Earnings from Branch in Country B	Dividend from Subsidiary in Country C	Dividend from Subsidiary in Country D
Branch/Subsidiary				
before-tax earnings		100.00	100.00	60.00
Foreign income taxes (30%/40%)		30.00	40.00	-0-
After-tax earnings		70.00	60.00	60.00
Dividend paid (50% of after-tax earnings)			30.00	30.00
Other foreign income	20.00			
Foreign withholding taxes (15%)	3.00		4.50	4.50
Net payment to parent	17.00		25.50	25.50
U.S. income	20.00	100.00[a]	30.00	30.00
Dividend gross-up (30/60 × 40)	___	___	20.00	-0-
Taxable income	20.00	100.00	50.00	30.00
U.S. tax (35%)	7.00	35.00	17.50	10.50
Foreign tax credit				
Paid	(3.00)	(30.00)	(4.50)	(4.50)
Deemed paid (30/60 × 40)	___	___	(20.00)	-0-
Total	(3.00)	(30.00)	(24.50)	(4.50)
U.S. tax (net)	4.00	5.00	(7.00)[b]	6.00
Foreign taxes	3.00	30.00	24.50	40.00[c]
Total taxes of U.S. taxpayer	7.00	35.00	17.50[d]	46.00

[a]Grossed up to include foreign taxes actually paid.

[b]Excess foreign tax credits can be carried back one year or carried forward 10 years to offset U.S. tax on other foreign source (not U.S. source) income. If unavailable, total taxes = 24.50.

[c]40% indirect sales tax on 100.00.

[d]Excludes deferred tax on undistributed earnings of affiliate.

In the second column of Exhibit 12-4, the foreign branch earnings of the U.S. parent are grossed up to include foreign income taxes paid of $30.00. U.S. taxes payable on this amount of $35.00 are offset by a foreign tax credit of $30.00, to yield a net U.S. tax payable of $5.00. As with the royalty payment, the effect of the foreign tax credit is to limit the total tax on foreign-source income to the higher of the two countries' taxes. In this example, the U.S. tax rate of 35 percent was higher than the foreign tax rate of 30 percent, yielding a total tax on royalty and branch earnings of 35 percent.

Further scrutiny of Exhibit 12-4 is instructive. A comparison of columns 2 and 3 suggests the importance of organizational form on international taxes. A branch operation, viewed as an extension of the parent company, is subject to the full tax rate of the home country. In our example, the foreign branch pays a total tax of $35: $30 of foreign income taxes and $5 of U.S. taxes. Thus, the foreign branch bears the full burden of the U.S. income tax rate. However, it is spared any withholding taxes on earnings distributions to the parent because only a foreign subsidiary can distribute its earnings. On the other hand, a foreign operation organized as a subsidiary is taxed only on earnings that it remits to the parent company. It can defer taxes on retained income, and thus compete on an equal tax footing with local companies.

Columns 3 and 4 illustrate how a system of worldwide taxation places a subsidiary at a competitive disadvantage when it is located in a country that relies primarily on an indirect tax for revenue. Note that the subsidiary in Country D has a higher total tax burden because the tax credit only relieves direct taxes, not indirect taxes. Similarly, the benefits of tax incentives granted by host governments may also be nullified.

Limits to Tax Credits

Home countries can tax foreign-source income in many ways. A country may elect to tax income from each separate national source. At the other extreme, all foreign-source income from any foreign source may be combined and taxed once. Some countries tax foreign-source income on a source-by-source basis, with the tax credit for foreign-source income limited to the corresponding domestic tax applicable to that income. As illustrated in columns 2 and 3 of Exhibit 12-4, the maximum tax liability will always be the higher of the tax rates in the host or home country. Other countries allow parent companies to pool income from many country sources by income type (e.g., dividends vs. interest vs. royalties). Excess tax credits from countries with high tax rates (column 3 of Exhibit 12-4) can offset taxes on income received from low-tax-rate countries (column 2 of Exhibit 12-4).

To prevent foreign tax credits from offsetting taxes on domestic-source income, many countries impose an overall limit on the amount of foreign taxes creditable in any year. The United States, for instance, limits the tax credit to the proportion of the U.S. tax that equals the ratio of the taxpayer's foreign-source taxable income to its worldwide taxable income for the year. Assume that Alpha Company earned $2,000 of foreign-source income and $3,000 of U.S.-source taxable income. Its foreign tax credit would be the lesser of the foreign income taxes paid or the foreign tax credit limitation computed as follows:

$$\text{Foreign tax credit limit} = \frac{\text{Foreign source taxable income}}{\text{Worldwide taxable income}} \times \text{U. S. tax before credits}$$

$$= (\$2{,}000/\$5{,}000) \times (\$5{,}000 \times 35\%)$$

$$= \$700$$

Thus, only $700 would be allowed as a tax credit, even if foreign taxes paid exceeded $700. Excess foreign taxes paid can be carried back one year and forward 10 years (see footnote b in Exhibit 12-4).

A separate foreign tax credit limitation applies to U.S. taxes on the foreign-source taxable income of each of the following types of income (or *baskets*):

- Passive income (e.g., investment-type income, such as dividends, interest, royalties, and rents)
- General income (all other types)[9]

---

[9]Before the American Jobs Creation Act of 2004, excess taxes paid could be carried back two years and forward five years. The act also reduced the number of income baskets from nine to two. Both changes were designed to improve tax breaks for multinational corporations.

Foreign-source taxable income is foreign-source gross income less expenses, losses, and deductions allocable to the foreign-source income, plus a ratable share of expenses, losses, and deductions that cannot be allocated definitely to any item or class of gross income. The interpretation of this provision is reportedly one of the major areas of dispute between taxpayers and the IRS.[10]

Tax Treaties

Although foreign tax credits shield foreign-source income from double taxation (to some extent), tax treaties go further. Signatories to such treaties generally agree on how taxes and tax incentives will be imposed, honored, shared, or otherwise eliminated on business income earned in one taxing jurisdiction by citizens of another. Thus, most tax treaties between home and host countries provide that profits earned by a domestic enterprise in the host country shall be subject to its taxes only if the enterprise maintains a permanent establishment there. Tax treaties also affect withholding taxes on dividends, interest, and royalties paid by the enterprise of one country to foreign shareholders. They usually grant reciprocal reductions in withholding taxes on dividends and often entirely exempt royalties and interest from withholding.

Foreign Exchange Considerations

The Tax Reform Act of 1986 introduced formal rules regarding the taxation of foreign currency gains or losses in the United States. In keeping with SFAS No. 52 (described in Chapter 6), all tax determinations must be made in the taxpayer's functional currency. The functional currency is assumed to be the U.S. dollar unless the foreign operation is an autonomous unit, or *qualified business unit*. In general, tax rules are similar but not necessarily identical to generally accepted accounting principles described in Chapter 6. Following are examples of tax treatments.[11]

Transaction gains or losses in currencies other than the functional currency are generally accounted for under the two-transactions perspective. Under this approach, any exchange gain or loss recognized when the foreign currency transaction is settled is treated as ordinary income and accounted for separately from the underlying transaction. However, gains or losses on transactions qualifying as hedges of certain foreign currency transactions can be integrated with the underlying transaction. For example, a gain or loss incurred on a forward exchange contract designated as an effective hedge of a foreign currency loan would offset the transaction gain or loss on the underlying obligation.

Foreign exchange gains or losses are generally allocated between U.S. and foreign sources by reference to the residence of the taxpayer on whose books the foreign currency asset or liability is reflected. Thus, for a U.S. corporation, the source of the gain or loss would be the United States.

Taxable profits for foreign branches are initially based on their functional currencies. The functional currency then is converted to U.S. dollars using the weighted average

---

[10]P. Bodner, "International Taxation," in *International Accounting and Finance Handbook*, ed. Frederick D. S. Choi, 3rd.ed. (New York: John Wiley, 2003), p. 30.11.
[11]Ibid., pp. 30.16–30.18.

exchange rate for the taxable period. Foreign income taxes paid are translated at the exchange rate in effect when the tax is paid and then added to foreign taxable income or grossed up. The foreign taxes paid are then claimed as a foreign tax credit for U.S. tax purposes.

For foreign subsidiaries, deemed distributions under Subpart F regulations (discussed in the next section) are translated using weighted average exchange rates for the foreign corporation's taxable year. Deemed-paid foreign taxes are translated into U.S. dollars using exchange rates in effect on the date the tax was paid.

TAX-PLANNING DIMENSIONS

In tax planning, multinational companies have a distinct advantage over purely domestic companies because they have more geographical flexibility in locating their production and distribution systems. This flexibility provides unique opportunities to exploit differences among national tax jurisdictions so as to lower the overall tax burden for the corporation. The shifting of revenues and expenses through intracompany ties also gives MNCs additional opportunities to minimize the global taxes paid. In response, national governments are constantly designing legislation to minimize arbitrage opportunities involving different national tax jurisdictions.

We begin our examination of tax-planning issues with two caveats:

- Tax considerations should never control business strategy. The financial or operating strength of a business transaction must stand on its own.
- Constant changes in tax laws limit the benefits of long-term tax planning.

Organizational Considerations

In taxing foreign-source income, many taxing jurisdictions focus on the organizational form of a foreign operation. A branch is usually considered an extension of the parent company. Accordingly, its income is immediately consolidated with that of the parent (an option not available to a subsidiary) and fully taxed in the year earned whether remitted to the parent company or not. Earnings of a foreign subsidiary are not generally taxed until repatriated. Exceptions to this general rule are described in the next section.

If initial operations abroad are forecast to generate losses, it may be tax-advantageous to organize initially as a branch. Once foreign operations turn profitable, operating them as subsidiaries may be attractive. For one thing, the corporate overhead of the parent company cannot be allocated to a branch, because the branch is viewed as part of the parent. Moreover, if taxes on foreign profits are lower in the host country than in the parent country, profits of a subsidiary are not taxed by the parent country until repatriated (see columns 2 and 3 of Exhibit 12-4). If the subsidiary were organized in a tax-haven country that imposes no taxes at all, tax deferral would be even more attractive. National governments know this phenomenon, and many have taken steps to minimize corporate abuse of it. One example is the U.S. treatment of Subpart F income.

Controlled Foreign Corporations and Subpart F Income

Recall that in the United States, like many other countries adopting the worldwide principle of taxation, income of foreign subsidiaries is not taxable to the parent until it is repatriated as a dividend—the so-called deferral principle. Tax havens give multinationals an opportunity to avoid repatriation—and home-country taxes—by locating transactions and accumulating profits in "brass plate" subsidiaries. These transactions have no real work or employment attached to them. The income earned on these transactions is *passive* rather than *active*.

The United States closed this loophole with the Controlled Foreign Corporation (CFC) and Subpart F Income provisions.[12] A CFC is a corporation in which U.S. shareholders (U.S. corporations, citizens, or residents) directly or indirectly own more than 50 percent of its combined voting power or fair market value. Only shareholders holding more than a 10 percent voting interest are counted in determining the 50 percent requirement. Shareholders of a CFC are taxed on certain income of the CFC (referred to as *tainted* income) even before the income is distributed.

Subpart F income includes certain *related-party* sales and services income. For example, if a Bahamian subsidiary of a U.S. corporation buys inventory from its U.S. parent and exports the inventory to the European Union, the profits booked by the Bahamian subsidiary are Subpart F income. On the other hand, if the Bahamian subsidiary sells the imported inventory in the Bahamas, income from the local sales is not Subpart F income. Subpart F income also includes passive income, such as dividends, interest, rents, and royalties; net gains on certain foreign exchange or commodities transactions; gains from the sale of certain investment property including securities; and certain insurance income.

Offshore Holding Companies

In some circumstances, a U.S.-based multinational parent company with operations in several foreign countries may find it advantageous to own its various foreign investments through a third-country holding company. The essential features of this structure are that the U.S. parent directly owns the shares of a holding company set up in one foreign jurisdiction, and the holding company, in turn, owns the shares of one or more operating subsidiaries set up in other foreign jurisdictions. The tax-related advantages of this holding company organizational form could include:

1. Securing beneficial withholding tax rates on dividends, interest, royalties, and similar payments
2. Deferring U.S. tax on foreign earnings until they are repatriated to the U.S. parent company (namely by reinvesting such earnings overseas)
3. Deferring U.S. tax on gains from the sale of the shares of the foreign operating subsidiaries

---

[12]CFC legislation was first enacted in the United States in 1962. It has now been introduced in most industrialized countries as an anti–tax-haven measure.

Realizing these advantages depends in large part on proper planning under complex U.S. tax rules (such as the Subpart F and foreign tax credit rules) and avoiding anti-treaty shopping rules found in many tax treaties.

Financing Decisions

The manner in which foreign operations are financed can also be shaped by tax considerations. Other things equal, the tax deductibility of debt, which increases the after-tax returns on equity, increases the attractiveness of debt financing in high-tax countries. Where local-currency borrowing is constrained by local governments that mandate minimum levels of equity infusion by the foreign parent, parent-company borrowing to finance this capital infusion could achieve similar ends, provided the taxing jurisdiction of the parent allows the interest to be deductible.

In other instances, offshore financing subsidiaries domiciled in a low-tax or tax-haven country also could be used as a financing vehicle. At one time, U.S. companies wishing to borrow funds in the eurodollar market were constrained from doing so because the U.S. government imposed a withholding tax on interest paid to foreign lenders. To lower the cost of financing, they formed offshore financing subsidiaries in the Netherlands Antilles, a country that has no withholding tax on interest to nonresidents.

As the following diagram illustrates, an offshore financing affiliate also can be used to transfer profits from a high-tax country in which either the parent or an affiliate is located to the low-tax jurisdiction of the financing affiliate.

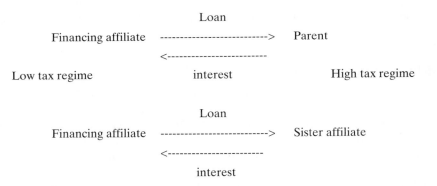

Pooling of Tax Credits

We mentioned earlier that some countries limit tax credits on a source-by-source basis. Pooling income from many sources allows excess credits generated from countries with high tax rates to offset taxes on income received from low-tax jurisdictions. Excess tax credits, for example, can be extended to taxes paid in connection with dividends distributed by second- and third-tier foreign corporations in a multinational network. The United States allows this treatment provided that the U.S. parent's indirect ownership in such corporations exceeds 5 percent. Forward planning in the use of such credits can produce worthwhile tax benefits. Assume, for example, that a U.S. parent owns 100 percent of the shares of Company X (a first-tier foreign corporation). Company X owns 100 percent of the voting stock of Company Y (a second-tier foreign corporation).

During the period, Company Y pays a dividend of 100 to Company X. Company X, in turn, remits a dividend of 100 to the U.S. parent as follows:

	U.S.Parent	Overseas Company X (First–tier Foreign Subsidiary)	Overseas Company Y (Second–tier Foreign Subsidiary)
1. Taxable earnings	100	200	200
2. Foreign income tax (15%/40%)		30	80
3. After-tax earnings		170	120
4. Dividends		100	100
5. Foreign taxes deemed paid	57	67	
	(100/170 × 97)	(100/120 × 80)	
6. Total taxes (2.+ 5.)		97	

Company X will be deemed to have paid 67 of the foreign income taxes paid by Company Y. In turn, the U.S. parent company will receive an indirect credit against U.S. taxes payable of 57 based on its share of taxes actually paid and deemed to have been paid by Company X (30 + 67). (Refer to our earlier discussion of the calculation of foreign credits.) In this illustration, a dividend from Company Y to Company X increases the allowable U.S. foreign tax credit attendant upon a dividend from Company X to the U.S. parent when the income taxes in Company Y's country of domicile exceed those in Company X's, and conversely.

Cost Accounting Allocations

Internal cost allocations among group companies are yet another vehicle to shift profits from high-tax to low-tax countries. The most common of these are allocations of corporate overhead expenses to affiliates in high-tax countries. The allocation of such service expenses as human resources, technology, and research and development will maximize tax deductions for affiliates in high-tax countries.

Location and Transfer Pricing

The locations of production and distribution systems also offer tax advantages. Thus, final sales of goods or services can be channeled through affiliates located in jurisdictions that offer tax shelter or deferral. Alternatively, a manufacturer in a high-tax country can obtain components from affiliates located in low-tax countries to minimize corporate taxes for the group as a whole. A necessary element of such a strategy is the prices at which goods and services are transferred between group companies. Profits for the corporate system as a whole can be increased by setting high *transfer prices* on components shipped from subsidiaries in relatively low tax countries, and low transfer prices on components shipped from subsidiaries in relatively high tax countries.

Transfer pricing has attracted increasing worldwide attention. The significance of the issue is obvious when we recognize that transfer pricing (1) is conducted on a relatively larger scale internationally than domestically, (2) is affected by more variables than are found in a strictly domestic setting, (3) varies from company to company, industry to industry, and country to country, and (4) affects social, economic, and political relationships in multinational business entities and, sometimes, entire countries. International transfer pricing is the most important international tax issue facing MNCs today.[13]

The impact of intracompany transfer pricing on international tax burdens cannot be examined in a vacuum; transfer prices can distort other parts of a multinational company's planning and control system. Cross-country transactions expose the multinational company to a host of strategic concerns that range from environmental risk to global competitiveness. These concerns often transcend tax considerations.

Integrating International Tax Planning

International tax planning should be integrally woven into corporate activities. Advises one tax attorney, "A tax plan should never be simply tacked on as an afterthought or bolted awkwardly on the side of a business or transaction."[14] To achieve integration of international tax planning, he recommends the following steps.

1. Seek competent tax advice in every relevant jurisdiction.
2. Communicate all the facts to each tax adviser. Tax conclusions are often based on fine distinctions among facts.
3. Appoint a single tax adviser to coordinate and reconcile the advice from the various jurisdictions.
4. Be sure that the plan fits the business. Sophisticated cross-border tax planning cannot be bought off-the-shelf.
5. Put all of the tax analysis in writing.
6. Be careful with the documentation of transactions. The audit battle is often won or lost based on the documents.
7. Obtain high-quality legal advice for any tax position that falls into a gray area or might be considered aggressive.
8. Consider how you would feel if your tax planning appeared in the local newspaper. If what you are doing might embarrass the company, don't do it.

Of these steps, 4 and 8 are the ones most frequently omitted, and the ones most likely to lead to trouble if they are not followed.[15]

INTERNATIONAL TRANSFER PRICING: COMPLICATING VARIABLES

The need for transfer pricing arises when goods or services are exchanged between organizational units of the same company. For example, it arises when one subsidiary of a corporation transfers inventory to another subsidiary or when the parent company charges a subsidiary for administrative and managerial services, royalties for intangibles rights, or interest on corporate-wide financing. The transfer price places a monetary value on

[13]Ernst & Young, *2005–2006 Global Transfer Pricing Surveys: Global Transfer Pricing Trends, Practices, and Analysis* (November 2005), p. 4 (www.ey.com).
[14]J. William Dantzler, Jr., as quoted in Fay Hansen, "Best Practices in Tax Planning," *Business Finance* (May 2004): 27.
[15]Ibid.

intracompany exchanges that occur between operating units and is a substitute for a market price. It is generally recorded as revenue by one unit and a cost by the other.

Transfer pricing is of relatively recent origin. Transfer pricing in the United States developed along with the decentralization movement that influenced many American businesses during the first half of the 20th century. Once a company expands internationally, the transfer pricing problem quickly becomes more serious. It is estimated that 60 percent of all international trade consists of transfers between related business entities. Cross-country transactions also expose the multinational company to a host of environmental influences that both create and destroy opportunities to increase enterprise profits by transfer pricing. Such variables as taxes, tariffs, competition, inflation rates, currency values, restrictions on fund transfers, political risks, and the interests of joint-venture partners complicate transfer pricing decisions tremendously. On top of these issues, transfer pricing decisions generally involve many trade-offs, often unforeseen and unaccounted for.

Tax Considerations

Unless counteracted by law, corporate profits can be increased by setting transfer prices so as to move profits from subsidiaries domiciled in high-tax countries to subsidiaries domiciled in low-tax countries. As an example, Blu Jeans–Hong Kong, a wholly owned manufacturing subsidiary of Global Enterprises (USA), ships 500,000 pairs of designer blue jeans to a related U.S. sales affiliate, Blu Jeans–USA (also wholly owned by Global Enterprises), for $6 per pair. They cost Blu Jeans–Hong Kong $4.20 per pair to produce. Assuming that each garment wholesales for $12 in the United States, consolidated profits (after eliminating intercompany sales and costs) and taxes would total $1,305,000 and $595,000, respectively. This scenario is shown in Exhibit 12-5.

Given a U.S. corporate tax rate of 35 percent versus 17.5 percent in Hong Kong, an increase in the transfer price of blue jeans from $6 to $8 per pair would increase total after-tax income as shown in Exhibit 12-6.

In this example, raising the transfer price charged by the Hong Kong affiliate increases taxable income in Hong Kong and reduces taxable income for the U.S. affiliate by $1,000,000. Because the corporate tax rate is lower in Hong Kong than in the United States, corporate income taxes for the system as a whole decrease by $175,000, with a corresponding increase in consolidated after-tax earnings.

EXHIBIT 12-5 Tax Effects of Transfer Pricing			
	Blu Jeans-HK	**Blu Jeans-USA**	**Global Enterprises**
Sales	$3,000,000[a]	$6,000,000	$6,000,000
Cost of sales	2,100,000	3,000,000[a]	2,100,000
Gross margin	$ 900,000	$3,000,000	$3,900,000
Operating expenses	500,000	1,500,000	2,000,000
Pretax income	$ 400,000	$1,500,000	$1,900,000
Income tax (17.5%/35%)[b]	70,000	525,000	595,000
Net income	$ 330,000	$ 975,000	$1,305,000

[a]Based on a transfer price of $6 per unit.
[b]Income tax rates: Hong Kong 17.5%, United States 35%.

EXHIBIT 12-6 Tax Effects of a Change in Transfer Prices

	Blu Jeans-HK	*Blu Jeans-USA*	*Global Enterprises*
Sales	$4,000,000[a]	$6,000,000	$6,000,000
Cost of sales	2,100,000	4,000,000[a]	2,100,000
Gross margin	$1,900,000	$2,000,000	$3,900,000
Operating expenses	500,000	1,500,000	2,000,000
Pretax income	$1,400,000	$ 500,000	$1,900,000
Income tax (17.5%/35%)[b]	245,000	175,000	420,000
Net income	$1,155,000	$ 325,000	$1,480,000

[a]*Based on a transfer price of $8 per unit.*

Unfortunately, such actions often create unanticipated problems. Governments often counteract such measures. In the United States, Section 482 of the Internal Revenue Code gives the Secretary of the Treasury authority to prevent a shifting of income or deductions between related taxpayers to exploit differences in national tax rates. This section states in part:

> In any case of two or more organizations, trades, or businesses (whether or not incorporated, whether or not organized in the United States, and whether or not affiliated) owned or controlled directly or indirectly by the same interests, the Secretary or his delegate may distribute, apportion, or allocate gross income, deductions, credits, or allowances between or among such organizations, trades, or businesses, if he determines that such distribution, apportionment, or allocation is necessary in order to prevent evasion of taxes or clearly to reflect the income of any such organizations, trades, or businesses.[16]

Section 482 essentially requires that intracompany transfers be based on an *arm's-length price*. An arm's-length price is one that an unrelated party would receive for the same or similar item under identical or similar circumstances. Acceptable arm's-length pricing methods include (1) comparable uncontrolled pricing, (2) resale pricing, (3) cost-plus pricing, and (4) other pricing methods. Severe penalties are imposed on valuation misstatements in connection with Section 482 adjustments. Penalties may be up to 40 percent of the additional taxes that result from income adjustments.

An emerging consensus among governments views arm's-length pricing as the appropriate standard in calculating profits for tax purposes. However, countries vary in how they interpret and implement arm's-length pricing. As a result, it is a somewhat fluid concept internationally. Multinational corporations are often "caught in the middle" when tax authorities from different jurisdictions disagree on a transfer price, each trying to maintain its "fair share" of taxes collected from the multinational. The resulting controversy can be time-consuming and expensive to resolve. The rigor applied in monitoring the transfer pricing policies of multinational companies still varies worldwide. Nevertheless, tax authorities around the world are drafting new transfer pricing rules

---

[16]Treasury Regulation, Sec, 1.482-1.

and stepping up enforcement efforts. In 1992, only two countries (Australia and the United States) had documentation rules for multinationals' transfer pricing policies. By 2003, 25 countries had such rules, and by 2006 the number had grown to 40.[17] Audits are also being carried out with regularity, and a high percentage of completed audits are leading to transfer price adjustments. Whereas in the past many multinationals simply set transfer prices without further complications, now they have to justify them and document them, or run the risk of severe noncompliance penalties. Thus, transfer pricing has become a major compliance burden.

Transfer pricing schemes designed to minimize global taxes often distort the multinational control system. When each subsidiary is evaluated as a separate profit center, such pricing policies can result in misleading performance measures that generally lead to conflicts between subsidiary and enterprise goals. In our earlier example, Blu Jeans–USA would report a lower profit than its sister affiliate in Hong Kong, even though the management of the U.S. subsidiary may be far more productive and efficient than the management in Hong Kong.

Tariff Considerations

Tariffs on imported goods also affect the transfer pricing policies of multinational companies. For example, a company exporting goods to a subsidiary domiciled in a high-tariff country can reduce the tariff assessment by lowering the prices of merchandise sent there.

In addition to the trade-offs identified, the multinational company must consider additional costs and benefits, both external and internal. Externally, an MNC would have three taxing authorities to contend with: the customs officials of the importing country and the income tax administrators of the exporting and importing countries. A high tariff paid by the importer would result in a lower tax base for income taxes. Internally, the enterprise would have to evaluate the benefits of a lower (higher) income tax in the importing country against a higher (lower) import duty, as well as the potentially higher (lower) income tax paid by the company in the exporting country.

To illustrate, let us revisit our blue jeans example depicted in Exhibits 12-5 and 12-6. In our revised example (see Exhibit 12-7), assume that the United States imposes an ad valorem import duty of 10 percent. Under a low transfer pricing policy, lower import duties are paid ($300,000 vs. $400,000), but the import duty advantage of a low transfer price is offset by the increased income taxes that must be paid ($490,000 vs. $280,000). Considering both import duties and income taxes, Global Enterprises is still $110,000 better off under a high transfer pricing policy.

Competitive Factors

To facilitate the establishment of a foreign subsidiary abroad, a parent company could supply the subsidiary with inputs invoiced at very low prices. These price subsidies could be removed gradually as the foreign affiliate strengthens its position in the foreign market. Similarly, lower transfer prices could be used to shield an existing operation from the effects of increased foreign competition in the local market or

---

[17]Ernst & Young, *2005–2006 Global Transfer Pricing Surveys: Global Transfer Pricing Trends, Practices, and Anaysis*, November 2005, p. 5 (www.ey.com).

EXHIBIT 12.7 Trade-Offs When Tariffs and Income Taxes are Considered

	Blu Jeans–HK	Blu Jeans–USA	Global Enterprises
Low Transfer Price			
Sales	$3,000,000	$6,000,000	$6,000,000
Cost of sales	2,100,000	3,000,000	2,100,000
Import duty at 10%	—	300,000	300,000
Gross margin	900,000	$2,700,000	$3,600,000
Operating expenses	500,000	1,500,000	2,000,000
Pretax income	400,000	1,200,000	1,600,000
Income tax (17.5%/35%)	70,000	420,000	490,000
Net income	$ 330,000	$ 780,000	$1,110,000
High Transfer Price			
Sales	$4,000,000	$6,000,000	$6,000,000
Cost of sales	2,100,000	4,000,000	2,100,000
Import duty at 10%	—	400,000	400,000
Gross margin	1,900,000	$1,600,000	$3,500,000
Operating expenses	500,000	1,500,000	2,000,000
Pretax income	1,400,000	100,000	1,500,000
Income tax (17.5%/35%)	245,000	35,000	280,000
Net income	$1,155,000	$ 65,000	$1,220,000

another market; in other words, profits earned in one country could subsidize the penetration of another market. Indirect competitive effects are also possible. To improve a foreign subsidiary's access to local capital markets, setting low transfer prices on its inputs and high transfer prices on its outputs could bolster its reported earnings and financial position. Sometimes, transfer prices could be used to weaken a subsidiary's competitors.

Such competitive considerations would have to be balanced against many offsetting disadvantages. Transfer prices may, for competitive reasons, invite antitrust actions by host governments or retaliatory actions by local competitors. Internally, pricing subsidies do little to instill a competitive mode of thinking in the minds of the managers whose companies gain from the subsidy. What begins as a temporary aid may easily become a permanent management crutch.

Environmental Risks

Whereas competitive considerations abroad might warrant charging low transfer prices to foreign subsidiaries, the risks of severe price inflation might call for the opposite. Inflation erodes the purchasing power of a firm's cash. High transfer prices on goods or services provided to a subsidiary facing high inflation can remove as much cash from the subsidiary as possible.

Balance-of-payment problems (often related to inflation) may prompt foreign governments to devalue their currencies, impose foreign exchange controls, and/or impose restrictions on the repatriation of profits from foreign-owned companies. Potential losses from exposures to currency devaluations may be avoided by shifting funds to the parent company (or related affiliates) through inflated transfer prices. With exchange controls (e.g., a government restricts the amount of foreign exchange available for importing a particular good), reduced transfer prices on the imported good would allow the affiliate affected by the controls to acquire more of the desired import. To circumvent repatriation restrictions, high transfer prices allow some cash to be returned to the parent company each time it sells a product or service to the foreign subsidiary.

Performance Evaluation Considerations

Transfer pricing policies are also affected by their impact on managerial behavior, and are often a major determinant of corporate performance. For example, if a foreign affiliate's mission is to furnish supplies for the rest of the corporate system, appropriate transfer prices enable corporate management to provide the affiliate with an earnings stream that can be used in performance comparisons. However, it is difficult for decentralized firms to set intracompany transfer prices that both (1) motivate managers to make decisions that maximize their unit's profits and are congruent with the goals of the company as whole, and (2) provide an equitable basis for judging the performance of managers and units of the firm. If subsidiaries are free to negotiate transfer prices, their managers may not be able to reconcile conflicts between what may be best for the subsidiary and what is best for the firm as a whole. However, the effect on subsidiary management may be even worse if corporate headquarters dictates transfer prices and sourcing alternatives that are seen as arbitrary or unreasonable. Moreover, the more decisions that are made by corporate headquarters, the less advantageous are decentralized profit centers, because local managers lose their incentive to act for the benefit of their local operations.

Accounting Contributions

Management accountants can play a significant role in quantifying the trade-offs in transfer pricing strategy. The challenge is to keep a global perspective when mapping out the benefits and costs associated with a transfer pricing decision. The effects of the decision on the corporate system as a whole must come first.

Quantifying the numerous trade-offs is difficult because environmental influences must be considered as a group, not individually. Consider, for example, the difficulties in measuring the trade-offs surrounding transfer pricing policies for a subsidiary located in a country with high income taxes, high import tariffs, price controls, a thin capital market, chronic high inflation, foreign exchange controls, and an unstable government. As we have seen, a high transfer price on goods or services provided to the subsidiary would lower the subsidiary's income taxes and remove excess cash to the parent company. However, a high transfer price might also result in higher import duties, impair the subsidiary's competitive position (due to higher input prices), worsen the rate of inflation, raise the subsidiary's capital costs, and even cause retaliation by the host government to protect its balance-of-payments position. To further complicate matters, all of these variables are changing constantly. One thing is clear: Superficial calculations of the effects of transfer pricing policy on individual units within a multinational system are not acceptable.

TRANSFER PRICING METHODOLOGY

In a world of perfectly competitive markets, it would not be much of a problem to set prices for intracompany resource and service transfers. Transfer prices could be based either on incremental cost or on market prices. Neither system would necessarily conflict with the other. Unfortunately, there are seldom external competitive markets for products or services transferred between related entities. Environmental influences on transfer prices also raise questions of pricing methodology. How are transfer prices established? Are standard market prices generally better than those based on some measure of cost, or are negotiated prices the only feasible alternative? Can a single transfer pricing methodology serve all purposes equally well? The following sections shed some light on these questions.

Market vs. Cost vs. . . . ?

The use of market-oriented transfer prices offers several advantages. Market prices show the opportunity cost to the transferring entity of not selling on the external market, and their use will encourage the efficient use of the firm's scarce resources. Their use is also said to be consistent with a decentralized profit center orientation. Market prices help differentiate profitable from unprofitable operations, and are easier to defend to taxing authorities as arm's-length prices.

The advantages of market-based transfer prices must be weighed against several shortcomings. One is that using market prices does not give a firm much room to adjust prices for competitive or strategic purposes. A more fundamental problem is that there is often no intermediate market for the product or service in question. Multinationals engage in transactions that independent enterprises do not undertake, such as transferring a valuable, closely held technology to an affiliate. Transactional relationships among affiliates under common control often differ in important and fundamental ways from potentially comparable transactions among unrelated parties.

Cost-based transfer pricing systems overcome many of these limitations. Moreover, they are (1) simple to use, (2) based on readily available data, (3) easy to justify to tax authorities, and (4) easily routinized, thus helping to avoid internal frictions that often accompany more arbitrary systems.

Of course, cost-based transfer pricing systems are not flawless either. For example, the sale of goods or services at actual cost may provide little incentive for sellers to control their costs. Production inefficiencies may simply be passed on to the buyer at inflated prices. Cost-based systems overemphasize historical costs, which ignore competitive demand-and-supply relationships, and do not allocate costs to particular products or services in a satisfactory manner. The problem of cost determination is compounded internationally because cost accounting concepts vary from country to country.

Arm's-Length Principle

The typical multinational is an integrated operation: Its subsidiaries are under common control and share common resources and goals. The need to declare taxable income in different countries means that multinationals must allocate revenues and expenses among subsidiaries and set transfer prices for intrafirm transactions.

Tax authorities around the world have developed complicated transfer-price and income allocation regulations as a part of their national income tax systems. Most are based on the *arm's-length principle*, which prices intrafirm transfers as if they took place between unrelated parties in competitive markets.[18] The OECD identifies several broad methods of ascertaining an arm's-length price. Resembling those specified by Section 482 of the U.S. Internal Revenue Code, they are (1) the comparable uncontrolled price method, (2) the comparable uncontrolled transaction method, (3) the resale price method, (4) the cost-plus method, (5) the comparable profit method, (6) the profit split method, and (7) other methods.

Comparable Uncontrolled Price Method

Under this approach, transfer prices are set by reference to prices used in comparable transactions between independent companies or between the corporation and an unrelated third party. It is appropriate when goods are sufficiently common that controlled sales are essentially comparable to sales on the open market. Commodity-type products ordinarily use this method for internal transactions.

Comparable Uncontrolled Transaction Method

This method applies to transfers of intangible assets. It identifies a benchmark royalty rate by referencing uncontrolled transactions in which the same or similar intangibles are transferred. Like the comparable uncontrolled price method, this method relies on market comparables.

Resale Price Method

This method calculates an arm's-length price by starting with the final selling price at which the item in question is sold to an uncontrolled party. An appropriate margin to cover expenses and a normal profit is then deducted from this price to derive the intracompany transfer price. This method is typically used when the unit buying the item is a distributor or sales subsidiary.

To illustrate this pricing method, assume that a company wishes to price a product sold by one of its operating units to one of its foreign distribution units. Income statement accounts and other related facts for the distribution unit are as follows:

1. Net sales (by the distribution unit) of 100,000 units at $300 per unit	$30,000,000
2. Other expenses (OE)	1,200,000
3. OE as a percentage of net sales	4.0%
4. Freight and insurance to import (FI)	$ 1.50/unit
5. Packaging costs (PC)	$ 2.00/unit
6. Customs duties (CD)	5.0%
7. Net sales price (NSP) by the distribution unit	$ 300/unit

---

[18]Of course, the result is only hypothetical because the parties are related and the markets normally are not competitive. See L. Eden, M. T. Dacin, and W. P. Wan, "Standards Across Borders: Cross-border Diffusion of the Arms-Length Standard in North America," *Accounting, Organizations and Society* (January 2001): 1–23.

The objective is to calculate a transfer price between the two units such that the distribution unit covers all costs and earns a normal profit. As we shall see, the resale price method is a *work backwards* approach. Assuming that the company requires a 5 percent additional margin to cover business risk and provide an appropriate profit, the total product margin would be computed as follows:

1. Other expenses		4.0%
2. Additional margin for risk and profit (AM)		5.0%
3. Total margin (TM)		9.0%

Here, the distribution unit must pay freight and insurance costs to import the product and customs duties in addition to the transfer price. (Thus, the distribution unit's cost to import differs from the transfer price.) Given the foregoing information, the transfer price (TP) per unit of product delivered to the distribution unit would be:

$$TP = \{[NSP \times (100\% - TM) - PC] / (100\% + CD)\} - FI$$
$$TP = \{[300 \times (100\% - 9\%) - \$2] / (100\% + 5\%)\} - \$1.50$$
$$TP = \$256.60$$

The foregoing calculation adjusts the net sales price for the total margin, packaging costs, freight and insurance costs, and customs duties to arrive at the transfer price. Specifically, the 1.05 factor adjusts the $271 cost-to-import price to a before-duties figure of $258.10. Other dutiable costs are subtracted from this figure to leave a transfer price of $256.60. The cost to import equals (1) the transfer price plus (2) freight and insurance, with duties applied to both. As a check on this result:

	Unit Cost
Transfer price	$256.60
+ Freight & Insurance	1.50
Subtotal	258.10
Duties (at 5%)	12.90
Cost to import	$271.00

To work backwards to the transfer price:

Net sales price	$300.00
Margin to cover expenses and normal profit (9%)	− 27.00
Packaging	− 2.00
Freight and insurance	− 1.50
Customs duties	− 12.90
Transfer price	$256.60

Cost-Plus Pricing Method

Cost-plus pricing is a *work forward* approach in which a markup is added to the transferring affiliate's cost in local currency. The markup typically includes (1) the imputed financing costs related to export inventories, receivables, and assets employed and (2) a percentage of cost covering manufacturing, distribution, warehousing, internal shipping, and other costs related to export operations. An adjustment is often made to reflect any government subsidies that are designed to make manufacturing costs competitive in the international marketplace.

This pricing method is especially useful when semifinished goods are transferred between foreign affiliates, or where one entity is a subcontractor for another. A major measurement issue involves calculating the cost of the transferred item and ascertaining an appropriate markup.

To see how a transfer price is derived employing the cost-plus method, assume that a manufacturing unit in Portugal wishes to price an intracompany transfer based on the following information:

1. Total manufacturing cost per unit (1,000 units)   € 200
2. Average net operating assets employed in manufacturing the item   €40,000
3. Average short-term interest rate in Portugal   8.0%
4. Financing cost as a percentage of total manufacturing cost
   ([8% × €40,000]/€200,000)   1.6%
5. Government subsidy based on final transfer price   6.0%
6. Credit terms to affiliates   90 days
7. Required profit and other expenses margin   8.0%

The cost-plus transfer price is that price which enables the transferring unit to earn a given percentage return above its production costs. That percentage return (the *plus* in cost-plus) is determined in the following manner:

1. Required margin before adjustments:
   Profit and other expenses   8.0%
   Financing cost   1.6%   9.60%
2. Government subsidy adjustment   6.00%
3. Adjusted margin with cash terms [(1.096/1.06) − 1]   3.39%
4. Adjusted margin with 90-day terms   5.46%[a]

[a] This figure is equal to the adjusted margin-cash terms multiplied by 1 plus the short-term interest rate for 90 days, or {1 .0339 × [1 + (0.08 × 90/360)]} − 1. It allows the transferring unit to earn imputed interest for carrying a receivable for 90 days.

This required margin of 5.46 percent, when multiplied by the transferred item's total manufacturing cost, yields the intracompany transfer price to be billed for that item. In this example, the transfer price is €210.92, the result of 1.0546 × €200. This transfer price causes the company to earn its required margin of 9.6 percent and an 8 percent (annualized compounded) return for carrying the affiliate's receivable for 90 days. As a check on this result:

$$\text{Compounded return} = \{1.096 \times [1 + (.08 \times 90/360)]\} - 1$$
$$= 11.79\%$$

Transfer price	=	€210.92
Cost		200.00
Margin		€ 10.92
Subsidy (6% x 210.92)		12.66
Total return		€ 23.58

$$\text{Return as a \% of cost} = (€23.58)/(€200.00) = 11.79\%$$

Comparable Profits Method

The comparable profits method supports the general notion that similarly situated taxpayers should earn similar returns over reasonable time periods.[19] Thus, intracompany profits on transactions between related parties should be comparable to profits on transactions between unrelated parties who engage in similar business activities under similar circumstances. *Return on capital employed* (ROCE) is a primary profit-level indicator. Under this approach, the operating income to average capital employed ratio of a benchmark entity is compared with the ROCE of the entity in question.

Application of this method will normally require adjustments for any differences between comparables. Factors requiring such adjustments include differing sales conditions, cost of capital differences, foreign exchange and other risks, and differences in accounting measurement practices.

Profit-Split Methods

Profit-split methods are used when product or market benchmarks are not available. Essentially they involve dividing profits generated in a related-party transaction between the affiliated companies in an arm's-length fashion. One variant of this approach, the *comparables profit-split method*, divides the profit generated by a related-party transaction using a percentage allocation of the combined profits of uncontrolled companies with similar types of transactions and activities.

A more sophisticated method, the *residual profit-split method*, employs a two-step approach. First, routine functions performed by affiliated entities—the parent and its subsidiary—are priced at each stage of the production process using relevant benchmarks. Any difference between total profits earned by the combined enterprise and those attributable to the routine functions is considered *residual profits*, essentially profits from nonroutine functions. This residual, which resembles a goodwill intangible, then is split on the basis of the relative value of each affiliated party's contribution to the intangible. This value can be determined using fair market value referents or the capitalized cost of developing the intangibles.

---

[19]The comparable profits method is similar to the transactional net margin method (TNMM) in the OECD guidelines. The key difference is that TNMM is applied on a transactional rather than a firm level. For more information on this and the profit-split method, see Victor H. Miesel, Harlow H. Higinbotham, and Chun W. Yi, "International Transfer Pricing: Practical Solutions for Intercompany Pricing: Part II," *International Tax Journal* (winter 2003): 1–40.

Other Pricing Methods

As existing pricing methodologies do not always reflect underlying circumstances, additional methodologies are allowed if they result in a more accurate measure of an arm's-length price. To quote the OECD:

> It has to be recognized that an arm's-length price will in many cases not be precisely ascertainable and that in such circumstances it will be necessary to seek a reasonable approximation to it. Frequently, it may be useful to take account of more than one method of reaching a satisfactory approximation to an arm's-length price in the light of the evidence available.[20]

Section 482 of the U.S. Internal Revenue Code specifies a *best methods rule* requiring the taxpayer to select the best transfer pricing method based on the facts and circumstances of the case. Argentina and Taiwan also have a best methods rule. Most countries with transfer pricing legislation prefer transaction-based methods (comparable uncontrolled price, comparable uncontrolled transaction, resale price, and cost-plus methods) to profit-based methods (comparable profit and profit-split methods). These countries include Belgium, Germany, Japan, the Netherlands, and the United Kingdom.[21] OECD guidelines specify that a *reasonable* method should be chosen, and also prefer transaction-based methods to profit-based methods.

It is not always possible to calculate a precise and accurate arm's-length price. Hence, documentation of any transfer price employed and its underlying rationale is important. This is true regardless of the tax jurisdiction and the transfer pricing methods it may prefer. An increasing number of countries now require companies to keep documentation substantiating the transfer pricing method(s) used for intracompany transactions. The following steps are helpful in setting transfer prices:

- Analyze the risks assumed, functions performed by the affiliated companies, and the economic and legal determinants that affect pricing.
- Identify and analyze benchmark companies and transactions. Document reasons for any adjustments made.
- Compare the financial results of the comparable companies and the taxpayer.
- If comparable transactions are available, note their similarities and differences with the taxpayer's transactions.
- Document why the chosen pricing method is the most reasonable and why the other methods are not.
- Update the information before filing the tax return.[22]

Advance Pricing Agreements

The acceptability of transfer prices to governments is a major concern. Aware that multinational enterprises use transfer prices to shift income, and worried about their economic and social consequences, governments are increasing their scrutiny of

---

[20]Organization for Economic Cooperation and Development, *Transfer Pricing and Multinational Enterprises* (Paris: OECD, 1979), p. 33.

[21]Deloitte, *Strategy Matrix for Global Transfer Pricing: Planning Methods, Documentation, Penalties and Other Issues* (2006), pp. 10–11 (www.deloitte.com).

[22]Alan Shapiro and Arnold McClellan, "New Transfer Pricing: New Rules Give Guidance on How to Avoid Penalties," *Deloitte Touche Tohmatsu International World Tax News* (March 1994): 2.

multinational operations. At the same time, the ambiguities and complexities of transfer pricing regulations make it likely that intracompany transactions will be the target of tax audits. Surveys of multinationals consistently show that they regard transfer pricing as their most important international tax issue and that facing a transfer pricing audit somewhere in the world is a near certainty.[23]

Advance pricing agreements (APAs) are a mechanism whereby a multinational and a taxing authority voluntarily negotiate an agreed transfer pricing methodology that is binding on both parties. These agreements reduce or eliminate the risk of a transfer pricing audit, saving time and money for both the multinational and the taxing authority. Introduced in the United States in 1991, APAs have been widely adopted by other countries.[24] The agreements are binding for a fixed period of time; for example, three years in the United States.

Exhibit 12-8 summarizes the transfer pricing requirements in the 10 countries discussed in Chapters 3 and 4.

EXHIBIT 12-8 Transfer Pricing Requirements in Selected Countries

	Preference for Transfer Pricing Method	*Statutory Requirements for Transfer Pricing Documentation[a]*	*Availability of APA*
China	Best method	Yes	Yes
Czech Republic	Transaction-based	Yes	Yes
France	Transaction-based	No	Yes
Germany	Transaction-based	Yes	Yes
India	Best method	Yes	No
Japan	Transaction-based	No	Yes
Mexico	Transaction-based	Yes	Yes
Netherlands	Transaction-based	Yes	Yes
United Kingdom	Transaction-based	Yes	Yes
United States	Best method	No	Yes

SOURCES: Compiled from Ernst & Young, *2005–2006 Global Transfer Pricing Surveys—Tax Authority Interviews: Perspectives, Interpretations, and Regulatory Changes* (2006), www.ey.com; Deloitte, *Strategy Matrix for Global Transfer Pricing* (2006), www.deloitte.com; Ernst & Young, *Transfer Pricing Global Reference Guide* (2006), www.ey.com.

[a]*Countries with no statutory requirements for maintaining transfer pricing documentation will require companies to produce documentation upon request, normally at the time of an audit. For example, taxpayers must produce such documentation within 30 days of the request in the United States and within 60 days in France. Given that a significant amount of documentation will need to be provided, companies are well advised to maintain the documentation in any event.*

---

[23]Ernst & Young, *Transfer Pricing 2003 Global Survey* (2003): 10–15 (www.ey.com).
[24]APAs go by different names. For example, they are called advance pricing arrangements in the United Kingdom and preconfirmation systems in Japan. For more on APAs around the world, see S. C. Borkowski, "Transfer Pricing Advance Pricing Agreements: Current Status by Country," *International Tax Journal* (spring 2000): 1–16. The U.S. APA program is the largest such program in the world.

TRANSFER PRICING PRACTICES

Multinational corporations obviously vary along many dimensions, such as size, industry, nationality, organizational structure, degree of international involvement, technology, products or services, and competitive conditions. Therefore, it is hardly surprising that a variety of transfer pricing methods are found in practice.[25] Most of the empirical evidence on transfer pricing practices is based on surveys. Because corporate pricing policies are often considered proprietary, such surveys should be interpreted cautiously. Given the dramatic effect of globalization on business operations since the 1990s, we are also cautious about whether transfer pricing surveys before the 1990s are still valid today.[26]

What factors influence the choice of transfer pricing methods? Are transfer pricing effects considered in the planning process? One study from the 1990s asked financial executives of U.S. multinationals to identify the three most important objectives of international transfer pricing.[27] Managing the tax burden dominated the other objectives, but operational uses of transfer pricing, such as maintaining the company's competitive position, promoting equitable performance evaluation, and motivating employees, were also important. Managing inflation, managing foreign exchange risk, and mitigating restrictions on cash transfers were relatively unimportant.

Another study asked a similar question of managers of multinationals from 19 nations.[28] In their responses, operational issues had a slightly higher priority than tax issues. The study also found that the operational and tax effects of transfer pricing are most often considered only after the strategic decisions have been made. However, a subsequent survey indicated that transfer pricing now plays a more important role in the multinational planning process.[29] The multinational corporations surveyed indicate that significantly more of them consider tax issues earlier in the business planning cycle than they did five years earlier. Transfer pricing is increasingly perceived as less of a compliance issue and more of a planning issue that contributes value.

---

[25]Cost-based transfer pricing methods appear to be used more often than market-based methods. It is also likely that a multinational uses more than one method, depending on the circumstances. See K. S. Cravens, "Examining the Role of Transfer Pricing as a Strategy for Multinational Firms," *International Business Review* 6, no. 2 (1997): 137–138.

[26]For example, one widely cited study [J. S. Arpan, "International Intracorporate Pricing: Non-American Systems and Views," *Journal of International Business Studies* (spring 1972): 1–18] found that U.S., French, British, and Japanese managers prefer cost-oriented transfer pricing methods, whereas Canadian, Italian, and Scandinavian managers prefer market-oriented methods; no particular preference was found for Belgian, Dutch, German, or Swiss managers. While we believe that nationality continues to influence the choice of transfer pricing methods, we question whether this particular conclusion is still valid.

[27]K. S. Cravens, "Examining the Role of Transfer Pricing as a Strategy of Multinational Firms," *International Business Review* 6, no. 2 (1997): 127–145.

[28]Ernst & Young, "1999 Global Transfer Pricing Survey," reprinted in R. Feinschreiber, *Transfer Pricing International: A Country-by-Country Comparison* (New York: John Wiley, 2000), pp. 35.1–35.49.

[29]Ernst & Young, *2005–2006 Global Transfer Pricing Surveys: Global Transfer Pricing Trends, Practices, and Analysis*, November 2005, p. 15 (www.ey.com).

THE FUTURE

Technology and the global economy are challenging many of the principles on which international taxation is based. One of these principles is that every nation has the right to decide for itself how much tax to collect from the people and businesses within its borders. Tax laws evolved in a world where transactions took place in clearly identifiable locations, but this is increasingly less true. Electronic commerce over the Internet ignores borders and physical location. Commercial events now take place in cyberspace—on a server anywhere in the world.[30]

The ability to collect taxes depends on knowing who should pay, but increasingly sophisticated encryption techniques make it harder to identify taxpayers. Anonymous electronic money is a reality. The Internet also makes it easy for multinationals to shift their activities to low-tax countries that may be a long way from customers but as close as a mouse click to access. It is becoming more difficult to monitor and tax international transactions. Further, there is a growing unease among governments that they are losing their grip on companies that increasingly can and do move their employees, know-how, capital, headquarters—and taxable profits—overseas.

Governments around the world require transfer pricing methods based on the arm's-length principle. That is, a multinational's businesses in different countries are taxed as if they were independent firms operating at arm's-length from each other. The complex calculation of arm's-length prices is less relevant today for global companies because fewer of them operate this way. Many multinationals now have global brands, global research and development, and regional profit centers. It is difficult to say exactly where their profits are generated. Moreover, companies are increasingly service-oriented and rely on brand names, intellectual property, and intangibles that are hard to price.[31]

What do these developments imply for international taxation? Are national taxes compatible with a global economy? We already see greater cooperation and information sharing by tax authorities around the world. This trend will continue. At the same time, many experts foresee greater tax competition. The Internet makes it easier to take advantage of tax havens. Some observers advocate a *unitary tax* as an alternative to using transfer prices to determine taxable income. Under this approach, a multinational's total profits are allocated to individual countries based on a formula that reflects the company's relative economic presence in the country. Each country would then tax its piece of the profit at whatever rate it sees fit. Clearly, taxation in the future faces many changes and challenges.[32]

---

[30]The digitization of tangible products is an example. A compact disc bought at a record store is a tangible item purchased at a physical location. Taxing this transaction is fairly simple because it is easy to identify the source of income. If it is downloaded online, it is an intangible purchased in cyberspace. Who can tax this transaction, and how, is less clear.

[31]The 2006 transfer pricing settlement between the pharmaceutical company GlaxoSmithKline and the U.S. Internal Revenue Service involved such issues. The settlement was the largest tax dispute in the history of the IRS. GlaxoSmithKline agreed to pay the IRS $3.4 billion.

[32]See "The Mystery of the Vanishing Taxpayer: A Survey of Globalisation and Tax," *Economist* (January 29, 2000): 1–22; S. James, "The Future International Tax Environment," *International Tax Journal* (winter 1999): 1–9; N. Warren, "Internet Challenges to Tax System Design," in *The International Taxation System*, ed. A. Lymer and J. Hasseldine (Boston: Kluwer Academic Publishers, 2002), pp. 61–82; "A Taxing Battle," *Economist* (January 31, 2004): 71–72.

SELECTED REFERENCES

Bodner, P., "International Taxation," in *International Accounting and Finance Handbook*, ed. Frederick D. S. Choi, 3rd ed., New York: John Wiley, 2003.

Borkowski, S., Transfer Pricing Advance Pricing Agreements: Current Status by Country, *International Tax Journal* (spring 2000): 1–16.

Bradley, W. E., and R .E. Nantz, "The Restructuring of U.S. International Tax Policy," *International Tax Journal* 28, no. 3 (summer 2002): 70–81.

Clausing, K. A., "Tax Holidays (and Other Escapes) in the American Jobs Creation Act," *National Tax Journal* (September 2005): 331–346.

Deloitte, *Strategy Matrix for Global Transfer Pricing: Planning for Methods, Documentation, Penalties and Other Issues* (2006), Deloitte Web site: www.deloitte.com.

Eden, L., M. T. Dacin, and W. P. Wan, "Standards Across Borders: Crossborder Diffusion of the Arm's-Length Standard in North America." *Accounting, Organizations and Society* (January 2001): 1–23.

Ernst & Young, *2005–2006 Global Transfer Pricing Surveys: Global Transfer Pricing Trends, Practices, and Analysis* (November 2005), Ernst & Young Web site: www.ey.com.

Ernst & Young, *2005–2006 Global Transfer Pricing Surveys: Tax Authority Interviews—Perspectives, Interpretations, and Regulatory Changes* (September 2006), Ernst & Young Web site: www.ey.com.

Ernst & Young, *Transfer Pricing Global Reference Guide* (June 2006), Ernst & Young Web site: www.ey.com.

Feinschreiber, R., "Transfer Pricing for Intercompany Transactions," in *International Accounting and Finance Handbook*, ed.

Frederick D. S. Choi, 3rd ed., New York: John Wiley, 2003.

Feinschreiber, R., *Transfer Pricing International: A Country-by-Country Guide*, New York: John Wiley, 2000.

Hansen, F., "Best Practices in Tax Planning," *Business Finance* (May 2004): 25–30.

Hines, J. R., "Lessons from Behavioral Responses to International Taxation," *National Tax Journal* (June 1999): 305–322.

James, S., "The Future International Tax Environment." *International Tax Journal* (winter 1999): 1–9.

Lymer, A., and J. Hasseldine, *The International Taxation System*, Boston: Kluwer Academic Publishers, 2002.

Meisel, V. H., H. H. Higinbotham, and C. W. Yi, "International Transfer Pricing: Practical Solutions for Intercompany Pricing," *International Tax Journal* 28, no. 4 (fall 2002): 1–22.

Meisel, V. H., H. H. Higinbotham, and C. W. Yi, "International Transfer Pricing: Practical Solutions for Intercompany Pricing—Part II," *International Tax Journal* 29, no. 1 (winter 2003): 1–40.

"The Mystery of the Vanishing Taxpayer: A Survey of Globalisation and Tax," *Economist* (January 29, 2000): 1–22.

Simmons, R. S., "Does Recent Empirical Evidence Support the Existence of International Corporate Tax Competition?" *Journal of International Accounting, Auditing and Taxation* 15, no. 1 (2006): 16–31.

Yancey, W. F., and K. S. Cravens, "A Framework for International Tax Planning for Managers," *Journal of International Accounting Auditing and Taxation* 7, no. 2 (1998): 251–272.

DISCUSSION QUESTIONS

1. What is tax neutrality? Are taxes neutral with regard to business decisions? Is this good or bad?
2. What philosophies and types of taxes exist worldwide?
3. What role do tax credits play in international taxation? What considerations might cause tax credits to not achieve their intended results?

4. Briefly describe the major advantages and disadvantages of the
   a. classical,
   b. split-rate, and
   c. imputation
   tax administration systems from the perspective of a multinational corporate taxpayer.

5. Consider the statement "National differences in statutory tax rates are the most obvious and yet least significant determinants of a company's effective tax burden." Do you agree? Explain.

6. Carried to its logical extreme, tax planning implies a conscientious policy of tax minimization. This mode of thinking raises an ethical question for international tax executives. Deliberate tax evasion is commonplace in many parts of the world. In Italy, for example, tax legislation is often honored only in the breach. Even when tax laws are enforced, actual tax settlements are usually subject to negotiation between the taxpayer and the tax collector. Should multinational corporations operating in such environments adopt a policy of "When in Rome do as the Romans do?" or should they adhere to the taxation norms of their domestic environments?

7. Compare and contrast the role of transfer pricing in national versus international operations.

8. Multinational transfer pricing causes serious concern for various corporate stakeholders. Identify potential concerns from the viewpoint of
   a. minority owners of a foreign affiliate,
   b. foreign taxing authorities,
   c. home-country taxing authorities,
   d. foreign-subsidiary managers, and
   e. headquarters managers.

9. The pricing of intracompany transfers is complicated by many economic, environmental, and organizational considerations. Identify six major considerations described in the chapter and briefly explain how they affect transfer pricing policy.

10. Identify the major bases for pricing intercompany transfers. Comment briefly on their relative merits. Which measurement method is best from the viewpoint of the multinational executive?

11. Explain the arm's-length price. Is the U.S. Internal Revenue Service alone in mandating such pricing of intracompany transfers? Would the concept of an arm's-length price resolve the measurement issue in pricing intracompany transfers?

12. What is an advance pricing agreement (APA)? What are the advantages and disadvantages of entering into an APA?

EXERCISES

1. You are an investment analyst domiciled in Country Z doing a cross-country comparison of the financial performance of two manufacturing companies in the pharmaceuticals industry. Both companies, X and Y (located in Countries X and Y), have similar expected sales of $600 million. Country X has a corporate income tax. Country Y has no income tax, but relies on indirect taxes. Selected data for companies X and Y are as follows:

	Company X	*Company Y*
Pretax income	$120 million	$72 million
Return on sales	12.0%	12.0%

Required: Determine which company promises to have the better financial performance? What tax considerations might affect your conclusions?

2. Using the facts in Exercise 1, assume that Companies X and Y have identical dividend payout ratios of 50 percent. Country Z, your country of domicile, has an income tax rate of 35 percent. Country Z has a tax treaty with countries X and Y so that no withholding taxes are assessed on dividends received. Furthermore, Country Z grants a tax credit for any direct foreign taxes paid.

Required: Show which company now promises the better after-tax investment performance, and why.

3. A Chinese manufacturing subsidiary produces items sold in Australia. The items cost the equivalent of $7.00 to produce and are sold to customers for $9.50. A Cayman Islands subsidiary buys the items from the Chinese subsidiary for $7.00 and sells them to the Australian parent for $9.50.

Required: Calculate the total amount of income taxes paid on these transactions. What are the implications for the company and the taxing authorities involved?

4. Kowloon Trading Company, a wholly-owned subsidiary incorporated in Hong Kong, imports macadamia nuts from its parent company in Honolulu for export to various duty-free shops in the Far East. During the current fiscal year, the company imported $2,000,000 worth of nuts and retailed them for $6,000,000. Local income taxes are paid at the rate of 17.5 percent. Profits earned by the Hong Kong subsidiary are retained for future expansion.

Required: Based on this information, calculate the U.S. parent company's U.S. tax liability under Subpart F provisions of the Internal Revenue Code.

5. A jewelry manufacturer domiciled in Amsterdam purchases gold from a precious metals dealer in Belgium for €2,400. The manufacturer fabricates the raw material into an item of jewelry and wholesales it to a Dutch retailer for €4,000.

Required: Compute the value-added tax from the jewelry manufacturer's activities if the Dutch value-added tax rate is 17.5 percent.

6. Sweden has a classical system of taxation. Calculate the total taxes that would be paid by a company headquartered in Stockholm that earns 1,500,000 Swedish krona (SEK) and distributes 50 percent of its earnings as a dividend to its shareholders. Assume that the company's shareholders are in the 40 percent tax bracket and that the company's income tax rate is 28 percent.

7. Alubar, a U.S. multinational, receives royalties from Country A, foreign-branch earnings from Country B, and dividends equal to 50 percent of net income from subsidiaries in Countries C and D. There is a 10 percent withholding tax on the royalty from Country A and a 10 percent withholding tax on the dividend from Country C. Income tax rates are 20 percent in Country B and 40 percent in Country C. Country D assesses indirect taxes of 40 percent instead of direct taxes on income. Selected data are as follows:

	Country A	Country B	Country C	Country D
Royalty from Country A operations	$20			
Pretax income		$90	$90	$54
Income taxes (20%/40%)		18	36	-0-
Net income		$72	$54	$54

Required: Calculate the foreign and U.S. taxes paid on each foreign-source income.

8. Global Enterprises has a manufacturing affiliate in Country A that incurs costs of $600,000 for goods that it sells to its sales affiliate in Country B. The sales affiliate resells these goods to final consumers for $1,700,000. Both affiliates incur operating expenses of

$100,000 each. Countries A and B levy a corporate income tax of 35 percent on taxable income in their jurisdictions.

Required: If Global Enterprises raises the aggregate transfer price such that shipments from its manufacturing to its sales affiliate increase from $1,000,000 to $1,200,000, what effect would this have on consolidated taxes?

9. Using the facts stated in Exercise 8, what would be the tax effects of the transfer pricing action if corporate income tax rates were 30 percent in Country A and 40 percent in Country B?

10. Drawing on the background facts in Exercises 8 and 9, assume that the manufacturing cost per unit, based on operations at full capacity of 10,000 units, is $60, and that the uncontrolled selling price of the unit in Country A is $120. Costs to transport the goods to the distribution affiliate in Country B are $16 per unit, and a reasonable profit margin on such cross-border sales is 20 percent of cost.

Now suppose that Country B levies a corporate income tax of 40 percent on taxable income (vs. 30 percent in Country A) and a tariff of 20 percent on the declared value of the imported goods. The minimum declared value legally allowed in Country B is $100 per unit with no upper limit. Import duties are deductible for income tax purposes in Country B.

Required:

a. Based on the foregoing information, formulate a transfer pricing strategy that would minimize Global Enterprise's overall tax burden.

b. What issues does your pricing decision raise?

11. Lumet Corporation, a manufacturer of cellular telephones, wishes to invoice a sales affiliate located in Fontainebleau for an order of 10,000 units. Wanting to minimize its exchange risk, it invoices all intracompany transactions in euros. Relevant facts on a per unit basis are as follows: net sales price, €450; other operating expenses, €63; freight and insurance, €1; packaging costs, €1.50. Customs duties are 5 percent, and Lumet Corporation wishes to earn a profit of 6 percent on the transaction.

Required: Determine the price at which Lumet would invoice its French affiliate for the cellular phones.

12. The partial income statement of the Lund Manufacturing Company, a Swedish-based concern producing pharmaceutical products, is presented here:

Sales	SEK 75,000,000
Cost of goods manufactured and sold:	
Finished goods, beginning inventory	-0-
Cost of goods manufactured: (100,000 units)	
Direct materials used	SEK 22,500,000
Direct labor	11,600,000
Overhead	6,000,000
Cost of goods available for sale	40,100,000
Finished goods, ending inventory	8,000,000
Cost of goods sold	32,100,000
Gross Margin	SEK 42,900,000

During the year, short-term interest rates in Sweden averaged 7 percent, while net operating assets averaged SEK 45,000,000. The company is entitled to a government subsidy of 5 percent. Its required margin to provide a profit and cover other expenses is 8 percent. All affiliates receive credit terms of 60 days.

Required: Based on this information, at what price would the Lund Manufacturing Company invoice its distribution affiliate in neighboring Finland?

Case 12-1   The Shirts Off Their Backs

Do accountants share the blame for Third World poverty? A report by the U.K.-based Christian Aid says so.[33] It attacks accounting firms for helping to perpetuate poverty in the developing world through their aggressive marketing of tax-avoidance schemes: "The tax avoidance industry [including accounting firms] has a very negative impact on developing countries and their ability to raise taxation — which is . . . critical for their escape from poverty."[34]

According to the report, the debate over how poor countries fund their escape from poverty has up to this point focused mainly on calls for debt cancellation and increases in aid.[35] While these factors are important, they are only pieces in a larger and more complicated puzzle. Solving this puzzle involves looking not only at the money that flows into poor countries, but also at money they can't get their hands on and the money that leaks away.

Taxation is facing a crisis in poorer countries. In the rich world, government revenue from taxation between 1990 and 2000 averaged 30 percent of gross domestic product (GDP). In sub-Saharan Africa, the average over the same period was 17.9 percent, in Latin America it was 15.1 percent, and in south Asia it was 10.5 percent. The low tax yield in poorer regions of the world limits the amount of domestically generated resources that are available to governments for essential public services, such as healthcare and education.

To quote the report:

It is not by accident that poor countries have been unable to increase the amount of revenue they raise through taxation. There are three specific tax strategies that have hindered them:

1. *Tax competition* between countries means poorer nations have been forced to lower corporate tax rates, often dramatically, in order to attract foreign investment.
2. *Trade liberalization* has deprived poorer countries of taxes on imports. In some cases, these had yielded up to one-third of their tax revenue.
3. *Tolerance of tax havens* has helped wealthy individuals and multinational companies (as well as criminals, corrupt leaders and terrorists) move their wealth and profits offshore to avoid paying taxes.[36]

Tax havens affect developing countries in a number of ways:

- Secret bank accounts and offshore trusts encourage wealthy individuals and companies to escape paying taxes by providing a place for untaxed earnings and profits to be banked.

- Many multinational corporations launder profits earned in developing countries by importing goods at

---

[33]Christian Aid, *The Shirts Off Their Backs: How Tax Policies Fleece the Poor* (September 2005), www.christianaid.org.uk.
[34]Andrew Pendleton, Christian Aid's senior policy officer, as quoted in Alice Nation, "Christian Aid Attacks Accountants over Tax Avoidance Schemes," *Accountancy* (October 2005): 11.
[35]Aid from the rich world is volatile and sometimes comes with strings attached.
[36]Christian Aid, *The Shirts Off Their Backs: How Tax Policies Fleece the Poor* (September 2005): 4 (www.christianaid.org.uk).

hugely inflated prices and exporting commodities at a fraction of their true value.[37] They do this through paper subsidiaries in tax havens, providing them with a significant tax advantage over their nationally based competitors and fleecing governments of tax revenue.

- Banking secrecy and trust services provided by globalized financial institutions operating offshore provide a secure cover for laundering the proceeds of political corruption, fraud, embezzlement, illicit arms trading and the global drugs trade.[38]

Who is to blame for this crisis? The study points the finger at international institutions like the International Monetary Fund and the World Bank, multinational corporations, banks, and accountants.

Accountancy firms . . . are champions of 'tax planning' whereby, along with their clients they organize networks of offshore subsidiaries to avoid paying tax. The collapse of Enron provided a rare insight into precisely how this works. The U.S. Senate report into the Enron case shows how accountants Andersen facilitated Enron's massive tax avoidance. The company paid no tax at all between 1995 and 1999.[39] Tax planning by accountants made this possible and involved setting up a global network of 3,500 companies, more than 440 of which were in the Cayman Islands. The subsequent Sarbanes-Oxley legislation in the US is intended to act as a deterrent, by making directors and shareholders more responsible for the consequences of such strategies. But it does little to lift the veil of secrecy surrounding tax havens.[40] ■

REQUIRED

1. Why should wealthy nations be concerned about seeing that poor ones collect their "fair share" of taxes?
2. Do you agree that accountants and accounting firms share the blame for perpetuating poverty in the developing world? Why or why not?
3. Is tax planning wrong?
4. Assume that you agree that new policies are needed to improve the ability of Third World countries to increase their tax yields. List policy recommendations that will achieve this result, and explain why you think these policies are needed.

---

[37]The report cites data that 45 to 50 percent of intracompany transfers are mispriced in Latin America and 60 percent are mispriced in Africa.
[38]Christian Aid, *The Shirts Off Their Backs: How Tax Policies Fleece the Poor* (September 2005): 11–12 (www.christianaid.org.uk).
[39]According to a 2004 U.S. Government Accountability Office report, 60 percent of U.S. corporations with at least $450 million in assets reported no federal tax liability for any of the years between 1996 and 2000.
[40]Christian Aid, *The Shirts Off Their Backs: How Tax Policies Fleece the Poor* (September 2005): 17 (www.christianaid.org.uk).

Case 12-2   Muscle Max: Your Very Own Personal Trainer

Muscle Max-Asia, a wholly owned affiliate of a French parent company, functions as a regional headquarters for operating activities in the Pacific Rim. It enjoys great autonomy from its French parent in conducting its primary line of business, the manufacture and sale of Muscle Max, a commercial-grade weight-lifting machine that can be used in athletic clubs or in the home. Muscle Max–Asia has manufacturing affiliates in Malaysia and Canton (China) and distribution outlets in Australia, Japan, New Zealand, South Korea, and Singapore. It plans to expand its operations to other Pacific Rim countries in the next several years.

Given the demand for weight-lifting equipment in Australia, the company's distribution affiliate there, Muscle Max–Australia, has been importing its equipment from both Canton and Malaysia, paying a customs duty of 5 percent. Competing suppliers of similar equipment have approached the Australian affiliate for orders. Prices quoted on such machinery have ranged between 650 to 750 Australian dollars (A$). Muscle Max–Australia, which currently retails the machine for A$1,349, recently complained to Muscle Max–Asia because of the differences in the prices it is being charged by its sister affiliates in Canton and Malaysia. Specifically, while the Malaysian affiliate charges a per unit price of A$675, the Canton supplier's price is 26 percent higher. Muscle Max–Asia explains that the transfer price, based on a cost-plus formula (production costs total A$540 per unit), reflects several considerations, including higher margins to compensate for credit risk, operating risk, and taxes. As for taxes, Muscle Max–Asia explains that the People's Republic of China provides fiscal incentives to enterprises that promote exports. Although normal corporate income tax rates are 33 percent, Cantonese tax authorities have agreed to a rate of 10 percent on all export-related earnings.

The manager of Muscle Max–Australia remains skeptical and believes that he is paying for the Cantonese manager's inefficiency. In his latest communication, he asks if he can consider alternative suppliers of weight-lifting equipment to preserve local market share. ■

REQUIRED

1. What issues does this case raise?

2. What courses of action would you recommend to resolve the issues you have identified?

Index

KEY

A = Appendix entries
E = Exhibits
n = notes